KT-557-938

Dewey Decimal Classification and Relative Index

Dewey Decimal Classification and Relative Index

Devised by Melvil Dewey

EDITION 22

Edited by

Joan S. Mitchell, Editor in Chief

Julianne Beall, Assistant Editor

Giles Martin, Assistant Editor

Winton E. Matthews, Jr., Assistant Editor

Gregory R. New, Assistant Editor

VOLUME 1

Manual ■ Tables

OCLC

OCLC Online Computer Library Center, Inc.

Dublin, Ohio

2003

Library of Congress Cataloging-in-Publication Data
Dewey, Melvil, 1851-1931.
Dewey decimal classification and relative index / devised by Melvil Dewey. — Ed. 22 / edited by Joan S. Mitchell, Julianne Beall, Giles Martin, Winton E. Matthews, Jr., Gregory R. New.
p. cm.
Contents: v. 1. Manual. Tables — v. 2. Schedules 000-599 — v. 3. Schedules 600-999 — v. 4. Relative index.
ISBN: 0910608709 (set : alk. paper)
1. Classification, Dewey decimal. I. Mitchell, Joan S. II. Beall, Julianne, 1946- III. Martin, Giles. IV. Matthews, Winton E. V. New, Gregory R. VI. Title.
Z696 .D52 2003
025.4'31—dc21 2003050872

OCLC Online Computer Library Center, Inc.
6565 Frantz Road
Dublin, OH 43017-3395 USA
www.oclc.org/dewey

The paper used in this publication meets the requirements of ANSI/NISO Z39.48-1992 (Permanence of Paper).

ISBN: (set) 0-910608-70-9

Recycled paper

Dedicated
to
Peter J. Paulson

Executive Director
OCLC Forest Press
1985–1998

Member
Decimal Classification Editorial Policy Committee
1983–1998

and

David A. Smith

Chief
Decimal Classification Division
Library of Congress
1987–2002

Contents

Volume 1

Volume 2

Volume 3

Volume 4

Foreword by the Decimal Classification Editorial Policy Committee

Work on Edition 22 of the Dewey Decimal Classification (DDC) system began in late 1996, immediately after the publication of Edition 21 and Abridged Edition 13. It is the culmination of the work of the editors, the Decimal Classification Editorial Policy Committee (EPC), and many advisors representing various fields and specific constituencies. Edition 22 reflects current thought in knowledge organization, and incorporates updates and changes identified during the life of Edition 21. A primary goal of this complex analytical process is to publish an edition that is committed to meeting the needs of both print and electronic users. To inform the planning for Edition 22, EPC held a planning retreat in 1997. The committee also commissioned George D'Elia (State University of New York at Buffalo) to conduct a market research survey of its American, Australian, Canadian, and United Kingdom users (the largest users of the English-language edition). The significant survey results were discussed during EPC meetings in 1997 and again in 1999.

Revisions and Development

For a classification system to maintain its relevancy, it must be continually revised and expanded. EPC reviews the entire Classification, from the schedules to the Manual and Relative Index, after the publication of an edition. Some portions of the DDC are revised more thoroughly than others. In certain areas, previously identified priorities drive the updating and revision process. In other cases, there is a perceived need to expand a discipline, provide for new topics, or improve the structure of the Classification. The committee is keenly aware that while relocations may improve the structure of the DDC, they also put a burden on those libraries that may not be able to reclassify that portion of their collection. A benefit to the user must be demonstrated before a change is approved.

EPC is often asked to react to proposals from the editors, but upon occasion, the committee initiates change. For example, EPC members thought the Manual notes were too long and too difficult to read. In response, the editors shortened and simplified the notes, dividing them into smaller sections for ease of reading and comprehension. Similarly, EPC urged the editors to consider user preference when classifying works on travel facilities. Users wanted these works located with travel numbers in 910. Taking this request seriously, the editors moved works on hotels and similar lodgings from home economics in 647 to travel numbers in 910.

Broadening of International Perspective via Outside Consultation

Because the DDC is the most widely used classification system in the world, EPC realizes it has responsibilities toward its diverse users. For example, EPC has supported and encouraged the previous edition's policy of removing Christian and western bias from the Classification. By continuing to be sensitive to cultural and social issues outside the United States, the Classification will remain relevant and useful to its many international users.

For this edition, the editors, on the advice of EPC, have continued to look for outside guidance and feedback on problematic or controversial areas of the DDC. EPC consulted with an increasing number of outside reviewers and experts in specific disciplines. Several subcommittees of the Subject Analysis Committee (American Library Association, Association for Library Collections & Technical Services, Cataloging and Classification Section) and the Chartered Institute of Library and Information Professionals (formerly the Library Association [United Kingdom]) were key players in analyzing the proposed revisions, expansions, and other suggested changes. The International Federation of Library Associations (IFLA) was consulted concerning changes to 340 Law. Colleagues and professors in Australia, England, and Italy provided extensive feedback on 510 Mathematics. Several national libraries participated in the process of updating the area tables and history of their countries. The Cataloging Committee of the Africana Librarians Council, African Studies Association, also provided valuable input.

Ross Trotter (Chair, Chartered Institute of Library and Information Professionals Dewey Decimal Classification Committee) served as an outside consultant in the revision of the Manual. EPC is grateful for his considerable Dewey expertise and his thoughtful analysis.

On a recommendation of EPC, practicing catalogers have begun to test a few selected areas of the DDC that have undergone extensive updating and revision. This testing has strengthened the Classification and assured that it remains both a useful and usable tool. Individuals at the Hong Kong Baptist University Library and the British Library tested Religion; Berkeley Public Library tested 305–306 Social groups and culture and institutions; Lucent Technologies, the British Library, and Deakin University Library tested 004–006 Computer science; and the University of Newcastle upon Tyne and Reading University Library tested 510 Mathematics.

New Emphasis on Research

In order to understand more fully the needs of Dewey users, early in the publication cycle of this edition, EPC became more involved in classification research. In addition to the international survey of Dewey users already mentioned, several EPC meetings included presentations by OCLC Office of Research knowledge organization experts, Diane Vizine-Goetz, Ed O'Neill, and Keith Shafer. In addition, the committee heard papers presented by library science professors Francis Miksa (University of Texas at Austin) and Nancy Williamson (University of Toronto).

During the preparation of this edition, the editors frequently searched the Internet to locate up-to-date research in areas such as mathematics and medicine. In addition, the editors relied heavily on searching electronic databases for literary warrant of specific portions of the Classification.

EPC Membership

The Decimal Classification Editorial Policy Committee was established in 1937 to serve as an advisory body to the Dewey Decimal Classification. Its role is to determine the direction and policy of the Classification. In 1953, it was reconstituted into a joint committee of the Lake Placid Foundation and the American Library Association. In 1988, when OCLC Online Computer Library Center, Inc., acquired the Dewey Decimal Classification, it reaffirmed the importance of EPC's advisory role to the DDC. The ten-member international board works closely with the DDC editors to suggest changes, facilitate innovations, and monitor the general development of the Classification.

EPC speaks for users of the Classification worldwide. EPC members come from public, special, and academic libraries, and from library schools. They represent the American Library Association, the Australian Committee on Cataloguing, the Chartered Institute of Library and Information Professionals, the Library of Congress, and the National Library of Canada.

Since the publication of Edition 21, EPC has consisted of the following members, listed with the positions they held or now hold as members:

David Ballati, Director, Bibliographic Services, National Library of Canada (Chair, 1996–1999)
Richard Baumgarten, Cataloger, Johnson County Library, Overland Park, KS
Pamela P. Brown, Information Technology Services Director, Suburban Library System, Burr Ridge, IL
Mary Carroll, Standards Librarian, National Library of Canada
Janice M. DeSirey, Youth Services Librarian, Hennepin County Library, Edina, MN
Lucy Evans, Collection Acquisition & Description, British Library
Jessica MacPhail, City Librarian, Racine Public Library, Racine, WI
Giles Martin, Cataloguing Department, University of Sydney
Peter J. Paulson, Executive Director, OCLC Forest Press
Anne Robertson, Representative of the Australian Committee on Cataloguing
Elaine Svenonius, Professor Emerita, Graduate School of Education and Information Studies, University of California, Los Angeles
Andrea L. Stamm, Head, Catalog Department, Northwestern University Library (Chair, 2000–2003)
Winston Tabb, Associate Librarian for Library Services, Library of Congress
Arlene G. Taylor, Professor, School of Information Sciences, University of Pittsburgh
Helena M. Van Deroef, Cataloging Coordinator, Lucent Technologies
Beacher Wiggins, Acting Associate Librarian for Library Services, Library of Congress
Susi Woodhouse, Westminster City Libraries, England

Other Acknowledgments

EPC is especially grateful to Joan S. Mitchell, Editor in Chief of the DDC, and Assistant Editors Julianne Beall, Giles Martin, Winton E. Matthews, Jr., and Gregory R. New, for their guidance, patience, and boundless energy during the course of this publication cycle.

We Welcome Your Feedback

The Decimal Classification Editorial Policy Committee commends to its readers this Edition 22 of the Dewey Decimal Classification. It represents the work of many individuals who are proud to have contributed to making this edition meet the needs of the user. Because the DDC long ago adopted a policy of continuous revision, work will begin immediately on Edition 23. DDC users are encouraged to send suggestions and comments to the EPC chair or the DDC editors via e-mail <dewey@loc.gov>.

Andrea L. Stamm
Chair, 2000–
Decimal Classification
Editorial Policy Committe

Preface and Acknowledgments

A new edition of the Dewey Decimal Classification is a significant event in the life of the world's most widely used knowledge organization tool. We stand on the shoulders of all who have gone before us in the 127 years of Dewey's continuous development, and we are mindful of our responsibility to current and future users to develop a structure that will ensure Dewey's future in the ever changing information environment.

We have developed Edition 22 during a period of many transitions. Some were external—the rising importance of the web, shifts in the world political situation, ongoing changes in knowledge, the expansion of our translation program. Others were closer to home—the move of the Forest Press office from Albany, N.Y., to OCLC headquarters in Dublin, Ohio; the retirement of the Forest Press imprint; changes in Dewey personnel. We are grateful to the many organizations and individuals for their help and support in meeting these challenges.

In preparation for Edition 22, we commissioned a survey of Dewey users. We thank the many users who participated in the survey—each respondent helped to shape the future of the DDC. Our users played a key part in reviewing the drafts of several major updates, and participated in testing the revised drafts. Committees appointed by the American Library Association (ALA) Subject Analysis Committee reviewed the following schedules: 004–006 Data processing Computer science; 300–307 Social sciences, sociology, and anthropology; 340 Law; and 510 Mathematics. The Chartered Institute of Library and Information Professionals (CILIP) appointed a review committee for 510 Mathematics. Members of these committees and others who reviewed the aforementioned schedules are listed below.

004–006 Data processing Computer science: Vivian Bliss (Microsoft); Ruth Bogan (Warren-Newport Public Library); April Davies (Iowa City Community School District); Lynn El-Hoshy (Library of Congress); Sara Shatford Layne (University of California, Los Angeles); Patricia Le Galèze (Bibliothèque nationale de France); Patricia Luthin (Western State University College of Law); Scott Opasik (Indiana University, South Bend); Tom Williamson (retired staff engineer, Intel).

300–307 Social sciences, sociology, and anthropology: Sophie Boganski (West Virginia University); April Davies (Iowa City Community School District); Daniel Joudry (University of Pittsburgh); Patricia Le Galèze (Bibliothèque nationale de France); Joseph Miller (H.W. Wilson Company); Dale Swenson (Brigham Young University).

340 Law: Abigail Ellsworth (Wilkes, Artis, Hedrick & Lane); John Hostage (Harvard Law School); Barbara Leiwesmeyer (Universitätsbibliothek Regensburg); Max Naudi (Bibliothèque nationale de France); Marie Whited (Yale Law School). In addition, the following people attended a special meeting at the International Federation of Library Associations and Institutions (IFLA) 2001 Conference to discuss the 340 Law schedule: Friedrich Geisselmann (Universitätsbibliothek Regensburg); Mauro Guerrini (University of Rome); Patrice Landry (National Library of Switzerland); Ia McIlwaine (University College London and editor in chief, Universal Decimal Classification); Max Naudi (Bibliothèque nationale de France). We are especially grateful to Jolande Goldberg (Library of Congress) for her advice on developments in international law, law of nations, comparative law, and intergovernmental law.

510 Mathematics: Tim Cole (University of Illinois at Urbana-Champaign); Philip Cooper (University of Huddersfield); Antonella De Robio (Università degli studi di Padova); Peter Donovan (University of New South Wales); John Hostage (Harvard Law School); Dorothy McGarry (University of California, Los Angeles); Alberto Marini (Istituto di Matematica Applicata e Tecnologie Informatiche); Merry Schellinger (Humboldt State University); Carol Speirs (University of Reading); Dale Swenson (Brigham Young University).

540 Chemistry: Bartow Culp (Purdue University); Cheri Folkner (Weyerhaeuser Company); Bernie Karon (University of Minnesota); Jane Keefer (West Chester University); Sara Shatford Layne and Marion Peters (University of California, Los Angeles); Anne-Marie Malaveille (Université Claude Bernard Lyon 1); Katherine Porter (Vanderbilt University).

After the drafts were revised, the following users tested the proposed schedules.

004–006 Data processing Computer science: Lisa Berry and Helena M. Van Deroef (Lucent Technologies); Steve Hodson and Emma Rogoz (British Library); Bernadette Houghton (Deakin University).

300–307 Social sciences, sociology, and anthropology: Margot Lucoff (Berkeley Public Library).

340 Law: Anna Gyngell (British Library).

510 Mathematics: Libby Matthewson (University of Newcastle upon Tyne); Carol Speirs (University of Reading Library).

In addition, Stephen Dingler (Hong Kong Baptist University) and Terrance Mann (British Library) tested 200 Religion.

National libraries throughout the world, our translation partners, and members of translation advisory committees made contributions throughout the tables and schedules, but especially in history, geography, language, and literature. We acknowledge the contributions of the following: Raymonde Couture-Lafleur (consultant to and coordinator of translations for ASTED); Bruno Béguet, Suzanne Jouguelet, and Patricia Le Galèze (Bibliothèque nationale de France); Magda-Heiner Freiling and Esther Scheven (Die Deutsche Bibliothek); David Farris, Pierre-Emile Grégoire, Paula Purcell, and Harry Walsh (National Library of Canada); Gudrun Karlsdottir (National and University Library of Iceland); Poori Soltani (National Library of the Islamic Republic of Iran); Margaret Callus (National Library of Malta); Unni Knutsen and Isabella Kubosch (National Library of Norway); Olof Osterman (National Library of Sweden); Patrice Landry (National Library of Switzerland); Margarita Amaya de Heredia (Rojas Eberhard Editores Ltda.); Ekaterina Zaitseva (Russian National Public Library for Science and Technology); Margit Sandner (University of Vienna). We are also grateful to the staffs of the British Library and State Library of South Africa, and to librarians in the United Kingdom and South Africa, for their contributions to the revision of the area tables for Great Britain and South Africa issued in print and electronic form in 1999.

We thank the following persons who contributed to the development of sign languages: Linda Alexander, Terry Chang, and Scott K. Liddell (Gallaudet University); Rosalee Connor and Eric Eldritch (Library of Congress). We also thank Venida S. Chenault (Haskell Indian Nations University) for advice about indexing indigenous peoples. The ALA Committee on Cataloging: Asian and African Materials and the Cataloging Committee of the Africana Librarians Council, African Studies Association, gave valuable advice on history, geography, languages, and religion.

We would be remiss if we did not also acknowledge the sizable contribution of Ross Trotter (Chair, CILIP Dewey Decimal Classification Committee) for his work on the streamlining of the Manual. Before his retirement from the British Library, Ross Trotter led efforts on the revision of the area table for Great Britain.

We have been fortunate to work with the dedicated representatives of our users on the Decimal Classification Editorial Policy Committee (EPC). EPC's guidance and critical review are essential in ensuring that the DDC remains a useful knowledge organization tool.

Many colleagues associated with the Dewey Decimal Classification at OCLC and the Library of Congress have made significant contributions to the development of Edition 22. I am grateful first and foremost to the assistant editors of the Dewey Decimal Classification, Julianne Beall (Library of Congress), Giles Martin (OCLC), Winton E. Matthews, Jr. (Library of Congress), and Gregory R. New (Library of Congress). Their scholarship, dedication, and commitment to our users are reflected throughout the Dewey Decimal Classification.

In December 1998, Peter J. Paulson, executive director of Forest Press, retired after thirteen years of service. Mr. Paulson led Forest Press through its acquisition by OCLC in 1988, and steered the Dewey Decimal Classification through a period of tremendous growth and constant change. In particular, Mr. Paulson was responsible for moving the DDC into the electronic environment and expanding international usage through the Dewey translation program. I thank him for his many years of support, dedication, and vision.

I am grateful to current and past OCLC staff members associated with the Dewey Decimal Classification: Suzanne Butte, Christy Carpenter, Libbie Crawford, Elizabeth Hansen, Judith Kramer Greene, Dawn Lawson, Judith Pisarski, Eliza Sproat, and Robert Van Volkenburg. The staff and management of OCLC have provided the support and resources to enable the DDC to grow as a knowledge organization system. Thanks particularly to Jay Jordan, President and CEO; his predecessor, Dr. K. Wayne Smith; and Gary Houk, Vice President, Cataloging and Metadata Services, for their support. I thank the Product Development Division, especially Marty Withrow, Viktoria Kushnir, and Dan Whitney, for the development and ongoing support of the editorial database management system. I am also grateful for the contributions of the following OCLC staff who support the ongoing development and updating of WebDewey, the electronic counterpart of this edition: Joe Abrams, Doug Allen, Joe Barna, Mel Beck, Janet Bickle, Eric Childress, Geoffrey Curtis, Larry Evans, Jonathan Fausey, Linda Gabel, Kristin Gain, Chris Grabenstatter, Larry Lambert, Heidi Laubenthal, Joanne Murphy, Doug Price, Catherine Savage, Joanne Shoemaker, Jim Simms, Kevin Skarsten, and David Whitehair. I thank Lorcan Dempsey, Vice President of the Office of Research, and his predecessor, Terry Noreault, for their ongoing support of knowledge organization research. I also acknowledge the many contributions of Office of Research staff, particularly Ed O'Neill and Jean Godby. I especially note the numerous and ongoing contributions of Diane Vizine-Goetz and the Knowledge Organization Group in the Office of Research: Carol Hickey, Andy Houghton, and Roger Thompson.

We are fortunate to have our editorial headquarters at the Library of Congress in the Decimal Classification Division, where editorial work on the DDC is performed under an agreement between OCLC and the Library of Congress. Until spring 2002, David A. Smith was chief of the Library of Congress Decimal Classification Division. Mr. Smith, Dennis M.

McGovern (current acting chief), and the Decimal Classification Division staff have continuously supported the editorial efforts by offering an expert view of new topics and areas requiring updating. In addition to the three assistant editors who are Library of Congress employees, present and past staff members who have contributed to the development of Edition 22 include: Teresa Baker, Darlene Banks, Mark Behrens, Victoria Behrens, Michael B. Cantlon, Larry Ceasar, Julia Clanton, Rosalee Connor, Eve M. Dickey, Ruth Freitag, Adrian Gore, Donald Hardy, Keith Harrison, Sarah Keller, Walter McClughan, Nobuko Ohashi, Letitia J. Reigle, Virginia A. Schoepf, Cosmo Tassone, Dorothy A. Watson, Ruby Woodard, and Susanne Welsh.

I will close by acknowledging once more the contributions of two key individuals who shaped the future of Dewey: Peter J. Paulson, retired executive director of OCLC Forest Press, and David A. Smith, retired chief, Decimal Classification Division. Their vision, advice, support, and colleagueship have been invaluable in the development of this new edition.

Joan S. Mitchell
Editor in Chief
Dewey Decimal Classification
OCLC, Inc.

New Features in Edition 22

Overview

Edition 22 is the first edition of the Dewey Decimal Classification to be produced in the context of the web environment. The web has enabled us to update the DDC continuously and provide those updates regularly to our users. The web has expanded our access to information sources and facilitated timely cooperation with our international user base. It has also challenged us to provide features that promote efficiency and accuracy in classification.

Continuous Updating

Edition 22 reflects the continuous updating policy in effect since the publication of Edition 21 in 1996. Edition 21 was the first DDC edition to be published in print and electronic form simultaneously. We have used the electronic versions and supplemental monthly web postings as our chief vehicles for delivering updates to our users. From 1996 through 2001, Dewey for Windows was issued annually. Since 2000, WebDewey has been the main source for updates and a fully updated version is released quarterly. Since 1997, we have also posted selected new numbers and changes to the DDC on a monthly basis on our web site (www.oclc.org/dewey). All of these updates have been incorporated into Edition 22.

New Numbers and Topics

Edition 22 contains many new numbers and topics. These range from new geographic provisions, e.g., the updating of administrative regions in Quebec, to new numbers throughout the DDC for emerging topics in fields such as computer science and engineering, sociology, medicine, and history. Many new built number entries and additional terms have been added to the Relative Index to cover sought topics and provide a wider base of entry vocabulary. We have waited for the publication of Edition 22 to introduce changes that have an impact across the DDC and substantial changes to disciplines.

International Cooperation

Edition 22 has benefited from the ongoing advice of the Decimal Classification Editorial Policy Committee (EPC) and our translation partners. Both groups provide a diverse outlook that is reflected in improvements to terminology throughout Edition 22, and in updated developments, particularly in geographic areas, law, political parties, language, literature, and historical periods.

Classifier Efficiency

Two striking changes in Edition 22, the removal of Table 7 and the streamlining of the Manual, have been motivated by a desire to promote classifier efficiency. We have removed Table 7 and replaced it with direct use of notation already available in the schedules and in notation 08 from Table 1. We have reviewed each Manual entry with an eye toward classifier efficiency. Information easily accommodated in notes in the tables and schedules has been transferred from the Manual, and redundant information already in the schedules and tables has been eliminated from the Manual. We have converted the Library of Congress Decimal Classification Division DDC application policies previously described in the Manual into standard Dewey practice. We have moved basic instructions on the use of the Dewey Decimal Classification to the Introduction, and background information to *Dewey Decimal Classification: Principles and Application.* We have revised the remaining Manual entries in a consistent style to promote quick understanding and efficient use.

Major Changes in Edition 22

In addition to the removal of Table 7 and the streamlining of the Manual, there are several major changes introduced in Edition 22. We have completely updated 004–006 Data processing Computer science. In Edition 21, we initiated a two-edition plan to reduce Christian bias in 200 Religion. Edition 22 contains the rest of the relocations and expansions in 200 Religion outlined in that plan. We have updated developments and terminology for social groups and institutions in 305–306, and removed many near duplicate provisions in that schedule. We have introduced several improvements to 340 Law that relate to the law of nations, human rights, and intergovernmental organizations. We have introduced a substantial update in 510 Mathematics, including the relocation of some topics to the new development at 518 Numerical analysis. We have updated and expanded 610 Medicine and health, and improved indexing for medical topics. We have moved facilities for travelers from 647.94 to 910.46 and to specific area numbers in 913–919, and introduced updated historical periods throughout 930–990. Likewise, we have updated Table 2 Geographic Areas, Historical Periods, Persons. We have changed the name of Table 5 from "Racial, Ethnic, National Groups" to "Ethnic and National Groups" to reflect the de-emphasis on race in current scholarship. We have also greatly expanded provisions for American native peoples and languages in Tables 5 and 6. A complete list of relocations, discontinuations, and reused numbers in Edition 22 is available immediately following Tables 1–6. A selected list of new numbers, revisions, and expansions in Edition 22 follows.

Selected List of Changes in Edition 22

Selected Changes in the Tables

TABLE 1. STANDARD SUBDIVISIONS

—029 Commercial miscellany
Subdivisions discontinued to —029 and reused immediately for geographic treatment

TABLE 2. GEOGRAPHIC AREAS, HISTORICAL PERIODS, PERSONS

—23 Collected persons treatment of members of specific ethnic and national groups
New number*

—29 Persons treatment of nonhumans
New number*

*Introduced in an interim update prior to the publication of Edition 22

—411–414	Scotland Revised and expanded*
—42	England and Wales Revised and expanded*
—431–436	Germany and Austria Revised and expanded
—437	Czech Republic and Slovakia Revised and expanded*
—438	Poland Revised and expanded*
—44	France and Monaco Revised and expanded*
—451–457	Italy Revised and expanded*
—541–548	India Revised and expanded
—54911	Federally Administered Tribal Areas Relocated from —54912*
—549149	Islāmābād Capital Territory Relocated from —549142
—5492	Bangladesh Revised and expanded
—55	Iran Revised and expanded
—5987	East Timor Relocated from —5986*
—624–629	Sudan Revised
—632–634	Ethiopia Revised*
—642–646 —648	Morocco Western Sahara Revised and expanded

*Introduced in an interim update prior to the publication of Edition 22

—669	Nigeria Revised
—6751	Democratic Republic of the Congo Revised*
—682–687	Republic of South Africa Revised and expanded*
—714	Quebec Revised and expanded
—719	Northern territories Revised and expanded*
—728537	Región Autónoma del Atlántico Norte Relocated from —728532
—7287	Panama Revised and expanded*
—78864	Broomfield County [of Colorado] Relocated from —78863, —78872 —78881, and —78884*
—7951	Western Oregon
—7955	Eastern Oregon
—7971	Eastern Washington
—7976	Western Washington New numbers*
—85	Peru Revised
—861	Colombia Revised and expanded*
—881	Guyana
—883	Suriname Revised and expanded

TABLE 3B. SUBDIVISIONS FOR WORKS BY OR ABOUT MORE THAN ONE AUTHOR

—30877	Picaresque fiction New number

*Introduced in an interim update prior to the publication of Edition 22

TABLE 3C. NOTATION TO BE ADDED WHERE INSTRUCTED IN TABLE 3B, 700.4, 791.4, 808–809

—32 Places
Travel relocated from —355

—35 Humanity
Revised and expanded

—36 Physical and natural phenomena
Agriculture, scientific themes, and comprehensive works on scientific and technical themes relocated from —356

—377 Magic and witchcraft
New number

TABLE 4. SUBDIVISIONS OF INDIVIDUAL LANGUAGES AND LANGUAGE FAMILIES

—31 Specialized dictionaries
Expanded

—5 Grammar of the standard form of the language Syntax of the standard form of the language
Expanded

—813 Spelling (Orthography) and pronunciation
New number

—89 Use of a spoken language or a manually coded form of a spoken language for communication with and by deaf persons
New number and subdivisions*

TABLE 5. ETHNIC AND NATIONAL GROUPS

"Racial" was removed from the name of this table

—05 Persons of mixed ancestry with ethnic origins from more than one continent
Relocated from —04

—09 Europeans and people of European descent
Relocated from —034

—97 North American native peoples
—98 South American native peoples
Revised and expanded

*Introduced in an interim update prior to the publication of Edition 22

TABLE 6. LANGUAGES

—395	North Germanic languages (Nordic languages)
—396	Old Norse (Old Icelandic), Icelandic, Faeroese
—397	Swedish
—398	Danish and Norwegian Revised*
—91469	Konkani New number*
—963989	Ndebele (South Africa) Relocated from —963977*
—97	North American native languages
—98	South American native languages Revised and expanded

TABLE 7. GROUPS OF PERSONS

This table was deleted and replaced by direct use of notation already available in the schedules and in notation 08 from Table 1. A complete list of revised add instructions is provided in the introduction to "Relocations" immediately following Tables 1–6

Selected Changes in the Schedules

005.18	Microprogramming and microprograms Relocated from 005.6
005.5	General purpose application programs Relocated from 005.3 and expanded
005.52	Word processing Relocated from 652.5
005.722	Character sets New number
006.74	Markup languages
006. 8	Virtual reality New numbers
011.37	[General bibliographies of] Audiovisual and visual media Expanded
011.384	[General bibliographies of] Audiobooks (Talking books)
011.39	[General bibliographies of] Electronic resources New numbers

*Introduced in an interim update prior to the publication of Edition 22

011.8	General bibliographies of works by specific kinds of authors Relocated from 013
027.42 027.652	Library outreach programs Legislative reference bureaus New numbers
070.57973	Web publications New number
150.1986 150.1987	Humanistic psychology Transpersonal psychology New numbers
152.44	Guilt and shame New number
174.2	[Ethics of] Medical professions Revised and expanded*
201–209	Specific aspects of religion Relocated from 291; revised and expanded
261.88	[Christianity and the] Environment New number; ecology relocated from 261.836
297.938	Sources [of Bahai Faith] Expanded
299.161 299.511	Specific aspects of Celtic religions Specific aspects of Chinese religions New numbers and subdivisions
299.6 299.7 299.8	Religions originating among Black Africans and people of Black African descent Religions of North American native origin Religions of South American native origin Revised and expanded
302.231	Digital media New number
305 306	Social groups Culture and institutions Revised and expanded
320.546 320.557 320.558 320.58	Black nationalism Islamic fundamentalism Black Muslim movement Environmentalist political ideologies New numbers

*Introduced in an interim update prior to the publication of Edition 22

324.243	Parties of Germany Expanded
330.155	Miscellaneous schools [of economics] Revised and expanded
331.21647	Profit sharing
331.21649	Employee stock ownership plans
331.2524	Pension funds
331.2552	Unemployment compensation
331.2554	Health services New numbers
331.256	Work environment New number and subdivisions
331.257	Hours Revised and expanded
331.88	Labor unions (Trade unions) Revised
332.024	Personal finance Revised and expanded
332.17522	Checking accounts
332.54	Barter
332.632283	[Stock] Options New numbers
332.645	Speculation Expanded
332.67	Investments in specific industries, in specific kinds of enterprise, by specific kinds of investors; international investment; investment guides Revised and expanded
333.9523	[Economics of] Nonnative species
333.9543	[Economics of] Nonnative animals New numbers
338.69	Worker control of industry
338.749	Government corporations New numbers

340	Law The heading at 341 was changed from "International law" to "Law of nations." Throughout 341, "International governmental organizations" was changed to "Intergovernmental organizations." A topic in either 341.4 or 341.7 that had a corresponding domestic law provision in 342–347 was relocated to the appropriate number in 342–347
342.0877	[Jurisdiction over] Age groups New number and subdivisions
343.012–.019 343.08	Military and defense law Regulation of commerce (trade) Revised
343.0939	Pipeline transportation New number and subdivisions
346.016	Marriage Expanded
346.0171	Unborn children New number
349.2	Law of regional intergovernmental organizations New number. Similar new numbers at 342.2, 343.2, 344.2, 345.2, 346.2, 347.2, and 348.2
362.1042584	Health maintenance organizations (HMOs) New number*
363.34926	Disasters caused by ice storms New number*
363.73849	Specific types of toxic chemicals New number and subdivisions
370.1528	[Educational psychology of] Behavior modification Relocated from 370.153
370.1529 370.1532 370.1534	[Educational psychology of] Intelligence [Educational psychology of] Personality [Educational psychology of] Emotions New numbers
371.895	School assemblies New number

*Introduced in an interim update prior to the publication of Edition 22

372.373	[Elementary education in] Nutrition and food
372.378	[Elementary education in] Substance abuse New numbers
378.121	Academic status [in higher education] Expanded
381	Commerce (Trade) Broadened to include comprehensive works on commerce, relocated here from 380.1, and domestic commerce
381.11	Shopping centers
381.177	Online auctions
381.186	Street fairs
381.347	Better business bureaus New numbers
394.2612	Kwanzaa
394.2628	Mother's Day New numbers
415	Grammar of standard forms of languages Syntax of standard forms of languages Expanded
419	Sign languages Revised and expanded*
439.5	North Germanic languages (Nordic languages)
439.6	Old Norse (Old Icelandic), Icelandic, Faeroese
439.7	Swedish
439.8	Danish and Norwegian Revised*
491.469	Konkani Relocated from 491.467*
495.17	Historical and geographic variations, modern nongeographic variations of Chinese Expanded
511.3	Mathematical logic (Symbolic logic) Revised and expanded
512.2	Groups and group theory
512.3	Fields
512.4	Rings
512.55	Topological and related algebras and groups Expanded

*Introduced in an interim update prior to the publication of Edition 22

512.6	Category theory, homological algebra, K-theory New number and subdivisions relocated from different parts of 510
512.78	Specific fields of numbers New number and subdivisions
512.94	Theory of equations Revised and expanded
515.353	Partial differential equations Expanded
515.39	Dynamical systems New number and subdivision relocated from 515.35
515.94	Functions of complex variables Expanded
516.15	Geometric configurations Expanded
518	Numerical analysis New number and subdivisions relocated from different parts of 510
519.236	Martingales Relocated from 519.287
519.6	Mathematical optimization Relocated from 519.3 and expanded
523.24	Extrasolar systems New number*
530.1433	Quantum electrodynamics Relocated from 537.67*
543	Analytical chemistry Revised; 544 Qualitative analysis, 545 Quantitative analysis, and 547.3 Analytical organic chemistry relocated here
547.2	Organic chemical reactions Relocated from 547.139
551.46	Hydrosphere and submarine geology Oceanography Revised and expanded
551.556	Ice storms Relocated from 551.559*

*Introduced in an interim update prior to the publication of Edition 22

560.41	Fossilization (Taphonomy)
560.43	Trace fossils
560.47	Micropaleontology New numbers
561.11	Stratigraphic paleobotany New number and subdivisions
569.9	Hominidae Expanded
578.62	[Biology of] Nonnative species New number. Similar new numbers at 581.62 and 591.62
579.171	Specific ecosystem processes of ecology
579.172	Specific factors affecting ecology New numbers and subdivisions. Similar new numbers and subdivisions at 581.71–.72 and 591.71–.72
591.57	Locomotion [of animals] New number
597.8	Amphibia (Amphibians) Expanded*
597.9	Reptilia (Reptiles) Expanded*
610.73	Nursing and services of allied health personnel Revised
611.01816	Physiological genetics Expanded
612.823	Emotions, conscious mental processes, intelligence New number and subdivisions
613.66	Self-defense Prevention of violent crimes for individuals relocated from 362.88
613.663	Rape prevention for individuals Relocated from 362.883
613.718	Stretching exercises, and exercises for muscles of specific parts of body New number and subdivisions

*Introduced in an interim update prior to the publication of Edition 22

613.72	Massage Relocated from 646.75
613.79	Relaxation, rest, sleep Expanded
614.1	Forensic medicine Expanded
614.3	Incidence of injuries and wounds New number
614.579	[Incidence of and public measures to prevent] Gram-positive bacterial infections New number and subdivisions
614.58	[Incidence of and public measures to prevent] Viral diseases Relocated from 614.575
615.822	Therapeutic massage Expanded
616.027	Experimental medicine Relocated from 619*
616.1–.9 617 618.1–.8	Specific diseases Miscellaneous branches of medicine Surgery Gynecology and obstetrics Add tables revised and expanded
616.372 616.515 616.517 616.6921 616.6922 616.772 616.773 616.775 616.839	Cystic fibrosis Photosensitivity disorders Urticaria (Hives) Male infertility Impotence Systemic lupus erythematosus Marfan syndrome Sjogren's syndrome Amyotrophic lateral sclerosis New numbers
616.8491	Headaches Expanded; migraine relocated from 616.857 to 616.84912
616.856	Diseases of cranial, spinal, peripheral nerves Relocated from 616.87

*Introduced in an interim update prior to the publication of Edition 22

616.8569	Diseases of autonomic nervous system Relocated from 616.88
616.8581	Personality disorders New number
616.85882	Autism Relocated from 616.8982
616.91	Virus diseases Relocated from 616.925; revised and expanded
616.929	Gram-positive bacterial infections New number and subdivisions
617.033	Self-help devices for persons with disabilities
617.057	Endoscopic surgery
617.058	Laser surgery
617.172	Cumulative trauma disorders
617.441	[Surgery of] Bone marrow
617.6922	Crowns
617.693	Dental implantation New numbers
617.919	Surgical complications; preoperative, intraoperative, postoperative care Expanded; surgical complications relocated from 617.01
617.95	Cosmetic and restorative plastic surgery, transplantation of tissue and organs, implantation of artificial tissue and organs Expanded
618.24	Prenatal care and preparation for childbirth Expanded
618.32686	Substance-related disorders
618.36	Pregnancy complications due to co-occurrence of pregnancy and disease in the mother New numbers and subdivisions
618.9202	Infants Relocated from 618.92000832 and expanded
621.38806	High-definition television (HDTV)
621.38807	Digital television New numbers

621.399	Devices for special computer methods
	Expanded
624.1526	Blasting
624.17725	Columns
	New numbers
624.21–.24	Specific kinds of bridges
	Relocated from 624.3–624.8
629.893	Specific kinds of robots
	New number and subdivisions
641.308	Food additives
641.532	Brunches
641.534	Box and bag lunches
641.536	Afternoon teas
641.538	Suppers
641.539	Snacks
641.5611	Cooking for one
641.5612	Cooking for two
641.56222	Cooking for infants
641.56318	[Cooking for] Persons with food allergies
641.56319	[Cooking for] Pregnant women
641.56323	Low-salt cooking
641.56383	Low-carbohydrate cooking
641.563837	Sugar-free cooking
641.56384	Low-fat cooking
641.563847	Low-cholesterol cooking
641.5686	Christmas cooking
641.5892	[Cooking with] Food processors
641.5893	[Cooking with] Blenders
641.774	Stir frying
641.8157	Muffins
641.819	Garnishes
641.8236	Chili
641.8248	Pizza
641.8642	Gelatins
641.8644	Puddings
641.86539	Cake decoration
	New numbers
642.56	[Meals in] Health care facilities
642.57	[Meals in] Schools
642.79	Napkin folding
	New numbers

643.2	Special kinds of housing Expanded
643.556	Swimming pools New number
645.12 645.32	Rugs Draperies New numbers
646.7247	Braiding [hair] New number
650.11	Time management New number
650.142	Résumés, cover letters, job applications New number; résumé writing relocated from 808.06665*
650.144	Employment interviewing New number
651.792	Intranets New number
657.837	[Accounting for] Hotels and restaurants Expanded
658.0412	Home-based business New number
658.16	Reorganization and dissolution of enterprises Expanded
658.3123 658.4058	Telecommuting Contracting out New numbers
658.8	Management of marketing Revised
659.144	Advertising in digital media New number
704.94343	[Iconography of] Flowers New number
736.96	Sand sculpture New number

*Introduced in an interim update prior to the publication of Edition 22

745.514	Woodburning (Pyrography) New number
745.59416	[Decorative objects related to specific] Holidays New number and subdivisions*
775	Digital photography New number
776	Computer art (Digital art) Relocated from 709.04 and expanded
794.72 794.73	Billiards Pocket billiards Revised and expanded*
796.046	Extreme sports New number*
796.5224	Sport climbing New number*
796.67	Street luge racing New number
796.939	Snowboarding New number*
810–890	Literatures of specific languages and language families Extended application of standard literary periods for affiliated literatures, i.e., for literature in English by authors not from the U.S., Canada, or Europe; and for literature in French, Spanish, and Portuguese by authors not from Europe*
839.5 839.6 839.7 839.8	North Germanic literatures (Nordic literatures) Old Norse (Old Icelandic), Icelandic, Faeroese literatures Swedish literature Danish and Norwegian literatures Revised*
891.469	Konkani literature New number*
910.46	Facilities for travelers Relocated from 647.94. Similar development at 06 in the 913–919 add table
936	Europe north and west of Italian Peninsula to ca. 499 New numbers for historical periods of Europe

*Introduced in an interim update prior to the publication of Edition 22

939.4	Middle East to 640
939.7	North Africa to ca. 640 New numbers for historical periods
940–990	General history of modern world, of extraterrestrial worlds New historical periods introduced throughout 940–990, e.g., 973.93 [United States in] 2001–
940.5318	Holocaust Expanded*
940.542	[World War II] Campaigns and battles by theater Revised and expanded
943	Central Europe Germany Numbers for historical periods revised and expanded*
945.85	Malta New numbers for historical periods*
948	Scandinavia Numbers for historical periods revised and expanded*
949.12	Iceland Numbers for historical periods revised and expanded*
951.2506	[Hong Kong in] 1997– New number*
951.26	Macau New numbers for historical periods*
959.6	Cambodia Numbers for historical periods revised and expanded*
959.87	East Timor Relocated from 959.86*
963.5	Eritrea Numbers for historical periods revised and expanded*
985	Peru
987	Venezuela Numbers for historical periods revised and expanded

*Introduced in an interim update prior to the publication of Edition 22

Introduction to the Dewey Decimal Classification

About the Introduction

1.1 This Introduction explains the basic principles and structure of the Dewey Decimal Classification (DDC) system.

1.2 The Introduction is intended to be used in conjunction with the Glossary and the Manual. The Glossary defines terms used in the Introduction and elsewhere in the Classification. The Manual offers advice on classifying in difficult areas, and explains how to choose between related numbers.

Classification: What It Is and What It Does

2.1 *Classification* provides a system for organizing knowledge. Classification may be used to organize knowledge represented in any form, e.g., books, documents, electronic resources.

2.2 *Notation* is the system of symbols used to represent the classes in a classification system. In the Dewey Decimal Classification, the notation is expressed in Arabic numerals. The notation gives both the unique meaning of the class and its relation to other classes. The notation provides a universal language to identify the class and related classes, regardless of the fact that different words or languages may be used to describe the class.

History, Current Use, and Development of the Dewey Decimal Classification

3.1 The Dewey Decimal Classification is a general knowledge organization tool that is continuously revised to keep pace with knowledge. The system was conceived by Melvil Dewey in 1873 and first published in 1876.

3.2 The DDC is published in full and abridged editions by OCLC Online Computer Library Center, Inc. The abridged edition is a logical truncation of the notational and structural hierarchy of the corresponding full edition on which it is based, and is intended for general collections of 20,000 titles or less. Both editions are issued in print and electronic versions; the electronic versions are updated frequently and contain additional index entries and mapped vocabulary. OCLC owns all copyright rights in the Dewey Decimal Classification, and licenses the system for a variety of uses.

3.3 The DDC is the most widely used classification system in the world. Libraries in more than 135 countries use the DDC to organize and provide access to their collections, and DDC numbers are featured in the national bibliographies of more than 60 countries. Libraries of every type apply Dewey numbers on a daily basis and share these numbers through a variety of means (including WorldCat, the OCLC Online

Union Catalog). Dewey is also used for other purposes, e.g., as a browsing mechanism for resources on the web.

3.4 The DDC has been translated into over thirty languages. Translations of recent full and abridged editions of the DDC are completed or underway in Arabic, Chinese, French, German, Greek, Hebrew, Icelandic, Italian, Korean, Norwegian, Russian, Spanish, and Vietnamese.

3.5 One of Dewey's great strengths is that the system is developed and maintained in a national bibliographic agency, the Library of Congress. The Dewey editorial office is located in the Decimal Classification Division of the Library of Congress, where classification specialists annually assign over 110,000 DDC numbers to records for works cataloged by the Library. Having the editorial office within the Decimal Classification Division enables the editors to detect trends in the literature that must be incorporated into the Classification. The editors prepare proposed schedule revisions and expansions, and forward the proposals to the Decimal Classification Editorial Policy Committee (EPC) for review and recommended action.

3.6 EPC is a ten-member international board whose main function is to advise the editors and OCLC on matters relating to changes, innovations, and the general development of the Classification. EPC represents the interests of DDC users; its members come from national, public, special, and academic libraries, and from library schools.

Overview of the Dewey Decimal Classification

CONCEPTUAL FRAMEWORK

4.1 The DDC is built on sound principles that make it ideal as a general knowledge organization tool: meaningful notation in universally recognized Arabic numerals, well-defined categories, well-developed hierarchies, and a rich network of relationships among topics. In the DDC, basic classes are organized by disciplines or fields of study. At the broadest level, the DDC is divided into ten *main classes,* which together cover the entire world of knowledge. Each main class is further divided into ten *divisions,* and each division into ten *sections* (not all the numbers for the divisions and sections have been used).

4.2 The main structure of the DDC is presented in the *DDC Summaries* in the beginning of volume 2. The *first summary* contains the ten main classes. The *second summary* contains the hundred divisions. The *third summary* contains the thousand sections. The headings associated with the numbers in the summaries have been edited for browsing purposes, and do not necessarily match the complete headings found in the schedules.

4.3 The ten main classes are:

000	Computer science, information & general works
100	Philosophy & psychology
200	Religion
300	Social sciences
400	Language
500	Science
600	Technology
700	Arts & recreation
800	Literature
900	History & geography

4.4 Class 000 is the most general class, and is used for works not limited to any one specific discipline, e.g., encyclopedias, newspapers, general periodicals. This class is also used for certain specialized disciplines that deal with knowledge and information, e.g., computer science, library and information science, journalism. Each of the other main classes (100–900) comprises a major discipline or group of related disciplines.

4.5 Class 100 covers philosophy, parapsychology and occultism, and psychology.

4.6 Class 200 is devoted to religion. Both philosophy and religion deal with the ultimate nature of existence and relationships, but religion treats these topics within the context of revelation, deity, and worship.

4.7 Class 300 covers the social sciences. Class 300 includes sociology, anthropology, statistics, political science, economics, law, public administration, social problems and services, education, commerce, communications, transportation, and customs.

4.8 Class 400 comprises language, linguistics, and specific languages. Literature, which is arranged by language, is found in 800.

4.9 Class 500 is devoted to the natural sciences and mathematics. The natural sciences describe and attempt to explain the world in which we live.

4.10 Class 600 is technology. Technology consists of utilizing the sciences to harness the natural world and its resources for the benefit of humankind.

4.11 Class 700 covers the arts: art in general, fine and decorative arts, music, and the performing arts. Recreation, including sports and games, is also classed in 700.

4.12 Class 800 covers literature, and includes rhetoric, prose, poetry, drama, etc. Folk literature is classed with customs in 300.

4.13 Class 900 is devoted to history and geography. When a work is a story of events that have transpired or an account of existing conditions in a particular place or region, it is classed in 900. A history of a specific subject is classed with the subject.

4.14 Since the parts of the DDC are arranged by discipline, not subject, a subject may appear in more than one class. For example, "clothing" has aspects that fall under several disciplines. The psychological influence of clothing belongs in 155.95 as part of the discipline of psychology; customs associated with clothing belong in 391 as part of the discipline of customs; and clothing in the sense of fashion design belongs in 746.92 as part of the discipline of the arts.

Notation

4.15 Arabic numerals are used to represent each class in the DDC. The first digit in each three-digit number represents the main class. For example, 500 represents science. The second digit in each three-digit number indicates the division. For example, 500 is used for general works on the sciences, 510 for mathematics, 520 for astronomy, 530 for physics. The third digit in each three-digit number indicates the section. Thus, 530 is used for general works on physics, 531 for classical mechanics, 532 for fluid mechanics, 533 for gas mechanics. The DDC uses the convention that no number should have fewer than three digits; zeros are used to fill out numbers.

4.16 A *decimal point,* or dot, follows the third digit in a class number, after which division by ten continues to the specific degree of classification needed. The dot is not a decimal point in the mathematical sense, but a psychological pause to break the monotony of numerical digits and to ease the transcription and copying of the class number. A number should never end in a 0 anywhere to the right of the decimal point.

Principle of Hierarchy

4.17 *Hierarchy* in the DDC is expressed through structure and notation.

4.18 *Structural hierarchy* means that all topics (aside from the ten main classes) are part of all the broader topics above them. The corollary is also true: whatever is true of the whole is true of the parts. This important concept is called *hierarchical force.* Certain notes regarding the nature of a class hold true for all the subordinate classes, including logically subordinate topics classed at coordinate numbers. (For a discussion of notes with hierarchical force, see paragraphs 7.10–7.17 and 7.20–7.22.)

Because of the principle of hierarchical force, hierarchical notes are usually given only once—at the highest level of application. For example, the scope note at 700 applies to 730, to 736, and to 736.4. The words "Description, critical appraisal . . ." found in the scope note at 700 also govern the critical appraisal of carving in 736 Carving and carvings, and of wood carving in 736.4 Wood. In order to understand the structural hierarchy, the classifier must read up and down the schedules (and remember to turn the page).

4.19 *Notational hierarchy* is expressed by length of notation. Numbers at any given level are usually *subordinate* to a class whose notation is one digit shorter; *coordinate* with a class whose notation has the same number of significant digits; and *superordinate* to a class with numbers one or more digits longer. The underlined digits in the following example demonstrate this notational hierarchy:

600	Technology (Applied sciences)
630	Agriculture and related technologies
636	Animal husbandry
636.7	Dogs
636.8	Cats

"Dogs" and "Cats" are more specific than (i.e., are subordinate to) "Animal husbandry"; they are equally specific as (i.e., are coordinate with) each other; and "Animal husbandry" is less specific than (i.e., is superordinate to) "Dogs" and "Cats."

4.20 Sometimes, other devices must be used to express the hierarchy when it is not possible or desirable to do so through the notation. Special headings, notes, and entries indicate relationships among topics that violate notational hierarchy. A dual heading is used when a subordinate topic is the major part of the subject; the subject as a whole and the subordinate topic as a whole share the same number (e.g., 599.9 Hominidae Homo sapiens). A see reference leads the classifier to subdivisions of a subject located outside the notational hierarchy. A centered entry (so called because its numbers, heading, and notes appear in the center of the page) constitutes a major departure from notational hierarchy. A centered entry is used to indicate and relate structurally a span of numbers that together form a single concept for which there is no specific hierarchical notation available. In the DDC, centered entries are always flagged typographically by the symbol > in the number column.

Classifying with the DDC

5.1 Classifying a work with the DDC requires determining the subject, the disciplinary focus, and, if applicable, the approach or form. (For a discussion of approach or form, see paragraph 8.3.)

DETERMINING THE SUBJECT OF A WORK

5.2 Classifying a work properly depends first upon determining the subject of the work in hand. A key element in determining the subject is the author's intent.

(A) The title is often a clue to the subject, but should never be the sole source of analysis. For example, *Who Moved My Cheese?* is a work on coping with change, not a work related to the culinary arts. Likewise, a title with specific terms that are subdivisions of a field may in fact use such terms symbolically to represent the broader topic. For example, titles containing terms like chromosomes, DNA, double helix, genes, and genomes may use these terms symbolically to represent the whole subject of biochemical genetics.

(B) The table of contents may list the main topics discussed. Chapter headings may substitute for the absence of a table of contents. Chapter subheadings often prove useful.

(C) The preface or introduction usually states the author's purpose. If a foreword is provided, it often indicates the subject of the work and suggests the place of the work in the development of thought on the subject. The book jacket or accompanying material may include a summary of the subject content.

(D) A scan of the text itself may provide further guidance or confirm preliminary subject analysis.

(E) Bibliographical references and index entries are sources of subject information.

(F) Cataloging copy from centralized cataloging services is often helpful by providing subject headings, classification numbers, and notes. Such copy appears in online services, and on the verso of the title page of many U.S., Australian, British, and Canadian books as part of Cataloging-in-Publication (CIP) data. Data from these sources should be verified with the book in hand, since the cataloging record is based on prepublication information.

(G) Occasionally, consultation of outside sources such as reviews, reference works, and subject experts may be required to determine the subject of the work.

DETERMINING THE DISCIPLINE OF A WORK

5.3 After determining the subject, the classifier must then select the proper discipline, or field of study, of the work.

5.4 The guiding principle of the DDC is that a work is classed in the discipline for which it is intended, rather than the discipline from which the work derives. This enables works that are used together to be found together. For example, a general work by a zoologist on agricultural pest control should be classed in agriculture, not zoology, along with other works on agricultural pest control.

5.5 Once the subject has been determined, and information on the discipline has been found, the classifier will turn to the schedules. The summaries are a good means of mental navigation. The headings and notes in the schedules themselves and the Manual provide much guidance. The Relative Index may help by suggesting the disciplines in which a subject is normally treated. (For a discussion of the summaries, see paragraph 7.1; for a discussion of the Manual, see paragraphs 10.1–10.6; for a discussion of the Relative Index, see paragraphs 11.1–11.15.)

5.6 If the Relative Index is used, the classifier must still rely on the structure of the Classification and various aids throughout to arrive at the proper place to classify a work. Even the most promising Relative Index citations must be verified in the schedules; the schedules are the only place where all the information about coverage and use of the numbers may be found.

More Than One Subject in the Same Discipline

5.7 A work may include multiple subjects treated separately or in relation to one another from the viewpoint of a single discipline. Use the following guidelines in determining the best placement for the work:

(A) Class a work dealing with interrelated subjects with the subject that is being acted upon. This is called the *rule of application*, and takes precedence over any other rule. For instance, class an analytical work dealing with Shakespeare's influence on Keats with Keats. Similarly, class a work on the influence of the Great Depression on 20th century American art with American art.

(B) Class a work on two subjects with the subject receiving fuller treatment.

(C) If two subjects receive equal treatment, and are not used to introduce or explain one another, class the work with the subject whose number comes first in the DDC schedules. This is called the *first-of-two rule*. For example, a history dealing equally with the United States and Japan, in which the United States is discussed first and is given first in the title, is classed with the history of Japan because 952 Japan precedes 973 United States.

Sometimes, specific instructions are given to use numbers that do not come first in the schedules. For example, at 598, the note "class comprehensive works on warm-blooded vertebrates in 599" tells the classifier to ignore the first-of-two rule and class a work on birds (598) and mammals (599) in 599, which is the comprehensive number for warm-blooded vertebrates.

Also disregard the first-of-two rule when the two topics are the two major subdivisions of a subject. For example, collection systems (628.142) and distribution systems (628.144) taken together constitute 628.14 Collection and distribution systems. Works covering both of these topics are classed in 628.14 (not 628.142).

(For a discussion of the first-of-two rule versus preference order, see paragraph 9.6; for a discussion of comprehensive numbers, see paragraphs 7.17 and 7.20–7.21.)

(D) Class a work on three or more subjects that are all subdivisions of a broader subject in the first higher number that includes them all (unless one subject is treated more fully than the others). This is called the *rule of three*. For example, a history of Portugal (946.9), Sweden (948.5), and Greece (949.5) is classed with the history of Europe (940).

(E) Subdivisions beginning with zero should be avoided if there is a choice between 0 and 1–9 at the same point in the hierarchy of the notation. Similarly, subdivisions beginning with 00 should be avoided when there is a choice between 00 and 0. This is called the *rule of zero*. For example, a biography of an American Methodist missionary in China belongs in 266 Missions. The content of the work can be expressed in three different numbers:

266.0092	biography of a missionary
266.02373051	foreign missions of the United States in China
266.76092	biography of a United Methodist Church missionary

The last number is used since it has no zero at the fourth position.

MORE THAN ONE DISCIPLINE

5.8 Treating a subject from the point of view of more than one discipline is different from treating several subjects in one discipline. Use the following guidelines in determining the best placement for the work:

(A) Use the *interdisciplinary number* provided in the schedules or Relative Index if one is given. An important consideration in using such an interdisciplinary number is that the work must contain significant material on the discipline in which the interdisciplinary number is found. For example, 305.231 (a sociology number) is provided for interdisciplinary works on child development. However, if a work that is interdisciplinary with respect to child development gives little emphasis to social development and a great deal of emphasis to the psychological and physical development of the child (155.4 and 612.65, respectively), class it in 155.4 (the first number in the schedules of the next two obvious choices). In short, interdisciplinary numbers are not absolute; they are to be used only when applicable. (For a discussion of interdisciplinary numbers, see paragraphs 7.17, 7.20–7.21, and 11.8–11.9.)

(B) Class works not given an interdisciplinary number in the discipline given the fullest treatment in the work. For example, a work dealing with both the scientific and the engineering principles of electrodynamics is classed in 537.6 if the engineering aspects are introduced primarily for illustrative purposes, but in 621.31 if the basic scientific theories are only preliminary to the author's exposition of engineering principles and practices.

(C) When classifying interdisciplinary works, do not overlook the possibilities of main class 000 Computer science, information & general works, e.g., 080 for a collection of interviews of famous people from various disciplines.

Any other situation is treated in the same fashion as those found in the instructions at More Than One Subject in the Same Discipline (paragraph 5.7).

Table of Last Resort

5.9 When several numbers have been found for the work in hand, and each seems as good as the next, the following table of last resort (in order of preference) may be used as a guideline in the absence of any other rule:

Table of last resort

(1) Kinds of things
(2) Parts of things
(3) Materials from which things, kinds, or parts are made
(4) Properties of things, kinds, parts, or materials
(5) Processes within things, kinds, parts, or materials
(6) Operations upon things, kinds, parts, or materials
(7) Instrumentalities for performing such operations

For example, surveillance by border patrols could be classed in either 363.285 Border patrols, or 363.232 Patrol and surveillance. Choose 363.285 since border patrols are a kind of police service, while patrol and surveillance are processes performed by police services.

5.10 Do not apply this table or any other guideline if it appears to disregard the author's intention and emphasis.

How DDC 22 Is Arranged

6.1 DDC 22 is composed of the following major parts in four volumes:

Volume 1

(A) New Features in Edition 22: A brief explanation of the special features and changes in DDC 22

(B) Introduction: A description of the DDC and how to use it

(C) Glossary: Short definitions of terms used in the DDC

(D) Index to the Introduction and Glossary

(E) Manual: A guide to the use of the DDC that is made up primarily of extended discussions of problem areas in the application of the DDC. Information in the Manual is arranged by the numbers in the tables and schedules

(F) Tables: Six numbered tables of notation that can be added to class numbers to provide greater specificity

(G) Lists that compare Editions 21 and 22: Relocations and Discontinuations; Reused Numbers

Volume 2

(H) DDC Summaries: The top three levels of the DDC

(I) Schedules: The organization of knowledge from 000–599

Volume 3

(J) Schedules: The organization of knowledge from 600–999

Volume 4

(K) Relative Index: An alphabetical list of subjects with the disciplines in which they are treated subarranged alphabetically under each entry

Key Features of the Schedules and Tables

SUMMARIES

7.1 *Summaries* provide an overview of the structure of classes. Three types of summaries appear in the DDC:

(A) DDC Summaries, the summaries of the top three levels of the DDC, are found in front of the schedules in volume 2. (For a discussion of DDC Summaries, see paragraphs 4.2–4.13.)

(B) Two-level summaries are provided for each main class and division of the schedules and main numbers of Table 2 with subdivisions that extend beyond forty pages. See the summaries at the beginning of Table 2 —4 Europe Western Europe and 370 Education for examples of two-level summaries.

(C) Single-level summaries in the schedules and tables provide an overview of classes whose subdivisions cover between four and forty pages. For example, 382 International commerce (Foreign trade) has the following summary:

SUMMARY

382.01–.09	**Standard subdivisions**
.1	**General topics of international commerce**
.3	**Commercial policy**
.4	**Specific products and services**
.5	**Import trade**
.6	**Export trade**
.7	**Tariff policy**
.9	**Trade agreements**

ENTRIES

7.2 Entries in the schedules and tables are composed of a DDC number in the number column (the column at the left margin), a heading describing the class that the number represents, and often one or more notes. DDC numbers are listed in groups of three digits for ease of reading and copying. All entries (numbers, headings, and notes) should be read in the context of the hierarchy. (For a discussion of the principle of hierarchy, see paragraphs 4.17–4.20.)

7.3 The first three digits of schedule numbers (main classes, divisions, sections) appear only once in the number column, when first used. They are repeated at the top of each page where their subdivisions continue. Subordinate numbers appear in the number column, beginning with a decimal point, with the initial three digits understood.

7.4 Table numbers are given in full in the number column of the tables, and are never used alone. There are six numbered tables in DDC 22:

T1 Standard Subdivisions

T2 Geographic Areas, Historical Periods, Persons

T3 Subdivisions for the Arts, for Individual Literatures, for Specific Literary Forms

T3A Subdivisions for Works by or about Individual Authors

T3B Subdivisions for Works by or about More than One Author

T3C Notation to Be Added Where Instructed in Table 3B, 700.4, 791.4, 808–809

T4 Subdivisions of Individual Languages and Language Families

T5 Ethnic and National Groups

T6 Languages

Except for notation from Table 1 (which may be added to any number unless there is an instruction in the schedules or tables to the contrary), table notation may be added only as instructed in the schedules and tables. (For a detailed discussion of the use of the six tables, see paragraphs 8.3–8.18.)

7.5 When a subordinate topic is a major part of a number, it is sometimes given as a part of a dual heading. For example:

—72 Middle America Mexico

599.9 Hominidae Homo sapiens

7.6 Some numbers in the schedules and tables are enclosed in parentheses or square brackets. Numbers and notes in parentheses provide options to standard practice. Numbers in square brackets represent topics that have been relocated or discontinued, or are unassigned. Square brackets are also used for standard subdivision concepts that are represented in another location. Bracketed numbers should never be used. (For a discussion of options, see paragraphs 12.1–12.7; for a discussion of relocations and discontinuations, see paragraphs 7.24–7.25; for a discussion of bracketed standard subdivisions, see paragraph 7.26.)

7.7 Standard subdivisions are also bracketed under a *hook number,* that is, a number that has no meaning in itself, but is used to introduce specific examples of a topic. Hook numbers have headings that begin with "Miscellaneous," "Other," or "Specific"; and do not contain add notes, including notes, or class-here notes. For example:

652.302 Specific levels of skill

[.302 01–.302 09] Standard subdivisions

Do not use; class in 652.3001–652.3009

NOTES

7.8 Notes are important because they supply information that is not obvious in the notational hierarchy or in the heading with regard to order, structure, subordination, and other matters. Notes may appear in the record for a number or a span of numbers. Notes may also appear at the beginning of a table. Footnotes are used for instructions that apply to multiple subdivisions of a class, or to a topic within a class. Individual entries in the Manual are also considered notes.

7.9 Notes in the schedules and tables generally appear in the following order: revision, former-heading, definition, number-built, standard-subdivisions-are-added, variant-name, scope, including, class-here, arrange, add (including subdivisions-are-added), build, preference, discontinued, relocation, class-elsewhere, see-reference, see-also reference, see-Manual, and option notes.

7.10 The notes below do the following: (A) describe what is found in the class and its subdivisions; (B) identify topics in *standing room*, i.e., topics with insufficient literature to have their own number; (C) describe what is found in other classes; and (D) explain changes in the schedules and tables. Other notes are described in the sections on number building (paragraphs 8.1–8.22), citation and preference order (paragraphs 9.1–9.6), the Manual (paragraphs 10.1–10.6), and options (paragraphs 12.1–12.5).

Notes in categories (A) and (C) have hierarchical force (i.e., are applicable to all the subdivisions of a particular number). Those in category (B) do not have hierarchical force.

(A) Notes That Describe What Is Found in a Class

7.11 *Definition notes* indicate the meaning of a term in the heading. For example:

364 Criminology

Crime and its alleviation

7.12 *Scope notes* indicate whether the meaning of the number is narrower or broader than is apparent from the heading. For example:

700 The arts Fine and decorative arts

Description, critical appraisal, techniques, procedures, apparatus, equipment, materials of the fine, decorative, literary, performing, recreational arts

7.13 *Number-built notes* identify and explain the source of built numbers included in the schedules and tables. Built numbers are occasionally included in the schedules or tables to provide additional information or to indicate exceptions to regular add instructions. For example:

353.132 63 Foreign service

Number built according to instructions under 352–354

Class here consular and diplomatic services

7.14 *Former-heading notes* are given only when the heading associated with a class number in the previous edition has been altered to such a degree that the new heading bears little or no resemblance to the previous heading, even though the meaning of the number has remained substantially the same. For example:

659.131 5 Industrial advertising

Former heading: Advertising directed to vocational uses

7.15 *Variant-name notes* are used for synonyms or near synonyms. For example:

332.32 Savings and loan associations

Variant names: building and loan associations, building societies, home loan associations, mortgage institutions

7.16 *Class-here notes* list major topics in a class. These topics may be broader or narrower than the heading, overlap it, or define another way of looking at essentially the same material. Topics in class-here notes are considered to *approximate the whole* of the class. For example:

371.192 Parent-school relations

Class here parent participation in schools; comprehensive works on teacher-parent relations

Standard subdivisions may be added for any topic in a class-here note. (For a detailed discussion of the use of standard subdivisions for concepts that approximate the whole of a class, see paragraphs 8.3–8.10 and the beginning of Table 1.)

7.17 Class-here notes are also used to indicate where interdisciplinary and comprehensive works are classed. *Interdisciplinary works* treat a subject from the perspective of more than one discipline. For example:

391 Costume and personal appearance

Class here interdisciplinary works on costume, clothing, fashion

Comprehensive works treat a subject from various points of view within a single discipline. Comprehensive works may be stated or implied in a class-here note. For example:

641.815 Breads and bread-like foods

Class here comprehensive works on baked goods *(stated)*

—411 5 Highland

Class here Scottish Highlands *(implied)*

(B) Including Notes (Notes That Identify Topics in Standing Room)

7.18 *Including notes* identify topics that have "standing room" in the number where the note is found. Standing room numbers provide a location for topics with relatively few works written about them, but whose literature may grow in the future, at which time they may be assigned their own number. For example:

362.16 Extended care medical facilities

Including convalescent homes, sanatoriums for persons suffering from chronic diseases

Standard subdivisions cannot be added for topics in standing room, nor are other number-building techniques allowed.

7.19 Entries in the taxonomic schedules in 579–590 may have two including notes. The first including note contains the scientific taxonomic names at or above the level of family. The second one contains common and genus names. For example:

593.55 Hydrozoa

Including Chondrophora, Hydroida, Milleporina, Pteromedusae, Siphonophora, Stylasterina, Trachylina

Including hydras, Portuguese man-of-war

(C) Notes That Describe What Is Found in Other Classes

7.20 *Class-elsewhere notes* lead the classifier to interrelated topics, or distinguish among numbers in the same notational hierarchy. They are used to show preference order, to lead to the comprehensive or interdisciplinary number, to override the first-of-two rule, or to lead to broader or narrower topics in the same hierarchical array that might otherwise be overlooked. They may point to a specific number, or to a concept scattered throughout the schedules. All notes that begin with the word "class" are class-elsewhere notes, except when they begin with "class here." For example:

791.43 Motion pictures

Class photographic aspects of motion pictures in 778.53; class made-for-TV movies, videotapes of motion pictures in 791.45

370.15 Educational psychology

Class interdisciplinary works on psychology in 150. Class psychology of a specific topic in education with the topic, plus notation 019 from Table 1, e.g., psychology of special education 371.9019

155.4 Child psychology

Class interdisciplinary works on child development in 305.231

7.21 *See references* lead from a stated or implied comprehensive number for a concept to the component (subordinate) parts of that concept in a different notational hierarchy. See references also lead from the interdisciplinary number for a concept to treatment of the concept in other disciplines. A see reference may point to a specific number, or to a concept scattered throughout the schedules. Each see reference begins with the word "For" and appears in italics. For example:

577.7 Marine ecology

Class here saltwater ecology

For salt lake ecology, see 577.639; for saltwater wetland and seashore ecology, see 577.69

305.4 Women

Class here interdisciplinary works on women, on females

For a specific aspect of women not provided for here, see the aspect, e.g., women's suffrage 324.623, legal status of women 346.0134

Throughout Table 2, see references (often in footnote form) lead from the implied comprehensive number for a jurisdiction, region, or feature to its subordinate parts in other classes. For example:

—411 5 Highland

Class here *Scottish Highlands

*For a specific part of this jurisdiction, region, or feature, see the part and follow instructions under —4–9

7.22 *See-also references* lead the classifier to related topics. They are reminders that minor differences in wording and context can imply differences in classification. Each see-also reference appears in italics. For example:

584.3 Liliidae

Class here Liliales, lilies

For Orchidales, see 584.4

See also 583.29 for water lilies

(D) Notes That Explain Changes or Irregularities in the Schedules and Tables

7.23 *Revision notes* warn users that there have been changes in the subdivisions of a class since the previous edition. A *complete* or *extensive revision* is always introduced by a revision note that appears first under the heading of the class affected. (There are no complete or extensive revision notes in DDC 22.)

7.24 *Discontinued notes* indicate that all or part of the contents of a number have been moved to a more general number in the same hierarchy, or have been dropped entirely. For example:

[306.853] Suburban family

Number discontinued; class in 306.85

616.852 23 Panic disorder

Use of this number for comprehensive works on anxiety disorders discontinued; class in 616.8522

7.25 *Relocation notes* state that all or part of the contents of a number have been moved to a different number. For example:

[624.5] Suspension and cable-stayed bridges

Relocated to 624.23

381.149 Discount stores

Discount stores that are outlet stores relocated to 381.15

The former number is usually given at the new number, either in the heading or in the appropriate note. For example:

624.23 Suspension and cable-stayed bridges [*both formerly* 624.5]

381.15 Outlet stores

Class here discount stores that are outlet stores [*formerly* 381.149] . . .

7.26 *Do-not-use notes* instruct the classifier not to use all or part of the regular standard subdivision notation or an add table provision, but instead to use a special provision or standard subdivision notation at a broader number. When the whole standard subdivision is removed from use, the note appears under a bracketed standard subdivision; when only part of the standard subdivision is *displaced*, the part displaced is specified. For example:

[374.809] Historical, geographic, persons treatment

Do not use; class in 374.9

320.409 Historical and persons treatment

Do not use for geographic treatment; class in 320.41–320.49

Number Building

8.1 The classifier will often find that to arrive at a precise number for a work it is necessary to build or synthesize a number that is not specifically listed in the schedules. Such *built numbers* allow for greater depth of content analysis. They are used only when instructions in the schedules make them possible (except for standard subdivisions, which are discussed in paragraphs 8.3–8.10). Number building begins with a base number (always stated in the instruction note) to which another number is added.

8.2 There are four sources of notation for building numbers: (A) Table 1 Standard Subdivisions; (B) Tables 2–6; (C) other parts of the schedules; and (D) add tables in the schedules.

(A) Adding Standard Subdivisions from Table 1

8.3 A *standard subdivision* represents a recurring physical form (such as a dictionary, periodical, or index) or approach (such as history or research) and thus is applicable to any subject or discipline that covers or approximates the whole of the meaning of the number. Here are a few examples with the standard subdivision concept underlined (in some cases an extra 0 precedes the standard subdivision according to instructions found in the schedules):

150.5	Periodical on psychology
230.003	Dictionary of Christianity
340.02573	Directory of lawyers in the U.S.
401	Philosophy of language
507.8	Use of apparatus and equipment in the study and teaching of science, e.g., science fair projects
624.0285	Computer applications in civil engineering
796.912092	Biography of a figure skater
808.0071	Teaching of rhetoric

Further instructions on using Table 1 are found at the beginning of Table 1. See also Manual notes on selected standard subdivisions.

8.4 Standard subdivisions are not usually listed in the schedules except where needed to fill out three-digit numbers, e.g., 605 Serial publications, and in a few other instances. Standard subdivisions may be listed in the schedules when the subdivisions have special meanings, when extended notation is required for the topic in question, or when notes are required. The rest of the standard subdivisions from Table 1 may be used with their regular meanings.

8.5 Notation from Table 1 Standard Subdivisions may be added to any number in the schedules unless there is a specific instruction to the contrary. The classifier should never use more than one zero in applying a standard subdivision unless instructed to do so. If more than one zero is needed, the number of zeros is always indicated in the schedules. When using standard subdivisions with numbers built by adding from Tables 2–6 or other parts of the schedules, be sure to check the table or schedule used for the segment preceding the standard subdivision for special instructions on the number of zeros.

8.6 Do not add multiple standard subdivisions to the same number except when specifically instructed to do so, and in the following instances. A second standard subdivision may be added to standard subdivisions that have changed or extended meanings. For example, notation 03 from Table 1, the standard subdivision for encyclopedias, may be added to 370.15 Educational psychology to represent encyclopedias of educational psychology 370.1503 because the regular meaning of 370.15 (scientific principles) has been discontinued to 370.1 and replaced by an extended meaning of the standard subdivision for psychological principles at this number. When standard subdivisions are displaced to nonzero numbers (usually for geographic treatment), the full range of standard subdivisions may be added, e.g., the management of penal institutions in Great Britain 365.941068.

8.7 Standard subdivisions should not be used where redundant, i.e., where the subdivision means the same as the base number, or where application of the standard subdivision would needlessly segregate material by aspects not emphasized by the author. For example, do not add notation 024694, which represents the subject for carpenters, to topics in 694, the number for carpentry, since works on a subject are written primarily for its practitioners. Likewise, do not add notation 0905, which represents the state-of-the-art, to general works on a subject because most users will expect to find such works in the main number. Special care should be taken in adding standard subdivisions to built numbers, since the standard subdivision applies to the whole number and not just to part of the number.

8.8 The table of preference at the beginning of Table 1 yields to two other rules, the rule of application and the rule of zero. By the rule of application, teaching financial management in hospital administration is classed in 362.110681, not 362.11071, even though notation 07 is above notation 068 in the table of preference. The rule of zero overrides the table of preference when standard subdivisions are displaced to nonzero positions, e.g., management of prisons in Great Britain 365.941068, not 365.068 as would be the case if prisons in Great Britain were classed in 365.0941. (For a discussion of the rule of application and rule of zero, see paragraph 5.7; for a discussion of displaced standard subdivisions, see paragraphs 7.26 and 8.6.)

8.9 *The most important caveat with respect to standard subdivisions is that they are added only for works that cover or approximate the whole of the subject of the number.* For example, a work on black widow spiders of California should be classed in the number for spiders 595.44 (not 595.4409794, the number for spiders in California). The classifier should not attempt to specify California because black widow spiders do not approximate the whole universe of spiders in California, and there is not a specific number available for black widows. Likewise, class a work on the De Havilland 98 Mosquito (a specific British World War II fighter-bomber) in the number for fighter-bombers 623.7463 (not 623.7463094109044, the number for British fighter-bombers in World War II).

8.10 *Standard-subdivisions-are-added notes* indicate which topics in a multiterm heading may have standard subdivisions added for them because the designated topics are considered to *approximate the whole* of the subject. For example:

639.2 Commercial fishing, whaling, sealing

Standard subdivisions are added for commercial fishing, whaling, sealing together; for commercial fishing alone

Standard-subdivisions-are-added notes do not have hierarchical force.

(B) Adding from Tables 2–6

8.11 The classifier may be instructed to add notation from Tables 2–6 to a base number from the schedules or to a number from a table. A summary of the use of each table follows. Further instructions on using Tables 2–6 are found at the beginning of each table. See also the Manual notes for Tables 2–6.

8.12 *Table 2 Geographic Areas, Historical Periods, Persons*. The major use of Table 2 is with notation 09 from Table 1, where it can be added to every number in the schedule unless there are specific instructions to the contrary. For example, reading instruction in the primary schools of Australia is 372.40994 (372.4 Reading instruction in primary schools + 09 Historical, geographic, persons treatment from Table 1 + 94 Australia from Table 2). Notation from Table 2 is also added through the use of other standard subdivisions from Table 1 (e.g., standard subdivisions 025, 074).

8.13 Area notation is sometimes added directly to schedule numbers, but only when specified in a note. For example:

373.3–373.9 Secondary education in specific continents, countries, localities

Add to base number 373 notation 3–9 from Table 2, e.g., secondary schools of Australia 373.94

8.14 *Table 3 Subdivisions for the Arts, for Individual Literatures, for Specific Literary Forms.* These subdivisions are used in class 800 as instructed, usually following numbers for specific languages in 810–890. Table 3C subdivisions are also added as instructed to numbers in Table 3B, 700.4, 791.4, and 808–809.

8.15 *Table 4 Subdivisions of Individual Languages and Language Families.* These subdivisions are used as instructed in class 400, following numbers for designated specific languages or language families in 420–490.

8.16 *Table 5 Ethnic and National Groups.* Notation from Table 5 is added through the use of standard subdivision 089 from Table 1, e.g., Ceramic arts of Chinese artists throughout the world is 738.089951 (738 Ceramic arts + 089 Ethnic and national groups from Table 1 + 951 Chinese from Table 5).

8.17 Table 5 notation may also be added directly to schedule numbers, but only when specified in a note. For example:

155.84 Specific ethnic groups

Add to base number 155.84 notation 05–9 from Table 5, e.g., ethnopsychology of African Americans 155.8496073

8.18 *Table 6 Languages.* The major uses of Table 6 notation are to provide the basis for building a specific language number in 490 (to which notation from Table 4 is sometimes added) and to provide the basis for building a specific literature number in 890 (to which notation from Table 3 is sometimes added). Table 6 notation is also used in Table 2 under —175 Regions where specific languages predominate, and at various points in the schedules.

(C) Adding from Other Parts of the Schedules

8.19 There are many instructions to make a direct addition to a number from another part of the schedules. For example:

809.935 Literature emphasizing subjects

Add to base number 809.935 notation 001–999, e.g., religious works as literature 809.9352, biography and autobiography as literature 809.93592

In this example, the 2 in 809.9352 comes from 200 Religion, the 92 in 809.93592 from 920 Biography, genealogy, insignia.

8.20 In many cases, part of a number may be added to another number upon instruction. For example:

372.011 Elementary education for specific objectives

Add to base number 372.011 the numbers following 370.11 in 370.111–370.119, e.g., character education 372.0114

In this example, 4 comes from 370.114 Moral, ethical, character education. Sometimes numbers are taken from more than one place in the schedules; in such cases the procedure for the second addition is the same as for the first.

(D) Adding from Tables Found in the Schedules

8.21 Add tables in the schedules provide numbers to be added to designated schedule numbers (identified by a symbol and accompanying footnoted instruction); these tables must be used only as instructed. For example:

616.973 *Contact allergies

Class here allergic contact dermatitis, allergies of skin

The asterisk in the entry above leads to the following footnote: "Add as instructed under 616.1–616.9." The add table at 616.1–616.9 is used only for diseases tagged with an asterisk or for diseases in class-here notes under headings tagged with an asterisk. Notation from the add table, such as 061 Drug therapy, may be used for 616.973 Contact allergies (tagged with an asterisk) and for allergic contact dermatitis and allergies of skin (in the class-here note).

8.22 *Subdivisions-are-added notes* indicate which terms in a multiterm heading may have subdivisions applied to them. For example:

616.51 *Dermatitis, photosensitivity disorders, urticaria

Subdivisions are added for dermatitis, photosensitivity disorders, urticaria together; for dermatitis alone

Citation and Preference Order

9.1 Citation and preference order must be considered when multiple aspects or characteristics of a subject (such as age, area, gender, historical periods, national origin) are provided for in the Classification, and a single work treats more than one of them.

Citation Order

9.2 Citation order allows the classifier to build or synthesize a number using two or more characteristics (*facets*) as specified in instruction notes. Success in building a DDC number requires determining which characteristics apply to a specific work, and then determining from the instructions in the schedule the sequence in which the facets will be ordered.

9.3 Citation order is always carefully detailed in number-building instructions. For example:

909.04 History with respect to ethnic and national groups

Add to base number 909.04 notation 05–9 from Table 5, e.g., world history of Jews 909.04924; then add 0 and to the result add the numbers following 909 in 909.1–909.8, e.g., world history of Jews in 18th century 909.0492407

For a work on the world history of the Jews in the 18th century, this note stipulates the following citation order for the individual facets of the full subject: world history + specific ethnic or national group + historical period. The historical period is introduced by the *facet indicator* 0.

PREFERENCE ORDER

9.4 If there is no provision to show more than one of the aspects or characteristics, it is a matter of preference (because a choice must be made among several characteristics). Preference notes supply either an instruction or table establishing the order in which to make the choice. An example of a preference instruction is found at 305.9:

305.9 Occupational and miscellaneous groups

Unless other instructions are given, class a subject with aspects in two or more subdivisions of 305.9 in the number coming last, e.g., unemployed librarians 305.9092 (not 305.90694)

In this case, the base subject is a group of persons; the two characteristics are employment status and occupational status. The occupation of librarian (305.9092) falls after unemployed status (305.90694) in the DDC hierarchy; following the instructions in the preference note, the characteristic that must be chosen is librarian (305.9092). (For an example of a preference instruction using a class-elsewhere note, see paragraph 7.20.)

9.5 An example of a table indicating preference order is found at 305:

305 Social groups

Unless other instructions are given, observe the following table of preference, e.g., African American male youths 305.235108996073 (*not* 305.3889607300835 or 305.896073008351):

Persons with disabilities and illnesses, gifted persons	305.908
Age groups	305.2
Groups by sex	305.3–.4
Social classes	305.5
Religious groups	305.6
Ethnic and national groups	305.8
Language groups	305.7
Occupational and miscellaneous groups (*except* 305.908)	305.9

9.6 Classifiers often must distinguish between preference order instructions and the first-of-two rule in the same schedule. If the work treats two subjects, apply the first-of-two rule. If the work treats two aspects of the same subject, apply the preference order instructions. When the preference order instruction is to class with the last, the first-of-two rule and the preference order instructions may lead the classifier in opposite directions. For example, a bibliography of newspapers and pamphlets giving equal treatment to each would be classed according to the first-of-two rule in 011.33 (bibliography of pamphlets) rather than 011.35 (bibliographies of newspapers). A bibliography of microform newspapers (i.e., newspapers in microform form) would be classed according to the preference note at 011.1–011.8: "Unless other instructions are given, class a subject with aspects in two or more subdivisions of 011.1–011.8 in the number coming last . . ."; thus, the bibliography of microform newspapers would be classed in 011.36 (bibliographies of microforms) rather than 011.35 (bibliographies of newspapers). (For a discussion of the first-of-two rule, see paragraph 5.7.)

The Manual

10.1 The Manual gives advice on classifying in difficult areas, and provides guidance on choosing between related numbers.

10.2 *See-Manual references* in the schedules and tables refer the classifier to the Manual for additional information about a certain number, range of numbers, or choice among numbers. In some cases, the see-Manual reference refers only to a portion of a longer Manual note, or topic narrower than the numbers in the heading, e.g., "See Manual at 930–990: Historic preservation." The see-Manual reference is repeated in the entries for each of the numbers or number spans covered in the Manual note. For example, "See Manual at 004.21 vs. 004.22, 621.392" is listed in the entries for 004.21, 004.22, and 621.392.

10.3 Brief Manual-like notes are sometimes given directly in the schedule or table entry. For example:

631.583 Controlled-environment agriculture

Most works on use of artificial light in agriculture will be classed in 635.0483 and 635.9826

Arrangement and Format of the Manual

10.4 The Manual is arranged by table and schedule numbers, with the broadest span coming before entries for narrower spans or individual numbers. Manual notes are entered under the preferred or "if-in-doubt" number. If there is no if-in-doubt number, prefer the interdisciplinary number.

10.5 The Manual note heading summarizes the contents of the note. The terms in the Manual note headings need not match the terms associated with the same number(s) in the tables and schedules if the note is narrower than the number, or the note refers to more than one number. For example:

510

Mathematics

510, T1—0151 vs. 003, T1—011

Systems

10.6 If the Manual note is very long, or part of the note focuses on a topic narrower than the heading, subheadings may be provided. For example:

T1—068 vs. 353–354

Public administration and management in specific fields

Exceptions *(subheading)*

The Relative Index

11.1 The Relative Index is so named because it relates subjects to disciplines. In the schedules, subjects are distributed among disciplines; in the Relative Index, subjects are arranged alphabetically, with terms identifying the disciplines in which they are treated subarranged alphabetically under them. For example:

Hospitals	362.11
accounting	657.832 2
American Revolution	973.376
animal husbandry	636.083 2
architecture	725.51
armed forces	355.72
Civil War (United States)	973.776
construction	690.551
energy economics	333.796 4
institutional housekeeping	647.965 1
landscape architecture	712.7
law	344.032 11
liability law	346.031
meal service	642.56
pastoral theology	206.1
Christianity	259.411
social theology	206.762 11
Christianity	261.832 11
social welfare	362.11
World War I	940.476
World War II	940.547 6
see also Health services	

In some cases the term implies rather than states the discipline. In the example above, the discipline of architecture is listed, but the discipline of military science is implied by "armed forces."

11.2 The Relative Index is primarily an index to the DDC as a system. It includes most terms found in the schedules and tables, and terms with literary warrant for concepts represented by the schedules and tables. The Relative Index is not exhaustive. If the term sought is not found, the classifier should try a broader term, or consult the schedules and tables directly. The schedules and tables should always be consulted before a number found in the Relative Index is applied.

ARRANGEMENT AND FORMAT OF THE RELATIVE INDEX

11.3 Index entries are arranged alphabetically word by word, e.g., Birth order precedes Birthday. Entries with the same word or phrase but with different marks of punctuation are arranged in the following order:

Term
Term. Subheading
Term (Parenthetical qualifier)
Term, inverted term qualifier
Term as part of phrase

Initialisms and acronyms are entered without punctuation and are filed as if spelled as one word. Hyphens are ignored and treated as a space. Terms indented below the main headings are alphabetized in one group even though they may be a mixture of disciplines, topical subheadings, and, to a limited extent, words that form phrases or inverted phrases when combined with the main heading.

11.4 Class numbers are listed in groups of three digits for ease of reading and copying. The spaces are not part of the numbers and do not represent convenient places to abridge the number.

11.5 See-also references are used for synonyms and for references to broader terms (but only when three or more new numbers will be found at the synonym or broader term), and for references to related terms (which may provide only one or two new numbers).

11.6 See-Manual references lead the classifier to relevant discussions in the Manual.

11.7 Numbers drawn from Tables 1–6 are prefixed by T1 through T6. (For a complete listing of table names and abbreviations, see paragraph 7.4.)

INTERDISCIPLINARY NUMBERS

11.8 The first class number displayed in an index entry (the unindented term) is the number for interdisciplinary works. If the term also appears in a table, the table number is listed next, followed by other aspects of the term. The discipline of the interdisciplinary number may be repeated as a subentry if the discipline is not clear. For example:

Adult education	374
	T1—0715
federal aid	379.121 5
law	344.074
public administrative support	353.84
public support	379.114
law	344.076 85
special education	371.904 75
university extension	378.175

11.9 Interdisciplinary numbers are not provided for all topics in the Relative Index. They are omitted when the index entry is ambiguous, does not have a disciplinary focus, or lacks literary warrant. In such cases, there is no number opposite the unindented entry. For example:

Coagulation	
blood	573.159
human physiology	612.115
physiology	573.159
see also Cardiovascular system	
water supply treatment	628.162 2

(For more information on interdisciplinary numbers, see paragraphs 5.8, 7.17, 7.20–7.21.)

TERMS INCLUDED IN THE RELATIVE INDEX

11.10 The Relative Index contains most terms found in the headings and notes of the schedules and tables, and synonyms and terms with literary warrant for concepts represented by the schedules and tables. The Relative Index also contains terms for the broad concepts covered in Manual notes.

Inverted phrases are avoided, except for personal and geographic names (see paragraphs 11.12–11.13). Qualifiers are used for homonyms, ambiguous terms, and most initialisms and abbreviations. The most common use of the term may not be qualified. Disciplinary qualifiers are avoided.

11.11 The following types of names from Table 2 Geographic Areas are included in the Relative Index: (A) names of countries; (B) names of the states and provinces of most countries; (C) names of the counties of the United States; (D) names of capital cities and other important municipalities; and (E) names of certain important geographic features.

11.12 Also included in the Relative Index are the personal names of the following groups of persons: heads of state used to identify historical periods, e.g., Louis XIV; founders or revealers of religions, e.g., Muḥammad; initiators of schools of thought when used to identify the school, e.g., Smith, Adam.

11.13 Place names and other proper names are generally given in the form specified by the second edition, 2002 revision, of the *Anglo-American Cataloguing Rules (AACR2)*, based on the names established in the Library of Congress authority files. If the *AACR2* form is not the common English name, an entry is also included under the familiar form of the name.

Plants and animals are indexed under their scientific and common names.

11.14 The choice of singular form versus plural form follows ISO 999:1996, *Guidelines for the content, organization and presentation of indexes.* Count nouns are generally in the plural; noncount nouns and abstract concepts are generally in the singular. Parts of the body are in the plural only when more than one occurs in a fully formed organism (e.g., ears, hands, nose). Plants and animals follow scientific convention in the choice of singular form versus plural form, with the decision based on whether the taxonomic class has more than one member (e.g., Horses, Lion, Lipizzaner horse). Where usage varies across disciplines, the index entry reflects the form preferred in the discipline where interdisciplinary works are classified.

TERMS NOT INCLUDED IN THE RELATIVE INDEX

11.15 Terms usually not included in the Relative Index are:

(A) Phrases beginning with the adjectival form of countries, languages, nationalities, religions, e.g., English poetry, French cooking, Italian architecture, Hindu prayer books.

(B) Phrases that contain general concepts represented by standard subdivisions such as education, statistics, laboratories, and management; e.g., Art education, Educational statistics, Medical laboratories, Bank management.

When there is strong literary warrant for such a phrase heading as a sought term, it may be included in the Relative Index, e.g., English literature. When the phrase heading is a proper name or provides the only form of access to the topic, it may also be included, e.g., English Channel, French horns, Amharic literature.

Options

12.1 Some devices are required to enable the DDC to serve needs beyond those represented in the standard English-language edition. At a number of places in the schedules and tables, *options* are provided to give emphasis to an aspect in a library's collection not given preferred treatment in the standard notation. In some cases, options are also suggested to provide shorter notation for the aspect.

12.2 Options are provided throughout the Classification to emphasize jurisdiction, ethnic or national group, language, topic, or other characteristic.

12.3 Options described in notes appear in parentheses and begin with "Option:". Options that apply to the full entry appear at the end of the entry; options to a specific instruction in the entry are indented under the appropriate note. For example, the following option appears at the end of the entry for 420–490:

> (Option B: To give local emphasis and a shorter number to a specific language, place it first by use of a letter or other symbol, e.g., Arabic language 4A0 [preceding 420], for which the base number is 4A. Option A is described under 410)

12.4 Some *optional numbers* are enumerated in the schedules and tables and appear in parentheses in the number column. A special optional arrangement (222)–(224) for books of the Bible as arranged in Tanakh appears as a subsection of the Manual note for 221.

12.5 *Arrange-alphabetically* and *arrange-chronologically notes* are not placed in parentheses, but are also options. They represent suggestions only; the material need not be arranged alphabetically or chronologically. An example of an arrange-alphabetically note is found at 005.133 Specific programming languages: "Arrange alphabetically by name of programming language, e.g., C++."

12.6 Some national libraries and central cataloging authorities assign a few optional numbers, e.g., the National Library of Canada uses C810 for Canadian literature in English and C840 for Canadian literature in French.

12.7 Most of the time, the responsibility for implementing an option rests with the local library. Libraries should weigh the value of using an option against the loss in interoperability of numbers. The library will not be able to use numbers assigned by other libraries, and other libraries will not be able to use the optional numbers assigned by the library. In addition, unless the option is widely used in a region, users may be confused by the alternate notation.

Close and Broad Classification

13.1 The Dewey Decimal Classification provides the basic option of close versus broad classification. *Close classification* means that the content of a work is specified by notation to the fullest extent possible. *Broad classification* means that the work is placed in a broad class by use of notation that has been logically abridged. For example, a work on French cooking is classed closely at 641.5944 (641.59 Cooking by place + 44 France from Table 2), or broadly at 641.5 (Cooking).

13.2 A library should base its decision on close versus broad classification on the size of its collection and the needs of its users. For example, a work on the sociology of sibling relationships in Canadian society would be most usefully classed in 306.8750971 (306.875 Sibling relationships + 09 Geographic treatment from Table 1 + 71 Canada from Table 2) in a research library or large public library. A small school library might prefer to class the same work in the broader number (306.875) without including the geographic facet in the notation. An engineering library might prefer close classification for works in engineering, but broad classification for disciplines outside science and technology.

13.3 The classifier should never reduce the notation to less than the most specific three-digit number (no matter how small the library's collection). A number also must never be reduced so that it ends in a 0 anywhere to the right of the decimal point.

13.4 One aid to logical abridgment of DDC numbers is the segmentation device provided by the Decimal Classification Division of the Library of Congress and some other centralized cataloging services.

13.5 The abridged edition of the Dewey Decimal Classification is another source for broad classification.

More Information

14.1 Classifiers desiring a more in-depth introduction to the Dewey Decimal Classification may consult *Dewey Decimal Classification: Principles and Application*, 3d ed., by Lois Mai Chan and Joan S. Mitchell (Dublin, Ohio: OCLC, 2003).

Glossary

The Glossary defines terms used in the Introduction and throughout the schedules, tables, and Manual. Fuller explanations and examples for many terms may be found in the relevant sections of the Introduction. An index to the Introduction and Glossary follows the Glossary.

Abridged edition: A shortened version of the Dewey Decimal Classification (DDC) system that is a logical truncation of the notational and structural hierarchy of the corresponding full edition on which it is based. The abridged edition is intended for general collections of 20,000 titles or less. *See also* **Broad classification; Full edition.**

Add note: A note instructing the classifier to append digits found elsewhere in the DDC to a given base number. *See also* **Base number.**

Add table: *See* **Tables (2).**

Application: *See* **Rule of application.**

Approximate the whole: When a topic is nearly coextensive with the full meaning of a DDC class, the topic is said to "approximate the whole" of the class. The term is also used to characterize topics that cover more than half the content of a class. When a topic approximates the whole of a class, standard subdivisions may be added. Topics that do not approximate the whole are said to be in "standing room" in the number. *See also* **Class-here note; Standard-subdivisions-are-added note; Standing room.**

Area table: An auxiliary table (Table 2) that gives geographic areas primarily, but also lists historical periods and several numbers for persons associated with a subject. Areas of the world are listed systematically, not alphabetically. Area table notation may be used with other numbers in the schedules and tables when explicit instructions permitting such use are given. *See also* **Tables.**

Arrange-alphabetically note: A note suggesting the option of alphabetical subarrangement when identification by specific name or other identifying characteristic is desired. *See also* **Option**.

Arrange-chronologically note: A note suggesting the option of chronological subarrangement when identification by date is desired. *See also* **Option**.

Artificial digit: A letter or other symbol used optionally as a substitute for digits 0–9 to provide a more prominent location or shorter notation for a jurisdiction, language, literature, religion, ethnic or national group, or other characteristic. *See also* **Option**.

Aspect: An approach to a subject, or characteristic (facet) of a subject. *See also* **Discipline; Facet; Subject.**

Attraction: *See* **Classification by attraction.**

Author number: *See* **Book number.**

Base number: A number of any length to which other numbers are appended. *See also* **Add note.**

Book number: The part of a call number that distinguishes a specific item from other items within the same class number. A library using the Cutter-Sanborn system can have D548d indicate David Copperfield by Dickens (where D stands for the D of Dickens, 548 stands for "ickens," and d stands for David Copperfield). *See also* **Call number; Cutter number; Work mark.**

Broad classification: The classification of works in broad categories by logical abridgment, even when more specific numbers are available, e.g., the use of 641.5 Cooking instead of 641.5972 Mexican cooking for a cookbook of Mexican recipes. Broad classification is the opposite of close classification. *See also* **Abridged edition; Close classification.**

Built number: A number constructed according to add instructions stated or implied in the schedules or tables. *See also* **Number building.**

Call number: A set of letters, numerals, or other symbols (in combination or alone) used by a library to identify a specific copy of a work. A call number may consist of the class number; book number; and other data such as date, volume number, copy number, and location symbol. *See also* **Book number; Class number.**

Caption: *See* **Heading.**

Category: *See* **Class** *(Noun).*

Centered entry: An entry representing a subject covered by a span of numbers, e.g., 372–374 Specific levels of education. The entry is called "centered" because the span of numbers appears in the center of the page in the print version of the DDC rather than in the number column on the left side of the page. Centered entries are identified by the symbol > in the number column.

Characteristic of division: *See* **Facet.**

Citation order: The order in which two or more characteristics (facets) of a class are to be combined in number building. When number building is not permitted or possible, instructions on preference order with respect to the choice of facets are provided. *See also* **Facet; Number building; Preference order.**

Class: (Noun) (1) A group of objects exhibiting one or more common characteristics, identified by specific notation. *See also* **Entry (1).** (2) One of the ten major groups of the DDC numbered 0–9. *See also* **Main class.** (3) A subdivision of the DDC of any degree of specificity. *See also* **Subdivision.** (Verb) To assign a class number to an individual work. *See also* **Classify.**

Class-elsewhere note: A note instructing the classifier about the location of interrelated topics. The note may show preference order, lead to the interdisciplinary or comprehensive number, override the first-of-two rule, or lead to broader or narrower numbers in the same hierarchical array that might otherwise be overlooked. *See also* **Comprehensive number; Interdisciplinary number; Preference order.**

Class-here note: A note that identifies topics that are equivalent to the whole of the class under which the note appears. The topic as a whole is classed in the number under which the note appears; parts of the topic are classed in the most appropriate subdivision of the number. Topics identified in class-here notes, even if broader or narrower than the heading, are said to "approximate the whole" of the number; therefore, standard subdivisions may be added for topics in class-here notes. Class-here notes also may identify the comprehensive or interdisciplinary number for a subject. *See also* **Approximate the whole; Comprehensive number; Interdisciplinary number.**

Class number: Notation that designates the class to which a given item belongs. *See also* **Call number.**

Classification: A logical system for the arrangement of knowledge.

Classification by attraction: The classification of a specific aspect of a subject in an inappropriate discipline, usually because the subject is named in the inappropriate discipline but not mentioned explicitly in the appropriate discipline.

Classified catalog: A catalog arranged according to the notational order of a classification system.

Classify: (1) To arrange a collection of items according to a classification system. (2) To assign a class number to an individual work.

Close classification: The classification of works to the fullest extent permitted by the notation. Close classification is the opposite of broad classification. *See also* **Broad classification; Full edition.**

Coextensive: Describes a topic equal in scope to the concept represented by the number.

Comparative table: A table provided for a complete or extensive revision that lists in alphabetical order selected topics accompanied by their previous number and their number in the current edition. *See also* **Equivalence table; Revision.**

Complete revision: *See* **Revision** *(Complete revision).*

Complex subject: A complex subject is a subject that has more than one characteristic. For example, "unemployed carpenters" is a complex subject because it has more than one characteristic (employment status and occupation). *See also* **Preference order.**

Comprehensive number: A number (often identified by a "Class here comprehensive works" note) that covers all the components of the subject treated within that discipline. The components may be in a span of consecutive numbers or distributed throughout the schedule or table. *See also* **Interdisciplinary number.**

Coordinate: Describes a number or topic at a level equal to another number or topic in the same hierarchy.

Cross classification: The accidental placement of works on the same subject in two different class numbers. This tends to happen when works being classified deal with two or more characteristics of a subject in the same class. Notes on preference order should prevent cross classification. *See also* **Preference order.**

Cross reference: *See* **Class-elsewhere note**; **See-also reference**; **See reference**.

Cutter number: The notation in a book number derived from the Cutter Three-Figure Author Table, the Cutter-Sanborn Three-Figure Author Table, or the OCLC Four-Figure Cutter Tables. The OCLC Four-Figure Cutter Tables are revised and expanded versions of the Cutter Three-Figure Author Table and the Cutter-Sanborn Three-Figure Author Table. *See also* **Book number.**

DDC: Dewey Decimal Classification.

DDC Summaries: A listing of the first three levels (main classes, divisions, and sections) of the Dewey Decimal Classification system. The headings associated with the numbers in the summaries have been edited for browsing purposes, and may not match the complete headings found in the schedules. *See also* **Division; Main class; Section; Summary.**

Decimal point: The dot that follows the third digit in a DDC number. In strict usage the word "decimal" is not accurate; however, common usage is followed in this edition's explanatory material.

Definition note: A note indicating the meaning of a term in the heading.

Digit: The smallest individual unit in a notational system. For example, the notation 954 has three digits: 9, 5, and 4.

Discipline: An organized field of study or branch of knowledge, e.g., 200 Religion, 530 Physics, 364 Criminology. In the DDC, subjects are arranged by disciplines. *See also* **Subject.**

Discontinuation: The shifting of a topic or the entire contents of a number to a more general number in the same hierarchy, or the complete removal of the topic or number. A topic or number is discontinued because the topic or concept represented by the number has a negligible current literature or represents a distinction that is no longer valid in the literature or common perception of the field. A note explaining its shift or removal accompanies a discontinued topic or number. Discontinued numbers appear in square brackets. *See also* **Relocation**; **Schedule reduction.**

Displaced standard subdivision: A standard subdivision concept given special notation in the schedule in place of its regular notation from Table 1. A do-not-use note is always provided at the regular location of the standard subdivision concept. *See also* **Do-not-use note; Standard subdivisions.**

Division: The second level of subdivision in the DDC, represented by the first two digits in the notation, e.g., 64 in 640 Home and family management. *See also* **DDC Summaries**; **Main class**; **Section.**

Do-not-use note: A note instructing the classifier not to use all or part of a regular standard subdivision notation or an add table provision, but instead to use a special provision or standard subdivision notation at a broader number. *See also* **Displaced standard subdivision.**

Document: A generic term for all media capable of conveying, coding, and preserving knowledge. Documents may be books, journals, electronic resources, reports, sound recordings, motion pictures, etc.

Dual heading: A heading with two separate terms, the first of which is the main topic and the second of which is a major subordinate topic, e.g., 570 Life sciences Biology. A dual heading is used when the subject as a whole and the subordinate topic as a whole share the same number and most of its subdivisions. Standard subdivisions may be added for either or both topics in a dual heading.

Dual provision: The inadvertent provision of more than one place in the DDC for the same aspect of a subject.

Entry: (1) In the schedules and tables, a self-contained unit consisting of a number or span of numbers, a heading, and often one or more notes. (2) In the Relative Index, a term or phrase usually followed by a DDC number. (3) In the Manual, a self-contained unit consisting of a number or group of numbers, the associated headings or topics, and an extended instruction or discussion.

Enumerative scheme: A classification system in which numbers for complex subjects are precombined and listed.

Equivalence table: A table provided for a complete or extensive revision that lists in numerical order the classes of the current edition with their equivalent numbers in the previous edition (and vice versa). *See also* **Revision.**

Expansion: The development of a class in the schedules or tables to provide further subdivisions. *See also* **Revision.**

Extensive revision: *See* **Revision** *(Extensive revision).*

Facet: Any of the various categories into which a given class may be divided, e.g., division of the class "people" into the categories of ethnicity, age, education, and language spoken. Each category contains terms based on a single characteristic of division, e.g., children, adolescents, and adults are characteristics of division of the "ages" category. *See also* **Citation order.**

Facet indicator: A digit used to introduce notation representing a characteristic of the subject. For example, "0" is often used as a facet indicator to introduce standard subdivision concepts.

First-of-two rule: The rule instructing that works dealing equally with two subjects that are not used to introduce or explain one another are classed in the number coming first in the schedules or tables.

Footnote: An instruction that applies to many subdivisions of a class, or to a topic within a class. The affected subdivision or topic is marked with a symbol such as an asterisk. In the print version of the DDC, the footnote is located at the bottom of the page. In the electronic version, the footnote is included in the notes section of each class to which the instruction applies.

Former-heading note: A note listing the heading associated with the class number in the previous edition. The note is used when the heading has changed so much that it bears little or no resemblance to the previous heading, even though the meaning of the number has remained substantially the same.

Full edition: The complete version of the Dewey Decimal Classification (DDC) system. *See also* **Abridged edition; Close classification.**

Heading: The word or phrase used as the description of a given class. Also called "caption."

Hierarchical force: The principle that the attributes of a class as defined in the heading and in certain basic notes apply to all the subdivisions of the class, and to all other classes to which reference is made.

Hierarchy: The arrangement of a classification system from general to specific. In the DDC, the length of the notation and the corresponding depth of indention of the heading usually indicate the degree of specificity of a class. Hierarchy may also be indicated by special headings, notes, and centered entries.

Hook number: A number in the DDC without meaning in itself, but used to introduce examples of the topic. Hook numbers have headings that begin with "Miscellaneous,"

"Specific," or "Other"; and do not contain add notes, including notes, or class-here notes. Standard subdivisions are always bracketed under hook numbers.

Including note: A note enumerating topics that are logically part of the class but are less extensive in scope than the concept represented by the class number. These topics do not have enough literature to warrant their own number. Standard subdivisions may not be added to the numbers for these topics. *See also* **Literary warrant**; **Standing room**.

Indention: Typographical setting of notes and subheadings below and to the right of the main entry term.

Influence: *See* **Rule of application**.

Interdisciplinary number: A number (often identified by a "Class here interdisciplinary works" note) to be used for works covering a subject from the perspective of more than one discipline, including the discipline where the interdisciplinary number is located, e.g., the interdisciplinary number for marriage is 306.81 in Sociology. *See also* **Comprehensive number.**

Literary form: A mode of literary expression such as poetry, drama, fiction, etc. Each form can be subdivided into kinds of forms, e.g., lyric poetry, comedy, science fiction, etc.

Literary warrant: Justification for the development of a class or the explicit inclusion of a topic in the schedules, tables, or Relative Index, based on the existence of a body of literature on the topic.

Main class: One of the ten major subdivisions of the DDC, represented by the first digit in the notation, e.g., 3 in 300 Social sciences. *See also* **DDC Summaries; Division; Section.**

Manual: A guide to the use of the DDC that is made up primarily of extended discussions of problem areas in the application of the DDC. In the schedules and tables, see-Manual references indicate where relevant discussions are located in the Manual. *See also* **Manual note**.

Manual note: An individual entry in the Manual. *See also* **Entry (3); Manual; See-Manual reference.**

Notation: Numerals, letters, and/or symbols used to represent the main and subordinate divisions of a classification scheme. In the DDC, Arabic numerals are used to represent the classes, e.g., notation 07 from Table 1 and 511.3 from the schedules.

Notational synthesis: *See* **Number building.**

Note: An instruction, definition, or reference that explains the contents and use of a class, or the relationship of the class to other classes. *See also* **Add note**; **Arrange-alphabetically note; Arrange-chronologically note; Class-elsewhere note; Class-here note; Definition note; Discontinuation; Do-not-use note; Footnote; Former-heading note**; **Including note; Manual note; Number-built note; Preference order; Relocation; Revision note; Scope note; See-also reference; See-Manual reference; See reference; Standard-subdivisions-are-added note; Subdivisions-are-added note.**

Number building: The process of constructing a number by adding notation from the tables or other parts of the schedules to a base number. *See also* **Base number; Citation order.**

Number-building note: *See* **Add note.**

Number-built note: A note that states where the number building instructions may be found for a built number that is explicitly listed in the schedules or tables. Typically, such built numbers are listed for two reasons: to provide an entry for a built number under which other notes are required; or to provide an entry for a three-digit built number.

Number column: In the print version of the DDC, the column of numbers that appears in the left margin of the schedules and tables, and to the right of the alphabetical entries in the Relative Index.

Option: An alternative to standard notation provided in the schedules and tables to give emphasis to an aspect in a library's collection not given preferred treatment in the standard notation. In some cases, an option may provide shorter notation for the aspect. *See also* **Optional number.**

Optional number: (1) A number listed in parentheses in the schedules or tables that is an alternative to the standard notation. (2) A number constructed by following an option. *See also* **Option.**

Order of preference: *See* **Preference order.**

Period table: A table giving chronological time periods with their notation. For many literatures, period tables are given in the schedules. For works not limited to a particular language, the period notation is taken from Table 1 —0901–0905. *See also* **Tables.**

Phoenix schedule: *See* **Revision** *(Complete revision).*

Preference order: The order indicating which one of two or more numbers is to be chosen when different characteristics of a subject cannot be shown in full by number building. A note (sometimes containing a table of preference) indicates which characteristic is to be selected for works covering more than one characteristic. When a notation can be synthesized to show two or more characteristics, it is a matter of citation order. *See also* **Citation order.**

Preference table: *See* **Preference order.**

Prime marks: *See* **Segmentation.**

Reduction of schedules: *See* **Schedule reduction.**

Regularization: The replacement of special developments for standard subdivision concepts by use of the regular standard subdivisions found in Table 1.

Relative Index: The index to the DDC. It is called "Relative" because it shows the connection between subjects and the disciplines in which they appear. In the schedules, subjects are arranged within disciplines. In the Relative Index, subjects are listed alphabetically. Under each subject, the disciplines in which the subject is found are listed alphabetically. In the print version of the DDC, the disciplines are indented under the subject. In the electronic version, the disciplines appear as subheadings associated with the subject.

Relocation: The shifting of a topic from one number to another number that differs from the old number in respects other than length. Notes at both ends of the relocation identify the new and former numbers. *See also* **Discontinuation.**

Retroactive citation order: In number building, the combination of characteristics (facets) of a class starting with a number coming later in the schedule as the base number, then adding as instructed from numbers earlier in the sequence.

Reused number: A number with a total change in meaning from one edition to another. Usually numbers are reused only in complete revisions or when the reused number has been vacant for two consecutive editions.

Revision: The result of editorial work that alters the text of any class of the DDC. There are three degrees of revision: *Routine revision* is limited to updating terminology, clarifying notes, and providing modest expansions. *Extensive revision* involves a major reworking of subdivisions but leaves the main outline of the schedule intact. *Complete revision* (formerly called a phoenix) is a new development; the base number remains unchanged from the previous edition, but virtually all subdivisions are changed. Changes for complete and extensive revisions are shown through comparative and equivalence tables rather than through relocation notes in the schedule or table affected. *See also* **Comparative table; Equivalence table.**

Revision note: A note that introduces a complete or extensive revision.

Routine revision: *See* **Revision** *(Routine revision).*

Rule of application: The rule instructing that works about the application of one subject to a second subject or the influence of one subject on another subject are classified with the second subject.

Rule of three: The rule instructing that works giving equal treatment to three or more subjects that are all subdivisions of a broader subject are classified in the first higher number that includes all of them.

Rule of zero: The rule instructing that subdivisions beginning with zero should be avoided if there is a choice between the 0 subdivision and subdivisions beginning with 1–9 in the same position in the notation. Similarly, subdivisions beginning with 00 should be avoided when there is a choice between 00 and 0.

Scatter note: A class-elsewhere, see-reference, or relocation note that leads to multiple locations in the DDC. *See also* **Class-elsewhere note; Relocation; See reference.**

Schedule reduction: The elimination of certain provisions of a previous edition, often resulting in discontinued numbers. *See also* **Discontinuation**.

Schedules: (1) Listings of subjects and their subdivisions arranged in a systematic order with notation given for each subject and its subdivisions. (2) The series of DDC numbers 000–999, their headings, and notes.

Scope note: A note indicating that the meaning of a class number is broader or narrower than is apparent from the heading.

Section: The third level of subdivision in the DDC, represented by the first three digits in the notation, e.g., 641 in 641 Food and drink. *See also* **DDC Summaries; Division; Main class.**

See-also reference: (1) In the schedules and tables, a note leading to classes that are tangentially related to the topic and therefore might be confused with it. (2) In the Relative Index, a note leading to a synonym, broader term, or related term. (3) In the Manual, a note leading to related Manual notes.

See-Manual reference: A note leading from an entry in the schedules or tables to additional information about the number in the Manual.

See reference: A note (introduced by the word "for") that leads from the stated or implied comprehensive or interdisciplinary number for a subject to component parts of the subject in numbers other than direct subdivisions of the original number or span. *See also* **Class-elsewhere note.**

Segmentation: The indication of logical breaks in a number by a typographical device, e.g., slash marks or prime marks. Segmentation marks indicate the end of an abridged number or the beginning of a standard subdivision.

Shelf mark: *See* **Call number.**

Standard subdivisions: Subdivisions found in Table 1 that represent frequently recurring physical forms (dictionaries, periodicals) or approaches (history, research) applicable to any subject or discipline. They may be used with any number in the schedules and tables for topics that approximate the whole of the number unless there are instructions to the contrary. *See also* **Tables.**

Standard-subdivisions-are-added note: A note indicating which topics in a multiterm heading may have standard subdivisions added to them. The designated topics are considered to approximate the whole of the number. *See also* **Approximate the whole.**

Standing room: A term characterizing a topic without sufficient literature to have its own number, and considerably narrower in scope than the class number in which it is included. Standard subdivisions cannot be added to a topic in standing room, nor are other number-building techniques allowed. Topics listed in including notes have standing room in the class number, as do minor unnamed topics that logically fall in the same place in the DDC. To have standing room is the opposite of approximating the whole. *See also* **Approximate the whole.**

Subdivision: (1) A subordinate member of a class, e.g., 518 Numerical analysis is a subdivision of class 510 Mathematics, and 518.5 Numerical approximation is a subdivision of 518. *See also* **Class (3).** (2) Notation that may be added to other numbers to make a class number appropriately specific to the work being classified. *See also* **Standard Subdivisions; Tables.**

Subdivisions-are-added note: A note used where subdivisions are provided by add instructions indicating which topics in a multiterm heading may have subdivisions added to them. The designated topics are considered to approximate the whole of the number. *See also* **Approximate the whole.**

Subject: An object of study. Also called topic. It may be a person or a group of persons, thing, place, process, activity, abstraction, or any combination of these. In the DDC, subjects are arranged by disciplines. A subject is often studied in more than one discipline, e.g., marriage is studied in several disciplines such as ethics, religion, sociology, and law. *See also* **Discipline.**

Subject catalog: An index to the contents of a collection. If access is provided alphabetically by words, it is called an alphabetical subject catalog. If access is provided by the notation of a classification system, it is called a classified catalog. *See also* **Classified catalog.**

Subordinate: Describes a number or topic at a lower (narrower) level than another number or topic in the same hierarchy. *See also* **Superordinate.**

Summary: A listing of the chief subdivisions of a class that provides an overview of its structure. *See also* **DDC Summaries**.

Superordinate: Describes a number or topic at a higher (broader) level than another number or topic in the same hierarchy. *See also* **Subordinate.**

Synthesis of notation: *See* **Number building.**

Table of preference: *See* **Preference order.**

Tables: In the DDC, lists of notation that may be added to other numbers to make a class number appropriately specific to the work being classified. The numbers found in a table are never used alone. There are two kinds of tables: (1) The six numbered auxiliary tables (Tables 1–6) representing standard subdivisions, geographic areas, languages, ethnic groups, etc. (2) Lists of special notation found in add notes under specific numbers throughout the schedules and occasionally in Tables 1–6. These lists are called add tables. *See also* **Add note**.

Topic: *See* **Subject.**

Unabridged edition: *See* **Full edition**.

Variant-name note: A note listing synonyms or near synonyms for a topic in a heading when it is awkward or inappropriate to include such information in the heading.

Word-by-word alphabetization: Refers to the filing of entries word by word, not letter by letter. For example, New York files before Newark in word-by-word alphabetization; Newark files before New York in letter-by-letter alphabetization.

Work: A distinct intellectual or artistic expression.

Work mark: The part of a book number that consists of a letter appended to the author (or biographee) designation to show the first letter of the title (or first letter of the surname of the biographer). *See also* **Book number**.

Index to the Introduction and Glossary

References to the Introduction are identified by paragraph numbers. References to the alphabetically arranged Glossary are identified by G.

Manual

Notes on Table Numbers

Table 1. Standard Subdivisions

T1—01

Philosophy and theory

The term philosophy and theory is treated as a single concept, covering the general or abstract principles applied to a field of activity or thought, such as science or art. Use T1—01 for a work discussing the discipline itself as a discipline, rather than its subject matter. Do not use T1—01 where theory constitutes the bulk of the subject matter of a field, e.g., nuclear physics. In philosophy subdivisions of 100, T1—01 itself is seldom used, though its subdivisions may be, and then only in the sense of theory and method of the topic.

Criticism

Use T1—01 for techniques and principles of criticism of a discipline. However, class the criticism itself in the same number as the subject of the criticism, e.g., criticism of Browning's poetry 821.8, of Frank Lloyd Wright's architecture 720.92, of Italian cooking 641.5945.

T1—015 vs. T1—0245–0246

Scientific principles vs. The subject for persons in scientific and technological occupations

Use the number for the technology plus notation 015 from Table 1 for the scientific principles of a technology, e.g., mathematical principles of engineering 620.00151. In such cases the table of contents will often be organized by concepts found in subdivisions of the technology or will follow the table of contents found in common treatises on thc technology. Conversely, use the number for the science plus notation 024 from Table 1 for the science if the work is written for technologists and engineers, e.g., mathematics for engineers 510.2462. In such cases the table of contents will be organized by concepts found in subdivisions of the science or will follow the table of contents found in common treatises on the science. If in doubt between science and technology, prefer the technology number.

When not to use cither subdivision

Do not use T1—015 and T1—024 in 500 and 600 when there is a direct relationship between a science and a corresponding technology, e.g., do not use 540.2466 for chemistry for chemical engineers, or 660.0154 for chemical principles in chemical engineering.

T1—0207 vs. T3B—7, T3A—8 + 02, T3B—802, T3B—8 + 02, T3A—8 + 07, T3B—807, T3B—8 + 07

Humor, satire, jokes

Any subject may be dealt with in a humorous or satirical manner. Use the number for the subject without T1—0207 for works where the humor involved is entirely incidental to the serious treatment of the subject, e.g., a joke inserted into a lecture to provide respite from a serious mood. Use the number for the subject plus notation 0207 from Table 1 for works where the author's intention is serious, but where humor or satire is used to convey the author's message, e.g., political satire grounded in genuine political criticism. Use numbers in literature, usually T3B—802 (or T3A—8 + 02 or T3B—8 + 02), only for works where the subject merely provides the occasion for humor, the author's primary concern being to amuse, e.g., a collection of jokes about cats. If in doubt between literature and the subject, prefer the subject. If in doubt whether to use T1—0207, prefer the subject without it.

Use T3B—802 (or T3A—8 + 02 or T3B—8 + 02) for jokes; use T3B—807 (or T3A—8 + 07 or T3B—8 + 07) for humorous literary works without identifiable literary form. Use T3B—7 only for collections of humor or satire in more than one literary form, including both verse and prose. (Class works in a particular literary form, e.g., drama or fiction, with the form; class works in multiple forms of literary prose with prose.)

T1—0222 vs. T1—0223

Pictures and related material vs. Maps, plans, diagrams

Use T1—0222 for charts that are basically pictures of things, T1—0223 for charts that are basically maps or diagrams. Use T1—0222 for designs that give a visual impression of what something does or will look like, e.g., architectural drawings; use T1—0223 for designs that show details on horizontal or vertical planes (often as a preliminary to construction), or the arrangement and relations of parts showing how something works. Use T1—0223 for atlases, which are usually compilations of maps, plans, or diagrams, unless they are compilations of pictorial material. Use T1—0222 for anatomical atlases, which are usually picture-like. Use 001–999 without adding either standard subdivision for atlases that are simply heavily illustrated texts on a subject.

Use T1—0222 for comprehensive works, e.g., architectural drawings and plans 720.222. If in doubt between T1—0222 and T1—0223, prefer T1—0222.

T1—024

The subject for persons in specific occupations

Use T1—024 for works that emphasize special instructions for persons in specific occupations that general readers would not find useful, e.g., mathematics for engineers 510.2462. Do not use T1—024 for works that draw examples from one broad discipline or for one kind of professional user, but effectively cover the subject for the general reader, e.g., use 616.12 (*not* 616.12002461073) for a textbook on cardiology for nurses that would be equally useful to patients, relatives, or social workers.

Do not use T1—024 when it is redundant, that is, when it is directed towards persons who would typically be expected to study the subject, e.g., engineering for engineers 620 (*not* 620.002462).

T1—025 vs. T1—029

Directories of enterprises and products

Use T1—025 for directories that describe business enterprises in a manner that serves people who run businesses; who invest in or lend money to businesses; or who want to sell ideas, products, and services to businesses. These directories typically emphasize organization, officers, and financial information. Use T1—029 for directories and catalogs designed to help customers obtain or evaluate products and services. If in doubt, prefer T1—025.

Directories of business and related enterprises

The guidelines in this section apply to directories that concentrate on enterprises and provide significant information about their organization, and sometimes also their officers, finances, and line of work. Use T1—025 with numbers from 001–999 for directories of persons and organizations that do not concentrate on enterprises, or that simply supply their names, addresses, and contact persons.

Limited to specific industries

Use T1—025 with subdivisions of 338.76 and related numbers for directories of enterprises in specific industries that emphasize organization, officers, and financial information. Related numbers are subdivisions of 338.8 that are divided by industry for business combinations; 332.1–.6 for financial institutions; 333.33 for real estate businesses; 334 for cooperative enterprises; 368 for insurance enterprises; and 380 for enterprises engaged in commerce, communications, and transportation.

Because "organization" is a basic element of 338.76 and related numbers, the guidelines in the Manual note T1—025 vs. T1—0601–0609 do not apply. Use notation 025 from Table 1 with these numbers for listings of companies, even if there is significant general information on the companies.

In most cases, the arrangement of a directory by enterprises points to use of T1—025 with subdivisions of 338.76 and related numbers, unless there is a predominance of detail on products and services. In that case, use T1—029 as instructed below. If in doubt, however, prefer T1—025.

Not limited to specific industries

Use T1—025 with 338.7, 338.8, and their general subdivisions (those not limited to specific industries) for directories of enterprises that are not limited to a specific industry, e.g., directories of all business enterprises in France, 338.702544, directories of multinational enterprises 338.88025.

Use 338.74025 only for directories explicitly limited to corporations. If the limitation is not explicitly stated, prefer 338.7025.

Use 338.767025 for directories of manufacturers that give financial and organizational information.

Use T1—025 with numbers in 381–382 for directories of merchants. Use 381.025 and 382.025 for chambers of commerce and boards of trade, even when the membership includes a wide cross section of business enterprises in an area.

Use T1—025 with numbers in 914–919 for telephone, city, and fax directories, and for business white pages (telephone directories largely limited to businesses) and yellow pages that are issued with general directories of people and organizations in an area. Use 338.7025, however, for business white pages and comprehensive fax directories of businesses that are not produced in connection with a directory of all people and organizations, and 338.02029 for yellow pages that are not produced in connection with a directory of all people and organizations.

Product and service directories and catalogs

Product and service directories may go by a variety of names, including trade catalogs and yellow pages. Yellow pages are usually not limited by specific industries. The guidelines in this section also apply to buyers' guides and consumer reports.

Limited to specific industries

Use T1—029 with numbers from 001–999 (other than 338.47 and related numbers) for directories of products and services in specific industries, e.g., information services 025.04029, chemical products of United States 660.02973, food and drink in Europe 664.00294. In all cases, use the number that represents making the products or producing the services, except when they are produced by three or more industries serving a single consumer industry. In such cases, use the number for the consumer industry, e.g., a directory of publishers, binders, and furniture makers serving libraries 020.29.

Not limited to specific industries

Use 338.4029 for wide-ranging product directories that emphasize products of secondary industries, or services and products of secondary industries. Use 338.02029 for wide-ranging directories that cover everything from farm produce and minerals to the output of secondary industries. If in doubt, prefer 338.4029.

Use 338.4029 (*not* 670.29) for directories of manufactured products, as they are then usefully classed with other comprehensive or wide-ranging directories.

Use 338.4700029 for comprehensive directories of services.

T1—025 vs. T1—0601–0609

Directories of persons and organizations vs. Organizations

Use T1—025 for works covering several or many organizations containing directory information, even if not called directories, i.e., works that supply addresses, key officers or contact people, phone numbers, and brief statements of purpose. These works may include directory information about component parts of individual organizations, and/or a limited amount of general information on structure and component parts. However, use T1—06 if there is significant general information (more than a page) per organization. Use T1—0601–0609 for works covering history, charters, regulations, membership lists, and administrative reports of an organization, and also for conference programs of an organization and organizational handbooks.

Use T1—06 for a combined organizational handbook and membership directory, even if the membership part predominates. However, use T1—025, plus the Table 2 notation for the area that the organization serves, if the organizational part consists of only a few preliminary pages followed by an extensive directory of members.

Use T1—025 for a membership list that includes addresses, as that is counted as a directory.

If in doubt, prefer T1—025.

See also discussion at T1—025 vs. T1—029.

T1—0285

Data processing   Computer applications

Use T1—0285 for comprehensive works on data processing applied to a subject. Also use T1—0285 if 004 is the interdisciplinary number for the applied concept, e.g., digital computers T1—0285. Do not use T1—02854 by itself, since the digit 4 simply repeats the meaning of notation 0285. However, it is not redundant to add to T1—0285 the notation for subdivisions of 004, e.g., digital microcomputers T1—0285416.

Do not add the digit 4 by itself to a number divided like 004–006 if the base number is limited to data processing and computer concepts, e.g., 651.8, 658.05.

Electronic resources and programs

Use T1—028553 for programs themselves and for works about programs, regardless of form (e.g., programs in electronic form, printed program listings bound into books). Do not use T1—0285 to indicate that a work is in electronic form, e.g., use 310 (*not* 310.285) for electronic census data.

Do not use T1—028553 for items that include both programs and data files, unless the data files are clearly of minor importance, e.g., small files intended merely to help beginners learn to use the programs.

If in doubt, do not use T1—028553.

T1—0601–0609

Organizations

Use subdivisions in T1—0601–0609 primarily for membership organizations and associations, but also for a selection of nonmembership institutions, foundations, and agencies that do not belong to the categories listed in class-elsewhere notes under T1—0601–0609. However, do not use T1—06 for nonmembership organizations if "organization" is inherent in the subject. For example, except as indicated below, do not use T1—06 with most subdivisions in 360 for social services. Under such numbers, use T1—09 for the basic organizations in specific areas, and for specific basic organizations, e.g., hospitals in China 362.110951. However, use T1—06 for associations that include the basic organizations and their staffs as members, e.g., hospital associations in China 362.1106051.

Use T1—06 also for administrative (in contrast to service) histories of institutions, e.g., administrative histories of hospitals (362.1106) or police agencies (363.206). Do not confuse these histories with how-to works on management, which are classed in T1—068.

Do not use T1—06 for membership organizations if "membership organization" is inherent in the subject, e.g., in 366 Associations or 061–068 General organizations. T1—06 is not used with numbers for a religion because of the ambiguity of membership organization in religion, e.g., 296.06 is bracketed, and a reference leads to 296.67 where membership is inherent in the organization number.

Selection of area number

For membership organizations, use the area that is the chief focus of the membership, e.g., American Medical Association 610.6073. For local affiliated associations or chapters that have their own name, use the area number of the local organization, e.g., Massachusetts Medical Association 610.60744. For offices and chapters that take the name of the parent body, use the number of the parent organization, e.g., the Washington office of the American Medical Association 610.6073 (*not* 610.60753).

For nonmembership organizations, institutions, foundations, and conferences, use the area number of the headquarters. Also use the number of the headquarters for membership organizations whose area cannot be determined.

T1—068

Management

The subdivisions of T1—068 parallel the subdivisions of 658. Use 658 as a guide to selecting the correct subdivision of T1—068, e.g., information management 658.4038, therefore information management applied to automobile manufacturing 629.2220684.

T1—068 vs. 353–354

Public administration and management in specific fields

Use numbers outside 350–354 plus notation 068 from Table 1 for the management or administration of organizations, public or private, that directly perform the work within their scope. Use numbers in 353–354 for agencies that regulate, control, or support organizations that provide the actual services. For example, use 363.2068 (*not* 353.36216) for management of city police departments; use 364.62068 (*not* 353.39) for management of parole boards; use 385.068 (*not* 354.767) for management of a nationalized railway system.

A given field may have both public administration and management aspects. For example, use 385.068 for managing railroads, but use 354.76728 for managing agencies that regulate railroads; use 025.1974 for administering public libraries, but use 353.73 for administering agencies that support public libraries.

Exceptions

Use 353–354 for administration of activities specific to government (such as licensing, taxing, and gathering census information, that is, activities found in 352 that are not also found in 658) when applied to specific fields of public administration.

Foreign affairs are among the few major activities for which administration of an actual operation is classed in 353–354. Use 353.13 (*not* 327.068 or numbers in 327.4–.9, plus notation 068 from Table 1) for foreign affairs management. Similarly, use 353.17 (*not* 327.12068 or numbers in 327.123–.129 plus notation 068 from Table 1) for foreign intelligence management.

If in doubt, prefer the number outside public administration.

T1—072 vs. T1—0601–0609

Research; statistical methods vs. Organizations

Use T1—072 for organizations that conduct research, e.g., agricultural research stations in the United States 630.72073; but use T1—06 for membership organizations that primarily promote research, e.g., the American Association for the Advancement of Science 506.073. If in doubt, prefer T1—072.

See also discussion at T1—07201–07209 vs. T1—0722–0724.

T1—07201–07209 vs. T1—0722–0724

Geographic treatment of research vs. Specific kinds of research

Use the geographic treatment span for works on research in progress or being planned, or for works that consist of general descriptions of research projects and do not emphasize the kind of research. Also use the geographic treatment span for works on research organizations that perform or sponsor all or most of the research in their fields, even if they have names like agricultural experiment stations.

Do not use numbers for kinds of research (descriptive, experimental, or historical research) if they are redundant, e.g., historical research in history, or experimental research in an experimental science such as chemistry.

However, use T1—0723 for surveys and data collection projects that concentrate on specific areas and concentrate on a single survey rather than on a number of projects.

If in doubt, prefer T1—07201–07209.

T1—074 vs. T1—029

Museums, collections, exhibits vs. Commercial miscellany

Use T1—074 for catalogs whose primary purpose is to promote knowledge or art, such as catalogs of collections; use T1—029 for catalogs whose primary purpose is to promote sale or distribution of products. Use T1—074 for catalogs of replicas, duplicates, and minor items when offered for sale in museum- or exhibit-like settings by noncommercial institutions. Also use T1—074 for auction catalogs (e.g., in art), and for catalogs of temporary exhibits of groups of artists, even if a succession of such exhibits provides most of the artists with their primary source of income. If in doubt, prefer T1—074.

T1—08 and 306.2–.6

Cultural institutions and social groups

Use the interdisciplinary number for a topic pertaining to a cultural institution plus notation 08 from Table 1 for works on social groups in relation to a cultural institution, e.g., racism in sports 796.089 (*not* 306.483), women in science 500.82 (*not* 306.45), police discrimination against minorities 363.208 (*not* 306.28). If the interdisciplinary number for the cultural institution falls in 306.2–.6, use the number for the institution or related topic plus notation 08 from Table 1, e.g., discrimination against retired women 306.38082.

T1—081 and T1—082, T1—08351, T1—08352, T1—08421, T1—08422

Men and women, Males twelve to twenty and females twelve to twenty, Young men and young women

Use subdivisions for men and women only if the works explicitly emphasize the sex of the people treated. For example, do not use 363.37081 for men as a group with respect to fire fighting unless the work makes clear that *male* fire fighters are being contrasted with *female* fire fighters, or 364.3608351 for juvenile delinquents (a term often implying young men under eighteen) unless *male* delinquents are being contrasted to *female* delinquents.

T1—0882 and 200

Religious groups and Religion

Use subdivisions of T1—0882 in 200 to represent official or semiofficial positions of denominations and sects, e.g., Catholic teachings on socioeconomic problems 261.8088282.

Do not use T1—0882 for works of an individual except in the rare cases in which an individual's view has become an official statement of a group. That is, use 261.8 (*not* 261.8088282) for writings on Christian attitudes towards socioeconomic problems by persons who happen to be Catholic.

T1—09

Historical and geographic treatment of subjects and disciplines

Different numbers are occasionally provided for the historical and geographic treatment of a subject and for the historical and geographic treatment of the discipline within which the subject is treated, e.g., 364.9 is provided for historical and geographic treatment of crime and its alleviation, while 364.09 is provided for comparable treatment of criminology. Use 364.9 for geographic treatment of offenses, offenders, causes, prevention, and treatment (when all are considered together). Use 364.09 for geographic treatment of criminology and of the principles and methods used in analyzing causes and remedies of crime. If in doubt, prefer the number for the historical and geographic treatment of the subject.

Use T1—09 for either or both aspects where the distinction is not made between the subject and the discipline.

T1—09 vs. T1—089

Historical, geographic, persons treatment vs. Ethnic and national groups

Use T1—09, not T1—089, to identify distinguishing characteristics of a subject in an area where a specific group of people lives, e.g., Arab architecture 720.9174927 (*not* 720.89927); French desserts 641.860944 (*not* 641.8608941).

Regions where specific ethnic groups predominate

Do not use T1—09174 (regions where specific ethnic groups predominate) for groups of persons treatment since such use would practically duplicate the group treatment numbers. For example, Arabs living in all areas where Arabs predominate constitute the overwhelming majority of all Arabs; therefore, use T1—089927 for treatment of Arabs as a group, and use T1—09174927 only for works about the area where they live, and works about styles prevailing in areas where they live.

T1—0901–0905

Historical periods

Do not use historical periods for subjects that have no significant history outside the period indicated, e.g., the history of railroads 385.09 (*not* 385.0903), but the history of railroads during the 19th century 385.09034. If in doubt, do not use periods.

Do not use the most recent period subdivision for works on current practice or the state of the art of a subject, since most users will expect to find these works in the base number. However, use the latest period number when the nature of the subject requires attention to the changing situation, e.g., 320.90511 for world political conditions in 2000–2009.

Use earlier historical periods only for retrospective works, not for contemporary works. For example, use 781.09032 for a current work on music theory of the baroque, but use 781 for a reprint of a treatise on music theory written in 1620 (when baroque music was in style).

T1—092

Persons

The following instructions apply also to notation 2 from Table 2 when numbers from Table 2 are added directly without the interposition of T1—09.

In the following notes the word "biography" is used for stylistic convenience; however, the instructions apply fully to description and critical appraisal as well as other persons aspects.

Do not use T1—092 for the actual works of a person except where instructed to do so at certain numbers in 700–779.

See also discussion at 913–919: Add table: 04: Biography; also at 920.008 vs. 305–306, 362; also at 920.009, 920.03–.09 vs. 909.09, 909.1–.8, 930–990; also at 930–990: Wars: Personal narratives; also at 930–990: Biography.

Comprehensive biography

Use the number for the subject of the person's most noted contribution for the comprehensive biography of the person. If the person made approximately equal contributions to a number of fields, use the number for the subject that provides the best common denominator, giving some extra consideration to the person's occupation. For example, use the university's area number under 378 for a physicist who became a science teacher, then head of a school of science, but went on to become a university president. Use 300.92 for a person who made significant contributions in political science, in university education, and the study of administrative and economic aspects of utility regulation, since that number provides the best common denominator for his work. However, use 610.92 for a famous woman doctor who also served as a feminist leader, wrote minor novels, and often served as a delegate to political conventions unless there is an obvious emphasis on her avocations. Give weight to designations listed first in biographical dictionaries, but make allowances for the tendency to list occupation first even when a career transcends occupation.

If in doubt between a number for a discipline and a number for a specific subject within the discipline, prefer the number for the discipline, e.g., use 620.0092 rather than 621.092 for a mechanical engineer who also did important work in transportation and construction engineering.

Public figures

Biographies of public figures frequently present difficulties because the person may have filled several positions that are given varying emphasis by different authors, or may have filled one position that had many facets. Use 930–990 for comprehensive works on persons who held such positions. However, use a number reflecting one position or interest of a person's career if a biography emphasizes this, e.g., use 362.1092 for a biography emphasizing Wayne Morse's promotion of the National Institutes of Health, even though he was a U.S. senator. (*See also Partial biography, below.*)

A public figure may exert a wide-ranging impact upon the history of the jurisdiction served. For example, Daniel Webster is most famous as a U.S. senator, although he served twice as secretary of state and was also a lawyer and orator. In all these roles he influenced the history of his time. Use 973.5092 for his biography, rather than 328.73092 for his senatorial service, 327.730092 for his foreign relations service, or 349.73092 for his legal activities. However, if a person in a high office of general responsibility concentrated on a single important field, consider a number that identifies that field. For example, William Wilberforce's chief interest while serving as a British Member of Parliament was the abolition of slavery. Thus use 326.8092 for his biography, rather than 941.073092 for his impact on the general history of his period or 328.41092 for his legislative work.

Give greatest weight to the highest office reached, unless there is a clear reason to do otherwise, using the following table of preference:

1. Use 930–990 for monarchs, presidents, other heads of state, prime ministers, vice presidents, and regents, using the number for the period during which they held office. Also use 930–990 for public figures of any position or combination of positions who had a significant impact upon general history, using the period numbers that best approximate their period of influence. Candidates of major parties for the highest office of a country are also assigned history numbers, generally using the number for the period during which they ran for office, e.g., use 973.68092 for Stephen Douglas, who ran against Lincoln in 1860. Sometimes a candidate defeated for party nomination made enough difference in the outcome to warrant a history number for his comprehensive biography, e.g., use 973.923092 for Eugene McCarthy, who ran unsuccessfully for the Democratic presidential nomination in 1968.

2. Use the number for the field of service for cabinet members, e.g., use 327.440092 for a foreign minister of France, use 336.092 for a secretary of the treasury.

3. Use 327.3–.9 for ambassadors and pre-World War II ministers plenipotentiary.

4. Use 328.4–.9 for legislators not warranting a specific subject number, e.g., a floor leader, whip, or member noted for promoting legislative work. Biographers tend to concentrate upon legislators who left their mark on general history; so always consider the number in 900 for the area the legislature served before assigning another. Only occasionally will a work focus on a legislator's own constituency.

5. Use 327.3–.9 for diplomats below the level of ambassador or pre-World War II minister plenipotentiary; however, if associated with notable events, use the number for the events.

6. Use the number for field of service for public administrators not holding cabinet positions, if their contribution to the service was significant, e.g., use 363.25092 for J. Edgar Hoover, director of the U.S. Federal Bureau of Investigation; otherwise use 352–354.

Use the same preference for public figures of state, provincial, and local jurisdictions. Usually national office takes preference over other levels, but consider the weight of contributions. For example, DeWitt Clinton, the famous governor of New York, was briefly U.S. senator, and was a minor party candidate for president, but use 974.703092 for New York State history of his time for his comprehensive biography. Fiorello La Guardia served fourteen years as U.S. representative, and briefly as chief of the U.S. Office of Civilian Defense and as director of the United Nations Relief and Rehabilitation Administration; but use 974.71042092 for his biography, as he is best known as mayor of New York City.

Systems and laws named after persons

Do not use T1—092 for a system or law named after a single individual, but *do* use it for treatment of the individual emphasizing biography, e.g., use 150.1952 for a work on Freudianism, but use 150.1952092 for a biography of Freud.

When an individual is named in a heading or notes, treat the system according to the standard rules for topics, but be liberal about adding notation 092 from Table 1 for treatment emphasizing the individual. For example, 576.52 (Laws of genetics) gives Mendel's laws in a class here note, so any subdivision may be added, e.g., use 576.5205 for serials on Mendel's laws, use 576.52092 for Mendel's biography. Conversely, 150.19434 (Neobehaviorism) gives systems of Guthrie, Hull, Skinner, Tolman in an including note, so standard subdivisions are not added, e.g., use 150.19434 for serials on systems of Skinner without addition of notation 05 from Table 1. However, use notation 092 for strictly persons treatment of any of these individuals, e.g., use 150.19434092 for a biography emphasizing Skinner's work on neobehaviorism.

Families and close associates of the famous

Class a history of the immediate or extended family of a famous person with the biography of that person if the work strongly emphasizes the famous person. The same rule applies to the biography of a single relative or close associate of a famous person. However, if the relative or associate is important in his or her own right, or if the famous person is not strongly featured, class the life of the relative in the subject warranted by his or her own work, e.g., use 269.2092 for a biography of evangelist Ruth Carter Stapleton, sister of President Jimmy Carter, that treats the president only incidentally. If in doubt, do not use the number assigned to a famous person for a relative or close friend; prefer a number warranted by the biographee's own activities. Class a general family history in 929.2.

Partial biography

Class each partial biography featuring a specific contribution of a person with the contribution. However, use the comprehensive biography number for a work about the portions of a person's life that preceded the activity with which the person is chiefly associated, unless the work has significant alternative subject emphasis. For example, use 796.42092 for British Member of Parliament Christopher Chataway's earlier life as an athlete; but use 954.045092 for the childhood of Indira Gandhi, the number for her period as prime minister of India.

Approximating the whole

Add T1—092 even in cases when a person's work may not approximate the whole of the most specific available number. Conversely, do not add T1—092 to extremely minute subjects, e.g., class ball players at the number for game they played, not in subordinate numbers for specific positions on the field, even if a player filled only one position.

Biography associated with place rather than subject

Class an individual biography in the number most nearly covering the history and civilization of the place and time of the activity emphasized when a work is not clearly associated with any subject but is clearly associated with a place, e.g., use 979.46104092 for the diary of a resident of San Francisco during the Gold Rush.

T1—0922

Collected persons treatment

Use T1—0922 for a work on two people collaborating in the same field, e.g., the Wright brothers 629.1300922, Pierre and Marie Curie 530.0922. However, use T1—092 when the focus is strongly on one of the two.

Do not use area subdivisions for collected biography of groups that have a strong collective personal identity, even though all the members are known to have come from one particular area, e.g., the Beatles 782.421660922 (*not* 782.42166092242 or 782.42166092242753).

T1—0922 vs. T1—093–099

Collected persons treatment vs. Geographic treatment

Persons treatment covers description and critical appraisal of work, and geographic treatment covers description by place, by specific instance of the subject. Prefer T1—0922 over T1—093–099 for material limited by persons but emphasizing area aspects. However, use T1—093–099 when the intent of the author or compiler is to describe works of art characteristic of an area, or simply to describe such works in an area (even though the works may be listed under their producers). When the title and front matter do not reveal the intent, any discussion of style is an important indicator. A discussion focusing on the character and style of the individual producers indicates persons treatment; one focusing on the characteristics of the place and times indicates geographic treatment. For example, use 730.92245 for a book on the style and character of sculptures by Cellini, Donatello, and Michelangelo, but use 730.94509024 for a book illustrating Italian Renaissance sculpture by describing the work of these same men. If in doubt, prefer T1—0922.

Use the area number if the text is largely confined to concise descriptions of works of technology or art (or to identifications and illustrations of them), even if persons are indicated in the title, e.g., descriptions of the works of six famous Italian sculptors 730.945.

However, use T1—092 without further subdivision for individual persons for all description and critical appraisal of works they have produced.

T1—093–099 and T2—3–9

Geographic treatment

Change of preference when area notation is added directly

When area notation from Table 2 is added directly in the schedules rather than through notation 09 from Table 1, the rule of zero changes the preference for areas with respect to other standard subdivisions. When there is no zero, areas move to the top of the table of preference from their normal position in the middle of the table.

The change of preference applies whenever the number of zeros differs, e.g., when areas remain in T1—09 but other subdivisions are displaced to 001–009.

When area notation from Table 2 is added directly in the schedules, standard subdivisions T1—01–091 can be added without restrictions, e.g., use 365.94405 for periodicals about penal institutions in France. Notation 092 for persons can be used, but only when the area notation is added directly while the persons notation remains in its standard subdivision position. If all of T1—09 is vacated, the preference for persons remains. For example, as all 365.09 is moved to 365.9, use 365.92 for all biography regardless of area, e.g., use 365.92244 for persons associated with penal institutions in France. But if only some of T1—09 is vacated, as when treatment by specific continents, countries, and localities is moved from 373.093–.099 to 373.3–.9, then notation 092 is added to area notation, e.g., use 373.40922 for secondary educators in Europe. Notation 093–099 can also be used when the base area notation specifies origin or style, while the added notation identifies the area in which the subject is found or practiced, e.g., use 641.5944 for French cooking, 641.59440973 for a work on the popularity of French cooking in America.

Differences in standard subdivisions added to area notation

A limited number of the subdivisions falling below T1—09 in the table of preference may be added in T1—09, overriding the rule that one standard subdivision is not added to another standard subdivision. Special tables in T1—09 show which may be used. The special table under T1—093–099 also allows T1—09 to be used to add historical periods and to add area notation to area notation in certain cases.

T1—0940902 vs. T1—0902

Medieval period in European history vs. 6th–15th centuries, 500–1499

Use T1—0940902 for works that are clearly focused on Europe in the Middle Ages and the medieval period, but use T1—0902 for works that attempt to cover the whole world during the period. However, the medieval record of many subjects outside Europe is poorly documented, so a work attempting worldwide coverage may in fact be predominantly about the subject in Europe. If in doubt, prefer T1—0940902.

Table 2. Areas, Periods, Persons

T2—162

Oceans and seas

Use T2—163–168 (*not* T2—3–9) for parts of oceans and noninland seas limited by either country or locality, e.g., use T2—16347 (*not* T2—752 or T2—7551) for Chesapeake Bay, an arm of the Atlantic Ocean that is almost surrounded by Maryland and Virginia.

Estuaries

Use the appropriate area number in T2—3–9 for estuaries that are parts of named rivers, but use T2—16 for estuaries that are parts of oceans and noninland seas, e.g., use T2—16347 (*not* T2—7553) for the York River, an estuary of the Chesapeake Bay.

Coastal waters

Use the number in T2—163–168 that includes the majority of the waters for comprehensive works on the coastal waters of a country, e.g., coastal waters of Russia T2—1632 (*not* T2—16334 or T2—16451), of the United States T2—1634 (*not* T2—16364 or T2—1643). If the areas are approximately equal in size, use the number coming first, e.g., coastal waters of Spain T2—16338 (*not* T2—16381), of Panama T2—16365 (*not* T2—1641).

T2—163 and T2—164, T2—165

Atlantic, Indian, and Pacific Oceans

Table 2 divides the world ocean into three parts—Atlantic, Indian, and Pacific Oceans. The Arctic Ocean is considered a sea of the Atlantic. There is no Antarctic Ocean, but provision is made in T2—167 for the extreme southern portions of the three oceans.

Divisions between the oceans are as follows:

Atlantic-Pacific: north, Bering Strait; south, a line drawn southeasterly from Cape Horn to the northern tip of Palmer Peninsula, Antarctica

Pacific-Indian: north, a line from Melville Island to Timor, thence through the islands of Indonesia to Singapore Strait; south, a line drawn south from Cape Howe, Victoria, Australia, on the 150° east meridian

Indian-Atlantic: north, Suez Canal; south, a line drawn south from Cape Agulhas, South Africa, on the 20° east meridian

Use notes and references to decide where to class connecting bodies of water, e.g., Bering Strait T2—16451 (*not* T2—16325 or T2—16327).

T2—4–9

Modern world; extraterrestrial worlds

General arrangement of Table 2

The general arrangement of Table 2 is geographic rather than by political units, e.g., Hawaii T2—969 under Oceania, separated from the rest of the United States in T2—73–79; the Asian parts of Russia T2—57, separated from the European portion of Russia in T2—471–474.

Physiographic features and regions

Class a specific feature or region not named in the area table and that is wholly or almost wholly contained within a political or administrative unit with the unit; however, do not add further notation. For example, use T2—7421 for Mount Washington, New Hampshire; T2—75793 for Lake Moultrie, South Carolina; 917.5793 (*not* 917.579304) for travel connected with Lake Moultrie.

Class a river with the political or administrative unit in which the river's mouth is located, e.g., Escanaba River, Michigan T2—77494. However, if the upper part of the river is more important politically, economically, or culturally, class the river with that part, e.g., Tigris and Euphrates Rivers T2—5674 (*not* T2—5675).

Class general treatment of a specific kind of feature or region limited to a specific continent, country or locality with the continent, country, or locality plus notation 091 from the table under T1—093–099 in Table 1, e.g., rivers of Europe T2—4091693, rivers of England T2—42091693. However, do not add notation 091 for individual features or regions, e.g., Nile River of Egypt T2—62 (*not* T2—62091693). Class treatment of a specific kind of feature or region not limited to a specific continent in T2—1, e.g., rivers T2—1693.

Cities, towns, villages

Cities are not named in Table 2, except:

1. Major world cities, either with their own numbers, e.g., Amsterdam T2—492352, or in a note, e.g., Mecca T2—538

2. Smaller cities given their own numbers early in the development of the DDC, e.g., Guelph, Ontario T2—71343

3. The capital and largest city of each state of the United States, e.g., Pierre and Sioux Falls, South Dakota, at T2—78329 and T2—783371 respectively

4. Independent cities, e.g., Alexandria, Virginia T2—755296

5. United States cities coextensive with their counties (or parishes), e.g., Philadelphia T2—74811, San Francisco T2—79461

6. Cities, towns, and villages named to indicate boundaries of units when the boundaries are not readily available in reference works, e.g., throughout Australia T2—94 and the western provinces of Canada T2—711–712

Class a metropolitan area with the central city, e.g., the metropolitan area of Chicago T2—77311. Standard subdivisions may be added if appropriate.

Class general treatment of urban regions limited to a specific continent, country or locality with the continent, country, or locality plus notation 091732 (derived from notation 091 from the table under T1—093–099), e.g., urban regions of Europe T2—4091732, urban regions of England T2—42091732. Class treatment of urban regions not limited to a specific continent in T2—1732.

See also discussion at T2—41 and T2—42; also at T2—713 and T2—714; also at T2—93.

T2—4–9 vs. T2—3

Modern world; extraterrestrial worlds vs. Ancient world

Use T2—4–9 for those parts of the world more or less known to classical antiquity (the "Ancient world") when considered after the period of "ancient history," as well as other areas such as America in both ancient and later times. Use T2—3 for only the "Ancient world" during the period of "ancient history." For example, use T2—51 for later China and T2—31 for ancient China; T2—5694 for later Palestine and T2—33 for ancient Palestine; T2—44 for France and T2—364 for ancient Gaul; but use T2—7265 for both ancient and later Yucatán. The demarcation date between "ancient" and "later" varies from place to place and can be determined by examination of the terminal dates in classes 931–939, e.g., 931 China to 420, 933 Palestine to 70, 936.4 Celtic regions to 486. If in doubt, prefer T2—4–9.

T2—41 and T2—42

Scotland and England

The lower level authorities of England and the unitary authorities of England and Scotland may be referred to by a number of different names, most commonly District, Borough, or City. The term "City" does not necessarily refer to an urban locality. The Districts, Boroughs, and Cities are often named after an urban locality either within or approximately the same as the jurisdiction. If the urban locality is approximately the same as the jurisdiction, the locality is given in a class-here note. For example, Exeter City, the jurisdiction, and Exeter, the urban locality, are coextensive; thus, the table entry:

T2—423 56 Exeter City

Class here Exeter

If the urban locality is not approximately the same as the jurisdiction, only the jurisdiction is given. The classifier can assume that were the locality to be given, it would be in an including note. For example, Canterbury City, the jurisdiction, and Canterbury, the urban locality, are not coextensive; thus, the table entry:

T2—422 34 Canterbury City

See also discussion at T2—4–9: Cities, towns, villages.

T2—713 and T2—714

Ontario and Quebec

In Ontario and Quebec, the jurisdiction directly below the Province is referred to by the names District, City, County, Municipality, Regional Municipality, or Regional County Municipality. The term "City" does not necessarily refer to an urban locality. A District, City, County, Municipality, Regional Municipality, or Regional County Municipality can be named after an urban locality within the jurisdiction. If the urban locality is approximately the same as the jurisdiction, the locality is given in a class-here note. For example, City of Québec, the jurisdiction, and Québec, the urban locality, are approximately the same; thus, the table entry:

T2—714 471 City of Québec

Former name: Quebec Urban Community

Class here Québec

If the urban locality is not approximately the same as the jurisdiction, only the jurisdiction is given. The classifier can assume that were the locality to be given, the locality would be in an including note. For example, City of Gatineau, the jurisdiction, and Gatineau, the urban locality, are not approximately the same; thus, the table entry:

T2—714 221 City of Gatineau

See also discussion at T2—4–9: Cities, towns, villages.

T2—73 vs. T2—71

United States vs. Canada

Use T2—73 if works about the United States and Canada are predominantly about the United States. Use T2—71 when Canada receives fuller treatment or the United States and Canada are given equal treatment. Use T2—7 only when the work also discusses areas in T2—72, even though Canada and the United States are assigned most of the numbers in the span. If in doubt, prefer T2—73.

T2—93

New Zealand

In New Zealand, the jurisdiction directly below the Region is referred to as either District or City. The term "City" does not necessarily refer to an urban locality. Districts and Cities are often named after an urban locality either within or approximately the same as the jurisdiction. If the urban locality is approximately the same as the jurisdiction, the locality is given in a class-here note. For example, Auckland City, the jurisdiction, and Auckland, the urban locality, are approximately the same; thus, the table entry:

T2—932 4 Auckland City

Class here Auckland

If the urban locality is not approximately the same as the jurisdiction, only the jurisdiction is given. The classifier can assume that were the locality to be given, it would be in an including note. For example, Dunedin City, the jurisdiction, and Dunedin, the urban locality, are not approximately the same; thus, the table entry:

T2—939 2 Dunedin City

See also discussion at T2—4–9: Cities, towns, villages.

T2—99 vs. T2—19

Extraterrestrial worlds vs. Space

Use T2—99 for the various bodies of the universe moving through space, e.g., moon rocks 552.09991. Use T2—19 only for space itself. If in doubt, prefer T2—99.

Table 3. Subdivisions for the Arts, for Individual Literatures, for Specific Literary Forms

Number building

Examples of basic number building for works in an individual language by or about individual authors (with use of Table 3A) and by or about more than one author (with use of Table 3B) are given in this entry. Use the following elements to build the numbers: base number; form; period; kind, scope, or medium; notation 08 Collections or notation 09 Criticism (plus additional 0s in some cases); subform; additional notation from Table 3C and other tables. Detailed instructions for number building appear in Tables 3A and 3B.

Note: in the following discussion, "T3" refers to both Table 3A (individual authors) and Table 3B (more than one author).

More than one form

1. Works by or about more than one author: not restricted by period or form (Table 3B)

Base no. + notation 08 or 09

81 + 08 = 810.8 (an anthology of American literature)

2. Works by or about more than one author: restricted to a specific period but not to a specific form (Table 3B)

Base no. + notation 08 or 09 + period

83 + 08 + 006 = 830.8006 (a collection of 18th-century German literature)

3. Works by or about more than one author: not restricted by form or period, place of authorship emphasized (Table 3B)

Base no. + notation 080 or 09 + 9 from Table 3C + area notation from Table 2

869 + 080 + 9 + 81 = 869.080981 (an anthology of literature in Portuguese by Brazilian authors)

Forms T3—1–7

1. Works by or about an individual author: restricted to a specific form and period (Table 3A)

Base no. + form + period

82 + 1 + 3 = 821.3 (Spenser's *Faerie Queene*)

2. Works by or about more than one author: restricted to a specific form but not to a specific period (Table 3B)

Base no. + form + notation 008 or 009

82 + 2 + 009 = 822.009 (criticism of English drama)

3. Works by or about more than one author: restricted to a specific form, to a specific kind, scope, or medium, and to a specific period (Table 3B)

Base no. + form + kind, scope, or medium + notation 08 or 09 + period

84 + 3 + 01 + 08 + 07 = 843.010807 (a collection of 19th-century French short stories)

4. Works by or about more than one author: restricted to a specific form but not to a specific kind, scope, or medium; restricted to a specific period (Table 3B)

Base no. + form + period + notation 08 or 09

83 + 2 + 914 + 09 = 832.91409 (criticism of German drama of the second half of the 20th century)

Form T3—8 Miscellaneous writings

1. Works by or about an individual author: restricted to a specific form, period, and subform (T3A—8)

   Base no. + form + period + subform

   81 + 8 + 4 + 02 = 818.402 (a collection of quotations of an individual American author of the later 19th century)

2. Works by or about more than one author: restricted to a specific form, period, and subform (T3B—8)

   Base no. + form + period + subform + notation 08 or 09

   84 + 8 + 914 + 02 + 08 = 848.9140208 (a collection of quotations of several French authors of the later 20th century)

Table 3A. Subdivisions for Works by or about Individual Authors

Comprehensive numbers for authors, and numbers for individual works

Follow the criteria given below on language, national affiliation, literary form, and literary period in order to determine the comprehensive number for collected works, critical evaluation, or biography of an author. Use the same national affiliation and literary period for comprehensive works and for all individual works of an author; however, use the language and form appropriate for each individual work, even if different from the language and form selected for the author's comprehensive number.

Language

Class an author with the language in which the author writes.

If an author changes place of residence or national affiliation to a country with a different language but continues to write in the same language, use the language in which the author writes, e.g., use 891.7344 for a novel in Russian by Solzhenit͡syn, even if the novel was written while he was living in the United States.

Class comprehensive works for an author who writes in more than one language with the language that the author used last, e.g., Samuel Beckett 848.91409. However, if another language is predominant, class with that language. Class individual works of such an author with the language in which they were originally written.

National affiliation

National affiliation affects the choice of number only for literature written in English (810 vs. 820) or if an option for identifying national literatures is used.

If an author changes national affiliation to a country with the same language as that in which the author has been writing, use the literature number appropriate for the author's adopted citizenship, e.g., class T. S. Eliot as a British author. Class all works of such an author, including individual works written before the change of citizenship, with the same national literature.

If an author changes place of residence, but not national affiliation, to another country with the same language as that in which the author has been writing, continue to use the literature number of the author's original country, e.g., class a Jamaican author living in London, but still retaining Jamaican citizenship, as a Jamaican author.

If information about an author's national affiliation is not readily available in the work being classed or in standard reference books, use the literature number of the author's country of origin, if known; or the literature number of the country in which the author's earlier works were published.

Literary form

For comprehensive works, use the form with which an author is chiefly identified, e.g., Jane Austen 823.7. If the author is not chiefly identified with one form, use T3A—8 Miscellaneous writings plus literary period plus notation 09 from the table at T3A—81–89, e.g., use 828.91409 for a late–20th-century English author who is equally famous as a novelist, dramatist, and poet. For an individual work, use the form in which the work is written.

Literary periods

Use only one literary period for an author and all of the author's works, including works that may have been published earlier or later than the dates covered by that period. Determine the literary period in accordance with scholarly consensus about when an author flourished. For example, class an author commonly regarded as an early-19th-century writer as such, even if the author published literary works at the end of the 18th century. In the absence of scholarly comment, use the weight of bibliographic evidence to determine when an author flourished. For example, class an author who published one novel in 1999, one novel in 2000, one in 2001, and one in 2002 in the literary period beginning with 2000. If the period when an author flourished cannot be determined, use the date of the author's earliest known separate literary publication, disregarding magazine contributions, isolated student works, and juvenilia.

Biography

Do not use notation 092 from Table 1 for biography. Class literary diaries and reminiscences in T3A—8 plus period subdivision plus subdivision 03, e.g., Hemingway's *A Moveable Feast* 818.5203.

Number building

Examples of number building are given in the Manual at the beginning of Table 3. Use the following flow chart as an aid to building numbers and as a supplement to the detailed instructions at Table 3A.

Flow chart A: Works by or about an individual author

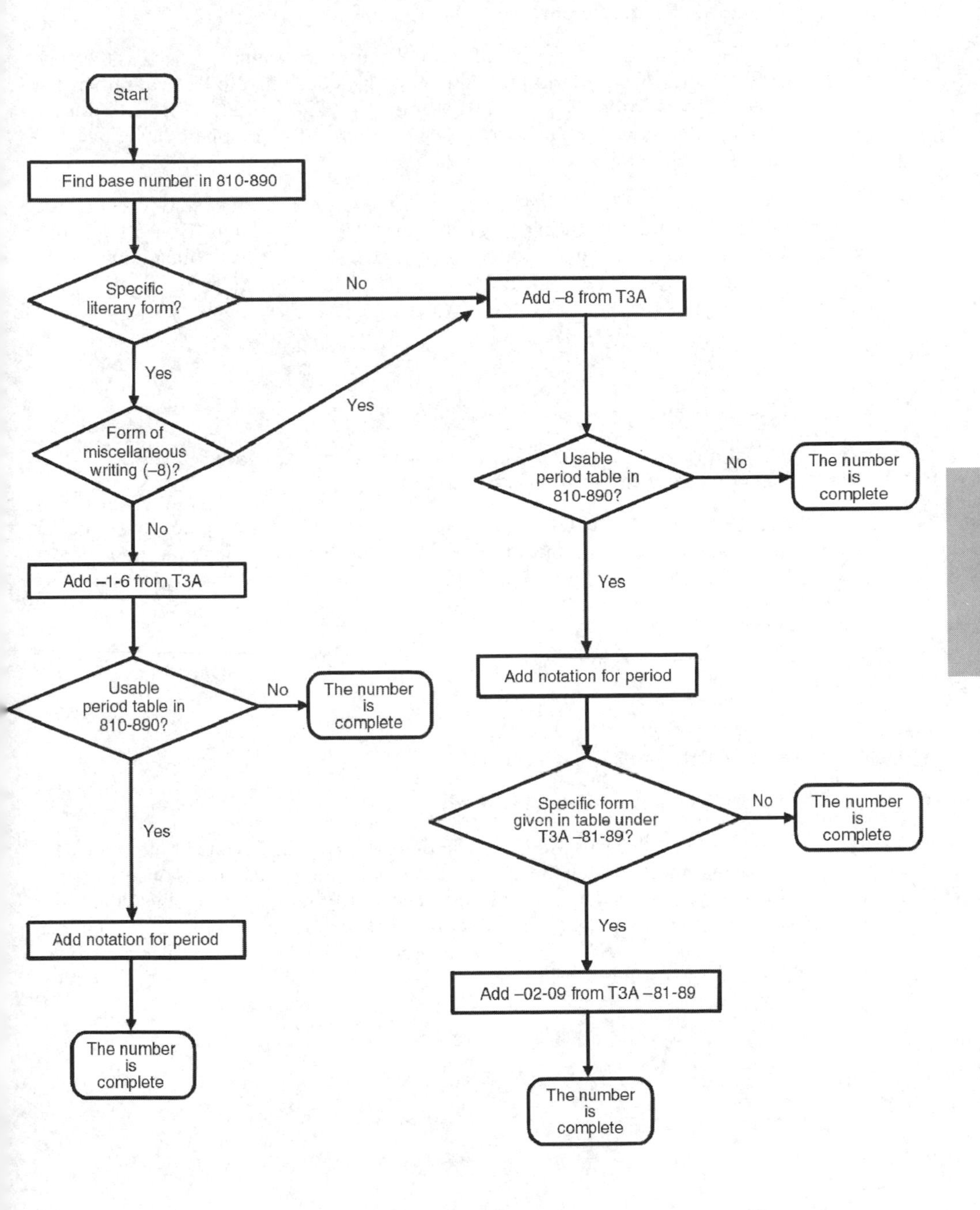

T3A—2, T3B—2 vs. T3A—1, T3B—102

Drama vs. Dramatic poetry

Use T3—2 for poetic plays intended for theatrical presentation, such as the plays of Shakespeare and Marlowe, and poetic plays designed to be read rather than acted, such as Milton's *Samson Agonistes*. Use T3A—1 and T3B—102 for poetry that employs dramatic form or some element of dramatic technique as a means of achieving poetic ends.

Use T3A—2 and T3B—2045 for monologues typically intended for use in theatrical presentations featuring only one actor. Use T3A—1 and T3B—102 for dramatic monologues that are poems in which the speaker is a fictional or historical character speaking to an identifiable but silent listener at a dramatic moment in the speaker's life, such as Robert Browning's "My Last Duchess."

If in doubt, prefer T3A—2 or T3B—2.

T3A—8 + 02, T3B—802, T3B—8 + 02 vs. 398.6, 793.735

Anecdotes, epigrams, graffiti, jokes, quotations vs. Riddles as folk literature vs. Riddles as entertainment

Use T3A—8 + 02, T3B—802, T3B—8 + 02 for riddles as jokes, even though they may not seem at home amid belles lettres, especially juvenile riddle jokes. Use 398.6 for riddles as folk literature, which are typically anonymous, and for interdisciplinary works on riddles. Use 793.735 for riddles as puzzles for indoor entertainment.

If in doubt, prefer in the following order: riddles as jokes (T3A—8 + 02, T3B—802, T3B—8 + 02), 398.6, 793.735.

T3A—8 + 03 and T3B—803, T3B—8 + 03

Diaries, journals, notebooks, reminiscences

Use T3A—8 + 03, T3B—803, and T3B—8 + 03 for diaries and reminiscences of literary authors in which the life of the author or authors as such is of key interest. However, class the diaries and reminiscences of literary authors that emphasize some other subject besides the general life of the author with the subject emphasized, e.g., use 940.5472 for a diary compiled while the author was in a prisoner-of-war camp during World War II.

Table 3B. Subdivisions for Works by or about More than One Author

Preference order

The preference order in case of conflict between literary forms is spelled out at the beginning of the 800 schedule and in Table 3B under T3B—1–8. There are also preference orders in case of conflict among other aspects. The preference order for the four aspects expressed by means of Table 3C is as follows:

Themes and subjects	T3C—3
Elements	T3C—2
Qualities	T3C—1
Persons	T3C—8–9

For example, use 811.0080358 (*not* 811.00809287) for a general anthology of poetry about war written by American women poets.

The preference given to literary period in relation to the four aspects expressed by means of Table 3C varies: for works treating more than two literatures or more than one form in one literature, literary periods have a lower priority than the aspects from Table 3C; for works treating a specific form in an individual literature, literary periods have a higher priority than the aspects from Table 3C.

Specific media, scopes, kinds consistently have preference over both period and the aspects from Table 3C. However, the preference given to scope in relation to kind varies: for drama, scope has a higher preference; but for fiction, kind has higher preference.

Preference orders are always the same for both collections of literary texts and criticism of the texts.

Sometimes elements low in the priority listings can be added to a number after the higher priority elements. For example, use 813.540932162 for a critical appraisal of later-20th-century American fiction about the sea: 813 (American fiction) + 54 (period: later 20th century) + 09 (critical appraisal) + 32162 (theme: the sea). The period comes first because it has higher priority than the theme; but the theme can also be expressed. Use the same preference order for these additional elements, e.g., for critical appraisal of later-20th-century American fiction about the sea by women, the theme of the sea would be expressed by means of Table 3C, but the authorship by a specific kind of person would not be expressed, because themes appear higher in the priority listing.

Sometimes aspects low in the priority listings can be expressed only by means of standard subdivision notation from Table 1. In the example above of a critical appraisal of later-20th-century American fiction about the sea by women, use notation 082 from Table 1 to express the aspect of women: 813.540932162082. For another example, use 808.83932173209034 for a collection of 19th-century fiction of several literatures about urban life: 808.839 (collection of fiction from more than two literatures displaying specific features) + 321732 (theme: urban life) + 09034 (standard subdivision for the historical period of the 19th century). In the priority listing, theme comes before period; and once the theme has been expressed, there is no way to express the period except by use of the standard subdivision.

See also discussion at T3B—08 and T3B—09; also at T3B—1; also at T3B—2; also at T3B—3; also at 808.8.

Number building

Examples of number building are given in the *Manual* at the beginning of Table 3. Use the following flow chart as an aid to building numbers and as a supplement to the detailed instructions at Table 3B.

Flow chart B: Works by or about more than one author

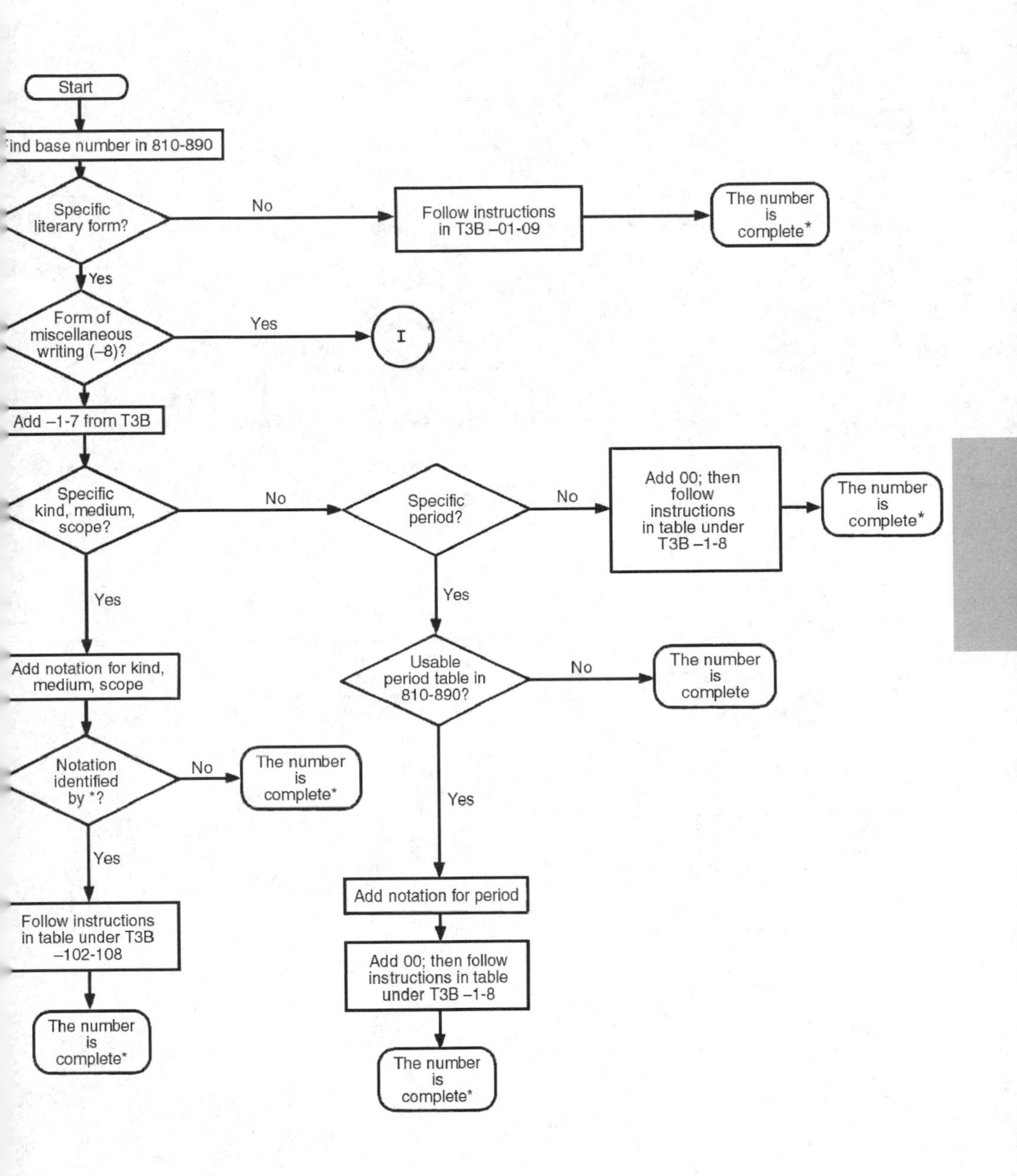

*If appropriate, standard subdivisions may be added

Flow chart B for notation 8 Miscellaneous writings

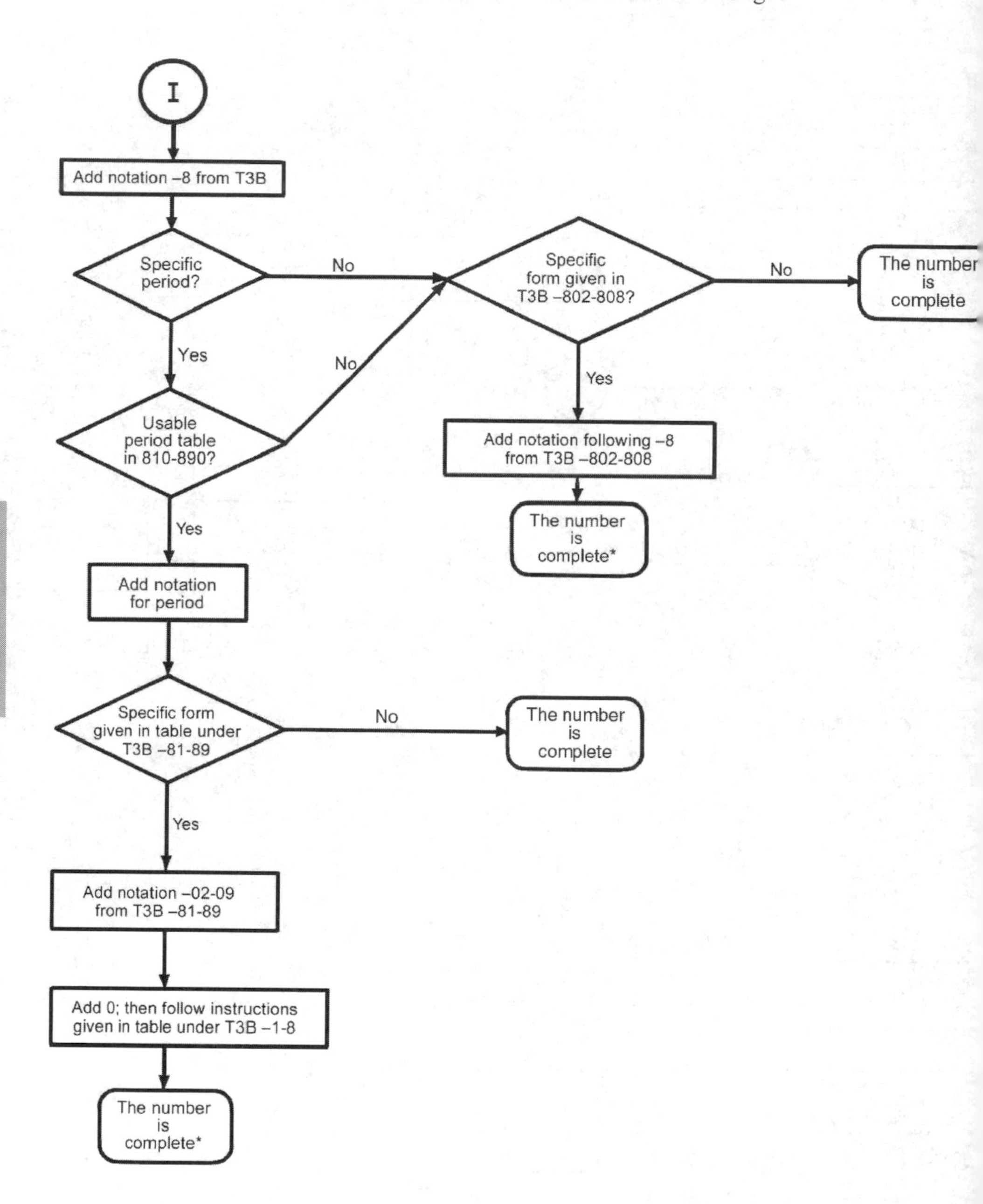

*If appropriate, standard subdivisions may be added

T3B—08 and T3B—09

Preference order for collections and criticism of literature in more than one form

Here are examples illustrating the preference order for collections of texts (T3B—08) in more than one form from an individual literature (American literature used for the examples). The preference order is the same for criticism (T3B—09).

1. Specific themes and subjects, e.g., 810.80382 (religion)
2. Specific elements, e.g., 810.8024 (plot)
3. Specific qualities, e.g., 810.8013 (idealism)
4. Works for and by specific kinds of persons, e.g., 810.809282 (for children)
5. Period, e.g., 810.8003 (19th century)

See also discussion at Table 3B: Preference order.

T3B—091–099 vs. T3B—09001–09009

Literature displaying specific features or emphasizing subjects, and for and by specific kinds of persons vs. Literature from specific periods

If there is no applicable literary period table, T3B—09001–09009 cannot be used; moreover, do not add notation 0901–0905 from Table 1 to T3B—09 to show period, e.g., 20th-century Macedonian literature 891.81909 (*not* 891.81909000904).

However, the rule of zero gives T3B—091–099 priority over T3B—09001–09009. If the provisions of T3B—091–099 are used, then do not add any otherwise applicable literary period table. Instead, add notation 0901–0905 from Table 1 to indicate period, regardless of whether there is a literary period table for that literature, e.g., use 810.93580904 for 20th-century American literature in English on historical and political themes, use 891.819093580904 for 20th-century Macedonian literature on historical and political themes.

T3B—1

Preference order for poetry

Here are examples illustrating the preference order for poetry (A) from more than two literatures and (B) from one or two literatures. The preference order is the same for collections and criticism.

A. Poetry from more than two literatures

(Collections used as example)

1. Specific kinds, e.g., 808.8142 (sonnets)
2. Specific themes and subjects, e.g., 808.819353 (friendship)

3. Specific elements, e.g., 808.81922 (description)
4. Specific qualities, e.g., 808.819145 (romanticism)
5. Period, e.g., 808.81033 (18th century)

B. Poetry from one or two literatures

(Criticism of American poetry used as example)

1. Specific kinds, e.g., 811.03209 (epic)
2. Period, e.g., 811.5409 (later 20th century)
3. Specific themes and subjects, e.g., 811.009353 (friendship)
4. Specific elements, e.g., 811.00922 (description)
5. Specific qualities, e.g., 811.009145 (romanticism)
6. Works for and by specific kinds of persons, e.g., 811.0098924 (by Jews)

See also discussion at Table 3B: Preference order.

T3B—102–107, T3B—205, T3B—308 vs. T3C—1, T3C—3

Genres of poetry, drama, fiction vs. Arts and literature displaying specific qualities of style, mood, viewpoint or dealing with specific themes and subjects

Use the numbers for specific kinds of poetry, drama, and fiction for works belonging to specific literary genres, e.g., the genres of historical drama T3B—20514 and realistic fiction T3B—3083. Often the themes and other characteristics that mark specific genres can also be expressed by means of notation 1 or 3 from Table 3C, e.g., works about historical themes T3C—358, works displaying realism T3C—12. Always prefer the genre number over the number derived from Table 3C for literary works belonging to a specific genre, e.g., a collection of historical drama T3B—2051408 (*not* T3B—20080358); criticism of realistic novels T3B—308309 (*not* T3B—300912). Add notation 1 or 3 from Table 3C to the genre number if it is not redundant, e.g., add T3C—358 for a discussion of historical themes in tragedy (T3B—2051209358), but not for a discussion of historical themes in historical drama.

Use notation 1 or 3 from Table 3C for literary works that display specific features and are not limited to a specific genre, e.g., a discussion of historical themes in serious and comic drama not limited by period T3B—2009358, a discussion of realistic elements in fiction of various kinds not limited by period T3B—300912. Use notation 1 or 3 from Table 3C also for literary works displaying specific features that might be regarded as marking a genre if no such genre is named for the relevant literary form in Table 3B, e.g., use T3B—20093278 for a discussion of western drama not limited by period as there is no mention of western drama under T3B—205 Specific kinds of drama. However, use genre notation 30874 from Table 3B for western fiction (*not* T3B—30093278).

If in doubt between Table 3B notation for genres and Table 3C notation, prefer the Table 3B notation.

Use notation from Table 3B only for literature (belles lettres); not for the arts, for films, or for radio or television programs. Use notation 1 and 3 from Table 3C to express genre for the arts, films, radio and television programs, e.g., use T3C—15 for science fiction in the arts, in films, in radio and television programs; but use T3B—308762 for science fiction as a genre of fiction. Use T3C—11 for experimental works in the arts, for experimental films, for experimental radio and television programs; but use T3B—807 for experimental literary works without identifiable literary form.

T3B—2

Preference order for drama

Here are examples illustrating the preference order for drama (A) from more than two literatures and (B) from one or two literatures. The preference order is the same for collections and criticism.

A. Drama from more than two literatures

(Criticism used as example)

1. Specific media, e.g., 809.225 (television)
2. Specific scopes, e.g., 809.241 (one-act plays)
3. Specific kinds, e.g., 809.2512 (tragedy)
4. Specific themes or subjects, e.g., 809.29351 (Faust)
5. Specific elements, e.g., 809.2925 (stream of consciousness)
6. Specific qualities, e.g., 809.29145 (romanticism)
7. Period, e.g., 809.204 (20th century)

B. Drama from one or two literatures

(Collections of American drama used as example)

1. Specific media, e.g., 812.025083548 (television plays on death)
2. Specific scopes, e.g., 812.04108 (one-act plays)
3. Specific kinds, e.g., 812.051208 (tragedy)
4. Period, e.g., 812.5408 (collection of later 20th century, no focus), 812.540809287 (20th century, by women)
5. Specific themes and subjects, e.g., 812.008036 (weather)
6. Specific elements, e.g., 812.008027 (characters)
7. Specific qualities, e.g., 812.008015 (symbolism)
8. Works for and by specific kinds of persons, e.g., 812.008092827 (for girls)

See also discussion at Table 3B: Preference order.

T3B—3

Preference order for fiction

Here are examples illustrating the preference order for fiction (A) from more than two literatures and (B) from one or two literatures. The preference order is the same for collections and criticism.

A. Fiction from more than two literatures

(Collections used as example)

1. Specific kinds, e.g., 808.8383 (sociological)
2. Specific scopes, e.g., 808.831 (short stories)
3. Specific themes and subjects, e.g., 808.839362 (animals)
4. Specific elements, e.g., 808.83922 (description)
5. Specific qualities, e.g., 808.83913 (idealism)
6. Period, e.g., 808.83034 (19th century)

B. Fiction from one or two literatures

(Criticism of American fiction used as example)

1. Specific kinds, e.g., 813.0876209 (science fiction)
2. Specific scopes, e.g., 813.0109358 (short stories about war)
3. Period, e.g., 813.5409 (later 20th century), 813.540932162 (later 20th century, about the sea)
4. Specific themes and subjects, e.g., 813.009351 (about King Arthur)
5. Specific elements, e.g., 813.00927 (characters)
6. Specific qualities, e.g., 813.00912 (naturalism)
7. Works for and by specific kinds of persons, e.g., 813.009896073 (fiction by African Americans)

See also discussion at Table 3B: Preference order.

Table 3C. Additional Notation for Arts and Literature

T3C—353–358 vs. T3C—352

Specific human, social, scientific, technical, artistic, literary, historical, political themes vs. Specific kinds of persons

Use T3C—353–358 for a specific theme or specific type of theme associated with a specific kind of person unless there is emphasis on the person as a person, e.g., T3C—358 rather than T3C—3528355 for a work about the theme of war associated with soldiers unless there is strong emphasis on the soldiers as persons.

Use T3C—352 for works on specific kinds of persons that treat no particular theme other than the person as a person, e.g., T3C—3522 for a work on women with no particular theme other than women. Also use T3C—352 for works on specific kinds of persons that treat multiple types of themes associated with the person, e.g., T3C—352 for a work on many types of themes associated with heroes. If in doubt, prefer T3C—353–358.

T3C—37 vs. T3C—15

The supernatural, mythological, legendary vs. Symbolism, allegory, fantasy, myth

Use T3C—37 for mythological themes closely tied to specific mythologies of the past, e.g., Roman mythology in Renaissance poetry. Use T3C—15 for abstract myths not tied to specific mythologies of the past, e.g., the myth of a search for lost innocence. If in doubt, prefer T3C—37.

Class specific mythological persons in T3C—351, specific kinds of mythological persons in T3C—352, mythology as a religious theme in T3C—382013.

T3C—93–99

Literature for and by persons resident in specific continents, countries, localities

Use notation 93–99 from Table 3C primarily for the following:

1. Literature in a language by persons from a certain area within a country, e.g., a collection of American literature by residents of Illinois 810.809773.

2. Literature in a language by persons in a country other than the traditional homeland of the dominant literature of the language, e.g., a collection of Spanish literature by Chilean authors 860.80983. The persons in a country other than the traditional homeland may be either native or nonnative residents of the country, e.g., a collection of English literature by non-Japanese residents of Japan 820.80952.

3. Literature in a language by residents of several countries on the same continent from more than one period (only for works in which the literature of one country does not predominate), e.g., French literature by residents of France, Switzerland, Belgium 840.8094; French literature by residents of Africa 840.8096.

Do not use T3C—93–99 for literature in a language by persons in the traditional homeland of the dominant literature of the language except for persons in only part of the country, e.g., a collection of Spanish literature by residents of Spain 860.8, but a collection of Spanish literature by residents of Madrid 860.8094641.

Do not use T3C—943 for German literature by residents of the Federal Republic of Germany, but use T3C—9436 for German literature by residents of Austria.

Do not use T3C—973 for literature in English by residents of the United States, but use T3C—971 for literature in English by residents of Canada.

T3C—93–99, T3C—9174 vs. T3C—8

Literature for and by persons resident in specific continents, countries, localities and Literature for and by persons resident in regions where specific ethnic and national groups predominate vs. Literature for and by persons of ethnic and national groups

Use T3C—93–99 rather than T3C—8 for groups that predominate in an area, e.g., a collection of English literature by persons of Irish ancestry in Australia 820.8089162094, but a collection of English literature by persons of Irish ancestry in Ireland 820.809415; a collection of Spanish literature by Mexican-Americans 860.8086872073, but a collection of Spanish literature by Mexicans 860.80972; a collection of French literature by Arabs in France 840.808927044, but a collection of French literature by Arabs in North Africa 840.80961.

Do not use T3C—8 for the ethnic or national group so closely associated with the language that specifying the group would be redundant, e.g., a collection of Arabic literature by Arabs 892.708 (*not* 892.70808927); thus use 892.7080944 (*not* 892.70808927044) for a collection of Arabic literature by Arabs residing in France.

Do not use T3C—9174 (regions where specific ethnic groups predominate) for groups of persons treatment since such use would practically duplicate the group treatment numbers. For example, Arabs who are residents of all areas where they predominate taken together constitute the overwhelming majority of all Arabs, so T3C—8927 would be used for them rather than T3C—9174927. However, in most cases use of T3C—8 would be redundant. For example, most books about literature by Arabs from all areas where they predominate are about literature in Arabic, so that expressing the ethnic group Arabs with either T3C—9174 or T3C—8 would be redundant.

If in doubt, prefer T3C—93–99 .

Table 4. Subdivisions of Individual Languages and Language Families

T4—1–5, T4—8 vs. T4—7

Description and analysis of the standard form of the language and Standard usage of the language (Prescriptive linguistics) Applied linguistics vs. Historical and geographic variations, modern nongeographic variations

A language may have multiple standard forms. Use T4—1–5 and T4—8 for any of the standard forms, e.g., use 421.52 (*not* 427.994) for a work on standard Australian English pronunciation. Use 427.994 for a work on Australian English pronunciation only if it stresses the distinctive characteristics that make Australian pronunciation different from British or American pronunciation. If in doubt, prefer T4—1–5 and T4—8.

T4—3 vs. T4—81

Dictionaries of the standard form of the language vs. Standard usage of words

Use T4—3 for works intended for ready reference. Specialized dictionaries may be arranged in other ways besides alphabetically (e.g., picture dictionaries in subject order, thesauri in classified order), but the order must be appropriate for ready reference.

Use T4—81 for works intended to be read or studied in full in order to learn vocabulary. The works may be informal and entertaining, e.g., narratives for small children, or formally organized into lessons with quizzes.

If in doubt, prefer T4—3.

T4—7

Historical and geographic variations, modern nongeographic variations

Use of standard subdivisions

Add notation from Table 1 to T4—7 and its subdivisions according to the usual limitations on use of standard subdivisions. For example, use notation 03 from Table 1 and notation 03 from the table under T1—093–099 in Table 1 for dictionaries, e.g., a dictionary of Old High German 437.0103, a dictionary of Northern Yemeni Arabic 492.7709533203.

Where a subdivision is provided for modern nongeographic variations, class comprehensive works on ephemera and slang in the subdivision, e.g., comprehensive works on English language slang 427.09. However, following the rule of zero, class ephemera and slang associated with a specific geographic area with the area, e.g., United States slang 427.973.

Where subdivisions are provided for early versions of a language, notes are used to override the rule of zero so that geographic variants of an early version of a language class with the early version, e.g., use 427.0209428 for Middle English dialects of northeast England. Use 427.8 for modern dialects of northeast England and comprehensive works on Middle English and modern English dialects of northeast England.

Pidgins and creoles

Class a specific pidgin or creole as a variation of the source language from which more of its vocabulary comes than from its other source language(s). Class a pidgin or creole, which is customarily associated with a specific geographic area, in T4—709 plus the area number from Table 2 or in one of the subdivisions of T4—7 for geographic variations where they are provided in 420–490, e.g., the Krio language of Sierra Leone 427.9664.

Table 5. Ethnic and National Groups

Nationality and language

Table 5 Ethnic and National Groups and Table 6 Languages are both based on the traditional sequence of languages in 420–490, and therefore most numbers are developed in parallel. But separate tables are needed because language and nationality do not always match, e.g., there are Canadian people (T5—11 in Table 5), but no Canadian language; there is a Yiddish language (T6—391 in Table 6) but no Yiddish people.

Ethnic group and nationality

The generally preferred citation order is ethnic group over nationality, as nationality is normally given a low priority, and citizens and noncitizens of a country class in the same number. However, a different and atypical citation order is given at some specific numbers in Table 5, e.g., for Canadians of French and British origin, the prescribed citation order is nationality first (T5—11 Canadians), then ethnic group: T5—112 for Canadians of British origin, T5—114 for Canadians of French origin. Use the numbers T5—21071 (T5—21 people of British Isles + T2—71 Canada) and T5—41071 (T5—41 French + T2—71 Canada) only for persons of British and French origin in Canada who are not Canadian citizens. But in the absence of specific instructions to the contrary use the citation order given at the beginning of the table, e.g., Canadians of Ukrainian descent T5—91791071 (*not* T5—11). Use this same number for both Canadians of Ukrainian descent and persons of Ukrainian descent who are in Canada but not Canadian citizens.

In general, use the same number for both the majority ethnic group of a nation and the total population viewed as a national group, e.g., T5—94541 for both ethnic Finns and all citizens of Finland viewed as a national group. Usually, priority between ethnic and national affiliation is an issue only for minority ethnic groups, e.g., use T5—39704897 (T5—397 Swedes + T2—4897 Finland) for Finnish citizens who are ethnic Swedes, a minority ethnic group, because their ethnic group takes priority over their nationality. Use T5—94541073 (T5—94541 Finns + T2—73 United States) for Finnish citizens who are ethnic Finns in the United States, but use T5—397073 (T5—397 Swedes + T2—73 United States) for Finnish citizens who are ethnic Swedes in the United States, which is the number for all persons of Swedish descent in the United States. Their Finnish national origin is not expressed because of the low priority given to nationality. The exception to this rule occurs when the class number to which Table 5 notation is added defines the present location of the group, as in 940–999, so that it is possible to express both the present and the past location of the group, e.g., use 973.0439704897 for ethnic Swedes from Finland in United States history.

Special developments that allow expression of both ethnic and national affiliation are typically made only for the majority ethnic group in a nation, under the heading "national group," e.g., T5—6887 expresses both Spanish American ethnicity and Venezuelan nationality, while T5—9697292 expresses both African ancestry and Jamaican nationality. However, there is no special development to express both African ancestry and Venezuelan nationality because African Venezuelans are a minority in Venezuela and cannot be called a "national group."

Therefore the number for African Venezuelans in England (T5—96042) is the same as the number for persons of African ancestry in general in England; and Venezuelan nationality is not expressed (*except* when it is possible to express both present and past location, e.g., African Venezuelans in English history 942.00496087). Conversely, Table 5 numbers for Venezuelans of Spanish origin in England (T5—6887042) and Jamaicans of African origin in England (T5—9697292042) always express the national origins.

In some cases, special developments for national groups lead to the number for a national group being clearly different from the number for the largest ethnic group of the country. For example, the number for the Bhutanese as a national group is T5—91418; but the Bhotia, the largest ethnic group, speak Tibetan dialects and class as an ethnic group with the Tibetans in T5—954. In some cases, the national group number for a country may not express the ethnicity of the majority of the population. For example, the national group numbers for all the modern nations of Latin America where Spanish is at least one of the official languages express Spanish-American ethnicity, though the majority of the population in some countries is of native American origin, e.g., Bolivia. Class works that discuss all the people of a nation in the national group number specified in the table. Class works that focus on a specific ethnic group with the ethnic group. Use the national group number for a work that focuses on a specific ethnic group if it expresses the appropriate ethnicity, e.g., use T5—6884 for works that discuss all the people of Bolivia and also for works that focus on the Bolivians who speak Spanish and follow Spanish-American customs; but use T5—98323084 for works that focus on the Quechua of Bolivia, T5—98324084 for works that focus on the Aymara of Bolivia.

Adding area notation

Area notation is normally added to a Table 5 number to signify location, e.g., sociology of Italians in England 305.851042. However, area notation is omitted whenever it is redundant, e.g., 973.046872 Mexican Americans in U.S. history (*not* 973.046872073).

African Americans

An atypical development for African Americans (T5—96073) gives extra emphasis to nationality for a minority group, while still preserving the usual citation order of ethnic group before nationality. The 073 signifies U.S. nationality rather than location; so area numbers can be added to it in the usual way, e.g., use T5—960730747 for U.S. citizens with African ancestry in New York State. However, this applies only to U.S. citizens; so use T5—960747 for noncitizens of African ancestry in New York State. There are no special developments for most ethnic groups in the United States, e.g., use T5—510747 for persons of Italian descent in New York State regardless of whether they are U.S. citizens. The Table 5 number for African Americans always expresses the U.S. national origin when used for areas outside the U.S., e.g., use T5—96073042 for African Americans in England. Conversely, the number for Italian Americans in England (T5—51042) is the same as for Italians in England (with the usual exception for history, e.g., Italian Americans in English history 942.00451073).

T5—112, T5—114 vs. T5—2, T5—41

Canadians of British origin and Canadians of French origin vs. British, English, Anglo-Saxons and French

Use T5—112 for Canadian citizens of British origin and T5—114 for Canadian citizens of French origin, even with numbers that already specify Canada, e.g., use 971.004112 for Canadian citizens of British ancestry in Canadian history. Use T5—112 or T5—114 for accounts of persons of British or French ancestry becoming Canadian citizens. Also use T5—112 and T5—114 for persons of British or French origin living in the territory that later became the nation of Canada if they are regarded as among the precursors of British or French Canadians or founders of the nation, e.g., the French in Canada 1600–1867 971.004114.

Use T5—2 and T5—41 for persons of British or French ancestry who were not and never became Canadian citizens, even though they may have resided in Canada or in the territory that later became Canada. For example, the inhabitants of the French colony Acadia in what is now Nova Scotia who were expelled in 1755 and became the Cajuns of today's Louisiana were never Canadian citizens; so use T5—410763 (*not* T5—1140763) for Louisiana Cajuns.

If in doubt, prefer T5—112 and T5—114.

T5—13 vs. T5—2073, T5—21073

People of United States ("Americans") vs. British, English, Anglo-Saxons in United States and People of British Isles in United States

Use T5—13 (*not* T5—2073 or T5—21073) for U.S. citizens of British ancestry, even with a number that already means United States, e.g., British Americans in U.S. history 973.0413. Use T5—13 for comprehensive works on both U.S. citizens and non-U.S. citizens of British ancestry in the United States. Use T5—13 for accounts of persons of British ancestry becoming U.S citizens. Use T5—2073 or T5—21073 for non-U.S. citizens of British ancestry in the United States. (Do not add notation 073 if T5—2 or T5—21 is used with a number that already means United States, as it would be redundant, e.g., all noncitizens of British ancestry in U.S. history 973.042.) If in doubt, prefer T5—13.

T5—201–209 vs. T5—2101–2109

British English Anglo-Saxons by area vs. People of British Isles by area

Use T5—201–209 for persons of British ancestry in an area when many of them are or have most recently been citizens of the United States, Canada, Australia, or New Zealand, e.g., persons from the United Kingdom, the United States, Canada, and Australia in the Third World T5—201724. Use T5—2101–2109 for persons of British ancestry in an area when they are or have most recently been citizens of the United Kingdom, e.g., persons from the United Kingdom in the Third World T5—2101724. If in doubt, prefer T5—201–209.

T5—9435

Turks

Use T5—9435 for (a) the people of Turkey as a national group; and (b) people who speak, or whose ancestors spoke, Turkish (Osmanli Turks and their descendants), including those who are not Turkish nationals, e.g., Turkish Cypriots T5—943505693.

T5—96073

African Americans (United States Blacks)

The 073 in T5—96073 signifies U.S. nationality rather than location. It is never omitted even where it would be redundant if it simply signified location, e.g., 973.0496073 African Americans in U.S. history (as distinct from 973.0496 for noncitizens of African ancestry in U.S. history). Area subdivisions are added to it in the usual way, e.g., 305.8960730747 sociology of African Americans in New York (as distinct from 305.8960747 sociology of non-U.S. citizens of African ancestry in New York).

Table 6. Languages

The source of information about language families most used in recent revisions of Table 6 is *Ethnologue*, 14th edition (Dallas, Texas: Summer Institute of Linguistics, 2000; also on the Internet http://www.sil.org/ethnologue/). However, Table 6 diverges from *Ethnologue* in many specific instances. Check Table 6 and the Relative Index first to find a specific language or group of languages. If nothing is found, consult *Ethnologue* to find the appropriate language family or group of languages.

T6—926

Minoan Linear A

It is not known what language is represented by the Minoan Linear A script. At one time the language was thought to be a West Semitic language, and works on the script have been classed in T6—926 Canaanite languages for many years. If the script is deciphered and the language identified as a non-Canaanite language, then Minoan Linear A will be moved to the appropriate place.

T6—9639

Bantu languages

Groups and zones of Bantu languages were originally based on Malcolm Guthrie's *Comparative Bantu; an Introduction to the Comparative Linguistics and Prehistory of the Bantu Languages*, 1967–1971. These groups and zones appear in a modified and updated form in *Ethnologue*, 14th edition (Dallas, Texas: Summer Institute of Linguistics, 2000; also on the Internet http://www.sil.org/ethnologue/). Most of the time, but not always, Table 6 follows *Ethnologue*. Check Table 6 and the Relative Index first to find a specific language or group of languages. If nothing is found, consult *Ethnologue*.

Notes on Schedule Numbers

001.9 and 130

Controversial knowledge and Parapsychology and occultism

Both 001.9 and 130 cover topics that cannot be disproved or be brought into the realm of certain and verifiable knowledge. Works that belong in either 001.9 or 130 include one or more of the following indicators:

1. A claim of access to secret or occult sources

2. A rejection of established authority

3. A pronounced reverence for iconoclasts, for laypersons-become-experts

4. An uncritical acceptance of lay observation of striking phenomena

5. A fixation on the unexplained, the enigmatic, the mysterious

6. A confidence verging on certainty in the existence of conspiracies and the working of malevolent forces

7. An acknowledgment of the powers of extraterrestrial beings or intelligences (other than religious beings)

Use 001.9 for phenomena not closely linked to humans. Use 130 for phenomena closely linked to human beings—the human mind, human capabilities and powers, human happiness. In case of doubt, and for interdisciplinary works, prefer 001.9.

004–006

Computer science

Here are key questions to guide in classifying works about computer science, with references to relevant Manual notes.

004–006 vs. other disciplines

1. Is the work (A) computer science per se (004–006), or (B) an application of computers to another discipline (T1—0285)?

A. Use 004–006 for works about computer science not applied to a specific discipline.

B. Use the number for the discipline plus notation 0285 from Table 1 for works about the application of computers in another discipline, e.g., the use of parallel computers in fluid dynamics 532.050285435.

See also discussion at T1—0285.

2. Is the work (A) predominantly about computer science (004–006), or (B) predominantly about the role of computers in society (300)?

A. Use 004–006 for works that are predominantly about computer science. Such works often have a chapter about the role of computers in society.

B. Use 300 for works about the role of computers in society, e.g., computers and social change 303.4834, computers and the right of privacy 323.448.

See also discussion at 303.483 vs. 306.45, 306.46.

3. If the work covers hardware topics, is it about (A) computer engineering (621.39), or (B) use of computer hardware (004), or hardware and software combined (004)?

A. Use 621.39 for works that discuss the engineering, manufacture or repair of computer hardware and say nothing about software.

B. Use 004–006 for works that discuss use of computers, or that discuss both hardware and software.

See also discussion at 004–006 vs. 621.39.

4. If the work is highly mathematical, is it (A) mathematics (510), or (B) mathematics applied to computer science (004–006 + T1—0151)?

A. Use 510 for mathematics per se, e.g., Turing machines 511.35.

B. Use 004–006 plus notation 0151 from Table 1 for mathematics applied to computers, e.g., the role of mathematical logic in computer science 004.015113.

See also discussion at 004.0151 vs. 511.1, 511.35; also at 005.101; also at 510, T1—0151 vs. 004–006, T1—0285.

5. If the work is about databases or information systems, is it (A) computer science (005.74–.75) or (B) information science (025.04–.06)?

A. Use 005.74 for computer science aspects of databases and information systems.

B. Use 025.04–.06 for information science aspects of databases and information systems.

6. If the work is about computer communications, is it about (A) computer science aspects (004–005) or (B) economic and related aspects (384.3)?

A. Use 004–005 for computer science aspects of computer communications, e.g., the Internet and how it works 004.678.

B. Use 384.3 for economic and related aspects, e.g., Internet access providers 384.33.

See also discussion at 004.6 vs. 384.3; also at 004.678 vs. 006.7, 025.04, 384.33.

Within 004–006

Once you have determined that the work belongs in 004–006 rather than in one of the alternative class numbers discussed above, you must decide whether the work is about a special computer method only (006); programming, programs, and data only (005); hardware only (004); or hardware plus programming, programs, data (004). Use 006 for both software (programming, programs, data) and hardware aspects of special computer methods.

The best way to approach the computer science schedule is to start at the end (006.8) and work backward toward 004. At 004, 005, and 006, there are instructions to class complex subjects with aspects in two or more subdivisions in the subdivision coming last in the schedule. Many works in computer science treat complex subjects to which these preference instructions apply.

The key questions are:

7. Is the work limited to a special computer method (006)?

   A. Yes: Go to question 13.

   B. No: Go to question 8.

8. Does the work cover 005 concepts only (programming, programs, data)?

   A. Yes: Go to question 12.

   B. No: Go to question 9.

9. Does the work cover both hardware (004) and computer programming, programs, data (005)?

   A. Yes: Go to question 11.

   B. No: Go to question 10.

Within 004

These questions apply only to works limited to 004 concepts.

10. Does the work cover more than one 004 concept?

    A. Yes: Are all the 004 concepts aspects of a single complex subject?

    i. Yes: Use the last number in 004 for a covered topic (following second note at 004), e.g., standards and protocols for local-area networks 004.68 (*not* 004.62).

    ii. No: Unless there are notes to the contrary, follow the first-of-two rule, e.g., distributed and parallel computing 004.35 (*not* 004.36).

    B. No: Use the appropriate subdivision of 004.

See also discussion at 004.1; also at 004.1 vs. 004.24; also at 004.1 vs. 004.3; also at 004.11–.16.

Within 004–005

This key question applies only to works that cover concepts expressed in both 004 (computer hardware) and 005 (computer programming, programs, data).

11. What is the relationship between the 004 concept(s) and the 005 concept(s)?

    A. Use 004 if the 004 and 005 concepts together constitute a single system, e.g., local-area networking, including both hardware and software aspects, with a specific computer program for distributed computer systems 004.68 (*not* 005.4476).

B. Use 005 if the information on the 004 concept is a brief supplement or background for the 005 concept, e.g., a work on microcomputer software with only brief treatment of hardware 005.36 (*not* 004.16).

C. Use 005 if the 005 concept is applied to the 004 concept, e.g., data security in client-server computer systems 005.8 (*not* 004.36).

D. Use 005 if the 004 concept is applied to the 005 concept. If the topic of the work approximates the whole of the class number, add T1—0285, e.g., a microprocessor for data encryption 005.8202854165 (*not* 004.165).

See also discussion at 004 vs. 005; also at 004.6 vs. 005.71.

Within 005

This key question applies only to works limited to 005 concepts (computer programming, programs, data).

12. Are all the 005 concepts aspects of a single complex subject?

A. Yes: Use the last number in 005 for a covered aspect, following the second note at 005, e.g., structured programming using a specific programming language on a specific microcomputer 005.265 (*not* 005.133 or 005.113).

B. No: Unless there are notes to the contrary, follow the first-of-two rule, e.g., operating systems for parallel and distributed computing 005.4475 (*not* 005.4476).

See also discussion at 004 vs. 005; also at 004.6 vs. 005.71; also at 005.1–.2 vs. 005.42; also at 005.1 vs. 005.3; also at 005.3; also at 005.3, 005.5 vs. 005.43–.45.

Within 006

This question applies only to works limited to special computer methods.

13. Does the topic in 006 have subdivisions for hardware, programming, and programs?

A. Yes: In choosing between subdivisions for hardware, programming, and programs in 006, the same distinctions are made as between 004 and 005 concepts; hence the questions about 004 and 005 are relevant to choosing between hardware and software subdivisions of 006.

B. No: Class in the appropriate topical subdivision.

004–006 vs. 621.39

Computer science vs. Computer engineering

Use 004–006 for works on (a) computer hardware from the user's viewpoint, (b) software or firmware, (c) comprehensive works on assembling the physical components and installing the software of a computer system, or (d) comprehensive works on the computer science and computer engineering aspects of a computer topic.

Use 621.39 for works that (a) treat computer hardware solely from the viewpoint of engineering, manufacturing, or repair and (b) do not treat software or the program aspect of firmware. Use 621.39 for works limited to assembling the physical components of a computer system, and for works treating the physical processes of manufacturing firmware chips, not discussing the programs embodied in those chips. Use 621.39 for works treating 004–006 concepts only if the 004–006 concepts are applied to 621.39 concepts, as in computer graphics programs to assist in design of computer circuitry 621.3950285668.

If in doubt, prefer 004–006.

004 vs. 005

Computer hardware and software

Use 004 for works on computer hardware and works treating both computer hardware and the "soft" aspects of computer systems—programs, programming, and data. Use 005 for works treating only these "soft" aspects. Use 005.1–.8 together with notation 0285 from Table 1 for works on hardware applied to topics named in 005.1–.8, e.g., parallel architectures for database machines 005.740285435. However, use 004.6 (*not* 005.71) for works on hardware for interfacing and data communications. If in doubt, prefer 004.

See also discussion at 004.6 vs. 005.71.

004.0151 vs. 511.1, 511.35

Computer mathematics

Use 004.0151 for works on how mathematics is used in practice on computers, and for comprehensive works on computer mathematics.

Use 511.1 for works on branches of mathematics in which objects can only have discrete or finite values, and hence can be represented on digital computers. These branches are often collectively referred to as "discrete mathematics" or "finite mathematics."

Use 511.35 for works on the theory of computer mathematics, without reference to practical implementations on real computers. Use 511.35 for works on Turing machines, because Turing machines are a theoretical concept. This subject is also called automata theory or machine theory.

If in doubt, prefer in the following order: 004.0151, 511.1, 511.35.

004.1

Computers and processors

In 004.1, its subdivisions, and similar numbers elsewhere in 004–006 and 621.39, computers and processors (central processing units) are treated for classification purposes as if they were the same. In fact they are not, but few works about processors can avoid discussing the other parts of the computer with which the processor must interact; hence works about specific types of computers and processors are typically not different enough to justify separate numbers.

Programmable calculators

Use 510.28541 rather than 004.1 for programmable calculators because they are limited-function computers, capable of working only with numbers, not alphabetic data.

004.1 vs. 004.24

Performance evaluation

Use 004.1 for general evaluations of computers, e.g., general evaluations of microcomputers 004.16, of a specific kind of microcomputer 004.165. Use 004.24 only for specialized works treating performance measurement and evaluation as an aid in designing or improving the performance of a computer system. If in doubt, prefer 004.1.

Add notation 029 from Table 1 to the number in 004.1 if the emphasis is on evaluation as a consideration in purchasing, e.g., evaluation and purchasing manuals for microcomputers 004.16029.

004.1 vs. 004.3

Processing modes

Many computers, processors, and computer systems can be classified either by type of computer as defined in 004.1 or by processing mode.

Use 004.1 for works that discuss a computer, processor or computer system in general. Use 004.3 only for works that emphasize the processing mode.

For example, the Intel Pentium® processor is a microprocessor that supports multiprogramming, interactive processing, and multiprocessing. Use 004.165 for works discussing the Pentium in general. Use 004.357 for Pentium-based multiprocessing computers.

If in doubt, prefer 004.1.

004.11–.16

Types of digital computers

Use 004.11–.16 and 621.3911–.3916 only for works that emphasize the specific type of computer. Use 004 and 621.39 for works that refer to a particular type as an illustration of what computers in general do. For example, use 004, not

004.12, for a general introduction to computers written at a time when the only computers were mainframes. If in doubt, prefer 004 or 621.39 without subdivision.

Specific computers

Here, "numbers for specific computers in 004–006" include 004.125, 004.145, 004.165, 005.265, and numbers in 004–006 built using these numbers, e.g., 006.7765.

Use numbers for specific computers in 004–006 for works treating more than one computer or processor only if:

1. The work treats a single series of very closely related computers or processors (e.g., the Intel Pentium® microprocessors 004.165); or

2. The work treats primarily one specific computer or processor but adds that it is also applicable to other similar machines (e.g., a work about programming the IBM PC® that says it can also be used as a guide to programming "IBM-compatible" computers 005.265).

Use numbers for specific computers in 004–006 for works that discuss a computer and its processor, e.g., a work about the Mac® series of computers and the PowerPC® series of microprocessors 004.165.

If in doubt, do not use numbers for specific computers in 004–006.

004.21 vs. 004.22, 621.392

Systems analysis and design vs. Computer architecture

Use 004.21 for works on computer-based systems involving a computer, application programs, and procedures, usually also other hardware, often a database and communications network, all working together to accomplish a task for the user. Use 004.21 for comprehensive works on systems analysis and design.

Use 004.22 for works focusing on the design and structure of the computer itself and on the computer in relation to its peripheral devices. Most works on computer architecture treat software or the program aspect of firmware as well as hardware; but in the discussion of programs, the focus is on system programs, which make the computer function properly, rather than on application programs, which accomplish user tasks. Use 004.22 for comprehensive works on computer architecture.

Use 621.392 for works that treat computer hardware but do not treat software or firmware.

If in doubt, prefer in the following order: 004.21, 004.22, 621.392.

004.6 vs. 005.71

Computer communications

Use 004.6 for comprehensive works on both the "hard" and "soft" aspects of computer interfacing and communications. Use 005.71 for comprehensive works on "soft" aspects—programming, programs, and data in interfacing and communications. Use 005.7–.8 for specific data aspects of interfacing and communications, e.g., error-correcting codes 005.72, data compression 005.746, data encryption 005.82. If in doubt, prefer 004.6.

004.6 vs. 384.3

Computer communication services

Use 004.6 for works on computer communication and its hardware in office and private use, works on computer science applied to the technological aspects of computer communication, practical works explaining how to use the hardware and software involved in computer communications, and interdisciplinary works.

Use 384.3 for works on economic and related aspects of providing computer communication services to the public, and works focusing on services and service providers, on broad issues of public good in relation to computer communication.

If in doubt, prefer 004.6.

004.6 vs. 621.382, 621.3981

Digital communications

Use 004.6 for works on digital communications that do not emphasize engineering, including works dealing with telecommunications and data communications engineering plus interfacing and communications in computer science.

Use 621.382 for works on digital telecommunications, or digital aspects of both telecommunications and data communications, that emphasize engineering. Use 621.3981 for works on computer data communications that emphasize engineering.

If in doubt, prefer in the following order: 004.6, 621.382, 621.3981.

See also discussion at 004.6 vs. 005.71; also at 004.6 vs. 384.3.

004.678 vs. 006.7, 025.04, 384.33

Internet and World Wide Web

The Internet and the World Wide Web (WWW) can be written about from various disciplinary viewpoints. Because the Dewey Decimal Classification is organized by disciplines, it is necessary to decide the focus of a particular work about the Internet or the WWW in order to choose the correct number.

Use 004.678 for works about the Internet or WWW if they contain a substantial amount of computer science material and at least some information about computer hardware, or if they include a comprehensive overview of the Internet as a system of hardware, software, communications protocols, and other aspects of computer communications included in 004.6.

Use 006.7 for general works about the use of HTML and XML to create hypertext documents on the World Wide Web, and works that discuss web page design or effective web pages.

Use 025.04 for:

1. Interdisciplinary works about the Internet and WWW that do not contain enough computer science material to be classified in 004.678, but that do contain some information science material

2. Information science works that emphasize search and retrieval, including use of web browsers and web search engines to facilitate search and retrieval on the Internet

3. Works that describe information resources available on the Internet or WWW, and on how to find information there

Use 384.33 for works on Internet access providers and works on economic and public policy issues concerning the Internet.

If in doubt, prefer in the following order: 004.678, 025.04, 006.7, 384.33.

005.1–.2 vs. 005.42

Application programming vs. Systems programming

Use 005.1–.2 for works on writing application programs and comprehensive works about writing both application and systems programs, including works about writing application programs that run on specific operating systems or user interfaces, e.g., writing application programs that run on the microcomputer operating system MS-DOS 005.268, writing application programs that run on the microcomputer graphical user interface Microsoft Windows 005.269. Use 005.42 for works about writing systems programs, e.g., writing operating systems 005.42, writing user interfaces 005.428. If in doubt, prefer 005.1–.2.

See also discussion at 005.3, 005.5 vs. 005.43–.45.

005.1 vs. 005.3

Programming vs. Programs

In this discussion, "other programming numbers" comprise 005.2, 005.42, 005.711, 005.712, 006.336, 006.337, 006.66 and 006.67. "Other numbers for programs" comprise 005.43, 005.5, 005.713, 006.338 and 006.68.

Use 005.1 and other programming numbers for works on writing programs, on software engineering, on modifying existing programs in ways that are typically done by computer programmers. Use 005.3 and other numbers for programs for works on using programs that have already been created by others, including works on writing macros of the kind that are typically written by end users of software packages.

Use 005.1 and other programming numbers for works on programming to achieve reliability, compatibility, portability, and other ideal qualities. Use 005.3 and other numbers for programs for works that discuss whether existing programs actually have these qualities.

Use 005.10218 and 005.150218 for standards for programs and program documentation that are aimed at programmers and documentation writers, to ensure that they produce good programs and documentation. Use 005.30218 and other numbers for programs for works that discuss standards to help users in selecting from among existing programs and documentation.

Use 005.14 for works on testing and measurement as part of program development. Use 005.30287 and other numbers for programs for works that discuss ways for users to test or measure programs as an aid in selection.

Use 005.1 or 005.2 for works devoted equally to programming and programs.

If in doubt, prefer 005.1 or other programming numbers.

005.101

Logic in computer programming

Use notation 01 from Table 1 only for specialized works with an intense focus on logical analysis. Typically such works treat symbolic (mathematical) logic; use notation 015113 for these works. Do not use notation 01 from Table 1 in 005.1–.2 for general discussions of logic in programming because logic is inherent in programming and is discussed in nearly every work about programming.

005.15 vs. 808.066005

Program documentation

Use 005.15 for comprehensive works on how to prepare program documentation; works on how to prepare the technical documentation needed by the personnel who will maintain, modify, and enhance the program (including such things as program source listings, program comments, flow charts, decision logic tables, file specifications, program function descriptions, program test history records, modification logs); works on how to prepare program users' manuals that focus on content rather than form; works on policies for program documentation.

Use 808.066005 for works that emphasize effective technical writing—that is, works that emphasize such things as organizing for clarity, writing appropriately for the intended audience, using good paragraph structure, preferring the active voice, using consistent terminology. Typically such works are concerned only with users' manuals.

If in doubt, prefer 005.15.

005.268 vs. 005.265, 005.269

Programming for specific operating systems, for specific computers, and for specific user interfaces

Numbers beginning with 005.26 are limited to microcomputers. Similar numbers for other types of computers, with instructions for building numbers by adding notation from 005.26 numbers, are found in 005.22–.24 and 005.27.

Use 005.268 (and similar numbers for other types of computers) for works on writing software that runs on specific operating systems. Use 005.265 (and similar numbers for other types of computers) for works on writing software that runs on specific computers. Use 005.269 (and similar numbers for other types of computers) for works on writing software that runs on specific user interfaces other than the native interface of the computer operating system.

See also discussion at 005.269 and 005.284, 005.3684, 005.384.

If two or three of these numbers are applicable to the same work, follow the preference note at 005 and class with the number coming last in the schedule (with the exception specified below). For example, if a work treats writing software that runs on a specific computer, on a specific operating system, and on a specific add-on user interface, prefer 005.269. Exception: If a specific computer has only one operating system, so that all programs that run on that computer also run on the operating system, e.g., the Mac® series of computers and Mac OS X®, class writing programs that run on that computer and operating system with the computer in 005.265. Earlier and later versions of the same operating system (e.g., Macintosh System 9® and Mac OS X®) count as one operating system, even though the differences between the earliest and the latest versions may be great.

If in doubt, prefer in the following order: 005.268 and similar numbers, 005.269 and similar numbers, 005.265 and similar numbers.

005.269 and 005.284, 005.3684, 005.384

User interfaces

The native interface of an operating system is the user interface bundled inseparably with the operating system.

005.3

Programs

Class a program or programs designed to run on two types of computers with the predominant type if there is one, e.g., a program that runs on five mainframe computers and one minicomputer 005.32. If neither of two types is predominant, class with the smaller type, e.g., a program for minicomputers and microcomputers 005.36.

Class programs for a specific application in computer science with the application in 005–006, but never in 004. Among the numbers most frequently used for software besides 005.3 and its subdivisions are 005.43 for systems software and operating systems, 005.5 for general purpose application software (such as word processing programs and spreadsheets), 005.713 for interfacing and data communications programs, 005.74 for database management systems, and 006.68 for computer graphics programs.

Programs applied to a particular subject or discipline are classed with the subject or discipline, plus notation 028553 from Table 1, e.g., programs for tax accounting 657.46028553.

See also discussion at T1—0285; also at 005.1 vs. 005.3.

005.3, 005.5 vs. 005.43–.45

Application programs vs. Systems programs

Use 005.3 for collections of or works about multiple kinds of application programs, and for comprehensive works on application programs and systems programs. Application programs are programs that do things users want done, for example, electronic spreadsheets, statistical packages, word processing programs, desktop publishing programs, computer games, educational programs, tax preparation programs, inventory control programs.

Use 005.5 for general purpose application programs, such as spreadsheets, statistical packages, word processing programs.

Use 001–999 for application programs employed in a specific discipline, e.g., application programs employed in library operations 025.0028553, computer games 794.8.

Use appropriate subdivisions of 005.3 for works about application programs that run on specific systems, e.g., application programs that run on a specific microcomputer operating system 005.3682.

Use 005.43–.45 for systems programs and works about them. Systems programs are programs that enable computers to function properly; in effect, they provide life support and housekeeping for computers. Systems programs accomplish little that interests users except to make it possible for application programs to run. Examples of systems programs are operating systems, utilities packages, user interfaces, and programming language translators.

If in doubt, prefer 005.3 and its subdivisions.

See also discussion at 005.3682 vs. 005.365, 005.3684.

005.3682 vs. 005.365, 005.3684

Programs for specific operating systems, for specific computers, and for specific user interfaces

Numbers beginning with 005.36 are limited to microcomputers. Similar numbers for other types of computers, with instructions for building numbers by adding notation from 005.36 numbers, are found in 005.32–.34 and 005.37.

Use 005.3682 (and similar numbers for other types of computers) for application programs that run on specific computer operating systems, and comprehensive works on application and systems programs that run on specific computer operating systems. Use 005.365 (and similar numbers for other types of computers) for application programs that run on specific computers, and comprehensive works on application and systems programs that run on specific computers. Use 005.3684 (and similar numbers for other types of computers) for application programs that run on specific user interfaces other than the native interface of the computer operating system, and comprehensive works on application and systems programs that run on specific user interfaces other than the native interface of the computer operating system.

See also discussion at 005.269 and 005.284, 005.3684, 005.384.

If two or three of these numbers are applicable to the same work, follow the preference note at 005 and class with the number coming last in the schedule (with the exception specified below). For example, if a work treats application programs that run on a specific computer, on a specific operating system, and on a specific add-on user interface, prefer 005.3684. Exception: If a specific computer has only one operating system, so that all programs that run on that computer also run on the operating system, e.g., the Mac® series of computers and Mac OS X®, class programs that run on that computer and operating system with the computer in 005.365. Earlier and later versions of the same operating system (e.g., Macintosh System 9® and Mac OS X®) count as one operating system, even though the differences between the earliest and the latest versions may be great.

If in doubt, prefer in the following order: 005.3682 and similar numbers, 005.3684 and similar numbers, 005.365 and similar numbers.

See also discussion at 005.3, 005.5 vs. 005.43–.45.

005.74 vs. 005.436

File managers and file organization

Use 005.74 or 005.75 for a file manager in the sense of software that manages data files, providing the ability to create, enter, change, query and produce reports on a data file or data files. Use 005.436 for a file manager in the sense of software that is used to manage files and directories on a computer, providing the ability to delete, copy, move, rename and view files and directories. A file manager in this latter sense may be part of an operating system or a separate utility program. Use 005.436 for comprehensive works on both kinds of file managers.

Use 005.741 for works on file organization in the sense of the structure of data within a single file that permits access to the data. Use 005.436 for works on file organization in the sense of the way that multiple files are organized on a disk or other storage medium.

If in doubt, prefer 005.74.

006.3 vs. 153

Cognitive science

Cognitive science is the interdisciplinary study of the mind and computers as information processing systems.

Use 006.3 for cognitive science if the goal is to produce computer systems with better artificial intelligence. Use 153 for cognitive science if the goal is to understand better how the human mind works. If in doubt, prefer 006.3.

006.37 vs. 006.42, 621.367, 621.391, 621.399

Computer vision, optical pattern recognition, and optical computers

Computer vision and optical pattern recognition

Computer vision and optical pattern recognition both involve recognition of forms, shapes, or other optical patterns for the purpose of classification, grouping, or identification; but computer vision makes extensive use of artificial intelligence for the complex interpretation of visual information, whereas optical pattern recognition involves only simple interpretation.

Use 006.37 or 006.42 for works on computer vision and optical pattern recognition that give substantial treatment to the computer programs needed to interpret optical patterns, and also for works treating computer-vision and optical-pattern-recognition devices from the user's point of view. Use 621.399 for works on designing and manufacturing the hardware for computer vision and optical pattern recognition. If in doubt, prefer 006.37 or 006.42.

Use 621.367 for works on devices that record and process optical signals while doing virtually no interpreting (either because interpretation is not needed or because interpretation is left to others—computers or humans), e.g., devices for image enhancement.

Optical computers

"Optical computers" is a term used to describe two different kinds of computers. Use 621.391 for works on optical computers that are general-purpose computers in which the central data processing mechanism is based on light (e.g., lasers). Use 006.37, 006.42, or 621.399 for works on optical computers that are special-purpose computers designed to process optical data, regardless of the type of central data processing mechanism.

011.39 vs. 005.3029, 016.0053, 025.04

Bibliographies of electronic resources

Use 011.39 for general bibliographies of electronic resources *not limited to computer programs (or software)*. Use 005.3029 for annotated lists of programs with lengthy reviews that are used as buyers' guides, e.g., a collection of reviews of microcomputer software 005.36029. Use 016.0053 for bibliographies and lists of programs and for annotated lists if the annotations are relatively brief. Use

025.04 for bibliographies of web sites, as they are normally indistinguishable from directories of web sites. If in doubt, prefer 011.39.

See also discussion at 025.04, 025.06 vs. 005.74.

016 vs. 026, T1—07

Bibliographies of specific subjects vs. Libraries on specific subjects vs. Table 1 notation for resources for education, research, related topics

Use 016 or 026 for works describing books, manuscripts, recordings, and the like, unless the works also describe kinds of resources not found in libraries and archives or emphasize how to use the library or archival resources for study, teaching, and research.

Use notation 07 from Table 1 for comprehensive works on resources for education, research, and related topics. Many of these resources are found in subdivisions of T1—07, e.g., schools and laboratories, collections of objects (such as botanical collections), and financial support.

Use 016 for works about resources in a field that describe individual works, such as books and articles. Use 016 also for inventories and calendars of archives. Use notation 07 from Table 1 in 016 if the resources being described treat education and research, e.g., a bibliography of material on education and research in mathematics 016.5107.

Use 026 for works about resources in a field that give broad descriptions of whole collections held by libraries, archives, and other information organizations. Such works often include directory information about the institutions and organizations.

If in doubt, prefer in the following order: 016, 026, T1—07.

025.04, 025.06 vs. 005.74

Data files and databases

Although there are technical differences between data files and databases, they are treated as the same for classification.

Use 025.04 or 025.06 for works on the information science aspects of the automated storage and retrieval systems that make databases available: that is, the kinds of things that users need to know about the systems in order to benefit fully from them.

Use 005.74 for computer science aspects of databases: that is, the narrowly technical issues of designing, programming, and installing databases and database management systems.

Use 001–999 for the subject content of databases (and works discussing that content) as if the databases were books, e.g., encyclopedic databases 030, bibliographic databases 010, nonbibliographic chemistry databases 540. Do not use notation 0285574 from Table 1 except for works that focus on the computer science aspects of the databases rather than the subject content.

If in doubt, prefer 025.04 and 025.06.

See also discussion at 011.39 vs. 005.3029, 016.0053, 025.04.

080 vs. 800

General collections vs. Literature (Belles-lettres) and rhetoric

Use 080 for essays and quotations collected for nonliterary purposes, e.g., quotations collected to answer reference questions about who said something familiar. Use 080 also for collections of writings, statements or quotations on a variety of topics, e.g., a collection of quotations by Winston Churchill on various topics 082. Use 800 for a collection of quotations if all or nearly all the quotations come from works of poetry, drama, or fiction. Also use 800 for a collection of essays or quotations if the intent of the collection, as revealed in prefatory matter, is clearly literary, e.g., to exhibit literary style. If in doubt, prefer 080.

081–089

General collections in specific languages and language families

Class collections originally written in one language or language family with that language or language family. Class collections originally written in two or more languages or language families with the predominant language or language family if there is one. If no original language or language family is predominant, but the work appears in one language as a result of translation, class it with the language in which it appears. Use 080 for collections in which the material appears in multiple languages with none predominant, even if accompanied by translations into the language of the intended audience.

130 vs. 200

Parapsychology and occultism vs. Religion

Use 130 for parapsychological and occult phenomena if they are not presented as religious, or if there is doubt as to whether they have been so presented. Use 200 for works about parapsychological or occult phenomena if the author describes them as religious, or the believers and practitioners consider them to be religious. If in doubt, prefer 130.

Use 130 for knowledge reputedly derived from secret and ancient religious texts but not applied for religious purposes; however, use 200 for editions of the texts, even if annotated from an occultist viewpoint, e.g., discussion of occult traditions derived from the Zohar 135.47, but the text of the Zohar 296.162.

152–158 vs. 150.19

Specific topics in psychology vs. Psychological systems, schools, viewpoints

Certain schools and systems draw their fundamental principles from a few selected psychological topics. When such topics are used to illustrate a system, class with the system in 150.19, e.g., the subconscious, fantasies, and dreams used to illustrate psychoanalytic principles 150.195 (*not* 154). If in doubt, prefer the specific topic in 152–158.

153 vs. 153.4

Conscious mental processes and intelligence vs. Thought, thinking, reasoning, intuition, value, judgment

Many works that claim to be about thought and thinking or reasoning also cover subjects such as memory, communication, perception, motivation, and intelligence. Use 153 (*not* 153.4) for these broader works. Use 153 (*not* 153.4) also for works on "cognitive psychology". Use 153.4 only for works that focus narrowly on thought and thinking, reasoning, intuition, value, judgment. If in doubt, prefer 153.

153.7 vs. 152.1

Perceptual processes vs. Sensory perception

Use 153.7 for comprehensive works on sensory perception and perceptual processes in general, and works that focus on the active, interpretative mental processes associated with perception in general. Also use 153.7 for types of perception that involve more than one sense, e.g., space perception that involves vision and touch 153.752. Use 152.1 for works that focus on the receptive aspects of sensory perception and comprehensive works on perception by a specific sense, e.g., visual perception 152.14. If in doubt, prefer 153.7.

155

Differential and developmental psychology

Some works on the psychology of sensory perception, movement, emotions, physiological drives (152) and conscious mental processes (153) use as research populations persons belonging to differential categories, or persons subject to environmental influences, that are given in 155.3–.9. Use 152–153 for works in which there is clearly little or no interest in the distinctiveness of the category or influence, or in which the researcher has simply used convenient samples. This is particularly applicable to ethnic and national groups (155.8), adults (155.6), and social environment (155.92).

Sex psychology

Use 155.3 for a study on sex psychology, drawing almost exclusively upon adult middle-class whites, but showing only marginal interest in the class, age, or ethnic group of the respondents. Use 155.3 also for discussion of the social class, national, or ethnic bias of such research, as the interest is in the validity of the findings about sex psychology.

155.89 vs. 155.84

National psychology vs. Psychology of specific ethnic groups in areas where they are not predominant

Use 155.89 for the psychology of nations taken as a whole, and the psychology of ethnic groups that are predominant in an area constituting an independent nation. Use 155.84 for the psychology of ethnic groups taken as a whole and the psychology of ethnic groups in areas where they are not predominant. For example, use 155.89595 for the national psychology of Malaysia or the psychology of Malays in Malaysia; but use 155.849928 for the psychology of Malays taken as a whole, 155.8499280593 for Malays in Thailand. If in doubt, prefer 155.89.

170.92 vs. 171

Persons associated with ethics vs. Ethical systems

Use 170.92 for biography, collected works, critical appraisal of the work of an individual moral philosopher if the ethical system represented by the philosopher cannot be determined. Use 171 for biography, collected works, critical appraisal if the ethical system can be determined, e.g., critical appraisal of the ethics of Jeremy Bentham 171.5092. If in doubt, prefer 170.92.

180–190

Historical, geographic, persons treatment of philosophy

Class single works by individual philosophers with the topic in philosophy. If there is no focus on a specific topic, class a work expressing primarily the philosopher's own viewpoint with the collected works of the philosopher in 180–190, e.g., use 193 for a general work by Hegel, such as *Phenomenology of Spirit*.

Class a work by an individual philosopher that is primarily a discussion of other philosophers' writings with the other philosophers' writings. For example, use 190 for a work by a western philosopher that is mostly a criticism of contemporary philosophers.

Use 100 for a work by an individual that takes a broad look at many questions in philosophy and does not seek to argue for the individual's own viewpoint.

200 vs. 100

Religion vs. Philosophy

Both religion and philosophy deal with the ultimate nature of existence and relationships, but religion treats them within the context of revelation, deity, worship. Philosophy of religion (210) does not involve revelation or worship but does examine questions within the context of deity.

Use 200 for any work that emphasizes revelation, deity, or worship, even if it uses philosophical methods, e.g., a philosophical proof of the existence of God 212.1. Use 180–190 for the thought of a religious tradition used to examine philosophical questions without reference to deity or religious topics, e.g., Jewish philosophy 181.06, Christian philosophy 190. However, use 200 for ethics based on a religion. If in doubt, prefer 200.

200.9 vs. 294, 299.5

Geographic treatment of religion vs. Religions of Indic and of East and Southeast Asian origin

Use 200.9 for works covering various religious traditions in an area, not just the religions that originated there, e.g., use 200.954 for the religions of India (including Christianity and Islam), use 200.951 for the religions of China (including Christianity and Buddhism). Use 294 and 299.5 for the religions that originated in particular geographic areas. Most of these religions have spread beyond the area where they originated. These areas also have adherents of religions that originated elsewhere, e.g., Buddhism (which originated in India) is present in China. If in doubt, prefer 200.9.

200.92 and 201–209, 292–299

Persons associated with religions other than Christianity

Persons associated with the religions in 292–299 are often identified with a number of religious functions and activities. For example, a Hindu guru may be thought of as a theologian, a teacher, a missionary, or a clergyman. If a religious leader cannot be identified primarily with one function, activity, or sect, class the leader's biography in the base number for the religion and add notation 092 from Table 1. Use 200.922 for collected biography of persons from many religions who are not identified with one function or activity. Use a number that corresponds to the number given in the table below for persons associated with a specific religion, e.g., a Buddhist member of a religious order 294.365092 (corresponds to 206.57092 in the table below). Use the following table of preference for comprehensive biographies of persons primarily identified with one function, activity, or sect:

Founders of religions	206.3
Founders of sects	209
Founders of religious orders	206.57092
Religious leaders (high ranking officials)	200.92
Of specific sects	209
Theologians	202.092
Moral theologians	205.092
Missionaries	207.2092
Martyrs, heretics, saints	200.92
Of specific sects	209
Teachers	207.5092
Members of religious orders	206.57092
Clergy	200.92
Of specific sects	209

Use the subdivisions of 206 for the nature, role, and function of religious leaders. Except for founders of religions (206.3) and founders and members of religious orders (206.57092), do not use the subdivisions of 206 for biography.

Class works dealing with only one aspect of a person's career with the aspect, e.g., Muḥammad as a moral theologian 297.5092 (*not* 297.63).

201–209 and 292–299

Comparative religion

Except for 296 Judaism and 297 Islam, the subdivisions of the various religions in 292–299 are based on 201–209. All topics in 201–209 are provided for under the separate religions in 292–299, either explicitly, by synthesis, or by implication, even if the order is sometimes different. What is said about 201–209, therefore, will also be true of 292–299.

Compare the topics in 201–209 with the subdivisions of Christianity for clues to placement of specific topics. A comparative list follows:

Social theologies	201.7	261
Doctrinal theologies	202	230
Public worship	203	246–247, 263–265
Religious experience, life, practice	204	242, 248
Religious ethics	205	241
Leaders and organizations	206	250, 262, 267
Pastoral theology and work	206.1	253
Missions, religious education	207	266, 268
Sources	208	220
Denominations, sects, reform movements	209	280

Denominations and sects

Class a denomination or sect with the religion to which its own members say it belongs.

Class the early history of a specific religion before its division into sects as general history of the religion, but class a comprehensive survey of the various sects in the number for the sects of the religion, e.g., the sects and reform movements of Buddhism 294.39. Class a work dealing with both early history and sects in the general number for history of the religion.

Class religious orders in 206.5 and similar numbers in 292–299, not with any sect within the religion to which the orders may belong.

203.6, 263.9, 292–299 vs. 394.265–.267

Customs associated with religious holidays

Use 203.6, 263.9, and similar numbers in 292–299 for the religious customs associated with religious holidays, e.g., sunrise Easter services 263.93, lighting the Hanukkah lamp 296.435. Use 394.265–.267 for the secular customs associated with religious holidays, e.g., Easter egg hunts 394.2667, eating latkes and spinning the Hanukkah top 394.267. If in doubt, prefer 203.6, 263.9, and similar numbers in 292–299.

207.5, 268 vs. 200.71, 230.071, 292–299

Religious education, Christian religious education vs. Education in religion, education in Christianity, in Christian theology

Use 207.5 (and similar numbers in 292–299, such as 294.575 Hindu religious education or 297.77 Islamic religious education) for works on how various religions educate their members (especially young members) to be good followers of their own religions, usually called "religious education." Such education stresses knowledge of the faith and living as a member of a religion, and is meant to instill the values of a particular religion, not to study it in a detached manner. Use 268 for religious education as a ministry of the Christian church for the purpose of confirming believers in Christian faith and life, and religious education programs sponsored by the local church.

Use 200.71 for works on education in and teaching of comparative religion, the religions of the world, and religion as an academic subject, usually called "religious studies." Use 230.071 for works on education in and teaching of Christianity as an academic subject, e.g., a course on Christianity in secular secondary schools 230.0712. Use a similar number in 292–299 for works on education in and teaching of another specific religion as an academic subject, e.g., a course on Hinduism in secular secondary schools 294.50712, on Islam 297.0712.

If in doubt as to which type of education is being treated, prefer 207.5 (or a similar number in 292–299) and 268.

Use 200.711 (*not* 207.5) for works on religious education at the level of higher education, and for works on the education of the clergy. Use 230.0711 (*not* 268) for works on higher education in both Christianity and Christian theology and for works on education of the clergy; all of this education usually takes place in divinity schools, theological seminaries, and graduate departments of theology or ministry in universities. Class education or training of the clergy for specialized work with the specialty, e.g., courses in Biblical studies 220.0711, programs in Christian pastoral counseling 253.50711. Use similar numbers from 292–299, e.g., university education in Islam 297.0711.

Class study and teaching of specific topics in comparative religion, Christianity, or the specific religions in 292–299, as follows:

> Class works on teaching a specific topic to children of elementary-school age with works on religious education of children in general, e.g., Christian religious education courses on the Bible for children 268.432; Jewish religious education courses on the Tanakh (scriptures) for children 296.68.
>
> Class works on teaching a specific topic to persons of secondary-school age and older with the topic using notation 071 from Table 1, e.g., study and teaching of Christian church history in secondary schools 270.0712; study of the Tanakh in Jewish colleges and universities 221.0711.

Use 268.434 for Christian religious education of adults, other than in the setting of formal higher education, e.g., works on adult education in parish religious education programs or Sunday schools.

220.92

Biography of individual persons in Bible

Class a comprehensive biography of a Biblical person with the book or books with which the person is most closely associated, usually the historical part of the Bible in which the person's life is narrated, e.g., Solomon, King of Israel, in 1st Kings 222.53092. Solomon's association with 223 Poetic books is weaker. However, some Biblical persons are more closely associated with nonhistorical books, e.g., class Isaiah and Timothy with the books that bear their names, 224.1092 and 227.83092, respectively. Although they appear briefly in historical narratives, their lives are not narrated in full there. Use 225.92 for the apostles John, Peter, and Paul, since each is associated with a number of books in the New Testament, but use 226.092 for the other apostles, associated primarily with Gospels and Acts.

See also discussion at 230–280.

221

Optional numbers for books of Old Testament (Tanakh)

Alphabetic index

Each of the books of the Old Testament (Tanakh) and the combination of them can have one of three different numbers depending on whether one chooses the preferred arrangement at 222–224 or one of the two optional arrangements. Optional numbers showing the books in the order found in Jewish Bibles appear as the second half of this entry (Option A) and at 296.11 (Option B). The following alphabetic listing gives the three numbers for each book or combination of books:

Book	Preferred	Option A	Option B
Amos	224.8	223.63	296.1143
Canticle of Canticles	223.9	224.41	296.11641
Chronicles	222.6	224.8	296.1168
Chronicles 1	222.63	224.81	296.11681
Chronicles 2	222.64	224.82	296.11682
Daniel	224.5	224.5	296.1165
Deuteronomy	222.15	222.5	296.1125
Ecclesiastes	223.8	224.44	296.11644
Exodus	222.12	222.2	296.1122
Esther	222.9	224.45	296.11645
Ezekiel	224.4	223.5	296.1139
Ezra	222.7	224.6	296.1166
Five scrolls	221.044	224.4	296.1164
Former Prophets	222	223.1	296.1131
Genesis	222.11	222.1	296.1121
Habakkuk	224.95	223.68	296.1148

Haggai	224.97	223.72	296.1152
Hosea	224.6	223.61	296.1141
Isaiah	224.1	223.3	296.1137
Jeremiah	224.2	223.4	296.1138
Job	223.1	224.3	296.1163
Joel	224.7	223.62	296.1142
Jonah	224.92	223.65	296.1145
Joshua	222.2	223.11	296.1132
Judges	222.32	223.12	296.1133
Ketuvim	223	224	296.116
Kings	222.5	223.14	296.1135
Kings 1	222.53	223.141	296.11351
Kings 2	222.54	223.142	296.11352
Kohelet	223.8	224.44	296.11644
Lamentations	224.3	224.43	296.11643
Later Prophets	224	223.2	296.1136
Leviticus	222.13	222.3	296.1123
Malachi	224.99	223.74	296.1154
Megillot	221.044	224.4	296.1164
Micah	224.93	223.66	296.1146
Minor Prophets	224.9	223.6	296.114
Nahum	224.94	223.67	296.1147
Nehemiah	222.8	224.7	296.1167
Nevi'im	224	223	296.113
Numbers	222.14	222.4	296.1124
Obadiah	224.91	223.64	296.1144
Pentateuch	222.1	222	296.112
Prophetic books	224	223	296.113
Proverbs	223.7	224.2	296.1162
Pslams	223.2	224.1	296.1161
Qohelet	223.8	224.44	296.11644
Ruth	222.35	224.42	296.11642
Samuel	222.4	223.13	296.1134
Samuel 1	222.43	223.131	296.11341
Samuel 2	222.44	223.132	296.11342
Song of Solomon	223.9	224.41	296.11641
Song of Songs	223.9	224.41	296.11641
Torah	222.1	222	296.112
Writings	223	224	296.116
Zechariah	224.98	223.73	296.1153
Zephaniah	224.96	223.71	296.1151

Optional numbers for books of Bible as arranged in Tanakh (Jewish Bible, Hebrew Bible) (Option A)

The following schedule is an optional arrangement for books of the Bible as found in Jewish Bibles. The preferred arrangement is at 222–224 in the regular schedule. Option B is given at 296.11 in the regular schedule. The see references and footnote instructions in this optional arrangement refer to numbers in the schedules, not to other numbers found in the Manual entries.

> **(222–224) Optional numbers for books of Bible as arranged in Tanakh (Jewish Bible, Hebrew Bible)**

Class comprehensive works in 221

For Apocrypha, pseudepigrapha, see 229

See Manual at 221: Optional numbers for books of Bible

(222) *Torah (Pentateuch)

(Optional number; prefer standard 222.1)

(.1) *Genesis

(Optional number; prefer standard 222.11)

(.2) *Exodus

(Optional number; prefer standard 222.12)

For Ten Commandments, see 222.6

(.3) *Leviticus

(Optional number; prefer standard 222.13)

(.4) *Numbers

(Optional number; prefer standard 222.14)

(.5) *Deuteronomy

(Optional number; prefer standard 222.15)

For Ten Commandments, see 222.6

(.6) *Ten Commandments (Decalogue)

(Optional number; prefer standard 222.16)

(223) *Prophetic books (Nevi'im)

(Optional number; prefer standard 224)

(.1) *Former Prophets (Nevi'im rishonim)

(Optional number; prefer standard 222)

(.11) *Joshua

(Optional number; prefer standard 222.32)

(.12) *Judges

(Optional number; prefer standard 222.32)

*Add as instructed under 221–229

Optional numbers for books of Bible as arranged in Tanakh (Jewish Bible, Hebrew Bible) (Option A)

(.13) *Samuel

(Optional number; prefer standard 222.4)

(.131) *Samuel 1

(Optional number; prefer standard 222.43)

(.132) *Samuel 2

(Optional number; prefer standard 222.44)

(.14) *Kings

(Optional number; prefer standard 222.5)

(.141) *Kings 1

(Optional number; prefer standard 222.53)

(.142) *Kings 2

(Optional number; prefer standard 222.54)

(.2) *Later Prophets (Nevi'im aḥaronim)

(Optional number; prefer standard 224)

For Isaiah, see 223.3; for Jeremiah, see 223.4; for Ezekiel, see 223.5; for Minor Prophets, see 223.6

(.3) *Isaiah

(Optional number; prefer standard 224.1)

(.4) *Jeremiah

(Optional number; prefer standard 224.2)

(.5) *Ezekiel

(Optional number; prefer standard 224.4)

(.6) *Minor prophets

(Optional number; prefer standard 224.9)

For Zephaniah, Haggai, Zechariah, Malachi, see 223.7

(.61) *Hosea

(Optional number; prefer standard 224.6)

*Add as instructed under 221–229

Optional numbers for books of Bible as arranged in Tanakh (Jewish Bible, Hebrew Bible) (Option A)

(.62) *Joel

(Optional number; prefer standard 224.7)

(.63) *Amos

(Optional number; prefer standard 224.8)

(.64) *Obadiah

(Optional number; prefer standard 224.91)

(.65) *Jonah

(Optional number; prefer standard 224.92)

(.66) *Micah

(Optional number; prefer standard 224.93)

(.67) *Nahum

(Optional number; prefer standard 224.94)

(.68) *Habakkuk

(Optional number; prefer standard 224.95)

(.7) *Zephaniah, Haggai, Zechariah, Malachi

(Optional number; prefer standard 224.9)

(.71) *Zephaniah

(Optional number; prefer standard 224.96)

(.72) *Haggai

(Optional number; prefer standard 224.97)

(.73) *Zechariah

(Optional number; prefer standard 224.98)

(.74) *Malachi

(Optional number; prefer standard 224.99)

(224) *Writings (Ketuvim)

(Optional number; prefer standard 223)

(.1) *Psalms

(Optional number; prefer standard 223.2)

*Add as instructed under 221–229

Optional numbers for books of Bible as arranged in Tanakh (Jewish Bible, Hebrew Bible) (Option A)

(.2) ***Proverbs**

(Optional number; prefer standard 223.7)

(.3) ***Job**

(Optional number; prefer standard 223.1)

(.4) ***Megillot (Five scrolls)**

(Optional number; prefer standard 221.044)

(.41) *Song of Solomon (Canticle of Canticles, Song of Songs)

(Optional number; prefer standard 223.9)

(.42) *Ruth

(Optional number; prefer standard 222.35)

(.43) *Lamentations

(Optional number; prefer standard 224.3)

(.44) *Ecclesiastes (Kohelet, Qohelet)

(Optional number; prefer standard 223.8)

(.45) *Esther

(Optional number; prefer standard 222.9)

(.5) ***Daniel**

(Optional number; prefer standard 224.5)

(.6) ***Ezra**

(Optional number; prefer standard 222.7)

(.7) ***Nehemiah**

(Optional number; prefer standard 222.8)

(.8) ***Chronicles**

(Optional number; prefer standard 222.6)

(.81) *Chronicles 1

(Optional number; prefer standard 222.63)

(.82) *Chronicles 2

(Optional number; prefer standard 222.64)

*Add as instructed under 221–229

230–280

Persons associated with Christianity

Use the following table of preference for comprehensive biographies:

Jesus Christ, Mary, Joseph, Joachim, Anne, John the Baptist	232.9
Other persons in the Bible	220
Founders of denominations	280
Founders of religious orders	271
Higher clergy (e.g., popes, metropolitans, archbishops, bishops) prior to 1054	270.1–.3
Higher clergy subsequent to 1054	280
Theologians	230
Moral theologians	241
Missionaries	266
Evangelists	269.2
Persons noted for participation in associations for religious work	267
Martyrs	272
Heretics	273
Saints	270
Saints prior to 1054	270.1–.3
Saints subsequent to 1054	280
Mystics	248.22
Hymn writers	264.23
Religious educators	268
Members of religious orders	271
Clergy prior to 1054	270.1–.3
Clergy subsequent to 1054	280
Members of the early church to 1054	270.1–.3
Members of denominations	280
Christian biography of persons who fall in none of the above categories	270

Add notation 092 from Table 1 as appropriate, e.g., collected biography of saints 270.0922; Pope Gregory the Great 270.2092.

Use numbers in the range 220–269 other than those listed in the table of preference above for comprehensive biographies of persons with specialized religious careers, or for works treating only one aspect of a person's life and work, e.g., a Biblical scholar 220.092.

Use subdivisions of 230 for biography and criticism of individual theologians, e.g., Saint Thomas Aquinas 230.2092. Use 230.044092 for Protestant theologians who are not connected with a specific denomination or who are important and influential enough to transcend their own denominations, e.g., Karl Barth 230.044092. Use 230.092 for theologians not connected with any specific type of theology. If in doubt, prefer 230.092. Class critical appraisal of an individual theologian's thought on a specific topic with the topic, e.g., on justification 234.7092.

Do not use 248.2 Religious experience or its subdivisions except 248.22 for comprehensive biographies, e.g., a biography of Teresa of Avila's religious life 282.092 (*not* 248.2092). However, use 248.2 for biographical accounts written for devotional purposes, not as comprehensive accounts of a person's life, e.g., the story of one's conversion 248.246092.

Do not use 253, 255, and 262.1 for biographies of the kinds of persons listed in the table of preference above.

Class biographies of members of specific denominations and sects with the main branch of the denomination rather than with the most specific organization or area, e.g., a biography of a member of the Lutheran Church in America 284.1092 (*not* 284.133092); a biography of a clergyman of the African Methodist Episcopal Church 287.8092 (*not* 287.83); a biography of a Russian clergyman of the Eastern Orthodox Church 281.9092 (*not* 281.947092); collected biography of Catholics in the United States 282.092273.

Use 280 without subdivision for members of nondenominational and interdenominational Christian churches. Also use 280 without subdivision if a person living after 1054 belongs to a Christian church, but it cannot be determined which denomination.

If a person does not belong to a church, or if it cannot be determined whether the person belongs to a church, use the historical period that most closely matches the individual's life span or the time period of the individual's greatest prominence in 270 and the country if known, e.g., biography of a 20th-century Christian 270.82092, biography of a 20th-century United States Christian 277.3082092.

See also discussion at 220.92.

231.7652 vs. 213, 500, 576.8

Relation of scientific and Christian viewpoints of origin of universe vs. Creation in philosophy of religion vs. Natural sciences and mathematics vs. Evolution

Evolution versus creation

Use 231.7652 for works on creation science or creationism written by Christians who assume that the Bible provides a chronology of natural history and who rely upon religious premises in responding to theories from the natural sciences. Similarly, use 231.7652 for works that attempt to refute creation science, unless they take the writings of creationists as a starting point from which to demonstrate the case for evolution. On the other hand, use 500 for works by creationist authors that attempt to refute evolution theory by examining the writings, hypotheses, and findings of scientists.

The difficulty stems from the fact that on the question of evolution the *pro* and *con* positions differ so radically that they normally belong in different disciplines, science and religion, respectively. However, when a religious author is trying to enlighten scientists on a specific scientific matter, class the work with science, while if a scientist is trying to enlighten the religious on a specific religious matter, class the work with religion. The correct classification is determined by the intent of the author, and the interest of the readers that the author is seeking to reach, not by the truth, falsity, or validity of interpretations and premises.

Use 231.7652 for comprehensive works including both religion and science.

Use 213 for works that consider the relation between divine creation and evolution as a philosophical problem, without appealing to a particular religion or scripture. If in doubt between 213 and 231.7652, prefer 231.7652.

The most common focus of interest of works belonging in 500 is on biological evolution. Use 576.8 for these works. Use 523.88 if the emphasis of a work is mainly on stellar evolution, 530 if on basic physical principles, 551.7 if on historical geology, and 560 if on paleontology. Use 500 if there is no clear emphasis on a specific branch of science.

241 vs. 261.8

Christian ethics vs. Christian social theology

Some topics are covered in both religious ethics and social theology, e.g., war and peace (241.6242, 261.873). Use 241 for works that focus on what conduct is right or wrong. Use 261.8 for works that may discuss right and wrong, but treat the topic in a broader context as a problem in society and discuss Christian attitudes toward and influence on the problem. Use 241 for works that emphasize what the individual should do. Use 261.8 for works that stress what the church's stance should be, what response the church or Christian community should make to alleviate the problem, or the church's view on problems transcending individual conduct. If in doubt, prefer 241.

260 vs. 251–254, 259

Christian social and ecclesiastical theology vs. Local church and Pastoral care of specific kinds of persons

The local church is the group in which individual believers can meet regularly face to face for worship, fellowship, and church activities—for example, a congregation, a college church group.

Among the more recent forms of the local church are the small groups called basic Christian communities or basic ecclesial communities. These are smaller than parishes or congregations, but, like other forms of the local church, are organized for the general religious welfare of their members, not just for special projects or functions. Class these in the same way as parishes, i.e., class comprehensive works in 250 (or in 262.26 when treated as part of ecclesiology), and class specific aspects with the aspect in the subdivisions of 250.

Use either 250 or 260 for activities undertaken by the church, depending on the context. Use 250 for works intended for the individual practitioner in the local setting. This may be as small as a parish youth group or as large as a counseling program that serves a metropolitan area. Use 261 for the church's attitude to cultural and social problems, and its activities regarding them, unless the context is limited to the local church, e.g., a practical work for the prison chaplain 259.5, but the church's attitude to the treatment of criminals 261.8336. If in doubt, prefer 260.

Use 260 for some activities that can be conducted by the local church, e.g., public worship (264–265), religious education (268), spiritual renewal and evangelism (269), as the context of works on these subjects is often broader than the local church.

Use 262 for church organization, unless the scope is limited to administration of the local church (254).

261.5

Christianity and secular disciplines

Use 261.5 for personal Christian views and church teachings about secular disciplines as a whole, their value, how seriously a Christian should take them, how far the disciplines should affect faith. Class Christian philosophy of a secular discipline with the discipline, e.g., a Christian philosophy of psychology 150.1. In some cases specific provision is made for use of secular disciplines for religious purposes, e.g., use of drama 246.72. If in doubt, class with the secular discipline.

270, 230.11–.14 vs. 230.15–.2, 281.5–.9, 282

Early church to 1054 vs. Eastern churches, Roman Catholic Church

Use 270.1–.3 (*not* 281.1–.4) for the history of the Church prior to 1054, because the early church is considered to be undivided by denominations until the schism of 1054. Use 274–279 for the history of specific churches prior to 1054.

Use 270.1–.3 or 274–279 for the history of the Eastern and Roman Catholic churches before 1054. Use 281.5–.9 or 282 for works on later history or works that cover both the early and later history. If in doubt for works about both Eastern and Roman Catholic churches, prefer 270. If in doubt for works about a specific denomination, prefer 281.5–.9 or 282.

Use 230.11–.14 for theology of Eastern and Roman Catholic churches before 1054. Use 230.15–.2 for later theology.

280.042 vs. 262.0011

Relations between denominations vs. Ecumenism

Use 280.042 for works on the ecumenical movement and interdenominational cooperation. Use 280.042 also for works on relations between two or more specific denominations having notation that differs in the first three digits, e.g., relations between Roman Catholics (282) and Lutherans (284.1). Class works about relations among denominations having the same notation in the first three digits in the most specific number that includes them all, e.g., relations among the various Baptist denominations, between Baptists and Disciples of Christ 286. Class works about relations between one denomination and several others with the denomination emphasized, e.g., relations between Baptists and other denominations 286. Class discussions among denominations on a specific subject with the subject, e.g., the Eucharist 234.163. Use 262.0011 for theoretical works on ecumenism. If in doubt, prefer 280.042.

283–289

Protestant and other denominations

Under the general name of some denominations, e.g., Presbyterian churches of United States origin 285.1, notation is provided for specific denominations, e.g., 285.13. The specific denominations are named church bodies uniting a number of individual local churches, e.g., the Presbyterian Church (U.S.A.) 285.137, the Associate Presbyterian Church of North America 285.13 (the latter denomination is not listed in the schedule). Along with notation for specific denominations, a span for treatment of the denomination by continent, country, or locality will also be provided, e.g., 285.14–.19. Use the notation for specific denominations if the denominations are treated with regard to all or nearly all the geographic area they cover, but use the span for treatment by continent, country, or locality for works on a specific denomination covering a smaller area, e.g., use 286.132 for the Southern Baptist Convention, but use 286.1768 for a state association of Southern Baptist churches in Tennessee (286.1 plus notation 768 for Tennessee from Table 2). Use the span for treatment by continent, country, or locality for individual local churches, regardless of the specific denomination to which they belong. Also use the span for treatment by continent, country, or locality for a work about several specific denominations in one country by area, e.g., a work describing the various Presbyterian denominations in the United States 285.173 (*not* 285.13).

Where the notation for specific denominations is limited to churches that originated in the United States or the British Commonwealth, e.g., the numbers following 284.1, 285.1, 285.2 and 287.5, use the span for treatment by continent, country, or locality for specific denominations in other areas, e.g., use 284.135 for the Evangelical Lutheran Church in America, but use 284.1485 (284.1 plus notation 485 for Sweden from Table 2) for the Lutheran Church of Sweden.

297.092

Persons associated with Islam

Use the following table of preference for comprehensive biographies of persons associated with an identifiable function, activity, or sect in Islam:

Muḥammad the Prophet	297.63
Muḥammad's family	297.64
Muḥammad's companions	297.648
Prophets prior to Muḥammad	297.246092
Other persons in Koran	297.122092
Founders of sects and reform movements	297.8
Founders of Sufi orders	297.48
Higher non-Sufi religious leaders	297.092
Of specific sects and movements	297.8
Theologians	297.2092
Moral theologians	297.5092
Da'wah workers	297.74
Leaders and members of Sufi orders	297.48
Other Sufis (mystics)	297.4
Religious educators	297.77092
Mosque officers	297.092
Of specific sects and movements	297.8
Members of sects and movements	297.8

Use 297.61 Leaders and their work for the role, function, and duties of religious leaders, not for biography of religious leaders.

Class works dealing with only one specialized aspect of a person's career or religious experience with the aspect, e.g., an account of conversion to Islam 297.574092.

Use 297.092 if a Muslim cannot be identified primarily with one function, activity, or sect.

297.26–.27

Islam and secular disciplines

Use numbers outside 200 for works that focus on issues of importance to practitioners of a secular discipline and for works that describe achievements of Muslims working within the discipline, but use 297.26–.27 for works that focus on Islamic theological issues in relation to secular disciplines. For example, class works describing achievements of Islamic arts with art, but use 297.267 for Islamic attitudes toward the arts, e.g., what kinds of music and visual arts are consistent with Islamic beliefs. Use 320.91767 (political situation and conditions in the Islamic world) or another subdivision of 320 for a work on Islam and politics that emphasizes issues primarily of concern to political scientists, but use

297.272 for a work on Islam and politics that emphasizes Islamic religious issues. If in doubt, prefer a number outside 297.

299.93

New Age religions

Class New Age perspectives on health and medicine, environmentalism, gardening, and other activities and areas of knowledge with the subject and discipline under discussion, even if the discussion rejects some of the main tenets of the discipline, e.g., using mental energy to cure illness 615.851.

Use 130 and its subdivisions for New Age literature mostly concerned with psychic and paranormal phenomena.

Use 201–209 for works on some aspects of religion from a New Age perspective if the works do not attempt to speak for a particular known religion or to establish a new religion or sect, e.g., use 204 for a New Age perspective on spirituality.

Use 299.93 for works concerned with several New Age religions, but use 200 if the work includes sects of the more established religions, e.g., sects of Buddhism, Hinduism, Native American religion, etc.

Use 299.93 for comprehensive works on the New Age as a whole or as a movement.

300–330, 355–390 vs. 342–347, 352–354

Bills, hearings, and legislative reports

Use 300–330 and 355–390 for:

General hearings and related reports, e.g., hearings on the state of the United States economy 330.973

Hearings and related reports on public policy

Oversight hearings and related reports that focus on whether present appropriations, laws, and public policies are meeting the needs of society

Hearings and related reports of legislative investigations not related to proposed legislation, e.g., investigations into political corruption 364.131

Military appropriation and authorization bills, hearings, and related reports

Use 342–347 for:

Bills, hearings, and reports relating to ordinary laws

Bills (including authorizations and appropriation bills) and related hearings and reports that establish government agencies. Use the number for the subject with which the agency deals, e.g., a bill to establish the U.S. Department of Education 344.73070262

Hearings on judicial nominations. Use numbers in 345 and 347, e.g., a hearing on a nomination to the U.S. Supreme Court 347.732634

Use 352–354 for:

Hearings and related reports on nonmilitary authorizations and appropriations that do not emphasize public policy and the needs of society. Use 352.49 plus notation 023 from the table under 352.493–.499 for general hearings and reports, e.g., hearings on appropriations in Germany 352.4943023. Use the number for a specific agency plus notation 249 from the table under 352–354 for hearings and reports on a specific agency, e.g., hearings on appropriations to support health facilities 353.68249, to support health care facilities in Germany 353.6824943023

Oversight hearings focusing on agency performance. Use the number for the agency, e.g., an oversight hearing on the U.S. Bureau of Indian Affairs 353.53497073

If in doubt, prefer in the following order: 300–330 and 355–390; 352–354; 342–347.

See also discussion at 300, 320.6 vs. 352–354: Nomination hearings.

300, 320.6 vs. 352–354

Social sciences and policy formulation vs. Specific topics of public administration

Public policy

Use 300–349, 355–399 for the public policy itself (what the policy is or should be, as distinct from how it is formulated or administered) in specific fields of social concern, e.g., economic development and growth policies 338.9, welfare policies 361.61. Use 353–354 for the public policy itself on other topics, e.g., art policy 353.77 (*not* 700). However, use 323 for policies with civil rights implications, e.g., religious policy 323.442 (*not* 200 or 353.7). Some exceptions are specified in the schedules, e.g., public policy for libraries 021.8.

Certain policies have names that suggest one discipline but actually concern another. For example, use 338.926 for technology policy, technology transfer policy, research and development (R and D) policy, and even science policy if formulated in terms of promoting economic growth and development.

Use 320.6 for interdisciplinary works on policy formulation, and works on how society as a whole makes up its mind. Governments usually, but not always, make up the leading parties in policy formulation, e.g., presidents, governors, courts, and legislatures at various levels. Use 320.6 for policy formulation led or mediated by agencies in two or more branches of government, but use 352.34 for policy formulation conducted by executive agencies, how an executive decides upon policies and gets them carried out. Class policy formulation in a specific field by "the government" or society with the policy as explained above, but class policy formulation by executive agencies in specific fields in 352–354, plus notation 234 derived from 352.34.

For example, use 323 for a work about what civil rights policies are or should be, and on how society as a whole decides what they should be; 353.48234 for a work on how a civil rights agency resolves policy issues; and 353.485 for a work on how to administer civil rights policies. Similarly, use 338.9 for a work on economic development, 354.27 for a report on an economic development agency, and 354.27234 for a work on policy making in an economic development agency.

If in doubt, prefer the number outside public administration.

Nomination hearings

Class all nomination hearings for executive officers in 352–354, because it is difficult to determine whether emphasis is on matters like personal qualifications and administrative issues or on the policies that the agency should carry out. Class nominations for the head of an agency in the field that the agency administers, plus notation 2293 from the table under 352–354, e.g., nomination hearing for an attorney general 353.42293.

See also discussion at T1—068 vs. 353–354.

300 vs. 600

Social sciences vs. Technology

Use 300 for works that discuss the social implications of a technology, e.g., the economic importance of lumbering 338.17498 (*not* 634.98). Use 300 for works on the social utilization, the social control, and the social effect of technology. Use 600 for works that discuss how to make, operate, maintain, or repair something, e.g., manufacture of motor vehicles 629.2.

Use 300 rather than 600 for the following categories of material:

1. Works that emphasize the social use of the topic rather than operating or processing it, e.g., tea drinking in England 394.12 (*not* 641.33720942 or 641.63720942)

2. Works that emphasize the overall perspective, e.g., the shift from coal to oil in American industry 333.82130973 (*not* 621.4023)

3. Works that emphasize the social control as opposed to the control exercised during the manufacturing process, e.g., standards of drug quality imposed by a government agency or a trade association 363.1946 (*not* 615.19)

4. Works that cite raw statistics, e.g., crop production, acreage, fertilizer consumption, farm size 338.1 (*not* 630)

Technical reports

Use 300 for technical and research reports that emphasize procedural technicalities and refer to economic, legal, administrative, or regulatory complexities. Consider the purpose of the writer and the mission of the agency authorizing the reports in determining the classification of a report series, and of individual reports in a series. Use 300 if the emphasis is on the exercise of social control over a process or the social aspects of technological processes, e.g., water quality monitoring systems 363.739463 (*not* 628.161), a work describing how railroads serve Argentina 385.0982 (*not* 625.100982); a report on fertilizer and rice studying production efficiency in developing countries 338.162 (*not* 633.1889).

Interdisciplinary works

Use 300 as the interdisciplinary number for a phenomenon of social significance; and as the place of last resort for general works on a subject lacking disciplinary focus, e.g., a work on industrial archaeology not emphasizing how things were made 338.47609 (*not* 609). However, use 600 for works that emphasize descriptions of products or structures, such as clocks, locomotives, and windmills.

Biography and company history

Use 600 for works on artisans, engineers, and inventors. However, use 338.7 for works on artisans, engineers, and inventors who are of more interest as entrepreneurs, e.g., Henry Ford 338.76292092.

Use 600 (or 700 if the interest is artistic) for works on the products of specific companies that emphasize the description and design of the products, e.g., Seth Thomas clocks or Ferrari automobiles. However, use 338.7 if the organization or history of the company receives significant attention, e.g., Seth Thomas clocks 681.113097461, but the Seth Thomas Clock Company and its clocks 338.7681113097461.

301–307 vs. 361–365

Sociology vs. Social problems and services

Use 301–307 only for works on social phenomena that deal exclusively, or almost exclusively, with the phenomenon in its pure state, i.e., its social background, its role in the social structure, its effects on society, its innate characteristics and inner structure.

Use 361–365 for works on social phenomena considered as social problems in connection with actual and potential remedies.

Examples:

1. Use 306.85 for the family as a social phenomenon.

2. Use 306.88 for a work discussing the effect of the changing social roles of men and women in the dissolution of the family.

3. Use 362.82 for a work that discusses actual and potential remedies for family dissolution.

If in doubt, prefer 301–307.

301–307 vs. 361.1, 362.042

Social problems

Use 301–307 for social problems primarily when they are discussed as social phenomena, rather than as matters that society should take action to solve. Use 361.1 for works about social problems discussed as a background to social action, especially if emphasis is clearly toward actual or potential remedies: these works can encompass any and all kinds of social problems from providing child care to supplying water. Use 362.042 for works on social problems thought of as social welfare problems, a narrower concept than 361.1. If in doubt, prefer in the following order: 301–307, 361.1, 362.042.

302–307 vs. 150, T1—019

Social psychology vs. Psychology

Use 302–307 for works that focus on group behavior, including those that discuss the role of the individual in group behavior. Use 150 for works that focus on the individual, including those that discuss the influence of group behavior on the individual. If in doubt, prefer 302–307.

Use 302–307 without adding notation 019 from Table 1 for application of social psychology to a subject, e.g., social psychology of religion 306.6. Use the number for the subject plus notation 019 from Table 1 for the application of psychology to a subject, e.g., individual psychology of religion 200.19. If in doubt, prefer 302–307.

302–307 vs. 156

Comparative psychology

Use 302–307 for works considering the social behavior of animals as a background to human social behavior. Use 156 for works on comparative social psychology when used to shed light on the behavior of the individual. If in doubt, prefer 302–307.

302–307 vs. 320

Specific topics in sociology and anthropology vs. Political science

Use 302–307 for works on social institutions, processes, and phenomena if they emphasize how the social topics are related to and manifested in political ones, even if they have a political cast. Only use 320 for works on political institutions, processes, and phenomena in which the political aspects are emphasized. For example, use 305.42 (*not* 324.623) for a work on the relation between the feminist movement and the enfranchisement of women. If in doubt, prefer 302–307.

303.483 vs. 306.45, 306.46

Social effects of science and technology

Use 303.483 for the effects of scientific discoveries and technological innovations upon society, e.g., a work on the transformation of religious, economic, and leisure institutions stemming from the development of electronic media 303.4833. Use 306.4 for the patterns of behavior of the individuals and groups engaged in scientific or technical endeavors, e.g., a description of the milieu that seems to be conducive to technological innovation 306.46. If in doubt, prefer 303.483.

305.6 vs. 305.92, 306.6

Sociology of religion and religious groups

Use 305.6 for the sociology of a group of people who are identified as belonging to a particular religion, especially if they are a minority group in a particular place, e.g., a work on the sociology of Christians in Indonesia 305.67598.

Use 305.92 for the sociology of a group of people whose occupation is religious, e.g., a work on the sociology of shamans 305.920144, a work on the sociology of people in Christian religious orders 305.9255.

Use 306.6 for the sociology of religious institutions considered from a secular viewpoint, e.g., a work on the sociology of the Christian Church 306.66.

If in doubt, prefer in the following order: 306.6, 305.6, 305.92.

305.9 vs. 305.5

Occupational and miscellaneous groups vs. Social classes

Use 305.9 for works on an occupational or miscellaneous group when either

1. there is little or no emphasis on class,
2. the group is well represented in two or more distinct classes, or
3. the group has an indefinite or transitional status.

Use 305.5 for works on an occupational or miscellaneous group considered in terms of its specific social status. If in doubt, prefer 305.9.

306 vs. 305, 909, 930–990

Social groups vs. Culture and institutions vs. History

Use 305 for social groups, e.g., women as a social category 305.4. Use 306 for social institutions, e.g., the family 306.85. Use the number for the institution in 306, plus notation 08 from Table 1, for the role of social groups in specific institutions of society, e.g., women in the family 306.85082.

Use 909 and 930–990 for the role of social groups in history, and for accounts of the major events shaping the history. In particular, use 909 and 930–990 for the history of ethnic and national groups.

If in doubt, prefer in the following order: 306, 305, 909, 930–990.

307

Communities

Use 307 for works on the community in a relatively restricted area as a social phenomenon and works on community planning, development, and redevelopment. These terms are used here in their ordinary meaning to imply the planning for and development of the community as a whole. Use 300 apart from 307 for works where specific subjects of community interest are addressed, e.g., economic development of the community 338.93–.99, developing hospitals for the community 362.11, planning community housing 363.5525, planning the city water supply 363.61, planning the education system 379.4–.9.

320 vs. 306.2

Politics of political institutions vs. Sociology of political institutions

Use 320 for works on the descriptive, comparative, historical, and theoretical study of political institutions and processes, in which the social environment is considered only as a background. Use 306.2 for works on the social dynamics of political institutions, the social sources (e.g., ethnic group, class, family) and the social processes of political institutions, or the impact of these institutions and their activity on the social environment. Use 306.2 also for works dealing with political institutions and processes as models for social institutions and processes. If in doubt, prefer 320.

320.557 vs. 297.09, 297.272, 322.1

Islamic fundamentalism

Use 320.557 for works on Islamic fundamentalism that emphasize political aspects from a secular viewpoint; and for works emphasizing the religiously oriented political ideologies of Islamic fundamentalism.

Use 297.09 and other subdivisions of 297 only for works that emphasize religious aspects of Islamic fundamentalism, such as a concern to maintain and hand down a pure version of the Islamic faith, a mindfulness to follow the strict letter of the Koran and Hadith, an attempt to generate a religious reawakening through preaching, teaching, and other forms of religious communication. Use 297.272 only for works that treat politics from the religious point of view.

Use 322.1 for works emphasizing the political role of Islamic fundamentalist organizations and groups in relation to the state.

If in doubt, prefer in the following order: 320.557; 322.1; a subdivision of 297.

320.9, 320.4 vs. 351

Government vs. Public administration

Government is limited to considerations of the nature, role, goals and structure of states; their political direction and control; and how central controls are exercised and balanced against each other. Public administration concentrates on executive agencies and the procedures used to carry out their goals, policies, and actions in various fields.

Use 320.9 for works that discuss the habitual conduct and methods of people in high office, even if they appear to cover the structure and functions of government.

Use 320.4 for works on the overall structure of governments, emphasizing their chief legislative, judicial, and executive organs, or for works that discuss typical activities of the different branches, e.g., regulating safety as an illustration of the police function. Use 320.4 also for comprehensive works on government and public administration of specific areas, but not for works emphasizing the work of carrying out goals and policies. Use 320 for interdisciplinary works on government and public administration not limited to specific areas.

Use 351 for works that emphasize agencies of the executive branch, or the usual components of administration: planning, organizing, staffing, financing, and equipping agencies to do a job.

If in doubt, prefer in the following order: 320.9, 320.4, 351.

322.1 vs. 201.72, 261.7, 292–299

Politics and religion

Use 322.1 for works discussing the relationships between religious organizations or movements and states or governments from a secular perspective. Use 201.72, 261.7, and similar numbers in 292–299 for works on the position that religious people and organizations take or should take toward political affairs (including the state). If in doubt, prefer 322.1.

324 vs. 320

The political process vs. Politics and government

Use 324 for works on party politics, but use 320 for comprehensive works on politics in the broad sense. "Politics" in the caption at 320 covers the concepts of adjusting relationships among individuals and groups in a political community, guiding and influencing the policy of government, and winning and holding control of society. If in doubt, prefer 324.

See also discussion at 909, 930–990 vs. 320.

324 vs. 320.5, 320.9, 909, 930–990

Political movements

Use 324 for works on the attempts of political movements to achieve power by nonviolent means and their ventures into electoral politics (even as splinter parties with scant chance of success). Use 320.5 for works concerning the thought and internal history or dynamics of political ideological movements. Use 320.5 also for comprehensive works on specific ideological movements. Use 320.9 for the impact of these movements on the political system and their interaction with other political forces. Use 909, 930–990 for works on movements that come to power or directly affect the major events of history. If in doubt, prefer in the following order: 324, 320.9, 320.5.

See also discussion at 909, 930–990 vs. 320.

324.2094–.2099 and 324.24–.29

Treatment of political parties in specific continents, countries, localities in modern world

Use 324.209 (or 324.21 for specific kind of party) for treatment of political parties by continent and by region larger than a specific country, e.g., political parties in Europe 324.2094; Conservative parties in Europe 324.214094.

Use 324.24–.29 for treatment of political parties by country, using area notation for country from Table 2, followed by notation to express the party, e.g., political parties in United Kingdom 324.241; the Conservative Party 324.24104.

Use the country number in 324.24–.29, followed by notation to express the party, plus notation 09 from Table 1, for treatment of political parties by locality within a country, since in most countries the local party is a branch of the national party, or, at least, a local organization of persons who regard themselves as members of a national party, e.g., the Conservative Party in Wales 324.2410409429 (*not* 324.242904). Use the same rule for works on regional and separatist parties, e.g., a separatist party in Wales 324.241098409429 (*not* 324.24290984). Use the national number, plus modified standard subdivision 009, for comprehensive works on parties of a specific part of a nation, e.g., parties of Wales 324.241009429, of Catalonia 324.246009467.

However, for Canada, the United States, and Australia, each of which has strong traditions of autonomy for state and provincial parties, the political parties of states and provinces are treated like "countries" rather than like "localities," e.g., political parties of New York State 324.2747 (*not* 324.273009747); the Democratic Party in New York State 324.274706 (*not* 324.273609747). Regions and localities are subordinated to national or state and provincial numbers, e.g., the Democratic Party in the Midwest 324.27360977, in New York City 324.274706097471.

330 vs. 650, 658

Business

Use 330 for works on business that present general information, economic conditions, financial information (such as interest rates), and reports on what certain companies are doing. Use 650 for works on business that emphasize practical managerial information and that cover 651 Office services as well as 658 General management. Use 658 if the work is limited to management. Use 330 for comprehensive works on 330 and 650. If in doubt, prefer 330.

331.120424 vs. 331.1377

Full employment policies vs. Prevention and relief of unemployment

Use 331.120424 for works on government labor policies and programs wider than simply combating unemployment, e.g., public service employment as a measure to provide both jobs for the unemployed and assistance to distressed areas and state and local governments. Use 331.1377 for works on government labor policies and programs that discuss them solely in terms of prevention and relief of unemployment. If in doubt, prefer 331.120424.

332, 336 vs. 339

Macroeconomics

Use 332 and 336 for works on economic topics considered in their own right, e.g., monetary activities of central banks 332.112. Use 339 if the topics are discussed in relation to the total economic picture of a country or region, since macroeconomics is the study of the economy as a whole, especially with reference to its general level of output and income and the interrelationships among sectors of the economy, e.g., activities of central banks undertaken primarily to carry out macroeconomic policy 339.53. If in doubt, prefer 332 and 336.

332 vs. 338, 658.15

Financial topics in production economics and financial management

Use 332 for works discussing financial topics from the viewpoint of people or organizations with money to invest and those who serve them—investors, bankers, stockbrokers, and the like. Use 338 for works discussing financial topics from the viewpoint of people concerned with the production of goods and services, or who are interested in capital because it is necessary for production. For example, use 332.6722 (domestic investment in specific types of enterprise) for a work discussing whether mining is a safe and profitable field of investment for the general public; but use 338.23 (financial aspects of extraction of minerals) for a work discussing whether the mining industry will attract enough investment to expand production. Use 658.15 (or the subject plus notation 0681 from Table 1) for works discussing financial topics from the viewpoint of an executive responsible for the financial management of an organization, or works that focus narrowly on managerial concerns. If in doubt, prefer 332.

332.632044 vs. 332.6323

Gilt-edged securities

Use 332.632044 for works on all types of gilt-edged securities. In American usage the term may refer to any security of exceptionally high quality, or it may refer primarily to high-quality bonds. Use 332.6323 for works only on bonds. Use 332.63232 also for British works on gilt-edged securities, as in British usage the term refers to government bonds. If in doubt, prefer 332.632044.

332.6322 vs. 332.6323

Stocks

Use 332.6322 for stocks in the sense of shares (American usage), but use 332.6323 for stocks in the sense of bonds (British usage). If in doubt, prefer 332.6322.

333.7–.9 vs. 363.1, 363.73, 577

Social aspects of ecology

Use numbers in 300 rather than 577 for works on ecology and specific natural environments that discuss public policy and resource economics rather than biology. Class works on natural resource management, environmental impacts and monitoring, risk assessment, development, conservation and biodiversity as follows:

1. Natural resource management: Use 333.7 or the number for the specific resource, e.g., management of wetlands 333.918.

2. Environmental impacts and monitoring:

A. The resource situation in general: Use 333.7 or the number for the specific resource (without adding any further subdivisions), e.g., monitoring biodiversity 333.95;

B. Environmental impacts: Use 333.714 or the number for the specific resource plus notation 14 from the table under 333.7–.9, e.g., monitoring the impact of reclamation projects on wetlands 333.91814;

C. Pollution levels: Use 363.7363 or the number for the specific kind of pollutant or environment plus notation 63 from table under 362–363, e.g., monitoring oil pollution 363.738263. (However, use 333.7–.9 as instructed under 2. B. above for the impact of pollution, e.g., monitoring the impact of oil pollution on wetlands 333.91814);

D. Potential environmental impacts: Class with the development whose impact is being studied, e.g., the potential impact of an oil pipeline on tundra ecology 388.55.

3. Risk assessment:

A. Generalized risks to the environment: Class as an impact study in 333.714 or the number for the specific resource plus notation 14 from the table under 333.7–.9, e.g., contemporary risks to wetlands of America 333.918140973;

B. Safety risks: Use the subdivision for the specific threat in 363.1 plus notation 72 from the table under 362–363, e.g., assessing the risk to humans of pesticides in food 363.19272;

C. Risks of specific developments: Class with the specific development as a study of potential impacts, e.g., assessing the risk of tourism to biodiversity in East Africa 916.7604.

4. Development: Use 333.715 or the number for the specific resource plus notation 15 from the table under 333.7–.9, e.g., hydroelectric power development 333.91415.

5. Conservation: Use 333.72 or the number for the specific resource plus notation 16 from the table under 333.7, e.g., conservation of biodiversity 333.9516.

6. Biodiversity: Use 333.95 (especially for works emphasizing its value or importance).

If in doubt, prefer in the following order: 333.7–.9, 363.1, 363.73.

See also discussion at 363.73 vs. 571.95, 577.27.

333.7–.9 vs. 363.6

Natural resources and energy vs. Public utilities

Use 333.7–.9 for comprehensive works on resources, projection of needs and supplies, development, conservation and protection of resources. Use 363.6 for works on problems and services related to utilities distributing and delivering the resources to users. Use 333.7–.9 for "supply" as a noun, but use 363.6 for "supply" as a verb. If in doubt, prefer 333.7–.9.

However, use 333.7932 for a work about distribution of electrical power by utilities if the work emphasizes the problems of developing the supply of electricity, says little about the problems of distributing the electricity to customers, and does not discuss prices without reference to production costs.

Use 333.717 or a number for a specific resource in 333.7–.9 plus notation 17 from the table under 333.7–.9 for works on the rationing of natural resources still in their natural state, but use 363 for works on the rationing of final products, e.g., wellhead allocation of natural gas for companies or jurisdictions 333.823317, but rationing of natural gas among consumers or classes of consumers at the other end of the line 363.63. If in doubt, prefer 333.717 and numbers for specific resources in 333.7–.9.

333.7–.9 vs. 508, 913–919, 930–990

National parks and monuments

Use 333.7–.9 for works on national parks where the main attraction is nature if the emphasis is on conservation and protection of natural resources, e.g., forest parks 333.784, game reserves 333.954916. Use 508 or other numbers in 500 if the emphasis is on description of and guides to natural phenomena, e.g., a comprehensive guide to the natural history of Yellowstone National Park 508.78752, a guide to the geology of Yellowstone 557.8752.

Use 913–919, plus notation 04 from the table under 913–919 followed by notation for the historical period when the guidebook was written, for general guidebooks to all the national parks of an area, e.g., a 1989 general guidebook to the national parks of South America 918.0438.

Class general works about historical monuments with the events commemorated. For example, class a battlefield national park with the battle, e.g., Gettysburg National Military Park 973.7349. Class a park associated with the life of an individual in the biography number for that individual, e.g., Lyndon B. Johnson National Historical Park 973.923092, George Washington Carver National Monument 630.92.

If in doubt, prefer in the following order: 333.7–.9; 508 and other numbers in 500; 930–990; 913–919.

See also discussion at 913–919: Historic sites and buildings; also at 913–919: Add table: 04: Guidebooks; also at 930–990: Wars; also at 930–990: Historic preservation.

333.72 vs. 304.28, 320.58, 363.7

Environmentalism

Use 333.72 for works on environmentalism discussing the broader concept of preserving and protecting the supply as well as the quality of natural resources and for works about the environmental movement that focus on the concerns it shares with the long established conservation movement. Use 304.28 for works that emphasize the effect upon society of overuse, misuse, or pollution of the environment. Use 320.58 for works that emphasize the political ideologies of environmentalism. Use 363.7 for works on preserving and restoring the quality of the social living space, i.e., taking care of wastes, pollution, noise, the dead, and pests. If in doubt, prefer in the following order: 333.72, 304.28, 363.7.

333.73–.78 vs. 333, 333.1–.5

Natural resources vs. Land economics

Use 333.73–.78 for works on land as a natural resource, as a source of economic goods (chiefly agricultural and mineral), and for works on the usage of the land and its resources. Use 333.73–.78, plus notation 17 from the add table under 333.7–.9, for works on control of usage regardless of who owns the land, e.g., price control, zoning. Use 333.73 for comprehensive works on land policy.

Use 333.73–.78 for land inventories, which often focus on land as a resource and land usage.

Use 333 for comprehensive works on land and on natural resources only if the works contain substantial discussion of ownership. It is more common for comprehensive works on land to contain substantial discussion of ownership than comprehensive works on other natural resources. Use 333.7–.9 for comprehensive works on natural resources that treat predominantly nonownership aspects. If in doubt, prefer 333.7–.9.

Use 333.1–.5 for land as property, where the central issues are the right to possession and use, and the right to transfer possession and use. Use 333.1–.5 for control of land only if the control is the kind that stems from ownership.

Use 333 for comprehensive works on both 333.1–.5 and 333.73–.78 with respect to land only if the works contain substantial discussion of ownership. Use

333.1–.5 for works on the right to use land and its resources. If in doubt, prefer in the following order: 333.73–.78, 333.1–.5, 333.

333.955–.959 vs. 639.97

Conservation and management of specific kinds of animals

Conservation and resource management are primarily economic concepts. Use 333.955–.959 for works on conservation of specific kinds of animals if the works discuss public policy and programs; give estimates or statistics of populations, abundance, harvest, catches, and kills; make appeals for resource management; and issue calls to protect an animal or save it from extinction. Use 639.97 for works that discuss agricultural methods and techniques and how to carry them out.

A few terms used in conservation work are troublesome because they may refer to either economics or technology. Use 333.955–.959 for works on rescue, reintroduction, management, and habitat improvement of specific kinds of animals, if the works are focused on programs and the rationale behind the activities. Use 639.97 only if the work is focused on hands-on activities where the animals are living.

If in doubt, prefer 333.955–.959.

335 vs. 306.345, 320.53

Socialism and related systems in economics, sociology, and political theory

Use 335 for interdisciplinary works on socialism and related systems, and works on their philosophic foundations, since they are based upon theories of how the economy does or should work. Use 335 also for wide-ranging works that do not fit within normal disciplinary boundaries but are clearly about socialism and related systems. Use 335 also for works discussing how another economic system should be reorganized into a socialist system.

Use 306.345 only for sociological studies of how socialist economic systems work out in practice.

Use 320.53 for works that emphasize how political movements intend to introduce socialism and what political forces they expect to harness to attain and keep power, or that discuss political movements and forces without in-depth discussion of the economic dynamics or theory.

Works in 320.53 and 335 may include material that is prescriptive, that says how society, the economy, or the political system ought to be organized. If in doubt, prefer 335.

337.3–.9 vs. 337.1

Foreign economic policies and relations of specific jurisdictions and groups of jurisdictions vs. Multilateral economic cooperation

Use 337.3–.9 for works on relations between a cooperative group treated as a whole and other countries or groups, e.g., economic relations of the European

Union with Japan 337.4052, economic relations of the European Union with the rest of the world 337.4. Use 337.1 for works on cooperative relations among the states of multistate groups, e.g., cooperation within the European Union 337.142. If in doubt, prefer 337.3–.9.

338.09 vs. 332.67309, 338.6042

Location of industry and investment

Use 338.09 for works showing where industry is in fact located, i.e., for works that consider location as a condition. Use 338.6042 for works on the rationale for and the process of locating business organizations, i.e., for works that consider location as an action.

Use 332.67309 for works describing the advantages and disadvantages of making international investments, including establishing international enterprises, in particular areas.

If in doubt, prefer 338.09.

338.092

Business biography

Use 338.0922 for collected biography of businessmen in many fields. Use 338.040922 for collected biography of entrepreneurs in many fields.

Use 338.1–.4 for biographies of business leaders not limited to a specific enterprise but limited to a specific field, e.g., business leaders in the automotive manufacturing industry 338.4762920922. Use 338.6–.8 for biographies of people associated with the development and operation of specific types of enterprises but not confined to a specific industry or group of industries, e.g., small-business owners 338.6420922, persons associated with trusts 338.850922. Use 338.70922 for biographies of company directors on the boards of companies in several industries or groups of industries. Use 338.76 for a biography of an entrepreneur or business leader associated with a specific business enterprise, e.g., the founder of a cosmetics manufacturing company 338.766855092.

338.1 vs. 631.558

Crop yields

Use 338.1 for works on crop yields that are compilations giving the total production of an area. Use 338.16 for works on yields per unit of area if they are taken as indicators of production efficiency, either of agricultural systems using various methods (e.g., crop rotation) or of agricultural systems prevailing in various areas. Use 631.558 only for works that have little or no economic or testing implications, e.g., lists of record yields of various crops. Class with the subject in agriculture if yield studies per unit of area are used in technical tests of varieties or specific production techniques, e.g., yield tests of fertilizer 631.80287. If in doubt, prefer 338.1.

338.926 vs. 352.745, 500

Science policy

Science policy generally focuses on what society should do to promote the utilization of science and the growth of industries and activities based on science. Use 338.926 for works on science policy regarded as a policy or program to promote economic development and growth (use similar numbers in 338.93–.99 for science policy for economic development in specific areas, e.g., Europe 338.9406). Use 352.745 (and similar numbers in 352–354, built with 352.745) for works on public administration of science policy. Use 354.274 for works that emphasize administration of economic development. In the absence of a focus on the social sciences, use 509 for natural science policy in an area. If in doubt, prefer 338.926.

340, 342–347 vs. 340.56

Civil law

Use 340 for comprehensive works that treat civil law as all law that is not law of nations or criminal law (342–344, 346–347). Contrast civil law in this sense with criminal law (345). Use 340.56 for works that treat civil law as a system of law derived from Roman law that is in use to a greater or lesser extent in most countries in the modern world, e.g., Germany, France, Japan, Brazil, and even in some subordinate jurisdictions of countries that otherwise use another system, e.g., the province of Quebec in Canada and the state of Louisiana in the United States. If in doubt, prefer 340.

340, 342–347 vs. 340.57

Common law

Use 340 and 342–347 for works that treat common law as the system of law of England and other countries, such as the United States, whose law is derived from English law, or that treat common law as the branch of English law that derives from the old English courts of common law as opposed to the branch of law known as equity that grew up in the Court of Chancery. Use 340.57 for works that treat common law as law that is not the result of legislation but rather of custom and judicial decision. If in doubt, prefer 340.

340 vs. 808.06634

Legal writing

Use the number for the subject in 340 for works on the composition of legal briefs, law reports, and other documents if the work emphasizes how to make the document comply with the law, e.g., how to draw up a legal contract 346.022. Use 808.06634 for works that emphasize techniques of composition. If in doubt, prefer 340.

340.02–.09 vs. 349

Geographic treatment of law

Use 340.02–.09 for works intended to be general in coverage, even if most examples are taken from a specific jurisdiction. Use 349 for works limiting the law to a specific jurisdiction. For example, use 340.03, general law dictionaries, (*not* 349.7303, dictionaries of American law), for *Black's Law Dictionary*, even though the majority of the cases cited are from the United States. Use 340.025752 for a directory of lawyers who can practice law not only in Maryland but also in other parts of the United States and whose place of residence is in Maryland, but use 349.752025 for a directory of lawyers who can practice in Maryland but whose place of residence need not be in Maryland. If in doubt, prefer 340.02–.09.

340.52

Law and indigenous peoples

Use 340.52 for laws of indigenous peoples that had legal systems of their own prior to their incorporation into the national systems of other groups, e.g., laws of North American native peoples before becoming a part of the United States 340.5273. Use 342–347, plus notation 089 from Table 1, for the laws of such groups on a specific subject, e.g., family law of North American native peoples 346.01508997.

Use 341 for the relations between indigenous peoples and a nation established in their territory before their incorporation into the nation, e.g., treaties between the United States and native American peoples on territorial matters 341.42026673008997.

Use the numbers of the specific jurisdiction in 342–349 for the relations between an indigenous people and a nation established in its territory after its incorporation into the nation, e.g., law regulating nursing services for Australian Aborigines 344.9404140899915, legal status of Australian Aborigines 346.94013.

340.9

Conflict of laws

Use 340.9 for works where the key issue is usually which jurisdiction's laws are to govern the case, e.g., whose laws will govern in the case of a Canadian citizen married in France to a citizen of Germany and later divorced in Mexico when a dispute arises as to the disposition of jointly owned personal property? Although usually called private international law, it is not the law governing the interrelationships of nations, but the law governing the conflicts and disputes between private citizens of different nations, and its material is drawn from private law.

341 vs. 327

Law of nations vs. International relations

Use 341 for works that discuss the standards and principles that it is commonly felt should govern international relations, or for works that discuss concrete events from the standpoint of the problems that they pose to this system of order. Use 341.026 for works on treaties and cases of international courts. Use 327 for works that discuss what is actually transpiring in international relations (including the theory as to why things happen as they do), and the effects of what has happened. If in doubt, prefer 341.

341.45 vs. 343.0962

Law of the sea vs. Law of ocean transportation

Use 341.45 for works emphasizing jurisdictional issues of law of the sea, i.e., works that discuss the problems that arise from the fact that the high seas are outside the jurisdiction of any nation. Use 343.0962 for works emphasizing transportation issues of maritime law or admiralty law that consider legal issues that could arise either within or outside a single national jurisdiction. If in doubt, prefer 341.45.

342–349

Geographic treatment of law

Class law limited by geographic area as follows:

1. For law limited to a specific jurisdiction: Use 349 or 342.3–.9 (and parallel numbers, e.g., 343.3–.9) plus the area number for that jurisdiction, e.g., law of Germany 349.43, railroad law of Germany 343.43095.

2. Class the laws of local jurisdictions (cities, counties, subprovincial jurisdictions) as follows:

For the laws of a specific local jurisdiction: Use 349 or 342.3–.9 (and parallel numbers, e.g., 343.3–.9) plus the area number for the local jurisdiction, e.g., tax laws of Bayreuth, Bavaria 343.4331504; by-laws relating to public parks in Sheffield, England 346.42821046783.

For the laws of all the localities of a given area: Use the area number for the jurisdiction that contains the localities, e.g., tax laws of the cities of Bavaria 343.43304, of the cities of Germany 343.4304, laws relating to the public parks of cities in the United Kingdom 346.41046783.

Do not observe the principle of approximating the whole for jurisdictions for which there is no specific area number, i.e., subdivisions may be added for a jurisdiction not having its own number, e.g., Flint, Michigan's and Mt. Morris, Michigan's ordinances governing mental health services to the addicted 344.77437044. (Flint is in an including note at T2—77437 in Table 2, which normally means subdivisions may not be added for it. Mt. Morris, a suburb of Flint, is not mentioned in the including note, but subdivisions may still be added).

3. For the application of law of a specific jurisdiction to a limited area within that jurisdiction: Use the number for the law of the jurisdiction plus notation 09 from the table under 342–347, e.g., German law as practiced in Bavaria 349.4309433, application of German railroad law in Bavaria 343.4309509433.

4. For law limited to a specific regional intergovernmental organization: Use 349.2 or 342.2 (and parallel numbers, e.g., 343.2) plus the area number for that organization, e.g., law of European Union 349.24, railroad law of European Union 343.24095.

5. Class the laws of more than one jurisdiction other than those of a specific regional intergovernmental organization as follows:

For a collection of laws from various jurisdictions located in a particular area: Use 349 or 342.3–.9 (and parallel numbers, e.g., 343.3–.9) plus the area number for that area, e.g., law of Germany, France, Italy 349.4, railroad laws of Germany, France, Italy 343.4095.

For laws that affect more than one jurisdiction: Use 341 or 342.3–.9 (and parallel numbers, e.g., 343.3–.9) plus the area number for the area affected, e.g., treaties among Germany, France, Italy 341.02644, international laws regulating disarmament in Germany, France, Italy 341.733094, international laws regulating railroads in Germany, France, Italy 343.4095.

See also discussion at 340.02–.09 vs. 349.

Law of countries with federal governments

In federally organized countries, e.g., the United States, Australia, Federal Republic of Germany, there are two sets of laws: those of the central jurisdiction (national laws) and those of subordinate jurisdictions (laws of the provinces or states). Use the area number for the subordinate jurisdiction for laws of an individual state or province, e.g., criminal law of Virginia 345.755, of New South Wales 345.944. However, use the area number for the federal jurisdiction for laws of the states or provinces taken as a whole, e.g., criminal laws of the states of the United States 345.73, of the states of Australia 345.94. Use the area number for the region for works on the state and provincial laws of a region, e.g., provincial criminal law of western Canada 345.712.

Use of area number for capital districts

Use the area number for the capital district if the laws are, in effect, local laws even though passed by the national legislature, e.g., use notation 753 from Table 2 for laws of Washington, D.C., even though the United States Congress passes some of these laws.

Jurisdiction in time

Class the laws of an area that was at some point not an independent jurisdiction as follows:

1. If the law is still operative in the now-independent jurisdiction, use the area number for the jurisdiction in question. For example, use notation 5491 from Table 2 for a law that is currently operative in Pakistan, even though it was enacted before Pakistan became independent, e.g., use 347.5491052 for the Limitation Act of 1908.

2. If the law is no longer operative in the now-independent jurisdiction, use the area number for the jurisdiction that was previously dominant. For example, use notation 54 from Table 2 for India for a law of 1908 no longer operative in Pakistan.

342.085 vs. 341.48

Civil rights vs. Human rights

Use 342.085 for works on the political and social rights of individuals that are recognized by the laws of a particular jurisdiction or group of jurisdictions. Use 341.48 for works on the political and social rights that are recognized by international agreements (such as the Universal Declaration of Human Rights) as the inherent and inalienable rights of all human beings. If in doubt, prefer 342.085

343.04–.06 vs. 336.2, 352.44

Tax law vs. Taxes and taxation vs. Revenue administration

Use 343.04–.06 for most works on taxes, especially popular works, because they usually explain what the law allows and prohibits, e.g., a work for taxpayers about U.S. income tax deductions 343.730523. Use 336.2 for works on the economics of taxes and interdisciplinary works on taxes, e.g., an economic and political analysis of U.S. tax policy 336.200973. Use 352.44 for works on tax administration, especially the administration of assessment and collection. If in doubt, prefer 343.04–.06.

343.078 vs. 343.08

Regulation of secondary industries and services vs. Regulation of commerce

Use 343.078 for works discussing regulations for topics such as production quotas, quality of the material produced, sizes of products specified, e.g., what services hotels are permitted to provide, how they are to provide them, and what rates they may charge 343.07864794. Use 343.08 for works discussing regulations for topics such as truth-in-labeling, advertising practices, and other aspects of marketing, e.g., how hotels may advertise 343.085564794. If in doubt, prefer 343.078.

345.02 vs. 346.03

Crimes (Offenses) vs. Torts (Delicts)

Use 345.02 for acts considered as criminal offenses, but use 346.03 if those acts are considered as torts (a part of civil law), e.g., libel and slander considered from the standpoint of criminal law or brought as a criminal action 345.0256, but considered as a tort or brought as a civil action 346.034. Whether a particular act is regarded as a crime or as a tort or as neither will often depend on the jurisdiction, e.g., adultery may be regarded as a crime for which the offender may be prosecuted, a tort for which the offender may be sued, or merely as a fact to be adduced in evidence in a divorce case. If in doubt, prefer 345.02.

347

Jurisdiction

The location of the court does not necessarily determine the jurisdiction involved in procedure and courts, e.g., use 347.744 for procedure in a court in Boston, Massachusetts, if it is a state court, but use 347.73 if it is a United States district court.

351 vs. 352.29

Organization and structure of government agencies

Use 351 for general descriptions of administrative agencies and their work if the descriptions cover a representative sample of the agencies of a jurisdiction, e.g., a work on the ministries of the Indian government 351.54. Use 352.29 only for works emphasizing the organizational aspects of departments and agencies, e.g., a work detailing the organizational patterns of agencies of the Indian government 352.290954. If in doubt, prefer 351.

See also discussion at 352–354: Add table: 22.

351.3–.9 vs. 352.13–.19

Administration in and of subordinate jurisdictions in specific areas

Use 351.3–.9 for descriptive works on administration of individual jurisdictions regardless of kind, e.g., administration of the government of Ontario 351.713, of Cook County (Illinois) 351.7731, of Northern Highland (Scotland) 351.41152. This approach ensures consistent classification of works on administration of specific subordinate jurisdictions, since a classifier does not need to decide to which category a specific government belongs, e.g., whether Cook County is urban, or Northern Highland is rural.

Also use 351.3–.9 for works on administration of an individual jurisdiction and its subordinate jurisdictions, e.g., administration of Ontario and its local authorities 351.713. Use 352.13–.19 plus notation 09 from Table 1 only for general treatises on subordinate jurisdictions or on specific kinds of subordinate jurisdictions, e.g., provincial administration in Canada 352.130971, county administration in Illinois 352.1509773, rural administration in United Kingdom 352.170941.

The distinction between 351.3–.9 and 352.13–.19 is carried over under specific topics of public administration in 352–354. Use 352–354 plus notation 093–099 from Table 1 for reports and practical works on the administration of a specific activity in a given jurisdiction or region, e.g., administration of social welfare in Ontario 353.509713. Use 352–354 plus notation 213–219 from the add table at 352–354 (and with notation 093–099 from Table 1) for theoretical and general descriptive works on how state (provincial) and local administration of a subject in a specific higher jurisdiction or region has been or should be conducted, e.g., local administration of social welfare in Ontario 353.521409713.

If in doubt, prefer 351.3–.9.

352–354

Specific topics of public administration

Agencies and their divisions

Use the same number for the administration of a function and the administration of an agency designated to perform that function. For example, use 354.50973 for both public administration of agriculture in the United States and administration of the United States Department of Agriculture. Also use the same number for an administrative report of a specific agency and an independent study of the functions that the agency performs. For example, use 354.5097305 for both the Annual Report of the United States Department of Agriculture and an independent journal on agricultural administration in the United States.

Use the number that best fits the responsibility of a specific agency. For example, use 352.5 for a general services agency having a wide range of miscellaneous functions, so long as the predominant duty concerns property administration (as is often the case), even if it has sections on archives and personnel training.

For works on a part of an agency, use the number that best fits the responsibility of that part of the agency, even if the number differs from the number for the agency as a whole. For example, use 352.53 for a procurement section in a general services agency, and 352.669 for a personnel training section in such an agency. For an archives section in the agency, use either 352.744 if it promotes archival activity or 026.93–.99 if it maintains general archives of the jurisdiction.

In some cases, the schedule gives a specific name of a generalized type of agency in a class-here note at a given number, referring to a typical agency with such a name. An agency with a similar name but a different function should be classed according to its function. Only when there is a conspicuous difference in the usage of different countries do notes in the schedule explain the difference. For example, at 353.3 one note reads "Class here home departments and ministries, European style interior ministries"; another note reads "See also 354.30973 for United States Department of the Interior."

Use the same number for two agencies that independently cover approximately the same field. However, use notation from the table under 352–354 for an agency that has a different relation to the subject. For example, use 354.760973 for the United States Department of Transportation, but use 354.76280973 for the former United States Interstate Commerce Commission (the ICC, which regulated transportation, not commerce). The base number for administration of transportation (354.76) and the final notation for area (T1—0973) are the same in both cases, but notation 28 for regulation is interposed between them for the ICC.

Use notation in 352–354 for agencies provided for in 352–354, even when the agencies are nominally subordinate to a nonexecutive branch of government. For example, use 352.430973 for the United States General Accounting Office, which is officially part of the legislative branch, but which performs a classical executive function of reviewing accounts and judging the effectiveness of expenditures throughout the government.

See also discussion at T1—068 vs. 353–354.

Add table

22

Organization and structure of government agencies

Use a number in 352–354 without adding notation 22 for general works on specific agencies, e.g., a work describing the Indian Home Ministry 353.30954. Use numbers in 352–354 plus notation 22 only for works emphasizing the organizational aspects of departments and agencies. If in doubt, prefer the number in 352–354 without notation 22.

See also discussion at 351 vs. 352.29.

2293

Heads of departments and agencies

Secretaries of state

Use notation 2293 for secretaries of state in the United Kingdom and countries in the Commonwealth of Nations, where the term is a generic one for heads of executive departments, often of cabinet level. (General works on this kind of secretary of state are classed in 352.293.)

Use 353.22930973 for the Secretary of State of the United States, a position equivalent to foreign minister or minister of foreign affairs in most other countries.

Do not use notation 2293 for secretaries of state in states of the United States. Most state secretaries of state may be classed in 352.387 plus notation 0973–0979 from Table 1 when their central duty is the authentication, maintenance, and preservation of important state papers and other records, and the compilation of organization manuals of the state government. When the office of a specific secretary of state has a range of duties that does not fit comfortably in the records management number, class the office in other numbers in 352–354.

Agencies named for their heads

Do not use notation 2293 from the add table with numbers in 352–354 for departments (usually quite small ones) named for their heads, e.g., offices of inspectors general or offices of ombudsmen. These agencies, and reports issued in the name of their heads, are classed in the number that most nearly approximates their duties, e.g., reports of inspectors general and ombudsmen 352.88, reports of ombudsmen in personnel agencies 352.6235.

27–28

Administration of supporting and controlling functions of government

Use notation 27 and 28 in fields where the role of government is commonly both supportive and regulatory. For example, use notation 27 throughout 354 in the special sense of administering development, or research and development, as explained under 354.27 in the schedule. Likewise, use notation 28 in much of 354 in the special sense of controlling public utilities, as explained under 354.428 and 354.728 in the schedule.

Do not use notation 27 in fields where the primary role of government is supportive, and do not use 28 in fields where the primary role of government is regulatory. For example, use 353.78 (*not* 353.7827) for administration of recreation agencies, because most recreation agencies support recreation; and use 353.9 (*not* 353.928) for administration of safety agencies, because the primary role of safety agencies is safety regulation. Use notation 27 and 28, however, for the less common function of these agencies, e.g., works on regulating recreation 353.7828, and works on administration of programs promoting safety 353.927.

352.13 vs. 352.15

State and provincial administration vs. Intermediate units of local administration

Use 352.13 for territorial subdivisions with an extent that places them distinctly above "local administration," regardless of what they are called. The following list indicates the major territorial units that can currently be regarded as equivalent to "states and provinces" as defined in the note at 352.13:

Argentina (provinces)
Australia (states)
Brazil (federal units)
Canada (provinces)
Chile (regions)
China (provinces, autonomous regions)
(former) Czechoslovakia (regions)
Ethiopia (federal states)
France (regions)
Germany (states)
India (states)
Indonesia (provinces)
Iran (provinces)
Italy (regions)
Japan (regions)
Korea (regions)
Mexico (states)
Nigeria (states)
Pakistan (provinces)
Peru (regions)
Philippines (regions)
Russia (provinces, territories, autonomous republics)
South Africa (provinces)
(former) Soviet Union (union republics)
Spain (autonomous communities)
Sudan (regions)
United States (states)
(former) Yugoslavia (republics, autonomous provinces)

Also use 352.13 for similar units that may be created in the future, and for "territories" in the sense of areas on the road to statehood, e.g., historic treatment of administration in territories of the United States 352.13097309.

Use 352.16 for general treatment of special urban units coordinate with states and provinces, e.g., administration of nationally controlled municipalities in China 352.160951.

Use 352.15 for all other units intermediate between the national governments and the primary units of local administration.

355–359 vs. 623

Military science vs. Military and nautical engineering

Use 623 for physical description, design, manufacture, operation, and repair of ordnance; use 355–359 for procurement and deployment, and also for the units and services that use the ordnance. Histories of the development of weapons emphasizing the interplay of human and social factors are regarded as procurement history, and are classed in 355.8 and similar numbers in 356–359 (e.g., 359.8, numbers built with notation 8 from add table under 356–359). If in doubt, prefer 355–359.

355.1409

Historical, geographic, persons treatment

Class uniforms of several participants in a particular war in the area number corresponding to the one used for the war in general history, e.g., uniforms of the Peninsular War (part of the Napoleonic Wars classed in 940.27) 355.14094, not 355.140946.

Class uniforms of a specific branch of the armed services with the branch, e.g., uniforms of the Royal Air Force 358.41140941.

359.32 vs. 359.83

Ships as naval units vs. Ships as transportation equipment and supplies

Use 359.32 or similar numbers in 359.9 (e.g., 359.933, 359.9435, 359.9853) when a work on ships focuses on matters normally covered by analogous works on regiments and other military units, e.g., the crew and its organization, duties, effectiveness, and history. Works about a specific ship will usually consider the ship as a naval unit (unless there is only one ship of a class). Use 359.83 or similar numbers in 359.9 (e.g., 359.9383, 359.94835, 359.98583) when the work focuses on development, procurement, operation, and actual or potential combat effectiveness of the hardware, or when discussion of personnel or personalities focuses on persons responsible for development and procurement of ships, e.g., Admiral Rickover's work in developing nuclear submarines 359.93834092. Use 359.83 also for comprehensive works. If in doubt, prefer 359.32.

Use notation 09 from Table 1 plus country numbers from Table 2 for either specific ships, or a number of ships of a specific class employed by a specific nation.

361–365

Social problems and services

Problems and services are often linked terms, and, where one is spelled out, the other is implied, e.g., addiction at 362.29 implies services to the addicted, and services of extended medical care facilities at 362.16 imply the problems that require such services.

See also discussion at 300 vs. 600.

361–365 vs. 353.5

Social problems and services vs. Public administration of social welfare

Much of the material on social problems and services consists of government reports or gives considerable emphasis to the political and legal considerations related to social services. Use 361–365 for reports about welfare programs and institutions or for works that focus on the problem or the service, e.g., a discussion of political obstacles to effective poverty programs 362.5, a discussion of the political maneuvering behind the adoption of an act of the United States Congress spelling out a new housing program 363.580973. Use 353.5 for reports concentrating on the administrative activities of agencies supporting and regulating the programs and institutions. If in doubt, prefer 361–365; however, prefer 353.5 for administrative annual reports of government agencies.

361 vs. 362–363

Social problems and social welfare in general vs. Specific social problems and services

Use 361 for comprehensive works on the whole range of problems and services found in 362–363, for works on principles and methods of assessing and solving the problems when the works do not address a specific problem, and for works on the principles and methods of welfare work in general. Use the number for a specific problem in 362–363, plus notation 5 from the table under 362–363, for works on the application of the principles and methods to a specific problem, e.g., social work with poor people 362.553, housing allocation to relieve discrimination 363.55. If in doubt, prefer 361.

362–363 vs. 364.1

Specific social problems and services vs. Criminal offenses

Use 362–363 for a human activity considered as a social problem, but use 364.1 for the activity treated as a crime, e.g., drug addiction as a social problem 362.29, but illegal use of drugs 364.177; suicide as a social problem 362.28, but suicide treated as a crime 364.1522. If in doubt, prefer 362–363.

362.1–.4 and 614.4–.5

Problems of and services to persons with illnesses and disabilities and Incidence of and public measures to prevent disease

Use 362.1 and 362.4 for works on the social provision of services to persons with physical illnesses or disabilities. Use 614.4–.5 for works on preventive measures, regardless of whether the emphasis is medical or social, e.g., social provision of immunization services and works on the medical aspects of immunization 614.47. Use 614.4–.5 for public measures strictly limited to preventive ones, e.g., fluoridation and programs advising people how to avoid cavities 614.5996; but programs to identify and treat people with cavities 362.19767. If in doubt, prefer 362.1.

Use 362.2 for works about the incidence and prevention of mental illness, mental illness as a social problem, and social provision of services to persons with mental illness.

Use 614.4–.5 for studies of epidemics and the incidence of physical disease (including mental retardation and physical disabilities) when treated solely from the medical standpoint. Use 362.1 and 362.3–.4 for works emphasizing diseases as social problems. If in doubt, prefer 614.4–.5.

362.1–.4 vs. 610

Biographies and case histories of persons with illnesses and disabilities, and biographies of medical personnel

Use 362.1–.4, plus notation 092 from Table 1, for biographies and memoirs of dying persons and persons with illnesses and disabilities if the works lack any other disciplinary focus, since such works typically illustrate the way society addresses itself to fundamental health problems and their solution. Use 001–999 for works that focus on a specific discipline, e.g., a work offering guidance in the Christian life with respect to health misfortunes 248.86, Christian meditations in times of illness 242.4. Use 362.1–.4, without adding notation 092 from Table 1, for studies of individual cases designed for the use of researchers, practitioners, and students in the social services, e.g., studies of services to patients with heart disease 362.19612. Use 616–618, plus notation 09 Case histories from the table under 616.1–.9, for studies of patients describing their illnesses in medical terms rather than their lives in social terms, e.g., case studies of heart disease 616.1209. If in doubt, prefer 362; however, prefer 616.8909, 616.890092, and similar numbers for psychiatric disorders (subdivisions of 616.852, 616.858, 616.89, 618.76), since the consideration of external circumstances is generally subordinated to the discussion of the state of mind of the patient.

Use 610 for most personal and biographical treatment of medical personnel, but use 362 for works on public health doctors or nurses emphasizing their influence on public health services and awareness, e.g., a biography of a doctor noted chiefly for promoting nursing homes 362.16092.

363 vs. 302–307, 333.7, 570–590, 600

Control of technology

Use 363, particularly 363.1 (safety) and 363.7 (environment), for works on control of technology addressing what must be done, regulating how it is to be done, inspecting to see whether or not it has been done, and investigating when it was not done. Use 600 only for works dealing with the technological procedures for carrying out a given operation. Use 363 for institutional breakdown (who let it break), but use 600 for machinery breakdown (finding out what broke).

Use 363 if the author or publishing agency is interested in social service and social need, 304.2 if interested in human ecology, 333.7 if interested in economics, 579–590 if interested in how organisms survive, 620–690 if interested in how to make things, 628.5 if interested in physical techniques for controlling pollution, 632–635 if interested in how crops survive.

Use 363 for comprehensive works and works oriented toward problems and their solution. Use 302–307 for works giving significant consideration to the social dynamics of the problem, use 333.7 for resource-oriented material, and use 600 for works emphasizing technology.

If in doubt, prefer in the following order: 363; other numbers in 300; 570–590; 600. Especially prefer numbers in 300 for most works produced by commercial publishers and environmental or safety advocacy groups.

See also discussion at 300 vs. 600; also at 301–307 vs. 361–365.

363 vs. 344.02–.05, 353–354

Other social problems and services vs. Law and public administration

Use 363 for the work of agencies by which the government carries out the detailed intent of the law in matters of population, safety, the environment, and provision of basic necessities, including most discussion of policy and most detailed procedures for enforcing law, policy, or regulation. Use 344.02–.05 for the law itself, draft laws, and enforcement of the law in courts with respect to these fields. Use 353–354 for the internal administration of agencies concerned with these fields, including their administrative annual reports. If in doubt, prefer 363.

Law enforcement

Use 363.23 for law enforcement by the police, but use 353–354 for enforcement of the law by government agencies in the sense of seeing that the requirements of the law are being met, e.g., activities of a department of education to ensure that the requirements of the law are being met in schools 353.8. However, use 340 for laws governing how such enforcement should be carried out, e.g., the law governing what measures police may use in enforcing the law 344.0523 (or 345.052 if the work treats matters of criminal investigation). If in doubt, prefer 363.23.

Class enforcement of the law through the courts in 342–347, plus notation 0269 from table under 342–347 where appropriate, e.g., court procedure that promotes the enforcement of tax law 343.040269.

363.1

Public safety programs

The meaning and scope of the word "safety" may vary. Use 363 if the scope covers most of the social services, or even 361 if sufficient 362 material is included. Use 363.2 if "safety" is used narrowly to comprise only the work of the police and fire departments.

Priority of safety

Use 363.1 or 363.3, rather than numbers elsewhere in 300, for those aspects of safety that society must deal with through investigations and programs (the topics in the add table at 362–363), e.g., railroad safety 363.122 (*not* 385.0289). However, use 353.9 for the public administration of safety.

363.1 vs. 600

Safety regulations

Use 363.1, plus subdivision 6 from the table under 362–363 if appropriate, for manuals written by or for safety agencies that discuss technical details useful as background for regulation and inspection of various operations while still focusing primarily on safety services. Use the 600 number for the technology involved for safety regulations that spell out operating and construction techniques in explicit detail, even if the regulations are in the form of an officially promulgated regulation by a safety authority. If in doubt, prefer 363.1.

363.31 vs. 303.376, 791.4

Censorship

Use 363.31 for censorship of movies and programs after being released or aired, e.g. use of v-chips by parents. Use 303.376 for theories of censorship and sociological studies of censorship of movies, radio, and television. Use 791.4 for censorship of films and programs as they are being produced, e.g., censorship through editing. If in doubt, prefer 363.31.

363.5, 363.6, 363.8 vs. 338

Housing, public utilities, and food supply vs. Production

363.5, 363.6, and 363.8 deal with the problems of providing the basic necessities of life, and each has economic implications. Use 363.5, 363.6, or 363.8 for social factors affecting the availability of housing, water, fuel and food, or for social measures to ensure an adequate supply. Use 338 for the effect of these topics on the economic aspects of society, or the impact of economic conditions on the availability of housing, water, fuel, or food. For example, use 363.81 for a study of the mismatch between the expected growth of the food supply and of the population, but use 338.19 for a study of the effect of a drop in farm prices on the food supply. If in doubt, prefer 363.5, 363.6, or 363.8.

363.5 vs. 307.336, 307.34

Housing

Use 363.5 for works on housing problems and solutions addressed specifically to housing. Use 307.336 for the descriptive analysis of housing patterns that treats problems in the context of the sociology of communities. Use 307.34 for works addressing housing problems in the context of restructuring whole communities. If in doubt, prefer in the following order: 363.5, 307.34, 307.336.

363.5 vs. 643.1

Housing vs. Houses

Use 363.5 for interdisciplinary works on housing that treat the social aspects of shelter, as the term "housing" normally refers to the provision of shelter considered in the abstract. Use 643.1 for interdisciplinary works on houses and their use and for the home economics aspects of either housing or houses, as the term "houses" normally refers to the buildings considered as physical objects. If in doubt, prefer 363.5.

363.61

Water reports

Use 363.61 for reports concentrating on the problem of treating and delivering water to consumers and for interdisciplinary reports on water supply. Use 333.91 for water supply reports concentrating on water used, or needed in the future; 363.7284 for reports concentrating on assuring that wastewaters are properly treated; 363.739472 for reports concentrating on protection of natural waters; and 553.7 for reports concentrating on the supply of water on hand. If in doubt, prefer 363.61.

Use 333.9116 for general works on monitoring to protect water quality; 553.7, plus notation 1–9 from Table 2 where appropriate, for reports that describe the present chemical and biological status of available water but do not not focus on a specific objective, e.g., a base-line study of the quality of French surface waters 553.780944; 363.61 for water quality monitoring reports as tools for assuring compliance with water supply standards; 363.739463 for such reports as tools for assuring compliance with wastewater pollution standards; 628.16 for reports as tools for determining plant loads and technical difficulties in water treatment; and 628.3 for reports as tools for checking the effectiveness of sewage treatment works.

363.73 vs. 571.95, 577.27

Pollution vs. Toxicology vs. Effects of humankind on ecology

Use 363.7363 or the number for the specific pollutant or environment in 363.738–.739, plus notation 63 from the table under 362–363, for pollution studies in which the growth and decline of biological indicator species is merely used to measure the extent and kind of pollution, and interpreted to suggest the need for, or sufficiency of, remedial measures, e.g., acid rain monitoring by use of indicator species 363.738663.

Use 571.95 for the pathological conditions caused by pollution and other agents in tissues of organisms. Use 577.27 or the number for the specific ecological environment (biome) in 577.3–.7, plus notation 27 derived from instructions under 577.3–.6 and 577.76–.79, for the more generalized effects of substances upon the community of organisms, e.g., the reduction of species counts (biodiversity) and the general health and vigor of surviving species.

If in doubt, prefer in the following order: 363.73, 571.95, 577.27.

See also discussion at 333.7–.9 vs. 363.1, 363.73, 577.

363.8 vs. 613.2, 641.3

Food supply vs. Dietetics vs. Food

Use 363.8 for works on meeting the food supply needs of society in general and of various social groups and for interdisciplinary works on nutrition. Use 613.2 for works emphasizing how to help individuals meet dietary requirements and maintain optimal balanced intake without gaining or losing weight, for material to help dietitians in planning diets for individuals, and for comprehensive works on personal aspects of nutrition. Use 641.3 for works emphasizing the food itself and for interdisciplinary works on food. If in doubt, prefer in the following order: 363.8, 641.3, 613.2.

371 vs. 353.8, 371.2, 379

School administration and policy

Use 371 for the basic operations and activities of schools and school systems. Use 353.8 only for administration of national and state or provincial departments of education that regulate and support local school systems. Use 371.2 for comprehensive works on school (or school-system) administration and for works covering both 371.2 and 353.8. Use 371.201–.207 and numbers to which reference is made under 371.201–.207 for specific topics in plant and system administration.

Use 379 for policy and debate on major policy issues in education, e.g., discussion of the role of government. Subdivisions are provided in 379 only for general works on support and control of public education, and for a limited selection of major, controversial issues in education. Use 370–378 for public policy and debate concerning all other issues in education (that is, all issues not specifically named in 379).

If in doubt, prefer in the following order: 371, 371.2, 379, 353.8.

371.01–.8 vs. 372–374, 378

Specific levels and topics of education

Use 371.01–.8 for specific topics relating to two or more levels of education, e.g., to elementary and secondary education, to secondary and higher education. Use

372–374 and 378 for any or all topics related to a specific level of education. There is specific provision at each level for each specific topic in 371.01–.8, usually in subdivision 1 under each level, e.g., in 372.1. If in doubt about whether a work relates to only one level, or to two or more levels, prefer 371.01–.8.

371.262 vs. 371.264

Standardized tests vs. Academic prognosis and placement

Use 371.262 for works that focus on particular tests and their use. Use 371.264 for general discussions of the use of results of standardized tests in prognosis and placement. Use 371.26 for works giving substantial treatment to both the tests in general and to their use in prognosis and placement. If in doubt, prefer 371.262.

372.24 and 373.23

Specific levels of elementary and secondary education

The following tables show some common combinations of grades or sublevels used in elementary and secondary education, and some names often associated with each combination. Use the pattern shown in the first table when individual grades are discussed. That table reflects the 3 3 3 3 plan used in the schedule. The other tables after the first show how other common American combinations of levels fit into the schedule.

Grades	Number
1–3 (Primary grades)	372.241
4–6 (Intermediate grades)	372.242
7–9 (Junior high school)	373.236
10–12 (Senior high school)	373.238

The 6-6 pattern:

Grades	Number
1–6 (Elementary school)	372
7–12 (High school)	373

The six-year elementary school is often called grammar school in the United States, and primary school in the United Kingdom.

The 8-4 pattern:

Grades	Number
1–8 (Elementary school)	372
9–12 (High school)	373

The 4-4-4 pattern:

Grades	Number
1–4 (Elementary school)	372
5–8 (Middle school)	373.236
9–12 (High school)	373

Use the higher level for other combinations of grades unless the majority of the grades are at the lower level, e.g., a K–2 infant school 372.241. Use 371 for schools extending from first to ninth grade or beyond.

These guidelines apply only to discussion of specific combinations of grades in general, e.g., junior high schools in the United States 373.2360973. Use the geographic span under the general number for elementary or secondary education (or 371.009) for specific schools, e.g., a specific junior high school in Atlanta, Georgia 373.758231.

378.4–.9 vs. 355.00711

College level military schools

Use 378.4–.9 (378 plus area notation of the place where it is found) for a college level military school that is not an official training academy, that is, those whose students (*except* in wartime) usually enter civilian occupations, e.g., Virginia Military Institute (Lexington, Virginia) 378.755853, The Citadel (Charleston, South Carolina) 378.757915.

Use 355.00711 plus the area notation of the country it serves for an official military service academy (or a similar number for an academy of a specific service), e.g., the Royal Military Academy (Sandhurst, England) 355.0071141, the United States Naval Academy (Annapolis, Maryland) 359.0071173.

If in doubt, prefer 378.4–.9.

380

Commerce, communications, transportation

Since 380 is part of 330, the table of preference under 330 also applies to subjects in 380. Commerce, communications and transportation take the same position in that table as production. Therefore, use 331.1251388 for a work on the labor market in transportation, but use 388.049 for a work on production economics of transportation.

Add table

09 vs. 065

Historical and geographic treatment vs. Business organizations

Use notation 09 for the system (facilities, activities, services) maintained by the company in a specific area, e.g., railroad transportation provided by the Union Pacific Railroad 385.0978. For international companies, use notation 09 only when coverage is limited to a specific area, e.g., comprehensive works on air transportation provided by United Airlines 387.7, air transportation in the United States provided by United Airlines 387.70973.

Use notation 065 for the corporate history of the company, e.g., the corporate history of the Union Pacific Railroad 385.06578. For international companies, use the area number for the country that is its home base, e.g., United Airlines 387.706573.

If in doubt, prefer 09.

384.54, 384.55, 384.8 vs. 791.4

Radio, television, and motion pictures

Use 384.54, 384.55, and 384.8 for for interdisciplinary works and for the various aspects of presenting a program to the general public, e.g., selecting the correct day and time to broadcast a television variety show 384.5531. Use 791.4 for the various aspects of producing an individual program, e.g., arranging the various acts of a television variety show 791.450232. If in doubt between 384 and 791.4, prefer 384.

Class the history of a radio, television, or motion picture company as follows:

1. Use 384, plus notation 09 from Table 1, for a general history of the organization, e.g., a history of NBC (National Broadcasting Company) Television Network 384.5540973, and the history of the system (facilities, activities, services) maintained by the organization, e.g., stations broadcasting NBC television programs 384.554530973.

2. Use 384, plus notation 065 from the add table under 380, for the corporate history of the organization, e.g., the corporate history of the NBC Television Network 384.55406573.

3. Use 791.4, plus notation 09 from Table 1, for the history and critical appraisal of the products of the organization, e.g., the history of the television programs provided by NBC 791.450973.

391 vs. 646.3, 746.92

Costume vs. Clothing

Use 391 for clothing customs, such as what was worn, what is now fashionable, national costumes, e.g., Edwardian fashion 391.0094109041, Lithuanian national costumes 391.0094793. Use 646.3 for home economics aspects of clothing, such as how to dress on a limited budget, select the best quality clothing, dress correctly for the business world. Use 746.92 for artistic aspects of clothing, such as clothing considered as a product of the textile arts, fashion design. If in doubt, prefer in the following order: 391, 746.92, 646.3.

398.2

Folk literature

Literary forms or collections cannot be specified for folk literature in 398.2. Disregard these aspects in classifying, and use the most specific number available.

Use notation 09 from Table 1 to distinguish literary criticism of collections of tales and lore, e.g., criticism of ghost stories 398.2509, criticism of French ghost stories 398.209440509. However, do not add notation 09 for individual tales or lore, e.g., literary criticism of a ghost story from France 398.2094405.

398.2 vs. 201.3, 230, 270, 292–299

Myths and legends

Use 398.2 for myths or mythology presented in terms of cultural entertainment or, especially, as representative of the early literary expression of a society, even if they are populated by gods and goddesses. Use 201.3 and similar numbers elsewhere in 200 for mythology presented from a strictly theological point of view or presented as an embodiment of the religion of a people. For example, use 398.2 for Greco-Roman myths retold for a juvenile audience; but use 294.382325 for Jataka tales illustrating the character of the Buddha.

Use 398.2 for mythology having a nonreligious basis that deals with beliefs and stories that can be referred to as superstitions, legends, fairy tales, etc., where the religious content or interest is not apparent. Use 201.3 and similar numbers elsewhere in 200 for mythology having a religious basis that deals with the most basic beliefs of people and with religious beliefs and practices.

Class specific myths and legends presented as examples of a people's religion with the subject in religion, e.g., legends of Jesus' coming to Britain 232.9.

Use 398.2 for interdisciplinary works on mythology, since this number includes folk narratives with a broader focus than religion alone. If in doubt, prefer 398.2.

398.2 vs. 398.3–.4

Folk literature

Use 398.2 for a folk tale on a specific subject and literary criticism of that tale. Use 398.3–.4 for comprehensive works on the history and criticism of the tale, e.g., tales of witches and wizards 398.21, a treatise on why in the tales witches are usually evil and wizards are usually good 398.45. If in doubt, prefer 398.2.

401 vs. 121.68, 149.94, 410.1

Philosophy and theory of language vs. Meaning, interpretation, hermeneutics in philosophy vs. Linguistic philosophies vs. Philosophy and theory of linguistics

Use 401 for works by philologists studying language, literature, and various other cultural issues, but with an emphasis on language, and for works where philologists with broader concerns than linguists reflect on their discipline and its methods. Use 401 also for broad works on the philosophy and theory of language and languages written by linguists and philologists.

Use 401.41 Semiotics or 401.43 Semantics for works in which linguists study semantics and semiotics to answer traditional questions about natural languages, often in relation to other topics in linguistic theory, such as grammar, lexicology, phonology. Use 410.1 for works in which linguists reflect on their discipline and its methods. *(See also discussion at 401.43 vs. 306.44, 401.9, 412, 415.)*

Philosophy of language

Use 149.94 for "linguistic philosophies"—viewpoints or schools of philosophy that put study of language at the center and use linguistic methods to study multiple questions in philosophy, such as metaphysics, aesthetics, logic, or ethics. Use 121.68 for philosophical writing on language investigating traditional concerns of epistemology (theory of knowledge), for example, truth and how truth can be determined.

If in doubt, prefer in the following order: 401, 410.1, 149.94, 121.68.

401.43 vs. 306.44, 401.9, 412, 415

Meaning

Use 401.43 for works on semantics dealing with meaning in language, covering topics such as synonymy, ambiguity, semantic truth (metalinguistic truth), and entailment. Semantics is particularly concerned with the underlying logical structure of natural language, i.e., what elements are necessary beyond correct grammar for statements to make sense. Use 412 for works on etymology that study the history of the meanings of individual words. Use 415 for works on grammar that are concerned with meaning only in relation to morphology and syntax. If in doubt, prefer 401.43.

Use 306.44 for works on the sociology of language concerned with meaning as affected by sociocultural context. Use 306.44 also for works on linguistic pragmatics that deal with language in its sociocultural context, but use 401.9 for works on pragmatics that focus on the individual psychological context. If in doubt, prefer 306.44.

407.1, T1—071 vs. 401.93, T4—019, 410.71, 418.0071, T4—80071

Education in language vs. Language acquisition

Use 407.1 for broad works on language education not limited to the prescriptive approach and comprehensive works on the study and teaching of both language and literature. Use 410.71 for works on the study and teaching of linguistics. Use 418.0071 for works on how to study or teach language using a prescriptive approach. The basic distinction between prescriptive and nonprescriptive linguistics is explained in the Manual note at 410. If in doubt, prefer 407.1.

Use notation for the specific language, plus notation 071 from Table 1 (which is incorporated in Table 4), for works on studying and teaching the linguistics of that language, broad works on studying and teaching the language that are not limited to the prescriptive approach, and comprehensive works on studying and teaching both the language and its literature, e.g., comprehensive works on studying and teaching French language and literature 440.71. Use notation 80071 from Table 4 for works on how to study or teach a specific language using a prescriptive approach, e.g., how to teach basic French 448.0071. If in doubt, prefer T1—071.

Use 401.93 for works on the psychology of learning language informally, as a child learns from its parents. Use T4—019 for the psychology of learning a specific language informally. Use 418.0071, or T4—80071 for a specific language, for the psychology of formal study and teaching of language. Use 401.93, or T4—019 for a specific language, for comprehensive works on the psychology of learning language both formally and informally. If in doubt, prefer 401.93 or T4—019.

410

Linguistics

Prescriptive linguistics

Use 410–417 and 419–490 plus notation 1–7 from Table 4 for works on nonprescriptive approaches to linguistics (e.g., descriptive and theoretical linguistics), which are concerned with describing or explaining language usage as it does or did exist, without regard to an ideal of correct usage. Use 418 and 419–490 plus notation 8 from Table 4 for works on prescriptive approaches, which are concerned with promoting standard or correct usage of language, i.e., trying to learn to speak or write like educated native users of a standard form of a language. For example, use 415 and notation 5 from Table 4 for descriptive works about grammar, but use 418 and notation 82 from Table 4 for prescriptive works about grammar, e.g., descriptive works on French grammar 445, prescriptive works on French grammar 448.2. However, use 413 and notation 3 from Table 4 for dictionaries, regardless of whether they are prescriptive or descriptive, e.g., French dictionaries 443.

Use the number for nonprescriptive approaches for comprehensive works containing both nonprescriptive and prescriptive linguistics, e.g., a collection containing both descriptive and prescriptive papers about grammar in general or the grammar of many different languages 415. If in doubt, prefer the number for nonprescriptive approaches.

Contrastive linguistics

Use 410 or other numbers not limited to applied linguistics for works of contrastive linguistics that are purely descriptive or theoretical, or a combination of applied and nonapplied linguistics. Use 418 and notation 8 from Table 4 for works of contrastive linguistics that focus on finding ways to prevent errors caused by interference or negative transfers from a first language in learning a second language or in translating into a second language. If in doubt, prefer the number not limited to applied linguistics.

Historical linguistics

Use 417.7 for works on general historical (diachronic) linguistics. Use notation 09 from Table 1 for general historical linguistics of a specific language, or for historical linguistics of a specific topic, if the work gives a history, but not if the work merely discusses the processes of change in a general way. For example, use 415 for a general description of grammatical change, 425.09 for a history of grammatical changes in the English language, and 420.9 for a history of all kinds of changes in the English language. Although no provision comparable to 417.7 exists for individual languages in Table 4, notation 7 is provided under specific languages for works that focus on the distinctive characteristics of specific early forms of the language, e.g., 427.02 Middle English.

Comparative linguistics

Class a comparison of two languages with the language requiring local emphasis (usually the language that is less common in the particular setting). For example, libraries in English-speaking countries will use 495.6 for a work comparing English and Japanese, but libraries in Japan will use 420. If no emphasis is required, class the work with the language coming later in Table 6.

Class a comparison of three or more languages in the most specific number that will contain them all; e.g., use 430 for a comparison of Dutch, German, and English, since all are Germanic languages; use 491.6 for a comparison of Gaelic, Welsh, and Breton, since all are Celtic languages.

Use 410 if there is no number that will contain all the languages, e.g., a comparison of French, Hebrew, and Japanese.

Use the same criteria for comparisons of just one feature of various languages, but do not add notation from Table 4 to the number for language families unless there are special instructions to do so. For example, libraries in English-speaking countries will use 495.65 for a comparison of English and Japanese grammar, but libraries in Japan will use 425. Use 415 for a comparison of French, Hebrew, and Russian grammar; use 430.045 for a comparison of Dutch, German, and English grammar (because at 430.04 there are instructions to add); but use 491.6 for a comparison of Gaelic, Welsh, and Breton grammar.

See also discussion at 407.1, T1—071 vs. 401.93, T4—019, 410.71, 418.0071, T4—80071.

420–490

Specific languages

Dialects

Sources may differ as to whether a particular tongue is a language or a dialect. Treat a tongue as a dialect if it is shown as such in the Dewey Decimal Classification even if it is treated as a language in the work being classified, and vice versa.

Language vs. subject

Class examples and collections of "text" whose purpose is to display and study a language with the language, even if limited to a specific subject, e.g., a grammar of scientific English 425. Class language analysis of a specific work with the number for the work. If in doubt, prefer the specific subject or work.

471–475, 478 vs. 477

Classical vs. Old, postclassical, Vulgar Latin

The dates of the Classical Age of Latin are 80 B.C. to 130 A.D. (the Ciceronian Age 80 B.C. to 43 B.C., the Golden Age of Augustan literature 43 B.C. to 18 A.D., the Silver Age 18 A.D. to 130 A.D.). Use 471–475 and 478 for formal or literary Latin written at any time after the Classical Age that conforms to the standards of that age, e.g., a linguistic study on Latin manuscripts of the monks of Iona. However, use 477 for works on Vulgar Latin, on Old Latin (80 B.C. or earlier), or on Postclassical Latin. The phrase "Postclassical Latin" refers to the nonclassical or vulgarized Latin used from the death of Juvenal (140 A.D.) until the period of renewed interest in the "pure" Latin of the Classical Age in the 11th and 12th centuries, and from the 14th century onward. If in doubt, prefer 471–475 and 478.

500 vs. 001

Natural sciences and mathematics vs. Knowledge

Use 500 for works about "science" that clearly imply emphasis on the natural sciences and mathematics. Use 001 for works that use the word "science" without implying emphasis on "natural science," for example, works that also cover the social sciences and the analytical aspects of other disciplines. Use 001.2 Scholarship and learning when the word "science" is used to cover disciplines outside 500. Use 001.4 Research rather than 507.2 for works on scientific method and scientific research with no clear emphasis on "natural science." However, use 509 for "history of science," as that term normally relates to the natural sciences and mathematics. If in doubt, prefer 500.

510

Mathematics

Elementary and secondary school topics

Use the following numbers for the mathematical topics presently taught in elementary and secondary schools of the United States:

Arithmetic	513
Algebra	512.9
Geometry	516.2
Trigonometry	516.24

Use caution, however, when classifying works with "precalculus" in the title. Use 510 for works that cover three or more of algebra, arithmetic, elementary calculus, geometry and trigonometry. Use 512 for works that predominantly cover algebra, or cover algebra and arithmetic. Use 515 for works that predominantly cover elementary calculus. If in doubt, prefer 510.

Combination of topics

Use the following instructions when classing in 512.1 Algebra combined with other branches of mathematics, 513.1 Arithmetic combined with other branches of mathematics, and 515.1 Analysis and calculus combined with other branches of mathematics and when using "Class here linear algebra combined with analytic geometry" at 512.5 Linear algebra:

1. Use these numbers for works that deal basically with one subject but have some information on another subject either added at the end of the work or interspersed throughout it. For example, use 512.12 Algebra and Euclidean geometry for a textbook with ten chapters on algebra and two on Euclidean geometry.

2. Use these numbers only for works that arc predominantly about the branch first named. For example, use 512.13 only for works about algebra with some trigonometry added; use 516.24 for works about trigonometry with some algebra added.

510, T1—0151 vs. 003, T1—011

Systems

Use 510 for works about purely mathematical systems, e.g., systems of equations. Careful examination may be required to determine whether a work is limited to purely mathematical systems, because the same or similar terms may be applied to both mathematical systems and mathematical descriptions of real-world systems; for example, a work on dynamical systems may discuss either mathematics (515.39) or real-world systems (003.85).

Use 003 for works on mathematics applied to real-world systems, even though they are highly mathematical, and even though a significant part is organized according to mathematical concepts. Use 003 if the work makes clear that the mathematics is intended as background for systems theory, and the systems part of the work will typically be organized according to specific applications, types of systems, or systems concepts such as control, stability, input-output, feedback, observability, or state estimation.

If in doubt, prefer 510.

Use notation 011 from Table 1 for works that clearly stress systems, modeling, forecasting, or other topics named in 003. Use notation 0151 from Table 1 for works lacking such stress. If in doubt, prefer T1—0151.

See also discussion at 519.5, T1—015195 vs. 001.422, T1—0727.

510, T1—0151 vs. 004–006, T1—0285

Mathematics and computer applications

Use 510 plus notation 0285 from Table 1 for the use or application of computers in mathematics, e.g., computer programs used for the numerical solution of ordinary differential equations 518.63028553. Use 004–006 plus notation 0151 from Table 1 for mathematics applied to computers, e.g., recursive functions used to explain how computers work 004.0151135. If in doubt, prefer 510 plus notation 0285 from Table 1.

If the application is in a third discipline, use notation 0285 from Table 1 for works that involve both the use of computers and the use of mathematics, e.g., a computer program for solving structural engineering calculations 624.1028553.

519.5, T1—015195 vs. 001.422, T1—0727

Statistics

The subject of statistics can be divided into three parts:

1. How to obtain and arrange statistical data
2. How to manipulate the data by mathematical means to produce information regarding the topic being examined
3. How to interpret the statistical results

Use 519.5, or the number in 001–999 for the subject, plus notation 015195 from Table 1, for works containing only 2, or 2 with 1 or 3 or both as incidental information. Use 001.422, or the number in 001–999 for the subject, plus notation 0727 from Table 1, for works giving equal treatment to 1, 2, and 3, or containing information about only 1 or 3 or both 1 and 3.

In many disciplines a word derived from the discipline name combined with -metrics or -statistics is used for statistical work, e.g., sociometrics, econometrics, biometrics, biostatistics. Commonly works on these subjects concentrate on 2 from the above list, with secondary treatment of 3 or 1 or both. Use the number in 001–999 for the subject plus notation 015195 from Table 1 for these works. Use the number in 001–999 for the subject plus notation 0727 from Table 1 for works of broader treatment, emphasizing 1 or 3 or both 1 and 3.

If in doubt, prefer 519.5 or T1—015195.

See also discussion at 510, T1—0151 vs. 003, T1—011.

520 vs. 500.5, 523.1, 530.1, 919.9

Outer space

Use 520 for popular works on astronomy that use the terms "space" and "outer space" while discussing the various interesting astronomical bodies and phenomena of the universe, and use 523.1 for works that use the terms as synonymous with the universe treated as a single unit.

Use 520 for works on exploring space or outer space that emphasize astronomical findings (or use a specific number in 523 if the work is limited to specific bodies, e.g., the solar system 523.2). Use 919.9 plus notation 04 from the table under 913–919 when the works refer to geographic exploration, that is, live humans going out on real or imaginary visits to the planets or stars.

Use 500.5 for a work on space sciences in general that has no particular reference to astronomical bodies. Use 530.1, where an including note mentions space, if the work refers simply to space with nothing in it.

If in doubt, prefer in the following order: 520, 523.1, 530.1, 500.5, 919.9.

520 vs. 523.1, 523.112, 523.8

Astronomy and allied sciences vs. The universe, galaxies, quasars vs. Galaxies vs. Stars

Use 520 for works describing the universe in its several distinct components, e.g., as individual planets, stars, galaxies. Use 523.1 for works treating the universe as a single unit. If in doubt, prefer 520.

Stars and galaxies

Use 523.8 for comprehensive works on stars and galaxies when they are treated as individual astronomical bodies. However, use 523.112 when the work considers stars primarily as components of galaxies. Use 523.1 if the work considers galaxies and stars primarily in the context of cosmological theories, with little discussion of individual stars or galaxies. Use 520 for works that discuss other astronomical bodies, e.g., planets and comets, as well as stars and galaxies.

If in doubt between 523.8 and 523.112, prefer 523.8.

523 vs. 559.9

Earth sciences in extraterrestrial worlds

Use 523 for phenomena of celestial bodies when the celestial body has no distinct lithosphere, since in such cases hydrosphere and meteorology are moot concepts, and thus the phenomena are not directly comparable to terrestrial phenomena. Use 559.9 and notation 0999 from Table 1 in 551–553 for phenomena of celestial bodies that have distinct lithospheres when the phenomena are directly comparable to terrestrial phenomena. For example, use 551.5099923 for the atmosphere of Mars (which has a lithosphere), but use 523.86 for the atmosphere of stars (which do not); use 523.45 for the red spot of Jupiter (a planet without a distinct lithosphere). If in doubt, prefer 523.

530.416 vs. 539.75

Responsive behavior and energy phenomena vs. Nuclear activities and interactions

Use 530.416 for works that study topics in responsive behavior, energy phenomena, nuclear activities, nuclear interactions in the context of the condensed (solid and liquid) state, i.e., in answer to the question, what is taking place in condensed matter that makes it behave the way it does. Use 539.75 for works that study these topics in the abstract, or in the context of nuclear structure, i.e., in answer to the question, what makes the atom and its particles behave the way they do. If in doubt, prefer 530.416.

530.475 vs. 530.12, 531.16

Brownian motion and particle mechanics

Use 530.475 (or the similar numbers 530.415, 530.425, 530.435) for treatment of particles in diffusion within various states of matter. Use 530.12 for comprehensive works on particle mechanics. Particle mechanics is a subject that exists in both classical and quantum physics, but is far more basic to the study of quantum physics, where the quanta can be considered particles. Use 531.16 only if the emphasis is clearly on classical mechanics. Use other numbers in modern physics if appropriate, e.g., orbits of subatomic particles 539.725. If in doubt, prefer in the following order: 530.475, 530.12, 531.16.

Use 530.475 for interdisciplinary works on Brownian motion, which usually refers to the random motion of microscopic particles. However, class with the subject the extension by analogy of the concept to a variety of similar random movements, e.g., of prices, of biological populations, of instrumental recordings.

Use 530.425 for works on Brownian motion with an emphasis (often unstated) on such motion in fluids.

541 vs. 546

Physical chemistry of specific chemicals

Use a subdivision of 546 for physical chemistry of a specific element or compound; however, use a subdivision of 541 when one or two examples drawn from large groupings like metals (546.3) or nonmetals (546.7) are used primarily to study or explain a specific topic in physical chemistry, e.g., hydrogen-ion concentration 541.3728 (*not* 546.2).

If in doubt, prefer 541.

548 vs. 530.41

Crystallography vs. Solid-state physics

Use 548 for works on crystals and crystallography when these terms are used to refer to discrete objects and abstract lattice patterns. Use 530.41 for works on crystallography and the crystalline state in their broad senses, i.e., when the terms are used to cover atomic arrangement in metals, ceramics, amorphous materials, or polymers. Use 530.41 as the comprehensive number. If in doubt, prefer 548 for works clearly emphasizing ordinary crystals.

549 vs. 546

Mineralogy vs. Inorganic chemistry

Use 549 numbers for topics of physical and theoretical chemistry pertaining to the structure and behavior of homogeneous crystalline solids. Use 546 numbers for comprehensive works on the chemistry and mineralogy of specific chemical types. If in doubt, prefer 549.

549 vs. 548

Mineralogy vs. Crystallography

Use 549 for the crystallography of specific minerals unless the minerals are used to study or explain a topic in 548, e.g., quartz, feldspar, and related crystals 549.68, but a study of isomorphism using quartz, feldspar, and related crystals 548.3. If in doubt, prefer 549.

550 vs. 910

Earth sciences vs. Geography and travel

Geophysics (550) is the analysis of the structure of the earth and the forces shaping it; physical geography (910.02) is the description of the resulting landscape. Use the number for a specific force or process in 551 for descriptions of the results of the specific force or process, e.g., earthquakes in Myanmar 551.2209591. Use the number for a specific land form in 551.41–.45 for the operation of all forces and processes that combined to create a specific topographic land form, e.g., formation of mountains in Myanmar 551.43209591. Use 554–559 for the operation of all the forces and processes taken as a whole in a specific area, especially if the work emphasizes solid geology, e.g., geophysical processes operating in Myanmar or the geology of Myanmar 555.91. However, use 910.02 or the specific area number in 913–919, plus notation 02 from the table at 913–919, when a work treats the geographic landscape with only minor consideration of geophysical processes, e.g., graphical description of surface features in Myanmar 915.9102. If in doubt, prefer 550.

Use 910 or the specific area number in 913–919, plus notation 04 from the table at 913–919, for descriptions of surface features for travelers. Such descriptions usually cover resort accommodations and the ambience as well as geographic features, e.g., contemporary tourist beaches in Myanmar 915.91045.

551.302–.307 vs. 551.35

Erosion and weathering, sediments and sedimentation, soil formation, mass movement vs. Geologic work of water

Use 551.302–.304 for works giving due coverage to the work of wind, glaciers, or frost, even if agents other than water take up only a small part of the text, since water is by far the most important agent in the erosion, transport, and deposit of geologic materials. Use 551.352–.354 only for works limited to the work of water or to materials transported by water.

Use 551.305 for the work of water in soil formation and 551.307 for the work of water in mass movement. Water is also the most important agent in these processes, but it almost always acts in conjunction with other agents to produce the processes, e.g., action of dissolved chemicals, temperature changes, or earthquake vibrations.

551.5 vs. 551.6

Meteorology vs. Climatology and weather

Meteorology analyzes and describes the properties and phenomena of the atmosphere, and thus explains climate and weather. Meteorology is also the comprehensive subject, encompassing consideration of climatology and weather. Use 551.5 for works called "climatology," "climate and weather," or simply "climate" or "weather," if they cover topics in meteorology. Use 551.6 only when the words are limited to four senses:

1. The description of phenomena of the atmosphere taken as a whole, weather usually being the short-range description, and climate the long-range description

2. The prediction of weather, climate, or specific meteorological phenomena, that is, weather forecasting and forecasts (551.63–.65)

3. The study of climate or meteorology in small areas, that is, microclimatology or micrometeorology (551.66)

4. The attempt to modify weather or any specific meteorological phenomena (551.68), which is actually a technology

Use 551.5 numbers for all other aspects, including description (weather reports) of specific phenomena, regardless of the terms used in the work in hand, e.g., a discussion of the factors that produce weather 551.5, reports of rainfall 551.577, a description of climate types of Asia 551.62095, forecasts of rainfall 551.6477, a forecast of a rainy day in Singapore 551.655957.

If in doubt, prefer 551.5.

551.7 vs. 560

Historical geology vs. Paleontology Paleozoology

Use 551.7 for works on historical geology, which studies the rocks and their strata, using paleontological facts to help date and interpret deposition, movement, and erosion. Use 560 for works on paleontology, which studies life in former geological ages through the interpretation of fossils. Paleontology utilizes the same material as historical geology, i.e., the geologic record, but only as a record of life and the environment in which life evolved. If in doubt, prefer 551.7.

571–575 vs. 630

Physiology, anatomy, and pathology of agricultural plants and animals

Use 571–575 for results of experimental work on basic physiology and pathology that utilize domestic plants and animals as models.

When domestic plants and animals are studied for agricultural purposes, observe the following guidelines:

Use 571.2 and 571.32 and similar numbers in 571.5–.8 and 575 for physiology and anatomy of agricultural plants, but use 636.0891–.0892 and similar numbers in 636.1–.8 for physiology and anatomy of agricultural animals.

Use 632 for comprehensive works on pathology and diseases of agricultural plants and animals, or for comprehensive works on pathology and diseases of plants. Use 633–635 plus notation 9 from the table under 633–635 for pathology and diseases of specific agricultural plants, e.g., diseases of cotton 633.519. Use 636.0896 for comprehensive works on pathology and diseases of agricultural animals. Use 636.1–.8 for pathology and diseases of specific kinds of agricultural animals plus notation 39 in add table under 636.1–.8 or notation 0896 as instructed in certain entries in the schedule, e.g., diseases of race horses 636.1239, diseases of horses 636.10896.

If in doubt, prefer 571–575.

See also discussion at 571–573 vs. 610.

571–573 vs. 610

Results of research in biology and medicine

Use 571–573 for results of physiological and anatomical research with animal models in 571–573. Use 615–618 for results of pharmacological, therapeutic, and pathological research if the medical relevance for humans is either stated or implied. If in doubt, prefer 571–573.

571.629 vs. 571.29

Cell biology vs. Physiology of microorganisms

Use 571.629 for works on microorganisms that go into details of internal structures, e.g., membranes and organelles, without also discussing details of reproduction. Use 571.29 for works that discuss only generalities of microorganisms or discuss cell reproduction of microorganisms in addition to their general cell biology. If in doubt, prefer 571.629.

571.8 vs. 573.6, 575.6

Reproduction, development, and growth vs. Reproduction in animals and in plants

Use 571.8 for comprehensive works on reproduction, development, and growth, and for works covering reproduction of both animals and plants. Use 571.81 for comprehensive works on reproduction, development, and growth in animals, but not for reproduction alone in animals. Use 571.82 for comprehensive works on reproduction, development, and growth in plants, but not for reproduction alone in plants. Use 573.6 for reproduction in animals as well as reproductive system in animals, and 575.6 for reproduction in plants as well as reproductive organs in plants. If in doubt, prefer 571.8.

Reproduction in other organisms

Use 571.829 for reproduction of fungi and algae. Although some fungi and algae have reproductive organs, e.g., mushrooms and seaweeds, most do not, and the organs are poorly developed at best.

Use 571.8429 (*not* 571.829) for reproduction of unicellular microorganisms, and 571.84529 for the sexual reproduction of unicellular microorganisms.

Vegetative reproduction

Use 571.89 for comprehensive works on vegetative reproduction. Use 571.829 for vegetative reproduction of microorganisms, and 575.49 for vegetative reproduction of plants.

573.44 vs. 571.74

Hormones

Use 573.44 for works that emphasize endocrine hormones or hormones in animals while giving relatively limited treatment to hormones outside the animal kingdom. Use 571.74 only for truly comprehensive works on hormones, e.g., works that give balanced treatment to hormones in plants and microorganisms as well as animals. If in doubt, prefer 573.44.

576.5 vs. 572.8

Genetics vs. Biochemical genetics

Use 576.5 for comprehensive works on genetics, for works that emphasize the somatic manifestations of genes, and works that do not emphasize the DNA-based chemical structure of genetic material. Use 572.8 for works on genetics that emphasize the chemical structure and processes, e.g., DNA, RNA, replication, errors in transcription, and crossing over. If in doubt, prefer 576.5.

576.8 vs. 560

Evolution vs. Paleontology

Use 576.8 for works that emphasize how paleontological findings are evidence for evolution and works that include significant nonpaleontological evidence. Use 560 for works on the evolution of extinct organisms and works on the history of life that emphasize the description of extinct organisms and ancient environments. If in doubt, prefer 576.8.

577.3–.7 vs. 578.73–.77

Ecology of specific kinds of environments vs. Biology of specific kinds of environment

Use 577.3–.7 for works emphasizing either the nature of an environment or the interrelationships among various kinds of organisms found in the environment. Use 578.73–.77 for descriptive accounts of organisms found in a specific kind of area, e.g., plants and animals found in wetlands 578.768; and for comprehensive works on the biology of a specific kind of area, e.g., marine biology 578.77. If in doubt, prefer 577.3–.7.

577.3–.7 vs. 579–590

Ecology of dominant organisms in a specific kind of environment

Use 577.3–.7 for the ecology of dominant organisms (usually plants) of a specific ecological environment (biome). For example, use 577.4 (*not* 584.917) for the role of grass in grasslands. Similarly, use 577.3 for the ecology of specific forest associations, e.g., ecology of coniferous forest associations in Canada 577.30971 (*not* 585.0971 or 585.170971); and use 577.686 (*not* 597.17686) for fishpond ecology.

Use 579–590 only for works that emphasize the biology of the dominant kind of organism, e.g., the biology of grass in grasslands 584.9 (*not* 584.917), the biology of fish found in fishponds 597.17636.

If in doubt, prefer 577.3–.7.

578 vs. 304.2, 508, 910

Natural history vs. Human ecology vs. Geography

Use 578 for works on nature that concentrate on nonhuman living organisms and their settings. Use 304.2 for works that emphasize the relationship between natural phenomena and human institutions. Use 508 for works on nature that give significant treatment to earth sciences phenomena, e.g., weather, water features, and mountains. Use 910 for works that describe human settlement as well as natural phenomena. If in doubt, prefer in the following order: 578, 508, 910, 304.2.

578.76–.77 vs. 551.46, 551.48

Biology of aquatic environments vs. Oceanography and hydrology

Use 578.76–.77 for works on aquatic and marine biology, including comprehensive works on biology and ecology of water bodies. These works may include significant consideration of land and sea waters as part of the lives of aquatic organisms, but do not usually include detailed physical description of water bodies. Use 551.46 and 551.48 for works limited to nonliving natural phenomena, and for comprehensive treatment of biological and physical phenomena of water bodies. If in doubt, prefer 578.76–.77.

579–590

Taxonomic nomenclature and sources of information

Taxonomic nomenclature

The notes below mention several of the commonly recognized taxonomic levels used in classifying organisms. The broadest is kingdom, followed (in order of increasing specificity) by phylum or division, class, order, family, genus, species.

In the schedules for specific kinds of organisms, scientific terms are preferred in headings for taxonomic numbers below the kingdom level. If there is an alternative scientific name still in current use, it is given in the heading in parentheses following the preferred term. If there are two or more alternative scientific names in current use, the preferred term is given in the heading, and the alternative names are given in a variant-name note. For example, Mycetozoa, Myxomycetes, Myxomycophyta, Myxomycota are given as variant names for Myxomycotina (slime molds) at 579.52. Most obsolete names have been dropped. If a common name is well established in the literature but does not have a clear-cut corresponding scientific term (or terms), the common name may be used alone, e.g., 598.412–.415 Ducks.

A scientific name given in a class-here note is usually that of a subordinate taxon that comprises all or most of the members of the group in the heading. For example, under 583.99 Asterales, the class here note gives Asteraceae (Compositae), the only family in the order.

Common names are linked to scientific names by parentheses when they are generally understood to be exact equivalents. When two common names are linked to a scientific name, a comma between them means that they are alternative common names, e.g., "(doves, pigeons)" after Columbidae in the class-here note at 598.65. An "and" means that the two groups with common names together comprise the scientific group, e.g., "(poplars and aspens)" after Populus in the including note at 583.65. Common names that simply refer to well-known members of a scientific class, however, are listed alphabetically in an including note.

With plants (and occasionally with animals), the familiar name for families consists of the name of a typical member or members plus the word "family," e.g., Ranunculaceae (buttercup family) at 583.34. The typical member may be a single species or a large genus with hundreds of species, but seldom approximates the whole of the family. Classifiers must not assume that if the family approximates the whole of an order, the typical members do also.

An illustration of two terminology problems appears at 583.23 Laurales. The main family of this order is Lauraceae, the laurel family, which encompasses over 85 percent of the species of the order. The family is therefore given in a class here note, signifying that subdivisions can be added to the number for works on the family because it approximates the whole of the order.

Only a few species of the laurel family, however, are individually known as laurels, while several plants of other orders are also called laurels. Since it is useful to know where to class comprehensive works on laurels, the including note reads, in part: "Including . . . comprehensive works on laurels." Being listed in an including note means that laurels (even in its broadest sense encompassing all plants called laurels) do not approximate the whole of the 2800 species in the order Laurales.

Some large classes of organisms have two including notes, for classifier convenience. The first including note lists the scientific names of families or higher taxa and their corresponding common names, the second the common names that do not correspond with the given scientific names. Genera are listed with the common names because so many have become common names.

Sources of taxonomic information

Taxonomic schedules usually follow the arrangement accepted in *The New Encyclopaedia Britannica*, 1989. Other works that often prove helpful are *Synopsis and Classification of Living Organisms* edited by Sybil P. Parker (McGraw-Hill, 1982), and *Webster's Third New International Dictionary*.

See also discussion at 579.24–.25; also at 579.3; also at 599.

579–590 vs. 571–575

Biology of whole organisms vs. Biology of internal processes

Use 579–590 for general and external biological phenomena of specific kinds of organisms. Use 571–575, plus notation 1 (for animals) or 2 (for plants and microorganisms) from various add instructions in 571–575, for internal biological processes and structures of specific kinds of organisms.

The distinction between the biology of whole organisms in 579–590 (the first biology) and the biology of internal processes in 571–575 (the second biology) is based upon the recognition of fundamental differences between the literature of the two biologies. While the distinction between the two is not absolute, there are a number of basic differences:

1. The first biology requires the study of whole organisms or taxonomic groups and their relationships to each other and the environment; the second requires the study of parts of organisms to find out how the various processes work.

2. The first biology is studied primarily in the field, where it usually involves descriptive research; the second is studied primarily in laboratories, where it usually involves experimental research. (Either kind of research, however, can be used in either biology.)

3. In the first biology, topics are usually seen as typical only of the specific kind of organism being studied, e.g., snail shells, reproductive behavior of sticklebacks, weaverbird nests. In the second biology, the process studied in one organism is usually seen as typical of all living organisms (or as typical of a large class of organisms such as animals, vertebrates, or mammals), e.g., cell division, blood circulation, immune reactions.

4. Natural history is at the core of the first biology, and approximates the whole of it; physiology is at the core of the second, and approximates the whole of it.

5. Most of the literature in the first biology is written by specialists named after kinds of organisms, e.g., ornithologists and ichthiologists, while most of the literature on the second biology is written by specialists named after the processes and structures they study, e.g., biochemists and cytologists. The biggest exception is ecology (a study of processes involving whole organisms, counted here in the first biology), where the specialists tend to concentrate on the ecology of different kinds of environments.

6. Finally, the first biology dominates the collections of general and small libraries, while the second is collected much more heavily in academic and research libraries.

If in doubt, prefer 579–590.

579.165 vs. 616.9041

Harmful organisms vs. Medical microbiology

Use 579.165 for the biology of pathogenic microorganisms. Use 616.9041 for the study of the microorganisms in relation to human diseases. If in doubt, prefer 579.165.

579.24–.25

Virus classification

Subdivisions for specific kinds of viruses in 579.24–.25 are based upon *Classification and Nomenclature of Viruses* by the International Committee on Taxonomy and Viruses, 1982.

579.3

Classification of bacteria

Subdivisions for specific kinds of bacteria in 579.3 are based upon sections of *Bergey's Manual of Systematic Bacteriology*, 1984–1989. In most cases the sections have names that are English phrases defining exactly what the section contains, e.g., "Anaerobic Gram-Negative Straight, Curved and Helical Rods." *Bergey's* does use some traditional Latin or Greek names. At 579.39, where it is clear that one of *Bergey's* names (Oxygenic photosynthetic bacteria) corresponds to two traditional names, the traditional names (Cyanobacteria and Prochlorales) are preferred in the heading, and *Bergey's* name is given as a definition.

Minor kinds of bacteria

Use 579.32 for bacteria described in sections 1–3, 6–11, 20–25, and 33 of *Bergey's Manual*.

Actinomycetes and related orders

Use 579.37 for bacteria described in sections 14–17 and 26–32 of *Bergey's Manual*.

580 vs. 582.13

Angiospermae (Flowering plants) vs. Plants noted for their flowers

Use 580 for works on the taxonomic group called "flowering plants," as found in 583–585. This group includes most plants that will be found in a typical vegetable garden. Use 582.13 for works largely limited to nondomesticated plants with attractive flowers. These are the kind of plants that are found in nature, but that might also find a place in flower gardens or flower books. If in doubt, prefer 580.

583–585 vs. 600

Interdisciplinary works on specific kinds of seed plants

Use 583–585 for works limited to the botany of useful plants, and for works giving significant treatment to species of no particular economic value. For example, use 583.34 for a work covering the 300 species of the buttercup family, and 583.952 for a work on peppers that covers all the species of Capsicum and other genera that are called peppers. Also use 583–585 when there are two or more uses in technology, or one such use offset by an obvious botanical interest, e.g., 583.46 for oaks because oaks are useful as ornamental trees as well as lumber trees, and 583.23 for laurels because the many wild species of interest to botanists usually outweigh the few species that are well known as ornamentals.

Use numbers in 600 for interdisciplinary works on most kinds of seed plants that have a single dominant use. For example, use 615.321 for medicinal plants, 633.2–.3 for forage plants, 635.9 for ornamental plants (635.933734 for roses), 641.33–.35 for food plants (641.3411 for apples), 674 for lumber plants, and 677 for textile plants (677.21 for cotton).

The interdisciplinary number for most common plants is given in the Relative Index as the number opposite the unindented term. Use 583–585 for interdisciplinary works on plants that are not indexed, unless they belong in categories like those mentioned in the preceding paragraph. If in doubt, prefer 583–585.

583–584

Classification and common names of Angiospermae (flowering plants)

The arrangement for specific kinds of dicotyledons in 583 is based upon the arrangement found in the article "Angiosperms" in *The New Encyclopedia Britannica*, 1989, volume 13, pages 627–835.

The subdivisions of monocotyledons in 584 are defined by reference to the same article in *The New Encyclopaedia Britannica*, but the basic outline from early editions of the Dewey Decimal Classification is retained.

Exercise caution in identifying orders and families of flowering plants by common names; many such names are used for plants in several unrelated taxonomic groups. Notes in the schedule linking the common names are not exhaustive.

598.824–.88

Families and common names of Oscines (Passeres, songbirds)

Use 598.8 for songbird families not given in 598.824–.88. Exercise caution in identifying families of songbirds by common names; many such names are used for birds of several different families.

599

Classification of mammals

In addition to the general sources of taxonomic information used throughout 579–590, *Walker's Mammals of the World*, 1991, is particularly helpful for genera and families.

See also discussion at 579–590.

599.94 vs. 611

Anthropometry vs. Human anatomy

Use 599.94 for works emphasizing variations of external features, shapes, and gross bone structure (e.g., the comparison of heavy-boned and thin-boned people, indexes of length and breadth of skeletal features). Use 611 for works emphasizing norms of overall structure, for detailed structure of bones, and for works on all other internal organs and structures. If in doubt, prefer 599.94.

604.7 vs. 660.2804

Hazardous chemicals

Use 604.7 for comprehensive consideration of hazardous chemicals that includes handling, transporting, and utilization outside the chemical industry. Use 660.2804 for consideration of hazardous chemicals during chemical engineering. If in doubt, prefer 604.7.

However, use numbers in 660 as comprehensive technology numbers for specific hazardous chemicals, e.g., processing, transportation, utilization of natural gas 665.73.

608 vs. 609

Inventions vs. History of technology

Use 608 for works on inventions that are primarily descriptive (and usually arranged topically). Use 609 for works that emphasize historical factors that led to inventions, or that consider inventions chronologically. If in doubt, prefer 608.

610 vs. 616

Medicine and health vs. Diseases

Use 610 for works containing separate treatment of health, pharmacology, and therapeutics, as well as of diseases. Use 616 for comprehensive works on the diseases listed in 616–618.

Use the table of contents as a guide in deciding whether a work belongs in 610 or 616. Use 610 if it reads like a summary of topics in 610.73–618; use 616 if it reads like a summary of topics in 616.02–.99 or in 616–618. Use 616 also if the whole of medicine is brought to bear on the concept of diseases in a single treatise that discusses group after group of diseases.

If in doubt, prefer 610.

Standard subdivisions

Use notation from Table 1 under 616 only for works works clearly limited to the concept of diseases or works focusing on topics named in the class-here note at 616: clinical medicine, evidence-based medicine, internal medicine. Use 610.3 for medical dictionaries, 610.711 for medical schools, 610.92 for doctors not having a distinct specialty. If in doubt, prefer 610 plus notation from Table 1.

610.92 vs. 615.534092

Biographies of chiropractors

Use 610.92 for biographies of chiropractors who do not limit their practice. Use 615.534092 for biographies of chiropractors who limit their practice to therapeutic manipulation (615.82) or to manipulation for diseases of the musculoskeletal system (616.7062). If in doubt, prefer 610.92.

612 vs. 611

Human physiology vs. Human anatomy, cytology, histology

Physiology deals with how organs work, while anatomy concerns their form and structure. Use 612 for works bearing the names of organs that emphasize their physiology or treat physiology as well as anatomy, unless they are limited to the cytological and histological level. Use 611.018 for treatment of anatomy, physiology, and pathology at the cytological and histological level. If in doubt, prefer 612.

612.1–.8

Physiology of specific functions, systems, organs

612.1–.8 contains the basic division of the human body into physiological systems. Parallel subdivisions 1–8 appear in shortened or slightly altered form under 611 for human anatomy; under 615.7 for pharmacokinetics; under 616 for diseases; and under 617.4 for surgery by system.

Use 612.1–.8 as a guide to classing an organ or function not provided for in one of the parallel arrays, e.g., use 615.74 Drugs affecting lymphatic and glandular systems for pharmacokinetics of the pituitary gland, as this is parallel to 612.4 Hematopoietic, lymphatic, glandular, urinary systems, where the pituitary gland is named at 612.492; use 615.73 Drugs affecting digestive system and metabolism for pharmacokinetics of the pancreas, as this is parallel to 612.3 Digestion, where the pancreas is named at 612.34. However, use 615.761, where the urinary system is given, for pharmacokinetics of the kidneys, even though kidney physiology is at 612.463, under 612.46, where the urinary system appears in the 612 schedule.

612.8 vs. 152

Physiology of nervous functions Sensory functions vs. Psychology of sensory perception, movement, emotions, physiological drives

Use 612.8 for works that emphasize the physical and chemical mechanisms and pathways of sensations, emotions, and movements, e.g., 612.8232 for studies using electrodes to determine how the brain processes emotions. Use 152 for works that emphasize awareness, sensation, intentions, meanings, and actions as experienced by the individual or observed and described without reference to the physics or chemistry of the nervous system, e.g., 152.47 for feeling anger. Use 152 for comprehensive works. If in doubt, prefer 612.8.

613 vs. 612, 615.8

Personal health and safety vs. Human physiology vs. Specific therapies and kinds of therapies

Topics in 613 also appear in 612, e.g., exercise 612.044 and 613.71, rest 612.76 and 613.79. Use 613 numbers for works on applied or "how to stay healthy" aspects; use 612 numbers for works on descriptive physiology or "how the body works" aspects. Use 612 for comprehensive treatment of descriptive physiology and promotion of personal health. Use 613 for works that give information about physiology as background for an emphasis on promotion of personal health. If in doubt, prefer 613.

Topics in 613 also appear in 615.8, e.g., breathing 613.192 and 615.836, diet 613.2 and 615.854, exercise 613.71 and 615.82. Use 613 numbers for works on preventive or "staying healthy" aspects; use 615.8 numbers for works on therapeutic or "regaining health" aspects. Use 613 for comprehensive works. If in doubt, prefer 613.

614.4

Epidemiology

The term "epidemiology" sometimes refers to a research technique with application outside 614, e.g., in determining etiologies, such as smoking as a cause of cancer 616.994071; in determining the dimensions of social service requirements, such as the boundaries of the mental retardation problem 362.32; in exploring the possible effectiveness of proposed preventive measures, such as in reducing traffic accidents 363.1257.

615.1 vs. 615.2–.3

Drugs (Materia medica) vs. Specific drugs and groups of drugs

Most drugs are organic (615.3). Use 615.1 for comprehensive works on drugs even if there is a strong predominance of organic drugs, as long as coverage of inorganic drugs is in proportion to their importance. However, use 615.321 for comprehensive works on crude drugs and simples (products that serve as drugs with minimal processing, e.g., medicinal teas). If in doubt, prefer 615.1.

615.1 vs. 615.7

Drugs (Materia medica) vs. Pharmacokinetics

The term "pharmacology" may be used in the titles of works mainly limited to pharmacokinetics. Use 615.1 if the table of contents is arranged by types of drugs. Also use 615.1 for comprehensive works on drugs. Use 615.7 if the table of contents is arranged by physiological systems or if the work emphasizes the physiological and therapeutic action of drugs. If in doubt, prefer 615.1.

615.2–.3 vs. 615.7

Specific drugs and groups of drugs vs. Pharmacokinetics

Use 615.2–.3 for drugs that have an effect on several physiological systems or are not known primarily for their effect on a single system, e.g., antibiotics 615.329. Use 615.7 for drugs known primarily for their effect on a single system, e.g., digitalis 615.711 Cardiotonic agents, or 616.129061 Drug therapy for heart failure (*not* 615.32395 Drugs derived from Scrophulariales); alcohol 615.7828 (*not* 615.32). If in doubt, prefer 615.2–.3.

615.53

General therapeutic systems

Use 615.53 only for historical or theoretical works about general therapeutic systems, e.g., a discussion of the theory of chiropractic 615.534. Use therapy numbers for works that discuss the application of these systems to therapy, e.g., the application of chiropractic 615.82. Use numbers in 616–618 when the therapies are applied to specific conditions, e.g., chiropractic in musculoskeletal diseases 616.7062.

Biography

Class biographies of founders of therapeutic systems with the system, e.g., use 615.533092 for a biography of Andrew Taylor Still, the founder of osteopathy. However, use 610.92 for other practitioners of a specific system.

See also discussion at 610.92 vs. 615.534092.

615.7 vs. 615.9

Pharmacokinetics vs. Toxicology

Use 615.704, or the number in 615.71–.78 for the system affected, for toxic effects and interactions of drugs primarily of pharmacokinetic interest. However, use 615.9 when a drug primarily of pharmacokinetic interest is considered a poison because it is so toxic that a single inadvertent ingestion would cause serious complications or death, e.g., the pharmacokinetics of atropine (belladonna) 615.7 (*not* in any specific subdivision because it affects several systems), but the toxicology of belladonna 615.9523952. If in doubt, prefer 615.7.

615.8

Specific therapies and kinds of therapies

Class the application of therapies listed in 615.8 to certain specific types of disorders with the disorder, even if the work takes the application for granted without highlighting it in the title, e.g., use 616.9940642 (*not* 615.842) for radiotherapy emphasizing cancer treatment; use 616.891654 (*not* 615.85154) for music therapy emphasizing psychiatric uses.

615.852 vs. 203.1, 234.131, 292–299

Religious and psychic therapy vs. Religious healing and Christian gift of healing

Use 615.852 for works on healing and medicine that focus on religious practices as a part of the medical practice. Use 203.1, 234.131, and similar numbers in 292–299 for works on healing as a religious practice, including such topics as religious beliefs about illness, rituals and prayers for healing, miraculous cures by charismatic leaders or saints, e.g., healing in religions of North American native peoples 299.7131 (number built with 31 from 203.1). Works on healing as a religious practice may also be concerned with emotional or spiritual healing as well as physical healing, or in place of physical healing. Use 615.8528 for works on the use of psychic and paranormal powers in healing that do not mention a religious context. If in doubt, prefer 615.852.

Class other works concerning illness or medicine and religion as follows:

Religion and the art and science of medicine	201.661
Christianity	261.561
Other religions	292–299
Religion and health and illness and the social questions and programs concerning them	201.7621
Christianity	261.8321
Other religions	292–299
Discussion of whether cures are miracles	202.117
Christianity	231.73
Philosophy of religion	212

616 vs. 612

Diseases vs. Human physiology

Use 616 for comprehensive works on diseases that move from a discussion of physiology to a more general consideration of causes of disease, complications, prevention, and therapy. Use 612 for comprehensive works on physiology (612) and pathological physiology (616.07). For example, use 616.1 for the physiology, pathology, and therapeutics of the circulatory system, but use 612.1 for the normal and pathological conditions of the circulatory system. If in doubt, prefer 616.

616 vs. 616.075

Clinical medicine

Use 616 for works on clinical medicine covering the application of all branches of medicine to the treatment of various diseases. Use 616.075 for works on clinical medicine limited to diagnosis or to the work of a clinical diagnostic laboratory. If in doubt, prefer 616.

616 vs. 617.4

Nonoperative therapies

Use numbers in 616 for most works on nonoperative therapies, e.g., therapeutic manipulations of muscles 616.74062 (*not* 617.473062). Use 617.4, which is primarily limited to operative surgery of systems, for nonoperative therapies only if they have some connection with operative surgery, e.g., electrotherapy by heart pacer 617.4120645, since the pacer must be surgically implanted (617.4120592). If in doubt, prefer 616.

616 vs. 618.92

Diseases vs. Pediatrics

Use 616 for diseases that are most often treated in children, but that remain lifetime problems or threats, e.g., congenital diseases 616.043, mumps 616.313. Use 618.92 only if the work in hand is limited to the occurrence of the disease in children, e.g., mumps in children 618.92313. If in doubt, prefer 616.

616.1–.9

Specific diseases

Add table

071 vs. 01

Etiology vs. Microbiology

Use notation 071 when a work considers multiple possible causes for a disease, e.g., genetic factors, environmental factors, and viruses as causes of cancer 616.994071. Use notation 01 or one of its subdivisions if the emphasis is on microorganisms or a specific type of microorganism, even when the cause of a disease is complex and not yet fully understood, e.g., oncogenic viruses 616.994019. If in doubt, prefer notation 071.

Use notation 01 without further subdivision when the etiological agent for a specific disease is known to be a single type of microorganism, unless predisposing and contributing factors are emphasized, e.g., Treponema pallidum causing syphilis 616.951301, but predisposing factors leading to severity of syphilis 616.9513071.

616.8583

Homosexuality

Use 616.8583 for homosexuality only when the work treats homosexuality as a medical disorder, or focuses on arguing against the views of those who consider homosexuality to be a medical disorder. Class works about gay men and lesbians in relation to other topics in medicine with the topic plus notation 08664 from Table 1, e.g., advice to gay men and lesbians about finding psychotherapy for a variety of psychiatric problems 616.891408664. Class most works about gay men and lesbians outside medicine, e.g., Christian attitudes to homosexuality 270.08664, interdisciplinary works on homosexuality 306.766, gay men and lesbians in armed forces 355.008664. If in doubt, prefer a number other than 616.8583.

616.86 vs. 158.1, 204.42, 248.8629, 292–299, 362.29

Recovery from addiction

Use 616.86 for self-help programs for individuals recovering from substance abuse and interdisciplinary works about recovery programs that focus on the individual's life with addiction, covering the individual's experience with both social and medical aspects. Use 204.42, 248.8629, and similar numbers in 292–299 for religious guides and inspirational works for the recovering addict. Use 362.29 for works on organizations providing recovery programs, including administration of the program, and interdisciplinary works that cover both organizational and therapeutic aspects of recovery programs. If in doubt, prefer 616.86.

Class works that treat recovery programs for persons recovering from a specific kind of substance abuse as a medical service with the substance in 616.86, plus notation 06 Therapy or notation 03 Rehabilitation from the table under 616.1–.9, whether the programs are run by professionals, such as psychiatrists or clinical psychologists, or whether they are self-help programs run by laypersons. Use notation 06 for programs to arrest the illness and begin recovery, e.g., twelve step programs. Use notation 03 for programs to help the individual remain in recovery. If in doubt, prefer notation 06.

Class works that treat recovery programs for those recovering from a specific kind of substance abuse as a social service, with the substance in 362.29, plus notation 86 Counseling and guidance from the table under 362–363. Such works typically emphasize the organizational or institutional aspects of the program.

For example, use 616.86103 for interdisciplinary works on life as a recovering alcoholic; 616.86106 for the twelve step Alcoholics Anonymous program; 204.42 for a general guide for a recovering alcoholic on how to live a religious life; 248.86292 for a guide for a recovering alcoholic on how to live a Christian life; 362.29286 for comprehensive works on Alcoholics Anonymous, the organization that provides the twelve step program and places for individuals in the program to meet.

Do not use 158.1 for works on recovery from addiction, because psychology applied to a medical problem is classed with the medical problem, not in 150.

616.89 vs. 150.195

Mental disorders vs. Psychoanalytic systems

Use 616.89 and similar numbers (616.852, 616.858, 618.76) for applications of a psychoanalytic system in psychiatry, e.g., 616.8917 for psychoanalytic treatment of mental illness. Use the appropriate subdivision of 150 for applications of a psychoanalytic system to specific topics or branches of normal psychology, or to specific topics or branches of both normal and abnormal psychology, e.g., 154.634 for Freudian theories of dream analysis. Use 150.195 for comprehensive works on a psychoanalytic system or its founder, e.g., 150.1952 for Freudian system. If in doubt, prefer 616.89.

617

Miscellaneous branches of medicine Surgery

Add table

06

Therapy

Do not use notation 06 by itself with numbers whose meaning is limited to surgery, since surgery is a therapy. Add subdivisions of 06 to surgery numbers for specific physical therapies used in preparation for or rehabilitation from operative surgery, or for branches of surgery not limited to operative surgery, e.g., drug therapy in treatment of burns 617.11061. Use notation 06 freely under numbers not limited to surgery, e.g., ophthalmologic therapy 617.706.

617.5

Regional medicine Regional surgery

This number brings together two different concepts: (1) regions, which incorporate parts of several physiological systems, e.g., the abdominal region 617.55; and (2) organs, which are parts of single systems, e.g., the stomach 617.553. Use numbers for regions in 617.5 for works covering regional medicine as well as regional surgery, but use notation 059 from the table under 617 for works limited to regional surgery, e.g., diseases of abdomen 617.55, abdominal surgery 617.55059. Use numbers for specific organs in 617.5 only for surgery, since nonsurgical treatment is given with the system in 616.1–.8, and do not add notation 059 by itself except for surgery utilizing specific instruments or techniques, e.g., diseases of stomach 616.33, cryosurgery of stomach 617.553059, but stomach surgery 617.553. Use notation 0592–0598 with numbers for specific organs for plastic surgery, transplantation of tissue and organs, implantation of artificial organs, implantation and removal of assistive devices for organs, endoscopic surgery, and laser surgery, e.g., liver transplantation 617.55620592. If in doubt for organs, prefer 616, or 617.6–.8 for teeth, eyes, and ears. If in doubt for regions, prefer 617.5.

618.92097 vs. 617

Regional medicine, ophthalmology, otology, audiology in pediatrics vs. Miscellaneous branches of medicine Surgery

Use 618.92097 for nonsurgical specialties given in 617.5 (regional medicine) and 617.7–.8 (ophthalmology, otology, audiology) when applied to children. Use 617.98 for comprehensive works on surgical specialties applied to children. Use the number for the subject in 617, plus notation 0083 from the table under 617 if appropriate, for works on surgery of a specific organ, system, disorder applied to children, e.g., medicine of the back for children 618.9209756, but surgery of the back for children 617.560083.

Use 617 for both nonsurgical and surgical aspects of topics given in 617.1–.2 when applied to children, e.g., pediatric sports medicine 617.1027083. Use 617.6 for both medical and surgical aspects of dentistry for children, e.g., comprehensive works 617.645, diseases of the teeth and gums 617.630083, dental surgery 617.605083.

If in doubt, prefer 618.92097.

618.977 vs. 617

Special branches of geriatric medicine vs. Miscellaneous branches of medicine Surgery

Use 618.9775–.9778 for nonsurgical specialties given in 617.5–.8 (regional medicine, dentistry, ophthalmology, otology, audiology) when applied to persons in late adulthood. Use 617.97 for comprehensive works on surgical specialties applied to persons in late adulthood. Use the number for the subject in 617, plus notation 00846 from the table under 617 if appropriate, for works on surgery of a specific organ, system, disorder applied to persons in late adulthood, e.g., medicine of the back for persons in late adulthood 618.97756, but surgery of the back for persons in late adulthood 617.5600846; diseases of the teeth and gums 618.97763, but dental surgery 617.6050846.

Use 617 for both nonsurgical and surgical aspects of topics given in 617.1–.2 when applied to persons in late adulthood, e.g., injuries in late adulthood 617.100846.

If in doubt, prefer 618.977.

622.22, 622.7 vs. 662.6, 669

In-situ processing and ore dressing vs. Chemical engineering of fuels and metallurgy

Use 622.22 or the number for the specific material in 622.3 for in-situ processing, which uses chemical techniques to get the target materials (or compounds containing the target materials) out of the ground and is usually considered as mining, e.g., solution mining of uranium 622.34932. However, class in-situ processing of a fossil fuel in the chemical engineering number for the material produced, as this usually transforms the fuel into another form, e.g., coal gasification 665.772.

Use 622.7 for ore dressing, which refers to physical means of separating more usable ore from the low-grade materials that are dug out of the ground, e.g., magnetic separation of iron ore 622.77. However, use a number in chemical engineering (usually metallurgy, 669) when physical means that effect substantial chemical change are applied, e.g., electrodeposition of iron from ores 669.14.

Class use of high temperatures that cause drastic chemical changes in chemical engineering, e.g., pyrometallurgy 669.0282.

If in doubt, prefer 622.22 or 622.7.

624 vs. 624.1

Civil engineering vs. Structural engineering

Use 624 for basic texts on civil engineering that discuss both (1) structural engineering (which treats the specific subdisciplines of civil engineering that have general applicability to all kinds of structures) and (2) the various types of structures to which the engineering is applied. Use 624.1 only for works that take a narrow view of structural engineering, and do not discuss the various types of structures. If in doubt, prefer 624.

624 vs. 690

Civil engineering vs. Buildings

Use 624 for works about "building" or "construction" in the sense of constructing all types of structures. Use 690 only for works limited to discussion of habitable structures (buildings). If in doubt, prefer 624.

629.046 vs. 388

Transportation equipment vs. Transportation

Use 629.046 and other vehicle numbers in 600 (e.g., 623.74, 623.82, 625.2, 629.1–.4, and 688.6) for:

1. Description of the vehicle, e.g., steam locomotives of the 1930s 625.26109043

2. Technology of the vehicle, e.g., design tests for ships 623.810287

3. Operation (technical) of the vehicle, e.g., piloting spacecraft 629.4582

4. Maintenance and repair of the vehicle, e.g., repairing motorcycles 629.28775

Use 385–388 for:

1. Services provided by the vehicle, e.g., transportation of passengers by trains 385.22

2. Operation (general) of the vehicle, e.g., duties of the ship's captain 387.54044

3. Economic and social aspects of the vehicle, e.g., a register of the airplanes owned by a company 387.73340216

Use 385–388 for interdisciplinary works. If in doubt, prefer 629.046 and other vehicle numbers in 600.

629.1366 vs. 387.740426

Air traffic control

Use 629.1366 for the equipment needed for air traffic control, e.g., radar devices, and the duties of the air traffic controllers. Use 387.740426 for general operational aspects, e.g., determining how many controllers are needed per airport; for economic and social aspects, e.g., the radio call letters of the control tower; and for interdisciplinary works. If in doubt, prefer 629.1366.

629.43, 629.45 vs. 559.9, 919.904

Space flight vs. Earth sciences of, geography of, and travel in extraterrestrial worlds

Use 629.43 and 629.45 for traveling to an extraterrestrial world and exploring it from space, e.g., Viking Mars Program 629.43543. Use 559.9 and notation 0999 from Table 1 in 551–553 for discoveries in extraterrestrial worlds emphasizing the "earth sciences" of the world, e.g., volcanic activity of Mars 551.21099923. Use 919.904 only for projected accounts about exploring the world, e.g., astronautics on Mars 919.92304. If in doubt, prefer 629.43 and 629.45.

630 vs. 579–590, 641.3

Agriculture and related technologies vs. Natural history of specific kinds of organisms vs. Food

Interdisciplinary numbers

Use numbers in 630 for interdisciplinary works on domestic plants and animals, or works discussing species known almost exclusively in agriculture. Use numbers in 630 as the interdisciplinary numbers for species if the work discusses varieties not known in nature. Use numbers in 579–590 for interdisciplinary works on plants and animals in general.

Use numbers in 630 for works that have material on where to find species in the wild, but concentrate on how to grow them, e.g., finding and growing wild flowers 635.9676 (*not* 582.13); where aquarium fishes are found and how to raise them 639.34 (*not* 597). Use numbers in 579–590 as the interdisciplinary numbers for species harvested in the wild, e.g., mushrooms, trees, and fishes, unless the species is best known for a single product, e.g., teak for lumber 674.144 (*not* 583.96).

Use 641.3 for interdisciplinary works on food. Use 641.3 (*not* 579–590 or 630) for works that discuss the utilization and food value as well as the agriculture and biology of edible plants and animals.

If in doubt, prefer in the following order: 630, 641.3, 579–590.

632.95 vs. 632.2–.8

Pesticides vs. Specific diseases and pests

Pesticides are an exception to the general rule that control of specific pests and diseases is classed with the disease or pest. Use 632.95 if a work concentrates on a pesticide, discussing the mechanism of action, the on-farm environmental effects, or the safety aspects, even if the pesticide is used only on a single kind of pest or disease.

Use 632.2–.8 if the work treats control of the pest or disease in crops, rather than emphasizing the pesticide and its toxicity. For example, use 632.951 for a work on how a rodenticide kills rats, or how it is a danger to local wildlife that eats poisoned rats, 632.9540289 for the safety hazards of herbicides; but use 632.69352 for a work on how to control rats by laying out rodenticides, 632.5 for a work on how to control weeds by spraying herbicides. If in doubt, prefer 632.95.

Use 632.95 for on-farm environmental effects of pesticides only if the work is limited to technical aspects. Use 363.7384 for interdisciplinary works on environmental effects of pesticides.

633–635

Specific plant crops

Certain plants have more than one number if they are important for two or more quite different crops. Some of the more important distinctions are:

Cereals versus cereal grasses (633.1 vs. 633.25)

Use 633.1 if the cereal is grown for grain (even if the fodder is an important byproduct), but use 633.25 if the whole plant is to be consumed by livestock (even if the grain is allowed to ripen).

Legumes (633.3 vs. 635.65)

Use 633.3 if the legume is grown for either the ripened seed or forage, but use 635.65 if the pod is to be picked green or unripened for human consumption.

Other crops

For crops that are listed in only one number, use that number if the difference in production techniques and the appearance of the crop produced by the farmer is minor, e.g., use 635.21 for potatoes whether grown for food, feed, or starch, as they are all grown in the same manner and look alike. However, use 634.9753 for hemlocks grown for lumber, but 635.97752 for hemlocks grown for landscaping, as they are grown in a quite different manner and look quite different when shipped. If the crop described in a work does not fit existing numbers where the plant is named, use the closest suitable number, e.g., a legume grown for hard fibers 633.58. If in doubt, prefer the existing number coming first in the schedule.

635.9 vs. 582.1

Flowers and ornamental plants in agriculture vs. Herbaceous and woody plants, plants noted for their flowers

Use 635.9 (often 635.97 Other groupings of ornamental plants) for works that emphasize plants to be cultivated or appreciated in human-made settings. Use 582.1 for works that emphasize the plants in nature or their biology. If in doubt, prefer 635.9.

See also discussion at 630 vs. 579–590, 641.3.

636.1–.8 vs. 636.088

Specific kinds of domestic animals vs. Animals for specific purposes

Use numbers in 636.1–.8 for terms used in subdivisions of 636.088 applied to specific kinds of domestic animals. Terms listed in 636.088 may apply to only one or a few kinds of animals provided for in 636.1–.8 and are therefore used primarily for number building. For example, the numbers for raising cows for milk and raising poultry for eggs are both derived in part from the eggs and milk number 636.08842. Notation 42 is added to 636.21 (cattle for specific purposes), giving 636.2142 for dairy farming, and to 636.51 (poultry for specific purposes), giving 636.5142 for egg production. 636.08842 itself will seldom be used, because there are few works on producing both milk and eggs or on producing milk from several kinds of animals. Use 636.5142 for works on producing eggs from several kinds of birds. If in doubt between a subdivision of 636.088 and a derived subdivision under 636.1–.8, prefer the latter.

636.72–.75

Specific breeds and groups of dogs

The main groupings used are those recognized by the American Kennel Club (AKC) in *The Complete Dog Book*, 1997. The roughly corresponding groupings of the Kennel Club of United Kingdom (KC) are given in class-here notes when the names differ materially. Most, but not all, of the breeds listed in the schedule are those recognized by the AKC. Class other breeds having pedigrees recognized in other nations that fit within the AKC or KC groupings with the groupings, e.g., European gundogs 636.752.

If in doubt about a breed not named in the schedule, class it in 636.7 (*not* 636.71).

Hounds

Use *Encyclopedia Americana* for help in separating gazehounds (636.7532) from scent hounds (636.7536).

636.82–.83

Specific breeds and kinds of domestic cats

Use David Taylor's *The Ultimate Cat Book*, 1989, for help in determining where a specific breed of cats should be classed.

643.29, 690.879, 728.79 vs. 629.226

Mobile and motor homes

Use 643.29 for interdisciplinary works on mobile homes and for mobile homes meant to serve as permanent homes. Use 629.226 (where campers, motor homes, trailers [caravans] are presented as types of motor land vehicles) only for what are essentially either automobiles with living accommodation, collapsible living accommodation to be used with trucks or trailers, or trailers with such limited living accommodation that they would not (even when hooked up) serve as permanent homes. Do not use 629.226 for mobile homes that must be towed and are meant to stay in one location for a long time. Use 690.879 for works on building mobile homes, and use 728.79 for works on the architecture of mobile homes. If in doubt, prefer 643.29.

647 vs. 647.068, 658.2, T1—0682

Institutional housekeeping vs. Plant management

Use 647 and subdivisions of 647.9 without the addition of the management notation from Table 1 for most works on the management of institutional households, because the term "management" often refers to the basic techniques of operating an establishment, i.e., to the topics found in 642–646 and 648 taken as a whole, when they apply to public facilities. Use 647.068 (or 647.94068, 647.95068, etc.) only when the work treats the kind of management topics found in 658.1–.8, e.g., financial management and marketing. If in doubt between 647 and 647.068, prefer 647.

Plant management covers some of the same topics as institutional housekeeping, e.g., utilities, equipment, maintenance. Use 647 (or other 640 numbers for specific aspects) if the emphasis is on doing the actual work, but use 658.2 if the emphasis is on making sure that the work is done, e.g., a how-to work on running utilities for restaurants 644, on hospital housecleaning 648.5; but a work on managing restaurant utilities 647.950682, on managing hospital housecleaning services 362.110682. If in doubt between 647 (or other 640 numbers for specific aspects) and 658.2 (or T1—0682), prefer 647.

658.04 vs. 658.114, 658.402

Management of enterprises of specific forms vs. Initiation of business enterprises by form of ownership organization vs. Internal organization

Use 658.04 for comprehensive works on management of enterprises of specific legal or ownership forms (e.g., corporations, partnerships). Use 658.114 for works that focus on initiating enterprises of specific legal or ownership forms—either starting a new business or converting an existing business to a new form, e.g., starting up a new individual proprietorship 658.1141, converting an individual proprietorship to a corporation 658.1145.

Use 658.402 for works on the internal managerial organization of an enterprise (how authority and responsibility are apportioned), not its legal or ownership organization. For example, in a line organization a single manager exercises final authority, either directly over production workers or over several supervisors who in turn supervise workers.

If in doubt, prefer in the following order: 658.04, 658.114, 658.402.

658.45 vs. 651.7, 808.06665

Communication in management vs. Communication as an office service vs. Business writing

Use 658.45 for works that focus on use of communication to achieve management goals. These works often emphasize the personal relations aspects of management communication.

Use 651.7 for works emphasizing such topics as the use of the telephone, techniques of dictation, how to use microcomputer software for form letters, mail-handling techniques—in short, the mechanics of communication. Do not use 651.7 for works that emphasize effective business writing style.

Use 808.06665 for style manuals on business writing and works on how to do effective business writing, whether aimed at secretaries or executives. Use 808.066651 for works on how to write a specific type of communication (e.g., business letters) and for model collections of a specific type intended to illustrate good writing style.

If in doubt, prefer in the following order: 658.45, 808.06665, 651.7.

669

Alloys

Use 669 for comprehensive works on alloys of a variety of metals. Use 669.1–.7 for comprehensive works on a specific alloy, or the alloys of a specific metal. Use 669.9 for the physical and chemical metallurgy of alloys, and the process of forming alloys.

Use the number for the chief constituent metal (if readily ascertainable) for an alloy not listed in 669, e.g., Monel®, a nickel alloy of about 67 percent nickel and 30 percent copper 669.7332 (*not* 669.3). If the chief constituent is not readily ascertainable, use the number for the metal coming first in the schedule, except use 669.142 for all alloys of steel.

671–679 vs. 680

Manufacture of products from specific materials vs. Manufacture of products for specific uses

In general, use 671–679 for primary products, and use 680 for final products from a given material, e.g., textiles 677, clothing 687. The distinction between 671–679 and 680 cannot be drawn consistently because some products from specific materials are in 680, e.g., leather and fur goods 685; and some products for specific uses are in 671–679, e.g., paper plates and cups 676.34. If in doubt, prefer 671–679.

680 vs. 745.5

Handicrafts

Use 680 for crafts in the sense of country crafts, and cottage industries and trades, such as those of the blacksmith (682) or harness maker (685.1). Also use 680 for handicrafts treated as the routine way of manufacturing secondary and final products. Use 745.5 for handicrafts when limited to artistic work. If in doubt, prefer 680.

690 vs. 643.7

Construction of buildings vs. Renovation, improvement, remodeling in home economics

Use 690.80286 or other numbers in 690 for works on home renovation and remodeling for professional builders. (Use the special standard subdivision notation 0286 for remodeling in 690 only with numbers drawn from 725–728; do not use a standard subdivision for this subject elsewhere in 690.) Use 643.7 and other numbers in 643 for a broad range of material intended for the do-it-yourself enthusiast, as indicated by the scope note at 643 reading "works for owner-occupants or renters covering activities by members of household." If in doubt, prefer 690.

700.92

Persons in the arts

The instructions for the classification of artists vary, either between major areas of the arts or within one division, e.g., use 730.92 for a sculptor, 730.092 for a sculptor who has also worked in one or more of the other plastic arts, 738.092 for a potter regardless of material or product.

Use either notation 092 from Table 1 or notation for period or place for works of an artist or artists as instructed under specific numbers, e.g., use 730.92 for works of a French sculptor, but use 741.944 for drawings by a French artist.

704.9 and 753–758

Iconography

Prefer iconography over historical and geographic treatment, e.g., a general work on Romanesque art 709.0216, Romanesque painting 759.0216, Romanesque art of Normandy 709.44209021, Romanesque painting of Normandy 759.4209021, but the Virgin Mary and Child in Romanesque art of Normandy 704.948550944209021, the Virgin Mary and Child in Romanesque painting of Normandy 755.550944209021. However, care should be taken in classifying schools and styles that are usually limited in subject matter, such as early Christian, Byzantine, and Romanesque schools, which usually treat religious themes. Use 704.9 or 753–758 only if a point is made that iconography or one of its aspects is the focus of the work.

Use of standard subdivisions

Add standard subdivisions to iconography numbers even if the topic does not approximate the whole of the heading. There are four exceptions: 704.9428 and 757.8 Pornography, 704.9434 and 758.5 Plants, 758.3 Animals, and notation from Table 2. For instance, if a work covers only roses in art or dogs in painting, a standard subdivision should not be added.

Add notation 09 from Table 1 plus notation 3–9 from Table 2 to show the nationality or locality of the artists rather than the location of the subject, e.g., Canadian portraits of British royal children 704.94250971, Canadian portrait paintings of British royal children 757.50971. Do not add notation 074 from the table under T1—093–099 in Table 1 unless the area covered by the work being classed approximates the whole of the area indicated by the notation from Table 2.

709.012–.05 vs. 709.3–.9

Periods of development of fine and decorative arts vs. Treatment by specific continents, countries, localities of fine and decorative arts

Class the works produced by an artistic school or in a particular style as follows:

1. From the same locality, with the locality in 709.3–.9

2. From various localities within a specific country, with the country in 709.3–.9

3. From two countries, with the country coming first in Table 2 in 709.3–.9

4. From three or more European countries, with the period when the school or style flourished in 709.012–.05

5. From three or more non-European countries within the same continent, with the continent in 709.3–.9

6. From three or more countries not within the same continent, with the period when the school or style flourished in 709.012–.05

If in doubt, prefer in the following order: 709.012–.05, the country number in 709.3–.9, the locality number in 709.3–.9.

709.2 vs. 381.457092

Art dealers

Use 709.2 for art dealers as a part of the art world, e.g., the artists the dealers knew and works of art they handled. Use 381.457092 for works about art dealers that focus on the economics of trading in art. If in doubt, prefer 709.2.

721 vs. 690.1

Architectural structure vs. Structural elements of buildings

Use 721 for descriptive details of buildings erected in the past or planned for the future. Use 690.1 for the principles of engineering design and construction of buildings, or actual instruction (e.g., for the builder) on how to put structural elements, shapes, and materials together. If in doubt, prefer 721.

729

Design and decoration of structures and accessories

Use 729 only for general works that focus specifically on architectural design. Use 690 for works that treat construction alone, and use 721 for works that treat design and construction together. Use 729 for works on decoration only when the subject is being treated as an aspect of architectural decoration rather than as an art object in itself, e.g., the use of murals as architectural decoration 729.4, but comprehensive works on murals 751.73.

731–735 vs. 736–739

Sculpture vs. Other plastic arts

Use 731–735 for products and techniques of sculpture. Use 736–739 for products and techniques of the plastic arts. For example, use 731.74 for a bronze figure that is a sculptured bust, but use 739.512 for a bronze figure that is part of a larger decorative work (such as a finial or handle). If in doubt, prefer 731–735.

741.6 vs. 800

Illustrations

Use 741.6 for illustration in general. Class a specific type of illustration with the art form represented if the type is emphasized, e.g., etchings. Use 800 for illustrations that merely accompany or enhance the literary text. If in doubt, prefer 741.6.

745.1

Antiques

Use the available number in 700 for a specific type of antique, e.g., gold coins 737.43, antique New England furniture 749.0974.

If there is no available number in 700–779, use the 600–699 number for a specific type of antique, e.g., antique passenger automobiles 629.222. If there are separate numbers in 600–699 for the use of the object and for its manufacture, prefer the use number, e.g., thimbles 646.19 (*not* 687.8).

If there is no available number in either 600–699 or 700–779 for a specific antique or collectible, class it with the subject with which it is most closely associated, e.g., Shirley Temple collectibles 791.43028092.

745.5928

Handcrafted models and miniatures

Class handcrafted miniatures and models as follows:

Use 700 for handcrafted models:

1. If there is a specific number in 700 for the model, e.g., paper airplanes 745.592.

2. If there is a specific number in 700 for the subject illustrated by the model, e.g., handcrafted miniature furniture 749.0228. (Use notation 0228 from Table 1 to indicate the model or miniature.)

3. If there is no number in 600 for the model or the subject illustrated by the model. In this case the most specific number possible is chosen.

Use 600 for handcrafted models and miniatures if there is no specific number in 700 *and* either of the following conditions is met:

1. If there is a specific number in 600 for the model, e.g., handcrafted model airplanes 629.133134.

2. If there is a specific number for the subject illustrated by the model, e.g., handcrafted miniature reciprocating steam engines 621.1640228. (Use notation 0228 from Table 1 to indicate the model or miniature.)

769.9

Historical, geographic, persons treatment of printmaking and prints

Use 769.92 for both printmakers who copy other artists and the artists being copied (if only prints are being discussed), e.g., prints after Gainsborough 769.92. Use 769.93–.99 for prints produced by a print workshop or a studio. If in doubt, prefer 769.92.

776 vs. 006.5–.7

Computer art

Use 776 for comprehensive works on computer art and for works on computer art where the computer itself displays the art object or creates the final art object. Use 700–780 plus notation 0285 from Table 1 or specific provisions in the schedule for works on computers used as tools or devices to create art objects, e.g., computers and the arts 700.285, computers in the graphic arts 760.0285, computer composition of music 781.34.

Use 006.5–.7 for works on the computer hardware and software used in computer arts, e.g., computer sound 006.5, computer graphics 006.6, multimedia systems 006.7. Such works will typically tell how to use the hardware or the software, and may include information on such topics as file compression.

If in doubt, prefer 776.

779 vs. 770.92

Photographs vs. Persons associated with photography

Use 779 and its subdivisions, plus notation 092 from Table 1, for collections of photographs by individuals. Use 779 and its subdivisions, plus notation 09 from Table 1 and notation 1–9 from Table 2, for collections of photographs by several artists from the same area to show the area where the photographers originated, e.g., collections of portrait photographs by French photographers 779.20944. Use 770.92 for biographies and critical appraisals, which may also contain some photographs. If in doubt, prefer 779.

780

Music

Building numbers

Building a number for a work that is classed in 780 is a four-step process:

1. Determine the various facets of the work.

2. Arrange the facets in the proper order.

3. Determine whether or not the topics belonging to the facets can be indicated.

4. Follow the add instructions.

For example, in building the number for a work entitled *Harmony in Beethoven's piano sonatas*, one takes the following steps:

1. *Determine the various facets of the work*: For the work being classed, there are four facets, or aspects: a general musical topic, harmony; the composer, Beethoven; the instrument, piano; and a musical form, sonata.

2. *Arrange the facets in proper order*: The usual arrangement is the executant (the voice or instrument that produces the music), here the piano at 786.2; the music form, here the sonata at 784.183; general principles, here harmony at 781.25; standard subdivisions, here a person associated with the music at 780.92 (in this case Beethoven). This arrangement obeys the general instruction at 780, which states: unless other instructions are given, class subjects with aspects in two or more subdivisions of 780 in the one coming last. The major exception to executant before form occurs with vocal music (*see 782 for complete details*). If one decided to follow the option of classing all works related to a composer in 789, the arrangement would then be composer, the executant, the musical form, general principles, other standard subdivisions.

3. *Determine whether or not the topics belonging to the facets can be indicated*: If the topic is given in a class-here note or is the same or approximately the same as a number's heading, a topic from another facet can be indicated. If the topic is given in an including note, topics in other facets cannot be indicated. Since the topics, piano, sonata, and harmony, are the headings at 786.2, 784.183, and 781.25, respectively, further topics can be indicated. (For *Har-*

mony in Chopin's mazurkas for piano, the topics harmony and Chopin cannot be indicated because mazurka is a part of the including note at 784.1884.)

4. *Follow the add instructions*: At 786.2 *Pianos, the * refers to the footnote, which instructs one to add as instructed in the add table under the centered entry at 784–788. The add instruction in the add table says that musical forms and instruments are shown by adding 1, then the numbers following 784.1 in 784.18–.19. Thus, facet indicator 1 plus 83 from 784.183 †Sonata form and sonatas added to 786.2 produces 786.2183 Piano sonatas. At 784.183, the † refers to the footnote, which instructs one to add as instructed in the add table under the centered entry at 781.2–.8, which says that in order to show general principles add 1 and then the numbers following 781 in 781.1–.7. The result of adding 1 and then 25 from 781.25 *Harmony is 786.2183125 harmony in piano sonatas. Even though the * at 781.25 indicates that further additions are possible, i.e., adding 092 to indicate Beethoven, the general add instruction at 780 forbids using 0 or 1 (alone or in combination) more than twice. (An option does allow further additions.) Thus, the class number for *Harmony in Beethoven's piano sonatas* is 786.2183125.

Examples

Works about music

New music vocabulary: a guide to notational signs	780.148
Music notation	780.148
Sound structure in music	781.234
Timbre	781.234
New life in country music	781.642
Western popular music	
Country	781.642
Wagner as man and artist	782.1092
Opera	782.1
General biography and criticism (from Table 1)	092
Voice production in choral technique	782.5143
Choral music	782.5
Facet indicator	1
Performance technique	43 (from 781.43)
Bartok orchestral music [criticism]	784.2092
Orchestra	784.2
Composer	092 (from Table 1)
Bartok. Concerto for orchestra [criticism]	784.2186
Orchestra	784.2
Facet indicator	1
Concerto form	86 (from 784.186)

Scoring for brass band	784.9138
Brass band	784.9
Facet indicator	1
Arrangement	38 (from 781.38)
Beethoven string quartets [criticism]	785.7194092
Chamber group-strings	785.7
Size of ensemble	19
Quartet	4 (from 785.14)
Composer	092 (from Table 1)
The fugue in piano music	786.21872
Piano	786.2
Facet indicator	1
Fugue	872 (from 784.1872)
Scientific piano tuning and servicing	786.21928
Piano	786.2
Facet indicator	1
Tuning	928 (from 784.1928)
The origins of bowing	787.1936909
Bowed stringed instruments	787
Facet indicator	1
Bowing	9369 (from 784.19369)
History	09 (from Table 1)
Pablo Casals; a biography	787.4092
Cello	787.4
Performers	092 (from Table 1)
Discography of zither music	016.78770266
Subject bibliography	016
Zither	787.7
Recordings	0266 (from 780.266)
The organs of London	786.519421
Organ	786.5
Facet indicator	19
London	421 (from Table 2)
The Story of "Silent Night"	782.281723
Carols	782.28
Facet indicator	1
Christmas music	723 (from 781.723)

Scores

Hymns for choirs, arranged for mixed voices and organ by David Willocks	782.527
Choral music for mixed voices	782.5
Hymns	27 (from 782.27)

Lees. Breathe on me, breath of God; anthem for 3-part female voice choir unaccompanied	782.6265
Choral music-women's voices	782.6
Anthems	265 (from 782.265)
Schubert song cycles	783.247
Solo voice	783.2
Song cycle	47 (from 782.47)
Brahms. Variations on the St. Anthony Chorale	784.21825
Orchestra	784.2
Facet indicator	1
Variations	825 (from 784.1825)
Berlioz. Romeo and Juliet; a dramatic symphony	784.22184
Orchestra with vocal parts	784.22
Facet indicator	1
Symphony form	84 (from 784.184)
Schuller. Trio: oboe, horn, viola	785.42193
Ensembles of woodwind, brass, strings	785.42
Size of ensemble	19
Trios	3 (from 785.13)
Chopin. Mazurka, piano	786.21884
Piano	786.2
Facet indicator	1
Mazurka form	884 (from 784.1884)

780.079 vs. 790.2

Music and the performing arts vs. The performing arts in general

Use 780.079 for works focusing on music in relation to the other performing arts. Use 790.2 for works on the performing arts as a whole. If in doubt, prefer 780.079.

780.26

Texts; treatises on music scores and recordings

Within 780, add 026 (from 780.26) to the number in 781–788 to indicate treatises about scores and recordings. (To distinguish scores and recordings themselves within 780, apply the optional provision given at 780.) However, when 780–788 numbers are added elsewhere in the schedules, add 026 for scores and recordings, as well as for treatises about them. For example:

Number	Used for
787.2	A treatise on violin music
787.2	Violin scores
787.2	Recordings of violin music
787.2026	A treatise on violin scores
787.20266	A treatise on recordings of violin music
016.7872	A bibliography of treatises on violin music
016.7872026	A bibliography of violin scores
016.7872026	A bibliography of treatises on violin scores
016.78720266	A discography of recordings of violin music
016.78720266	A bibliography of treatises on recordings of violin music

780.92 and 791.092

Persons associated with public performances

Use the number for the activity with which the person's career is chiefly identified for the biography of a performer, e.g., the biography of an opera singer 782.1092. If the person's career involves more than one kind of public performance with no particular predominance, use the activity that comes first in the following table of preference:

Music	780
Dancing	792.8
Stage	792
Motion pictures	791.43
Television	791.45
Radio	791.44

For example, use 792.028092 for the biography of a stage actor who has also done considerable work in television. Give preference to activities listed in the above table over all other activities listed in 791.

780.92

Musicians and composers

Musicians

Comprehensive works on musicians are classed in the most specific number that describes their careers. Use 780.92 only for musicians who are equally known for both their vocal and instrumental work, e.g., Ludwig van Beethoven 780.92. Use

782–783 for musicians known primarily for vocal music, e.g., Richard Wagner, an opera composer, 782.1092; Elvis Presley, a rock singer, 782.42166092. Use 784–788 for musicians known primarily for instrumental music, e.g., Sir Thomas Beecham, a conductor, 784.2092; Nicolò Paganini, a violinist, 787.2092. (*See also 781.6 for discussion of musicians associated with traditions of music other than classical.*)

See also discussion at 784–788: Add table: 092.

Composers

Use notation 092 from Table 1 to indicate a biography, a general criticism of the composer, an analysis of a composer's contribution to the development of some aspect of music (such as Haydn's role in the development of the concerto form), critical works on the body of a composer's work (such as a critique of the piano music of Ravel), and a collection of analyses of the individual pieces of music. Do not use notation 092 for criticism of an individual work by a composer.

The citation order for music requires that general criticism of a composer's works in a specific form and criticism of a single aspect of the works be separated because the aspect is shown by adding from 781. For example, use 784.2184092 for general criticism of Brahms's symphonies, but use 784.2184125 for criticism of harmony in Brahms's symphonies. However, if a library wishes to keep all criticism of a composer's works in the same number, it is optional not to add from 781, e.g., criticism of Brahms's symphonies and of harmony in Brahms's symphonies both 784.2184092.

See also discussion at 784–788: Add table: 092.

781.38

Arrangements

Add 138 (the arrangement notation derived from 781.38) to the number in 782–788 for a voice, instrument, or ensemble to indicate arrangements in general either of or for the voice, instrument, or ensemble. For example, use 787.2138 for both violin music arranged for various instruments and music of several instruments arranged for the violin, 787.2 (violin music) plus 138 (arrangements).

Add 1382–1388 (the arrangement notation derived from 781.382–.388) to the number in 782–788 for a voice, instrument, or ensemble for which the music was arranged in order to indicate the original voice, instrument, or ensemble. Use 781.382–.388 only for building other numbers; never use these numbers by themselves. For example, use 786.213872 for an arrangement of violin music for piano, that is, 786.2 (piano music) plus 13872 (arrangements of violin music).

781.47

Accompaniment

For treatises, add 147 (the accompaniment notation derived from 781.47) to indicate how to accompany the work, e.g., how to accompany violin music 787.2147.

(Option: For scores, add notation 147 to indicate the presence of accompaniment, e.g., accompanied violin music 787.2147, unaccompanied violin music 787.2.)

781.6

Nonclassical musicians

Comprehensive works on nonclassical musicians (musicians of a tradition other than classical music) are classed in the most specific number that describes their careers. Use numbers in 781.62–.66 and in 781.69 for musicians that are equally known for both their vocal and instrumental work, e.g., Louis Armstrong, a jazz trumpeter, singer, and band leader, 781.65092. Use 782–783 for musicians known primarily for vocal music, e.g., Ella Fitzgerald, a jazz singer, 782.42165092. Use 784–788 for musicians known primarily for instrumental music, e.g., John Coltrane, a jazz tenor-saxophonist, 788.74092. Add 162–166 or 169 (the traditions-of-music notation derived from 781.62–.66 and 781.69) to the number in 782–788 before adding notation 092 from Table 1.

See also discussion at 784–788: Add table: 092.

781.62 vs. 780.89

Folk music vs. Music with respect to specific ethnic and national groups

Use 781.62 for music indigenous to an ethnic or national group, e.g., African American music 781.6296073. Use 780.89 for the group in relation to music in general, e.g., a work about African American composers, opera singers, jazz conductors 780.8996073. If in doubt, prefer 781.62.

782

Vocal music

Use 782.1 for dramatic vocal scores, e.g., opera scores 782.1, scores of musical plays 782.14. Use 782.5–.9 and 783 for nondramatic vocal scores. (Use 792.5 for staging dramatic music.)

For nondramatic vocal music (782.2–783), classification is determined by whether an item is a treatise or a recording, on the one hand, or a score, on the other. A person interested in reading about or listening to a singer or a piece of music will usually not know the singer's vocal range or the vocal requirements of that piece of music. In contrast, a person interested in scores will know the type of voice or voices involved, e.g., a song cycle sung by a soprano, or a mass sung by a tenor and male chorus. Therefore, use 782.2–.4 for treatises about and recordings of singers and nondramatic vocal forms, but use 782.5–783 for scores and texts.

The following flow chart will help users select the correct section of vocal music.

Flow chart for vocal music

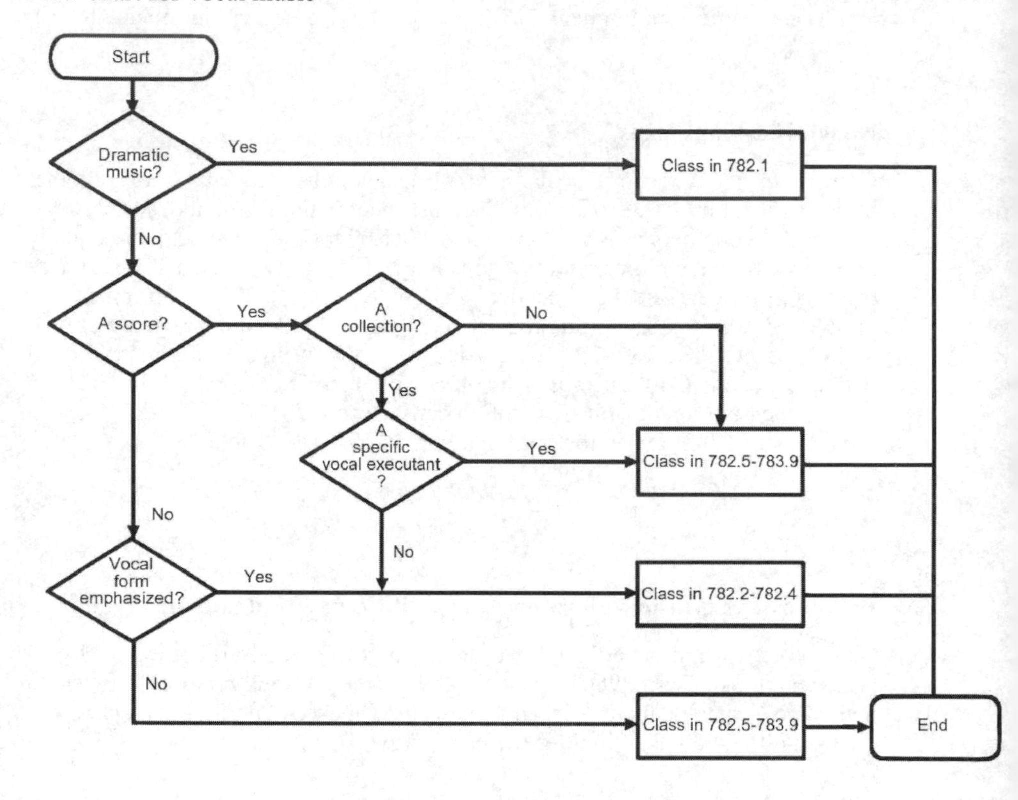

Examples (from applying the flow chart):

Soprano arias from opera [scores]	782.1
Soprano airs not from opera [scores]	783.66
Sacred songs by sopranos [recordings]	782.25
Women's soprano voice [treatise]	783.66

Vocal scores

With scores, kind of voice and size of vocal ensemble must be considered. The distinction between 782.5–.9 and 783 is based upon the number of voices per part. Use 782.5–.9 for music having several voices per part (what is usually meant by choral music). Use 783 for music having one voice per part (part songs and solos). Observe the following preference order for scores and parts of non-dramatic vocal music:

Size of vocal ensemble (including solos)
Type of voice, e.g., male, high, soprano, child's
Vocal forms

Size of vocal ensemble parallels the primary division in the instrument portion of the schedule. Choral music is analogous to orchestral music (more than one voice/instrument per part in some parts); music for single voices in combination is analogous to chamber music (only one voice/instrument per part); and music for solo voice is analogous to music for solo instrument.

Type of voice also parallels the instrument portion of the schedule, in that specifying the sex and range of the voice is analogous to specifying the kind and type of instrument. Different kinds of voice are distinguished first by sex and age (women, children, men) and second by range.

For example:

Secular song for male voice choir	782.842
Male voice choir	782.8
Secular song	42 (from 782.42)
Carols for single voices in combination	783.11928
Single voices in combination	783.1
Nondramatic vocal forms	19
Carols	28 (from 782.28)

782.1 vs. 792.5, 792.6

Dramatic vocal forms

Use 782.1 for dramatic vocal forms as a type of vocal music, including such topics as tempos, plots, singers, conducting. Use 792.5 and 792.6 for dramatic vocal forms as a type of stage presentation, including such topics as costumes, sets, direction. For example, use 782.1 for operas as vocal music, 792.5 for staging of operas; use 782.14 for musical plays as vocal music, 792.6 for staging of musical plays. Use 792.509 for an opera house and its productions, e.g., a history of La Scala, Milan 792.5094521. If in doubt, prefer 782.1.

784–788

Instruments and their music

Add table

092

Persons associated with instruments and their music

For persons associated with an instrument and its music <u>and</u> for persons associated with the music for the instrument, add notation 092 from Table 1 directly to the number for the instrument and its music, e.g., Nicolò Paganini (a violinist and composer) <u>and</u> Isaac Stern (a violinist) 787.2092. However, for persons interested only in the instrument, add 19 (the instrument notation derived from 784.<u>19</u>) before adding notation 092 from Table 1, e.g., Antonio Stradivari (a violin maker) 787.2<u>19</u>092.

For persons associated with a specific tradition of music other than western art music, add 162–166 or 169 (the traditions-of-music notation derived from 781.62–.66 and 781.69) before adding notation 092 from Table 1, e.g., a country music violinist 787.2<u>1642</u>092. If the person is associated with more than one tradition, do not add to show the tradition.

791.43, 791.45 vs. 778.5

Motion pictures and television

Use 791.43 and 791.45 for motion pictures and television as art forms and for comprehensive works on producing them. Use 778.5 for the technical aspects of making motion pictures and videos. For example, use 791.43025 for the use of lighting techniques to enhance the mood of the scene and for a comprehensive work on lighting, but use 778.5343 for how to determine what kind of lighting apparatus to use while filming in bright sunlight. If in doubt, prefer 791.43 and 791.45.

791.437 and 791.447, 791.457, 792.9

Films, radio programs, television programs, stage productions

A production recorded in a different medium than the original production is classed with the recording, not with the production, e.g., a staged opera recorded for television 791.4572 (a television program), *not* 792.542 (a staged opera).

793.932 vs. 794.822

Computer adventure and fantasy games vs. Arcade games

Use 793.932 for computer adventure games that present the player with a situation and a goal (or goals). These goals may involve solving a mystery or problems and accumulating points. The player must think as opposed to making reflex actions, and is projected into an interactive story. An example is *Myst*®.

Use 793.932 also for computer fantasy role-playing games that involve reaching a goal by solving intellectual problems, but require reflex actions because of the fighting or athletic action, and in which outcomes are decided by the computer. Examples are *Final Fantasy*® and *SimCity*®.

Use 794.822 for arcade games that emphasize quick reflexes, as opposed to intellectual decisions. The term refers to a type of game, not just those games played in video arcades, and may include fighting, space flight, shooting, pinball, mazes, space shootouts, and strategy. Examples are *Tekken*® and *PacMan*®.

If in doubt, prefer 793.932.

795.015192 vs. 519.27

Games of chance

Use 795.015192 for the probabilities, or "odds," of winning "games of chance" in the recreational sense, i.e., any games in which chance, not skill, is the most important factor in determining the outcome, e.g., craps, poker, solitaire. Use 519.27 for "games of chance" in the mathematical sense, which are limited to games played by a single player to determine the optimal policy or strategy of winning the games and are a part of the theory of controlled probabilities. If in doubt, prefer 795.015192.

796.08 vs. 796.04

History and description of sports and games with respect to kinds of persons vs. General kinds of sports and games

Use numbers in 796.08 or notation 08 from Table 1 added to numbers for specific sports or games for works on the participation of specific kinds of persons if the sports or games are not modified to allow their participation. Use either 796.04 or the number for the modified version if the sports or games have been modified to allow participation of specific kinds of persons. Numbers for the modified versions of a sport are usually given in the "specific types" or "variants" subdivisions of the sport, e.g., baseball 796.357, Little League baseball 796.35762, indoor baseball 796.3578. If these subdivisions are not provided, use the number for the type of sport as a whole. For example, use 796.3520873 for works on how persons who have lost a leg can play golf, as they can usually play without a major change to the rules of golf. However, in order to participate in other sports, the person who has lost a leg may require a wheelchair. Use 796.0456 for comprehensive works on wheelchair sports. Class the wheelchair version of a specific sport with variants of the sport, e.g., wheelchair basketball 796.3238. If in doubt, prefer 796.08 or the number for the specific sport or game with use of notation 08 from Table 1.

The name of a variant of the sport may give the impression that it is for only one type of person when any type can play it. For example, women's basketball before 1971 was a variant of basketball in which there were six players per team and the three forwards played in the forecourt. Use 796.3238 (*not* 796.323082) for this variant because it can be played by either men or women.

Some sports and games have similar sounding names, but the rules are so different as to create separate, though related, sports and games. For example, American football, Canadian football, and Australian-rules football are similar sports, but they each have their own separate rules and are classed in 796.332, 796.335, and 796.336, respectively.

796.092

Sports personnel

Use the general number for the sport for the biography of sports personnel, regardless of position played or type of game, e.g., a quarterback in American professional football 796.332092 (*not* 796.33225092 or 796.33264092).

796.15 vs. 629.0460228

Play with remote-control models, kites, similar devices vs. Models and miniatures of transportation equipment

Use 796.15 for both play with remote-control vehicles and for interdisciplinary works on remote-control vehicles, e.g., flying and building remote-control airplanes 796.154. Use 629.0460228 and similar numbers in 620 for the design and construction of model vehicles, e.g., building model airplanes 629.133134. If in doubt, prefer 796.15.

Use 790.133 for comprehensive works on play with all types of model railroads and trains, because most play with model railroads and trains does not involve remote-control vehicles.

800

Literature (Belles-lettres)

This entry uses notation from Table 3 to illustrate the application of principles to various literatures, e.g., "T3—1" is used to discuss poetry in specific literatures rather than "811, 821, 831, 841, etc." The notation "T3—1" refers to both T3A—1 from Table 3A (individual authors) and T3B—1 from Table 3B (more than one author). Difficulties arise with the notation for T3—8 Miscellaneous writings because the literary period comes between T3—8 and its various subdivisions. In the entry this form is expressed as T3—8 + the notation for the subdivision, e.g., diaries T3—8 + 03.

Choice between literature and nonliterary subject

The discipline of literature is restricted to: (1) works of the imagination that are written in the various literary forms, e.g., fiction, poetry; (2) literary criticism and description; (3) literary history and biography. Class works of the imagination intended to delight in 800, but class works that are essentially informational with the subject in other disciplines, regardless of their literary form. For example, class Jonathan Swift's *The Drapier's Letters* as a work on monetary policy in 332.49415 (*not* as a collection of the author's letters).

Essays, speeches, letters, and diaries are commonly used for nonliterary purposes. If in doubt whether to class a work in one of these forms as literature in 800 or with a subject elsewhere in the schedule, prefer the subject.

Class nonfiction novels that use the techniques of fiction writing to tell the story of actual people and actual events as follows. Class an account of a true event or series of events using the names of the people involved, not inventing characters or distorting facts to enhance an intended artistic effect, and not going beyond the information available to the author from investigation and interviews, in the discipline appropriate to the facts described. For example, class Truman Capote's *In Cold Blood*, a true account of a multiple murder, in 364.1523. If, however, the author goes beyond what is learned from investigation and interviews in describing conversations, feelings, thoughts, or states of mind of the people depicted in the book, class the work as fiction, e.g., Norman Mailer's *The Executioner's Song* 813.54. If in doubt, class as fiction.

Other kinds of fiction, and poetry and drama, are sometimes used as vehicles for conveying factual information, e.g., biographies written in verse, fiction employed to teach the fundamentals of mathematics. Use 800 for poetry, drama, and fiction unless the form is incidental to the explanation of a specific subject, e.g., Harvey's *Circulation of the Blood* (written in Latin verse) 612.13 (*not* 871.04). Make an exception for certain ancient works that have long been classed as literature regardless of their content, e.g., Hesiod's *Works and Days* 881.01 (*not* 630), even though it deals with practical agriculture.

Class a collection of literary texts or excerpts from literary texts that is meant to serve as a model for studying another discipline with the discipline illustrated. For example, use 307 for a collection meant to explain what a community is.

Class a literary study of nonliterary works in 809.935, e.g., the Bible as literature 809.93522.

Language

Class literary works by language, not by country of origin. However, class works in English originating in North America, South America, Hawaii, and geographically associated islands in 810 (*not* 820). Class works in English from Europe, Africa, Asia, Australia, and New Zealand, and comprehensive works on English literature in 820. In certain cases, use Table 3C to indicate country of origin. *(See also discussion at T3C—93–99.)*

Class literary works in the language in which they were originally written, e.g., an English translation of a work originally written in Spanish 860 (*not* 820).

Literature of two or more languages

Works treating literature of two or more languages are usually collections or works of criticism. If two languages are involved, use the number coming first in 820–890, except where there are different instructions. For example, use 820 (*not* 860) for English and Spanish, but use 880 (*not* 870) for Greek and Latin. If more than two languages are involved, but the languages all belong to a particular language family, use the most specific number that will contain all the languages. For example, use 830 for a work covering English, German, and Dutch, since they are all Germanic languages. Do not use 820–890 for broad groupings such as Indo-European literature. For example, use 808 for collections covering English, French, and Russian (all Indo-European languages), 809 for criticism, 800 for a combination of collections and criticism. Similarly, use 800, 808, or 809 for a work about literature in more than two languages when the languages are unrelated except that they belong to a broad grouping such as nonwestern or Asian languages. For example, use 808 (*not* 890) for a collection of Arabic, Persian, and Turkish literary texts. If any one language is predominant, class with that language.

Literary form

In literature there are two basic modes of expression: poetry and prose. Class drama, whether in poetry or prose, with drama in T3—2. Class epigrams with miscellaneous writings in T3—8 + 02, regardless of mode. Class works in other forms with poetry in T3—1 if written in verse. Class prose works in T3—3 Fiction, T3—4 Essays, T3—5 Speeches, T3—6 Letters, and T3—8 Miscellaneous writings. Use the subdivision for prose literature, T3—8 + 08, only for prose works in more than one literary form. Class prose works in a specific form with the form.

Use notation 7 Humor and satire only for collections in, or works of criticism about, two or more forms including both verse and prose, because humor and satire are categories of writing rather than a form or mode. Class literary works exhibiting humor and satire in a particular form (T3—1–6 and T3—8) with the form. Table 3A for individual authors has no notation parallel to T3B—7; class a collection of works by an individual author in more than one form exhibiting humor and satire in T3A—8 + 09.

Literary period

Use the period tables supplied under various languages for the literature of that language from throughout the world and for the literatures of individual countries. For example, use 843.912 for French-language fiction of the early 20th century from throughout the world and for French-language fiction of the early 20th century from France. Use the same periods for affiliated literatures (literatures in the same language, but from countries other than the traditional homeland), e.g., use 843.912 for Belgian, Swiss, Canadian, and Senegalese French-language fiction of the early 20th century. However, there is an exception to the general rule for American literature in English, which has two period tables. Use one period table for Canada; use the other period table for countries of North, Middle, and South America other than Canada, and for comprehensive works on American literature in English. (Optional periods are sometimes provided for use with a country other than the traditional homeland of the literature if some special device is used to set such literature apart from the literature in general. The options are described at 810–890 in the schedule.) In certain cases, use Table 3C to indicate country of origin of affiliated literatures. *(See also discussion at T3C—93–99.)*

In literary period tables, the name for a particular century is given if the span of years in the heading is less than 75 years, e.g., the 19th century in English literature is given in a class-here note under notation 8 Victorian period, 1837–1899, in the period table for English literature at 820.1–828. The name for the century is usually not given if the span of years in the heading is 75 or more years, e.g., the 20th century in English literature is not given under notation 91, which covers the span 1900–1999, in the period table for English literature.

Other elements

If appropriate, add notation 08 from Table 3B (or notation 8 from table under T3B—1–8, notation 08 from table under T3B—102–107) for collections of works by or about more than one author, and notation from Table 3C, to express features such as literary themes or subjects, literary elements (e.g., dialogue), literary qualities (e.g., romanticism), and specific kinds of persons for whom or by whom the literature is written.

Literary criticism

Class criticism with the literature being criticized. Class criticism of a specific work in the same number as the work itself, e.g., a critical analysis of Hemingway's *For Whom the Bell Tolls* 813.52. Class general criticism of the work of an author in the comprehensive number for the author, e.g., criticism of Hemingway 813.52.

Use 809 and notation 09 from Table 3B (or notation 9 from table under T3B—1–8, notation 09 from table under T3B—102–107) for criticism of all kinds of literature except the works of individual authors. Use 809 for criticism of several literatures as a whole, 809.3 for criticism of fiction from several literatures. Use 810.9 for criticism of the English-language literature of the United States in general, 813.009 for criticism of English-language fiction of the United

States in general, 813.5209 for criticism of early 20th-century American fiction in English.

Use 809.1–.7 for criticism of literature in a specific form from more than two literatures. Use 808.1–.7 for critical works in which the emphasis is on the various forms of literature as such, not on the various authors and literatures that may be used as examples. If in doubt between 808.1–.7 and 809.1–.7, prefer 809.1–.7.

Use 801.95 for the theory and technique of literary criticism. Use 808.1–.7 for the theory and technique of criticism of specific literary forms. If in doubt between 801.95 and 808.1–.7, prefer 801.95.

Class appreciation of literature in the same manner as other criticism.

Class textual criticism of literature in the same manner as other criticism. However, use 801.959 (*not* 808.1–.7) for the theory and technique of textual criticism of specific literary forms.

Class criticism of criticism with the criticism being criticized and hence with the original subject of criticism, e.g., criticism of Hemingway and a criticism of that criticism by a third person, both 813.52.

Class works about critics in the same manner as works about other authors, i.e., class critics with the kind of literature that they chiefly criticize, e.g., a man who devoted the major part of his life to criticizing the works of Hemingway 813.52; a critic of Spanish literature 860.9.

Class criticism and critics with the language of the literature they are criticizing, not with the language in which the criticism is written, e.g., a French critic writing in French but criticizing American literature 810.9.

Adaptations

An adaptation may alter the form of a work or modify the content to such an extent in language, scope, or level of presentation that it can no longer be considered a version of the original. Class an adaptation in the number appropriate to the adaptation, e.g., Lamb's *Tales from Shakespeare* 823.7.

However, class a prose translation of poetry (which is merely a change in mode) in the number for the original work, e.g., Dante's *Divine Comedy* translated into German prose 851.1.

Excerpts

Class a collection of excerpts from different literary works as a collection.

800, T3C—362 vs. 398.245, 590, 636

Literature (Belles-lettres) and pets as specific subjects in literature vs. Folk literature of animals vs. Animals vs. Animal husbandry

Class literary accounts of animals, whether fictional or true, with the appropriate form in literature, e.g., poetry. Use subdivisions of T3—8 Miscellaneous writings for literary accounts of actual animals in the form of anecdotes or personal reminiscences, T3—8 + 02 for anecdotes, T3—8 + 03 for reminiscences, diaries, journals; or T3—8 + 07 for works without identifiable literary form.

Use T3C—362 for collections of literary works that treat pets as a specific subject or theme, e.g., a collection of English fiction about cats 823.00803629752.

Class works about animals intended to contribute to some discipline other than literature in the relevant discipline. Use 398.245 for folk literature of animals. Use 590 for animal stories in which the author's emphasis is on the habits and behavior of the animal. Use 636 where the emphasis is on the care and training of the animal.

If in doubt, prefer 800.

800 vs. 398.2

Literature (Belles-lettres) vs. Folk literature

Anonymous classics are not considered to be folk literature. Despite the fact that their authorship is unknown, such works have a recognized literary merit, are almost always lengthy, and form a part of the literary canon. Use 800 for them, e.g., *Chanson de Roland* 841.1, *Cantar de mio Cid* 861.1, *Kalevala* 894.54111. Folk literature consists of brief works in the oral tradition. Whatever literary individuality the folk literature may once have had has been lost to the anonymity that the passage of time brings. Use 398.2 for folk literature. If in doubt, prefer 800.

Some legendary or historical events or themes form the basis for original works in many literatures, periods, and forms, e.g., the search for the Holy Grail or the battle of Roland with the Saracens. Medieval works involving them are often anonymous. Class each retelling of the event or theme with the literature, form, and period in which it was written, e.g., Mary Stewart's Merlin trilogy 823.914. Use 809.933 for works about a specific theme treated in several literatures.

If in doubt, prefer 800.

808.8

Collections of literary texts from more than two literatures

Here are examples illustrating the preference order for collections of texts in more than one form from more than two literatures. The preference order is the same for criticism (809).

1. Specific themes and subjects, e.g., 808.80382 (religion)
2. Specific elements, e.g., 808.8024 (plot)
3. Specific qualities, e.g., 808.8013 (idealism)
4. For and by specific kinds of persons, e.g., 808.899282 (children)
5. Period, e.g., 808.80033 (18th century)

See also discussion at Table 3B: Preference order.

808.81–.88 and 809.1–.7

Specific kinds of poetry, drama, fiction, speeches

The add instructions at 808.812–.818 Specific kinds of poetry, which allow the addition of the numbers following T3B—10 in notation 102–107 from Table 3B, also permit further addition at that point, since numbers in the range T3B—102–107 have a footnote that leads to an add table under a centered entry: "Add as instructed under T3B—102–107."

Do not add notation 08 Collections of literary texts from the add table under T3B—102–107 by itself, since it would be redundant because 808.8 already means collections of literary texts, e.g., collections of narrative poetry 808.813 (*not* 808.81308). However, add notation 08 if it serves as a link for adding further notation from Table 3C, e.g., collections of narrative poetry about political themes 808.81308358.

Apply the same policy for collections of specific kinds of drama, fiction, and speeches, e.g., a collection of short stories 808.831 (*not* 808.83108), but a collection of short stories about political themes 808.83108358.

Apply a similar policy for history and criticism of specific kinds of poetry, drama, fiction, speeches. Do not add notation 09 History, description, critical appraisal by itself to numbers in 809 History, description, critical appraisal of more than two literatures, e.g., history and criticism of narrative poetry 809.13 (*not* 809.1309). However, add notation 09 if it serves as a link for adding further notation from Table 3C, e.g., history and criticism of narrative poetry about political themes 809.1309358.

808.82 vs. 791.437, 791.447, 791.457, 792.9

Texts of plays vs. Production scripts

Use 808.82 and similar numbers built with T3A—2 or T3B—2 for texts of plays. Use 791.437, 791.447, 791.457, and 792.9 for production scripts. A production script contains a variety of directions, e.g., where the furniture is to be placed, where the actors are to stand. For example, use 812.52 for the text of Thornton Wilder's *Our Town*, but use 792.92 for the production script for a staged production of *Our Town*. If in doubt, prefer 808.82 and similar numbers.

900

History

Use 900 for the story of events that have transpired, or an account of the conditions that have prevailed, in a particular place or region. Use 001–899 for the history of a specific subject, e.g., a history of political developments (such as internal developments in government) without respect to their effect upon the larger society and place where they occur 320.9, history of economic events in France 330.944, history of warfare 355.0209, history of clocks 681.11309.

The general arrangement of Table 2, which determines the number assigned to the history of a particular place, is geographic rather than by political units, because although political affiliation may change, position on the earth's surface does not, e.g., history of Hawaii 996.9 under Oceania (*not* under United States history).

History includes the present (situation and conditions), but not the future (projected events). Use 303.49 for projected events.

Historic events vs. nonhistoric events

Depending upon their impact, class specific events either in 900 or in specific disciplines in 001–899. Use 930–990 for events that are important enough to affect the general social life and history of the place, regardless of any discipline involved, e.g., the sinking of the Lusitania 940.4514; the assassination of Abraham Lincoln 973.7092; the 1906 San Francisco earthquake 979.461051.

Use 001–899 for the history of the discipline for other specific events. For example, use 364 for the history of a crime, e.g., the Whitechapel murders committed by Jack the Ripper 364.1523. Use 796–799 for a sporting accident, e.g., a fatal accident during an automobile race 796.72.

However, take into account the author's purpose or point of view. For example, use 364.1524092 (*not* 973.922092) for a work about the assassination of John F. Kennedy that focuses on the modus operandi of the crime, the detective work involved in solving it, or both.

Use 300 for events that emphasize social aspects. Use 363 (*not* any other discipline involved) if safety factors are stressed, e.g., use 363.12365 for a study of the wreck of the Andrea Doria to determine what the causes of the accident were or what preventive measures might be mandated as a result of the incident.

Use 001–899 for collected accounts of events pertaining to one discipline, e.g., scientific travel 508. Use 904 for collected events without such focus.

909, 930–990 vs. 320

History and politics

Political history

Use 909 and 930–990 for political history that emphasizes major political events typified by the "battles, kings, and dates" school of history. Use 320.9 for political history that emphasizes the mechanics of give and take of political forces and movements and their internal development. Use 909 and 930–990 if the forces and movements come to power or bring about major changes in society. If in doubt, prefer 909 and 930–990.

See also discussion at 909, 930–990 vs. 320.4, 321, 321.09.

Political activities

Use 909 and 930–990 for the sum total of political activity of a specific period or place. Use 320 for specific important political activities presented in terms of the discipline political science, but consider 909 and 930–990 whenever an activity is discussed in a manner that highlights its influence on general events. Use 909 and 930–990 for important events and leaders with wide-ranging responsibilities, unless considered primarily in the context of a specific subject. If in doubt, prefer 909 and 930–990.

Special consideration of 320.9, 324, and 328 follows:

320.9: Use 320.9 for habitual activities and styles of leading political figures as a group, and activities reflecting the adjustment of political forces or the status of political parties and movements. Use 909 and 930–990 for the activities analyzed in terms of their effect on general events.

324: Use 324.2 for party histories; use 324.5 and 324.24–.29, plus notation 015, for histories of nomination campaigns; and use 324.9 for histories of election campaigns, but only when they treat largely internal events of the parties and campaigns, or report winners, losers, and votes. Use 930–990 for the history of how a party or candidate came to power (or almost did), or how party and campaign events move nations (or other areas) in certain directions.

328: Use 328.4–.9 for histories of specific legislative bodies, but only when they are largely limited to what happened within or to the bodies, without significant consideration of what the legislative body did for the political unit it served. Use 328 for reports of proceedings of a legislature (i.e., its motions, debates, actions). Use 930–990 for the accomplishments of a given legislative session, but use 328 if the work concentrates on the body's internal history.

909, 930–990 vs. 320.4, 321, 321.09

Change of government

Use 909 and 930–990 for the history of changes in government or for particular coups and revolutions in specific areas, e.g., revolutions in the 20th century 909.82, the Russian Revolution 947.0841. Use 320.4 for political treatment of systems of government that precede or follow changes in a specific country, e.g., the government of the Soviet Union after the 1917 revolution 320.4470904. Use 321 numbers other than 321.09 for works on particular systems or kinds of systems and general political treatment of a specific system of government preceding or following changes, e.g., new republics 321.86. Use 321.09 primarily for studies of *the process* of change, rather than for works on particular changes. If in doubt, prefer in the following order: 909 or 930–990; 320.4; all subdivisions of 321 except 321.09; 321.09.

909, 930–990 vs. 910

History vs. Geography and travel

Use 909 or 930–990 if a work deals with both geography and civilization or with both travel and civilization. However, use 910 if the treatment of geography or travel is predominant. If in doubt, prefer 909 or 930–990

Use 910.02 or 913–919, plus notation 02 from table under 913–919, if the work deals only with the description of the physical earth.

913–919

Geography of and travel in ancient world and specific continents, countries, localities in modern world; extraterrestrial worlds

Historic sites and buildings

Works describing historic sites and buildings should be classed with the discipline that is emphasized.

Class a work about a building or historic site that has or had a specific purpose with the purpose of the building or site unless some other discipline is emphasized, e.g., a work about a Benedictine monastery in Lower Austria that emphasizes the history of the religious order in that place 271.1043612, a guide to the New York Stock Exchange building 332.64273. Class works about buildings that are associated with the life of an individual with the biography number for that person, e.g., the home of Thomas Wolfe in Asheville, North Carolina 813.52. Class works about a site that is famous for a historic event with the history of the event, e.g., Gettysburg National Military Park 973.7349.

Use 720.9 or 725–728 for works on a building or buildings in an area that emphasize the architecture of the building or buildings, e.g., a work on a church in Paris that emphasizes architectural history 726.50944361. Also use 725–728 for comprehensive works on the art history of a building and its contents, including the architecture of the building and the art works it contains.

Use 930–990 for a work that describes the buildings in an area for the purpose of illustrating the history of the area. (See the discussion at 930–990: Historic preservation.)

Use 913–919 for works when no specific purpose or discipline is evident. (See the discussion below under 04 Travel on Guidebooks.)

See also discussion at 333.7–.9 vs. 508, 913–919, 930–990.

Add table

The following flow chart is offered as an aid to building numbers and as a supplement to the detailed directions at 913–919.

Flow chart for geography and travel

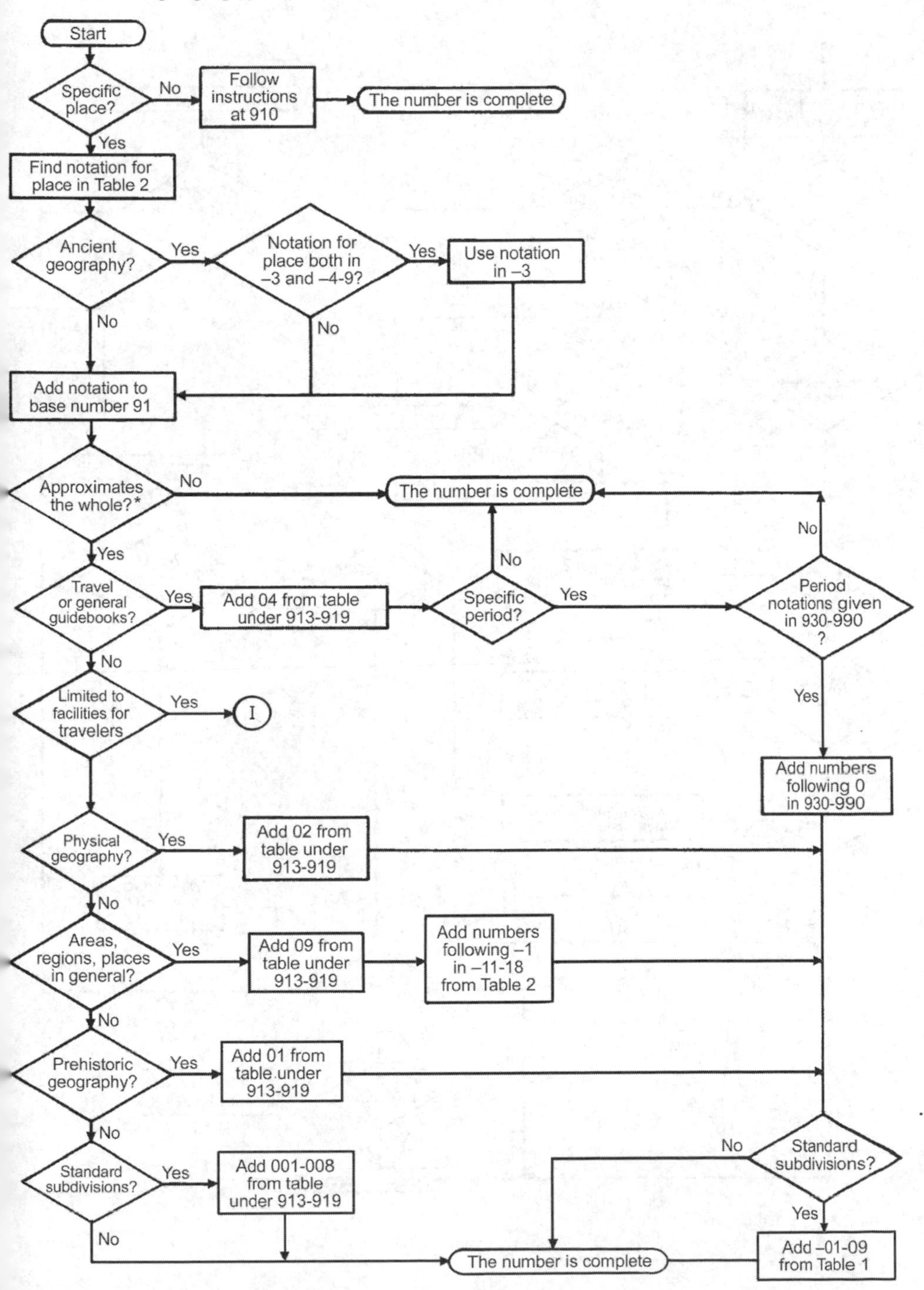

*See also Introduction and Glossary for information about "Approximates the whole"

Flow chart for travelers

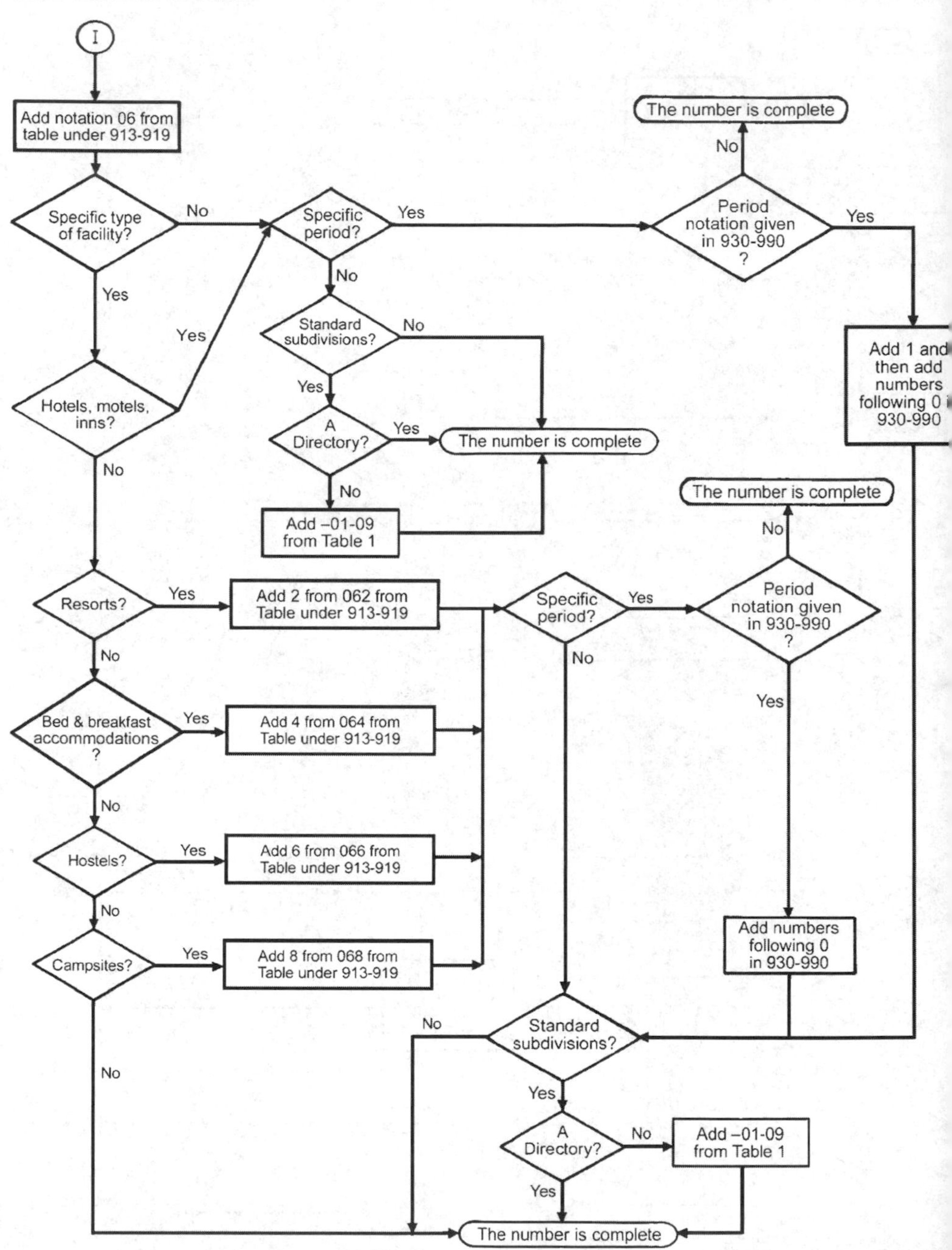

04

Travel

Use 04 for accounts of travel that emphasize events of the trip, places stopped at, accommodations, modes of transportation. If the work is purely a description of the area visited, with none, or very few, of these accompaniments, use subdivision 02 for physical geography. Use 930–990 for civilization and social conditions of the place visited and for works by a person who has lived in the area for several years.

Works on travel normally do not cover the whole of any given area. Class accounts according to the widest span covered, e.g., travel from Marseilles to Paris 914.404, travel from New York to San Francisco 917.304, travel in 1981 from New York City to Buffalo, New York 917.470443. Standard subdivisions may be added.

Discovery and exploration

Use 04 for works describing excursions into previously unknown or little known areas, e.g., the Lewis and Clark expedition 917.8042, Byrd's expedition to the South Pole 919.8904. However, use 930–990 if the initial exploration of a place forms an important part of its early history, e.g., early exploration of North America 970.01.

Use 930.1 for accounts of archaeological expeditions.

Guidebooks

A guidebook can be either a residential guidebook (i.e., a guide for the permanent resident or long-term visitor) or a tourist guidebook (i.e., a guide for the short-term visitor). Residential guidebooks cover not only the tourist attractions but also the other parts of the area, such as banks, churches, grocery stores, real estate agencies, and residential neighborhoods, and normally give a snapshot view of the history of the area. Use 940–990, plus the notation for the period during which it was written, for a residential guidebook, e.g., use 975.3042 for a residential guidebook to Washington, D.C., written in 2003. Tourist guidebooks provide detailed information about the area through which tourists travel, telling them what to see, where to stay, and where to eat. If in doubt whether the book is a residential or a tourist guidebook, class it as a tourist guidebook.

Use 913–919, plus notation 04 from the table at 913–919, for tourist guidebooks, e.g., guidebooks to the United States 917.304. For individual guidebooks, add the notation for the historical period during which it was written, e.g., use 917.530442 for a tourist guidebook to Washington, D.C., written in 2003. Use 913 for guidebooks written before ca. 499, e.g., use 913.85049 for Pausanias' guide to Attica written ca. 130. Use the corresponding number in 914–919 for modern guidebooks to ancient areas, e.g., a 2003 guide to the ruins of Rome 914.56320493.

A guidebook that is limited to an aspect of the trip is classed with that aspect, e.g., a guide to London's underground rail system 388.42809421, restaurants of Hawaii 647.95969, lodgings for tourists in London 914.2106, bed and breakfast establishments of London 914.21064. In addition, guidebooks emphasizing a specific subject are classed with the subject, e.g., a guidebook to holy places in Spain 263.04246, a skiing guide to Aspen, Colorado 796.930978843. (For guidebooks to historic sites and buildings, see the discussion in the section above, Historic sites and buildings.)

Use the number for the attraction in 001–999 for a guidebook to a locality that is usually visited for only one type of attraction. For example, most people go to Orlando, Florida, in order to visit its theme parks: Walt Disney World, Sea World of Florida, and Universal Studios Florida. Therefore, use 791.06875924 for both guidebooks to the theme parks and to Orlando in general. However, use 913–919, plus notation 04 from the table at 913–919, for a guidebook that covers more than one locality, e.g., a guide to central Florida that covers not only Orlando but also Cape Canaveral, Daytona Beach, and Tampa 917.59204.

See also discussion at 333.7–.9 vs. 508, 913–919, 930–990; also at 913–919 vs. 796.51.

Biography

Add notation 092 from Table 1 to subdivisions 041–049 for biographies of discoverers, explorers, and travelers, but not for general geographers nor for first-person accounts of travel. Use the area without further subdivision for biographies of general geographers. Use subdivisions 041–049 for first-person accounts of travel, but do not add notation 092.

913–919 vs. 796.51

Walkers' guides

Walkers' guides can be written for either the hiker or the tourist. Both types of guides give detailed instructions on how to get from point A to point B, e.g., at the fork turn left, and a general description of the route to help the walker to choose one route over another, such as distance, what can be seen. Guides for the tourist also give detailed description of things en route, e.g., the type of vegetation, the history of the wayside shrine. Use 913–919, plus notation 04 from the table at 913–919, for guides for the tourist and for walking guides to an urban area, e.g., walking guides to San Francisco 917.946104. Use 796.51 for guides for the hiker in non-urban areas. If in doubt, prefer 913–919.

Use 001–999 for a guide limited to one topic, e.g., a walker's guide to the geology of Yosemite National Park 557.9447, a walking tour of the skyscrapers of San Francisco 720.4830979461.

920.008 vs. 305–306, 362

History and description of biography as a discipline with respect to kinds of persons; general collections of biography by kind of person vs. Social groups and social welfare problems and services

Use 920.008 for collected biographies of a social group. However, use 305 or 306, plus notation 0922 from Table 1, for biographies that focus on the sociological aspects of the group. Use 362, plus notation 0922 from Table 1, for biographies that focus on the social problems of a group and their solutions. If in doubt, prefer 920.008.

For example, use 920.0086642 for a collection of biographies of gay men. However, use 306.76620922 if the biographies focus on these men as leaders in the gay-rights movements and or on other sociological aspects. Use 920.00871 for a collection of biographies of famous persons who are blind. However, use 362.410922 if the biographies focus on the problems of being blind and social services provided.

Apply the same policy for collected biographies of members of a specific ethnic or national group; however, use 920.0092 (*not* 920.0089). Apply the same policy also for collected biographies of men and of women; however, use 920.71 and 920.72, respectively (*not* 920.0081 or 920.0082).

920.009, 920.03–.09 vs. 909.09, 909.1–.8, 930–990

Biography vs. History

Use 920.009 and 920.03–.09 for collected biographies that contain both (a) biographies of historians and public figures who had a significant impact upon the general history of the place or time and (b) biographies of other public figures and/or biographies of persons of various occupations. Use 909.09, 909.1–.8, and 930–990 for collected biographies limited to biographies of historians and public figures who had a significant impact upon the general history of the place or time. For example, use 920.009033 for a collected biography of the famous persons of the 18th century that includes not only biographies of the kings and queens but also biographies of the bishops, scientists, artists, and athletes; 920.04 for a similar biography limited to Europe; and 920.044 for one limited to France. However, use 909.70922 for a collected biography of the heads of state of the 18th century; 940.099 for a collected biography of the kings and queens of Europe; and 944.0099 for a collected biography of the kings and queens of France. If in doubt, prefer 920.009 and 920.03–.09.

929.2

Family histories

Do not use numbers that are too specific for family histories, since families disperse from their place of origin. Use the area number for the country in which the family lives, not for the state, province, or smaller area, e.g., the history of a Florida family 929.20973 (*not* 929.209759). Treat England, Scotland, Wales, and Northern Ireland as separate countries.

Class a family history with the country in which the family presently lives, not with the country from which the family's ancestors came, e.g., the Duponts, a United States family of French origin, 929.20973 (*not* 929.20944).

Class family histories that give historical information about the area in which the family is located with the history of the area, e.g., prominent families in New York City 974.71.

930–990

History of ancient world; of specific continents, countries, localities; of extraterrestrial worlds

Wars

In most instances, use the number for the history of the country or region in which most of the fighting took place for the history of a war, e.g., the Napoleonic wars 940.27, the Vietnam War 959.7043, the 1982 Falkland Islands War 997.11024. However, use the number for the region where the war began or the history of one of the principal participants for some wars. For example, class World War II with European history (the area where the war began) in 940.53 (*not* with world history in 909.824); class the Spanish-American War with United States history in 973.89. Class a war with the history of the country as a whole, even when it was fought within a limited portion of a country, e.g., the Second Seminole War, which was fought against the Seminole Indians in Florida, 973.57 (*not* 975.904).

Use the number for the war, not the number for the place where the action occurred, for specific battles or actions of a war, e.g., a battle occurring in the Philippines during the Spanish-American War 973.8937 (*not* 959.9031); air raids on Tokyo in World War II 940.5425 (*not* 952.135033).

Two kinds of wartime history are not classed in the war numbers (unless the number for the area covered coincides with the number for the war). Use the number for the area for routine history of the everyday events of an area, even if during wartime, e.g., the history of Maryland during the Civil War 975.203 (*not* 973.709752). Use the number for the history of a place for the effect of military action on the everyday life and civilization of the place, e.g., the effect of Civil War military actions on Maryland 975.203 (*not* 973.709752). However, use the war number for the participation of an area in that war, e.g., Maryland's participation in the Civil War 973.709752 (*not* 975.203). Use the war number for national histories covering a time of war that emphasize the country's participation, e.g., British participation in World War II 940.5341. However, use the nation's history number if there is no such emphasis, e.g., a history of Britain during George VI's reign 941.084.

See also discussion at 333.7–.9 vs. 508, 913–919, 930–990; also at 930–990 vs. 355.009, 355–359.

Wars: Occupied countries

Use the war number for the history of the occupation of a country during time of war, e.g., occupation of countries in World War II 940.5336. Use 355.49 for military administration of the government of an occupied country during or following the war. Use 341.66 for international law concerning occupation.

Wars: Military units

Use the numbers for military units under history of the particular war for the history of specific military units in that war, e.g., military units in World War I 940.412–.413. Use the number for military operations if there is no specific number for military units, e.g., military units in the Vietnam War 959.70434.

Use 355.3 (or similar numbers in 355–359, e.g., 358.4131, 359.31, 359.933) for comprehensive works on specific military units and for military units in peacetime.

Wars: Personal narratives

Class personal narratives of participants in a war in the appropriate subdivision of the history numbers for the specific war, e.g., personal narratives of American soldiers in World War II 940.548173. Class narratives that focus on a specific campaign, battle, or other subject with the subject, e.g., a personal account of the Battle of Berlin 940.54213155092, of Axis intelligence operations in World War II 940.5487092.

Class the narrative of a person's experiences during time of war, if it does not focus on the war as such, as biography and not in the number for the war, e.g., an actor's personal experiences of performing during 1940–1942 in Scotland 792.092 (*not* 940.53088792092).

See also discussion at 930–990: Biography; also at 930–990 vs. 355.009, 355–359.

Historic preservation

Use 363.69 for comprehensive works on historic preservation and lists of preservation projects to be undertaken. However, use 930–990 if the list is primarily devoted to inventorying or describing the sites; use 720 if the list is primarily a description of buildings at the site.

Use 353.77 for administrative annual reports of agencies promoting the preservation of historical sites.

Use 720.288 (or numbers in 721–729, plus notation 0288 from Table 1) for works on historic preservation in an architectural context.

See also discussion at 333.7–.9 vs. 508, 913–919, 930–990.

Biography

Add notation 092 from Table 1 to subdivisions 01–09 for biographies of persons who lived during the historical period and also for biographies of historians and historiographers of that period, e.g., biographies of Abraham Lincoln and of Bruce Catton, Civil War historian, 973.7092. Add notation 092 even if the life span of the person or the time during which the person impacted upon the history of the country or locality does not approximate the whole of the period, e.g., biography of Rajiv Gandhi 954.052092. Use subdivision 0099 (which is limited to collected treatment) *only* for works not limited to a specific period, e.g., biographies of the kings and queens of Great Britain 941.0099. If subdivisions 01–09 for historical periods are not given in the schedule, do not add subdivision 0099 either for collected biographies limited to a specific period or for individual biographies, e.g., biographies of the 20th-century princes and princesses of Monaco and a biography of Grace, Princess of Monaco 944.949 (*not* 944.9490099). However, add subdivision 0099 for collected biographies *not* limited to a specific period, e.g., biographies of the princes and princesses of Monaco 944.9490099. Use subdivision 007202 for biographies of historians and historiographers whose works are not limited to a specific period, e.g., biographies of historians of British history 941.007202.

See also discussion at T1—092: Comprehensive biography: Public figures; also at 920.009, 920.03–.09 vs. 909.09, 909.1–.8, 930–990.

Add table

The following flow chart is offered as an aid to building numbers and as a supplement to the detailed instructions at 930–990.

Flow chart for history

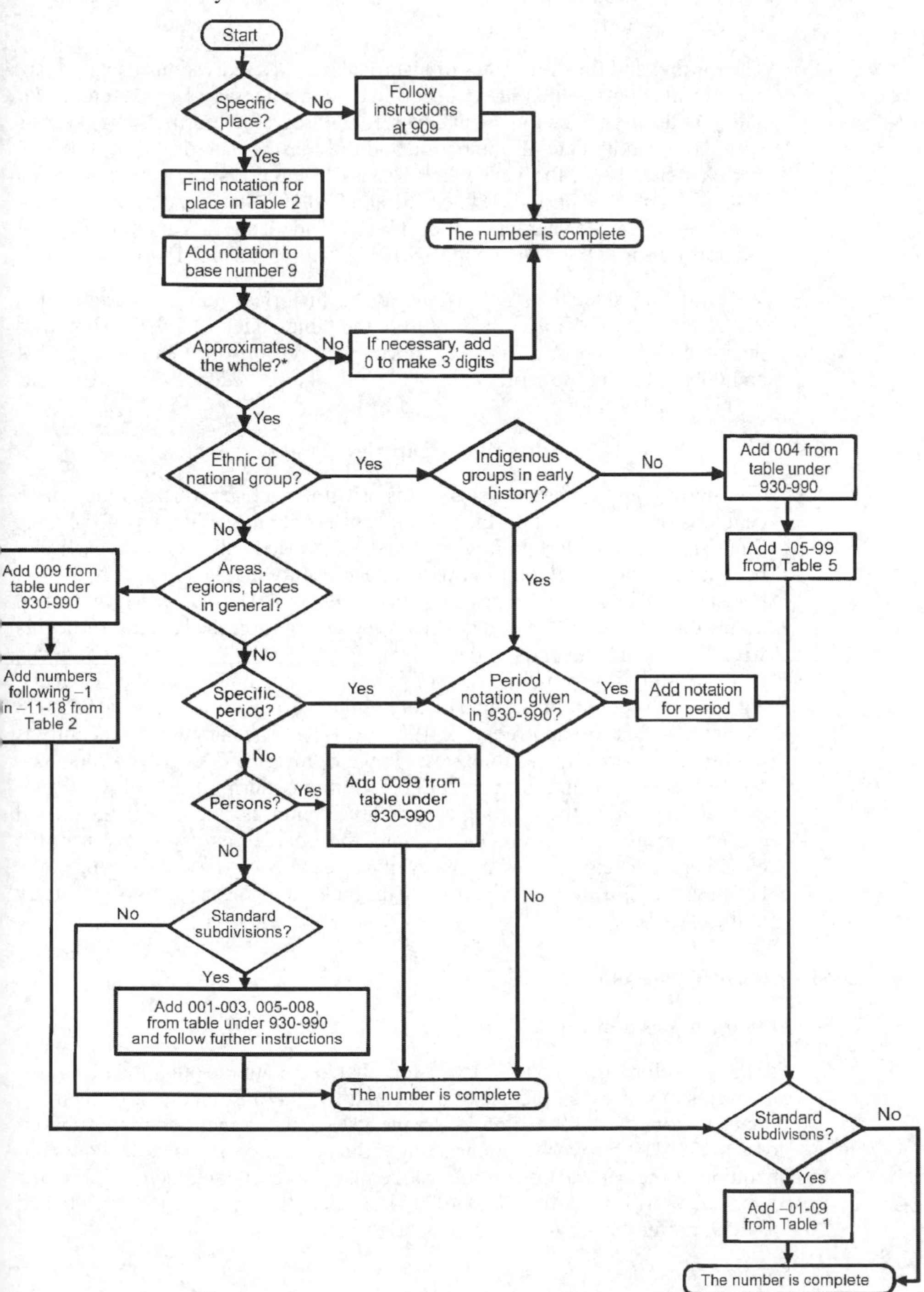

*See also Introduction and Glossary for information about "Approximates the whole"

01–09

Historical periods

The starting and finishing dates of historical period subdivisions usually mark significant events, which rarely occurred on either January 1 or December 31. The year during which the event occurred will therefore normally be given as both the finishing date of one period and the starting date of the next period. For example, 1861, the year when Kansas became a state, appears at both 978.102 Territorial period, 1803–1861 and 978.103 Statehood period, 1861–. Similarly, 1945, the year when World War II ended, appears at both 978.1032 [Kansas during] 1918–1945 and 978.1033 [Kansas during] 1945–.

When adding standard subdivisions to the historical periods, use notation 01–09 from Table 1 (*not* 001–009 from the table under 930–990). However, do not use T1—089 and T1—091, since the provisions for them given at 004 and 0091–0098 in the table under 930–990 take precedence over provisions for historical periods.

Add table: Centuries

The starting and finishing dates of historical period subdivisions may mark centuries or decades rather than significant events in the history of the area. Since such periods start on January 1 and end on December 31, the year either beginning or ending the period will appear in only one heading, e.g., 978.02 [Western United States during] 1800–1899 and 978.03 [Western United States during] 1900–. (The DDC uses the convention that a century begins with the year 00 and ends with the year 99.) In 940–990, the name for a particular century is given if the span of years in the heading is less than 75 years, e.g., the 15th century in German history is given in a class-here note at 943.028 Reigns of Albert II and Frederick III, 1438–1493. The name for the century is not usually given if the span of years in the heading is 75 or more years, e.g., the 17th century is not given at 943.04 [Germany during] 1618–1705. However, if the span in the heading covers three centuries, and the first and third century are given in the including note, the middle century is given in the class-here note, e.g., the 947.03 entry of Russian history has 1240–1462 in the heading, the 13th and 15th centuries in the including note, and the 14th century in the class here note.

930–990 vs. 355.009, 355–359

Military topics and war

Use 930–990 for works on military history that deal with the outcome of significant events in wars, e.g., the use of tanks on the Eastern Front and how their use affected various battles 940.54217. Use the historical treatment standard subdivisions in 355–359 for works emphasizing military history or topics without consideration of the general course of a war, e.g., changes in tank tactics during the course of World War II 358.18409044. If in doubt between 930–990 and 355–359, prefer 930–990.

See also discussion at 930–990: Wars.

Persons

Use 930–990 for comprehensive works on soldiers chiefly associated with the history of a specific war, e.g., William Tecumseh Sherman 973.73092. Use 355.0092 for comprehensive works on soldiers associated with more than one war, or who had long and varied careers, e.g., Douglas MacArthur. If in doubt, prefer 930–990.

941

History of the British Isles

Use 941 for works on the United Kingdom (England, Wales, Scotland, and Northern Ireland), a political entity, and on Great Britain (England, Wales, and Scotland), a geographic entity. Use 942 only for works dealing with England alone, or with England and Wales. Histories of the period since 1603 (or including this period) will seldom deal with England or England and Wales alone. Histories of the period before 1603 may deal with England or England and Wales alone. Works on the civilization of this area may deal with any combination. Use 941 for the following combinations of two areas: England and Scotland, England and Ireland, Ireland and Wales.

Tables

Table 1. Standard Subdivisions

The following notation is never used alone, but may be used as required with any regular schedule number, e.g., workbooks (—076 in this table) in arithmetic (513): 513.076. When adding to a number from the schedules, always insert a decimal point between the third and fourth digits of the complete number. (Full instructions on the use of standard subdivisions are found in the Introduction to the Dewey Decimal Classification)

Standard subdivisions should be added only when the work in hand covers the whole, or approximately the whole, subject of the number in the schedules

When standard subdivision notation from Table 1 is listed in Tables 2 through 6 and in the schedules, all of its subdivisions as given in this table may be used. Other Table 1 notation that is not listed in the schedules may also be used. For example, the fact that 610.7 is listed does not exclude the use of 610.71 or 610.8

Do not add one standard subdivision to another standard subdivision unless specially instructed. Numbers in the schedules that look as though they were built with notation from this table but have headings with a broader or different meanings are not considered "standard" subdivisions. Hence notation from Table 1 may be added to such schedule numbers

If the 0 subdivisions of a number in a schedule are used for special purposes, use 001–009 for standard subdivisions; if the 00 subdivisions also are used for special purposes, use 0001–0009 for standard subdivisions

(continued)

Table 1. Standard Subdivisions (continued)

Unless other instructions are given, observe the following table of preference, e.g., language and communication in education and research —07 (*not* —014):

Special topics	—04
Persons	—092
Auxiliary techniques and procedures; apparatus, equipment, materials	—028
Education, research, related topics (*except* —074, —075)	—07
Management	—068
Philosophy and theory	—01
The subject as a profession, occupation, hobby	—023
The subject for persons in specific occupations	—024
Directories of persons and organizations	—025
Patents and identification marks	—027
Commercial miscellany	—029
Organizations	—0601–0609
Organizations (without subdivision)	—06
History and description with respect to kinds of persons	—08
Treatment by specific continents, countries, localities; extraterrestrial worlds	—093–099
Treatment by areas, regions, places in general	—091
Maintenance and repair	—0288
Historical periods	—0901–0905
Forecasting and forecasts	—0112
Museums, collections, exhibits	—074
Museum activities and services Collecting	—075
Review and exercise	—076
Programmed texts	—077
Illustrations, models, miniatures	—022
Tabulated and related materials	—021
Synopses and outlines	—0202
Humorous treatment	—0207
Audiovisual treatment	—0208
Language and communication	—014
Dictionaries, encyclopedias, concordances	—03
Historical and geographic treatment (without subdivision)	—09
Serial publications	—05

SUMMARY

— 01	**Philosophy and theory**
— 02	**Miscellany**
— 03	**Dictionaries, encyclopedias, concordances**
— 04	**Special topics**
— 05	**Serial publications**
— 06	**Organizations and management**
— 07	**Education, research, related topics**
— 08	**History and description with respect to kinds of persons**
— 09	**Historical, geographic, persons treatment**

—01 Philosophy and theory

Including value

Class here methodology, schools of thought

Class interdisciplinary works on philosophy in 100

See Manual at T1—01

—011 Systems

Class here models (simulation), operations research

Add to base number —011 the numbers following 003 in 003.1–003.8, e.g., computer modeling and simulation —0113, forecasting and forecasts —0112; however, for short term forecasts (ten years or less) in a specific historical period, see —0901–0905, plus notation 01 from table under —0901–0905, e.g., forecasts for 2000–2010 —09051101; for forecasts in a specific continent, country, locality, see —093–099, plus notation 01 from table under —093–099, e.g., forecasts for United States —097301

Class models (simulations) in study and teaching in —078

See Manual at 510, T1—0151 vs. 003, T1—011

—012 Classification

Class classification of bibliographic material in 025.42; class classification of bibliographic material on a specific subject in 025.46; class interdisciplinary works on classification in 001.012

—[013] Value

Number discontinued; class in —01

—014 Language and communication

Including content analysis, semiotics; etymology; pronunciation, spelling

Class here terminology

Class subject headings and thesauri in information retrieval in 025.49001–025.49999; class interdisciplinary works on communication, semiotics in 302.2; class interdisciplinary works on language in 400; class interdisciplinary works on terminology in 401.4; class interdisciplinary works on etymology in 412. Class aspects of linguistics not provided for here with the aspect in 400, e.g., translating 418.02; class readers for nonnative speakers of a specific language intended to instill a knowledge of the special vocabulary of that language for a specific subject or discipline with the language in 400, plus notation 864 from Table 4, e.g., engineering readers (in a language other than Spanish) for Spanish-speaking people —8646102462, English-language engineering readers for Spanish-speaking people 428.646102462

For dictionaries, see —03

—[014 2] Etymology

Number discontinued; class in —014

—014 8 Abbreviations and symbols

Symbols classed here are limited to conventional or standard signs such as those used in mathematics, chemistry, flow charts, circuit diagrams, maps, road signs

Including acronym dictionaries

Class interdisciplinary works on symbols in 302.2223; class interdisciplinary works on abbreviations in 411; class interdisciplinary dictionaries of abbreviations in 413.1

—015 Scientific principles

Use of science to analyze and describe the subject, to support or attack its validity, to carry out operations in the subject, to provide information needed in a subject

Add to base number —015 the numbers following 5 in 510–590, e.g., mathematics —0151, meteorology —015515

Class scientific method in —072; class statistical methods in —0727; class interdisciplinary works on natural sciences and mathematics in 500

For psychological principles, see —019

See Manual at T1—015 vs. T1—0245–0246; also at 510, T1—0151 vs. 003, T1—011; also at 510, T1—0151 vs. 004–006, T1—0285; also at 519.5, T1—015195 vs. 001.422, T1—0727

—(016) Bibliographies, catalogs, indexes

(Optional number; prefer 016)

—019 Psychological principles

Use for applications of individual psychology only, not for applications of social psychology

Including psychology of learning specific subjects

Class social psychology in 302; class psychology of learning a specific subject at elementary level in 372.3–372.8; class interdisciplinary works on psychology in 150

See Manual at 302–307 vs. 150, T1—019

—02 Miscellany

SUMMARY

— 020 2–020 8 [Synopses and outlines, humorous treatment, audiovisual treatment]
— 021 Tabulated and related materials
— 022 Illustrations, models, miniatures
— 023 The subject as a profession, occupation, hobby
— 024 The subject for persons in specific occupations
— 025 Directories of persons and organizations
— 027 Patents and identification marks
— 028 Auxiliary techniques and procedures; apparatus, equipment, materials
— 029 Commercial miscellany

—020 2 Synopses and outlines

Including chronologies

Class works called synopses and outlines that are regular treatises or introductions to a subject in 001–999 without use of notation 0202 from Table 1; class interdisciplinary chronologies in 902.02

—020 7 Humorous treatment

See Manual at T1—0207 vs. T3B—7, T3A—8 + 02, T3B—802, T3B—8 + 02, T3A—8 + 07, T3B—807, T3B—8 + 07

—020 8 Audiovisual treatment

—021 Tabulated and related materials

Including statistics, statistical graphs

Class interdisciplinary collections of statistics in 310

See also —0727 for analysis of statistical data; also —0728 for methods of presenting statistical data

—021 2 Formulas and specifications

Class here tables of values for use in formulas and specifications

—021 6 Lists, inventories, catalogs

Not provided for elsewhere

Class directories of persons and organizations in —025; class lists and catalogs of products and services offered for sale, lease, or free distribution in —029; class catalogs of collections and exhibits in —074; class price trends for collectors in —075; class bibliographic catalogs on specific subjects in 016; class directories of databases on specific subjects in 016.02506

—021 8 Standards

Add to base number —0218 notation 1–9 from Table 2, e.g., standards in Israel —02185694; however, for persons treatment, see —092

Class interdisciplinary works on standardization in 389.6; class interdisciplinary collections of standards in 602.18

For specifications, see —0212

—022 Illustrations, models, miniatures

Including graphs

Class statistical graphs in —021

—[022 1] Drafting illustrations

Provision discontinued because without meaning in context

—022 2 Pictures and related illustrations

Class here cartoons, drawings, pictorial charts and designs, sketches

Class interdisciplinary works on cartoons in 741.5

For humorous cartoons, see —0207

See Manual at T1—0222 vs. T1—0223

—022 3 Maps, plans, diagrams

Class comprehensive works on historical maps and atlases in 911; class interdisciplinary works on maps, plans, diagrams; on maps, plans, diagrams of geography, travel, and roads in general and in specific areas in 912

See Manual at T1—0222 vs. T1—0223

—022 8 Models and miniatures

Class simulation models in —011; class model and miniature educational exhibits in —074; class interdisciplinary works in 688.1

—023 The subject as a profession, occupation, hobby

Class here vocational guidance, choice of vocation, career opportunities, occupational specialties, professional relationships; the subject as a profession, occupation, hobby for specific kinds of persons

Add to base number —023 notation 1–9 from Table 2, e.g., the subject as a profession in Great Britain —02341; however, for persons treatment, see —092

Class interdisciplinary works on professional relationships in 331.7; class interdisciplinary works on vocational guidance, choice of vocation, career opportunities, occupational specialties in 331.702; class interdisciplinary works on hobbies in 790.13

—024 The subject for persons in specific occupations

Add to base number —024 notation 001–999, e.g., the subject for engineers —02462

Notation 001–999 replaces notation 09–99 from Table 7 with the result that many numbers have been reused with new meanings

See Manual at T1—024; also at T1—015 vs. T1—0245–0246

—025 Directories of persons and organizations

Class here directories of public officials and employees; membership lists containing directory information, e.g., employment and education

Add to base number —025 notation 1–9 from Table 2, e.g., directories of Ohio —025771; however, for persons treatment, see —092

Class directories giving biographical information in —0922

See also —029 for directories of products and services; also 016.02506 for directories of databases on specific subjects

See Manual at T1—025 vs. T1—029; also at T1—025 vs. T1—0601–0609

—(026) Law

(Optional number; prefer 341–347)

Add to base number —026 notation 1–9 from Table 2, e.g., law of Australia —02694; however, for persons treatment, see —092

A special development of —026 covering treaties and cases in law of nations is given in centered entry at 341.2–341.7 for use with Subdivisions in 341.2–341.7; another special development of —026 covering laws, regulations, cases, procedures, courts in the rest of law is given in centered entry at 342–347 for use with subdivisions in 342–347

—027 Patents and identification marks

—027 2 Patents

Add to base number —0272 notation 1–9 from Table 2, e.g., patents of Japan —027252; however, for persons treatment, see —092

Class interdisciplinary works on patents in 346.0486; class interdisciplinary collections of patents in 608

> —027 5–027 8 Identification marks

Class comprehensive works in —027

—027 5 Trademarks and service marks

Class comprehensive works on trademarks generally found on products rather than identifying services in 602.75; class interdisciplinary works on trademarks and service marks in 929.95

—027 7 Ownership marks

—027 8 Artists' and craftsmen's marks

Class interdisciplinary works in 700.278

—028 Auxiliary techniques and procedures; apparatus, equipment, materials

—028 4 Apparatus, equipment, materials

Limited to apparatus, equipment, materials used in a subject

Class here instruments, instrumentation

Class apparatus, equipment, materials used in a specific auxiliary technique or procedure in —0285–0289; class collectibles, memorabilia in —075; class use of apparatus and equipment in study and teaching in —078; class products of a subject in 001–999 without adding notation 0284 from Table 1

> —028 5–028 9 Auxiliary techniques and procedures

Class laboratory manuals in —078; class comprehensive works in —028

For research techniques, statistical methods, see —072

—028 5 Data processing Computer applications

Class here data processing in research

Unless it is redundant, add to base number —0285 the numbers following 00 in 004–006, e.g., digital microcomputers —0285416, but digital computers —0285 (*not* —02854)

Class computer modeling and simulation in —0113; class interdisciplinary works on data processing in 004

See Manual at T1—0285; also at 510, T1—0151 vs. 004–006, T1—0285

—028 6 Waste technology

Class here environmental engineering, pollution control technology

Class interdisciplinary works on environmental engineering in 628; class interdisciplinary works on waste technology in 628.4; class interdisciplinary works on pollution control technology in 628.5

—028 7 Testing and measurement

Use this subdivision only with numbers denoting fabrication, manufacture, construction, installation, not with numbers denoting use, operation, or application when these are different, e.g., testing and measurement of textile manufacturing machinery 681.76770287 (*not* 677.02850287), of tools 621.900287

Class here laboratory manuals for testing, mensuration

Class aptitude tests in a specific field in 153.94; class technology of testing and measuring instruments in 681.2; class interdisciplinary works on measurement and mensuration in 530.8

For educational testing, see —076

—028 8 Maintenance and repair

Use this subdivision only with numbers denoting fabrication, manufacture, construction, installation, not with numbers denoting use, operation, or application when these are different, e.g., maintenance and repair of textile manufacturing machinery 681.76770288 (*not* 677.02850288), of tools 621.900288

Class here conservation, preservation, restoration

Class conservation in the sense of environmental engineering and waste technology in —0286; class maintenance and repair in specific areas in —09; class interdisciplinary works on maintenance and repair in 620.0046; class interdisciplinary works on artistic conservation, preservation, restoration in 702.88

See also —0682 for management of maintenance

—028 9 Safety measures

Use only for personal safety and safety engineering

Class interdisciplinary works on safety in 363.1; class interdisciplinary works on personal safety in 613.6; class interdisciplinary works on safety engineering in 620.86

See Manual at 363.1

—029 Commercial miscellany

Including estimates of labor, time, materials; price trends

Class here listings of products and services offered for sale, lease, or free distribution

Class house organs in —05; class interdisciplinary commercial miscellany in 381.029; class noncurrent offers for sale used primarily to illustrate civilization and customs of an earlier period in 900

For price trends for collectors, see —075; for catalogs of bibliographic materials on specific subjects, see 016

See also —074 for listings of noncommercial collections and exhibits

See Manual at T1—025 vs. T1—029; also at T1—074 vs. T1—029

—029 1 Commercial miscellany of area, regions, places in general

Add to base number —0291 the numbers following —1 in notation 11–19 from Table 2, e.g., commercial miscellany of Western Hemisphere —0291812

—029 3 Commercial miscellany of the ancient world

Add to base number —0293 the numbers following —3 in notation 31–39 from Table 2, e.g., commercial miscellany of ancient Egypt —02932

—029 4 Commercial miscellany of Europe

Use of this number for trade catalogs and directories discontinued; class in —029

Add to base number —0294 the numbers following —4 in notation 41–49 from Table 2, e.g., commercial miscellany of England —02942

—029 5 Commercial miscellany of Asia

Add to base number —0295 the numbers following —5 in notation 51–59 from Table 2, e.g., commercial miscellany of Japan —02952

—029 6 Commercial miscellany of Africa

Use of this number for buyers' guides and consumer reports discontinued; class in —029

Add to base number —0296 the numbers following —6 in notation 61–69 from Table 2, e.g., commercial miscellany of Egypt —02962

—029 7 Commercial miscellany of North America

Use of this number for evaluation and purchasing manuals discontinued; class in —029

Add to base number —0297 the numbers following —7 in notation 71–79 from Table 2, e.g., commercial miscellany of Mexico —02972

—029 8 Commercial miscellany of South America

Add to base number —0298 the numbers following —8 in notation 81–89 from Table 2, e.g., commercial miscellany of Argentina —02982

—029 9 Commercial miscellany of other parts of world

Use of this number for estimates of labor, time, materials discontinued; class in —029

Add to base number —0299 the numbers following —9 in notation 93–99 from Table 2, e.g., commercial miscellany of New Zealand —02993

—03 Dictionaries, encyclopedias, concordances

Including thesauri (synonym dictionaries)

Class acronym dictionaries in —0148; class biographical dictionaries in —0922; class interdisciplinary encyclopedias in 030; class interdisciplinary dictionaries in 413

See also 025.49 for thesauri (controlled vocabularies)

—04 Special topics

Use this subdivision only when it is specifically set forth in the schedules. Add other standard subdivisions —01–09 to it and its subdivisions as required, e.g., participatory democracy in France 323.0420944

—05 Serial publications

Regardless of form (print or electronic) or frequency

Class here house organs, magazines, newspapers, yearbooks

Class monographic series in 001–999 without adding notation 05 from Table 1; class interdisciplinary serial publications in 050; class interdisciplinary newspapers in 071–079

For a special kind of serial publication, see the kind, e.g., directories in serial form —025, administrative reports of organizations —06

—06 Organizations and management

> —060 1–060 9 Organizations

Class here Greek-letter societies, student organizations; history, charters, regulations, membership lists, administrative reports

Class directories of organizations, membership lists with directory information in —025; class organizations engaged in education, research, related topics in —07; class business enterprises in 338.7; class government administrative and military organizations in 350; class nonadministrative proceedings and reports in 001–999 without adding notation 06 from Table 1; class comprehensive works on organizations active in a subject in —06; class interdisciplinary works on organizations in 060

See Manual at T1—0601–0609; also at T1—025 vs. T1—0601–0609; also at T1—072 vs. T1—0601–0609

—060 1 International organizations

Class guides to national organizations of the world in —06

—060 3–060 9 National, state, provincial, local organizations

Add to base number —060 notation 3–9 from Table 2, e.g., national organizations in France —06044

—068 Management

Class management in the sense of carrying out ordinary activities of a subject in 001–999 without adding notation 068 from Table 1, e.g., management of patients 616 (*not* 616.0068); class interdisciplinary works in 658

See Manual at T1—068; also at T1—068 vs. 353–354

(Option: Class management of specific enterprises in 658.9)

—068 1 Organization and financial management

Including fund raising, initiation of business enterprises

For internal organization, see —0684

See also —079 for fund raising for competitions, festivals, awards, financial support

—068 2 Plant management

Including equipment and utilities; maintenance

Class here comprehensive works on energy management

For a specific aspect of energy management, see the aspect, e.g., energy conservation in production management —0685

See also —0288 for technology of maintenance

See Manual at 647 vs. 647.068, 658.2, T1—0682

—068 3 Personnel management (Human resource management)

Including management of fringe benefits, of in-service training and residency, of wages and salaries

Class comprehensive works on in-service training and residency in —07155; class interdisciplinary works on labor relations in 331.88

For management of executive personnel, see —0684

See also 331.21 for wages; also 331.255 for fringe benefits

—068 4 Executive management

Including contracting out, internal organization, safety management

For contracting out a specific activity in management, see the activity, e.g., contracting out financial management —0681; for a specific aspect of safety management, see the aspect, e.g., personnel safety —0683

—068 5 Management of production

Class factory operations engineering in 670.42

—068 7 Management of materials

Including physical distribution, procurement of office equipment

See also —029 for evaluation and purchasing manuals

—068 8 Management of distribution (Marketing)

Including market research, personal selling

Class financial aspects of marketing management in —0681; class results of market research in 381

For physical distribution, see —0687; for advertising, see 659.1

—07 Education, research, related topics

Including programmed texts

Class here subject-oriented study programs; comprehensive works on education and research, on resources for education and research

Class psychology of learning specific subjects in —019

For a specific resource not provided for here, see the resource, e.g., directories —025, bibliographies 016, libraries 026

See Manual at 016 vs. 026, T1—07

SUMMARY

—070 1–070 9 Geographic treatment

Add to base number —070 notation 1–9 from Table 2, e.g., education and research in France —07044

—071 Education

Class here curricula, study (education), teaching, vocational education

Class student organizations in —0601–0609; class religious education to inculcate religious faith and values in 207.5 (*not* 200.71); class religious education to inculcate Christian faith and values in 268 (*not* 230.071); class textbooks, school activities in a subject in 001–999 without adding notation 071 from Table 1; class comprehensive works on education and research in —07; class interdisciplinary works on education in 370; class interdisciplinary works on teaching in 371.102

For review and exercise, see —076; for use of apparatus and equipment in education, see —078; for competitions, festivals, awards, financial support in education, see —079; for special education in specific subjects, see 371.9

See Manual at 407.1, T1—071 vs. 401.93, T4—019, 410.71, 418.0071, T4—80071

—071 01–071 09 Geographic treatment

Class here treatment of any two levels of education, e.g., secondary and higher education

Add to base number —0710 notation 1–9 from Table 2, e.g., education in Argentina —071082

> —071 1–071 5 Specific levels of education

Class comprehensive works in —071

For education in specific subjects at elementary level, see 372.3–372.8

—071 1 Higher education

Class here professional education

Add to base number —0711 notation 1–9 from Table 2, e.g., universities in Japan —071152; however, for persons treatment, see —092

For extension departments and services, see —0715

—071 2 Secondary education

Add to base number —0712 notation 1–9 from Table 2, e.g., secondary schools in rural regions —07121734; however, for persons treatment, see —092

—071 5 Adult education and on-the-job training

Class here continuing, further, lifelong, permanent, recurrent education; correspondence schools and courses, distance education; extension departments and services; institutes and workshops; occupational and vocational training; radio and television classes

—071 55 On-the-job training

Class here apprenticeship, in-service training, residency

Class management of on-the-job training by employers in —0683; class interdisciplinary works in 331.2592

—072 Research; statistical methods

Class here laboratory manuals used in research, research and scientific techniques not provided for elsewhere in Table 1, comprehensive works on scientific method

Class operations research in —011; class financial support of research in —079; class results of research in 001–999 without adding notation 072 from Table 1; class interdisciplinary works on research in 001.4

For scientific method used in systems analysis, see —011. For a specific research or scientific technique provided for elsewhere in Table 1, see the technique, e.g., mathematical techniques —0151, data processing —0285, testing —0287

See Manual at T1—072 vs. T1—0601–0609

—072 01–072 09 Geographic treatment of research and statistical methods together, of research alone

Add to base number —0720 notation 1–9 from Table 2, e.g., research in England —072042

See Manual at T1—07201–07209 vs. T1—0722–0724

> —072 2–072 4 Specific kinds of research

Avoid notation for a specific kind of research when it is redundant, e.g., historical research in history 907.2 (*not* 907.22)

Class statistical methods used in specific kinds of research in —0727; class comprehensive works in —072

See Manual at T1—07201–07209 vs. T1—0722–0724

—072 2 Historical research

Including use of case studies

Class here historiography

It is redundant to use the final digit of —0722 in history (900); stop at —072, e.g., historical research in European history 940.072

Class interdisciplinary works on historical research in 001.432; class interdisciplinary works on historiography in 907.2

—072 3 Descriptive research

Including sampling techniques

Class here data collection, surveys and survey methodology

Class management of information collection in —0684; class collection of operational data in 001–999 without adding notation 0723 from Table 1; class interdisciplinary works on data collection in research in 001.433

For analysis of statistical data, see —0727; for presentation of statistical data, see —0728

See also —075 for collection of objects

—072 4 Experimental research

Class models (simulation) in —011

—072 7 Statistical methods

Class statistical methods used in systems analysis in —011; class interdisciplinary works on statistical methods in 001.422

For data collection, see —0723; for presentation of statistical data, see —0728

See also —021 for works containing the statistics themselves

See Manual at 519.5, T1—015195 vs. 001.422, T1—0727

—072 8 Presentation of statistical data

Class here graphic presentation

Class the statistics themselves (no matter how presented) in —021

—074 Museums, collections, exhibits

Class here exhibitions, fairs; catalogs, lists regardless of whether or not articles are offered for sale; guidebooks, history and description

Add to base number —074 notation 1–9 from Table 2 for the area in which museums, collections, exhibits are found, e.g., museums in Pennsylvania —074748

Class comprehensive works on museology of a subject in —075; class interdisciplinary works on museums, collections, exhibits in 069; class interdisciplinary works on exhibitions, fairs in 907.4

For collections of books and related informational materials in specific subjects, see 016. For collections representing a specific time period, see the period in —0901–0905, plus notation 074 from table under —0901–0905, e.g., collections from 19th century —09034074; for collections representing a specific kind of area, region, place, see the kind of area, region, place in —091, plus notation 074 from table under —093–099, e.g., collections from Mediterranean region —091822074; for treatment by area represented in the collections, see the area in —093–099, plus notation 074 from table under —093–099, e.g., collections of Brazilian objects —0981074, collections of Brazilian objects in Pennsylvania —0981074748

See Manual at T1—074 vs. T1—029

—075 Museum activities and services Collecting

Class here museology, collectibles, memorabilia, price trends for collectors

Class interdisciplinary works on museum activities and services in 069; class interdisciplinary works on museum collecting in 069.4; class interdisciplinary works on recreational collecting in 790.132

For activities and services of or relating to specific museums, collections, exhibits, see —074. For a specific museological technique not provided for here, see the technique in —028, e.g., maintenance and repair of collected objects —0288

—[075 3–075 5] Organizing and preparing collections and exhibits, service to patrons

Numbers discontinued; class in —075

—076 Review and exercise

Including workbooks with problems, questions, answers; civil service examinations; testing, test construction and evaluation

Class programmed texts with problems, questions, answers in —07; class interdisciplinary works on civil service examinations in 351.076; class interdisciplinary works on examinations and tests in 371.26

For review and exercise using apparatus and equipment, see —078

See also 153.94 for aptitude tests in a specific field

(Option: Class civil service examinations in specific subjects in 351.076)

—[077] Programmed texts

Number discontinued; class in —07

—078 Use of apparatus and equipment in study and teaching

Class here laboratory manuals, student projects and experiments

Class interdisciplinary works on teaching aids in 371.33

For laboratory manuals used in testing, see —0287; for laboratory manuals used in research, see —072

—078 5 Computer-assisted instruction

Unless it is redundant, add to base number —0785 the numbers following 00 in 004–006, e.g., use of digital microcomputers —0785416, but digital computers —0785 (*not* —07854); interactive video —078567

Class interdisciplinary works on computer-assisted instruction in 371.334

—079 Competitions, festivals, awards, financial support

Including fund raising to support such activities; judging competitions

Class here bursaries, fellowships and scholarships, grants, honorary titles, prizes

Add to base number —079 notation 4–9 from Table 2, e.g., competitions in California —079794

Subdivisions are added for any or all topics in heading

Class description of works that are entered into competitions and festivals, that receive awards, or that are the results of financial support in 001–999 without adding notation 079 from Table 1; class interdisciplinary works on awards in 929.81

See also —0681 for financial management aspects of fund raising

—08 History and description with respect to kinds of persons

Class here discrimination, minorities

Add to each subdivision identified by * as follows:

01	Forecasting and forecasts
02	Statistics and illustrations
021	Statistics
022	Illustrations
03	Dictionaries, encyclopedias, concordances
05	Serial publications
07	Museums and collecting
074	Museums, collections, exhibits Add to 074 notation 4–9 from Table 2, e.g., collections in Pennsylvania 074748
075	Collecting objects
09	Historical and geographic treatment Add to 09 notation 01–9 from Table 2, e.g., the kind of person in Japan 0952

If a standard subdivision is not given in the table above, do not add its notation to the kind of person in —081–089

Class ethnic and national minorities in —089; class treatment of specific kinds of persons as individuals in —092

See Manual at T1—08 and 306.2–306.6

SUMMARY

— 080 1–080 9	**Forecasting, statistics, illustrations, dictionaries, encyclopedias, concordances, serials, museums and collecting, historical and geographic treatment**
— 081	**Men**
— 082	**Women**
— 083	**Young people**
— 084	**Persons in specific stages of adulthood**
— 085	**Relatives Parents**
— 086	**Persons by miscellaneous social characteristics**
— 087	**Persons with disabilities and illnesses, gifted persons**
— 088	**Occupational and religious groups**
— 089	**Ethnic and national groups**

—080 1–080 9 Forecasting, statistics, illustrations, dictionaries, encyclopedias, concordances, serials, museums and collecting, historical and geographic treatment

Add to base number —080 the numbers following 0 in notation 01–09 from table under —08, e.g., statistics —08021

> —081–088 Miscellaneous specific kinds of persons

Unless other instructions are given, class a subject with aspects in two or more subdivisions of —081–088 in the number coming last, e.g., children with disabilities —087 (*not* —083)

Class comprehensive works in —08

—081 *Men

Class here males

See Manual at T1—081 and T1—082, T1—08351, T1—08352, T1—08421, T1—08422

—082 *Women

Class here females; feminist views of a subject, e.g., feminist Christian theology 230.082

For women with characteristics of another group (other than a specific ethnic or national group), see the group, e.g., unmarried mothers —086947, but Chinese women —082, not —089951

See Manual at T1—081 and T1—082, T1—08351, T1—08352, T1—08421, T1—08422

—083 *Young people

Class here children

For young people with characteristics of another group (other than a specific ethnic or national group), see the group, e.g., abandoned children, abused children, children born out of wedlock, orphans —086945, but Chinese children —083, not —089951

—083 2 *Infants

Children from birth through age two

—083 3 *Children three to five

Class here preschool children

—083 4 *Children six to eleven

Class here school children

For school children over eleven, see —0835

—083 41 *Boys six to eleven

—083 42 *Girls six to eleven

*Add as instructed under —08

—083 5 *Young people twelve to twenty

Variant names: adolescents, teenagers, young adults, youth

Class youth twenty-one and over, comprehensive works on young adults in —0842

—083 51 *Males twelve to twenty

See Manual at T1—081 and T1—082, T1—08351, T1—08352, T1—08421, T1—08422

—083 52 *Females twelve to twenty

See Manual at T1—081 and T1—082, T1—08351, T1—08352, T1—08421, T1—08422

—084 Persons in specific stages of adulthood

Class comprehensive works on adults in 001–999 without adding notation 084 from Table 1

—084 2 *Young adults

Aged twenty-one and above

Class here comprehensive works on young adults

For young adults under twenty-one, see —0835

—084 21 *Young men

See Manual at T1—081 and T1—082, T1—08351, T1—08352, T1—08421, T1—08422

—084 22 *Young women

See Manual at T1—081 and T1—082, T1—08351, T1—08352, T1—08421, T1—08422

—084 4 *Persons in middle adulthood

—084 6 *Persons in late adulthood

—085 *Relatives Parents

Class here adoptive and foster parents, stepparents

—085 1 *Fathers

—085 2 *Mothers

For unmarried mothers, see —086947

—085 3 *Grandparents

Including great grandparents of any degree (ancestors)

—085 4 *Progeny

Class here children considered in relation to parents

*Add as instructed under —08

—085 5 *Siblings

Brothers and sisters by blood, adoption, foster care, remarriage of parents

—086 *Persons by miscellaneous social characteristics

Not provided for elsewhere

—086 2 *Persons by social and economic levels

Class here social classes

Class groups with special social status in —0869

—086 21 *Upper classes

Including nobility, royalty, wealthy

Class here elites

For reigning monarchs and their regents, see —08835223

—086 22 *Middle classes (Bourgeoisie)

Including entrepreneurs, managers, professionals

Class here moderately well-to-do persons

For lower middle classes, see —08623

—086 23 *Lower middle classes

Class here moderate-income persons, working class in developed areas, blue collar workers

—086 24 *Lower classes

Including migrant workers, unskilled workers

Class blue collar workers in —08623; class peasants, sharecroppers in —08863

For slaves, serfs, peons, see —08625; for the poor, see —086942

—086 25 *Slaves, serfs, peons

—086 3 *Persons by level of cultural development

—086 31 *Persons of high cultural development

Class here intellectuals

—[086 32] Persons of medium cultural development

Number discontinued; class in —0863

—086 33 *Persons of low cultural development

Including nonliterate persons

Class here culturally disadvantaged persons

*Add as instructed under —08

—086 5 *Persons by marriage status

Including unmarried couples

—086 52 *Single persons

For separated and divorced persons, see —08653; for widowed persons, see —08654

—086 523 *Engaged persons

—086 53 *Separated and divorced persons

Subdivisions are added for either or both topics in heading

—086 54 *Widowed persons

—086 55 *Married persons

Including persons married in common law

For polygamous persons, see —08659

—086 59 *Polygamous persons

—086 6 *Persons by sexual orientation

Including persons with no sexual orientation, transsexuals

—086 62 *Heterosexuals

—086 63 *Bisexuals

—086 64 *Gays

—086 642 *Gay men

—086 643 *Lesbians

—086 9 *Persons with special social status

—086 91 *Persons with status defined by changes in residence

Class here aliens, expatriates, foreigners

Class migrant workers in —08624; class runaway children in —086923; class tramps in —086942; class persons of a specific ethnic or national group in —089

—086 912 *Immigrants

Class displaced persons, refugees in —086914

—086 914 *Displaced persons

Class here exiles, refugees

—086 918 *Nomads

*Add as instructed under —08

—086 92 *Antisocial and asocial persons

Subdivisions are added for either or both topics in heading

See also —086942 for tramps

—086 923 *Juvenile delinquents and predelinquents

Subdivisions are added for either or both topics in heading

—086 927 *Offenders

Class here convicts, criminals

Class juvenile delinquents in —086923

—086 93 *Nondominant groups

Class a specific nondominant group with the group, e.g., serfs —08625

—086 94 *Socially disadvantaged persons

Class here alienated and excluded classes

Class a specific kind of persons socially disadvantaged for a reason not provided for here with the kind, e.g., addicts in recovery —0874

—086 941 *Unemployed persons

Class poverty-stricken and destitute unemployed persons in —086942

—086 942 *The poor

Including homeless persons, tramps

—086 945 *Abandoned children, abused children, children of unmarried parents, orphans

See also —086923 for runaway children

—086 947 *Unmarried mothers

—086 949 *Victims of war and crime

Including inmates of concentration or internment camps

—086 96 *Retired persons

—086 97 *Veterans of military service

—087 *Persons with disabilities and illnesses, gifted persons

Including persons with learning disabilities

Class here persons with physical disabilities

*Add as instructed under —08

—087 1 *Persons with blindness and visual impairments

Class here persons who are blind-deaf

Subdivisions are added for either or both topics in heading

—087 2 *Persons with hearing impairments

Class here persons who are deaf

Class persons who are deaf-blind in —0871

—087 3 *Persons with mobility impairments

Class persons with mobility impairments resulting from developmental disabilities in —0875

—087 4 *Persons with mental illness and disabilities

Including addicts, addicts in recovery, alcoholics

—087 5 *Persons with developmental disabilities

Class persons with congenital visual disabilities in —0871; class persons with congenital hearing disabilities in —0872

For persons with mental developmental disabilities, see —0874

—087 7 *Shut-in persons (Housebound persons)

Class here persons with physical illnesses not provided for elsewhere, comprehensive works on persons with physical illnesses

Class a specific kind of shut-in persons with the kind, e.g., shut-in persons with developmental disabilities —0875

—087 9 *Gifted persons

—088 Occupational and religious groups

—088 001–088 999 Specific occupational and religious groups

Add to base number —088 notation 001–999, e.g., nondominant religious groups —0882, Catholic teachings on socioeconomic problems 261.8088282; however, forecasting, statistics, illustrations, serials, museums and collecting, historical and geographic treatment for comprehensive works on occupational and religious groups discontinued from —088001–088009 to —088

Notation 001–999 replaces notation 09–99 from Table 7 with the result that many numbers have been reused with new meanings

Class works on the subject for persons in specific occupations in —024

See Manual at T1—0882 and 200

*Add as instructed under —08

—089 Ethnic and national groups

Class here ethnic and national minorities; racial groups, racism

Class persons treatment (e.g., biography) of members of a specific ethnic or national group in —0923; class treatment with respect to specific ethnic and national groups in places where they predominate in —091–099. Class treatment with respect to miscellaneous specific kinds of persons of a specific ethnic or national group with the kind of person in —081–088, e.g., Chinese children —083

See Manual at T1—09 vs. T1—089

—089 001–089 009 Forecasting, statistics, illustrations, dictionaries, encyclopedias, concordances, serials, museology, historical and geographic treatment

Add to base number —08900 the numbers following 0 in notation 01–09 from table under —08, e.g., statistics —0890021

—089 05–089 9 Specific ethnic and national groups

Add to base number —089 notation 05–9 from Table 5, e.g., the subject with respect to Chinese —089951, with respect to Chinese in United States —089951073

—09 Historical, geographic, persons treatment

Class historiography in —0722; class historical and geographic treatment of museums, collections, exhibits representing the whole subject in —074; class historical and geographic treatment of museum activities and services representing the whole subject in —075

See Manual at T1—09; also at T1—0601–0609: Selection of area number; also at T1—09 vs. T1—089

SUMMARY

— 090 05 Serial publications
— 090 1–090 5 Historical periods
— 091 Treatment by areas, regions, places in general
— 092 Persons
— 093–099 Treatment by specific continents, countries, localities; extraterrestrial worlds

—090 05 Serial publications

> —090 1–090 5 Historical periods

Add to each subdivision identified by * as follows:

01 Short term forecasts
  Ten years or less
  Class long term forecasts (more than ten years) in —0112
02 Statistics and illustrations
021 Statistics
022 Illustrations
03 Dictionaries, encyclopedias, concordances
05 Serial publications
07 Museums, collections, exhibits; collecting objects
074 Museums, collections, exhibits
  Add to 074 notation 4–9 from Table 2, e.g., collections in Pennsylvania 074748, collections of ancient objects in Pennsylvania —0901074748
075 Collecting objects

If a standard subdivision is not given in the table above, do not add its notation to the historical period notation in —0901–0905

Class historical periods in specific areas, regions, places in general in —091; class historical periods in specific continents, countries, localities in —093–099; class comprehensive works in —09

See Manual at T1—0901–0905

—090 1 *To 499 A.D.

The ancient period when the coverage is not limited to areas provided for in —093

—090 12 *To 4000 B.C.

Class here comprehensive works on prehistoric periods

For a specific prehistoric period not provided for here, see the period, e.g., 3999–1000 B.C. —09013

—090 13 *3999–1000 B.C.

—090 14 *999–1 B.C.

—090 15 *1st-5th centuries, 1–499

—090 2 *6th–15th centuries, 500–1499

Class here Middle Ages (Medieval period)

See Manual at T1—0940902 vs. T1—0902

—090 21 *6th–12th centuries, 500–1199

*Add as instructed under —0901–0905

—090 22 *13th century, 1200–1299

—090 23 *14th century, 1300–1399

—090 24 *15th century, 1400–1499

—090 3 *Modern period, 1500–

For 20th century, see —0904; for 21st century, see —0905

—090 31 *16th century, 1500–1599

—090 32 *17th century, 1600–1699

—090 33 *18th century, 1700–1799

—090 34 *19th century, 1800–1899

—090 4 *20th century, 1900–1999

—090 41 *1900–1919

Class here early 20th century

For 1920–1929, see —09042; for 1930–1939, see —09043; for 1940–1949, see —09044

—090 42 *1920–1929

—090 43 *1930–1939

—090 44 *1940–1949

Class here period of World War II

For 1939, see —09043

—090 45 *1950–1959

Class here late 20th century, post World War II period

For 1945–1949, see —09044; for 1960–1969, see —09046; for 1970–1979, see —09047; for 1980–1989, see —09048; for 1990–1999, see —09049

—090 46 *1960–1969

—090 47 *1970–1979

—090 48 *1980–1989

—090 49 *1990–1999

—090 5 *21st century, 2000–2099

—090 51 *2000–2019

—090 511 *2000–2009

—090 512 *2010–2019

*Add as instructed under —0901–0905

—091 Treatment by areas, regions, places in general

History and description

Add to base number —091 the numbers following —1 in notation 11–19 from Table 2, e.g., Torrid Zone —0913; then add further as instructed under —093–099, e.g., conservation and preservation in tropical areas —0913028

Class history and description with respect to kinds of persons in —08; class persons regardless of area, region, place in —092; class treatment by specific continents, countries, localities in —093–099

—092 Persons

Biography, autobiography, description and critical appraisal of work, diaries, reminiscences, correspondence of persons regardless of area, region, or place who are part of the subject or who study the subject, e.g., biographers, collectors, leaders and followers, practitioners and clients, scholars

Class here treatment of individuals

Class treatment with respect to kinds of persons in —08; class biography not clearly related to any specific subject in 920; class belletristic diaries, reminiscences, correspondence in 800

Observe instructions not to use —092 (or 92 or —2 from Table 2 when the standard subdivision has been displaced) that apply to 180–190, 759, 809, 810–890. (The instructions for 810–890 are found under notation 09 from Table 3B)

Do not use —092 for a person whose name is used in a schedule heading, e.g., class Muḥammad the Prophet in 297.63 (*not* 297.63092)

See Manual at T1—092; also at 913–919: Add table: 04: Biography; also at 930–990: Wars: Personal narratives; also at 930–990: Biography

(Option A: Class biography in 920.1–928

(Option B: Class individual biography in 92, or B

(Option C: Class individual biography of men in 920.71, of women in 920.72)

—092 2 Collected persons treatment

Add to base number —0922 notation 3–9 from Table 2, e.g., collected biography of a subject in Italy —092245

Class collectibles and memorabilia related to more than one person in —075; class collected treatment of persons of specific areas when not limited to a specific subject in 920.03–920.09

For collected persons treatment of members of specific ethnic and national groups, see —0923

See Manual at T1—0922; also at T1—0922 vs. T1—093–099

(Option: Class collected biography in 92, or 920 without subdivision)

—092 3 Collected persons treatment of members of specific ethnic and national groups

Add to base number —0923 notation 05–9 from Table 5, e.g., biography of Irish-Americans —09239162073

Class collected persons treatment of members of specific ethnic and national groups in areas where they predominate with the group in a specific area in —0922, e.g., biography of Irish in Ireland —0922415

—092 9 Persons treatment of nonhumans

Use this number for animals and plants treated as individuals, e.g., a biography of Secretariat 798.400929

—093–099 Treatment by specific continents, countries, localities; extraterrestrial worlds

History and description by place, by specific instance of the subject

Add to base number —09 notation 3–9 from Table 2, e.g., the subject in North America —097, in Brazil —0981; then add further as follows:

01 Forecasts
02 Statistics, illustrations; conservation, preservation, restoration
021 Statistics
022 Illustrations
Class maps, plans, diagrams in 912
028 Conservation, preservation, restoration
Class here maintenance and repair; conservation, preservation, restoration projects
03 Dictionaries, encyclopedias, concordances
05 Serial publications
07 Museums, collections, exhibits; collecting objects
074 Museums, collections, exhibits
Add to 074 notation 4–9 from Table 2, e.g., collections in Pennsylvania 074748, collections of Brazilian objects in Pennsylvania —0981074748
075 Collecting objects
09 Historical and geographic treatment
Add to 09 the numbers following —09 in notation 090–099 from Table 1, e.g., 20th century 0904, rural regions 091734
Use 093–099 to add notation for a specific continent, country, locality when first area notation is used to specify area of origin, while second one identifies area in which subject is found or practiced, e.g., Polish political refugees 325.2109438, Polish political refugees in Canada 325.21094380971

In the table above, observe preference as given at beginning of Table 1, e.g., a periodical of statistics 021 (*not* 05); however, class museums, collections, exhibits of the subject in an area in 074 regardless of historical period, e.g., collections of 20th-century Brazilian art 709.81074 (*not* 709.810904)

If a standard subdivision is not given in the table above, do not add its notation to the Table 2 notation

(Option: Add historical period numbers that appear in subdivisions of 930–990, using one 0 in all cases except 00 for North America and South America, e.g., United States during Reconstruction —097308, Brazil during Empire —098104, North America in 20th century —097005. If option is used, do not use notation 090 from table above. An extra zero is used for the balance of notation from table above, e.g., statistics of Brazil —09810021)

Class history and description with respect to kinds of persons regardless of continent, country, locality in —08; class treatment by areas, regions, places not limited by continent, country, locality in —091; class persons treatment regardless of continent, country, locality in —092

See Manual at T1—0922 vs. T1—093–099; also at T1—093–099 and T2—3–9; also at T1—0940902 vs. T1—0902

Table 2. Geographic Areas, Historical Periods, Persons

The following numbers are never used alone, but may be used as required (either directly when so noted or through the interposition of notation 09 from Table 1) with any number from the schedules, e.g., wages (331.29) in Japan (—52 in this table): 331.2952; railroad transportation (385) in Brazil (—81 in this table): 385.0981. They may also be used when so noted with numbers from other tables, e.g., notation 025 from Table 1. When adding to a number from the schedules, always insert a decimal point between the third and fourth digits of the complete number

SUMMARY

— 001–009	**Standard subdivisions**
— 01–05	**Historical periods**
— 1	**Areas, regions, places in general; oceans and seas**
— 11	**Frigid zones**
— 12	**Temperate zones (Middle latitude zones)**
— 13	**Torrid zone (Tropics)**
— 14	**Land and landforms**
— 15	**Regions by type of vegetation**
— 16	**Air and water**
— 17	**Socioeconomic regions**
— 18	**Other kinds of terrestrial regions**
— 19	**Space**
— 2	**Persons**
— 22	**Collected treatment**
— 3	**The ancient world**
— 31	**China**
— 32	**Egypt**
— 33	**Palestine**
— 34	**India**
— 35	**Mesopotamia and Iranian Plateau**
— 36	**Europe north and west of Italian Peninsula**
— 37	**Italian Peninsula and adjacent territories**
— 38	**Greece**
— 39	**Other parts of ancient world**
— 4	**Europe Western Europe**
— 41	**British Isles**
— 42	**England and Wales**
— 43	**Central Europe Germany**
— 44	**France and Monaco**
— 45	**Italian Peninsula and adjacent islands Italy**
— 46	**Iberian Peninsula and adjacent islands Spain**
— 47	**Eastern Europe Russia**
— 48	**Scandinavia**
— 49	**Other parts of Europe**

—5 Asia Orient Far East
—51 China and adjacent areas
—52 Japan
—53 Arabian Peninsula and adjacent areas
—54 South Asia India
—55 Iran
—56 Middle East (Near East)
—57 Siberia (Asiatic Russia)
—58 Central Asia
—59 Southeast Asia

—6 Africa
—61 Tunisia and Libya
—62 Egypt and Sudan
—63 Ethiopia and Eritrea
—64 Northwest African coast and offshore islands Morocco
—65 Algeria
—66 West Africa and offshore islands
—67 Central Africa and offshore islands
—68 Southern Africa Republic of South Africa
—69 South Indian Ocean islands

—7 North America
—71 Canada
—72 Middle America Mexico
—73 United States
—74 Northeastern United States (New England and Middle Atlantic states)
—75 Southeastern United States (South Atlantic states)
—76 South central United States Gulf Coast states
—77 North central United States Lake states
—78 Western United States
—79 Great Basin and Pacific Slope region of United States Pacific Coast states

—8 South America
—81 Brazil
—82 Argentina
—83 Chile
—84 Bolivia
—85 Peru
—86 Colombia and Ecuador
—87 Venezuela
—88 Guiana
—89 Paraguay and Uruguay

—9 Other parts of world and extraterrestrial worlds Pacific Ocean islands
—93 New Zealand
—94 Australia
—95 Melanesia New Guinea
—96 Other parts of Pacific Ocean Polynesia
—97 Atlantic Ocean islands
—98 Arctic islands and Antarctica
—99 Extraterrestrial worlds

—001–008 Standard subdivisions

—009 Historical treatment

If "historical" appears in the heading for the number to which notation 009 could be added, this notation is redundant and should not be used

—[009 01–009 9] Historical periods, geographic and persons treatment

Do not use; class in —01–9

—01–05 **Historical periods**

Add to base number —0 the numbers following —090 in notation 0901–0905 from Table 1, e.g., 20th century —04

—1 Areas, regions, places in general; oceans and seas

Not limited by continent, country, locality

Class persons regardless of area, region, place in —2; class specific continents, countries, localities in —3–9

(Option: Add to each number in —1 as follows:

03–09 Treatment by continent, country, locality

Add to 0 notation 3–9 from Table 2, e.g., Asia 05, Torrid Zone of Asia —1305, rivers of Asia —169305, cities of Asia —173205

Prefer —3–9)

SUMMARY

—11	**Frigid zones**
—12	**Temperate zones (Middle latitude zones)**
—13	**Torrid zone (Tropics)**
—14	**Land and landforms**
—15	**Regions by type of vegetation**
—16	**Air and water**
—17	**Socioeconomic regions**
—18	**Other kinds of terrestrial regions**
—19	**Space**

> **—11–17 Zonal, physiographic, socioeconomic regions**

Unless other instructions are given, class a subject with aspects in two or more subdivisions of —11–17 in the number coming last, e.g., forested plateaus in north temperate zone —152 (*not* —123 or —143)

Class comprehensive works in —1

—11 **Frigid zones**

Class here polar regions

—113 North frigid zone

—116 South frigid zone

—12 **Temperate zones (Middle latitude zones)**

—123 North temperate zone

—126 South temperate zone

—13 **Torrid zone (Tropics)**

—14 **Land and landforms**

—141 Continents

Including continental shelves

—142 Islands

Including atolls, coral reefs

—143 Elevations

Including mountains, plateaus, hills, slopes

—144 Depressions and openings

Including canyons, chasms, gorges, gulches, ravines, valleys; craters; caves, karsts

—145 Plane regions

Including plains

Pampas, prairies, steppes, tundras relocated to —153

—146 Coastal regions and shorelines

Including beaches, deltas

—148 Soil

—15 Regions by type of vegetation

—152 Forests

—153 Grasslands

Class here grassland plains (pampas, prairies, steppes, tundras [*all formerly also* —145], savannas)

—154 Deserts

Class here semiarid lands

—16 Air and water

SUMMARY

— 161	**Atmosphere**
— 162	**Oceans and seas**
— 163	**Atlantic Ocean**
— 164	**Pacific Ocean**
— 165	**Indian Ocean**
— 167	**Antarctic waters**
— 168	**Special oceanographic forms and inland seas**
— 169	**Fresh and brackish waters**

—161 Atmosphere

—161 2 Troposphere

—161 3 Stratosphere

—161 4 Ionosphere

—162 Oceans and seas

For Atlantic Ocean, see —163; for Pacific Ocean, see —164; for Indian Ocean, see —165; for Antarctic waters, see —167; for special oceanographic forms and inland seas, see —168

See also —182 for ocean and sea basins

See Manual at T2—162

—163 Atlantic Ocean

See Manual at T2—162; also at T2—163 and T2—164, T2—165

—163 1 North Atlantic Ocean

Area north of a line drawn from Strait of Gibraltar to Straits of Florida

For Arctic Ocean, see —1632; for northeast Atlantic Ocean, see —1633; for northwest Atlantic Ocean, see —1634

—163 2 Arctic Ocean (North Polar Sea)

—163 24 European sector

Including Denmark Strait; Barents, Greenland, Norwegian, White Seas

—163 25 Asian sector

Including Chukchi, East Siberian, Kara, Laptev Seas

For Bering Strait, see —16451

—163 27 American sector

Including Beaufort and Lincoln Seas, seas of Canadian Arctic Archipelago, Baffin and Hudson Bays

For Bering Strait, see —16451

—163 3 Northeast Atlantic Ocean

—163 34 Baltic Sea

Including Gulfs of Bothnia, Finland, Riga; Great and Little Belts; Kattegat, Oresund

—163 36 North Sea and English Channel

Including Firth of Forth, Skagerrak, Strait of Dover

—163 37 Western waters of British Isles

Including Firth of Clyde, Irish Sea, North and Saint George's Channels, Solway Firth

—163 38 French, Spanish, and Portugese coastal waters to Strait of Gibraltar

Including Bay of Biscay

For Strait of Gibraltar, see —16381

—163 4 Northwest Atlantic Ocean

—163 42 Davis Strait

—163 43 Labrador Sea

—163 44 Gulf of Saint Lawrence and coastal waters of Newfoundland and eastern Nova Scotia

—163 45 North American coastal waters from Bay of Fundy to Massachusetts Bay

Including Cape Cod Bay

—163 46 United States coastal waters from Cape Cod to Cape Charles

Including Long Island, Nantucket, Rhode Island, Sounds; Buzzards, Delaware, Narragansett, New York Bays

—163 47 Chesapeake Bay

—163 48 United States coastal waters from Cape Henry to Straits of Florida

Including Albemarle, Pamlico Sounds; Biscayne Bay; Biscayne National Park

For Straits of Florida, see —16363

—163 5 South Atlantic Ocean

Area south of a line drawn from Strait of Gibraltar to Straits of Florida

For southwest Atlantic Ocean, see —1636; for southeast Atlantic Ocean, see —1637; for Atlantic sector of Antarctic waters, see —1673

—163 6 Southwest Atlantic Ocean

Class here west Atlantic Ocean

For northwest Atlantic Ocean, see —1634

—163 62 Sargasso Sea

—163 63 Bahama waters

Including Straits of Florida

—163 64 Gulf of Mexico

Including Yucatán Channel

For Straits of Florida, see —16363

—163 65 Caribbean Sea

Including Gulfs of Darien, Honduras, Venezuela

For Yucatán Channel, see —16364

—163 66 South American coastal waters from Gulf of Paria to Cape São Roque

—163 67 Brazilian coastal waters southward from Cape São Roque

—163 68 Uruguayan and Argentine coastal waters

Including Bahía Blanca Estuary, Rio de la Plata

—163 7 Southeast Atlantic Ocean

Class here east Atlantic Ocean

For northeast Atlantic Ocean, see —1633; for Mediterranean Sea, see —1638

—163 72 African coastal waters from Cape of Good Hope to Congo River

—163 73 Gulf of Guinea

African coastal waters from Congo River to Cape Palmas

—163 75 West African coastal waters from Cape Palmas to Strait of Gibraltar

For Strait of Gibraltar, see —16381

—163 8 Mediterranean Sea

—163 81 Western Mediterranean

Strait of Gibraltar to Strait of Sicily

For waters between Spain and Sardinia-Corsica, see —16382; for Tyrrhenian Sea, see —16383

—163 82 Waters between Spain and Sardinia-Corsica

Including Balearic and Ligurian Seas, Gulf of Lions

—163 83 Tyrrhenian Sea

For Strait of Messina, see —16386

—163 84 Eastern Mediterranean

East of Strait of Sicily

For Adriatic Sea, see —16385; for Ionian Sea, see —16386; for Mediterranean east of Crete, see —16387; for Sea of Crete and Aegean Sea, see —16388; for Black Sea, see —16389

—163 85 Adriatic Sea

Including Gulf of Venice

163 86 Ionian Sea

Including Strait of Messina, Gulf of Taranto

For Strait of Otranto, see —16385

—163 87 Mediterranean east of Crete

—163 88 Sea of Crete and Aegean Sea

For Dardanelles, see —16389

—163 89 Black Sea

Including Bosporus, Dardanelles, Seas of Azov and Marmara

—164 Pacific Ocean

See Manual at T2—162; also at T2—163 and T2—164, T2—165

—164 1 Southeast Pacific Ocean

American coastal waters from Strait of Magellan to Mexico-United States boundary

Including Gulfs of California, Guayaquil, Panama, Tehuantepec

For Strait of Magellan, see —1674

—164 2 East Pacific Ocean

For southeast Pacific Ocean, see —1641; for northeast Pacific Ocean, see —1643

—164 3 Northeast Pacific Ocean

North American coastal waters from California to tip of Alaska

—164 32 United States waters

Including Monterey and San Francisco Bays, Puget Sound, Strait of Juan de Fuca

For Alaskan waters, see —16434

—164 33 Canadian waters

Including Dixon Entrance, Hecate and Queen Charlotte Straits, Queen Charlotte Sound, Strait of Georgia

Class here Inside Passage

For Strait of Juan de Fuca, see —16432

—164 34 Alaskan waters

Including Bristol Bay, Cook Inlet, Gulf of Alaska, Norton Sound, Shelikof Strait

For Dixon Entrance, see —16433

—164 4 North Pacific Ocean

American and Asian coastal waters located in an arc from Mexico-United States boundary to southern tip of Philippines, excluding South China Sea and inner seas of the Philippines

For northeast Pacific Ocean, see —1643; for northwest Pacific Ocean, see —1645

—164 5 Northwest Pacific Ocean

—164 51 Bering Sea

Including Bering Strait

—164 52 Coastal waters of southeast Kamchatka

—164 53 Sea of Okhotsk

Including La Perouse Strait

—164 54 Sea of Japan

Including Korea, Tatar, Tsugaru Straits

For La Perouse Strait, see —16453

—164 55 Eastern coastal waters and inner seas of Japan

Including Inland Sea (Seto-naikai)

—164 56 Yellow Sea

—164 57 East China Sea

Including Formosa Strait

For Korea Strait, see —16454

—164 58 Philippine Sea

Including Luzon Strait

—164 6 West Pacific Ocean

For northwest Pacific Ocean, see —1645; for southwest Pacific Ocean, see —1647

—164 7 Southwest Pacific Ocean

—164 71 Inner seas of Philippines

For Sulu Sea, see —16473

—164 72 South China Sea

Including Gulf of Thailand, Singapore Strait

For Formosa Strait, see —16457; for Luzon Strait, see —16458

—164 73 Inner seas of Malay Archipelago

Including Celebes, Ceram, Molucca, Sulu Seas; Makasar Strait

For seas adjoining southern Sunda Islands, see —16474

—164 74 Seas adjoining southern Sunda Islands

Including Bali, Banda, Flores, Java, Savu Seas

For Karimata Strait, see —16472

—164 75 Arafura Sea

For Torres Strait, see —16476

—164 76 Coral Sea and seas adjoining Melanesia

Including Bismarck and Solomon Seas, Torres Strait; eastern Queensland coastal waters

—164 77 Fiji Sea

—164 78 Tasman Sea

Including New South Wales coastal waters, Cook Strait

For Tasmanian coastal waters, see —16576

—164 79 Eastern coastal waters of New Zealand

—164 8 South Pacific Ocean

American coastal waters from Mexico-United States boundary to Strait of Magellan; coastal water of Antarctica, New Zealand, Australia, and New Guinea; waters of Melanesia; coastal waters west and south of Philippines, including South China Sea and inner seas of Philippines

For southeast Pacific Ocean, see —1641; for southwest Pacific Ocean, see —1647; for Pacific sector of Antarctic waters, see —1674

—164 9 Central Pacific Ocean

American and Asian non-coastal waters; waters of Polynesia and isolated islands of Pacific, such as Wake and Easter Island

Including coastal waters of Hawaii

—165 Indian Ocean

For Indian Ocean sector of Antarctic waters, see —1675

See Manual at T2—162; also at T2—163 and T2—164, T2—165

—165 2 Southwest Indian Ocean

Class here west Indian Ocean

For northwest Indian Ocean, see —1653

—165 23 Eastern coastal waters of Madagascar

—165 24 Coastal waters of south and southeast Africa

From Cape of Good Hope to and including Delagoa Bay

—165 25 Mozambique Channel

—165 26 Coastal waters of east Africa

From Cape Delgado to Cape Guardafui (tip of the "Horn")

—165 3 Northwest Indian Ocean

—165 32 Gulf of Aden

Including ‘Bab el Mandeb

—165 33 Red Sea

Including Gulfs of Aqaba and Suez

Suez Canal relocated to —6215

For ‘Bab el Mandeb, see —16532

—165 35 Persian Gulf

Including Strait of Hormuz

—165 36 Gulf of Oman

For Strait of Hormuz, see —16535

—165 37 Arabian Sea

Including Laccadive Sea

—165 6 Northeast Indian Ocean

—165 64 Bay of Bengal

—165 65 Andaman Sea

Including Gulf of Martaban, Strait of Malacca

For Singapore Strait, see —16472

—165 67 Coastal waters of southern Sumatra, Java, Lesser Sunda Islands

For Timor Sea, see —16574

—165 7 Southeast Indian Ocean

Class here east Indian Ocean

For Arafura Sea, see —16475; for northeast Indian Ocean, see —1656

—165 74 Northwest Australian coastal waters

From Melville Island to Northwest Cape

Including Timor Sea

—165 75 West Australian coastal waters

From Northwest Cape to Cape Leeuwin

—165 76 South Australian coastal waters

From Cape Leeuwin to Cape Howe

Including Bass Strait, Great Australian Bight, Tasmanian coastal waters

—167 Antarctic waters

See Manual at T2—162; also at T2—163 and T2—164, T2—165

—167 3 Atlantic sector

Including Drake Passage, Scotia and Weddell Seas

For Strait of Magellan, see —1674

—167 4 Pacific sector

Including Amundsen, Bellingshausen, Ross Seas; Strait of Magellan

—167 5 Indian Ocean sector

—168 Special oceanographic forms and inland seas

Including coastal pools, saltwater lagoons

Class specific inland seas in —4–9

See Manual at T2—162

—169 Fresh and brackish waters

> —169 2–169 4 Surface waters

Class comprehensive works in —169

—169 2 Lakes, ponds, freshwater lagoons

—169 3 Rivers and streams

—169 4 Waterfalls

—169 8 Groundwaters (Subsurface waters)

—17 Socioeconomic regions

—171 Socioeconomic regions by political orientation

—171 2 Noncontiguous empires and political unions

Add to base number —1712 notation 3–9 from Table 2 for "mother country", e.g., French Community —171244

Class Roman Empire in —37

—171 3 Western bloc

—171 6 Unaligned blocs

—171 65 Afro-Asian bloc

—171 7 Former communist bloc

—171 8 Wartime groupings

—171 82 Belligerents

—171 83 Nonbelligerents and neutrals

—171 9 Non-self-governing territories

—172 Socioeconomic regions by degree of economic development

—172 2 Developed regions

—172 4 Developing regions

—173 Socioeconomic regions by concentration of population

—173 2 Urban regions

—173 3 Suburban regions

—173 4 Rural regions

Including rural villages

—174 Regions where specific ethnic and national groups predominate

Add to base number —174 notation 05–99 from Table 5, e.g., regions where Arabs predominate —174927

—175 Regions where specific languages predominate

Add to base number —175 notation 1–9 from Table 6, e.g., regions where Spanish language predominates —17561

—176 Regions where specific religions predominate

—176 1 Christianity

—176 12 Catholicism

—176 14 Protestantism

—176 2–176 9 Other religions

Add to base number —176 the numbers following 29 in 292–299, e.g., regions where Islam predominates —1767

Notation 292–299 replaces notation 292–299 from Table 7 with the result that many numbers have been reused with new meanings

—177 Nations belonging to specific international organizations

Including nations belonging to Organization of Petroleum Exporting Countries

Arrange alphabetically by name of organization

—18 Other kinds of terrestrial regions

—181 Hemispheres

Class zonal, physiographic, socioeconomic regions in a specific hemisphere in —11–17

—181 1 Eastern Hemisphere

—181 2 Western Hemisphere

Portion of world between 20° west longitude and 160° east longitude, including North and South America, most of North Atlantic Ocean (excluding northeastern portion), Southwest Atlantic Ocean, Northeast Pacific Ocean, and most of South Pacific Ocean (excluding southwestern portion)

Class land portion of North and South America in —7; class geography of Western Hemisphere in 917; class history of Western Hemisphere in 970

—181 3 Northern Hemisphere

—181 4 Southern Hemisphere

—182 Ocean and sea basins

The totality of continents facing and islands in specific major bodies of water

Class ocean and sea waters in —162; class zonal, physiographic, socioeconomic regions in a specific ocean or sea basin in —11–17

—182 1 Atlantic region Occident

Class here western world

See also —729 for Caribbean Area

—182 2 Mediterranean region

—182 3 Pacific region

—182 4 Indian Ocean region

—19 Space

Class extraterrestrial worlds in —99

See Manual at T2—99 vs. T2—19

—2 Persons

Regardless of area, region, place

Class here description and critical appraisal of work, biography, autobiography, diaries, reminiscences, correspondence of persons associated with the subject, e.g., elementary educators 372.92

All notes for notation 092 from Table 1 and its subdivision are applicable here

—22 Collected treatment

Add to base number —22 notation 3–9 from Table 2, e.g., collected biography of persons from Italy —2245

For collected persons treatment of members of specific ethnic and national groups, see —23

—23 Collected persons treatment of members of specific ethnic and national groups

Add to base number —23 notation 05–9 from Table 5, e.g., biography of Irish-Americans —239162073

—29 Persons treatment of nonhumans

Use this number for animals and plants treated as individuals

> —3–9 Specific continents, countries, localities; extraterrestrial worlds

Class here specific instances of the subject

An area is classed in its present number even if it had a different affiliation at the time under consideration, e.g., Arizona under Mexican sovereignty —791 (*not* —72)

Class areas, regions, places not limited by continent, country, locality in —1; class parts of oceans and noninland seas limited by country or locality in —163–168; class persons regardless of area, region, place in —2; class comprehensive works in 001–999, without adding notation from Table 2

See Manual at T1—093–099 and T2—3–9; also at T2—162; also at T2—4–9 vs. T2—3

(Option: Class areas and regions limited by continent, country, locality in —1)

—3 Ancient world

Class a specific part of ancient world not provided for here in —4–9

See Manual at T2—4–9 vs. T2—3

(Option: Class specific parts in —4–9 as detailed below)

SUMMARY

—31	**China**
—32	**Egypt**
—33	**Palestine**
—34	**India**
—35	**Mesopotamia and Iranian Plateau**
—36	**Europe north and west of Italian Peninsula**
—37	**Italian Peninsula and adjacent territories**
—38	**Greece**
—39	**Other parts of ancient world**

—31 China

(Option: Class in —51)

—32 Egypt

Including Alexandria, Giza, Memphis, Abydos, Karnak, Luxor, Thebes

(Option: Class Egypt in —62; class Alexandria in —621; class Giza, Memphis in —622; class Abydos, Karnak, Luxor, Thebes in —623)

—33 Palestine

Including Israel, Judah; Galilee, Judaea, Samaria; Jerusalem

(Option: Class Palestine, Israel in —5694; class Jerusalem in —569442; class Galilee in —56945; class Judah, Judaea in —56949; class Jordanian part of Palestine in —5695; class Samaria in —56953)

—34 **India**

(Option: Class in —54)

—35 **Mesopotamia and Iranian Plateau**

Including Media, Elam, Persia, Assyria, Babylonia, Sumer; Ecbatana, Susa, Pasargadae, Persepolis, Ashur, Nineveh, Babylon, Ur

Class here Seleucid Empire

Class central Asia in —396

(Option: Class Iranian Plateau in —55; class Media, Ecbatana in —555; class Elam, Susa in —556; class Persia, Pasargadae, Persepolis in —5572; class Mesopotamia, Seleucid Empire in —567; class Assyria, Ashur, Nineveh in —5674; class Babylonia, Sumer, Babylon, Ur in —5675)

—36 **Europe north and west of Italian Peninsula**

Class here comprehensive works on Europe, western Europe

For a specific part of Europe or western Europe not provided for here, see the part, e.g., Greece —38

(Option: Class in —4)

—361 British Isles Northern Britain and Ireland

Add to base number —361 the numbers following —41 in notation 411–419 of this table, e.g., ancient Border Country —36137

For southern Britain, see —362

(Option: Class British Isles in —41; class northern Britain in —411; class Ireland in —415)

—362 Southern Britain England

Add to base number —362 the numbers following —42 in notation 421–429 of this table, e.g., ancient Chester —362714

Class comprehensive works on British Isles in —361

(Option: Class in —42)

—363 Germanic regions

Including Vindelicia, Noricum, Raetia

For British Isles, see —361

(Option: Class Germanic regions in —43; class Vindelicia in —433; class Noricum in —436; class Raetia in —4364; class Scandinavia in —48)

—364 Celtic regions

Including Germania Superior, Lugdunensis, Aquitania, Narbonensis, Germania Inferior, Belgica, Helvetia

Class here Gaul (Gallia Transalpina)

For British Isles, see —361

See also —372 for Gallia Cisalpina

(Option: Class Celtic regions, Gaul [Gallia Transalpina] in —44; class Germania Superior in —4439; class Lugdunensis in —445; class Aquitania in —447; class Narbonensis in —448; class Germania Inferior in —492; class Belgica in —493; class Helvetia in —4943)

—366 Iberian Peninsula and adjacent islands

Including Tarraconensis, Baetica, Lusitania

Subdivisions are added for Iberian Peninsula and adjacent islands together, for Iberian Peninsula alone

(Option: Class Iberian Peninsula and adjacent islands, Tarraconensis in —46; class Baetica in —468; class Lusitania in —469)

—37 Italian Peninsula and adjacent territories

Class here Roman Empire

Subdivisions are added for Italian Peninsula and adjacent territories together, for Italian Peninsula alone

For a specific part of Roman Empire not provided for here, see the part, e.g., Britain —361

(Option: Class in —45)

—371 Liguria

(Option: Class in —4518)

—372 Gallia Cisalpina

(Option: Class in —451)

—373 Venetia and Istria

(Option: Class Venetia in —453; class Istria in —4972)

—374 Region northeast of Rome

Including Umbria, Picenum; Volsinii (Orvieto)

(Option: Class Umbria in —4565; class Volsinii [Orvieto] in —45652; class Picenum in —4567)

—375 Etruria

(Option: Class in —455)

—376 Latium

Including Volsinii Novi (Bolsena), Ostia, Veii

Class here Rome

(Option: Class Latium in —4562; class Volsinii Novi [Bolsena] in —45625; class Ostia, Veii in —4563; class Rome in —45632)

—377 Southern Italy

Including Samnium, Campania, Apulia, Calabria, Lucania, Bruttium

Including Naples, Herculaneum, Pompeii, Stabiae, Brundusium

(Option: Class Southern Italy in —457; class Samnium in —4571; class Campania in —4572; class Naples, Herculaneum, Pompeii, Stabiae in —4573; class Apulia, Calabria, Brundusium in —4575; class Lucania in —4577; class Bruttium in —4578)

—378 Sicily and Malta

Including Syracuse

Subdivisions are added for Sicily and Malta together, for Sicily alone

(Option: Class Sicily in —458; class Syracuse in —45814; class Malta in —4585)

—379 Sardinia and Corsica

(Option: Class Corsica in —4499; class Sardinia in —459)

—38 Greece

Class here comprehensive works on Greece and the Roman Empire; the Hellenistic World; southern Europe

For Roman Empire, see —37. For a specific part of Greece, Hellenistic World, southern Europe not provided for here, see the part, e.g., Ptolemaic Egypt —32, Aegean Islands —391

(Option: Class southern Europe in —4; class Greece in —495)

—381 Macedonia

(Option: Class in —4956)

—382 Thessaly, Epirus, adjacent Ionian Islands

Class here comprehensive works on Ionian Islands

For Ithaca Island, see —383; for southern Ionian Islands, see —386

(Option: Class Epirus in —4953; class Thessaly in —4954; class Ionian Islands, northern Ionian Islands in —4955)

—383 Aetolia, Acarnania, Doris, Locris, Malis, Phocis; Ithaca Island

Including Amphissa, Delphi

(Option: Class Doris, Locris, Malis, Phocis, Amphissa, Delphi in —49515; class Aetolia, Acarnania in —49518; class Ithaca Island in —4955)

—384 Boeotia, Megaris; Euboea Island

Including Chalcis, Thebes

(Option: Class Boeotia, Euboea Island, Chalcis, Thebes in —49515; class Megaris in —49522)

—385 Attica

Including Marathon

Class here Athens

(Option: Class Attica, Athens, Marathon in —49512)

—386 Peloponnesus and adjacent Ionian Islands

Subdivisions are added for Peloponnesus and adjacent Ionian Islands together, for Peloponnesus alone

For divisions of Peloponnesus, see —387–389

(Option: Class Peloponnesus in —4952; class southern Ionian Islands in —4955)

> —387–389 Divisions of Peloponnesus

Class comprehensive works in —386

—387 Achaea and Corinth

(Option: Class Corinth in —49522; class Achaea in —49527)

—388 Arcadia, Argolis, Elis

Including Mycenae, Olympia, Phigalia, Tiryns

(Option: Class Arcadia, Argolis, Mycenae, Tiryns in —49522; class Elis, Olympia, Phigalia in —49527)

—389 Laconia and Messenia

Class here Sparta

(Option: Class in —49522)

—39 Other parts of ancient world

SUMMARY

— 391	**Aegean Islands**
— 392	**Western Asia Minor**
— 393	**Eastern Asia Minor and Cyprus**
— 394	**Middle East**
— 395	**Black Sea and Caucasus regions**
— 396	**Central Asia**
— 397	**North Africa**
— 398	**Southeastern Europe**

—391 Aegean Islands

Class here Sporades

(Option: Class comprehensive works in —4958)

—391 1 Northern Aegean Islands

Including Northern Sporades (including Skyros Island), Thasos Island, Samothrace Island, Lemnos Island; Imbros, Tenedos islands

(Option: Class Skyros Island in —49515; class Northern Sporades in —4954; class Samothrace Island, Thasos Island in —4957; class Lemnos Island in —49582; class Imbros, Tenedos islands in —562)

—391 2 Lesbos

(Option: Class in —49582)

—391 3 Chios

(Option: Class in —49582)

—391 4 Samos

(Option: Class in —49582)

—391 5 Southwestern Aegean Islands

Class here Cyclades

(Option: Class in —49585)

—391 6 Southern Sporades

Including Dodecanese, Rhodes

For Karpathos, see —3917

(Option: Class in —49587)

—391 7 Karpathos

(Option: Class in —49587)

—391 8 Crete

Including Knossos

(Option: Class in —4959)

—392 Western Asia Minor

Class here comprehensive works on Asia Minor

For eastern Asia Minor, see —393

(Option: Class in —561)

—392 1 Mysia and Troas

Including Pergamum, Troy

(Option: Class in —562)

—392 2 Lydia

Including Sardis

(Option: Class in —562)

—392 3 Ionia

Including Ephesus, Magnesia ad Maeandrum, Miletus, Smyrna

For Aegean Islands, see —391

(Option: Class in —562)

—392 4 Caria

Including Halicarnassus

(Option: Class in —562)

—392 5 Bithynia

(Option: Class in —563)

—392 6 Phrygia

(Option: Class in —562)

—392 7 Pisidia

(Option: Class in —564)

—392 8 Lycia

(Option: Class in —564)

—392 9 Pamphylia

(Option: Class in —564)

—393 Eastern Asia Minor and Cyprus

Subdivisions are added for eastern Asia Minor and Cyprus together, for eastern Asia Minor alone

(Option: Class eastern Asia Minor in —561)

> —393 1–393 6 Eastern Asia Minor

Class comprehensive works in —393

—393 1 Paphlagonia

(Option: Class in —563)

—393 2 Galatia

(Option: Class in —563)

—393 3 Pontus

(Option: Class in —565)

—393 4 Cappadocia

(Option: Class in —564)

—393 5 Cilicia

(Option: Class in —564)

—393 6 Commagene

(Option: Class in —564)

—393 7 Cyprus

(Option: Class in —5693)

—394 Middle East

For a specific part of Middle East not provided for here, see the part, e.g., Egypt —32, Palestine —33

(Option: Class in —56)

—394 3 Syria

Including Antioch, Palmyra, Ebla, Ugarit, Damascus

For Phoenicia, see —3944

(Option: Class Antioch in —564; class Syria in —5691; class Palmyra in —56912; class Ebla, Ugarit in —56913; class Damascus in —569144)

—394 4 Phoenicia

Including Coelesyria; Baalbek, Byblos, Sidon, Tyre

(Option: Class in —5692)

—394 6 Edom and Moab

(Option: Class Edom in —56949; class Moab in —56956)

—394 7 Arabia Deserta

(Option: Class in —567)

—394 8 Arabia Petraea

Including Sinai Peninsula; Petra

(Option: Class Arabia Petraea in —53; class Sinai Peninsula in —531; class Petra in —569577)

—394 9 Arabia Felix

Class here comprehensive works on Arabia

For Arabia Deserta, see —3947; for Arabia Petraea, see —3948

(Option: Class Arabia Felix, Arabia in —53)

—395 Black Sea and Caucasus regions

Including Albania, Colchis, Iberia, Sarmatia

(Option: Class Caucasus in —475; class Albania in —4754; class Colchis, Iberia in —4758; class Black Sea region, Sarmatia in —477)

—395 1 Scythia

(Option: Class in —4983)

—395 5 Armenia

(Option: Class in —5662)

—396 Central Asia

Including Hyrcania, Ariana, Bactria, Margiana, Sogdiana; Parthia

(Option: Class Hyrcania in —5523; class Central Asia in —58; class Ariana, Bactria, Parthia in —581; class Margiana in —585; Sogdiana in —587)

—397 North Africa

For Egypt, see —32

(Option: Class in —61)

—397 1 Mauretania

Including Mauretania Caesariensis, Mauretania Tingitana

(Option: Class Mauretania Tingitana in —64; class Mauretania Caesariensis, comprehensive works on Mauretania in —65)

—397 2 Numidia

(Option: Class in —655)

—397 3 Carthage

(Option: Class in —611)

—397 4 Tripolis

Including Leptis Magna, Oea, Sabrata

(Option: Class in —612)

—397 5 Cyrenaica

(Option: Class in —612)

—397 6 Marmarica

(Option: Class in —612)

—397 7 Gaetulia

(Option: Class —657)

—397 8 Nubia

Class here Ethiopia (a part of what is now modern Sudan, not modern Ethiopia), Kush

(Option: Class in —625)

—398 Southeastern Europe

Including Pannonia, Thrace, Illyria, Dacia, Moesia; Constantinople

For Greece, see —38; for Black Sea region, see —395

(Option: Class Pannonia in —439; class Thrace in —4957; class southeastern Europe in —496; class Constantinople in —49618; class Illyria in —497; class Dacia in —498; class Moesia in —499)

> —4–9 Modern world; extraterrestrial worlds

Class comprehensive works on specific jurisdictions, regions, or features extending over more than one country, state, county, or other unit and identified by * with the unit where noted in this table, e.g., Rocky Mountain National Park —78869, Lake Huron —774, Appalachian Mountains —74. For works on a part of such a jurisdiction, region, or feature, see the specific unit where the part is located, e.g., Rocky Mountain National Park in Larimer County —78868, Lake Huron waters and shores in Ontario —7132, Cumberland Mountains —7691, Cumberland Mountains in Bell County, Kentucky —769123

Class comprehensive works in 001–999, without adding notation from Table 2

See Manual at T2—4–9; also at T2—4–9 vs. T2—3

(Option: Class here specific parts of ancient world; prefer —3

(Option: To give local emphasis and a shorter number to a specific country, place it first under its own continent or major region by use of a letter or other symbol, e.g., Pakistan —5P [preceding —51]; then subarrange each such number like the corresponding number in this table, e.g., Peshawar —5P23. Apply like any other area notation, e.g., geology of Peshawar 555.P23, history of Pakistan since 1971 95P.05, history of medical sciences in Pakistan 610.95P)

—4 Europe Western Europe

Class here nations belonging to the Council of Europe, southern Europe

Class Eurasia in —5

(Options: Class here ancient Europe, western Europe; prefer —36. Class here ancient southern Europe; prefer —38)

SUMMARY

—41	**British Isles**
—411	**Scotland**
—412	**Northeastern Scotland**
—413	**Southeastern Scotland**
—414	**Southwestern Scotland**
—415	**Ireland**
—416	**Ulster Northern Ireland**
—417	**Republic of Ireland (Eire)**
—418	**Leinster**
—419	**Munster**
—42	**England and Wales**
—421	**Greater London**
—422	**Southeastern England**
—423	**Southwestern England and Channel Islands**
—424	**Midlands of England**
—425	**East Midlands of England**
—426	**Eastern England East Anglia**
—427	**Northwestern England and Isle of Man**
—428	**Northeastern England**
—429	**Wales**
—43	**Central Europe Germany**
—431	**Northeastern Germany**
—432	**Saxony and Thuringia**
—433	**Bavaria (Bayern)**
—434	**Southwestern Germany**
—435	**Northwestern Germany**
—436	**Austria and Liechtenstein**
—437	**Czech Republic and Slovakia**
—438	**Poland**
—439	**Hungary**
—44	**France and Monaco**
—441	**Brittany (Bretagne) and Pays de la Loire**
—442	**Basse-Normandie, Haute-Normandie, Picardie, Nord-Pas-de-Calais**
—443	**Champagne-Ardenne, Ile-de-France, Lorraine, Alsace**
—444	**Burgundy and Franche-Comté**
—445	**Centre, Rhône-Alpes, Auvergne**
—446	**Poitou-Charentes and Limousin**
—447	**Aquitaine and Midi-Pyrénées**
—448	**Languedoc-Roussillon**
—449	**Provence-Côte d'Azur, Monaco, Corsica**
—45	**Italian Peninsula and adjacent islands Italy**
—451	**Northwestern Italy Piedmont (Piemonte) region**
—452	**Lombardy (Lombardia) region**
—453	**Northeastern Italy Veneto region**
—454	**Emilia-Romagna region and San Marino**
—455	**Tuscany (Toscana) region**
—456	**Central Italy and Vatican City**
—457	**Southern Italy**
—458	**Sicily and adjacent islands**
—459	**Sardinia**

—46	**Iberian Peninsula and adjacent islands Spain**
—461	**Northwestern Spain Galicia autonomous community**
—462	**Western Spain León region**
—463	**Castile**
—464	**New Castile region Castilla-La Mancha autonomous community**
—465	**Northeastern Spain**
—466	**País Vasco autonomous community**
—467	**Eastern Spain and Andorra**
—468	**Andalusia autonomous community and Gibraltar**
—469	**Portugal**
—47	**Eastern Europe Russia**
—471	**Northern area of European Russia**
—472	**Western area of Russia**
—473	**West central area of Russia**
—474	**Eastern area of European Russia**
—475	**Caucasus**
—476	**Moldova**
—477	**Ukraine**
—478	**Belarus**
—479	**Lithuania, Latvia, Estonia**
—48	**Scandinavia**
—481	**Norway**
—482	**Southeastern Norway (Østlandet)**
—483	**Sørlandet and Vestlandet**
—484	**Trøndelag and Nord-Norge**
—485	**Sweden**
—486	**Southern Sweden (Götaland)**
—487	**Central Sweden (Svealand)**
—488	**Northern Sweden (Norrland)**
—489	**Denmark and Finland**
—49	**Other parts of Europe**
—491	**Northwestern islands**
—492	**Netherlands**
—493	**Southern Low Countries Belgium**
—494	**Switzerland**
—495	**Greece**
—496	**Balkan Peninsula**
—497	**Serbia and Montenegro, Croatia, Slovenia, Bosnia and Hercegovina, Macedonia**
—498	**Romania**
—499	**Bulgaria**

—41 British Isles

Class here Great Britain, United Kingdom

For England and Wales, see —42

See Manual at T2—41 and T2—42

(Option: Class here ancient British Isles; prefer —361)

SUMMARY

—411	**Scotland**
—412	**Northeastern Scotland**
—413	**Southeastern Scotland**
—414	**Southwestern Scotland**
—415	**Ireland**
—416	**Ulster Northern Ireland**
—417	**Republic of Ireland (Eire)**
—418	**Leinster**
—419	**Munster**

—411 Scotland

For northeastern Scotland, see —412; for southeastern Scotland, see —413; for southwestern Scotland, see —414

(Option: Class here ancient northern Britain; prefer —3611)

—411 1 Northern Scotland

For divisions of northern Scotland, see —4113–4115

—[411 2] Islands authorities

Relocated to —4113

\> —411 3–411 5 Divisions of northern Scotland

Class comprehensive works in —4111

—411 3 Orkney and Shetland Islands

Class here comprehensive works on Islands authorities [*formerly* —4112]

For Eilean Siar, see —4114

—411 32 Orkney Islands

Former name: Orkney Islands Authority

—411 35 Shetland Islands

Former name: Shetland Islands Authority

—411 4 Eilean Siar (Outer Hebrides)

Former name: Western Isles Islands Authority

Class here comprehensive works on Hebrides

For Inner Hebrides, see —41154

—411 5 Highland

Former name: Highland Region

Class here *Scottish Highlands

*For a specific part of this jurisdiction, region, or feature, see the part and follow instructions under —4–9

—411 52 Northern Highland

Area north of and including Dornoch Firth, Carron River, Loch Broom

Including former Caithness District, former Sutherland District, Kincardine, Wick [*all formerly* —4116]; Ullapool [*formerly* —41172]

—411 54 Skye and adjacent islands

Including Canna, Eigg, Muck, Rhum [*all formerly* —41185]

Class here former *Skye and Lochalsh District [*formerly* —41182]; Inner Hebrides [*formerly* —4118]

Subdivisions are added for Skye and adjacent islands together, for Skye alone

—411 56 Western Highland

Area west of and including Great Glen; south of Dornoch Firth, Carron River, Loch Broom; excluding Skye and adjacent islands

Including former *Inverness District, former *Ross and Cromarty District, Inverness, Great Glen, Loch Ness [*all formerly* —4117]; former *Lochaber District, Fort William [*both formerly* —41185]

—411 58 Eastern Highland

Area east of Great Glen

Including former Badenoch and Strathspey District, former Nairn District, *Spey River [*all formerly* —4119]; *Grampian Mountains [*formerly* —4121]

For Fort William, see —41156

—[411 6] Former Caithness District, former Sutherland District, Kincardine, Wick

Relocated to —41152

—[411 7] Former Inverness District, former Ross and Cromarty District, Inverness, Great Glen, Loch Ness

Relocated to —41156

—[411 72] Ullapool

Relocated to —41152

—[411 8] Western districts of former Highland Region

Provision discontinued because without meaning in context

Inner Hebrides relocated to —41154

*For a specific part of this jurisdiction, region, or feature, see the part and follow instructions under —4–9

—[411 82] Former Skye and Lochalsh District

Relocated to —41154

—[411 85] Former Lochaber District

Former Lochaber District, Fort William relocated to —41156; Canna, Eigg, Muck, Rhum relocated to —41154

—[411 9] Former Badenoch and Strathspey District, former Nairn District, Spey River

Relocated to —41158

—412 Northeastern Scotland

—[412 1] Former Grampian Region

Former Grampian Region relocated to —4124; Grampian Mountains relocated to —41158

—412 2 Moray

Former name: Moray District

Use of this number for northern districts of Grampian discontinued because without meaning in context

—[412 23] Former Moray District

Number discontinued; class in —4122

—[412 25] Former Banff and Buchan District, Deveron River

Relocated to —4124

—412 3 Aberdeen City

Class here Aberdeen

Use of this number for central districts of Grampian discontinued because without meaning in context

—[412 32] Former Gordon District, Don River

Relocated to —4124

—[412 35] Former Aberdeen City

Number discontinued; class in —4123

—412 4 Aberdeenshire

Including former Banff and Buchan District, *Deveron River [*both formerly* —41225]; former Gordon District, Don River [*both formerly* —41232]; former Kincardine and Deeside District; *Cairngorm Mountains; *Dee River

Class here former *Grampian Region [*formerly* —4121]

*For a specific part of this jurisdiction, region, or feature, see the part and follow instructions under —4–9

—[412 5] Former Tayside Region

Former Tayside Region relocated to —4128; Strathmore relocated to —4126

—412 6 Angus

Including Monifieth [*formerly* —4127]

Class here *Strathmore [*formerly* —4125]; former Angus District

—412 7 Dundee City

Class here Dundee

Monifieth relocated to —4126

—412 8 Perth and Kinross

Class here former *Tayside Region [*formerly* —4125], former Perth and Kinross District; *Ochil Hills; *Tay River

—412 9 Fife

Former name: Fife Region

Including former Dunfermline District, former Kirkcaldy District, former North East Fife District

—[412 92–412 98] Former Dunfermline District, former Kirkcaldy District, former North East Fife District

Numbers discontinued; class in —4129

—413 Southeastern Scotland

Class here *Lowlands

—413 1 Stirling, Clackmannanshire, Falkirk

Former name: Central Region

Class here *Forth River

See also —16336 for Firth of Forth

—413 12 Stirling

Former name: Stirling District

Class here *Lennox Hills

—413 15 Clackmannanshire

Former name: Clackmannan District

—413 18 Falkirk

Former name: Falkirk District

*For a specific part of this jurisdiction, region, or feature, see the part and follow instructions under —4–9

—[413 2] Former Lothian Region

Relocated to —4133

—413 3 West Lothian

Former name: West Lothian District

Class here former *Lothian Region [*formerly* —4132]

—413 4 Edinburgh City

Class here Edinburgh

—413 5 Midlothian

Former name: Midlothian District

Class here *Pentland Hills

—413 6 East Lothian

Former name: East Lothian District

Class here *Lammermuir Hills

—413 7 Scottish Borders

Former name: Borders Region

Including former Berwickshire District, former Roxburgh District [*both formerly* —4139]; former Ettrick and Lauderdale District, former Tweeddale District [*both formerly* —4138]

Class here *Border Country, *Southern Uplands; *Tweed River

—[413 8] Former Ettrick and Lauderdale District, former Tweeddale District

Relocated to —4137

—[413 9] Former Berwickshire District, former Roxburgh District

Relocated to —4137

—414 Southwestern Scotland

Class here former Strathclyde Region; *Clyde River

See also —16337 for Firth of Clyde

—[414 1] Former Strathclyde Region

Number discontinued; class in —414

*For a specific part of this jurisdiction, region, or feature, see the part and follow instructions under —4–9

—414 2 Argyll and Bute

Including western part of former Dumbarton District; Campbeltown, Dunoon, Helensburgh, Oban; Loch Lomond

Class here former Argyll and Bute District

Use of this number for northwestern districts of Strathclyde discontinued because without meaning in context

—[414 23] Former Argyll and Bute District

Number discontinued; class in —4142

—[414 25] Former Dumbarton District

Use of this number for western part of former Dumbarton District discontinued; class in —4142

Eastern part of former Dumbarton District, comprehensive works on former Dumbarton District, Alexandria, Dumbarton relocated to —41432

—[414 28] Former Inverclyde District

Relocated to —41431

—414 3 Inverclyde, West Dunbartonshire, East Dunbartonshire, Renfrewshire, East Renfrewshire

Use of this number for north central districts of Strathclyde discontinued because without meaning in context

—414 31 Inverclyde

Former name: Inverclyde District [*formerly* —41428]

—414 32 West Dunbartonshire

Including eastern part of former Dumbarton District, comprehensive works on former Dumbarton District, Alexandria, Dumbarton [*all formerly* —41425], Clydebank

Class here former Clydebank District

For western part of former Dumbarton District, see —4142

—[414 34] Former Bearsden and Milngavie District

Relocated to —41436

—414 36 East Dunbartonshire

Including former Bearsden and Milngavie District [*formerly* —41434]; Kirkintilloch

Class here former *Strathkelvin District

Muirhead, Stepps relocated to —41452

*For a specific part of this jurisdiction, region, or feature, see the part and follow instructions under —4–9

—414 37 Renfrewshire

Including Paisley, Renfrew [*both formerly* —41441]

Class here former *Renfrew District [*formerly* —41441]

—[414 38] Former Cumbernauld and Kilsyth District

Relocated to —41452

—414 39 East Renfrewshire

Including Barrhead [*formerly* —41441], Newton Mearns [*formerly* —41451]

Class here former Eastwood District [*formerly* —41451]

—414 4 Glasgow City

Class here Glasgow

Use of this number for central districts of Strathclyde discontinued because without meaning in context

—[414 41] Former Renfrew District

Former Renfrew District, Paisley, Renfrew relocated to —41437; Barrhead relocated to —41439

—[414 43] Glasgow City, Cambuslang, Rutherglen

Use of this number for Glasgow City discontinued; class in —4144

Cambuslang, Rutherglen relocated to —41457

—[414 46] Former Monklands District, Airdrie, Coatbridge

Relocated to —41452

—[414 49] Former Motherwell District

Relocated to —41452

—414 5 North Lanarkshire and South Lanarkshire

Use of this number for south central districts of Strathclyde discontinued because without meaning in context

—[414 51] Former Eastwood District, Newton Mearns

Relocated to —41439

—414 52 North Lanarkshire

Including former Cumbernauld and Kilsyth District [*formerly* —41438]; former Monklands District, Airdrie, Coatbridge [*all formerly* —41446]; former Motherwell District [*formerly* —41449]; Muirhead, Stepps [*both formerly* —41436]

*For a specific part of this jurisdiction, region, or feature, see the part and follow instructions under —4–9

—[414 54] Former East Kilbride District

Relocated to —41457

—414 57 South Lanarkshire

Including former Clydesdale District [*formerly* —41469]; former East Kilbride District [*formerly* —41454]; Cambuslang, Rutherglen [*both formerly* —41443]; former Hamilton District

—414 6 North Ayrshire, South Ayrshire, East Ayrshire

Class here former Ayrshire

Use of this number for southern districts of Strathclyde discontinued because without meaning in context

—414 61 North Ayrshire

Former name: Cunninghame District

—[414 63] Former Kilmarnock and Loudoun District

Relocated to —41467

—414 64 South Ayrshire

Former name: Kyle and Carrick District

—414 67 East Ayrshire

Including former Kilmarnock and Loudoun District [*formerly* —41463], former Cumnock and Doon Valley District

—[414 69] Former Clydesdale District

Relocated to —41457

—414 7 Dumfries and Galloway

Former name: Dumfries and Galloway Region

Including former Annandale and Eskdale District, former Nithsdale District, *Nith River [*all formerly* —4148]; former Stewartry District, former Wigtown District [*both formerly* —4149]

See also —16337 for Solway Firth

—[414 8] Former Annandale and Eskdale District, former Nithsdale District, Nith River

Relocated to —4147

—[414 9] Former Stewartry District, former Wigtown District

Relocated to —4147

*For a specific part of this jurisdiction, region, or feature, see the part and follow instructions under —4–9

—415 Ireland

For divisions of Ireland, see —416–419

(Option: Class here ancient Ireland; prefer —3615)

> —416–419 Divisions of Ireland

Class comprehensive works in —415

—416 Ulster Northern Ireland

Class here *Bann River, *Lough Neagh

> —416 1–416 7 Northern Ireland

Class comprehensive works in —416

—416 1 Northeast area of Northern Ireland

Class here former *Antrim county

—416 12 Antrim Borough

—416 13 Ballymena Borough

—416 14 Ballymoney Borough

—416 15 Moyle District

—416 16 Larne Borough

—416 17 Carrickfergus Borough

—416 18 Newtownabbey Borough

—416 19 Lisburn Borough

> —416 2–416 4 Western area of Northern Ireland

Class comprehensive works in —4162

—416 2 Western area of Northern Ireland

Class here former Londonderry (Derry) county; *Sperrin Mountains

For Fermanagh District, see —4163; for west central area, see —4164

—416 21 City of Derry

Class here Derry (Londonderry)

—416 25 Limavady District

—416 27 Coleraine Borough

*For a specific part of this jurisdiction, region, or feature, see the part and follow instructions under —4–9

—416 29 Magherafelt District

—416 3 Fermanagh District

—416 4 West central area of Northern Ireland

Class here former Tyrone county

—416 41 Strabane District

—416 43 Cookstown District

—416 45 Dungannon District

—416 47 Omagh District

—416 5 Southeast area of Northern Ireland

Class here former Down county

—416 51 Castlereagh Borough

—416 53 North Down Borough

—416 54 Ards Borough

Class here *Strangford Lough

—416 56 Down District

—416 57 Banbridge District

—416 58 Newry and Mourne District

Class here *Mourne Mountains

—416 6 Southern area of Northern Ireland

Class here former *Armagh county

—416 61 Armagh District

—416 64 Craigavon Borough

—416 7 City of Belfast

Class here Belfast, *Greater Belfast

—416 9 Counties of Republic of Ireland in Ulster

—416 93 Donegal County

—416 97 Monaghan County

—416 98 Cavan County

*For a specific part of this jurisdiction, region, or feature, see the part and follow instructions under —4–9

—417 Republic of Ireland (Eire)

Class here *Shannon River

For counties in Ulster, see —4169; for Leinster, see —418; for Munster, see —419

—417 1 Connacht

For divisions of Connacht, see —4172–4176

> —417 2–417 6 Divisions of Connacht

Class comprehensive works in —4171

—417 2 Sligo County

—417 25 Sligo

—417 3 Mayo County

—417 4 Galway County

—417 45 Galway

—417 48 Aran Islands

—417 5 Roscommon County

—417 6 Leitrim County

—418 Leinster

Class here *Barrow River

—418 1 Northwest Leinster

—418 12 Longford County

—418 15 Westmeath County

—418 2 Northeast Leinster

—418 22 Meath County

Class here *Boyne River

—418 25 Louth County

—418 256 Drogheda

—418 3 Dublin County

Class here *Liffey River

—418 35 Dublin

—418 38 Dún Laoghaire

—418 4 Wicklow County

*For a specific part of this jurisdiction, region, or feature, see the part and follow instructions under —4–9

—418 5 Kildare County

Class here *Bog of Allen

—418 6 Offaly County

—418 7 Laois County

—418 8 Southeast Leinster

—418 82 Carlow County

—418 85 Wexford County

—418 856 Wexford

—418 9 Kilkenny County

Class here *Nore River

—419 Munster

—419 1 Waterford County

Class here *Suir River

—419 15 Waterford

—419 2 Tipperary County

—419 25 Clonmel

—419 3 Clare County

—419 4 Limerick County

—419 45 Limerick

—419 5 Cork County

Class here *Blackwater River

—419 56 Cork

—419 6 Kerry County

—419 65 Killarney

—42 England and Wales

Subdivisions are added for England and Wales together, for England alone

See Manual at T2—41 and T2—42

(Option: Class here ancient southern Britain, England; prefer —362)

*For a specific part of this jurisdiction, region, or feature, see the part and follow instructions under —4–9

SUMMARY

—421	**Greater London**
—422	**Southeastern England**
—423	**Southwestern England and Channel Islands**
—424	**Midlands of England**
—425	**East Midlands of England**
—426	**Eastern England East Anglia**
—427	**Northwestern England and Isle of Man**
—428	**Northeastern England**
—429	**Wales**

> —421–428 England

Class comprehensive works in —42

—421 Greater London

—421 2 City of London

—421 3 West London

—421 32 Westminster City

—421 33 Hammersmith and Fulham London Borough

—421 34 Kensington and Chelsea Royal Borough

—421 4 North London

—421 42 Camden London Borough

—421 43 Islington London Borough

—421 44 Hackney London Borough

—421 5 Tower Hamlets London Borough

—421 6 South London

—421 62 Greenwich London Borough

—421 63 Lewisham London Borough

—421 64 Southwark London Borough

—421 65 Lambeth London Borough

—421 66 Wandsworth London Borough

—421 7 Eastern Outer London

Class here Outer London

For northwestern Outer London, see —4218; for southwestern Outer London, see —4219

—421 72 Waltham Forest London Borough

—421 73 Redbridge London Borough

—421 74 Havering London Borough

—421 75 Barking and Dagenham London Borough

—421 76 Newham London Borough

—421 77 Bexley London Borough

—421 78 Bromley London Borough

—421 8 Northwestern Outer London

Class here former Middlesex

—421 82 Hounslow London Borough

—421 83 Hillingdon London Borough

—421 84 Ealing London Borough

—421 85 Brent London Borough

—421 86 Harrow London Borough

—421 87 Barnet London Borough

—421 88 Haringey London Borough

—421 89 Enfield London Borough

—421 9 Southwestern Outer London

—421 91 Croydon London Borough

—421 92 Sutton London Borough

—421 93 Merton London Borough

—421 94 Kingston upon Thames London Borough

—421 95 Richmond upon Thames London Borough

—422 Southeastern England

Class here *Home Counties; *Thames River; comprehensive works on southern England

For Greater London, see —421; for southwestern England and Channel Islands, see —423

—422 1 Surrey

—422 11 Runnymede Borough

—422 12 Spelthorne Borough

—422 13 Surrey Heath Borough

—422 14 Woking and Elmbridge Boroughs

—422 142 Woking Borough

Class here Woking

*For a specific part of this jurisdiction, region, or feature, see the part and follow instructions under —4–9

—422 145 Elmbridge Borough

—422 15 Epsom and Ewell Borough

—422 16 Guildford Borough and Mole Valley District

—422 162 Guildford Borough

—422 165 Mole Valley District

—422 17 Reigate and Banstead Borough

—422 18 Tandridge District

—422 19 Waverley Borough

—422 3 Kent and Medway Borough

Class here *North Downs

Subdivisions are added for Kent and Medway Borough together, for Kent alone

—422 31 Dartford and Gravesham Boroughs

—422 312 Dartford Borough

—422 315 Gravesham Borough

—422 32 Medway Borough

Unitary authority

Including former Rochester upon Medway City, former Gillingham Borough

—[422 323] Former Rochester upon Medway City

Number discontinued; class in —42232

—[422 325] Former Gillingham Borough

Number discontinued; class in —42232

—422 33 Swale Borough

—422 34 Canterbury City

—422 35 Dover and Thanet Districts

—422 352 Dover District

Class here *Cinque Ports

—422 357 Thanet District

—422 36 Sevenoaks District

—422 37 Tonbridge and Malling, and Maidstone Boroughs

—422 372 Tonbridge and Malling Borough

*For a specific part of this jurisdiction, region, or feature, see the part and follow instructions under —4–9

—422 375 Maidstone Borough

—422 38 Tunbridge Wells Borough

—422 39 Ashford Borough and Shepway District

—422 392 Ashford Borough

—422 395 Shepway District

—422 5 East Sussex, and Brighton and Hove

Class here former Sussex; the *Weald

Subdivisions are added for East Sussex, and Brighton and Hove together; for East Sussex alone

For West Sussex, see —4226

—422 51 Wealden District

—422 52 Rother District

—[422 54] Former Hove Borough

Relocated to —42256

—422 56 Brighton and Hove

Unitary authority

Including former Hove Borough [*formerly* —42254]

Class here former Brighton Borough; Brighton

—422 57 Lewes District

—422 58 Eastbourne Borough

Class here Eastbourne

—422 59 Hastings Borough

Class here Hastings

—422 6 West Sussex

Class here *South Downs

—422 61 Crawley Borough

Class here Crawley

—422 62 Chichester District

—422 64 Horsham District

—422 65 Mid Sussex District

—422 67 Arun District

*For a specific part of this jurisdiction, region, or feature, see the part and follow instructions under —4–9

—422 68 Worthing Borough

Class here Worthing

—422 69 Adur District

—422 7 Hampshire, Southampton City, Portsmouth City

Subdivisions are added for Hampshire, Southampton City, Portsmouth City together; for Hampshire alone

—422 71 Basingstoke and Deane Borough

—422 72 Hart District and Rushmoor Borough

—422 723 Hart District

—422 725 Rushmoor Borough

—422 73 Test Valley Borough and Winchester City

—422 732 Test Valley Borough

Class here *Test River

—422 735 Winchester City

—422 74 East Hampshire District

—422 75 New Forest District

—422 76 Southampton City

Unitary authority

Class here Southampton

—422 77 Eastleigh and Fareham Boroughs

—422 772 Eastleigh Borough

—422 775 Fareham Borough

Including Fareham

—422 78 Gosport Borough

Class here Gosport

—422 79 Portsmouth City and Havant Borough

—422 792 Portsmouth City

Unitary authority

Class here Portsmouth

—422 795 Havant Borough

*For a specific part of this jurisdiction, region, or feature, see the part and follow instructions under —4–9

—422 8 Isle of Wight

Unitary authority

Including former Medina and South Wight Boroughs

—[422 82] Former Medina Borough

Number discontinued; class in —4228

—[422 85] Former South Wight Borough

Number discontinued; class in —4228

—422 9 Unitary authories created from Berkshire

Class here former Berkshire

—422 91 West Berkshire District

Former name: Newbury District

Unitary authority

—422 93 Reading Borough

Unitary authority

Class here Reading

—422 94 Wokingham District

Unitary authority

—422 96 Windsor and Maidenhead Royal Borough

Unitary authority

—422 97 Slough Borough

Unitary authority

Class here Slough

—422 98 Bracknell Forest Borough

Unitary authority

—423 Southwestern England and Channel Islands

—423 1 Wiltshire and Swindon Borough

Subdivisions are added for Wiltshire and Swindon Borough together, for Wiltshire alone

—423 12 North Wiltshire District

—423 13 Swindon Borough

Former name: Thamesdown Borough

Unitary authority

—423 15 West Wiltshire District

—423 17 Kennet District

—423 19 Salisbury District

Class here *Salisbury Plain; *East Avon River

—423 3 Dorset, Poole Borough, Bournemouth Borough

Class here *Stour River

Subdivisions are added for Dorset, Poole Borough, Bournemouth Borough together; for Dorset alone

—423 31 West Dorset District

—423 32 North Dorset District

—423 34 East Dorset District

—423 35 Weymouth and Portland Borough

—423 36 Purbeck District

—423 37 Poole Borough

Unitary authority

Class here Poole

—423 38 Bournemouth Borough

Unitary authority

Class here Bournemouth

—423 39 Christchurch Borough

—423 4 Channel Islands

—423 41 Jersey

For Minquiers, see —42348; for Dirouilles, Ecrehous, Paternosters, see —42349

—423 42 Guernsey

For Jethou, see —42347; for Lihou, Lihoumel, see —42349

—423 43 Alderney

For Burhou, see —42347; for Casquets, see —42348

—423 45 Sark

For Brecqhou, see —42347

—423 46 Herm

—423 47 Brecqhou, Burhou, Jethou

For a specific part of this jurisdiction, region, or feature, see the part and follow instructions under —4–9

—423 48 Casquets, Chausey Islands, Minquiers

Chausey Islands are under French jurisdiction

—423 49 Other islands

Including Barnouic, Dirouilles, Ecrehous, Lihou, Lihoumel, Paternosters, Roches Douvres

Roches Douvres are under French jurisdiction

—423 5 Devon, Plymouth City, Torbay

Class here *Exe River, *Tamar River

Subdivisions are added for Devon, Plymouth City, Torbay together; for Devon alone

—423 51 Torridge District

—423 52 North Devon District

—423 53 West Devon Borough

Class here *Dartmoor

—423 54 Mid Devon District

—423 55 Teignbridge District

—423 56 Exeter City

Class here Exeter

—423 57 East Devon District

—423 58 Plymouth City

Unitary authority

Class here Plymouth

—423 59 South Hams District and Torbay

—423 592 South Hams District

Class here *Dart River

—423 595 Torbay

Former name: Torbay Borough

Unitary authority

Class here Torbay

—423 7 Cornwall and Scilly Isles

Subdivisions are added for Cornwall and Scilly Isles together, for Cornwall alone

*For a specific part of this jurisdiction, region, or feature, see the part and follow instructions under —4–9

—423 71 North Cornwall District

—423 72 Restormel Borough

—423 74 Caradon District

—423 75 Penwith District

—423 76 Kerrier District

—423 78 Carrick District

Class here *Fal River

—423 79 Scilly Isles

—423 8 Somerset

—423 81 Sedgemoor District

—423 83 Mendip District

Class here *Mendip Hills

—423 85 West Somerset District

Class here *Exmoor; *Quantock Hills

—423 87 Taunton Deane District

Class here *Blackdown Hills

—423 89 South Somerset District

—423 9 Unitary authories created from Avon

Class here former Avon; *Lower (Bristol) Avon River

—423 91 South Gloucestershire

Unitary authority

Including former Kingswood Borough [*formerly* —42394], former Northavon District

—423 93 Bristol City

Unitary authority

Class here Bristol

—[423 94] Former Kingswood Borough

Relocated to —42391

—423 96 North Somerset

Former name: Woodspring District

Unitary authority

*For a specific part of this jurisdiction, region, or feature, see the part and follow instructions under —4–9

—[423 97] Former Wansdyke District

Relocated to —42398

—423 98 Bath and North East Somerset District

Unitary authority

Including former Wansdyke District [*formerly* —42397], former Bath City

Class here Bath

—424 Midlands of England

Class here West Midlands; *Welsh Marches (Welsh Borders); *Severn River

For East Midlands, see —425

—424 1 Gloucestershire

—424 12 Tewkesbury Borough

—424 13 Forest of Dean District

—424 14 Gloucester City

Class here Gloucester

—424 16 Cheltenham Borough

Class here Cheltenham

—424 17 Cotswold District

Class here *Cotswold Hills

—424 19 Stroud District

—424 2 Herefordshire

Unitary authority

Including former Hereford City [*formerly* —42446], former Leominster District [*formerly* —42444], former South Herefordshire District, Ross-on-Wye [*both formerly* —42445], western part of former Malvern Hills District, Bromyard, Ledbury [*all formerly* —42447]

For parts of former Leominster District in Malvern Hills District, see —42447

—424 4 Worcestershire

Class here former Hereford and Worcester; *Upper (Warwickshire) Avon River

For Herefordshire, see —4242

—424 41 Wyre Forest District

*For a specific part of this jurisdiction, region, or feature, see the part and follow instructions under —4–9

—424 42 Bromsgrove District

—424 43 Redditch Borough

Class here Redditch

—[424 44] Former Leominster District

Former Leominster District relocated to —4242; Tenbury Wells relocated to —42447

—[424 45] Former South Herefordshire District, Ross-on-Wye

Relocated to —4242

—[424 46] Former Hereford City

Relocated to —4242

—424 47 Malvern Hills District

Including Tenbury Wells [*formerly* —42444], Malvern, Upton upon Severn

Western part of former Malvern Hills District, Bromyard, Ledbury relocated to —4242

—424 48 Worcester City

Class here Worcester

—424 49 Wychavon District

—424 5 Shropshire, and Telford and Wrekin

Subdivisions are added for Shropshire, and Telford and Wrekin together, for Shropshire alone

—424 51 Oswestry Borough

—424 53 North Shropshire District

—424 54 Shrewsbury and Atcham Borough

—424 56 Telford and Wrekin

Former name: The Wrekin District

Unitary authority

—424 57 South Shropshire District

—424 59 Bridgnorth District

—424 6 Staffordshire and Stoke-on-Trent City

Subdivisions are added for Staffordshire and Stoke-on-Trent City together, for Staffordshire alone

—424 61 Staffordshire Moorlands District

—424 62 Newcastle-under-Lyme Borough

—424 63 Stoke-on-Trent City

Unitary authority

Class here Stoke-on-Trent

—424 64 Stafford Borough

—424 65 East Staffordshire Borough

—424 66 South Staffordshire District

—424 67 Cannock Chase District

—424 68 Lichfield District

—424 69 Tamworth Borough

Class here Tamworth

—424 8 Warwickshire

—424 81 North Warwickshire Borough

—424 83 Nuneaton and Bedworth Borough

—424 85 Rugby Borough

—424 87 Warwick District

—424 89 Stratford-on-Avon District

—424 9 Metropolitan boroughs created from West Midlands Metropolitan County

Class here former West Midlands Metropolitan County; Black Country

—424 91 Wolverhampton Metropolitan Borough

Class here Wolverhampton

—424 92 Walsall Metropolitan Borough

Including Walsall

—424 93 Dudley Metropolitan Borough

—424 94 Sandwell Metropolitan Borough

—424 96 Birmingham City

Class here Birmingham

—424 97 Solihull Metropolitan Borough

—424 98 Coventry City

Class here Coventry

—425 East Midlands of England

Class here *Chiltern Hills; *Trent River

SUMMARY

—425 1	**Derbyshire and Derby City**
—425 2	**Nottinghamshire and Nottingham City**
—425 3	**Lincolnshire**
—425 4	**Leicestershire, Leicester City, Rutland County**
—425 5	**Northamptonshire**
—425 6	**Bedfordshire and Luton Borough**
—425 7	**Oxfordshire**
—425 8	**Hertfordshire**
—425 9	**Buckinghamshire and Milton Keynes**

—425 1 Derbyshire and Derby City

Class here *Derwent River of Derbyshire

Subdivisions are added for Derbyshire and Derby City together, for Derbyshire alone

—425 11 High Peak Borough

Class here *Peak District

—425 12 Chesterfield Borough

—425 13 Derbyshire Dales District

Class here *Dove River

—425 14 North East Derbyshire District

—425 15 Bolsover District

—425 16 Amber Valley Borough

—425 17 Derby City

Unitary authority

Class here Derby

—425 18 Erewash Borough

—425 19 South Derbyshire District

—425 2 Nottinghamshire and Nottingham City

Subdivisions are added for Nottinghamshire and Nottingham City together, for Nottinghamshire alone

—425 21 Bassetlaw District

—425 23 Mansfield District

*For a specific part of this jurisdiction, region, or feature, see the part and follow instructions under —4–9

—425 24 Newark and Sherwood District

Class here *Sherwood Forest

—425 25 Ashfield District

—425 26 Broxtowe Borough

—425 27 Nottingham City

Unitary authority

Class here Nottingham

—425 28 Gedling Borough

—425 29 Rushcliffe Borough

—425 3 Lincolnshire

Class here *Lincoln Heath; *the Wash; *Witham River

—425 31 West Lindsey District

Class here former *Parts of Lindsey

—425 32 East Lindsey District

Class here *Lincoln Wolds

—425 34 Lincoln City

Class here Lincoln

—425 35 North Kesteven District

Class here former Parts of Kesteven

For South Kesteven, see —42538

—425 37 Boston Borough

—425 38 South Kesteven District

—425 39 South Holland District

Class here former Parts of Holland; *Welland River

For Boston Borough, see —42537

—425 4 Leicestershire, Leicester City, Rutland County

Subdivisions are added for Leicestershire, Leicester City, Rutland County together; for Leicestershire alone

—425 41 Blaby District

*For a specific part of this jurisdiction, region, or feature, see the part and follow instructions under —4–9

—425 42 Leicester City

Unitary authority

Class here Leicester

—425 43 Oadby and Wigston Borough

—425 44 Harborough District

—425 45 Rutland County

Former name: Rutland District

Unitary authority

—425 46 Melton Borough

—425 47 Charnwood Borough

—425 48 North West Leicestershire District

—425 49 Hinckley and Bosworth Borough

—425 5 Northamptonshire

Class here *Nene River

—425 51 Corby Borough

—425 52 Kettering Borough

—425 54 East Northamptonshire District

—425 56 Daventry District

Class here *Northampton Uplands

—425 57 Northampton Borough

Class here Northampton

—425 58 Wellingborough Borough

—425 59 South Northamptonshire District

—425 6 Bedfordshire and Luton Borough

Subdivisions are added for Bedfordshire and Luton Borough together, for Bedfordshire alone

—425 61 Bedford Borough

—425 63 Mid Bedfordshire District

—425 65 South Bedfordshire District

*For a specific part of this jurisdiction, region, or feature, see the part and follow instructions under —4–9

—425 67 Luton Borough

Unitary authority

Class here Luton

—425 7 Oxfordshire

—425 71 West Oxfordshire District

—425 73 Cherwell District

—425 74 Oxford City

Class here Oxford

—425 76 Vale of White Horse District

—425 79 South Oxfordshire District

—425 8 Hertfordshire

—425 81 North Hertfordshire District

—425 82 Stevenage Borough

Class here Stevenage

—425 83 East Hertfordshire District

—425 84 Dacorum Borough

—425 85 St. Albans City and District

—425 86 Welwyn Hatfield District

—425 87 Broxbourne Borough

—425 88 Three Rivers District

—425 89 Watford and Hertsmere Boroughs

—425 892 Watford Borough

Class here Watford

—425 895 Hertsmere Borough

—425 9 Buckinghamshire and Milton Keynes

Subdivisions are added for Buckinghamshire and Milton Keynes together, for Buckinghamshire alone

—425 91 Milton Keynes

Former name: Milton Keynes Borough

Unitary authority

Class here Milton Keynes

—425 93 Aylesbury Vale District

—425 95 Wycombe District

—425 97 Chiltern District

—425 98 South Bucks District

—426 Eastern England East Anglia

Class here *The Fens; *Great Ouse River

> —426 1–426 5 East Anglia

Class comprehensive works in —426

—426 1 Norfolk

Class here *Yare River

—426 12 North Norfolk District

—426 13 King's Lynn and West Norfolk Borough

—426 14 Breckland District

—426 15 Norwich City

Class here Norwich

—426 17 Broadland District

Class here *Norfolk Broads

—426 18 Great Yarmouth Borough

—426 19 South Norfolk District

Class here *Waveney River

—426 4 Suffolk

—426 41 Waveney District

—426 43 Forest Heath District

—426 44 Saint Edmundsbury Borough

—426 45 Mid Suffolk District

—426 46 Suffolk Coastal District

—426 48 Babergh District

—426 49 Ipswich Borough

Class here Ipswich

—426 5 Cambridgeshire and Peterborough City

Subdivisions are added for Cambridgeshire and Peterborough City together, for Cambridgeshire alone

*For a specific part of this jurisdiction, region, or feature, see the part and follow instructions under —4–9

—426 51 Peterborough City

Unitary authority

—426 53 Fenland District

Class here Isle of Ely

See also —42656 for Ely

—426 54 Huntingdonshire District

—426 56 East Cambridgeshire District

Including Ely

See also —42653 for Isle of Ely

—426 57 South Cambridgeshire District

—426 59 Cambridge City

Class here Cambridge

—426 7 Essex, Thurrock, Southend-on-Sea Borough

Subdivisions are added for Essex, Thurrock, Southend-on-Sea Borough together; for Essex alone

—426 71 Uttlesford and Braintree Districts

—426 712 Uttlesford District

—426 715 Braintree District

—426 72 Colchester Borough and Tendring District

—426 723 Colchester Borough

—426 725 Tendring District

—426 73 Harlow District

Class here Harlow

—426 74 Epping Forest District

—426 75 Chelmsford Borough and Maldon District

—426 752 Chelmsford Borough

—426 756 Maldon District

—426 76 Brentwood Borough

—426 77 Basildon and Rochford Districts

—426 772 Basildon District

Including Basildon

—426 775 Rochford District

—426 78 Thurrock

Former name: Thurrock Borough

Unitary authority

Including Thurrock

—426 79 Castle Point and Southend-on-Sea Boroughs

—426 792 Castle Point Borough

—426 795 Southend-on-Sea Borough

Unitary authority

Class here Southend-on-Sea

—427 Northwestern England and Isle of Man

Class here comprehensive works on northern England

Subdivisions are added for northwestern England and Isle of Man together, for northwestern England alone

For northeastern England, see —428

—427 1 Cheshire, Halton Borough, Warrington Borough

Subdivisions are added for Cheshire, Halton Borough, Warrington Borough together; for Cheshire alone

—427 12 Crewe and Nantwich Borough

—427 13 Congleton Borough

—427 14 Chester City

—427 15 Vale Royal Borough

—427 16 Macclesfield Borough

—427 17 Ellesmere Port and Neston Borough

—427 18 Halton Borough

Unitary authority

—427 19 Warrington Borough

Unitary authority

—427 3 Metropolitan boroughs created from Greater Manchester Metropolitan County

Class here former Greater Manchester Metropolitan County

—427 31 Trafford Metropolitan Borough

—427 32 Salford City

—427 33 Manchester City

Class here Manchester

—427 34 Stockport Metropolitan Borough

—427 35 Tameside Metropolitan Borough

—427 36 Wigan Metropolitan Borough

—427 37 Bolton Metropolitan Borough

—427 38 Bury Metropolitan Borough

—427 39 Rochdale and Oldham Metropolitan Boroughs

—427 392 Rochdale Metropolitan Borough

—427 393 Oldham Metropolitan Borough

—427 5 Metropolitan boroughs created from Merseyside Metropolitan County

Class here former Merseyside Metropolitan County; *Mersey River

—427 51 Wirral Metropolitan Borough

—427 53 Liverpool City

Class here Liverpool

—427 54 Knowsley Metropolitan Borough

—427 57 St. Helens Metropolitan Borough

—427 59 Sefton Metropolitan Borough

—427 6 Lancashire, Blackburn with Darwen Borough, Blackpool Borough

Subdivisions are added for Lancashire, Blackburn with Darwen Borough, Blackpool Borough together; for Lancashire alone

—427 61 West Lancashire District and Chorley Borough

—427 612 West Lancashire District

—427 615 Chorley Borough

—427 62 Blackburn with Darwen Borough and Hyndburn Borough

—427 623 Blackburn with Darwen Borough

Former name: Blackburn Borough

Unitary authority

—427 625 Hyndburn Borough

—427 63 Rossendale Borough

—427 64 Burnley and Pendle Boroughs

—427 642 Burnley Borough

—427 645 Pendle Borough

*For a specific part of this jurisdiction, region, or feature, see the part and follow instructions under —4–9

—427 65 Blackpool Borough

Unitary authority

Class here Blackpool

—427 66 Fylde and Preston Boroughs

—427 662 Fylde Borough

Class here *The Fylde

—427 665 Preston Borough

—427 67 South Ribble Borough

—427 68 Wyre and Ribble Valley Boroughs

—427 682 Wyre Borough

—427 685 Ribble Valley Borough

Class here *Forest of Bowland; *Ribble River

—427 69 Lancaster City

—427 8 Cumbria

Class here Lake District; Cumbrian Mountains

—427 81 Barrow-in-Furness Borough

—427 83 South Lakeland District

—427 84 Copeland Borough

—427 86 Eden District

Class here *Eden River

—427 87 Allerdale District

See also —16337 for Solway Firth

—427 89 Carlisle City

—427 9 Isle of Man

—428 Northeastern England

Class here the *Pennines

—428 1 Metropolitan boroughs created from West Yorkshire Metropolitan County

Class here former West Yorkshire Metropolitan County; former *Yorkshire

—428 12 Calderdale Metropolitan Borough

—428 13 Kirklees Metropolitan Borough

*For a specific part of this jurisdiction, region, or feature, see the part and follow instructions under —4–9

—428 15 Wakefield City

Class here *Aire River

—428 17 Bradford City

—428 19 Leeds City

—428 2 Metropolitan boroughs created from South Yorkshire Metropolitan County

Class here former South Yorkshire Metropolitan County

—428 21 Sheffield City

—428 23 Rotherham Metropolitan Borough

—428 25 Barnsley Metropolitan Borough

—428 27 Doncaster Metropolitan Borough

—428 3 Unitary authorities created from Humberside

Class here former Humberside; *Yorkshire Wolds; *Humber River

—[428 31] Former Scunthorpe Borough

Relocated to —42832

—428 32 North Lincolnshire

Unitary authority

Including former Scunthorpe Borough [*formerly* —42831], southern part of former Boothferry Borough, Crowle, Isle of Axholme [*all formerly* —42835], former Glanford Borough

—[428 33] Former Cleethorpes Borough

Relocated to —42834

—428 34 North East Lincolnshire

Unitary authority

Including former Cleethorpes Borough [*formerly* —42833], former Great Grimsby Borough

—[428 35] Former Boothferry Borough

Southern part of former Boothferry Borough, Crowle, Isle of Axholme relocated to —42832; northern part of former Boothferry Borough, comprehensive works on former Boothferry Borough, Goole, Howden relocated to —42839

—[428 36] Former Beverley Borough

Relocated to —42839

*For a specific part of this jurisdiction, region, or feature, see the part and follow instructions under —4–9

—428 37 Kingston upon Hull City

Unitary authority

Class here Hull

—[428 38] Former Holderness Borough

Relocated to —42839

—428 39 East Riding of Yorkshire

Unitary authority

Including former Beverley Borough [*formerly* —42836]; former Holderness Borough [*formerly* —42838]; northern part of former Boothferry Borough, comprehensive works on former Boothferry Borough, Goole, Howden [*all formerly* —42835]; former East Yorkshire Borough

For southern part of former Boothferry Borough, see —42832

—428 4 North Yorkshire and York City

Class here *Yorkshire Dales; *Derwent River of Yorkshire, *Ouse River

Subdivisions are added for North Yorkshire and York City together, for North Yorkshire alone

—428 41 Craven District

—428 42 Harrogate Borough

—428 43 York City

Unitary authority

Class here York

—428 45 Selby District

—428 46 Ryedale District

Class here *North Yorkshire Moors

—428 47 Scarborough Borough

—428 48 Richmondshire District

Class here *Swale River, *Ure River

—428 49 Hambleton District

Class here *Cleveland Hills

—428 5 Unitary authorities created from Cleveland

Class here former Cleveland; *Tees River

*For a specific part of this jurisdiction, region, or feature, see the part and follow instructions under —4–9

—428 51 Stockton-on-Tees Borough

Unitary authority

—428 53 Middlesbrough

Former name: Middlesbrough Borough

Unitary authority

—428 54 Redcar and Cleveland Borough

Former name: Langbaurgh-on-Tees Borough

Unitary authority

—428 57 Hartlepool Borough

Unitary authority

—428 6 Durham and Darlington Borough

Class here *Wear River

Subdivisions are added for Durham and Darlington Borough together, for Durham alone

—428 61 Teesdale District

—428 62 Sedgefield Borough

—428 63 Darlington Borough

Unitary authority

—428 64 Wear Valley District

—428 65 Durham City

—428 67 Easington District

—428 68 Derwentside District

—428 69 Chester-le-Street District

—428 7 Metropolitan boroughs created from Tyne and Wear Metropolitan County

Class here former Tyne and Wear Metropolitan County; *Tyne River

—428 71 Sunderland Metropolitan Borough

—428 73 Gateshead Metropolitan Borough

—428 75 South Tyneside Metropolitan Borough

—428 76 Newcastle upon Tyne City

Class here Newcastle upon Tyne

—428 79 North Tyneside Metropolitan Borough

*For a specific part of this jurisdiction, region, or feature, see the part and follow instructions under —4–9

—428 8 Northumberland

Class here *Cheviot Hills

—428 81 Tynedale District

—428 83 Castle Morpeth Borough

—428 84 Blyth Valley Borough

—428 86 Wansbeck District

—428 87 Alnwick District

Class here *Coquet River

—428 89 Berwick-upon-Tweed Borough

—429 Wales

Class here *Cambrian Mountains

—429 1 North Wales

For northwestern Wales, see —4292; for northeastern Wales, see —4293

—429 2 Northwestern Wales

Class here former Gwynedd County

—429 21 Isle of Anglesey County

Former name: Ynys Môn Borough

—[429 23] Former Dwyfor District

Relocated to —42925

—429 25 Gwynedd

Including former Dwyfor District [*formerly* —42923], former Meirionnydd District [*formerly* —42929], former Arfon Borough

Class here *Snowdonia

—429 27 Conwy County Borough

Including former *Colwyn Borough, Abergele, Colwyn Bay [*all formerly* —42931]; former Aberconwy Borough

—[429 29] Former Meirionnydd District

Relocated to —42925

—429 3 Northeastern Wales

Class here former Clwyd County

*For a specific part of this jurisdiction, region, or feature, see the part and follow instructions under —4–9

—[429 31] Former Colwyn Borough, Abergele, Colwyn Bay

Relocated to —42927

—[429 32] Former Rhuddlan Borough, Prestatyn, Rhyl

Relocated to —42937

—429 33 Flintshire County

Including former Alyn and Deeside District [*formerly* —42936], former Delyn Borough

—[429 36] Former Alyn and Deeside District

Relocated to —42933

—429 37 Denbighshire County

Including former Rhuddlan Borough, Prestatyn, Rhyl [*all formerly* —42932]; Denbigh, Llangollen

Class here former Glyndŵr District

Parts of former Glyndŵr District now in Wrexham County Borough relocated to —42939; parts of former Glyndŵr District now in Powys County relocated to —42951

—429 39 Wrexham County Borough

Including parts of former Glyndŵr District [*formerly* —42937]

Class here former Wrexham Maelor District

—429 4 South Wales

For Powys County, see —4295; for southwestern Wales, see —4296; for central southern Wales, see —4297; for City and County of Swansea, Neath Port Talbot County Borough, Cardiff County, Vale of Glamorgan, see —4298; for southeastern Wales, see —4299

—429 5 Powys County

Class here *mid Wales; *Wye River

—429 51 Northern Powys County

Area north of Wye River

Including former *Radnor District, Llandrindod Wells [*both formerly* —42954], parts of former Glyndŵr District [*formerly* —42937]; Machynlleth, Newtown, Welshpool; Severn River in Wales

Class here former Montgomery District

—[429 54] Former Radnor District, Llandrindod Wells

Relocated to —42951

*For a specific part of this jurisdiction, region, or feature, see the part and follow instructions under —4–9

—429 56 Southern Powys County

Area south of Wye River

Including Brecon, Builth Wells, Llanwrtyd Wells

Class here former Brecknock Borough

—429 6 Southwestern Wales

Class here former Dyfed County

—429 61 Ceredigion County

Former name: Ceredigion District

—429 62 Pembrokeshire County

Including former South Pembrokeshire District [*formerly* —42963], former Preseli District

—[429 63] Former South Pembrokeshire District

Relocated to —42962

—429 65 Carmarthenshire County

Including former Dinefwr Borough [*formerly* —42968], former Llanelli Borough [*formerly* —42967], former Carmarthen District

—[429 67] Former Llanelli Borough

Relocated to —42965

—[429 68] Former Dinefwr Borough

Relocated to —42965

—429 7 Central southern Wales

Class here former county of *Mid Glamorgan

For City and County of Swansea, Neath Port Talbot County Borough, Cardiff County, Vale of Glamorgan, see —4298

—429 71 Bridgend County Borough

Including Porthcawl

Class here former *Ogwr Borough

St. Bride's Major relocated to —42989

—[429 72] Former Rhondda Borough

Relocated to —42978

—[429 73] Former Cynon Valley Borough, Aberdare

Relocated to —42978

*For a specific part of this jurisdiction, region, or feature, see the part and follow instructions under —4–9

—429 75 Merthyr Tydfil County Borough

Former name: Merthyr Tydfil Borough

—429 76 Caerphilly County Borough

Including former Islwyn Borough [*formerly* —42993], former Rhymney Valley District

—429 78 Rhondda Cynon Taff County Borough

Including former Cynon Valley Borough, Aberdare [*both formerly* —42973]; former Rhondda Borough [*formerly* —42972]; former *Taff-Ely Borough; Llantrisant, Pontypridd

Creigiau, Pentyrch relocated to —42987

—429 8 City and County of Swansea, Neath Port Talbot County Borough, Cardiff County, Vale of Glamorgan

—[429 81] Former county of West Glamorgan

Relocated to —42982

—429 82 City and County of Swansea

Including western part of former Lliw Valley Borough, comprehensive works on former Lliw Valley Borough, Pontarddulais [*all formerly* —42983]; Swansea; Gower Peninsula

Class here former county of *West Glamorgan [*formerly* —42981]

For eastern part of former Lliw Valley Borough, see —42985

—[429 83] Former Lliw Valley Borough

Western part of former Lliw Valley Borough, comprehensive works on former Lliw Valley Borough, Pontarddulais relocated to —42982; eastern part of former Lliw Valley Borough, Gwaun-cae-Gurwen relocated to —42985

—[429 84] Former Neath Borough

Relocated to —42985

—429 85 Neath Port Talbot County Borough

Including eastern part of former Lliw Valley Borough, Gwaun-cae-Gurwen [*both formerly* —42983]; former Neath Borough [*formerly* —429894]; former Afan Borough

—[429 86] Former county of South Glamorgan

Relocated to —42987

*For a specific part of this jurisdiction, region, or feature, see the part and follow instructions under —4–9

—429 87 Cardiff County

Including Creigiau, Pentyrch [*both formerly* —42978]

Class here former county of *South Glamorgan [*formerly* —42986]; Cardiff

—429 89 Vale of Glamorgan

Including St. Bride's Major [*formerly* —42971], Barry, Cowbridge, Penarth

Class here former Vale of Glamorgan Borough

—429 9 Southeastern Wales

Class here former *Gwent, former *Monmouthshire

—429 91 Newport County Borough

Former name: Newport Borough

—[429 93] Former Islwyn Borough

Relocated to —42976

—429 95 Blaenau Gwent County Borough

Including Abertillery, Ebbw Vale, Tredegar

Class here former *Blaenau Gwent Borough

Clydach, Gilwern relocated to —42998

—429 97 Torfaen County Borough

Former name: Torfaen Borough

—429 98 Monmouthshire County

Including Clydach, Gilwern [*both formerly* —42995], Abergavenny, Chepstow, Usk

Class here former Monmouth District

—43 Central Europe Germany

Class here *Holy Roman Empire

For Switzerland, see —494

(Option: Class here ancient Germanic regions; prefer —363)

*For a specific part of this jurisdiction, region, or feature, see the part and follow instructions under —4–9

SUMMARY

> —431–435 Germany

Class comprehensive works in —43

> —431–432 Eastern Germany

This development reflects the political divisions established in 1990–1996. Relatively minor changes between this development and the Edition 21 development, which reflects the previous political divisions, are not indicated

Class comprehensive works in —431

—431 Northeastern Germany

Class here former German Democratic Republic (East Germany); *Elbe River

For Saxony and Thuringia, see —432

—431 5 Brandenburg and Berlin

Subdivisions are added for Brandenburg and Berlin together, for Brandenburg alone

---

> —431 51–431 54 Brandenburg

Class comprehensive works in —4315

—431 51 Southern Brandenburg

Including Dahme-Spreewald, Elbe-Elster, Oberspreewald-Lausitz, Spree-Neisse counties (Landkreise); Cottbus

Class here former *Cottbus district (Cottbus Bezirk)

*For a specific part of this jurisdiction, region, or feature, see the part and follow instructions under —4–9

—431 53 Eastern Brandenburg

Including Barnim, Märkisch-Oderland, Oder-Spree, Uckermark counties (Landkreise)

Class here former *Frankfurt an der Oder district (Frankfurt an der Oder Bezirk)

—431 532 Frankfurt an der Oder

—431 54 Western Brandenburg

Including Havelland, Oberhavel, Ostprignitz-Ruppin, Potsdam-Mittelmark, Prignitz, Teltow-Fläming counties (Landkreise); Brandenburg an der Havel

Class here former *Potsdam district (Potsdam Bezirk) [*formerly* —43157]

—431 546 Potsdam

—431 55 Berlin

—431 552 Eastern Berlin

Class here former East Berlin

—431 554 Western Berlin

Class here former West Berlin

—[431 57] Former Potsdam district (Potsdam Bezirk)

Relocated to —43154

—431 7 Mecklenburg-Vorpommern

Class here former Mecklenburg

—431 72 Eastern Mecklenburg

Including Demmin, Mecklenburg-Strelitz, Müritz counties (Landkreise); Neubrandenburg

Class here former *Neubrandenburg district (Neubrandenburg Bezirk)

Southern part of German Pomerania, formerly part of Neubrandenburg district, relocated to —43178

—431 74 Central Mecklenburg

Including Bad Doberan, Güstrow counties (Landkreise)

Class here former *Rostock district (Rostock Bezirk)

Northern part of German Pomerania, formerly part of Rostock district, relocated to —43178

—431 745 Rostock

*For a specific part of this jurisdiction, region, or feature, see the part and follow instructions under —4–9

—431 76 Western Mecklenburg

Including Ludwigslust, Nordwestmecklenburg, Parchim counties (Landkreise); Schwerin, Wismar

Class here former *Schwerin district (Schwerin Bezirk)

—431 78 German Pomerania (Vorpommern)

Including southern part of German Pomerania [*formerly* —43172]; northern part of German Pomerania [*formerly* —43174]; Nordvorpommern, Ostvorpommern, Rügen, Uecker-Randow counties (Landkreise); Greifswald, Stralsund

—431 8 Saxony-Anhalt (Sachsen-Anhalt)

Class here former Prussian Saxony

—431 82 Magdeburg district (Magdeburg Regierungsbezirk)

Including *Harz Mountains

Northern part of Dessau district, formerly part of Magdeburg district, relocated to —43186

—431 822 Magdeburg

—431 84 Halle district (Halle Regierungsbezirk)

Class here *Saale River

Southern part of Dessau district, formerly part of Halle district, relocated to —43186

—431 848 Halle

—431 86 Dessau district (Dessau Regierungsbezirk)

Including northern part of Dessau district [*formerly* —43182]

Class here southern part of Dessau district [*formerly* —43184], Anhalt

—432 Saxony and Thuringia

—432 1 Saxony (Sachsen)

—432 12 Leipzig district (Leipzig Regierungsbezirk)

—432 122 Leipzig

—432 14 Dresden district (Dresden Regierungsbezirk)

—432 142 Dresden

—432 16 Chemnitz district (Chemnitz Regierungsbezirk)

Former heading: Karl-Marx-Stadt district (Karl-Marx-Stadt Bezirk)

Class here Erzgebirge in Germany

*For a specific part of this jurisdiction, region, or feature, see the part and follow instructions under —4–9

—432 162 Chemnitz

—432 2 Thuringia (Thüringen)

—432 22 Eastern Thuringia

Including Altenburger Land, Greiz, Saale-Holzlandkreis, Saale-Orla-Kreis, Saalfeld-Rudolstadt counties (Landkreise); Gera, Jena

Class here former *Gera district (Bezirk)

—432 24 Northern Thuringia

Including Eichsfeld, Gotha, Kyffhäuserkreis, Nordhausen, Sömmerda, Unstrut-Hainich-Kreis, Weimarer Land counties (Landkreise)

Class here former *Erfurt district (Erfurt Bezirk)

—432 241 Weimar

—432 248 Erfurt

—432 26 Southern Thuringia

Including Hildburghausen, Ilm-Kreis, Schmalkalden-Meiningen, Sonneberg, Wartburgkreis counties (Landkreise); Eisenach, Suhl; Thuringian Forest

Class here former *Suhl district (Suhl Bezirk)

—433 Bavaria (Bayern)

Class here Franconian Jura; *Danube River in Germany

(Option: Class here ancient Vindelicia; prefer —363)

—433 1 Upper Franconia (Oberfranken)

—433 11 Coburg

—433 15 Bayreuth

—433 18 Bamberg

—433 2 Middle Franconia (Mittelfranken)

—433 22 Erlangen

—433 24 Nuremberg (Nürnberg)

—433 3 Lower Franconia (Unterfranken)

—433 31 Aschaffenburg

—433 36 Schweinfurt

—433 39 Würzburg

—433 4 Upper Palatinate (Oberpfalz)

*For a specific part of this jurisdiction, region, or feature, see the part and follow instructions under —4–9

—433 47 Regensburg

—433 5 Lower Bavaria (Niederbayern)

Class here *Bavarian Forest, *Bohemian Forest in Germany

Class comprehensive works on Bohemian Forest in —43714

—433 55 Passau

—433 58 Landshut

—433 6 Upper Bavaria (Oberbayern)

Class here *Bavarian Alps

—433 62 Ingolstadt

—433 64 Munich (München)

—433 7 Swabia district (Schwaben Regierungsbezirk)

Comprehensive works on Swabia relocated to —4346

—433 75 Augsburg

—434 Southwestern Germany

Class here *Main, *Rhine Rivers

—434 1 Hesse (Hessen)

—434 12 Kassel district (Kassel Regierungsbezirk)

—434 124 Kassel

—434 14 Giessen district (Giessen Regierungsbezirk)

Including *Lahn River

—434 16 Darmstadt district (Darmstadt Regierungsbezirk)

Including *Taunus Mountains

—434 163 Offenbach am Main

—434 164 Frankfurt am Main

—434 165 Wiesbaden

—434 167 Darmstadt

—434 2 Saarland

Class here *Saar River

—434 21 Saarbrücken

*For a specific part of this jurisdiction, region, or feature, see the part and follow instructions under —4–9

—434 3 Rhineland-Palatinate (Rheinland-Pfalz)

Class here Rhine Province (Rhenish Prussia); *Moselle River

For Saarland, see —4342; for North Rhine-Westphalia, see —4355

—434 31 Trier district (Trier Regierungsbezirk)

—434 313 Trier

—434 32 Koblenz district (Koblenz Regierungsbezirk)

—434 323 Koblenz

—434 35 Rheinhessen-Pfalz district (Rheinhessen-Pfalz Regierungsbezirk)

Class here Palatinate; Pfälzerwald Mountains

For Upper Palatinate, see —4334

—434 351 Mainz

—434 352 Worms

—434 353 Ludwigshafen am Rhein

—434 6 Baden-Württemberg

Class here comprehensive works on Swabia [*formerly* —4337]; *Black Forest

For Swabia district of Bavaria, see —4337; for Stuttgart and Tübingen districts, see —4347

—434 62 Freiburg district (Freiburg Regierungsbezirk)

Including *Lake of Constance (Bodensee)

—434 626 Südlicher Oberrhein Region

Including Breisgau-Hochschwarzwald, Emmendingen, Ortenaukreis counties (Landkreise)

—434 626 2 Freiburg im Breisgau

—434 64 Karlsruhe district (Karlsruhe Regierungsbezirk)

Class here former *Baden

—434 643 Mittlerer Oberrhein Region

Including Karlsruhe, Rastatt counties (Landkreise); Baden-Baden

—434 643 6 Karlsruhe

*For a specific part of this jurisdiction, region, or feature, see the part and follow instructions under —4–9

—434 645 Unterer Neckar Region

Including Neckar-Odenwald-Kreis, Rhein-Neckar-Kreis counties (Landkreise)

Class here *Neckar River

—434 645 2 Mannheim [*formerly* —434646]

—434 645 4 Heidelberg

—[434 646] Mannheim

Relocated to —4346452

—434 7 Stuttgart and Tübingen districts

Class here former *Württemberg

—434 71 Stuttgart district (Stuttgart Regierungsbezirk)

Class here Stuttgart Region

—434 715 Stuttgart

—434 73 Tübingen district (Tübingen Regierungsbezirk)

Including former *Hohenzollern

Class here *Swabian Jura

—435 Northwestern Germany

—435 1 Schleswig-Holstein and Hamburg

—435 12 Schleswig-Holstein

Including North Friesland; *North Frisian Islands

—435 123 Kiel

—435 125 Lübeck

—435 15 Hamburg

—435 2 Bremen

Class here Bremen city

—435 21 Bremerhaven

—435 5 North Rhine-Westphalia (Nordrhein-Westfalen)

Class here *Ruhr River

For Münster, Arnsberg, Detmold districts, see —4356

—435 51 Cologne district (Köln Regierungsbezirk)

—435 511 Aachen

*For a specific part of this jurisdiction, region, or feature, see the part and follow instructions under —4–9

—435 514	Cologne (Köln)
—435 518	Bonn
—435 53	Düsseldorf district (Düsseldorf Regierungsbezirk)
—435 532	Wuppertal
—435 534	Düsseldorf
—435 535	Mönchengladbach and Krefeld
—435 535 3	Mönchengladbach
—435 535 7	Krefeld
—435 536	Duisburg
—435 537	Mülheim an der Ruhr and Oberhausen
—435 537 3	Mülheim an der Ruhr
—435 537 7	Oberhausen
—435 538	Essen
—435 6	Münster, Arnsberg, Detmold districts
	Class here Westphalia; *Lippe River
—435 61	Münster district (Münster Regierungsbezirk)
	Class here *Münsterland
—435 614	Münster
—435 618	Gelsenkirchen
—435 63	Arnsberg district (Arnsberg Regierungsbezirk)
—435 632	Bochum
—435 633	Dortmund
—435 635	Hagen
—435 65	Detmold district (Detmold Regierungsbezirk)
	Class here *Teutoburg Forest
—435 655	Bielefeld
—435 9	Lower Saxony (Niedersachsen)
	Class here *Weser River
—435 91	Weser-Ems district (Weser-Ems Regierungsbezirk)
—435 911	Osnabrück
—435 914	Oldenburg

*For a specific part of this jurisdiction, region, or feature, see the part and follow instructions under —4–9

—435 917 East Friesland region

Including Aurich, Friesland, Leer, Wittmund counties (Landkreise); Emden, Wilhelmshaven; *East Frisian Islands

—435 93 Lüneburg district (Lüneburg Regierungsbezirk)

—435 95 Hannover district (Hannover Regierungsbezirk)

—435 954 Hannover

—[435 958] Hildesheim

Number discontinued; class in —43595

—435 97 Braunschweig district (Braunschweig Regierungsbezirk)

Class here former *Braunschweig state

—435 976 Braunschweig

—436 Austria and Liechtenstein

Class here *Austrian Empire, *Dual Monarchy of Austria-Hungary

Subdivisions are added for Austria and Liechtenstein together, for Austria alone

(Option: Class here ancient Noricum; prefer —363)

—436 1 Eastern Austria

—436 12 Lower Austria (Niederösterreich)

Class here *Danube River in Austria

—436 13 Vienna (Wien)

—436 15 Burgenland

—436 2 Upper Austria (Oberösterreich)

—436 24 Linz

—436 3 Salzburg province (Salzburg Land)

—436 32 Salzburg

—436 4 Western Austria, and Liechtenstein

Subdivisions are added for western Austria, and Liechtenstein together; for western Austria alone

Class here *Alpine region of Austria, *Eastern Alps

For Salzburg province, see —4363

(Option: Class here ancient Raetia; prefer —363)

—436 42 Tyrol (Tirol)

*For a specific part of this jurisdiction, region, or feature, see the part and follow instructions under —4–9

—436 424 Innsbruck

—436 45 Vorarlberg

—436 48 Liechtenstein

Independent principality

—436 5 Styria (Steiermark)

—436 55 Graz

—436 6 Carinthia (Kärnten)

—437 Czech Republic and Slovakia

Class here Czechoslovakia

—437 1 Czech Republic

Including Sudetenland

Class here Bohemia

For Moravia, see —4372

—437 11 Středočeský Region (Středočeský Kraj)

—437 12 Prague (Praha)

—437 13 Jihočeský Region (Jihočeský Kraj)

Former name: Budějovický Region (Budějovický Kraj)

—437 14 Plzeňský Region (Plzeňský Kraj)

Class here former *Západočeský Region (Západočeský Kraj), *Bohemian Forest (Český Les)

—437 15 Karlovarský Region (Karlovarský Kraj)

Including *Erzgebirge

—437 16 Ústecký Region (Ústecký Kraj)

Class here former *Severočeský Region (Severočeský Kraj)

—437 17 Liberecký Region (Liberecký Kraj)

—437 18 Královéhradecký Region (Královéhradecký Kraj)

Class here former *Východočeský Region (Východočeský Kraj)

—437 19 Pardubický Region (Pardubický Kraj)

—437 2 Moravia

—437 22 Vysočina Region (Vysočina Kraj)

Former name: Jihlavský Region (Jihlavský Kraj)

*For a specific part of this jurisdiction, region, or feature, see the part and follow instructions under —4–9

—437 24 Jihomoravský Region (Jihomoravský Kraj)

Former name: Brněnský Region (Brněnský Kraj)

—437 25 Zlínský Region (Zlínský Kraj)

—437 27 Olomoucký Region (Olomoucký Kraj)

—437 28 Moravskoslezský Region (Moravskoslezský Kraj)

Former name: Ostravský Region (Ostravský Kraj)

Class here Czech Silesia, former *Severomoravský Region (Severomoravský Kraj)

—437 3 Slovakia

Class here *Carpathian Mountains in Slovakia

—437 31 Bratislava Region (Bratislava Kraj)

Class here Bratislava

—437 32 Trnavský Region (Trnavský Kraj)

—437 33 Nitriansky Region (Nitriansky Kraj)

Class here former *Západoslovenský Region (Západoslovenský Kraj)

—437 34 Banskobystrický Region (Banskobystrický Kraj)

Class here former *Banskobystrický Region (Banskobystrický Kraj)

—437 35 Košický Region (Košický Kraj)

Class here former *Východoslovenský Region (Východoslovenský Kraj)

—437 36 Prešovský Region (Prešovský Kraj)

—437 37 Žilinský Region (Žilinský Kraj)

—437 38 Trenčianský Region (Trenčianský Kraj)

—438 Poland

—438 1 Northwestern Poland

Former Słupsk Province (Słupsk Voivodeship) relocated to —43822

—438 12 Lubuskie Province (Lubuskie Voivodeship)

Including former *Gorzów Wielkopolski, *Zielona Góra provinces (voivodeships)

*For a specific part of this jurisdiction, region, or feature, see the part and follow instructions under —4–9

—438 16 Zachodniopomorskie Province (Zachodniopomorskie Voivodeship)

Including former Koszalin, Szczecin provinces (voivodeships)

Class here *Pomerania, *Polish Pomerania

For German Pomerania, see —4317

—438 2 North central Poland

Class here *West Prussia

Former Elbląg Province (Elbląg Voivodeship) relocated to —43832

—438 22 Pomorskie Province (Pomorskie Voivodeship)

Including former *Słupsk Province (Słupsk Voivodeship) [*formerly* —4381], Gdańsk Province (Gdańsk Voivodeship)

Class here Pomerelia

—438 26 Kujawsko-Pomorskie Province (Kujawsko-Pomorskie Voivodeship)

Including former Bydgoszcz, *Toruń, Włocławek provinces (voivodeships)

—438 3 Northeastern Poland

—438 32 Warmińsko-Mazurskie Province (Warmińsko-Mazurskie Voivodeship)

Including former *Elbląg Province (Elbląg Voivodeship) [*formerly* —4382]; former Olsztyn, *Suwałki provinces (voivodeships)

Class here comprehensive works on East Prussia

For Kaliningrad province of Russia, see —4724

—438 36 Podlaskie Province (Podlaskie Voivodeship)

Including former Białystok, *Łomża provinces (voivodeships)

—438 4 Central Poland

Former Tarnobrzeg Province (Tarnobrzeg Voivodeship) relocated to —43866

—438 41 Mazowieckie Province (Mazowieckie Voivodeship)

Including former *Ciechanów, *Ostrołęka, *Płock, Radom, *Siedlce, Warsaw provinces (voivodeships)

—438 43 Lubelskie Province (Lubelskie Voivodeship)

Including former *Biała Podlaska, Chełm, Lublin, Zamość provinces (voivodeships)

—438 45 Świętokrzyskie Province (Świętokrzyskie Voivodeship)

Including former *Kielce Province (Kielce Voivodeship)

*For a specific part of this jurisdiction, region, or feature, see the part and follow instructions under —4–9

—438 47 Łódzkie Province (Łódzkie Voivodeship)

Including former Łódź, *Piotrków Trybunalski, Sieradz, *Skierniewice provinces (voivodeships)

—438 49 Wielkopolskie Province (Wielkopolskie Voivodeship)

Including former *Kalisz, Konin, *Leszno, *Piła, Poznań provinces (voivodeships)

—438 5 Southwestern Poland

Class here Silesia

For Czech Silesia, see —4372

—438 52 Dolnośląskie Province (Dolnośląskie Voivodeship)

Including former Jelenia Góra, Legnica, Wałbrzych, Wrocław provinces (voivodeships)

—438 55 Opolskie Province (Opolskie Voivodeship)

Class here former Opole Province (Opole Voivodeship)

—438 58 Śląskie Province (Śląskie Voivodeship)

Including former *Bielsko Province (Bielsko Voivodeship) [*formerly* —4386]; former *Częstochowa, *Katowice provinces (voivodeships)

—438 6 Southeastern Poland Polish Galicia

Class here Galicia

Former Bielsko Province (Bielsko Voivodeship) relocated to —43858

For East Galicia, see —4779

—438 62 Małopolskie Province (Małopolskie Voivodeship)

Including former Kraków, Nowy Sącz, *Tarnów provinces (voivodeships)

—438 66 Podkarpackie Province (Podkarpackie Voivodeship)

Including former *Tarnobrzeg Province (Tarnobrzeg Voivodeship) [*formerly* —4384]; former *Krosno, Przemyśl, Rzeszów provinces (voivodeships)

—439 Hungary

(Option: Class here ancient Pannonia; prefer —398)

*For a specific part of this jurisdiction, region, or feature, see the part and follow instructions under —4–9

—439 1 Pest county and Budapest

Variant name: Pest Megye

Subdivisions are added for Pest county and Budapest together, for Pest county alone

—439 12 Budapest

—439 7 Hungary west of Danube

Including Baranya, Fejér, Győr-Moson-Sopron, Komárom-Esztergom, Somogy, Tolna, Vas, Veszprém, Zala counties (megyek)

For Pest county, see —4391

—439 8 Hungary east of Danube

Including Bács-Kiskun, Csongrád, Heves, Jász-Nagykun-Szolnok, Nógrád counties (megyek)

For Pest county, see —4391; for easternmost Hungary, see —4399

—439 9 Easternmost Hungary

Including Békés, Borsod-Abaúj-Zemplén, Hajdú-Bihar, Szabolcs-Szatmár-Bereg counties (megyek)

—44 France and Monaco

Subdivisions are added for France and Monaco together, for France alone

For a specific overseas department of France, see the department, e.g., Martinique —72982

(Option: Class here ancient Celtic regions, Gaul [Gallia Transalpina]; prefer —364)

SUMMARY

— 441 Brittany (Bretagne) and Pays de la Loire
— 442 Basse-Normandie, Haute-Normandie, Picardie, Nord-Pas-de-Calais
— 443 Champagne-Ardenne, Ile-de-France, Lorraine, Alsace
— 444 Burgundy and Franche-Comté
— 445 Centre, Rhône-Alpes, Auvergne
— 446 Poitou-Charentes and Limousin
— 447 Aquitaine and Midi-Pyrénées
— 448 Languedoc-Roussillon
— 449 Provence-Côte d'Azur, Monaco, Corsica

—441 Brittany (Bretagne) and Pays de la Loire

Class here northwestern France

Subdivisions are added for Brittany (Bretagne) and Pays de la Loire together, for Brittany (Bretagne) alone

---

> —441 1–441 5 Brittany (Bretagne)

Class comprehensive works in —441

—441 1 Finistère department

—441 12 Brest

—441 2 Côtes-d'Armor department

Former name: Côtes-du-Nord department

—441 3 Morbihan department

—[441 4] Loire-Atlantique department

Relocated to —44167

—441 5 Ille-et-Vilaine department

—441 54 Rennes

—441 6 Pays de la Loire

Class here *Maine

For Sarthe department, see —4417; for Maine-et-Loire department, see —4418

—441 62 Mayenne department

—441 67 Loire-Atlantique department [*formerly* —4414]

—441 675 Nantes

—441 69 Vendée department [*formerly* —4461]

—441 7 Sarthe department

—441 8 Maine-et-Loire department

Class here *Anjou

—441 84 Angers

—442 Basse-Normandie, Haute-Normandie, Picardie, Nord-Pas-de-Calais

Class here Normandy (Normandie)

> —442 1–442 5 Normandy (Normandie)

Class comprehensive works on Normandy (Normandie) in —442

—442 1 Basse-Normandie

For Calvados department, see —4422; for Orne department, see —4423

—442 12 Manche department

For Chausey Islands, see —42348; for Roches Douvres, see —42349

*For a specific part of this jurisdiction, region, or feature, see the part and follow instructions under —4–9

—442 2 Calvados department

—442 24 Caen

—442 3 Orne department

—442 4 Haute-Normandie

For Seine-Maritime department, see —4425

—442 42 Eure department

—442 5 Seine-Maritime department

Former name: Seine-Inférieure department

—442 52 Rouen

—442 6 Picardy (Picardie)

—442 62 Somme department

—442 625 Amiens

—442 64 Oise department [*formerly* —4435]

—442 66 Aisne department [*formerly* —44345]

—442 7 Nord-Pas-de-Calais

Class here *northern France

For Nord department, see —4428

—442 72 Pas-de-Calais department

Class here Artois

—442 8 Nord department

Class here French Flanders

—442 84 Lille

—443 Champagne-Ardenne, Ile-de-France, Lorraine, Alsace

Class here *Marne River; northeastern France

—443 1 Champagne-Ardenne

Class here *Champagne

For Marne department, see —4432; for Aube and Haute-Marne departments, see —4433

—443 12 Ardennes department

—443 2 Marne department

—443 22 Reims

*For a specific part of this jurisdiction, region, or feature, see the part and follow instructions under —4–9

—443 3 Aube and Haute-Marne departments

—443 31 Aube department

—443 32 Haute-Marne department

—[443 4] Ile-de-France

Relocated to —4436

—[443 45] Aisne department

Relocated to —44266

—[443 5] Oise department

Relocated to —44264

—443 6 Ile-de-France [*formerly also* —4434]

Class here Région parisienne; former Seine-et-Oise department; Paris metropolitan area; *Seine River

Class Paris department in —44361

For Seine-et-Marne department, see —4437

—443 61 Paris department (Paris)

Class here *former Seine department

Class Paris metropolitan area in —4436

—443 62 Seine-Saint-Denis department

—443 63 Val-de-Marne department

—443 64 Hauts-de-Seine department

—443 65 Essonne department

—443 66 Yvelines department

—443 663 Versailles

—443 67 Val-d'Oise department

—443 7 Seine-et-Marne department

—443 8 Lorraine

—443 81 Meuse department

Including *Argonne

—443 82 Meurthe-et-Moselle department

—443 823 Nancy

Use of this number for Meurthe-et-Moselle department discontinued; class in —44382

*For a specific part of this jurisdiction, region, or feature, see the part and follow instructions under —4–9

—[443 825] Moselle department

Relocated to —44385

—[443 83] Alsace region

Relocated to —4439

—443 85 Moselle department [*formerly* —443825]

—443 853 Metz

—443 89 Vosges department [*formerly* —4439]

Including *Vosges Mountains

—443 9 Alsace [*formerly* —44383]

Vosges department relocated to —44389

For territory of Belfort, see —44455

(Option: Class here ancient Germania Superior; prefer —364)

—443 93 Haut-Rhin department

—443 933 Mulhouse

—443 95 Bas-Rhin department

—443 954 Strasbourg

—444 Burgundy and Franche-Comté

Class here *eastern France, *Saône River

—444 1 Burgundy (Bourgogne)

For Côte-d'Or department, see —4442; for Saône-et-Loire department, see —4443

—444 12 Yonne department

—444 16 Nièvre department [*formerly* —4456]

—444 2 Côte-d'Or department

—444 26 Dijon

—444 3 Saône-et-Loire department

—[444 4] Ain department

Relocated to —44583

—444 5 Franche-Comté

Class here *Jura Mountains in France

For Doubs department, see —4446; for Jura department, see —4447

*For a specific part of this jurisdiction, region, or feature, see the part and follow instructions under —4–9

—444 53 Haute-Saône department

—444 55 Territory of Belfort

—444 6 Doubs department

—444 66 Besançon

—444 7 Jura department

—[444 8] Savoie department

Relocated to —44585

—[444 9] Haute-Savoie department

Relocated to —44584

—445 Centre, Rhône-Alpes, Auvergne

Class here *Loire River; central France

(Option: Class here ancient Lugdunensis; prefer —364)

—445 1 *Centre

Class here *Orléanais

—445 12 Eure-et-Loir department

—445 124 Chartres

—445 2 Loiret department

—445 27 Orléans

—445 3 Loir-et-Cher department

Including *Sologne

—445 4 Indre-et-Loire department

Class here Touraine

For Indre and Cher departments, see —4455

—445 45 Tours

—445 5 Indre and Cher departments

Class here Berry

—445 51 Indre department

—445 52 Cher department

—445 525 Bourges

—[445 6] Nièvre department

Relocated to —44416

*For a specific part of this jurisdiction, region, or feature, see the part and follow instructions under —4–9

—[445 7] Allier department

Relocated to —44597

—445 8 Rhône-Alpes

Class here *Alps in France [*formerly* —449]; *Rhône River

—445 81 Loire department

Class comprehensive works on Lyonnais in —44582

—445 817 Saint-Etienne

—445 82 Rhône department

Class here Lyonnais

For Loire department, see —44581

—445 823 Lyon

—445 83 Ain department [*formerly* —4444]

—445 84 Haute-Savoie department [*formerly* —4449]

Class comprehensive works on Savoy in —44585

—445 85 Savoie department [*formerly* —4448]

Including Vanoise National Park

Class here Savoy

For Haute-Savoie department, see —4449

—445 86 Isère department [*formerly* —4499]

Class here Dauphiné [*formerly* —4496]

For Drôme department, see —44587; for Hautes-Alpes department, see —4497

—445 865 Grenoble

—445 87 Drôme department [*formerly* —4498]

—445 88 Valréas [*formerly* —4492]

Enclave of Vaucluse department

—445 89 Ardèche department [*formerly* —4482]

—445 9 Auvergne

Class here *Massif Central

—445 91 Puy-de-Dôme department

—445 914 Clermont-Ferrand

*For a specific part of this jurisdiction, region, or feature, see the part and follow instructions under —4–9

—445 92 Cantal department

—445 95 Haute-Loire department [*formerly* —44813]

—445 97 Allier department [*formerly* —4457]

Class here *Bourbonnais

—446 Poitou-Charentes and Limousin

Class here Poitou, *western France

Subdivisions are added for Poitou-Charentes and Limousin together, for Poitou-Charentes alone

—[446 1] Vendée department

Relocated to —44169

—446 2 Deux-Sèvres department

—446 3 Vienne department

—446 34 Poitiers

—446 4 Charente-Maritime department

Former name: Charente-Inférieure

Including Aunis

Class here *Saintonge

—446 42 La Rochelle

—446 5 Charente department

Class here *Angoumois; *Charente River

—446 6 Limousin

For Corrèze department, see —4467; for Creuse department, see —4468

—446 62 Haute-Vienne department

—446 624 Limoges

—446 7 Corrèze department

—446 8 Creuse department

Class here *Marche

—447 Aquitaine and Midi-Pyrénées

Class here *Guyenne; *Garonne River; southwestern France

(Option: Class here ancient Aquitania; prefer —364)

*For a specific part of this jurisdiction, region, or feature, see the part and follow instructions under —4–9

—447 1 Aquitaine

For Dordogne department, see —4472

—447 14 Gironde department

—447 144 Bordeaux

—447 15 Landes department [*formerly* —44772]

—447 16 Pyrénées-Atlantiques department [*formerly* —4479]

Class here Béarn, Pays Basque

—447 18 Lot-et-Garonne department [*formerly* —4476]

—447 2 Dordogne department

Class here *Périgord

—447 3 *Midi-Pyrénées [*formerly* —4486]

Class here *Gascony (Gascogne) [*formerly* —4477]; *Pyrenees Mountains in France [*formerly* —4489]

—447 33 Lot department

—447 35 Ariège department [*formerly* —4488]

Class here *Foix

—447 36 Haute-Garonne department [*formerly* —4486]

—447 367 Toulouse

—447 37 Tarn department [*formerly* —4485]

—447 4 Aveyron department

Class here *Rouergue

—447 5 Tarn-et-Garonne department

—[447 6] Lot-et-Garonne department

Relocated to —44718

—447 7 Gers department

Gascony (Gascogne) relocated to —4473

—[447 71] Gers department

Number discontinued; class in —4477

—[447 72] Landes department

Relocated to —44715

*For a specific part of this jurisdiction, region, or feature, see the part and follow instructions under —4–9

—447 8 Hautes-Pyrénées department

Including *Pyrenees National Park

—[447 9] Pyrénées-Atlantiques department

Relocated to —44716

—448 Languedoc-Roussillon

Class here *Languedoc; *southern France

See also —16382 for Gulf of Lions

(Option: Class here ancient Narbonensis; prefer —364)

—448 1 Lozère department

Including *Cévennes National Park; *Cévennes Mountains

—[448 13] Haute-Loire department

Relocated to —44595

—[448 15] Lozère department

Number discontinued; class in —4481

—[448 2] Ardèche department

Relocated to —44589

—448 3 Gard department

—448 37 Nîmes

—448 4 Hérault department

—448 42 Montpellier

—[448 5] Tarn department

Relocated to —44737

—[448 6] Haute-Garonne department

Midi-Pyrénées relocated to —4473; Haute-Garonne department relocated to —44736

—448 7 Aude department

—[448 8] Ariège department

Relocated to —44735

—448 9 Pyrénées-Orientales department

Class here Roussillon

Comprehensive works on Pyrenees Mountains in France relocated to —4473

*For a specific part of this jurisdiction, region, or feature, see the part and follow instructions under —4–9

—449 Provence-Côte d'Azur, Monaco, Corsica

Class here Provence; southeastern France

Subdivisions are added for Provence-Côte d'Azur, Monaco, Corsica together; for Provence-Côte d'Azur alone

Comprehensive works on Alps in France relocated to —4458

—449 1 Bouches-du-Rhône department

—449 12 Marseilles (Marseille)

—449 18 Arles

—449 2 Vaucluse department

Valréas relocated to —44588

—449 22 Avignon

—449 3 Var department

Including Port Cros National Park

—449 4 Alpes-Maritimes department and Monaco

Including *Mercantour National Park

Class here Nice (county); *Riviera (Côte d'Azur)

Subdivisions are added for Alpes-Maritimes department and Monaco together, for Alpes-Maritimes department alone

Class Nice (city) in —44941

—449 41 Nice (city)

Use of this number for Alpes-Maritimes department discontinued; class in —4494

Class Nice (county) in —4494

—[449 414] Nice

Number discontinued; class in —44941

—[449 45] Corsica (Corse)

Relocated to —4499

—449 49 Monaco

Independent principality, enclave in Alpes-Maritimes

—449 5 Alpes de Haute-Provence department

—[449 6] Dauphiné

Relocated to —44586

*For a specific part of this jurisdiction, region, or feature, see the part and follow instructions under —4–9

—449 7 Hautes-Alpes department

Including *Ecrins National Park

—[449 8] Drôme department

Relocated to —44587

—449 9 Corsica (Corse) [*formerly* —44945]

Isère department relocated to —44586

(Option: Class here ancient Corsica; prefer —379)

—449 92 Corse-de-Sud department

—449 96 Haute-Corse department

—45 Italian Peninsula and adjacent islands Italy

Class here *Apennines

Subdivisions are added for Italian Peninsula and adjacent islands, Italy together; for Italian Peninsula alone; for Italy alone

(Option: Class here ancient Italian Peninsula and adjacent territories, Roman Empire; prefer —37)

SUMMARY

—451 Northwestern Italy Piedmont (Piemonte) region
—452 Lombardy (Lombardia) region
—453 Northeastern Italy Veneto region
—454 Emilia-Romagna region and San Marino
—455 Tuscany (Toscana) region
—456 Central Italy and Vatican City
—457 Southern Italy
—458 Sicily and adjacent islands
—459 Sardinia

—451 Northwestern Italy Piedmont (Piemonte) region

Class here *Alps in Italy

(Option: Class here ancient Gallia Cisalpina; prefer —372)

—451 1 Valle d'Aosta region

Class here Aosta

> —451 2–451 7 Piedmont (Piemonte) region

Class comprehensive works in —451

—451 2 Turin (Torino) province

Class here Turin

*For a specific part of this jurisdiction, region, or feature, see the part and follow instructions under —4–9

—451 3 Cuneo province

—451 4 Alessandria province

—451 5 Asti province

—451 6 Novara and Verbania provinces

Subdivisions are added for Novara and Verbania provinces together, for Novara province alone

—451 65 Verbania (Verbano-Cusio-Ossola) province

Including *Lake Maggiore

—451 7 Vercelli and Biella provinces

Subdivisions are added for Vercelli and Biella provinces together, for Vercelli province alone

—451 76 Biella province

—451 8 Liguria region

Class here *Italian Riviera

See also —16382 for Ligurian Sea

(Option: Class here ancient Liguria; prefer —371)

—451 82 Genoa (Genova) province

Class here Genoa

—451 83 La Spezia province

—451 84 Savona province

—451 87 Imperia province

—452 Lombardy (Lombardia) region

Class here *Po River

—452 1 Milan (Milano) and Lodi provinces

Class here Milan

Subdivisions are added for Milan (Milano) and Lodi provinces together, for Milan (Milano) province alone

—452 19 Lodi province

—452 2 Varese province

—452 3 Como and Lecco provinces

Class here Como

Subdivisions are added for Como and Lecco provinces together, for Como province alone

*For a specific part of this jurisdiction, region, or feature, see the part and follow instructions under —4–9

—452 37 Lecco province

—452 4 Bergamo province

Class here Bergamo

—452 5 Sondrio province

—452 6 Brescia province

Including *Lake Garda

Class here Brescia

—452 7 Cremona province

Class here Cremona

—452 8 Mantua (Mantova) province

Class here Mantua

—452 9 Pavia province

—453 Northeastern Italy Veneto region

See also —16385 for Gulf of Venice

(Option: Class here ancient Venetia; prefer —373)

> —453 1–453 7 Veneto region

Class comprehensive works in —453

—453 1 Venice (Venezia) province

Class here Venice

—453 2 Padua (Padova) province

Class here Padua

—453 3 Rovigo province (Polesine)

—453 4 Verona province

Class here Verona

—453 5 Vicenza province

Class here Vicenza

—453 6 Treviso province

Class here Treviso

—453 7 Belluno province

—453 8 Trentino-Alto Adige region

*For a specific part of this jurisdiction, region, or feature, see the part and follow instructions under —4–9

—453 83 Bolzano province (Alto Adige)

Class here South Tyrol

—453 85 Trento province

Including Trento

—453 9 Friuli-Venezia Giulia region

—453 91 Udine province

—453 92 Gorizia province

—453 93 Trieste province

Class here Trieste

—453 94 Pordenone province

—454 Emilia-Romagna region and San Marino

Subdivisions are added for Emilia-Romagna region and San Marino together, for Emilia-Romagna region alone

—454 1 Bologna province

Class here Bologna

—454 2 Modena province

Class here Modena

—454 3 Reggio Emilia (Reggio nell'Emilia) province

—454 4 Parma province

Class here Parma

—454 5 Ferrara province

Class here Ferrara

—454 6 Piacenza province

—454 7 Ravenna province

Class here Ravenna

—454 8 Forlì province

—454 9 San Marino

Independent state

—455 Tuscany (Toscana) region

(Option: Class here ancient Etruria; prefer —375)

—455 1 Florence (Firenze) and Prato provinces

Class here Florence

Subdivisions are added for Florence (Firenze) and Prato provinces together, for Florence (Firenze) province alone

—455 19 Prato province

—455 2 Pistoia province

—455 3 Lucca province

—455 4 Massa-Carrara (Massa e Carrara) province

—455 5 Pisa province

Class here Pisa

—455 6 Livorno province

Including Elba island

—455 7 Grosseto province

Class here *Maremma

—455 8 Siena province

Class here Siena

—455 9 Arezzo province

—456 Central Italy and Vatican City

Class here former *Papal States (States of the Church)

Subdivisions are added for central Italy and Vatican City together, for central Italy alone

—456 2 Lazio region

For Rome province, see —4563

(Option: Class here ancient Latium; prefer —376)

—456 22 Frosinone province

—456 23 Latina province

Including Pontine Islands

Class here Pontine Marshes

—456 24 Rieti province

—456 25 Viterbo province

Class here Viterbo

(Option: Class here ancient Volsinii Novi [Bolsena]; prefer —376)

—456 3 Rome (Roma) province and Vatican City

Subdivisions are added for Rome (Roma) province and Vatican City together, for Rome (Roma) province alone

(Option: Class here ancient Ostia, Veii; prefer —376)

*For a specific part of this jurisdiction, region, or feature, see the part and follow instructions under —4–9

—456 32 Rome

(Option: Class here ancient Rome; prefer —376)

—456 34 Vatican City

Independent papal state, enclave in Rome

—456 5 Umbria region

(Option: Class here ancient Umbria; prefer —374)

—456 51 Perugia province

Class here Perugia

—456 52 Terni province

(Option: Class here ancient Volsinii [Orvieto]; prefer —374)

—456 7 Marches (Marche) region

(Option: Class here ancient Picenum; prefer —374)

—456 71 Ancona province

Including Ancona

—456 73 Macerata province

—456 75 Ascoli Piceno province

—456 77 Pesaro e Urbino province

—457 Southern Italy

For Sicily, see —458

(Option: Class here ancient southern Italy; prefer —377)

—457 1 Abruzzo and Molise regions

Subdivisions are added for Abruzzo and Molise regions together, for Abruzzo region alone

(Option: Class here ancient Samnium; prefer —377)

> —457 11–457 17 Abruzzo region

Class comprehensive works in —4571

—457 11 Aquila (L'Aquila) province

Including L'Aquila

—457 13 Chieti province

—457 15 Teramo province

—457 17 Pescara province

—457 19 Molise region

—457 192 Campobasso province

Including Campobasso

—457 194 Isernia province

—457 2 Campania region

For Naples province, see —4573; for Salerno province, see —4574

(Option: Class here ancient Campania; prefer —377)

—457 21 Avellino province

—457 23 Benevento province

—457 25 Caserta province

—457 3 Naples (Napoli) province

Including Capri, Ischia Islands

Class here Naples

(Option: Class here ancient Naples, Herculaneum, Pompeii, Stabiae; prefer —377)

—457 4 Salerno province

Class here Salerno

—457 5 Puglia (Apulia) region

See also —16386 for Gulf of Taranto

(Option: Class here ancient Apulia, Calabria, Brundusium; prefer —377)

—457 51 Bari province

Class here Bari

—457 53 Lecce province

—457 54 Brindisi province

Class here Brindisi

—457 55 Taranto province

—457 57 Foggia province

—457 7 Basilicata (Lucania) region

See also —16386 for Gulf of Taranto

(Option: Class here ancient Lucania; prefer —377)

—457 71 Potenza province

—457 72 Matera province

—457 8 Calabria region

See also —16386 for Gulf of Taranto, Strait of Messina

(Option: Class here ancient Bruttium; prefer —377)

—457 81 Catanzaro province

Vibo Valentia province, formerly part of Catanzaro province, relocated to —45782; Crotone province, formerly part of Catanzaro province, relocated to —45787

—457 82 Vibo Valentia province [*formerly* —45781]

—457 83 Reggio di Calabria province

Class here Reggio di Calabria

—457 85 Cosenza province

—457 87 Crotone province [*formerly* —45781]

—458 Sicily and adjacent islands

Subdivisions are added for Sicily and adjacent islands together, for Sicily alone

(Option: Class here ancient Sicily; prefer —378)

> —458 1–458 2 Sicily region

Class comprehensive works in —458

—458 1 Eastern Sicily

—458 11 Messina province

Including Lipari Islands

Class here Messina

See also —16386 for Strait of Messina

—458 12 Enna province

—458 13 Catania province

Including Mount Etna

Class here Catania

—458 14 Syracuse (Siracusa) province

Class here Syracuse

(Option: Class here ancient Syracuse; prefer —378)

—458 15 Ragusa province

—458 2 Western Sicily

—458 21 Caltanissetta province

—458 22 Agrigento province

Including Pelagian Islands

Class here Agrigento

—458 23 Palermo province

Class here Palermo

—458 24 Trapani province

Including Egadi Islands

—458 5 Malta

Independent state

(Option: Class here ancient Malta; prefer —378)

—459 Sardinia

Region of Italy

(Option: Class here ancient Sardinia; prefer —379)

—459 1 Cagliari province

Class here Cagliari

—459 2 Nuoro province

—459 3 Sassari province

—459 4 Oristano province

—46 Iberian Peninsula and adjacent islands Spain

Subdivisions are added for Iberian Peninsula and adjacent islands, Spain together; for Iberian Peninsula alone; for Spain alone

(Option: Class here ancient Iberian Peninsula and adjacent islands, Tarraconensis; prefer —366)

SUMMARY

— 461	**Northwestern Spain Galicia autonomous community**
— 462	**Western Spain León region**
— 463	**Castile**
— 464	**New Castile region Castilla-La Mancha autonomous community**
— 465	**Northeastern Spain**
— 466	**País Vasco autonomous community**
— 467	**Eastern Spain and Andorra Cataluña autonomous community**
— 468	**Andalusia autonomous community and Gibraltar**
— 469	**Portugal**

> —461–468 Spain

Class comprehensive works in —46

For Ceuta and Melilla, see —641; for Canary Islands, see —649

—461 Northwestern Spain Galicia autonomous community

> —461 1–461 7 Galicia autonomous community

Class comprehensive works in —461

—461 1 La Coruña province

Including Santiago de Compostela

—461 3 Lugo province

—461 5 Orense province

—461 7 Pontevedra province

—461 9 Asturias autonomous community (Asturias province)

Class here Oviedo

—462 Western Spain León region

Class here Castilla-León autonomous community; *Cantabrian Mountains

For Burgos province, see —46353; for Soria province, see —46355; for Segovia province, see —46357; for Avila province, see —46359

> —462 1–462 5 León region

Class comprehensive works in —462

—462 1 León province

—462 2 Palencia province

—462 3 Valladolid province

Class here Valladolid

—462 4 Zamora province

—462 5 Salamanca province

—462 6 Extremadura autonomous community

For Badajoz province, see —4627; for Cáceres province, see —4628

—462 7 Badajoz province

Including Mérida

—462 8 Cáceres province

Class here *Tagus River in Spain

*For a specific part of this jurisdiction, region, or feature, see the part and follow instructions under —4–9

—463 Castile

For New Castile region, see —464

—463 5 Old Castile region

For Palencia province, see —4622; for Valladolid province, see —4623

—463 51 Cantabria autonomous community (Cantabria province)

Including Santander

—463 53 Burgos province

For Treviño, see —4667

—463 54 La Rioja autonomous community (La Rioja province)

Including Logroño

—463 55 Soria province

—463 57 Segovia province

Class here Segovia

—463 59 Avila province

—464 New Castile region Castilla-La Mancha autonomous community

Class here La Mancha

—464 1 Madrid autonomous community (Madrid province)

Class here Madrid

> —464 3–464 8 Castilla-La Mancha autonomous community

Class comprehensive works in —464

—464 3 Toledo province

Class here Toledo

—464 5 Ciudad Real province

—464 6 Albacete province

—464 7 Cuenca province

—464 9 Guadalajara province

—465 Northeastern Spain

Class here *Pyrenees Mountains, *Ebro River

For Cataluña autonomous community, see —467

*For a specific part of this jurisdiction, region, or feature, see the part and follow instructions under —4–9

—465 2 Navarra autonomous community (Navarra province)

Including Pamplona

—465 5 Aragon autonomous community

—465 51 Teruel province

—465 53 Zaragoza (Saragossa) province

Class here Zaragoza

—465 55 Huesca province

—466 País Vasco autonomous community

Class here territory of the Basque people

For Pyrénées-Atlantiques department of France, see —44716; for Navarra autonomous community, see —4652

—466 1 Guipúzcoa

Class here San Sebastián

—466 3 Vizcaya (Biscay)

Class here Bilbao

For Orduña, see —4669

—466 5 Alava

Including Vitoria

—466 7 Treviño

Enclave of Burgos province in Alava province

—466 9 Orduña

Enclave of Vizcaya province between Alava and Burgos provinces

—467 Eastern Spain and Andorra

Class here Cataluña autonomous community

Subdivisions are added for eastern Spain and Andorra together, for eastern Spain alone

---

> —467 1–467 4 Cataluña autonomous community

Class comprehensive works in —467

—467 1 Gerona province

—467 2 Barcelona province

Class here Barcelona

—467 3 Tarragona province

—467 4 Lérida province

—467 5 Baleares autonomous community (Balearic Islands)

—467 52 Minorca (Menorca)

—467 54 Majorca (Mallorca)

—467 542 Palma

—467 56 Formentera and Ibiza

—467 6 Valencia autonomous community

—467 61 Castellón province

—467 63 Valencia province

Class here Valencia

—467 65 Alicante province

—467 7 Murcia autonomous community (Murcia province)

Including Cartagena

Class here former Murcia region

For Albacete province, see —4646

—467 9 Andorra

Independent state

—468 Andalusia autonomous community and Gibraltar

Class here *Guadalquivir River

Subdivisions are added for Andalusia autonomous community and Gibraltar together, for Andalusia autonomous community alone

(Option: Class here ancient Baetica; prefer —366)

> —468 1–468 8 Andalusia autonomous community

Class comprehensive works in —468

—468 1 Almería province

—468 2 Granada province

Class here Granada

—468 3 Jaén province

—468 4 Córdoba province

Class here Córdoba

*For a specific part of this jurisdiction, region, or feature, see the part and follow instructions under —4–9

—468 5 Málaga province

Class here Málaga

For Melilla, see —641

—468 6 Seville province

Class here Seville

—468 7 Huelva province

—468 8 Cádiz province

For Ceuta, see —641

—468 9 Gibraltar

British crown colony

—469 Portugal

(Option: Class here ancient Lusitania; prefer —366)

—469 1 Historic province of Entre Douro e Minho

—469 12 Modern province of Minho

Including Braga and Viana do Castelo districts

—469 15 Modern province of Douro Litoral

Including Porto district

For Viseu district, see —46931; for Aveiro district, see —46935

—469 2 Historic province of Trás-os-Montes Modern province of Trás-os-Montes e Alto Douro

Including Bragança and Vila Real districts

For Guarda and Viseu districts, see —46931

—469 3 Historic province of Beira

For modern province of Douro Litoral, see —46915; for modern province of Trás-os-Montes e Alto Douro, see —4692

—469 31 Modern province of Beira Alta

Including Guarda and Viseu districts

For Coimbra district, see —46935

—469 33 Modern province of Beira Baixa

Including Castelo Branco district

For Coimbra district, see —46935; for Santarém district, see —46945

—469 35 Modern province of Beira Litoral

Including Aveiro and Coimbra districts

For Leiria district, see —46942; for Santarém district, see —46945

—469 4 Historic province of Estremadura

For modern province of Beira Litoral, see —46935; for modern province of Baixo Alentejo, see —46955

—469 42 Modern province of Estremadura

Including Leiria and Setúbal districts

—469 425 Lisbon (Lisboa) district

Class here Lisbon

—469 45 Modern province of Ribatejo

Including Santarém district

Class here *Tagus River

For Lisbon district, see —469425; for Portalegre district, see —46952

—469 5 Historic province of Alentejo

—469 52 Modern province of Alto Alentejo

Including Evora and Portalegre districts

—469 55 Modern province of Baixo Alentejo

Including Beja district

For Setúbal district, see —46942

—469 6 Algarve province (Faro district)

—469 8 Madeira (Funchal district)

Islands in Atlantic Ocean

—469 9 Azores

Islands in Atlantic Ocean

Including Angra do Heroísmo, Horta, Ponta Delgada districts

—47 Eastern Europe Russia

Class here Commonwealth of Independent States, former Union of Soviet Socialist Republics (Soviet Union)

For Balkan Peninsula, see —496; for Commonwealth of Independent States in Asia, see —58

*For a specific part of this jurisdiction, region, or feature, see the part and follow instructions under —4–9

SUMMARY

—471	**Northern area of European Russia**
—472	**Western area of Russia**
—473	**West central area of Russia**
—474	**Eastern area of European Russia**
—475	**Caucasus**
—476	**Moldova**
—477	**Ukraine**
—478	**Belarus**
—479	**Lithuania, Latvia, Estonia**

> —471–474 Russia

Class comprehensive works in —47

For Caucasus area of Russia, see —4752; for Siberia (Asiatic Russia), see —57

—471 Northern area of European Russia

For Komi republic, see —4743

See also —16324 for White Sea

—471 1 Nenets autonomous district (Nenet͡skiĭ avtonomnyĭ okrug)

—471 3 Murmansk province (Murmanskai͡a oblastʹ)

Including Kola Peninsula

—471 5 Karelia republic

Including Lakes *Ladoga and *Onega

—471 7 Arkhangelʹsk province (Arkhangelʹskai͡a oblastʹ)

For Franz Josef Land, see —985; for Novaya Zemlya, see —986

—471 9 Vologda province (Vologodskai͡a oblastʹ)

—472 Western area of Russia

—472 1 Leningrad province (Leningradskai͡a oblastʹ)

Class here Saint Petersburg (Leningrad); Baltic Sea area of Russia

For Novgorod province, see —4722; for Pskov province, see —4723; for Kaliningrad province, see —4724

See also —16334 for Baltic Sea

—472 2 Novgorod province (Novogrodskai͡a oblastʹ)

—472 3 Pskov province (Pskovskai͡a oblastʹ)

—472 4 Kaliningrad province (Kaliningradskai͡a oblastʹ)

*For a specific part of this jurisdiction, region, or feature, see the part and follow instructions under —4–9

—472 5 Bryansk province (Brīanskaīa oblast´)

—472 6 Kaluga province (Kaluzhskaīa oblast´)

—472 7 Smolensk province (Smolenskaīa oblast´)

—472 8 Tver´ province (Tverskaīa oblast´)

Variant name: Kalinin province (Kalininskaīa oblast´)

—473 West central area of Russia

—473 1 Moscow province (Moskovskaīa oblast´)

Class here Moscow

—473 2 Yaroslavl´ province (ÎAroslavskaīa oblast´)

—473 3 Ivanovo province (Ivanovskaīa oblast´), Kostroma province (Kostromskaīa oblast´), Ryazan province (Rīazanskaīa oblast´), Vladimir province (Vladimirskaīa oblast´)

—473 4 Tula province (Tul´skaīa oblast´)

—473 5 Central Black Earth Region

Including Belgorod (Belgorodskaīa), Kursk (Kurskaīa), Lipetsk (Lipet͡skaīa), Orel (Orlovskaīa), Tambov (Tambovskaīa), Voronezh (Voronezhskaīa) provinces (oblasti)

—474 Eastern area of European Russia

Class here *Volga River

See also —57 for Asiatic Russia (eastern half of Russia)

—474 1 Nizhegorod province (Nizhegorodskaīa oblast´)

Variant name: Nizhniy Novgorod province

—474 2 Kirov province (Kirovskaīa oblast´)

—474 3 Ural Mountains region

Including Chelyabinsk (Chelīabinskaīa), Orenburg (Orenburgskaīa), Perm´ (Permskaīa), Sverdlovsk (Sverdlovskaīa) provinces (oblasti); Bashkortostan (Bashkiriīa), Komi republics; Komi-Permīak autonomous district (Komi-Permīat͡skiĭ avtonomnyĭ okrug)

Class here *Ural Mountains

—474 4 Samara province (Samarskaīa oblast´)

—474 5 Tatarstan republic

—474 6 Penza province (Penzenskaīa oblast´), Saratov province (Saratovskaīa oblast´), Ul´yanovsk province (Ul´īanovskaīa oblast´); Chuvashia (Chuvashiīa) republic, Mari El republic, Mordvinia (Mordoviīa) republic, Udmurtia (Udmurtiīa) republic

*For a specific part of this jurisdiction, region, or feature, see the part and follow instructions under —4–9

—474 7 Volgograd province (Volgogradskaia͡ oblastʹ)

—474 8 Astrakhan province (Astrakhanskaia͡ oblastʹ), Kalmykia (Kalmykii͡a) republic

—474 9 Rostov province (Rostovskaia͡ oblastʹ)

Class here *Don River

—475 Caucasus

Class here *Caspian Sea

(Option: Class here ancient Caucasus; prefer —395)

—475 2 Caucasus area of Russia

Including Krasnodar (Krasnodarskiĭ), Stavropolʹ (Stavropolʹskiĭ) territories (kraia͡); Adygea, Chechnya (Chechnia͡), Dagestan, Ingushetia (Ingushetnia͡), Kabardino-Balkaria (Kabardino-Balkarii͡a), Karachay-Cherkessia (Karachaevo-Cherkesii͡a), North Ossetia (Severnaia͡ Osetii͡a) republics

See also —16389 for Sea of Azov

> —475 4–475 8 Transcaucasus

Class comprehensive works in —475

—475 4 Azerbaijan

Including Nagorno-Karabakh, Nakhichevan autonomous republics

Class comprehensive works on Azerbaijan region in —553

(Option: Class here ancient Albania; prefer —395)

—475 6 Armenia

Class comprehensive works on Armenia region in —5662

—475 8 Georgia

Including Abkhazia, Ajaria autonomous republics; South Osset autonomous region

(Option: Class here ancient Colchis, Iberia; prefer —395)

—476 Moldova

Class here *Bessarabia

Class comprehensive works on Moldavia in —4981

*For a specific part of this jurisdiction, region, or feature, see the part and follow instructions under —4–9

—477 Ukraine

Including *Dnieper River

Class here *Black Sea area of Commonwealth of Independent States

See also —16389 for Black Sea

(Option: Class here ancient Black Sea region, Sarmatia; prefer —395)

—477 1 Crimea province (Krymskaîa oblast´)

—477 2 Odessa province (Odes´ka oblast´)

—477 3 Kherson province (Khersons´ka oblast´), Mykolayiv province (Mykolaïvs´ka oblast´), Zaporizhzhya province (Zaporiz´ka oblast´)

See also —16389 for Sea of Azov

—477 4 *Donets Basin

Including Dnepropetrovsk (Dnipropetrovs´ka), Donets´k (Donets´ka), Luhans´k (Luhans´ka) provinces (oblasti)

Class here *Donets River

—477 5 Kharkiv province (Kharkivs´ka oblast´)

—477 6 Cherkasy province (Cherkas´ka oblast´), Chernihiv province (Chernihivs´ka oblast´), Kirovohrad province (Kirovohrads´ka oblast´), Poltava province (Poltavs´ka oblast´), Sumy province (Sums´ka oblast´)

—477 7 Kiev province (Kyïvs´ka oblast´)

—477 8 Khmel´nyts´kyy province (Khmel´nyts´ka oblast´), Vinnytsa province (Vinnyts´ka oblast´), Zhytomyr province (Zhytomyrs´ka oblast´)

—477 9 Western Ukraine

Including Chernivtsy (Chernivets´ka), Ivano-Frankivs´k (Ivano-Frankivs´ka), L´viv (L´vivs´ka), Rivne (Rivnens´ka), Ternopil´ (Ternopil´s´ka), Volyn (Volyns´ka), Transcarpathia (Zakarpats´ka) provinces (oblasti); North Bukovina

Class here East Galicia; *Carpathian Mountains, *Dniester River

—478 Belarus

Variant names: Belorussia, Byelarus

Including *Pripet Marshes

—478 1 Homelâ province (Homel´skaîa voblasts´)

—478 2 Mahilîoŭ province (Mahilîoŭskaîa voblasts´)

—478 4 Vitebsk province (Vitebskaîa voblasts´)

*For a specific part of this jurisdiction, region, or feature, see the part and follow instructions under —4–9

—478 6 Minsk province (Minskaı͡a voblastsʹ)

—478 8 Hrodzen province (Hrodzenskaı͡a voblastsʹ)

—478 9 Brėst province (Brėstskaı͡a voblastsʹ)

—479 Lithuania, Latvia, Estonia

Class here Baltic States

See also —16334 for Baltic Sea; also —485 for comprehensive works on Baltic Sea Region

—479 3 Lithuania

—479 6 Latvia

Including Courland

—479 8 Estonia

Class here Livonia

For Latvia, see —4796

See also —16334 for Gulf of Finland

—48 Scandinavia

Class here northern Europe

For northwestern islands, see —491

(Option: Class here ancient Scandinavia; prefer —363)

SUMMARY

—481	**Norway**
—482	**Southeastern Norway (Østlandet)**
—483	**Southwestern Norway (Sørlandet and Vestlandet)**
—484	**Central and northern Norway (Trøndelag and Nord-Norge)**
—485	**Sweden**
—486	**Southern Sweden (Götaland)**
—487	**Central Sweden (Svealand)**
—488	**Northern Sweden (Norrland)**
—489	**Denmark and Finland**

—481 Norway

For divisions of Norway, see —482–484; for Svalbard, see —981; for Jan Mayen Island, see —983

> —482–484 Divisions of Norway

Class comprehensive works in —481

—482 Southeastern Norway (Østlandet)

See also —16336 for Skagerrak

—482 1 Oslo county (Oslo fylke)

Class here Oslo

—482 2 Akershus county (Akershus fylke)

—482 3 Østfold county (Østfold fylke)

—482 4 Hedmark county (Hedmark fylke)

—482 5 Oppland county (Oppland fylke)

—482 6 Buskerud county (Buskerud fylke)

—482 7 Vestfold county (Vestfold fylke)

—482 8 Telemark county (Telemark fylke)

—483 Sørlandet and Vestlandet

Subdivisions are added for Sørlandet and Vestlandet together, for Sørlandet alone

See also —16336 for Skagerrak

> —483 1–483 2 Counties of Sørlandet

Class comprehensive works in —483

—483 1 Aust-Agder county (Aust-Agder fylke)

Use of this number for Sørlandet discontinued; class in —483

—483 2 Vest-Agder county (Vest-Agder fylke)

—483 3 Vestlandet

For counties of Vestlandet, see —4834–4839

> —483 4–483 9 Counties of Vestlandet

Class comprehensive works in —4833

—483 4 Rogaland county (Rogaland fylke)

—483 6 Hordaland county (Hordaland fylke)

—483 8 Sogn og Fjordane county (Sogn og Fjordane fylke)

—483 9 Møre og Romsdal county (Møre og Romsdal fylke)

—484 Trøndelag and Nord-Norge

Subdivisions are added for Trøndelag and Nord-Norge together, for Trøndelag alone

---

> —484 1–484 2 Counties of Trøndelag

Class comprehensive works in —484

—484 1 Sør-Trøndelag county (Sør-Trøndelag fylke)

Use of this number for Trøndelag discontinued; class in —484

—484 2 Nord-Trøndelag county (Nord-Trøndelag fylke)

—484 3 Nord-Norge

Class here northern Norway

For counties of Nord-Norge, see —4844–4846

> —484 4–484 6 Counties of Nord-Norge

Class comprehensive works in —4843

—484 4 Nordland county (Nordland fylke)

Including Lofoten, Vesterålen islands

—484 5 Troms county (Troms fylke)

—484 6 Finnmark county (Finnmark fylke)

—485 Sweden

Class here *Baltic Sea Region

For divisions of Sweden, see —486–488

See also —16334 for Baltic Sea; also —479 for Baltic States

> —486–488 Divisions of Sweden

Class comprehensive works in —485

—486 Southern Sweden (Götaland)

Including Älvsborg, Blekinge, Göteborg och Bohus, Gotland, Halland, Jönköping, Kalmar, Kristianstad, Kronoberg, Malmöhus, Östergötland, Skaraborg counties (länet)

Including Öland Island

See also —16334 for Baltic Sea, Kattegat

—487 Central Sweden (Svealand)

Including Gävleborg, Kopparberg, Örebro, Södermanland, Uppsala, Värmland, Västmanland counties (länet)

—487 3 Stockholm county (Stockholms län)

Class here Stockholm

*For a specific part of this jurisdiction, region, or feature, see the part and follow instructions under —4–9

—488 Northern Sweden (Norrland)

Including Jämtland, Norrbotten, Västerbotten, Västernorrland counties (länet)

See also —16334 for Gulf of Bothnia

—489 Denmark and Finland

Subdivisions are added for Denmark and Finland together, for Denmark alone

---

> —489 1–489 5 Denmark

Class comprehensive works in —489

For Greenland, see —982

—489 1 Zealand (Sjælland) island

Including Frederiksborg, Roskilde, Storstrøms, Vestsjælland counties (amts)

For Falster and Lolland islands portion of Storstrøms county, see —4893

See also —16334 for Great Belt, Oresund

—489 13 Copenhagen

Including Frederiksberg

See also —48914 for Copenhagen county (Københavns amt)

—489 14 Copenhagen county (Københavns amt)

See also —48913 for Copenhagen

—489 2 Bornholm island

Class here Bornholms county (Bornholms amt)

—489 3 Falster and Lolland islands

Class comprehensive works on Storstrøms county in —4891

—489 4 Fyn and Langeland islands

Class here Fyns county (Fyns amt)

See also —16334 for Great and Little Belts

—489 5 Jutland peninsula

Including Århus, Nordjylland, Ribe, Ringkøbing, Sonderjylland, Vejle, Viborg counties (amts)

See also —16336 for Skagerrak

—489 7 Finland

See also —16334 for Gulf of Finland

—489 71 Southern Finland

Including Kymi, Uusimaa provinces (läänit); Helsinki

—489 73 Southwestern Finland

Including Ahvenanmaa, Häme, Keski-Suomi, Turku ja Pori, Vaasa provinces (läänit); Åland Islands

—489 75 Southeastern Finland

Including Kuopio, Mikkeli, Pohjois-Karjala provinces (läänit)

—489 76 Oulu province (Oulu lääni)

—489 77 Lappi province (Lappi lääni)

Class here Lapland

For Murmansk province of Russia, see —4713; for northern Norway, see —4843; for northern Sweden, see —488

—49 Other parts of Europe

SUMMARY

— 491	**Northwestern islands**
— 492	**Netherlands**
— 493	**Southern Low Countries Belgium**
— 494	**Switzerland**
— 495	**Greece**
— 496	**Balkan Peninsula**
— 497	**Serbia and Montenegro, Croatia, Slovenia, Bosnia and Hercegovina, Macedonia**
— 498	**Romania**
— 499	**Bulgaria**

—491 Northwestern islands

—491 2 Iceland

—491 5 Faeroes

—492 Netherlands

Class here comprehensive works on Low Countries, on Benelux countries

For southern Low Countries, see —493; for Netherlands Antilles, see —72986

(Option: Class here ancient Germania Inferior; prefer —364)

—492 1 Northeastern provinces of Netherlands

—492 12 Groningen

—492 13 Friesland

Including *West Frisian Islands

*For a specific part of this jurisdiction, region, or feature, see the part and follow instructions under —4–9

—492 15 Drenthe

—492 16 Overijssel

Including North East Polder

—492 18 Gelderland

Including Arnhem, Nijmegen

Class here *IJssel River

—492 2 Flevoland (Zuidelijke IJsselmeerpolders) and Markerwaard

Including Almere, Dronten, Lelystad, Zeewolde

Class here *IJssel Lake (Zuider Zee)

—492 3 Northwestern provinces of Netherlands

—492 32 Utrecht

Class here Utrecht

—492 35 North Holland (Noord-Holland)

Including Haarlem; Wieringermeer

—492 352 Amsterdam

—492 38 South Holland (Zuid-Holland)

Including Delft, Leiden

—492 382 The Hague

—492 385 Rotterdam

—492 4 Southern provinces of Netherlands

Class here *Meuse (Maas) River

—492 42 Zeeland

—492 45 North Brabant (Noord-Brabant)

Including Eindhoven

—492 48 Limburg

Including Maastricht

—493 Southern Low Countries Belgium

(Option: Class here ancient Belgica; prefer —364)

> —493 1–493 4 Belgium

Class comprehensive works in —493

*For a specific part of this jurisdiction, region, or feature, see the part and follow instructions under —4–9

—493 1 Northwestern provinces of Belgium

Class here Flanders

For French Flanders region, see —4428

—493 12 West Flanders

—493 122 Bruges (Brugge)

—493 14 East Flanders

—493 142 Ghent (Gent)

—493 2 Northern provinces of Belgium

—493 22 Antwerp

—493 222 Antwerp (Anvers)

—493 24 Limburg

—493 3 Brabant province

—493 32 Brussels

—493 4 Southern provinces of Belgium (Wallonia)

—493 42 Hainaut

—493 44 Namur

—493 46 Liège

Class here *Meuse (Maas) River in Belgium

—493 48 Luxembourg

Class here *Ardennes

—493 5 Luxembourg

Grand duchy

—494 Switzerland

Class here *Rhine River in Switzerland

—494 3 Jura region cantons

Class here *Jura Mountains, *Birs River

(Option: Class here ancient Helvetia; prefer —364)

—494 32 Basel-Stadt (Bâle-Ville)

Class here Basel, former Basel canton

For Baselland, see —49433

—494 33 Baselland

*For a specific part of this jurisdiction, region, or feature, see the part and follow instructions under —4–9

—494 35 Solothurn

—494 36 Jura

—494 38 Neuchâtel

Class here *Lake of Neuchâtel

—494 5 Mittelland cantons

—494 51 Geneva

Class here Geneva

—494 52 Vaud

Class here *Lake Geneva (Lake Léman)

—494 524 Lausanne

—494 53 Fribourg (Freiburg)

—494 54 Bern

Class here *Bernese Alps, *Aar River

—494 542 Bern

—494 55 Luzern

Class here *Lake Lucerne (Vierwaldstätter See)

—494 56 Aargau

Including *Reuss River

—494 57 Zurich

Including *Lake of Zurich

—494 572 Zurich

—494 58 Schaffhausen (Schaffhouse)

—494 59 Thurgau

Class here *Lake of Constance (Bodensee) in Switzerland, *Thur River

—494 7 Alpine region cantons

Class here *Alps

—494 71 Appenzell Ausser-Rhoden and Appenzell Inner-Rhoden

Class here former Appenzell canton

—494 712 Appenzell Ausser-Rhoden

—494 714 Appenzell Inner-Rhoden

*For a specific part of this jurisdiction, region, or feature, see the part and follow instructions under —4–9

—494 72 Saint Gall

—494 73 Graubünden (Grisons)

Including Swiss National Park, *Rätikon Mountains, *Rhaetian Alps

—494 74 Glarus

Class here *Glarner Alps

—494 75 Schwyz and Zug

—494 752 Schwyz

—494 756 Zug

—494 76 Nidwalden and Obwalden

—494 762 Nidwalden

—494 764 Obwalden

—494 77 Uri

—494 78 Ticino

Including *Lake of Lugano

Class here *Lepontine Alps

—494 79 Valais (Wallis)

Class here *Rhône River in Switzerland, *Pennine Alps

—495 Greece

See also —16388 for Aegean Sea

(Option: Class here ancient Greece; prefer —38)

—495 1 Attica and Central Greece regions and Aetolia and Acarnania department

—495 12 Attica region (Attikē periphereia)

Class here Athens

For Kythēra Island, Peloponnesus portion of Attica region, see —4952

(Option: Class here ancient Attica, Athens, Marathon; prefer —385)

*For a specific part of this jurisdiction, region, or feature, see the part and follow instructions under —4–9

—495 15 Central Greece region (Sterea Hellada periphereia)

Including Boeotia (Voiōtia), Euboea (Euvoia), Eurytania, Phocis (Phōkis), Phthiōtis departments (nomes); Euboea, Skyros Islands

(Options: Class here ancient Doris, Locris, Malis, Phocis, Amphissa, Delphi; prefer —383. Class here ancient Boeotia, Euboea Island, Chalcis, Thebes; prefer —384. Class here ancient Skyros Island; prefer —3911)

—495 18 Aetolia and Acarnania department (Aitōlia kai Akarnania nome)

(Option: Class here ancient Aetolia, Acarnania; prefer —383)

—495 2 Peloponnesus and Isthmus of Corinth

Including Peloponnesus portion of Attica region, Kythēra Island

Subdivisions are added for Peloponnesus and Isthmus of Corinth together, for Peloponnesus alone

See also —16386 for Gulf of Corinth; also —49522 for Peloponnesus region (Peloponnēsos periphereia)

(Option: Class here ancient Peloponnesus; prefer —386)

—495 22 Peloponnesus region (Peloponnēsos periphereia)

Including Arcadia (Arkadia), Argolis, Corinth (Korinthia), Laconia (Lakōnia), Messēnia departments (nomes); Isthmus of Corinth

See also —4952 for Peloponnesus

(Options: Class here ancient Megaris; prefer —384. Class here ancient Corinth; prefer —387. Class here ancient Arcadia, Argolis, Mycenae, Tiryns, —388. Class here ancient Laconia, Messenia, Sparta; prefer —389)

—495 27 Western Greece region (Dytikē Hellada periphereia)

Including Achaea (Achaia), Elis (Ēleia) departments (nomes)

For Aetolia and Acarnania department, see —49518

(Options: Class here ancient Achaea; prefer —387. Class here ancient Elis, Olympia, Phigalia; prefer —388)

—495 3 Epirus region (Ēpeiros periphereia)

Including Arta, Iōannina, Preveza, Thesprōtia departments (nomes)

Class here comprehensive works on Epirus; *Pindus Mountains

For Albanian Epirus, see —4965

(Option: Class here ancient Epirus; prefer —382)

*For a specific part of this jurisdiction, region, or feature, see the part and follow instructions under —4–9

—495 4 Thessaly region (Thessalia periphereia)

Including Karditsa, Larisa, Magnēsia, Trikala departments (nomes); Northern Sporades

For Skyros Island, see —49515

(Options: Class here ancient Thessaly; prefer —382. Class here ancient Northern Sporades; prefer —3911)

—495 5 Ionian Islands region (Ionioi Nēsoi periphereia)

Including Cefalonia (Kephallēnia), Corfu (Kerkyra), Leukas, Zante (Zakynthos) departments (nomes); Ithaca Island

Class here Ionian Islands

(Options: Class here ancient northern Ionian Islands, comprehensive works on Ionian Islands; prefer —382. Class here ancient Ithaca Island; prefer —383. Class here ancient southern Ionian Islands; prefer —386)

—495 6 Former Macedonia region (Makedonia periphereia)

Class here comprehensive works on Macedonia region

For country of Macedonia, see —4976; for Macedonia in Bulgaria, see —4998

(Option: Class here comprehensive works on ancient Macedonia; prefer —381)

—495 62 Western Macedonia region (Dytikē Makedonia periphereia)

Including Flórina (Phlorina), Grevena, Kastoria, Kozanē departments (nomes)

—495 65 Central Macedonia region (Kentrikē Makedonia periphereia)

Including Chalkidikē, Hematheia (Ēmathia), Kilkis, Pella, Pieria, Serrai, Thessalonikē departments (nomes); Mount Athos

—495 7 Eastern Macedonia and Thrace region (Anatolikē Makedonia kai Thrakē periphereia)

Including Drama, Evros, Kavala, Rodopē (Rhodope), Xanthē departments (nomes); Samothrace, Thasos Islands

Class here comprehensive works on Thrace

For Eastern Thrace, see —4961; for Bulgarian Thrace, see —4995

(Options: Class here ancient Samothrace Island, Thasos Island; prefer —3911. Class here ancient Thracia; prefer —398)

—495 8 Former Aegean Islands region (Aigaio Nēsoi periphereia)

Class here *Aegean Islands, *Sporades

See also —16388 for Aegean Sea

(Option: Class here ancient Aegean Islands, Sporades; prefer —391)

—495 82 Northern Aegean region (Voreio Aigaio periphereia)

Including Chios, Lesvos (Lesbos), Samos departments (nomes)

(Options: Class here ancient Lemnos Island; prefer —3911. Class here ancient Lesbos; prefer —3912. Class here ancient Chios; prefer —3913. Class here ancient Samos; prefer —3914)

—495 85 Cyclades department (Kyklades nome)

Class here Southern Aegean region (Notio Aigaio periphereia)

For Dodecanese department, see —49587

(Option: Class here ancient Cyclades; prefer —3915)

—495 87 Dodecanese department (Dōdekanēsos nome)

Class here Southern Sporades

(Options: Class here ancient Southern Sporades, Dodecanese, Rhodes; prefer —3916. Class here ancient Karpathos; prefer —3917)

—495 9 Crete region (Krētē periphereia)

Including Chania (Canea), Hērakleion, Lasithi, Rethymnē departments (nomes)

(Option: Class here ancient Crete; prefer —3918)

—496 *Balkan Peninsula

Class here *Danube River

See also —56 for Ottoman Empire

(Option: Class here ancient southeastern Europe; prefer —398)

—496 1 Turkey in Europe (Eastern Thrace)

Including Edirne (Adrianople), Kırklareli, Tekirdağ provinces (illeri); European portion of Çanakkale Province (Çanakkale İli)

Class comprehensive works on Çanakkale Province (Çanakkale İli) in —563

See also —16389 for Dardanelles, Sea of Marmara

*For a specific part of this jurisdiction, region, or feature, see the part and follow instructions under —4–9

—496 18 İstanbul Province (İstanbul İli)

Class here Istanbul (Constantinople)

For Asian portion of İstanbul Province, see —563

See also —16389 for Bosporus

(Option: Class here ancient Constantinople; prefer —398)

—496 5 Albania

—497 Serbia and Montenegro, Croatia, Slovenia, Bosnia and Hercegovina, Macedonia

Class here Yugoslavia (1918–1991), comprehensive works on former Yugoslavia

Class Yugoslavia (1991–2003) in —4971

(Option: Class here ancient Illyria; prefer —398)

—497 1 Serbia

Including Belgrade, Kosovo i Metohija, Voivodina, Yugoslav Banat

Class here Serbia and Montenegro, Yugoslavia (1991–2003)

Use of this number for comprehensive works on former Yugoslavia discontinued; class in —497

For Montenegro, see —49745

—497 2 Croatia

Including Dalmatia, *Istria, Slavonia

(Option: Class here ancient Istria; prefer —373)

—497 3 Slovenia

—497 4 Bosnia and Hercegovina, Montenegro

—497 42 Bosnia and Hercegovina

Including Sarajevo

—497 45 Montenegro

—497 6 Macedonia

Class here Vardar River

Class comprehensive works on Macedonia region in —4956

*For a specific part of this jurisdiction, region, or feature, see the part and follow instructions under —4–9

—498 Romania

(Option: Class here ancient Dacia; prefer —398)

—498 1 Northeast Romania

Including Bacău, Botoşani, Brăila, Galaţi, Iaşi, Neamţ, Suceava, Vaslui, Vrancea districts (judeţe)

Class here *Moldavia

—498 2 Walachia (Southeast Romania)

Including Argeş, Bucureşti, Buzău, Călăraşi, Dîmboviţa, Giurgiu, Ialomiţa, Olt, Prahova, Teleorman, Vîlcea districts (judeţe)

Including Ploieşti

For Black Sea area, see —4983

—498 3 Black Sea area

Including Constanţa, Tulcea districts (judeţe)

Class here *Dobruja

For South Dobruja, see —4994

See also —16389 for Black Sea

(Option: Class here ancient Scythia; prefer —3951)

—498 4 Central and west Romania

Including Alba, Arad, Bihor, Bistriţa-Năsăud, Braşov, Caraş-Severin, Cluj, Covasna, Dolj, Gorj, Harghita, Hunedoara, Maramureş, Mehedinţi, Mureş, Sălaj, Satu Mare, Sibiu, Timiş districts (judeţe)

Including Oltenia, Transylvania

Class here *Bukovina, comprehensive works on *Banat

For North Bukovina, see —4779; for Yugoslav Banat, see —4971

—499 Bulgaria

Class here *Balkan Mountains

(Option: Class here ancient Moesia; prefer —398)

—499 1 Montana region (Montana oblast)

—499 2 Lovech region (Loveshka oblast)

—499 3 Ruse region (Rusenska oblast)

—499 4 Varna region (Varnenska oblast)

Including South Dobruja

*For a specific part of this jurisdiction, region, or feature, see the part and follow instructions under —4–9

—499 5 Burgas region (Burgaska oblast)

Including Bulgarian Thrace

—499 6 Khaskovo region (Khaskovska oblast)

—499 7 Plovdiv region (Plovdivska oblast)

Class here *Rhodope Mountains

—499 8 Sofia region (Sofiĭska oblast)

Including Bulgarian Macedonia

—499 9 Sofia city

Class here comprehensive works on historic region of Sofia

For parts of historic region of Sofia in Sofia region (Sofiĭska oblast), see —4998

—5 Asia Orient Far East

Class here Eurasia

For Europe, see —4

SUMMARY

— 51 **China and adjacent areas**
— 52 **Japan**
— 53 **Arabian Peninsula and adjacent areas**
— 54 **South Asia India**
— 55 **Iran**
— 56 **Middle East (Near East)**
— 57 **Siberia (Asiatic Russia)**
— 58 **Central Asia**
— 59 **Southeast Asia**

—51 China and adjacent areas

Class here People's Republic of China

Subdivisions are added for China and adjacent areas together, for China alone

(Option: Class here ancient China; prefer —31)

—511 Northeastern China

Class here Northern Region; *Yellow River (Huang He)

For Inner Mongolia Autonomous Region, see —5177; for Manchuria, see —518

See also —16456 for Yellow Sea

—511 3 Shanghai Municipality and Jiangsu Province

—511 32 Shanghai Municipality (Shanghai Shi)

*For a specific part of this jurisdiction, region, or feature, see the part and follow instructions under —4–9

—511 36 Jiangsu Province (Jiangsu Sheng)

Including Nanjing

—511 4 Shandong Province (Shandong Sheng)

—511 5 Hebei Province and Tianjin and Beijing municipalities

—511 52 Hebei Province (Hebei Sheng)

—511 54 Tianjin Municipality (Tianjin Shi)

—511 56 Beijing Municipality (Beijing Shi)

—511 7 Shanxi Province (Shanxi Sheng)

—511 8 Henan Province (Henan Sheng)

—512 Southeastern China and adjacent areas

Class here Eastern and Central-Southern Regions; *Yangtze River

Subdivisions are added for southeastern China and adjacent areas together, for southeastern China alone

For Shanghai Municipality, see —51132; for Jiangsu Province, see —51136; for Shandong Province, see —5114; for Henan Province, see —5118

—512 1 Hubei and Hunan provinces

—512 12 Hubei Province (Hubei Sheng)

—512 15 Hunan Province (Hunan Sheng)

—512 2 Jiangxi and Anhui provinces

—512 22 Jiangxi Province (Jiangxi Sheng)

—512 25 Anhui Province (Anhui Sheng)

—512 4 East China Sea area

See also —16457 for East China Sea

—512 42 Zhejiang Province (Zhejiang Sheng)

—512 45 Fujian Province (Fujian Sheng)

See also —16457 for Formosa Strait

—512 49 Taiwan (Formosa) and adjacent islands

Republic of China (Nationalist China)

Subdivisions are added for Taiwan (Formosa) and adjacent islands together, for Taiwan (Formosa) alone

See also —16457 for Formosa Strait

—512 5 Hong Kong

*For a specific part of this jurisdiction, region, or feature, see the part and follow instructions under —4–9

—512 6 Macau

—512 7 Guangdong Province (Guangdong Sheng)

—512 75 Guangzhou (Canton)

—512 8 Guangxi Zhuangzu Autonomous Region (Guangxi Zhuangzu Zizhiqu)

See also —16472 for Gulf of Tonkin

—512 9 Hainan Province (Hainan Sheng)

—513 Southwestern China (South-Western Region)

For Tibet, see —515

—513 4 Guizhou Province (Guizhou Sheng)

—513 5 Yunnan Province (Yunnan Sheng)

—513 8 Sichuan Province (Sichuan Sheng)

Including Chongqing

—514 Northwestern China (North-Western Region)

For Xinjiang Uygur Autonomous Region, see —516; for Ningsia Huizu Autonomous Region, see —5175

—514 3 Shaanxi Province (Shaanxi Sheng)

—514 5 Gansu Province (Gansu Sheng)

—514 7 Qinghai Province (Qinghai Sheng)

—515 Tibet Autonomous Region (Xizang Zizhiqu)

—516 Xinjiang Uygur Autonomous Region (Xinjiang Uygur Zizhiqu)

Including *Tien Shan

—517 Mongolia

—517 3 Outer Mongolia (Mongolian People's Republic)

Independent state

Including *Gobi Desert; *Altai Mountains

—517 5 Ningxia Huizu Autonomous Region (Ningxia Huizu Zizhiqu)

—517 7 Inner Mongolia Autonomous Region (Nei Monggol Zizhiqu)

—518 Manchuria

Class here North-Eastern Region

—518 2 Liaoning Province (Liaoning Sheng)

—518 4 Heilongjiang Province (Heilongjiang Sheng)

*For a specific part of this jurisdiction, region, or feature, see the part and follow instructions under —4–9

—518 8 Jilin Province (Jilin Sheng)

—519 Korea

See also —16456 for Yellow Sea

—519 3 North Korea (People's Democratic Republic of Korea)

—519 5 South Korea (Republic of Korea)

—52 Japan

—521 Honshū (Honsyū)

—521 1 Tōhoku region (Tōhoku chihō)

See also —16454 for Tsugaru Strait

—521 12 Aomori prefecture (Aomori-ken)

Including *Towada Lake

—521 13 Akita prefecture (Akita-ken)

—521 14 Iwate prefecture (Iwate-ken)

—521 15 Miyagi prefecture (Miyagi-ken)

—521 16 Yamagata prefecture (Yamagata-ken)

—521 17 Fukusima prefecture (Fukusima-ken)

—521 3 Kantō region (Kantō chihō)

Including *Tone River

—521 31 Ibaraki prefecture (Ibaraki-ken)

—521 32 Tochigi prefecture (Tochigi-ken)

—521 33 Gumma prefecture (Gumma-ken)

—521 34 Saitama prefecture (Saitama-ken)

—521 35 Tōkyō prefecture (Tōkyō-to)

Class here Tokyo

For Bonin (Ogasawara) Islands, see —528

—521 36 Kanagawa prefecture (Kanagawa-ken)

—521 364 Yokohama

—521 37 Chiba prefecture (Chiba-ken)

—521 5 Hokuriku region (Hokuriku chihō)

*For a specific part of this jurisdiction, region, or feature, see the part and follow instructions under —4–9

—521 52 Niigata prefecture (Niigata-ken)

Class here *Shinano River

—521 53 Toyama prefecture (Toyama-ken)

—521 54 Ishikawa prefecture (Ishikawa-ken)

—521 55 Fukui prefecture (Fukui-ken)

—521 6 Chūbu region (Chūbu chihō)

Including *Akaishi Mountains

For Hokuriku region, see —5215

—521 62 Gifu prefecture (Gifu-ken)

—521 63 Nagano prefecture (Nagano-ken)

—521 64 Yamanashi prefecture (Yamanashi-ken)

—521 65 Shizuoka prefecture (Shizuoka-ken)

For Mount Fuji, see —52166

—521 66 Mount Fuji (Fuji-san, Fujiyama)

—521 67 Aichi prefecture (Aichi-ken)

—521 674 Nagoya

—521 8 Kinki region (Kinki chihō)

—521 81 Mie prefecture (Mie-ken)

—521 82 Wakayama prefecture (Wakayama-ken)

—521 83 Ōsaka prefecture (Ōsaka-fu)

Class here *Yodo River

—521 834 Ōsaka

—521 84 Nara prefecture (Nara-ken)

—521 85 Shiga prefecture (Shiga-ken)

—521 86 Kyōto prefecture (Kyōto-fu)

—521 864 Kyōto

—521 87 Hyōgo prefecture (Hyōgo-ken)

—521 874 Kōbe

—521 9 Chūgoku region (Chūgoku chihō)

See also —16455 for Inland Sea (Seto-naikai)

*For a specific part of this jurisdiction, region, or feature, see the part and follow instructions under —4–9

—521 93 Tottori prefecture (Tottori-ken)

—521 94 Okayama prefecture (Okayama-ken)

—521 95 Hiroshima prefecture (Hiroshima-ken)

—521 954 Hiroshima

—521 96 Shimane prefecture (Shimane-ken)

—521 97 Yamaguchi prefecture (Yamaguchi-ken)

—522 Kyusyu region (Kyūshū chihō)

> —522 2–522 8 Kyusyu (Kyūshū) island

Class comprehensive works in —522

—522 2 Fukuoka prefecture (Fukuoka-ken)

—522 3 Saga prefecture (Saga-ken)

—522 4 Nagasaki prefecture (Nagasaki-ken)

—522 44 Nagasaki

—522 5 Kumamoto prefecture (Kumamoto-ken)

—522 6 Kagoshima prefecture (Kagoshima-ken)

—522 7 Miyazaki prefecture (Miyazaki-ken)

—522 8 Ōita prefecture (Ōita-ken)

—522 9 Okinawa prefecture (Okinawa-ken)

Class here Ryukyu Islands

—522 94 Okinawa island

—523 Shikoku

—523 2 Ehime prefecture (Ehime-ken)

—523 3 Kōchi prefecture (Kōchi-ken)

—523 4 Tokushima prefecture (Tokushima-ken)

—523 5 Kagawa prefecture (Kagawa-ken)

—524 Hokkaidō

Including Etorofu, Kunashiri (islands claimed by both Japan and Russia)

See also —16453 for La Perouse Strait; also —16454 for Tsugaru Strait

—528 Bonin (Ogasawara) Islands

—53 Arabian Peninsula and adjacent areas

Class here Persian Gulf region

Subdivisions are added for Arabian Peninsula and adjacent areas together, for Arabian Peninsula alone

For Iran, see —55; for Iraq, see —567

See also —16533 for Red Sea; also —16535 for Persian Gulf

(Options: Class here ancient Arabia Petraea ; prefer —3948. Class here ancient Arabia, Arabia Felix; prefer —3949)

—531 Sinai Peninsula

Including Janūb Sīnā', Shamāl Sīnā' provinces; Gaza Strip

Class Suez Canal in —6215

(Option: Class here ancient Sinai Peninsula; prefer —3948)

—533 Yemen

Class here Republic of Yemen

—533 2 Northern Yemen

Class here Yemen Arab Republic

—533 5 Southern Yemen

Class here Federation of South Arabia, People's Democratic Republic of Yemen

—535 Oman and United Arab Emirates

—535 3 Oman

See also —16536 for Gulf of Oman

—535 7 United Arab Emirates

Including Abu Dhabi, ʻAjmān, Dubai, Fujairah, Ras al Khaimah, Shārjah, Umm al-Qaiwain

—536 Persian Gulf States

For Oman and United Arab Emirates, see —535

—536 3 Qatar

—536 5 Bahrain

—536 7 Kuwait

—538 Saudi Arabia

Including Hejaz, Nejd; Mecca; *Rubʻal-Khali, Syrian Desert in Saudi Arabia

*For a specific part of this jurisdiction, region, or feature, see the part and follow instructions under —4–9

—54 South Asia India

For southeast Asia, see —59

(Option: Class here ancient India; prefer —34)

SUMMARY

— 541	**Northeastern India**
— 542	**Uttar Pradesh**
— 543	**Madhya Pradesh**
— 544	**Rajasthan**
— 545	**Punjab region of India**
— 546	**Jammu and Kashmir**
— 547	**Western India**
— 548	**Southern India**
— 549	**Other jurisdictions**

> —541–548 India

Class comprehensive works in —54

—541 Northeastern India

Including *Ganges River

—541 2 Bihar and Jharkhand

—541 23 Bihar

—541 27 Jharkhand

—541 3 Orissa and Chhattīsgarh

—541 33 Orissa

—541 37 Chhattīsgarh [*formerly* —543]

—541 4 West Bengal

Class here former province of Bengal

For former East Bengal, see —5492

—541 47 Calcutta

—541 5 Tripura

—541 6 Far northeast of India

Class here *Brahmaputra River in India

For Manipur, see —5417

—541 62 Assam

—541 63 Arunāchal Pradesh

*For a specific part of this jurisdiction, region, or feature, see the part and follow instructions under —4–9

—541 64 Meghalaya

—541 65 Nāgāland

—541 66 Mizoram

—541 67 Sikkim

—541 7 Manipur

—542 Uttar Pradesh

Uttaranchal, formerly part of Uttar Pradesh, relocated to —5451

—543 Madhya Pradesh

Chhattīsgarh, formerly part of Madhya Pradesh, relocated to —54137

—544 Rajasthan

Class here *Thar (Great Indian) Desert

—545 Northwestern India

Class here former province of Punjab

For Jammu and Kashmir, see —546; for Punjab Province of Pakistan, see —54914

—545 1 Uttaranchal [*formerly* —542]

—545 2 Himachal Pradesh

—545 5 Punjab and Haryana

Class here former Punjab state

—545 52 Punjab

Including Chandīgarh

—545 58 Haryana

—545 6 Delhi

Class here Delhi, New Delhi

—546 Jammu and Kashmir

Class here comprehensive works on Kashmir

Including *Karakoram Range

For area of Kashmir controlled by Pakistan, see —54913

—547 Western India

—547 5 Gujarat

—547 6 Dādra and Nagar Haveli [*formerly* —54796]

*For a specific part of this jurisdiction, region, or feature, see the part and follow instructions under —4–9

—547 7 Daman and Diu [*formerly* —54799]

Class comprehensive works on Portuguese India in —5478

—547 8 Goa [*formerly* —54799]

Class here Portuguese India

For Daman and Diu, see —5477

—547 9 Maharashtra

—547 92 Bombay (Mumbai)

Use of this number for Maharashtra discontinued; class in —5479

—[547 923] Bombay (Mumbai)

Number discontinued; class in —54792

—[547 96] Dādra and Nagar Haveli

Relocated to —5476

—[547 99] Goa, Daman and Diu

Daman and Diu relocated to —5477; Goa relocated to —5478

—548 Southern India

Class here *Deccan

—548 1 Lakshadweep

—548 2 Tamil Nadu

Including Madras

—548 3 Kerala

—548 4 Andhra Pradesh

Including Hyderabad

Class here former state of Hyderabad

For Maharashtra, see —54792; for Karnataka, see —5487

—548 6 Pondicherry

—548 7 Karnataka

—548 8 Andaman and Nicobar Islands

—549 Other jurisdictions

Class here Pakistan (West and East, 1947–1971)

—549 1 Pakistan

Class here *Indus River

*For a specific part of this jurisdiction, region, or feature, see the part and follow instructions under —4–9

—549 11 Federally Administered Tribal Areas [*formerly* —54912]

—549 12 North-West Frontier Province

Federally Administered Tribal Areas relocated to —54911

—549 122 Districts and agencies north of Peshawar

Including Chitrāl, Dīr, Kalam, Swat

—549 123 Peshawar District

Class here Peshawar

—549 124 Districts south of Peshawar

Including Dera Ismāīl Khān District

—549 13 Northern Areas and Azad Kashmir

Class here area of Kashmir controlled by Pakistan

Class comprehensive works on Kashmir in —546

—549 132 Northern Areas

—549 138 Azad Kashmir

—549 14 Punjab Province and Islāmābād Capital Territory

Including Multān, Sargodha Districts

Subdivisions are added for Punjab Province and Islāmābād Capital Territory together, for Punjab Province alone

For Bahāwalpur District, see —54916

—549 142 Rāwalpindi District

Islāmābād Capital Territory relocated to —549149

—549 143 Lahore District

Class here Lahore

—549 149 Islāmābād Capital Territory [*formerly* —549142]

Class here Islāmābād

—549 15 Baluchistan Province

Class here comprehensive works on Baluchistan

For Iranian Baluchistan, see —5583

—549 152 Quetta District

—549 153 Kalāt District

—549 16 Bahāwalpur District

—549 17 Khairpūr District

—549 18 Sindh Province

For Khairpūr District, see —54917

—549 182 Hyderabad District

Class here Hyderabad

—549 183 Karachi District

Class here Karachi

—549 2 Bangladesh

Class here comprehensive works on *Brahmaputra River

—549 22 Dhaka Division

Class here Dhaka

—549 23 Chittagong Division

Class here Chittagong

Sylhet Division, formerly part of Chittagong Division, relocated to —54927; Chittagong Hill Tracts Region, formerly part of Chittagong Division, relocated to —54929

—549 24 Rājshāhi Division

—549 25 Khulna Division

Barisāl Division, formerly part of Khulna Division, relocated to —54926

—549 26 Barisāl Division [*formerly* —54925]

—549 27 Sylhet Division [*formerly* —54923]

—549 29 Chittagong Hill Tracts Region [*formerly* —54923]

—549 3 Sri Lanka

Including Colombo

—549 5 Maldives

—549 6 Nepal

Class here *Himalaya Mountains

—549 8 Bhutan

—55 Iran

(Option: Class here ancient Iranian Plateau; prefer —35)

—551 Ardabīl, Gīlān, Zanjān, Qazvīn provinces

—551 2 Ardabīl province [*formerly* —553]

*For a specific part of this jurisdiction, region, or feature, see the part and follow instructions under —4–9

—551 4 Gīlān province

—551 6 Zanjān province

—551 8 Qazvīn province

—552 Golestān, Māzandarān, Semnān, Tehran, Qum, Markazī provinces

—552 2 Golestān province [*formerly* —5523]

—552 3 Māzandarān province

Golestān province, formerly part of Māzandarān province, relocated to —5522; Semnān province relocated to —5524

(Option: Class here ancient Hyrcania; prefer —396)

—552 4 Semnān province [*formerly* —5523]

—552 5 Tehran province

Class here Tehran

—552 6 Qum province [*formerly* —5527]

—552 7 Markazī province

Qum province, formerly part of Markazī province, relocated to —5526

—553 East Azerbaijan (Āzarbāyjān-i Khāvarī) province

Class here Azerbaijan region

Ardabīl province, formerly part of East Azerbaijan province, relocated to —5512

For country of Azerbaijan, see —4754; for West Azerbaijan province of Iran, see —554

—554 West Azerbaijan (Āzarbāyjān-i Bākhtarī) province

—555 Hamadān, Kordestān, Kermānshāhān, Īlām provinces

(Option: Class here ancient Media, Ecbatana; prefer —35)

—555 2 Hamadān province

Kermānshāhān province relocated to —5556; Īlām province relocated to —5558

—555 4 Kordestān province

Class comprehensive works on Kurdistan in —5667

—555 6 Kermānshāhān province [*formerly* —5552]

—555 8 Īlām province [*formerly* —5552]

—556 Lorestān, Khūzestān, Boyer Ahmadī va Kohkīlūyeh provinces

(Option: Class here ancient Elam [Susiana], Susa; prefer —35)

—556 2 Lorestān province

—556 4 Khūzestān province

—556 8 Boyer Ahmadī va Kohkīlūyeh province

—557 Fārs, Būshehr, Hormozgān provinces

—557 2 Fārs province

(Option: Class here ancient Persia, Pasargadae, Persepolis; prefer —35)

—557 4 Būshehr province [*formerly* —5575]

—557 5 Hormozgān province

Būshehr province relocated to —5574

—558 Kermān and Sīstān va Balūchestān provinces

—558 2 Kermān province

—558 3 Sīstān va Balūchestān province

Class comprehensive works on Baluchistan in —54915

—559 Khorāsān, Yazd, Eṣfahān, Chahār Mahāll va Bakhtīarī provinces

—559 2 Khorāsān province

—559 4 Yazd province [*formerly* —5595]

—559 5 Eṣfahān province

Yazd province relocated to —5594; Chahār Mahāll va Bakhtīarī province relocated to —5597

—559 7 Chahār Mahāll va Bakhtīarī province [*formerly* —5595]

—56 *Middle East (Near East)

Class here *Ottoman Empire

(Option: Class here ancient Middle East; prefer —394)

*For a specific part of this jurisdiction, region, or feature, see the part and follow instructions under —4–9

SUMMARY

—561 Turkey

Class here Asia Minor

For divisions of Turkey, see —562–566

(Options: Class here ancient Asia Minor, western Asia Minor; prefer —392. Class here ancient eastern Asia Minor; prefer —393)

> —562–566 Divisions of Turkey

Class comprehensive works in —561

For Turkey in Europe, see —4961

—562 Western Turkey

Including Afyon, Aydın, Balıkesir, Burdur, Çanakkale, Denizli, İzmir, Kütahya, Manisa, Muğla, Uşak provinces (illeri)

Including Bozca (Tenedos) and İmroz (Imbros) islands

For European portion of Çanakkale Province, see —4961

See also —16389 for Dardanelles

(Options: Class here ancient Imbros and Tenedos islands; prefer —3911. Class here ancient Mysia and Troas; prefer —3921. Class here ancient Lydia; prefer —3922. Class here ancient Ionia; prefer —3923. Class here ancient Caria; prefer —3924. Class here ancient Phrygia; prefer —3926)

—563 North central Turkey

Including Amasya, Ankara, Bartın, Bilecik, Bolu, Bursa, Çankırı, Çorum, Eskişehir, Karbük, Kastamonu, Kırıkkale, Kocaeli, Sakarya, Samsun, Sinop, Yalova, Yozgat, Zonguldak provinces (illeri); Asian portion of İstanbul Province (İstanbul İli)

Class comprehensive works on İstanbul Province (İstanbul İli) in —49618

See also —16389 for Bosporus, Sea of Marmara

(Options: Class here ancient Bithynia; prefer —3925. Class here ancient Paphlagonia; prefer —3931. Class here ancient Galatia; prefer —3932)

—564 South central Turkey

Including Adana, Aksaray, Antalya, Gaziantep, Hatay, İçel, Isparta, Karaman, Kayseri, Kilis, Kırşehir, Konya, Nevşehir, Niğde, Osmaniye provinces (illeri); Taurus Mountains

(Options: Class here ancient Pisidia; prefer —3927 for Pisidia. Class here ancient Lycia; prefer —3928. Class here ancient Pamphylia —3929. Class here ancient Cappadocia; prefer —3934. Class here ancient Cilicia; prefer —3935. Class here ancient Commagene; prefer —3936. Class here ancient Antioch; prefer —3943)

—565 East central Turkey

Including Adıyaman, Bayburt, Giresun, Gümüşhane, Kahramanmaraş, Malatya, Ordu, Sivas, Tokat, Trabzon, Urfa provinces (illeri)

(Option: Class here ancient Pontus; prefer —3933)

—566 Eastern Turkey

—566 2 Northeastern Turkey

Including Ağrı, Ardahan, Artvin, Erzurum, Hakkâri, Iğdır, Kars, Rize, Van provinces (illeri)

Class here comprehensive works on Armenia region

Former southeastern portion of Hakkâri Province (İli) relocated to —5667

For country of Armenia, see —4756

(Option: Class here ancient Armenia; prefer —3955)

—566 7 Southeast central Turkey

Including former southeastern portion of Hakkâri Province (İli) [*formerly* —5662]; Batman, Bingöl, Bitlis, Diyarbakır, Elazığ, Erzincan, Mardin, Muş, Siirt, Şirnak, Tunceli provinces (illeri)

Class here comprehensive works on Kurdistan

For Iranian Kurdistan, see —5554; for Iraqi Kurdistan, see —5672

—567 Iraq

Class here Mesopotamia

(Options: Class here ancient Mesopotamia, Seleucid Empire; prefer —35. Class here ancient Arabia Deserta; prefer —3947)

—567 2 Kurdish Autonomous Region

Including Dahūk, Irbīl, Sulaymānīyah provinces

Class comprehensive works on Kurdistan in —5667

—567 4 Upper Mesopotamia

Including Anbār, Diyālá, Nīnawá (Nineveh), Ṣalāḥ ad-Dīn, Ta'mim provinces; Mosul; Syrian Desert in Iraq

(Option: Class here ancient Assyria, Ashur, Nineveh; prefer —35)

—567 47 Baghdād Province

Class here Baghdad

—567 5 Lower Mesopotamia

Including Bābil, Baṣrah, Dhī Qār, Karbalā', Maysān, Muthanná, Najaf, Qādisīyah, Wāsiṭ (Kūt) provinces

(Option: Class here ancient Babylonia, Sumer, Babylon, Ur; prefer —35)

—569 Syria, Lebanon, Cyprus, Israel, Jordan

Class here *Syrian Desert

—569 1 Syria

(Option: Class here ancient Syria; prefer —3943)

—569 12 Desert provinces of Syria

Including Dayr al-Zawr, Ḥasakah, Ḥimṣ, Raqqah

Class here Syrian Desert in Syria

(Option: Class here ancient Palmyra; prefer —3943)

—569 13 Northwest provinces of Syria

Including Aleppo (Ḥalab), Ḥamāh, Idlib, Latakia, Ṭarṭūs

(Option: Class here ancient Ebla, Ugarit; prefer —3943)

—569 14 Southwest provinces of Syria and city of Damascus

Including Damascus (Dimashq), Dar'ā, Qunayṭirah, Suwaydā' provinces; *Anti-Lebanon

Subdivisions are added for southwest provinces and city of Damascus together, for southwest provinces alone

—569 144 City of Damascus

(Option: Class here ancient Damascus; prefer —3943)

—569 2 Lebanon

(Option: Class here ancient Phoenicia, Coelesyria, Baalbek, Byblos, Sidon, Tyre; prefer —3944)

—569 25 Beirut

*For a specific part of this jurisdiction, region, or feature, see the part and follow instructions under —4–9

—569 3 Cyprus

(Option: Class here ancient Cyprus; prefer —3937)

—569 4 Palestine Israel

Palestine: area covering Israel, Gaza Strip, and West Bank of Jordan

Including *Jordan River; *Dead Sea

For Gaza Strip, see —531; for West Bank, see —56951–56953

(Option: Class here ancient Palestine, Israel; prefer —33)

—569 44 Jerusalem district

—569 442 Jerusalem

(Option: Class here ancient Jerusalem; prefer —33)

—569 45 Tsafon district

Class here Galilee

(Option: Class here ancient Galilee; prefer —33)

—569 46 Haifa district

—569 47 Merkaz district

—569 48 Tel Aviv district

Class here Tel Aviv

—569 49 Darom district

Class here Negev

(Options: Class here ancient Judah, Judaea; prefer —33. Class here ancient Edom; prefer —3946)

—569 5 Jordan and West Bank

Subdivisions are added for Jordan and West Bank together, for Jordan alone

(Option: Class here Jordanian part of ancient Palestine; prefer —33)

> —569 51–569 53 West Bank

Class comprehensive works in —56953

—569 51 Hebron district

—569 52 Jerusalem district

Class city of Jerusalem in —569442

*For a specific part of this jurisdiction, region, or feature, see the part and follow instructions under —4–9

—569 53 Nablus district

Class here comprehensive works on West Bank, area administered by Palestinian National Authority

For Gaza Strip, see —531; for Hebron district, see —56951; for Jerusalem district, see —56952

(Option: Class here ancient Samaria; prefer —33)

> —569 54–569 59 Jordan

Class comprehensive works in —5695

—569 54 Irbid, ‘Ajlūn, Jarash provinces

—569 542 Irbid Province

—569 546 ‘Ajlūn Province

—569 548 Jarash Province

—569 55 Balqā’ Province

—569 56 Ma’dabā, Karak, Ṭafīlah provinces

(Option: Class here ancient Moab; prefer —3946)

—569 562 Ma’dabā Province [*formerly* —56958]

—569 563 Karak Province

—569 567 Ṭafīlah Province

—569 57 ‘Aqabah and Ma‘ān provinces

—569 572 ‘Aqabah Province

—569 577 Ma‘ān Province

(Option: Class here ancient Petra; prefer —3948)

—569 58 Amman Province

Class here Amman

Ma’dabā Province, formerly part of Amman Province relocated to —569562

—569 59 Zarqā’ and Mafraq provinces

Class here *Syrian Desert in Jordan

—569 593 Zarqā’ Province

—569 597 Mafraq Province

*For a specific part of this jurisdiction, region, or feature, see the part and follow instructions under —4–9

—57 **Siberia (Asiatic Russia)**

—573 Western Siberia

Including Kemerovo (Kemerovskaia͡), Kurgan (Kurganskaia͡), Novosibirsk (Novosibirskaia͡), Omsk (Omskaia͡), Tomsk (Tomskaia͡), Tyumen (Ti͡umenskaia͡) provinces (oblasti); Altay territory (Altaĭskiĭ kraĭ); Gorno-Altay (Gorno-Altaĭ) republic; Khantia-Mansia (Khanty-Mansiĭskiĭ), Yamal-Nenets (Yamal-Nenetskiĭ) autonomous districts (avtonomnyĭ okruga)

For Chelyabinsk, Sverdlovsk provinces, see —4743

—575 Eastern Siberia

Including Chita (Chitinskaia͡), Irkutsk (Irkutskaia͡) provinces (oblasti); Krasnoyarsk territory (Krasnoi͡arskiĭ kraĭ); Buryatia (Buri͡atii͡a), Khakassia (Khakasskaia͡), Sakha (Yakutia, I͡Akutii͡a), Tuva republics; Agin Buri͡at (Agin Buri͡atskiĭ), Evenki (Evenskiĭ), Taĭmyr (Taĭmyrskiĭ), Ust-Orda Buri͡at (Ust-Orda Buri͡atskiĭ) autonomous districts (avtonomnyĭ okruga); *Sayan Mountains

For Far Eastern Siberia, see —577; for Severnaya Zemlya, see —987; for New Siberian Islands, see —988

—577 Far Eastern Siberia

Including Amur (Amurskaia͡), Kamchatka (Kamchatskaia͡), Magadan (Magadanskaia͡), Sakhalin (Sakhalinskaia͡ provinces (oblasti); Khabarovsk (Khabarovskiĭ), Primor´ye (Primorskiĭ) territories (kraia͡); Jewish autonomous region (Evreĭskaia͡ avtonomnaia͡ oblast, Yevrey avtonomnaia͡ oblast); Chukchi (Chukotskiĭ), Koraia͡k (Koraia͡kskiĭ) autonomous districts (avtonomnyĭ okruga); Komandorski, Kuril, Wrangel Islands; *Amur River

See also —16451 for Bering Strait; also —16453 for Sea of Okhotsk; also —16454 for Tatar Strait

—58 **Central Asia**

(Option: Class here ancient Central Asia; prefer —396)

—581 Afghanistan

Class here *Hindu Kush

(Option: Class here ancient Ariana, Bactria, Parthia; prefer —396)

—584 Turkestan

Class Sinkiang in —516

For Turkmenistan, see —585; for Tajikistan, see —586; for Uzbekistan, see —587

*For a specific part of this jurisdiction, region, or feature, see the part and follow instructions under —4–9

—584 3 Kyrgyzstan

Including *Tien Shan

—584 5 Kazakhstan

—585 Turkmenistan

(Option: Class here ancient Margiana; prefer —396)

—586 Tajikistan

Including Gorno-Badakhshan autonomous province (oblast)

Class here *Pamir

—587 Uzbekistan

Including Karakalpak autonomous republic; *Aral Sea

(Option: Class here ancient Sogdiana; prefer —396)

—59 Southeast Asia

Class here *Indochina (southeast peninsula of Asia)

Class works about "Indochina" when used to equate with French Indochina in —597

—591 Myanmar

—593 Thailand

See also —16472 for Gulf of Thailand

—594 Laos

—595 Commonwealth of Nations territories Malaysia

—595 1 Peninsular Malaysia (Malaya, West Malaysia)

Including states of Johor, Kedah, Kelantan, Malacca (Melaka), Negeri Sembilan, Pahang, Perak, Perlis, Pinang (Pulau Pinang), Selangor, Terengganu; Kuala Lumpur

Class here *Malay Peninsula

—595 3 Sabah

State of Malaysia

Including Labuan

Class here northern Borneo, East Malaysia

For Sarawak, see —5954; for Brunei, see —5955

—595 4 Sarawak

State of Malaysia

*For a specific part of this jurisdiction, region, or feature, see the part and follow instructions under —4–9

—595 5 Brunei

—595 7 Singapore

Independent republic

See also —16472 for Singapore Strait

—596 Cambodia

—597 Vietnam

Including *Mekong River

Class here *French Indochina (Indochina)

Class works about "Indochina" when used to equate with the southeast peninsula of Asia in —59

—598 Indonesia and East Timor

Class here Malay Archipelago, Sunda Islands

Subdivisions are added for Indonesia and East Timor together, for Indonesia alone

For Philippines, see —599; for Papua, see —951

See also —16473 for inner sea of Malay Archipelago; also —16474 for seas adjoining southern Sunda Islands

---

> —598 1–598 6 Indonesia

Class comprehensive works in —598

—598 1 Sumatra

—598 2 Java and Madura

Subdivisions are added for Java and Madura together, for Java alone

—598 22 Jakarta (Djakarta)

—598 3 Kalimantan

Class here Borneo

For northern Borneo, see —5953

—598 4 Celebes (Sulawesi)

—598 5 Maluku (Moluccas)

—598 6 Lesser Sunda Islands (Nusa Tenggara)

Including Bali, Flores, Lombok, Sumba, Sumbawa, West Timor; *Timor Island

East Timor relocated to —5987

*For a specific part of this jurisdiction, region, or feature, see the part and follow instructions under —4–9

—598 7 East Timor [*formerly* —5986]

—599 Philippines

See also —16471 for inner seas of Philippines

—599 1 Luzon and adjacent islands

Including Abra, Albay, Bataan, Batanes, Batangas, Benguet, Bulacan, Cagayan, Camarines Norte, Camarines Sur, Catanduanes, Cavite, Ifugao, Ilocos Norte, Ilocos Sur, Isabela, Kalinga-Apayao, La Union, Laguna, Marinduque, Mountain, Nueva Ecija, Nueva Vizcaya, Pampanga, Pangasinan, Quezon, Rizal, Sorsogon, Tarlac, Zambales provinces

Subdivisions are added for Luzon and adjacent islands together, for Luzon alone

See also —16458 for Luzon Strait

—599 16 Manila

—599 3 Mindoro and adjacent islands

Including Occidental Mindoro, Oriental Mindoro provinces

Subdivisions are added for Mindoro and adjacent islands together, for Mindoro alone

—599 4 Palawan and adjacent islands (Palawan province)

Subdivisions are added for Palawan and adjacent islands together, for Palawan Island alone

—599 5 Visayan Islands

Including Aklan, Antique, Bohol, Capiz, Cebu, Eastern Samar, Iloilo, Leyte, Masbate, Negros Occidental, Negros Oriental, Northern Samar, Romblon, Southern Leyte, Western Samar provinces

Including Cebu, Leyte, Negros, Panay, Samar Islands

—599 7 Mindanao and adjacent islands

Including Agusan del Norte, Agusan del Sur, Basilan, Bukidnon, Camiguin, Davao del Norte, Davao del Sur, Davao Oriental, Lanao del Norte, Lanao del Sur, Maguindanao, Misamis Occidental, Misamis Oriental, North Cotabato, South Cotabato, Sultan Kudarat, Surigao del Norte, Surigao del Sur, Zamboanga del Norte, Zamboanga del Sur provinces

Including Basilan, Dinagat Islands

Subdivisions are added for Mindanao and adjacent islands together, for Mindanao Island alone

—599 9 Sulu Archipelago

Including Sulu and Tawitawi provinces

See also —16473 for Sulu Sea

—6 Africa

SUMMARY

—61	**Tunisia and Libya**
—62	**Egypt and Sudan**
—63	**Ethiopia and Eritrea**
—64	**Northwest African coast and offshore islands Morocco**
—65	**Algeria**
—66	**West Africa and offshore islands**
—67	**Central Africa and offshore islands**
—68	**Southern Africa Republic of South Africa**
—69	**South Indian Ocean islands**

—61 Tunisia and Libya

Class here *Barbary States, *North Africa

(Option: Class here ancient North Africa; prefer —397)

—611 Tunisia

Including Bizerte, Tunis

(Option: Class here ancient Carthage; prefer —3973)

—612 Libya

Including Banghāzī, Tripoli; *Libyan Desert

(Options: Class here ancient Tripolis, Leptis Magna, Oea, Sabrata; prefer —3974. Class here ancient Cyrenaica; prefer —3975. Class here ancient Marmarica; prefer —3976)

—62 Egypt and Sudan

Class here Federation of Arab Republics, *Nile River

Subdivisions are added for Egypt and Sudan together, for Egypt alone

For Syria, see —5691; for Libya, see —612

(Option: Class here ancient Egypt; prefer —32)

> —621–623 Egypt

Class comprehensive works in —62

For Sinai, see —531

*For a specific part of this jurisdiction, region, or feature, see the part and follow instructions under —4–9

—621 Lower Egypt

Including Alexandria, Buḥayrah, Damietta (Dumyāṭ), Daqahlīyah, Gharbīyah, Kafr al-Shaykh, Marsá Maṭrūḥ (Maṭrūḥ), Minūfīyah, Mudīrīyat al-Sharqīyah (Sharqīyah), Qalyūbīyah provinces

Class here Nile River Delta

(Option: Class here ancient Alexandria; prefer —32)

—621 5 Isthmus of Suez

Including Suez Canal [*formerly* —16533]; Ismailia, Port Said (Būr Sa'īd), Suez (Suways) provinces

See also —16533 for Gulf of Suez

—621 6 Cairo (Qāhirah) province

Class here Cairo

—622 Middle Egypt

Including Asyūṭ, Banī Suwayf, Fayyūm, Jīzah, Minyā, Wādī al-Jadīd provinces; *Western Desert, *Qattara Depression

(Option: Class here ancient Giza, Memphis; prefer —32)

—623 Upper Egypt

Including Aswān, Bahr al Ahmar, Qinā, Sūhāj provinces; *Eastern (Arabian) Desert; *Lake Nasser

(Option: Class here ancient Abydos, Karnak, Luxor, Thebes; prefer —32)

—624 Sudan

For states of Sudan, see —625–629

> —625–629 States of Sudan

Class comprehensive works in —624

—625 Northern states of Sudan

Including Kassalā, Northern (Shamālīyah), Qaḍārif, Red Sea (Baḥr al-Aḥmar), River Nile (Nahr an Nīl) states (wilāyat); Port Sudan

See also —16533 for Red Sea

(Option: Class here ancient Nubia, Ethiopia, Kush; prefer —3978)

—626 Khartoum state and east central states of Sudan

—626 2 Khartoum state (Wilāyat al-Kharṭūm)

Class here Khartoum

*For a specific part of this jurisdiction, region, or feature, see the part and follow instructions under —4–9

—626 4 East central states of Sudan

Including Blue Nile (Nīl al-Azraq), Gezira (Jazīrah), Sinnār, White Nile (Nīl al-Abyaḍ) states (wilāyat)

Class here *Blue Nile River

Class comprehensive works on White Nile River in —6293

—627 Darfur region

Including Northern Darfur (Shamāl Dārfūr), Southern Darfur (Janūb Dārfūr), Western Darfur (Gharb Dārfūr) states (wilāyat)

—628 Kordofan region

Including Northern Kordofan (Shamāl Kurdufān), Southern Kordofan (Janūb Kurdufān), Western Kordofan (Gharb Kurdufān) states (wilāyat)

—629 Southern states of Sudan

—629 3 Upper Nile states

Including Junqalī, Upper Nile (A'ālī al-Nīl), Waḥdah states (wilāyat)

Class here *White Nile River

See also —6264 for White Nile state

—629 4 Southwestern states of Sudan

Including Lakes (Buḥayrāt), Northern Bahr al Ghazal (Shamāl Baḥr al Ghazāl), Warab, Western Bahr al Ghazal (Gharb Baḥr al Ghazāl) states (wilāyat)

—629 5 Equatoria states

Including Baḥr al Jabal, East Equatoria (Sharq al-Istiwā'īyah), West Equatoria (Gharb al-Istiwā'īyah) states (wilāyat)

—63 Ethiopia and Eritrea

Class here Horn of Africa

Subdivisions are added for Ethiopia and Eritrea together, for Ethiopia alone

For Djibouti and Somalia, see —677

See also —3978 for ancient Ethiopia (a part of what is now modern Sudan, not modern Ethiopia)

*For a specific part of this jurisdiction, region, or feature, see the part and follow instructions under —4–9

> —632–634 Ethiopia

This development reflects the political divisions established in 1994. Changes between this development and the Edition 21 development, which reflects the previous political divisions, are not indicated. The comprehensive location of a former province whose parts are now in more than one notation is identified by *

Class comprehensive works in —63

—632 Central and eastern Ethiopia

Including Dirē Dawa Administrative Region (Dirē Dawa Āwraja); Hārerī Hizb, Oromiyā, Somali federal states (keleloch); former Ārsī, Balē, *Hārergē, *Sīdamo provinces (Kifle hāgeroch)

—633 Western Ethiopia

Including Addis Ababa administrative region (Addis Ababa Āwraja); Benishangul-Gumuz Federal State (Benishangul-Gumuz kelel); Southern Nations, Nationalities, and Peoples Federal State (YaDabub behér béhérasbočenā hezboč kelel); Gambella Federal State (Gambēla Āstedader Ākababī); former Gamo Gofa, *Gojam, *Īlubabor, *Kefa, *Shewa (Shoa), *Welega provinces (Kifle hāgeroch)

Class Oromiyā federal state (kelel) in —632

—634 Northern Ethiopia

Including 'Afār, 'Amāra, Tigray federal states (keleloch); former Gonder (Bagēmder), Tigray, Welo provinces (kifle hāgeroch)

—635 Eritrea

Including Asmara

—64 Northwest African coast and offshore islands Morocco

Class here *Atlas Mountains

Subdivisions are added for northwest African coast and offshore islands, Morocco together; for northwest African coast alone; for Morocco alone

(Option: Class here ancient Mauretania Tingitana; prefer —3971)

—641 Ceuta and Melilla [*both formerly* —642]

Autonomous communities of Spain

> —642–646 Morocco

Class Western Sahara, claimed by Morocco, in —648; class comprehensive works in —64

*For a specific part of this jurisdiction, region, or feature, see the part and follow instructions under —4–9

—642 Tangier-Tétouan region

Including Chefchaouen (Chaouen), Larache, Tétouan provinces; Tangier-Assilah, Fahs-Beni Makada prefectures; former Tangier Province

Class here former *Spanish Morocco

Ceuta and Melilla relocated to —641; Hoceïma province, Rif Mountains relocated to —6432; Nador province relocated to —6433

—643 Northern regions of Morocco

Ifrane, Khénifra provinces, former Meknès province relocated to —645; Jadīda province relocated to —6462

For Tangier-Tétouan region, see —642

—643 2 Taza-Al Hoceïma-Taounate region

Including Hoceïma province, *Rif Mountains [*both formerly* —642]; Taounate, Taza provinces

—643 3 Oriental region

Including Nador province [*formerly* —642]; Berkane, Jerada, Figuig, Taourirt provinces; Oujda-Angad prefecture; former Oujda province

—643 4 Fès-Boulemane region

Including Boulemane, Sefrou provinces; Fez-Jdid Dar-Dbibegh, Fez-Medina, Zouagha-Moulay Yacoub prefectures; former Fès (Fez) province

—643 5 Gharb-Chrarda-Béni Hsen region

Including Kénitra, Sidi Kacem provinces

—643 6 Rabat-Salé-Zemmour-Zaër region

Including Khémisset province; Rabat, Salé, Skhirate-Témara prefectures; former Rabat-Salé prefecture; Rabat

—643 8 Grand Casablanca region

Including Aïn Chok-Hay Hassani, Aïn Sebaâ-Hay Mohamed, Ben M'sik-Sidi Othmane, Casablanca-Anfa, Fida-Derb Soltane, Méchouar de Casablanca, Mohammedia, Sidi Bernoussi-Zenata prefectures; former Mohamedia-Znata prefecture; Casablanca

—643 9 Chaouia-Ouardigha region

Including Ben Slimane, Khouribga, Settat provinces

—644 Tadla-Azilal region

Including Azilal, Béni Mellal provinces

Class here *High Atlas Mountains

*For a specific part of this jurisdiction, region, or feature, see the part and follow instructions under —4–9

—645 Meknès-Tafilalt region

Including Ifrane, Khénifra provinces; former Meknès province [*all formerly* —645]; Errachidia (Rachidia), Hajeb provinces; Meknès-El Menzeh, Ismaïlia prefectures

—646 Southwestern regions of Morocco

For regions in Western Sahara, claimed by Morocco, see —648

—646 2 Doukkala-Abda region

Including Jadīda province [*formerly* —643], Safi province

—646 4 Marrakech-Tensift-El Haouz region

Including Chichaoua, Haouz, Kelâat Es-Sraghna (Kelaa des Srarhna), Essaouira provinces; Marrakech-Médina, Marrakech-Ménara, Sidi-Youssef-Ben-Ali prefectures; former Marrakech province

—646 6 Souss Massa-Draâ region

Including Ouarzazate, Taroudant, Tiznit, Zagora provinces; Agadir Idda Outanane, Chtouka-Aït Baha, Inezgane-Aït Melloul prefectures; former Agadir province

—646 8 Guelmim-Es Semara region

Including Assa-Zag, Guelmim, Tan-Tan, Tata provinces

For Es Semara (Smara) province, see —648

—648 Western Sahara

Claimed by Morocco

Including Oued Eddahab-Lagouira, Laâyoune-Bojador-Sakia El-Hamra regions; Ad Dakhla, Bojador (Boujdour), Es Semara (Smara), Laâyoune provinces

—649 Canary Islands

Including Las Palmas and Santa Cruz de Tenerife provinces of Spain

—65 Algeria

(Option: Class here ancient Mauretania Caesariensis, comprehensive works on Mauretania; prefer —3971)

—651 Northwestern provinces of Algeria

Including Aïn Temouchent, Mascara, Mostaganem, Oran, Relizane, Saïda, Sidi Bel Abbès, Tiaret, Tissemsilt, Tlemcen

—653 North central provinces of Algeria

Including Aïn Defla, Algiers (Jaza'ir), Blida (Boulaida), Bouira, Boumerdes, Cheliff (Chlef, El Asnam, Orléansville), Djelfa, Médéa, Tipaza, Tizi-Ouzou

—655 Northeastern provinces of Algeria

Including Annaba (Bône), Batna, Bejaïa (Bougie), Biskra, Bordj Bou Arréridj, Constantine (Qacentina), Guelma, Jījil (Jijel), Khenchela, Mila, M'Sila, Oum el Bouaghi, Sétif, Skikda, Souk Ahras, Tarf, Tébessa

(Option: Class here ancient Numidia; prefer —3972)

—657 Sahara provinces of Algeria

Including Adrar, Bayadh, Béchar, Ghardaia, Illizi, Laghouat, Naâma, Ouargla, Oued, Tamanrasset, Tindouf

(Option: Class here ancient Gaetulia; prefer —3977)

—66 West Africa and offshore islands

Class here *Sahara Desert, *Sahel

Subdivisions are added for west Africa and offshore islands together, for west Africa alone

SUMMARY

— 661	**Mauritania**
— 662	**Mali, Burkina Faso, Niger**
— 663	**Senegal**
— 664	**Sierra Leone**
— 665	**Gambia, Guinea, Guinea-Bissau, Cape Verde**
— 666	**Liberia and Côte d'Ivoire**
— 667	**Ghana**
— 668	**Togo and Benin**
— 669	**Nigeria**

—661 Mauritania

Including Nouakchott

—662 Mali, Burkina Faso, Niger

Class here *Niger River

—662 3 Mali

Including Bamako

—662 5 Burkina Faso

Including Bobo-Dioulasso, Ouagadougou

—662 6 Niger

Including Niamey

*For a specific part of this jurisdiction, region, or feature, see the part and follow instructions under —4–9

—663 Senegal

Including Dakar, Diourbel, Fatick, Kaolack, Kolda, Louga, Saint-Louis, Tambacounda, Thiès, Ziguinchor regions

Class here Senegambia

For Gambia, see —6651

—664 Sierra Leone

Including Freetown

—665 Gambia, Guinea, Guinea-Bissau, Cape Verde

Class here *Upper Guinea area

—665 1 Gambia

Including Banjul

Class here *Gambia River

—665 2 Guinea

Including Conakry, Kankan

—665 7 Guinea-Bissau

Including Bissau

—665 8 Cape Verde

Including Praia

Class here Cape Verde Islands

—666 Liberia and Côte d'Ivoire

—666 2 Liberia

Including Monrovia

—666 8 Côte d'Ivoire (Ivory Coast)

Including Abidjan, Bouaké, Yamoussoukro

—667 Ghana

Including Accra, Kumasi; British Togoland

Class here *Volta River

—668 Togo and Benin

*For a specific part of this jurisdiction, region, or feature, see the part and follow instructions under —4–9

—668 1 Togo

Including Lomé

Class here French Togoland, comprehensive works on Togoland

For British Togoland, see —667

—668 3 Benin

Including Cotonou, Porto-Novo

—669 Nigeria

—669 1 Lagos State

Class here Lagos

—669 2 Western states of Nigeria

—669 23 Ogun State

—669 25 Oyo State

Including Ibadan

—669 26 Osun State

—669 27 Ekiti State [*formerly* —66928]

—669 28 Ondo State

Ekiti State, formerly part of Ondo State, relocated to —66927

—669 3 Bendel states

—669 32 Edo State

Including Benin City

—669 36 Delta State

—669 4 Eastern states of Nigeria

—669 41 Bayelsa State [*formerly* —66942]

—669 42 Rivers State

Including Port Harcourt

Bayelsa State, formerly part of Rivers State, relocated to —66941

—669 43 Akwa Ibom State

—669 44 Cross River State

Including Calabar

—669 45 Abia State

Southern part of Ebonyi State, formerly part of Abia State, relocated to —66947

—669 46 Imo State

—669 47 Ebonyi State

Including southern part of Ebonyi State, formerly part of Abia State [*formerly* —66945], northern part of Ebonyi State, formerly part of Enugu State [*formerly* —66949]

—669 48 Anambra State

—669 49 Enugu State

Including Enugu

Northern part of Ebonyi State, formerly part of Enugu State, relocated to —66947

—669 5 Plateau, Nassarawa, Benue, Kwara states

—669 52 Plateau State

Including Jos

Nassarawa State, formerly part of Plateau State, relocated to —66953

—669 53 Nassarawa State [*formerly* —66952]

—669 54 Benue State

Including Makurdi

—669 56 Kogi State

—669 57 Kwara State

Including Ilorin

—669 6 Zamfara, Sokoto, Kebbi, Niger states and Federal Capital Territory

—669 61 Zamfara State [*formerly* —66962]

—669 62 Sokoto State

Including Sokoto

Zamfara State, formerly part of Sokoto State, relocated to —66961

—669 63 Kebbi State

—669 65 Niger State

Including Minna

—669 68 Federal Capital Territory

Class here Abuja

—669 7 Kaduna, Katsina, Jigawa, Kano states

—669 73 Kaduna State

Including Kaduna

—669 76 Katsina State

—669 77 Jigawa State

—669 78 Kano State

Including Kano

—669 8 Bauchi, Gombe, Borno, Yobe, Adamawa, Taraba states

—669 82 Bauchi State

Gombe State, formerly part of Bauchi State, relocated to —66984

—669 84 Gombe State [*formerly* —66982]

—669 85 Borno State

Including Maiduguri

—669 87 Yobe State

—669 88 Adamawa State

—669 89 Taraba State

—67 Central Africa and offshore islands

Class here *Black Africa, *Sub-Saharan Africa (Africa south of the Sahara)

Subdivisions are added for central Africa and offshore islands together, for central Africa alone

SUMMARY

— 671 Cameroon, Sao Tome and Principe, Equatorial Guinea
— 672 Gabon and Republic of the Congo
— 673 Angola
— 674 Central African Republic and Chad
— 675 Democratic Republic of the Congo, Rwanda, Burundi
— 676 Uganda and Kenya
— 677 Djibouti and Somalia
— 678 Tanzania
— 679 Mozambique

—671 Cameroon, Sao Tome and Principe, Equatorial Guinea

Class here Islands of Gulf of Guinea, *Lower Guinea area

See also —16373 for Gulf of Guinea

—671 1 Cameroon

Including Douala, Yaoundé

—671 5 Sao Tome and Principe

Including São Tomé

—671 8 Equatorial Guinea

—671 83 Río Muni

*For a specific part of this jurisdiction, region, or feature, see the part and follow instructions under —4–9

—671 86 Bioko (Fernando Po) and Annobón (Pagalu) islands

Including Malabo

—672 Gabon and Republic of the Congo

—672 1 Gabon

Including Libreville

—672 4 Republic of the Congo

Including Brazzaville

See also —6751 for Democratic Republic of the Congo

—673 Angola

—673 1 Cabinda province

Exclave of Angola

—673 2 Northern provinces of Angola

Including Bengo, Cuanza Norte, Cuanza Sul, Luanda, Uíge, Zaire; Luanda (capital city)

For Cabinda province, see —6731

—673 4 Central provinces of Angola

Including Benguela, Bié, Huambo, Lunda Norte, Lunda Sul, Malanje, Moxico

—673 5 Southern provinces of Angola

Including Cuando Cubango (Kuando Kubango), Cunene (Kunene), Huíla, Namibe

—674 Central African Republic and Chad

—674 1 Central African Republic

Including Bangui

—674 3 Chad

Including Djamena

—675 Democratic Republic of the Congo, Rwanda, Burundi

—675 1 Democratic Republic of the Congo

Former name: Zaire

Class here *Congo (Zaire) River

See also —6724 for Republic of the Congo

—675 11 Bas-Congo and Bandundu provinces and Kinshasa

*For a specific part of this jurisdiction, region, or feature, see the part and follow instructions under —4–9

—675 112 Kinshasa

Former name: Leopoldville

—675 114 Bas-Congo province

Former name: Bas-Zaïre region

—675 116 Bandundu province

—675 12 Kasaï-Occidental and Kasaï-Oriental provinces

—675 123 Kasaï-Occidental province

—675 126 Kasaï-Oriental province

—675 13 Équateur province

—675 15 Orientale province

Former name: Haute-Zaïre region

—675 17 Maniema, Nord-Kivu, Sud-Kivu provinces

Including *Lake Kivu

Class here former Kivu region

—675 18 Katanga province

Former name: Shaba region

Including Lubumbashi; *Lake Mweru

—675 7 Rwanda and Burundi

—675 71 Rwanda

Including Kigali

—675 72 Burundi

Including Bujumbura

—676 Uganda and Kenya

Class here *East Africa, *Great Rift Valley

—676 1 Uganda

Including Kampala

—676 2 Kenya

—676 22 North-Eastern Province

—676 23 Coast Province

Including Mombasa

—676 24 Eastern Province

*For a specific part of this jurisdiction, region, or feature, see the part and follow instructions under —4–9

—676 25 Nairobi

—676 26 Central Province

—676 27 Rift Valley Province

Including *Lake Turkana (Rudolf)

—676 28 Western Province

—676 29 Nyanza Province

—677 Djibouti and Somalia

Class here Somaliland

—677 1 Djibouti

Including Djibouti (city)

—677 3 Somalia

Including Mogadishu

—678 Tanzania

—678 1 Zanzibar and Pemba regions

Including Pemba North, Pemba South, Zanzibar Central/South, Zanzibar North, Zanzibar Urban/West

—678 2 Mainland regions of Tanzania

Former name: Tanganyika

—678 22 Tanga Region

—678 23 Dar es Salaam and Pwani regions

Variant name for Pwani Region: Coast Region

—678 232 Dar es Salaam Region

Class here Dar es Salaam

—678 24 Lindi and Mtwara regions

—678 25 South central regions of Tanzania

Including Iringa, Morogoro, Ruvuma

—678 26 North central regions of Tanzania

Including Arusha, Dodoma, Kilimanjaro, Singida; *Mount Kilimanjaro; Kilimanjaro National Park

*For a specific part of this jurisdiction, region, or feature, see the part and follow instructions under —4–9

—678 27 Regions of Tanzania adjacent to Lake Victoria

Including Kagera (West Lake, Ziwa Magharibi), Mara, Mwanza; Serengeti National Park

Class here *Lake Victoria

—678 28 Western regions of Tanzania

Including Kigoma, Mbeya, Rukwa, Shinyanga, Tabora; *Lake Tanganyika

—679 Mozambique

Including *Zambezi River

—679 1 Maputo province

Class here Maputo; *Komati River; Pongola River (Rio Maputo) in Mozambique

—679 2 Gaza province

Class here *Limpopo River

—679 3 Inhambane province

—679 4 Manica and Sofala provinces

—679 5 Tete province

—679 6 Zambézia province

—679 7 Nampula province

—679 8 Cabo Delgado province

—679 9 Niassa province

—68 Southern Africa Republic of South Africa

SUMMARY

— 682	**Gauteng, North-West, Limpopo, Mpumalanga, former homelands (national states) of Republic of South Africa**
— 684	**KwaZulu-Natal**
— 685	**Free State**
— 687	**Northern Cape, Western Cape, Eastern Cape**
— 688	**Namibia, Botswana, Lesotho, Swaziland**
— 689	**Zimbabwe, Zambia, Malawi**

> —682–687 Republic of South Africa

Class comprehensive works on Republic of South Africa in —68; class comprehensive works on Orange River in —687

*For a specific part of this jurisdiction, region, or feature, see the part and follow instructions under —4–9

—682 Gauteng, North-West, Limpopo, Mpumalanga, former homelands (national states) of Republic of South Africa

Class here former Transvaal; *Highveld regions of South Africa; *Vaal River

—[682 1] Heidelberg, Vanderbijlpark, Vereeniging districts; Vaal Triangle

Relocated to —68223

—682 2 Gauteng

Former name: Pretoria-Witwatersrand-Vereeniging (PWV)

Class here Witwatersrand

Delmas district relocated to —68277

—682 21 Johannesburg district

Including Soweto

Class here Johannesburg

—682 22 Krugersdorp, Oberholzer, Randfontein, Roodepoort, Westonaria districts

Class here *West Rand, Far Western Rand

—682 23 Heidelberg, Vanderbijlpark, Vereeniging districts [*all formerly* —6821]

Class here *Vaal Triangle [*formerly* —6821]

—682 24 Brakpan, Nigel, Springs districts

Class here *East Rand

—682 25 Alberton, Benoni, Boksburg, Germiston, Kempton Park districts

—682 26 Randburg district

—682 27 Pretoria district [*formerly* —68235]

Class here Pretoria, *Tshwane

—682 28 Soshanguve district [*formerly* —6823] and Wonderboom district [*formerly* —68235]

—682 29 Bronkhorstspruit and Cullinan districts [*both formerly* —6823]

—[682 3] Central districts

Soshanguve district relocated to —68228; Bronkhorstspruit and Cullinan districts relocated to —68229; Brits and Rustenburg districts relocated to —68241; Marico and Swartruggens districts, Marico River relocated to —68248; Warmbaths district relocated to —68251; Groblersdal district relocated to —68275

*For a specific part of this jurisdiction, region, or feature, see the part and follow instructions under —4–9

—[682 35] Pretoria and Wonderboom districts

Pretoria district relocated to —68227; Wonderboom district relocated to —68228

—682 4 North-West

Class here former *Bophuthatswana [*formerly* —68294]

—682 41 Brits and Rustenburg districts [*both formerly* —6823]; Bafokeng, Moretele I, Odi districts [*all formerly* —68294]

See also —68275 for Moretele II district

—682 42 Koster, Potchefstroom, Ventersdorp districts

—682 43 Klerksdorp district

—682 44 Ditsobotla district [*formerly* —68294]; Coligny, Delareyville, Lichtenburg districts

—682 45 Bloemhof, Christiana, Schweizer-Reneke, Wolmaransstad districts

—682 46 Ganyesa, Kudumane (Thlaping Tlaro), Taung districts [*all formerly* —68294]; Vryburg district [*formerly* —68711]

—682 47 Molopo district [*formerly* —68294]

—682 48 Northern districts of North-West

Including Marico and Swartruggens districts, *Marico River [*all formerly* —6823]; Lehurutshe district, Madikwe district, Mankwe district, Pilanesberg National Park [*all formerly* —68294]

—682 5 Limpopo

Former names: Northern Province, Northern Transvaal

Class here *Limpopo River in South Africa

—682 51 Warmbad district [*formerly* —6823] and Thabazimbi district

—682 53 Mokerong district [*formerly* —68293]; Ellisras, Potgietersrus, Waterberg districts

Including *Mogalakwena River [*formerly* —68293]

—682 55 Nebo, Sekhukhuneland, Thabamoopo districts [*all formerly* —68293]

Including Sekhukhuneberg Range [*formerly* —68293]

Class here former *Lebowa [*formerly* —68293]

—682 56 Bochum and Seshego districts [*both formerly* —68293]; Polokwane (Pietersburg) district

*For a specific part of this jurisdiction, region, or feature, see the part and follow instructions under —4–9

—682 57 Northeastern districts of Limpopo

Including Dzanani, Mutale, Thohoyandou, Vuwani districts [*all formerly* —68291]; Hlanganani and Malamulele districts [*both formerly* —68292]; Sekgosese district [*formerly* —68293]; Messina and Soutpansberg districts

Class here former Venda [*formerly* —68291]; Soutpansberg

—682 59 Southeastern districts of Limpopo

Including Letaba, Lulekani, Phalaborwa districts [*all formerly* —6826]; Giyani, Mapulaneng, Mhala, Namakgale, Ritavi districts [*all formerly* —68292]; Bolobedu and Naphuno districts [*both formerly* —68293]

Class here *Lowveld regions of South Africa [*formerly* —6826]; former *Gazankulu [*formerly* —68292]

—[682 6] Eastern districts

Letaba district, Lulekani district, Phalaborwa district, Lowveld regions of South Africa relocated to —68259; Pelgrimsrus 1 (Pilgrim's Rest 1) and Witrivier (White River) districts, Lebombo Mountains, Crocodile River, Sabie River, Kruger National Park relocated to —68271; Barberton district, Komati River in South Africa relocated to —68272; Nelspruit district relocated to —68273; Lydenburg and Pelgrimsrus 2 (Pilgrim's Rest 2) districts relocated to —68274

—682 7 Mpumalanga

Former name: Eastern Transvaal

Class here *Drakensberg Mountains in former Transvaal

Simdlangentsha district relocated to —6842

—682 71 Pelgrimsrus 1 (Pilgrim's Rest 1) and Witrivier (White River) districts [*both formerly* —6826]; Nsikazi district [*formerly* —68296]

Including *Lebombo Mountains; *Crocodile, *Sabie Rivers [*all formerly* —6826]

Class here *Kruger National Park [*formerly* —6826]

See also —68274 for Pelgrimsrus 2 (Pilgrim's Rest 2) district

—682 72 Barberton district [*formerly* —6826]; Eerstehoek and Nkomazi (Kamhlushwa) districts [*both formerly* —68296]

Including *Komati River in South Africa [*formerly* —6826]

Class here former KaNgwane [*formerly* —68296]

For Nsikazi district, see —68271

—682 73 Nelspruit district [*formerly* —6826]

*For a specific part of this jurisdiction, region, or feature, see the part and follow instructions under —4–9

—682 74 Lydenburg and Pelgrimsrus 2 (Pilgrim's Rest 2) districts [*formerly* —6826], Belfast and Waterval-Boven districts

See also —68271 for Pelgrimsrus 1 (Pilgrim's Rest 1) district

—682 75 Northwestern districts of Mpumalanga

Including Groblersdal district [*formerly* —6823]; Mortele II district [*formerly* —68294]; Kwamhlanga, Mbibana, Mdutjana, Mkobola, Moutse districts [*all formerly* —68295]

Class here former KwaNdebele [*formerly* —68295]

See also —68241 for Moretele I district

—682 76 Middelburg and Witbank districts

—682 77 Delmas district [*formerly* —6822], Balfour, Hoëveldrif (Highveld Ridge), Kriel districts

—682 78 Bethal, Carolina, Ermelo districts

—682 79 Southern districts of Mpumalanga

Including Amersfoort, Piet Retief, Standerton, Volksrust, Wakkerstroom districts

—682 9 Former homelands (Former national states)

Use only if the work covers pre-1997 periods

For a specific homeland or part of a homeland, see the homeland or the part, e.g., Ciskei —68755

—[682 91] Former Venda

Former Venda; Dzanani, Mutale, Thohoyandou, Vuwani districts relocated to —68257

—[682 92] Former Gazankulu

Hlanganani and Malamulele districts relocated to —68257; former Gazankulu; Giyani, Mapulaneng, Mhala, Namakgale, Ritavi districts relocated to —68259

—[682 93] Former Lebowa

Mokerong district, Mogalakwena River relocated to —68253; former Lebowa, Nebo district, Sekhukhuneland district, Thabamoopo district, Sekhukhuneberg Range relocated to —68255; Bochum and Seshego districts relocated to —68256; Sekgosese district relocated to —68257; Bolobedu and Naphuno districts relocated to —68259

—[682 94] Former Bophuthatswana

Former Bophuthatswana relocated to —6824; Bafokeng, Moretele I, Odi districts relocated to —68241; Ditsobotla district relocated to —68244; Ganyesa, Kudumane (Thlaping Tlaro), Taung districts relocated to —68246; Molopo district relocated to —68247; Lehurutshe district, Madikwe district, Mankwe district, Pilanesberg National Park relocated to —68248; Mortele II district relocated to —68275; Thaba Nchu district relocated to —6855

—[682 95] Former KwaNdebele

Former KwaNdebele; Kwamhlanga, Mbibana, Mdutjana, Mkobola, Moutse districts relocated to —68275

—[682 96] Former KaNgwane

Nsikazi district relocated to —68271; Former KaNgwane; Eerstehoek and Nkomazi (Kamhlushwa) districts relocated to —68272

—684 KwaZulu-Natal

Former name: Natal

Province of Republic of South Africa

Class here former KwaZulu; Zululand; *Tugela River

—684 1 Northwestern districts of KwaZulu-Natal

Including Dannhauser, Dundee, Glencoe, Newcastle, Utrecht districts

Class here *Blood River

—684 2 North central districts of KwaZulu-Natal

Including Simdlangentsha district [*formerly* —6827, —68491]; Nqutu district [*formerly* —68491]; Babanango, Ngotshe, Paulpietersburg, Vryheid districts; *Pongola River

For Pongola River (Rio Maputo) in Mozambique, see —6791

—684 3 Northeastern districts of KwaZulu-Natal

Including Ingwavuma, Mhlabatini, Nongoma, Ubombo districts [*all formerly* —68491]; Hlabisa, Lower Umfolozi, Mtonjaneni districts

Including Maputaland, Tongaland; Hluhluwe, Mkuze, Ndumu, Umfolozi Game Reserves [*all formerly* —68491], Greater Saint Lucia Wetland Park

—684 4 *North Coast districts

Including Mapumulu and Ndwedwe districts [*both formerly* —68491], Eshowe, Inanda, Lower Tugela, Mtunzini districts

—684 5 Southern coastal districts of KwaZulu-Natal

Including Umbumbulu and Umlazi districts [*both formerly* —68491]; Chatsworth, Pinetown, Port Shepstone, Umzinto districts; Oribi Gorge Nature Reserve

Class here *South Coast (area south of Durban to Port Edward)

—684 55 Durban district

Including Amanzimtoti, Kingsburgh

Class here Durban; *Durban-Pinetown industrial area

*For a specific part of this jurisdiction, region, or feature, see the part and follow instructions under —4–9

—684 6 Alfred and Mount Currie districts

Class here *Griqualand East

—684 7 Natal Midlands districts

Including Msinga and Nkandla districts [*both formerly* —68491]; Bergville, Camperdown, Estcourt, Impendle, Ixopo, Kliprivier, Kranskop, Lions River, Mooirivier, New Hanover, Polela, Richmond, Umvoti, Underberg, Weenen districts

Including Natal Drakensberg Park, Royal Natal National Park; Giant's Castle Game Reserve; *Mgeni River

Class here *Drakensberg Mountains

—684 75 Pietermaritzburg district

Including Albert Falls and Nature Reserve

—[684 9] Homelands (National states)

Number discontinued; class in —684

—[684 91] Former KwaZulu

Use of this number for comprehensive works on former KwaZulu discontinued; class in —684

A specific part of former KwaZulu relocated to the part in —6841–6847, e.g., Umbombo district and Umfolozi Game Reserve —6843

—685 Free State

Former name: Orange Free State

Province of Republic of South Africa

—685 1 Northeastern districts of Free State

Including Witsieshoek district [*formerly* —68591]; Bethlehem, Ficksburg, Fouriesburg, Frankfort, Harrismith, Lindley, Reitz, Senekal, Vrede districts

Including former homelands of Orange Free State [*formerly* —6859], former Qwaqwa [*formerly* —68591]; Golden Gate Highlands National Park

Class here *Northeastern Orange Free State

—685 2 Northern districts of Free State

Including Bothaville, Heilbron, Koppies, Kroonstad, Parys, Viljoenskroon, Vredefort districts

Class here *Northern Orange Free State

—685 25 Sasolburg district

*For a specific part of this jurisdiction, region, or feature, see the part and follow instructions under —4–9

—685 3 North central districts of Free State

Including Brandfort, Bultfontein, Hennenman, Hoopstad, Odendaalsrus, Theunissen, Ventersburg, Virginia, Wesselsbron, Winburg districts; Willem Pretorius Game Reserve

—685 35 Welkom district

—685 4 Bloemfontein district

—685 5 East central districts of Free State

Including Thaba Nchu district [*formerly* —68294]; Clocolan, Excelsior, Ladybrand, Marquard districts

—685 6 Southeastern districts of Free State

Including Botshabelo, Dewetsdorp, Reddersburg, Rouxville, Smithfield, Wepener, Zastron districts

Class here *Caledon River

For Caledon River in Lesotho, see —6885

—685 7 Southwestern districts of Free State

Including Bethulie, Edenburg, Fauresmith, Jagersfontein, Petrusburg, Philippolis, Trompsburg districts

—685 8 Boshof, Jacobsdal, Koffiefontein districts

—[685 9] Homelands (National states)

Relocated to —6851

—[685 91] Qwaqwa, Witsieshoek district

Relocated to —6851

—687 Northern Cape, Western Cape, Eastern Cape

Provinces of Republic of South Africa

Class here former Cape of Good Hope

—687 1 Northern Cape

Class here *Orange River

—687 11 Northeastern districts of Northern Cape

Including Barkly West, Hartswater, Hay, Herbert, Kimberley, Kuruman, Postmasburg, Warrenton districts; Vaalbos National Park; *Harts River

Class here *Kalahari Desert in South Africa

Class comprehensive works on Kalahari Desert in —6883

Vryburg district relocated to —68246

*For a specific part of this jurisdiction, region, or feature, see the part and follow instructions under —4–9

—687 12 Gordonia, Kenhardt, Prieska districts

Including Augrabies, Kalahari Gemsbok National Parks

—687 13 Eastern Upper Karoo districts

Including Britstown, Colesberg, De Aar, Hanover, Hopetown, Noupoort, Philipstown, Richmond districts; *Vanderkloof (P. K. le Roux) Dam

Class here *Upper Karoo

Albert, Steynsburg, Venterstad districts relocated to —68756

For western Upper Karoo districts, see —68717

—[687 14] Cape Midlands districts

Jansenville and Steytlerville districts relocated to —68751; Somerset East district relocated to —68753; Cradock district, Graaff-Reinet district, Middelburg district, Pearston district, Mountain Zebra National Park relocated to —68754; Tarka district relocated to —68755; Hofmeyr district relocated to —68756

—[687 15] Great Karoo districts

Beaufort West district, Laingsburg district, Murraysburg district, Prince Albert district, Karoo National Park, the Karoo, Great Karoo relocated to —68739; Willowmore district relocated to —68751; Aberdeen district relocated to —68754

—[687 16] Little Karoo; Calitzdorp, Ladismith, Oudtshoorn districts

Relocated to —68738

—687 17 Western Upper Karoo districts

Including Calvinia, Carnarvon, Fraserburg, Sutherland, Victoria West, Williston districts; Tankwa-Karoo National Park; *Bokkeveld, *Nuweveld, *Roggeveld Ranges

—687 19 Namaqualand district [*formerly* —6872]

Including Richtersveld National Park

—[687 2] Namaqualand, Clanwilliam, Vanrhynsdorp, Vredendal districts

Namaqualand district relocated to —68719; Clanwilliam, Vanrhynsdorp, Vredendal districts relocated to —68731

—687 3 Western Cape

—687 31 Clanwilliam, Vanrhynsdorp, Vredendal districts [*formerly* —6872]

Class here *Cedarberg

—687 32 West central districts of Western Cape

Including Hopefield, Malmesbury, Moorreesburg, Piquetberg, Vredenburg districts; West Coast National Park

*For a specific part of this jurisdiction, region, or feature, see the part and follow instructions under —4–9

—687 33 North central districts of Western Cape

Including Ceres, Montagu, Robertson, Tulbagh, Worcester districts

—687 34 Paarl, Somerset West, Stellenbosch, Strand, Wellington districts

Including *Boland

—687 35 Cape Peninsula districts

Including Bellville, Goodwood, Kuils River, Mitchell's Plain, Simonstown, Wynberg districts; Crossroads; Cape of Good Hope; Robben Island

Class here Cape Metroplitan Area

—687 355 Cape district

Including Kirstenbosch Botanic Gardens, Table Mountain

Class here Cape Town

—687 36 South central districts of Western Cape

Including Bredasdorp, Caledon, Heidelberg, Hermanus, Swellendam districts; Bontebok National Park; Overberg

—687 37 Southeastern districts of Western Cape

Including George district, Knysna district, Mosselbaai (Mossel Bay) district, Knysna Lakes National Park, Wilderness National Park [*all formerly* —6874]; Riversdale district

Class here *Garden Route [*formerly* —6874]

—687 38 Little Karoo [*formerly* —68716]

Including Calitzdorp, Ladismith, Oudtshoorn districts [*all formerly* —68716]; Uniondale district [*formerly* —6874]

—687 39 Great Karoo districts [*formerly* —68715]

Including Beaufort West, Laingsburg, Murraysburg, Prince Albert districts; Karoo National Park

Class here *Great Karoo, the *Karoo

—[687 4] Southern districts

George district, Knysna district, Mosselbaai (Mossel Bay) district, Wilderness National Park, Garden Route relocated to —68737; Uniondale district relocated to —68738; Hankey district, Humansdorp district, Joubertina district, Tsitsikamma Forest and Coastal National Park relocated to —68751

—687 5 Eastern Cape

Class here homelands (national states [South Africa]) [*formerly* —6879]; Kaffraria

*For a specific part of this jurisdiction, region, or feature, see the part and follow instructions under —4–9

—687 51 Southwestern districts of Eastern Cape

Including Jansenville and Steytlerville districts [*both formerly* —68714]; Willowmore district [*formerly* —68715]; Hankey district, Humansdorp district, Joubertina district, Tsitsikamma Forest and Coastal National Park [*all formerly* —6874]

—687 52 Port Elizabeth and Uitenhage districts

Class here Port Elizabeth-Uitenhage-Despatch industrial area

—687 53 Southeastern districts of Eastern Cape

Including Somerset East district [*formerly* —68714]; Adelaide, Albany, Alexandria, Bathurst, Bedford, Fort Beaufort, Kirkwood districts; Addo Elephant National Park, Zuurberg National Park

—687 54 Northwestern districts of Eastern Cape

Including Cradock district, Graaff-Reinet district, Middelburg district, Pearston district, Mountain Zebra National Park [*all formerly* —68714]; Aberdeen district [*formerly* —68715]

—687 55 Central districts of Eastern Cape

Including Tarka district [*formerly* —68714]; Molteno district, *Stormberg [*both formerly* —6876]; Hewu, Keiskammahoek, Mdantsane, Middledrift, Mpofu, Ntabethemba, Peddie, Victoria East, Zwelitsha districts [*all formerly* —68792]; Cathcart, King William's Town, Komga, Queenstown, Sterkstroom, Stutterheim districts

Class here former Ciskei [*formerly* —68792]

—687 555 East London district

—687 56 North central districts of Eastern Cape

Including Albert, Steynsburg, Venterstad districts [*all formerly* —68713]; Hofmeyr district [*formerly* —68714]; Aliwal North, Lady Grey districts [*both formerly* —6876]; Sterkspruit (Herschel) district [*formerly* —68791]

—687 57 Northeastern districts of Eastern Cape

Including Barkly East, Elliot, Indwe, Maclear, Wodehouse districts [*formerly* —6876]

*For a specific part of this jurisdiction, region, or feature, see the part and follow instructions under —4–9

—687 58 Former Transkei [*formerly* —68791]

Including Butterworth, Cala, Cofimvaba, Elliotdale, Engcobo, Idutywa, Kentani, Lady Frere, Libode, Mqanduli, Ngqeleni, Nqamakwe, Port St. Johns, Qumbu, Tsolo, Tsomo, Umtata, Willowvale districts; *Great Kei River

Class here Pondoland

For Sterkspruit, see —68756; for Bizana, Flagstaff, Lusikisiki, Maluti, Mount Ayliff, Mount Fletcher, Mount Frere, Tabankulu, Umzimkulu districts, see —68759

—687 59 Eastern districts of Eastern Cape [*formerly* —68791]

Including Bizana, Flagstaff, Lusikisiki, Maluti, Mount Ayliff, Mount Fletcher, Mount Frere, Tabankulu, Umzimkulu districts

—[687 6] Northeastern districts

Molteno district, Stormberg relocated to —68755; Aliwal North, Lady Grey districts relocated to —68756; Barkly East, Elliot, Indwe, Maclear, Wodehouse districts relocated to —68757

—[687 9] Homelands (National states)

Relocated to —6875

—[687 91] Former Transkei

Sterkspruit (Herschel) district relocated to —68756; former Transkei relocated to —68758; eastern districts (Bizana, Flagstaff, Lusikisiki, Maluti, Mount Ayliff, Mount Fletcher, Mount Frere, Tabankulu, Umzimkulu districts) relocated to —68759

—[687 92] Former Ciskei

Former Ciskei; Hewu, Keiskammahoek, Mdantsane, Middledrift, Mpofu, Ntabethemba, Peddie, Victoria East, Zwelitsha districts relocated to —68755

—688 Namibia, Botswana, Lesotho, Swaziland

—688 1 Namibia

Including Windhoek

—688 3 Botswana

Including Gaborone

Class here *Kalahari Desert

—688 5 Lesotho

Including Maseru

*For a specific part of this jurisdiction, region, or feature, see the part and follow instructions under —4–9

—688 7 Swaziland

Including Mbabane

—689 Zimbabwe, Zambia, Malawi

—689 1 Zimbabwe

Including Manicaland, Mashonaland Central, Mashonaland East, Mashonaland West, Masvingo, Matabeleland North, Matabeleland South, Midlands provinces; Bulawayo, Harare; Victoria Falls

For Victoria Falls in Zambia, see —6894

—689 4 Zambia

Including Central, Copperbelt, Eastern, Luapula, Lusaka, North-Western, Northern, Southern, Western provinces; Lusaka

—689 7 Malawi

Including Blantyre, Lilongwe

Class here *Lake Nyasa (Lake Malawi)

—69 South Indian Ocean islands

—691 Madagascar

Including Antananarivo, Antsiranana, Fianarantsoa, Mahajanga, Toamasina, Toliara provinces; Antananarivo (capital city)

—694 Comoro Islands

—694 1 Comoros (Federal and Islamic Republic of the Comoros)

Including Moroni

—694 5 Mayotte

—696 Seychelles

Including Victoria; Aldabra, Mahé islands

—697 Chagos Islands

—698 Réunion and Mauritius

Class here Mascarene Islands

—698 1 Réunion

Overseas department of France

Including Saint-Denis

—698 2 Mauritius

Including Port Louis; Cargados Carajos Shoals, Rodrigues Island

—699 Isolated islands

Including Amsterdam, Cocos (Keeling), Crozet, Kerguelen, Prince Edward, Saint Paul

*For a specific part of this jurisdiction, region, or feature, see the part and follow instructions under —4–9

—7 North America

Class here comprehensive works on North and South America

Class Western Hemisphere (North and South America, plus parts of Atlantic and Pacific Oceans) in —1812

For South America, see —8

SUMMARY

—71 Canada
—711 British Columbia
—712 Prairie Provinces
—713 Ontario
—714 Quebec
—715 Atlantic Provinces Maritime Provinces
—716 Nova Scotia
—717 Prince Edward Island
—718 Newfoundland and Labrador, Saint Pierre and Miquelon
—719 Northern territories

—72 Middle America Mexico
—721 Northern states of Mexico
—722 Lower California peninsula
—723 Central Pacific states of Mexico
—724 Central states of Mexico
—725 Valley of Mexico
—726 Southern Gulf states of Mexico
—727 Southern Pacific states of Mexico
—728 Central America
—729 West Indies (Antilles) and Bermuda

—73 United States

—74 Northeastern United States (New England and Middle Atlantic states)
—741 Maine
—742 New Hampshire
—743 Vermont
—744 Massachusetts
—745 Rhode Island
—746 Connecticut
—747 New York
—748 Pennsylvania
—749 New Jersey

—75 Southeastern United States (South Atlantic states)
—751 Delaware
—752 Maryland
—753 District of Columbia (Washington)
—754 West Virginia
—755 Virginia
—756 North Carolina
—757 South Carolina
—758 Georgia
—759 Florida

— 76 South central United States Gulf Coast states
— 761 Alabama
— 762 Mississippi
— 763 Louisiana
— 764 Texas
— 766 Oklahoma
— 767 Arkansas
— 768 Tennessee
— 769 Kentucky

— 77 North central United States Lake states
— 771 Ohio
— 772 Indiana
— 773 Illinois
— 774 Michigan
— 775 Wisconsin
— 776 Minnesota
— 777 Iowa
— 778 Missouri

— 78 Western United States
— 781 Kansas
— 782 Nebraska
— 783 South Dakota
— 784 North Dakota
— 786 Montana
— 787 Wyoming
— 788 Colorado
— 789 New Mexico

— 79 Great Basin and Pacific Slope region of United States Pacific Coast states
— 791 Arizona
— 792 Utah
— 793 Nevada
— 794 California
— 795 Oregon
— 796 Idaho
— 797 Washington
— 798 Alaska

—71 Canada

See Manual at T2—73 vs. T2—71

—711 British Columbia

Class here *Canadian Cordillera; *Rocky Mountains in Canada; *Rocky Mountain Trench

*For a specific part of this jurisdiction, region, or feature, see the part and follow instructions under —4–9

—711 1 Northern coastal region of British Columbia

Coastal mainland and Coast Mountains from Alaska border to Powell River

Including Central Coast, Skeena-Queen Charlotte Regional Districts; mainland parts of Comox-Strathcona, Mount Waddington Regional Districts; Kitimat-Stikine Regional District south of 54°30′ N

Including Bella Coola, Kitimat, Ocean Falls, Prince Rupert; Cortes, Hardwicke, Maurelle, Read, East and West Redonda, Sonora, East and West Thurlow Islands; Bella Coola River

Class here comprehensive works on Kitimat-Stikine Regional District; *Pacific Coast in Canada; *Coast Mountains

For coasts of southwestern British Columbia, see —7113; for Kitimat-Stikine Regional District north of 54°30′ N, see —71185

See also —16433 for Dixon Entrance, Hecate Strait, Inside Passage, Queen Charlotte Sound

—711 12 Queen Charlotte Islands

—711 2 Vancouver Island

Including Alberni-Clayoquot, Nanaimo, Cowichan Valley Regional Districts; parts of Comox-Strathcona, Mount Waddington Regional Districts on Vancouver Island

Including Nanaimo; comprehensive works on Comox-Strathcona, Mount Waddington Regional Districts; Pacific Rim National Park; Denman, Hope, Hornby, Malcolm, Nigei, Quadra Islands; Koksilah River; Shawnigan Lake

For mainland parts of Comox-Strathcona, Mount Waddington Regional Districts, see —7111

See also —16433 for Strait of Georgia, Queen Charlotte Strait

—711 28 Victoria region

Including Capital Regional District (Vancouver Island south of San Juan and Koksilah Rivers and Shawnigan Lake)

Including Central Saanich, Esquimalt, Metchosin, North Saanich, Oak Bay, Port Renfrew, Saanich, Sidney, Sooke, Victoria; Saanich Peninsula; *Gulf Islands; San Juan River; Sooke Lake

See also —16432 for Strait of Juan de Fuca

—711 3 Southwestern region of British Columbia

Class here *Fraser River, *Lillooet River

*For a specific part of this jurisdiction, region, or feature, see the part and follow instructions under —4–9

—711 31 Southern coastal region of British Columbia

Mainland coast from Powell River to Howe Sound

Including Powell River, Squamish-Lillooet, Sunshine Coast Regional Districts

Including Lillooet, Pemberton, Powell River, Squamish, Whistler; *Garibaldi Provincial Park; Desolation Sound Provincial Marine Park; Anvil, Gambier, Hernando, Keats, Lasqueti, Texada Islands; Malaspina Peninsula; Bridge River; Carpenter, Lillooet Lakes

—711 33 Greater Vancouver Regional District

Including Maple Ridge, Pitt Meadows [*both formerly* —71137]; Burnaby, Coquitlam, Delta, Langley, Lions Bay, New Westminster, North Vancouver, Port Coquitlam, Port Moody, Richmond, Surrey, West Vancouver, White Rock; Bowen Island

Class here Vancouver

—711 37 Fraser Valley Regional District

Including former Central Fraser Valley, Dewdney-Alouette, Fraser-Cheam Regional Districts

Including Abbotsford, Chilliwack, Hope, Mission; Golden Ears Provincial Park; Fraser Canyon; Coquihalla, Nahatlatch, *Pitt Rivers; Harrison Lake

Maple Ridge, Pitt Meadows relocated to —71133

—711 5 Okanagan-Similkameen region

Including Central Okanagan, North Okanagan, Okanagan-Similkameen Regional Districts

Including Armstrong, Enderby, Kelowna, Osoyoos, Penticton, Princeton, Vernon; Manning Provincial Park; Shuswap, Tulameen Rivers; Okanagan Lake

Class here *Cascade Mountains in British Columbia

—711 6 Southeastern region of British Columbia

Class here *Columbia River in British Columbia

—711 62 West Kootenay region

Including Central Kootenay, Kootenay Boundary Regional Districts

Including Castlegar, Creston, Grand Forks, Greenwood, Nelson, Rossland, Trail; *Monashee Mountains; *Granby, *Kettle, *West Kettle Rivers; Upper and Lower Arrow, Slocan, Kootenay Lakes

*For a specific part of this jurisdiction, region, or feature, see the part and follow instructions under —4–9

—711 65 East Kootenay Regional District

Approximately the area drained by the upper Columbia and Kootenay Rivers

Including Cranbrook, Invermere, Kimberley; Kootenay National Park

Class here *Purcell Mountains; *Kootenay River

—711 68 Columbia-Shuswap Regional District

Including Golden, Revelstoke, Salmon Arm; Glacier, Mount Revelstoke, Yoho National Parks; Hamber Provincial Park; Illecillewaet, Seymour, Spillimacheen Rivers; *Kinbasket (McNaughton), Shuswap Lakes

Class here *Selkirk Mountains

—711 7 Central interior region of British Columbia

Class here *Cariboo Mountains

—711 72 Thompson-Nicola Regional District

Approximately the area drained by the Thompson and Nicola Rivers

Including Cache Creek, Chase, Clinton, Kamloops, Lytton, Merritt; Wells Gray Provincial Park; Bonaparte, Clearwater, Coldwater, Nicola, North and South Thompson, Thompson Rivers; Adams Lake

—711 75 Cariboo Regional District

Approximately the central Fraser Valley and the area drained by the Chilcotin, Nazko, and Quesnel Rivers

Including Anahim Lake, Barkerville, 100 Mile House, Quesnel, Wells, Williams Lake; Bowron Lake Provincial Park; Adams, Chilcotin, Chilko, Horsefly, Nazko, Quesnel, Taseko, West Road Rivers; Quesnel Lake

Class here *Fraser Plateau

—711 8 Northern region of British Columbia

—711 82 North central region of British Columbia

Approximately the corridor formed by the Bulkley, Nechako, and upper Fraser valleys

Including Bulkley-Nechako, Fraser-Fort George Regional Districts

Including Mackenzie, McBride, Prince George, Smithers, Valemount, Vanderhoof; Mount Robson, *Tweedsmuir Provincial Parks; *Bulkley, Chilako, McGregor, Morice, Nation, *Omineca, Parsnip Rivers; Morice, Takla Lakes; Nechako Reservoir

Class here *Nechako Plateau; Nechako River

*For a specific part of this jurisdiction, region, or feature, see the part and follow instructions under —4–9

—711 85 Northwestern region of British Columbia

Including Stikine Region, parts of Kitimat-Stikine Regional District north of 54°30′ N

Including Hazelton, Stewart, Terrace; *Hazelton, *Omineca Mountains; Gataga, Kechika, Nass, Osilinka, Skeena, Spatsizi, *Stikine, Sustut Rivers

Class here *Cassiar, *Skeena Mountains

—711 87 Northeastern region of British Columbia

Including Northern Rockies (Fort Nelson-Liard), Peace River Regional Districts

Including Dawson Creek, Fort Nelson, Fort St. John, Tumbler Ridge; Finlay, Fort Nelson, Ingenika, Mesilinka, Murray, Pine, Sukunka Rivers; *Williston Lake

Class here Peace River in British Columbia, *Liard River

—712 Prairie Provinces

Class here *western Canada

—712 3 Alberta

—712 31 Northwestern region of Alberta

Area north of 55° N, and west of 114° W

Including Grande Prairie, Peace River; Lesser Slave Lake

Class here *northern Alberta; *Peace River

—712 32 Northeastern region of Alberta

Area north of 55° N, and east of 114° W

Including Fort McMurray

Class here *Wood Buffalo National Park; *Athabaska River

—712 33 Central region of Alberta

Area between 55° N and 51° N

Including Drumheller, Red Deer; Elk Island National Park; Lac La Biche

Class here *Rocky Mountains in Alberta; *Bow, *North Saskatchewan, *Red Deer Rivers

*For a specific part of this jurisdiction, region, or feature, see the part and follow instructions under —4–9

—712 332 Rocky Mountain parks region

Including Banff; Banff, Jasper National Parks; Peter Lougheed Provincial Park; Willmore Wilderness Provincial Park; Kananaskis Country

See also —71234 for Waterton Lakes National Park

—712 334 Edmonton

—712 338 Calgary

—712 34 Southern region of Alberta

Area south of 51° N to international boundary

Including Crowsnest Pass, Fort Macleod, Medicine Hat; Waterton Lakes National Park

—712 345 Lethbridge

—712 4 Saskatchewan

—712 41 Northern region of Saskatchewan

Area north of 55° N

Class here *Lake Athabasca

—712 42 Central region of Saskatchewan

Area between 55° N and 51° N

Including Battlefords, Lloydminster, Prince Albert, Yorkton; *Lake Diefenbaker

Class here *Saskatchewan, *South Saskatchewan Rivers

For parts of Lloydminster in Alberta, see —71233

—712 425 Saskatoon

—712 43 Southwestern region of Saskatchewan

Area south of 51° N, and west of 106° W

Including Swift Current; *Cypress Hills

—712 44 Southeastern region of Saskatchewan

Area south of 51° N, and east of 106° W

Including Fort Qu'Appelle, Melville, Moose Jaw

—712 445 Regina

—712 7 Manitoba

*For a specific part of this jurisdiction, region, or feature, see the part and follow instructions under —4–9

—712 71 Northern region of Manitoba

Area north of 55° N

Including Churchill, Port Nelson, Thompson

Class here *Churchill, *Nelson Rivers

—712 72 Central region of Manitoba

Area between 55° N and 50°30′ N

Including Dauphin, Flin Flon, The Pas; Interlake region; Lakes *Manitoba, Winnipegosis, *Winnipeg

Class here *Canadian Shield in Manitoba

—712 73 Southwestern region of Manitoba

Area south of 50°30′ N, and west of 98° W

Including Brandon, Minnedosa, Portage la Prairie

Class here *Assiniboine River

—712 74 Southeastern region of Manitoba

Area south of 50°30′ N, and east of 98° W

Including Selkirk; Whiteshell Provincial Park

Class here *Red River of the North in Manitoba

—712 743 Winnipeg

—713 Ontario

Including *Niagara Escarpment

Class here *eastern Canada; *Great Lakes in Canada

See Manual at T2—713 and T2—714

—713 1 Northern Ontario and Georgian Bay regions

Including Patricia portion of Kenora District

Class here Canadian Shield in Ontario, northern Ontario

Subdivisions are added for either or both topics in heading

See also —16327 for Hudson, James Bays

> —713 11–713 14 Northern Ontario region

Class comprehensive works in —7131

*For a specific part of this jurisdiction, region, or feature, see the part and follow instructions under —4–9

—713 11 Northwestern Ontario

Including *Lake of the Woods in Canada

For Thunder Bay District, see —71312

—713 112 Kenora District

For Patricia portion of Kenora District, see —7131

—713 117 Rainy River District

—713 12 Thunder Bay District

Class here *Lake Superior in Ontario

—713 13 Northeastern Ontario

For clay belt, see —71314; for Parry Sound District, see —71315; for District Municipality of Muskoka, see —71316

—713 132 Algoma District

Including *North Channel

—713 133 Sudbury District

Class here City of Greater Sudbury (Regional Municipality of Sudbury)

—713 135 Manitoulin District

—713 14 Clay belt

—713 142 Cochrane District

Including *Lake Abitibi

—713 144 Timiskaming District

—713 147 Nipissing District

Including Algonquin Provincial Park; *Lake Nipissing

> —713 15–713 18 Georgian Bay region

Class comprehensive works in —7131

—713 15 Parry Sound District

Class here *Georgian Bay

—713 16 District Municipality of Muskoka

—713 17 Simcoe County

—713 18 Grey County

*For a specific part of this jurisdiction, region, or feature, see the part and follow instructions under —4–9

> —713 2–713 8 Southern Ontario

Class comprehensive works in —713

For Simcoe County, see —71317; for Grey County, see —71318

—713 2 Lake Huron region

Class here *Southwestern Ontario; *Lake Huron in Ontario

—713 21 Bruce County

—713 22 Huron County

—713 23 Perth County

—713 25 Middlesex County

For London, see —71326

—713 26 London

—713 27 Lambton County

Including *Saint Clair River in Ontario

—713 3 Lake Erie region

Class here *Lake Erie in Ontario

—713 31 Essex County

Including *Lake Saint Clair in Ontario

For Windsor, see —71332

—713 32 Windsor

—713 33 Municipality of Chatham-Kent

Former name: Kent County

—713 34 Elgin County

—713 36 Norfolk County

Class here former Regional Municipality of Haldimand-Norfolk

Haldimand County relocated to —71337

—713 37 Haldimand County [*formerly* —71336]

—713 38 Regional Municipality of Niagara

Including Niagara Falls (city); Niagara River; Welland Canal

Class here *Niagara Peninsula

For Niagara Falls (physiographic feature), see —71339; for Niagara River in New York, see —78798

*For a specific part of this jurisdiction, region, or feature, see the part and follow instructions under —4–9

—713 39 Niagara Falls

Physiographic feature

For Niagara Falls in New York, see —74799

—713 4 West central region of Ontario

—713 41 Dufferin County

—713 42 Wellington County

For Guelph, see —71343

—713 43 Guelph

—713 44 Regional Municipality of Waterloo

For Kitchener, Waterloo (city), see —71345

—713 45 Kitchener-Waterloo

Including Waterloo (city)

Class here Kitchener

—713 46 Oxford County

—713 47 Brant County

—713 5 Lake Ontario region

Class here *Lake Ontario in Ontario

—713 52 City of Hamilton

Former name: Regional Municipality of Hamilton-Wentworth

Class here former Wentworth County; Hamilton

—713 53 Halton and Peel Regional Municipalities

—713 533 Regional Municipality of Halton

—713 535 Regional Municipality of Peel

—713 54 City of Toronto and Regional Municipality of York

Class here former York County

—713 541 City of Toronto

Former name: Metropolitan Toronto

Including East York, Etobicoke, North York, Scarborough, York

Class here Toronto

—713 547 Regional Municipality of York

—713 56 Regional Municipality of Durham

*For a specific part of this jurisdiction, region, or feature, see the part and follow instructions under —4–9

—713 57 Northumberland County

Including *Rice Lake

—713 58 Hastings and Prince Edward Counties

—713 585 Hastings County

—713 587 Prince Edward County

—713 59 Lennox and Addington County

—713 6 East central region of Ontario

—713 61 Haliburton County

—713 64 City of Kawartha Lakes

Former name: Victoria County

Class comprehensive works on Kawartha Lakes (physiographic feature) in —71367

—713 67 Peterborough County

Class here *Kawartha Lakes

See also —71364 for City of Kawartha Lakes

—713 7 Saint Lawrence River region

Class here *Eastern Ontario; *Thousand Islands in Ontario; *Saint Lawrence River in Ontario; *Saint Lawrence Seaway in Ontario

—713 71 Frontenac County

For Kingston, see —71372

—713 72 Kingston

—713 73 United Counties of Leeds and Grenville

—713 75 United Counties of Stormont, Dundas and Glengarry

—713 8 Ottawa River region

Class here *Ottawa River

—713 81 Renfrew County

—713 82 Lanark County

—[713 83] City of Ottawa

Relocated to —71384

*For a specific part of this jurisdiction, region, or feature, see the part and follow instructions under —4–9

—713 84 City of Ottawa [*formerly* —71383]

Former name: Regional Municipality of Ottawa-Carleton

Class here Ottawa; comprehensive works on National Capital Region

For National Capital Region in Quebec province, see —714221

—713 85 United Counties of Prescott and Russell

—714 Quebec

Class here *Canadian Shield; *Saint Lawrence River; *Saint Lawrence Seaway

This development reflects the regional county municipalites established in 1980 and any reorganization of them between 1980 and 2002. Relatively minor changes between this development and the development for the previous counties, as given in Editions 20 and 21, are not indicated

See also —16344 for Gulf of Saint Lawrence

See Manual at T2—713 and T2—714

—714 1 Northern region of Quebec

—714 11 Nord-du-Québec region

Former name: New Quebec

Class here former Nouveau-Québec Administrative Region

See also —7182 for Labrador

—714 111 Extreme northern region of Quebec

Area north of 55° N

Including Hudson Bay and Ungava Bay regions

Class here Kativik Regional Administration, Nunavik region

See also —16327 for Hudson, Ungava Bays

—714 115 James Bay region

Including Baie-James, Chibougamau, Lebel-sur-Quévillon, Matagami

Class here mid-northern region of Quebec

Use of this number for former Nouveau-Québec Administrative Region discontinued; class in —71411

Caniapiscau Regional County Municipality, Gagnon, Schefferville relocated to —714117

*For a specific part of this jurisdiction, region, or feature, see the part and follow instructions under —4–9

—714 117 Caniapiscau Regional County Municipality [*formerly* —714115]

Including Gagnon, Schefferville [*formerly* —714115]

—714 13 Abitibi-Témiscamingue regional county municipalities and City of Rouyn-Noranda

—714 132 Abitibi-Ouest Regional County Municipality

—714 134 Abitibi Regional County Municipality

—714 136 City of Rouyn-Noranda

Former name: Rouyn-Noranda Regional County Municipality

—714 137 Témiscamingue Regional County Municipality

—714 139 Vallée-de-l'Or Regional County Municipality

—714 14 Lac-Saint-Jean regional county municipalities

Class here *Saguenay-Lac-Saint-Jean Administrative Region

—714 142 Le Domaine-du-Roy Regional County Municipality

Including Ashuapmushuam Wildlife Reserve (Chibougamau Wildlife Reserve)

—714 145 Maria-Chapdelaine Regional County Municipality

—714 148 Lac-Saint-Jean-Est Regional County Municipality

—714 16 City of Saguenay and Le Fjord-du-Saguenay Regional County Municipality

Class here *Saguenay River

—714 162 City of Saguenay

Including Chicoutimi, Jonquière

—714 165 Le Fjord-du-Saguenay Regional County Municipality

—714 17 Côte-Nord regional county municipalities

See also —7182 for Labrador

—714 172 La Haute-Côte-Nord Regional County Municipality

—714 174 Manicouagan Regional County Municipality

—714 176 Sept-Rivières Regional County Municipality

—714 178 Minganie Regional County Municipality

Class here Basse-Côte-Nord region

—714 178 2 Anticosti Island

*For a specific part of this jurisdiction, region, or feature, see the part and follow instructions under —4–9

—714 2 Western region of Quebec

Class here *Ottawa River in Quebec Province

—714 21 Pontiac Regional County Municipality

La Vérendrye Wildlife Reserve relocated to —714224

—714 22 Outaouais regional county municipalities

For Pontiac Regional County Municipality, see —71421

—714 221 City of Gatineau

Former name: Outaouais Regional Community

Including National Capital Region in Quebec province

Les Collines-de-l'Outaouais Regional County Municipality relocated to —714223; La Vallée-de-la-Gatineau Regional County Municipality, Gatineau River relocated to —714224

Class comprehensive works on National Capital Region in —71384

—714 223 Les Collines-de-l'Outaouais Regional County Municipality [*formerly* —714221]

Class here Gatineau Park

—714 224 La Vallée-de-la-Gatineau Regional County Municipality [*formerly* —714221]

Class here *La Vérendrye Wildlife Reserve [*formerly* —71421]; *Gatineau River [*formerly* —714221]

—[714 225] Antoine-Labelle Regional County Municipality

Relocated to —714241

—714 227 Papineau Regional County Municipality

—714 23 Argenteuil Regional County Municipality

—714 24 Laurentides regional county municipalities

Class here *Laurentians region (Laurentides region); *lower Laurentian Mountains

Les Moulins Regional County Municipality relocated to —714412

Class comprehensive works on Laurentian Mountains in —7144

—714 241 Antoine-Labelle Regional County Municipality [*formerly* —714225]

Class here *Papineau-Labelle Wildlife Reserve

—714 242 Les Laurentides Regional County Municipality

—714 244 Les Pays-d'en-Haut Regional County Municipality

*For a specific part of this jurisdiction, region, or feature, see the part and follow instructions under —4–9

—714 246 La Rivière-du-Nord Regional County Municipality

—714 248 Thérèse-De Blainville Regional County Municipality

—714 25 Deux-Montagnes Regional County Municipality and City of Mirabel

—714 252 Deux-Montagnes Regional County Municipality

—714 254 City of Mirabel

Former name: Mirabel Regional County Municipality

—714 26 Vaudreuil-Soulanges Regional County Municipality

—714 27 Montréal Metropolitan Community

Class here Montréal region

For a specific part of Montréal Metropolitan Community not provided for here, see the part, e.g., City of Montréal —71428, La Vallée-du-Richelieu Regional County Municipality —714365

—714 271 City of Laval

Class here Jésus Island

—714 28 City of Montréal

Class here former Montreal Urban Community; Montréal Island

For City of Laval, see —714271; for City of Longueuil, see —71437

—714 3 Southwestern region of Quebec

Area south of Saint Lawrence River, and Richelieu River valley and westward

Class here *Montérégie region; Richelieu River

—714 31 Le Haut-Saint-Laurent Regional County Municipality

—714 32 Beauharnois-Salaberry Regional County Municipality

—[714 33] Former Châteauguay County

Relocated to —71434

—714 34 Roussillon Regional County Municipality

Class here former *Châteauguay County [*formerly* —71433], former *Laprairie County

—714 35 Les Jardins-de-Napierville Regional County Municipality

—714 36 Lajemmerais and La Vallée-du-Richelieu regional county municipalities

—714 362 Lajemmerais Regional County Municipality

*For a specific part of this jurisdiction, region, or feature, see the part and follow instructions under —4–9

—714 365 La Vallée-du-Richelieu Regional County Municipality

Class here former *Chambly County [*formerly* —71437]

—714 37 City of Longueuil

Former name: Champlain Regional County Municipality

Former Chambly County relocated to —714365

—714 38 Le Haut-Richelieu Regional County Municipality

Class here former Iberville County [*formerly* —71461], former Saint-Jean County

—714 39 Le Bas-Richelieu Regional County Municipality [*formerly* —71451]

—714 4 North central region of Quebec

Area north of Saint Lawrence River from Montréal to Saguenay River

Class here *Laurentian Mountains

—714 41 Lanaudière regional county municipalities

—714 412 Les Moulins Regional County Municipality [*formerly* —71424]

—714 415 Montcalm Regional County Municipality

—714 416 L'Assomption Regional County Municipality

—714 418 Matawinie Regional County Municipality

Class here *Mont-Tremblant National Park

—714 42 Joliette Regional County Municipality

—714 43 D'Autray Regional County Municipality

—714 44 Maskinongé Regional County Municipality

—714 45 Mauricie regional county municipalities

Class here *Saint-Maurice River

—714 451 City of Trois-Rivières

Including Cap-de-la-Madeleine [*formerly* —714455]

Class here former Francheville Regional County Municipality

City of Shawinigan relocated to —714453; Les Chenaux Regional County Municipality relocated to —714455

—714 453 City of Shawinigan [*formerly* —714451]

Former name: Le Centre-de-la-Mauricie Regional County Municipality

Including *La Mauricie National Park

*For a specific part of this jurisdiction, region, or feature, see the part and follow instructions under —4–9

—714 455 Les Chenaux Regional County Municipality [*formerly* —714451]

Class here former *Champlain County

Cap-de-la-Madeleine relocated to —714451

—714 457 Mékinac Regional County Municipality

—714 459 Le Haut-Saint-Maurice Regional County Municipality

—714 46 Portneuf Regional County Municipality

Including Portneuf Wildlife Reserve

—714 47 *Québec Metropolitan Community

Class here *Capitale-Nationale region

—714 471 City of Québec

Former name: Quebec Urban Community

Class here Québec

—714 474 La Jacques-Cartier Regional County Municipality

Class here *Jacques-Cartier River

—714 476 L'Île-d'Orléans Regional County Municipality [*formerly* —71448]

Class here Isle of Orléans

—714 48 La Côte-de-Beaupré Regional County Municipality

Class here *Laurentides Wildlife Reserve (Laurentides Provincial Park)

L'Île-d'Orléans Regional County Municipality relocated to —714476

—714 49 Charlevoix regional county municipalities

—714 492 Charlevoix Regional County Municipality

Including Île aux Coudres

—714 494 Charlevoix-Est Regional County Municipality

—714 5 South central region of Quebec

Area south of Saint Lawrence River, and east of Richelieu River valley

Class here *Centre-du-Québec region

Saint-François River relocated to —7146

For southern border area, see —7146

—[714 51] Le Bas-Richelieu Regional County Municipality

Relocated to —71439

*For a specific part of this jurisdiction, region, or feature, see the part and follow instructions under —4–9

—714 52 Les Maskoutains and Acton regional county municipalities

—714 523 Les Maskoutains Regional County Municipality

—714 525 Acton Regional County Municipality

—714 53 Rouville Regional County Municipality

—714 54 Nicolet-Yamaska Regional County Municipality

—714 55 Bécancour Regional County Municipality

—714 56 Drummond and Arthabaska regional county municipalities

—714 563 Drummond Regional County Municipality

—714 565 Arthabaska Regional County Municipality

Class here *Bois-Francs region

—714 57 Asbestos and L'Érable regional county municipalities

—714 573 Asbestos Regional County Municipality

Former name: L'Or-Blanc Regional County Municipality

L'Amiante Regional County Municipality relocated to —714712

—714 575 L'Érable Regional County Municipality

—714 58 Lotbinière Regional County Municipality

—714 59 City of Lévis

Including former Les Chutes-de-la-Chaudière, former Desjardins Regional County Municipalities

—714 6 Southern region of Quebec

Southern border area east of Richelieu River valley

Class here *Saint-François River [*formerly* —7145]; *Eastern Townships (Cantons-de-l'Est), *Estrie Administrative Region

—[714 61] Former Iberville County

Relocated to —71438

—714 62 Brome-Missisquoi Regional County Municipality

—714 63 La Haute-Yamaska Regional County Municipality

—714 64 Memphrémagog Regional County Municipality

Class here *Lake Memphrémagog

—714 65 Le Val-Saint-François Regional County Municipality

*For a specific part of this jurisdiction, region, or feature, see the part and follow instructions under —4–9

—714 66 City of Sherbrooke

Former names: La Région-Sherbrookoise Regional County Municipality, Sherbrooke Regional County Municipality

—714 67 Coaticook Regional County Municipality

—714 68 Le Haut-Saint-François Regional County Municipality

—714 69 Le Granit Regional County Municipality

—714 7 Eastern region of Quebec

Area south of Saint Lawrence River from Lévis to Gulf of Saint Lawrence

Class here *Notre-Dame Mountains

—714 71 L'Amiante, Beauce-Sartigan, Robert-Cliche, La Nouvelle-Beauce regional county municipalities

Class here *Beauce, *Chaudière-Appalaches regions; *Chaudière River

—714 712 L'Amiante Regional County Municipality [*formerly* —714573]

—714 714 Beauce-Sartigan Regional County Municipality

—714 716 Robert-Cliche Regional County Municipality

—714 718 La Nouvelle-Beauce Regional County Municipality

—714 72 Les Etchemins Regional County Municipality

—714 73 Bellechasse and Montmagny regional county municipalities

—714 733 Bellechasse Regional County Municipality

—714 735 Montmagny Regional County Municipality

Including Île aux Grues, Grosse Île

—714 74 L'Islet Regional County Municipality

—714 75 Kamouraska Regional County Municipality

—714 76 Témiscouata, Rivière-du-Loup, Les Basques regional county municipalities

Class here *Bas-Saint-Laurent region

—714 762 Témiscouata Regional County Municipality

—714 764 Rivière-du-Loup Regional County Municipality

Including Île Verte

—714 766 Les Basques Regional County Municipality

*For a specific part of this jurisdiction, region, or feature, see the part and follow instructions under —4–9

—714 77 Gaspé Peninsula regional county municipalities

Class here Gaspésie region; Gaspésie-Îles-de-la-Madeleine Administrative Region, former Bas-Saint-Laurent-Gaspésie Administrative Region; *Gaspé Peninsula

For Bas-Saint-Laurent region, see —71476; for Avignon and Bonaventure regional county municipalities, see —71478; for Gaspé regional county municipalities and Municipality of Les Îles-de-la-Madeleine, see —71479

—714 771 Rimouski-Neigette Regional County Municipality

La Mitis Regional County Municipality relocated to —714773

—714 773 La Mitis Regional County Municipality [*formerly* —714771]

—714 775 Matane Regional County Municipality

La Matapédia Regional County Municipality relocated to —714778

—714 778 La Matapédia Regional County Municipality [*formerly* —714775]

—714 78 Avignon and Bonaventure regional county municipalities

—714 783 Avignon Regional County Municipality

—714 785 Bonaventure Regional County Municipality

—714 79 Gaspé regional county municipalities and Municipality of Les Îles-de-la-Madeleine

—714 791 La Haute-Gaspésie Regional County Municipality

Former name: Denis-Riverin Regional County Municipality

Class here *Gaspésie National Park

—714 793 La Côte-de-Gaspé Regional County Municipality

Including Forillon National Park

—714 795 Le Rocher-Percé Regional County Municipality

Former name: Pabok Regional County Municipality

—714 797 Municipality of Les Îles-de-la-Madeleine

Former name: Îles-de-la-Madeleine Regional County Municipality

Class here Magdalen Islands

—715 Atlantic Provinces Maritime Provinces

For Nova Scotia, see —716; for Prince Edward Island, see —717; for Newfoundland and Labrador, see —718

See also —16344 for Gulf of Saint Lawrence, Northumberland Strait

*For a specific part of this jurisdiction, region, or feature, see the part and follow instructions under —4–9

—715 1 New Brunswick

For eastern counties, see —7152; for southern counties, see —7153; for central counties, see —7154; for western counties, see —7155

> —715 11–715 12 Northern counties of New Brunswick

Class comprehensive works in —7151

—715 11 Restigouche County

Including *Restigouche River

—715 12 Gloucester County

Including Bathurst

—715 2 Eastern counties of New Brunswick

—715 21 Northumberland County

Class here *Miramichi River

—715 22 Kent County

—715 23 Westmorland County

Including Sackville

—715 235 Moncton

—715 3 Southern counties of New Brunswick

See also —16345 for Bay of Fundy

—715 31 Albert County

—715 32 Saint John County

—715 33 Charlotte County

Including Grand Manan Island; *Saint Croix River in New Brunswick

—715 4 Central counties of New Brunswick

—715 41 Kings County

—715 42 Queens County

—715 43 Sunbury County

—715 5 Western counties of New Brunswick

Class here *Saint John River

—715 51 York County

*For a specific part of this jurisdiction, region, or feature, see the part and follow instructions under —4–9

—715 515 Fredericton

—715 52 Carleton County

—715 53 Victoria County

—715 54 Madawaska County

—716 Nova Scotia

—716 1 Northern counties of Nova Scotia

—716 11 Cumberland County

Including Amherst

—716 12 Colchester County

Including Truro

—716 13 Pictou County

Including New Glasgow, Pictou

—716 14 Antigonish County

—716 2 Southern counties of Nova Scotia

—716 21 Guysborough County

—716 22 Halifax Regional Municipality

Former name: Halifax County

—716 225 Halifax-Dartmouth metropolitan area

Class here Dartmouth, Halifax

716 23 Lunenburg County

—716 24 Region of Queens Municipality

Former name: Queens County

—716 25 Shelburne County

—716 3 Bay of Fundy counties

See also —16345 for Bay of Fundy

—716 31 Yarmouth County

—716 32 Digby County

—716 33 Annapolis County

Including Kejimkujik National Park

For Kejimkujik National Park in Queens County, see —71624

—716 34 Kings County

Including Wolfville

—716 35 Hants County

Including Windsor

—716 9 Cape Breton Island and Sable Island

Class here *Bras d'Or Lake

Subdivisions are added for Cape Breton Island and Sable Island together, for Cape Breton Island alone

---

> —716 91–716 98 Cape Breton Island

Class comprehensive works in —7169

—716 91 Inverness County

Including Cape Breton Highlands National Park

For Cape Breton Highlands National Park in Victoria County, see —71693

—716 93 Victoria County

—716 95 Cape Breton Regional Municipality

Former name: Cape Breton County

—716 955 Louisbourg

Class here Fortress of Louisbourg National Historic Site

—716 98 Richmond County

—716 99 Sable Island

—717 Prince Edward Island

—717 1 Prince County

—717 4 Queens County

For Charlottetown, see —7175

—717 5 Charlottetown

—717 7 Kings County

—718 Newfoundland and Labrador, Saint Pierre and Miquelon

Class here Newfoundland

See also —16344 for Grand Banks of Newfoundland

—718 1 St. John's

—718 2 Labrador

*For a specific part of this jurisdiction, region, or feature, see the part and follow instructions under —4–9

—718 8 Saint Pierre and Miquelon

Overseas territory of France

—719 Northern territories

Class here Canadian Arctic

See also —16327 for Beaufort Sea, Canadian Arctic waters, Northwest Passage

—719 1 Yukon Territory

Including Dawson, Whitehorse

—719 2 *Northwest Territories (1870–1999)

Nunavut relocated to —7195

See also —7193 for Northwest Territories (1999–)

—719 3 Northwest Territories (1999–)

Including Inuvik region [*formerly* —7196], *Fort Smith Region

Including *Thelon Game Sanctuary [*formerly* —7194]; Holman [*formerly* —7197]; Aklavik, Colville Lake, Déline (Fort Franklin), Fort Simpson, Fort Smith, Hay River, Inuvik, Lutselk'e, Paulatuk, Pine Point, Rae Lakes, Reliance, Sachs Harbour, Tuktoyaktuk, Tulita (Fort Norman), Wrigley, Yellowknife; Nahanni, Tuktut Nogait National Parks; Cape Baring, Cape Wollaston; Banks, *Borden, *Mackenzie King Islands; Mackenzie Mountains; Slave River; Great Bear, Great Slave Lakes

Class here former *Mackenzie District; Mackenzie River

See also —7192 for Northwest Territories (1870–1999)

—[719 4] Keewatin Region (Kivallik Region)

Thelon Game Sanctuary relocated to —7193; Keewatin Region (Kivallik Region) relocated to —71958

—719 5 Nunavut [*formerly* —7192]

*For a specific part of this jurisdiction, region, or feature, see the part and follow instructions under —4–9

—719 52 Baffin Region (Qikiqtaaluk Region)

Baffin, Bylot, Mansel, Nottingham, Salisbury, Somerset, Wales Islands; Ellesmere Island and all other islands east of 106° W and north of M'Clure Strait and Viscount Melville and Lancaster Sounds; all islands in Hudson, James, and Ungava Bays and Hudson Strait; Melville Peninsula

Including Arctic Bay (Tununirusiq), Cape Dorset (Kinngait), Grise Fiord (Ausuittuq), Hall Beach (Sanirajak), Igloolik (Iglulik), Iqaluit, Pangnirtung (Pannirtuuq), Pond Inlet (Mittimatalik), Resolute (Qausuittuq), Sanikiluaq; Auyuittuq National Park

Class here former Franklin District; *Canadian Arctic Archipelago

See also —16327 for Hudson, James, Ungava Bays

—719 55 Kitikmeot Region [*formerly* —7197]

Mainland within Nunavut north of 66° N and west of 87° W; King William, Prince of Wales, *Victoria Islands

Including Bathurst Inlet (Kingaok), Cambridge Bay (Ikaluktutiak), Coppermine (Kugluktuk), Gjoa Haven (Oqsuqtooq), Pelly Bay (Aqvilgjuaq), Spence Bay (Talurqjuak), Umingmaktok; Boothia, Simpson Peninsulas; *Contwoyto Lake

—719 58 Keewatin Region (Kivallik Region) [*formerly* —7194]

Mainland within Nunavut between 60° N and 66° N, and east of 106° W; land surrounding Repulse Bay; Coats, Southampton Islands

Including Baker Lake (Qamani'tuaq), Chesterfield Inlet (Igluligaarjuk), Coral Harbour (Salliq), Rankin Inlet (Kangiqsliniq), Repulse Bay (Naujaat); *Dubawnt Lake; *Thelon River

Class here former Keewatin District

—[719 6] Inuvik Region

Relocated to —7193

—[719 7] Kitikmeot Region

Kitikmeot Region relocated to —71955; Holman relocated to —7193

—72 Middle America Mexico

*For a specific part of this jurisdiction, region, or feature, see the part and follow instructions under —4–9

SUMMARY

> —721–727 Mexico

Class comprehensive works in —72

—721 Northern states of Mexico

Class here *Mexican-American Border Region

For Lower California peninsula, see —722

—721 2 Tamaulipas

—721 3 Nuevo León

—721 4 Coahuila

—721 5 Durango

—721 6 Chihuahua

—721 7 Sonora

Class here *Sonoran Desert

See also —1641 for Gulf of California

—722 Lower California peninsula

See also —1641 for Gulf of California

—722 3 Baja California Norte

—722 4 Baja California Sur

—723 Central Pacific states of Mexico

—723 2 Sinaloa

—723 4 Nayarit

—723 5 Jalisco

—723 6 Colima

—723 7 Michoacán

*For a specific part of this jurisdiction, region, or feature, see the part and follow instructions under —4–9

—724	Central states of Mexico
	For Valley of Mexico, see —725
—724 1	Guanajuato
—724 2	Aguascalientes
—724 3	Zacatecas
—724 4	San Luis Potosí
—724 5	Querétaro
—724 6	Hidalgo
—724 7	Tlaxcala
—724 8	Puebla
—724 9	Morelos
—725	*Valley of Mexico
—725 2	Mexico state
—725 3	Distrito Federal
	Class here Mexico City
—726	Southern Gulf states of Mexico
—726 2	Veracruz
—726 3	Tabasco
—726 4	Campeche
—726 5	Yucatán
—726 7	Quintana Roo
—727	Southern Pacific states of Mexico
—727 3	Guerrero
—727 4	Oaxaca
—727 5	Chiapas
—728	Central America

*For a specific part of this jurisdiction, region, or feature, see the part and follow instructions under —4–9

SUMMARY

—728 1 Guatemala

—728 11 Guatemala department

Class here Guatemala City

—728 12 Petén department

—728 13 Izabal and Zacapa departments

—728 131 Izabal department

—728 132 Zacapa department

—728 14 Southeastern departments of Guatemala

—728 141 Chiquimula department

—728 142 Jalapa department

—728 143 Jutiapa department

—728 144 Santa Rosa department

—728 15 North central departments of Guatemala

—728 151 Alta Verapaz department

—728 152 Baja Verapaz department

—728 153 El Progreso department

—728 16 South central departments of Guatemala

—728 161 Chimaltenango department

—728 162 Sacatepéquez department

—728 163 Escuintla department

—728 164 Sololá department

—728 165 Suchitepéquez department

—728 17 Huehuetenango and Quiché departments

—728 171 Huehuetenango department

—728 172 Quiché department

—728 18 Southwestern departments of Guatemala

—728 181 Totonicapán department

—728 182 Quezaltenango department

—728 183 Retalhuleu department

—728 184 San Marcos department

—728 2 Belize

—728 21 Corozal District

—728 22 Belize District

—728 23 Stann Creek District

—728 24 Toledo District

—728 25 Cayo District

—728 26 Orange Walk District

—728 3 Honduras

—728 31 Northern departments of Honduras

—728 311 Cortés

—728 312 Atlántida

—728 313 Colón

—728 314 Yoro

—728 315 Islas de la Bahía

—728 32 Gracias a Dios department

—728 33 Olancho department

—728 34 El Paraíso department

—728 35 Southern departments of Honduras

—728 351 Choluteca

—728 352 Valle

—728 36 La Paz department

—728 37 Central departments of Honduras

—728 371 Francisco Morazán

Class here Tegucigalpa

—728 372 Comayagua

—728 38 Western departments of Honduras

—728 381 Intibucá

—728 382 Lempira

—728 383 Ocotepeque

—728 384 Copán

—728 385 Santa Bárbara

—728 4 El Salvador

—728 41 Western departments of El Salvador

—728 411 Ahuachapán

—728 412 Santa Ana

—728 413 Sonsonate

—728 42 Central departments of El Salvador

—728 421 Chalatenango

—728 422 La Libertad

—728 423 San Salvador

Class here San Salvador

—728 424 Cuscatlán

—728 425 La Paz

—728 426 Cabañas

—728 427 San Vicente

—728 43 Eastern departments of El Salvador

—728 431 Usulután

—728 432 San Miguel

—728 433 Morazán

—728 434 La Unión

—728 5 Nicaragua

—728 51 Pacific departments of Nicaragua

—728 511 Chinandega

—728 512 León

—728 513 Managua

Class here Managua

—728 514 Masaya

—728 515 Granada

—728 516 Carazo

—728 517 Rivas

Class here *Lake Nicaragua

*For a specific part of this jurisdiction, region, or feature, see the part and follow instructions under —4–9

—728 52 Central departments of Nicaragua

—728 521 Nueva Segovia

—728 522 Jinotega

—728 523 Madriz

—728 524 Estelí

—728 525 Matagalpa

—728 526 Boaco

—728 527 Chontales

—728 53 Atlantic region of Nicaragua

—728 531 Río San Juan department

—728 532 Región Autónoma del Atlántico Sur

Class here former Zelaya department

Región Autónoma del Atlántico Norte, part of former Zelaya department relocated to —728537

—728 537 Región Autónoma del Atlántico Norte [*formerly* —728532]

—728 6 Costa Rica

—728 61 Limón province

—728 62 Cartago province

—728 63 San José province

Class here San José

—728 64 Heredia province

—728 65 Alajuela province

—728 66 Guanacaste province

—728 67 Puntarenas province

—728 7 Panama

See also —1641 for Gulf of Panama

—728 71 Western Panama

—728 711 Chiriquí province

Southwestern part of Ngöbe Buglé comarca, formerly part of Chiriquí province, relocated to —728717

—728 712 Bocas del Toro province

Northern part of Ngöbe Buglé comarca, formerly part of Bocas del Toro province, relocated to —728717

—728 717 Ngöbe Buglé comarca

Including southwestern part of Ngöbe Buglé comarca [*formerly* —728711]; northern part of Ngöbe Buglé comarca [*formerly* —728712]; southeastern part of Ngöbe Buglé comarca [*formerly* —728722]

—728 72 Central Panama

For Panama and Colón provinces, see —72873

—728 721 Coclé province

—728 722 Veraguas province

Southeastern part of Ngöbe Buglé comarca, formerly part of Veraguas province, relocated to —728717

—728 723 Los Santos province

—728 724 Herrera province

—728 73 Panamá and Colón provinces

Kuna Yala comarca, formerly part of Panamá and Colón provinces, relocated to —728772

For Canal Area, see —72875

—728 731 Panamá province

Class here Panama City

Kuna de Madungandí comarca, formerly part of Panamá province, relocated to —728773

—728 732 Colón province

—[728 74] Darién province

Kuna de Wargandi comarca, formerly part of Darién province, relocated to —728774; Emberá comarca, formerly part of Darién province, relocated to —728776; Darién province relocated to —728778

—728 75 Canal Area

Class here Panama Canal

—728 77 Eastern Panama

—728 772 Kuna Yala comarca [*formerly* —72873]

Former name: San Blas comarca

—728 773 Kuna de Madungandí comarca [*formerly* —728731]

—728 774 Kuna de Wargandi comarca [*formerly* —72874]

—728 776 Emberá comarca [*formerly* —72874]

—728 778 Darién province [*formerly* —72874]

—729 West Indies (Antilles) and Bermuda

Class here *Caribbean Area

Subdivisions are added for West Indies (Antilles) and Bermuda together, for West Indies (Antilles) alone

See also —16365 for Caribbean Sea

SUMMARY

—729 1	**Cuba**
—729 2	**Jamaica and Cayman Islands**
—729 3	**Dominican Republic**
—729 4	**Haiti**
—729 5	**Puerto Rico**
—729 6	**Bahama Islands**
—729 7	**Leeward Islands**
—729 8	**Windward and other southern islands**
—729 9	**Bermuda**

> —729 1–729 5 Greater Antilles

Class comprehensive works in —729

—729 1 Cuba

—729 11 Pinar del Río province

—729 12 Ciudad da La Habana province (Havana), Havana province, Isla de la Juventud

—729 123 Ciudad da La Habana province (Havana)

—729 124 Havana province

—729 125 Isla de la Juventud

—729 13 Matanzas province

—729 14 Villa Clara, Cienfuegos, Sancti Spíritus provinces

—729 142 Villa Clara province

—729 143 Cienfuegos province

—729 145 Sancti Spíritus province

—729 15 Ciego de Avila and Camagüey provinces

—729 153 Ciego de Avila province

—729 156 Camagüey province

—729 16 Eastern Cuba

—729 162 Las Tunas province

*For a specific part of this jurisdiction, region, or feature, see the part and follow instructions under —4–9

—729 163 Granma province

—729 164 Holguín province

—729 165 Santiago de Cuba province

—729 167 Guantánamo province

—729 2 Jamaica and Cayman Islands

—729 21 Cayman Islands

—729 3 Dominican Republic

Class here comprehensive works on Hispaniola

For Haiti, see —7294

—729 32 Southwestern provinces of Dominican Republic

—729 323 Pedernales

—729 324 Barahona

—729 325 Independencia

—729 326 Baoruco (Bahoruco)

—729 34 Western provinces of Dominican Republic

—729 342 San Juan

—729 343 Elísa Piña

Former name: La Estrelleta

—729 345 Dajabón

—729 35 Northwestern provinces of Dominican Republic

—729 352 Monte Cristi

—729 353 Santiago Rodríguez

—729 356 Santiago

—729 357 Valverde

—729 358 Puerto Plata

—729 36 North central provinces of Dominican Republic

—729 362 Espaillat

—729 363 Salcedo

—729 364 María Trinidad Sánchez

—729 365 Samaná

—729 367 Duarte

—729 368 Sánchez Ramírez

—729 369 Monseñor Nouel and La Vega provinces

—729 369 3 Monseñor Nouel

—729 369 7 La Vega

—729 37 South central provinces of Dominican Republic

—729 372 Azua

—729 373 Peravia

—729 374 San Cristóbal

—729 375 Distrito Nacional

Class here Santo Domingo

—729 377 Monte Plata

—729 38 Eastern provinces of Dominican Republic

—729 381 Hato Mayor

—729 382 San Pedro de Macorís

—729 383 La Romana

—729 384 El Seibo

—729 385 La Altagracia

—729 4 Haiti

—729 42 Nord-Ouest département

Including Ile de la Tortue

—729 43 Nord and Nord-Est départements

—729 432 Nord département

—729 436 Nord-Est département

—729 44 Centre and Artibonite départements

—729 442 Centre département

—729 446 Artibonite département

—729 45 Ouest and Sud-Est départements

—729 452 Ouest département

Class here Port-au-Prince

—729 456 Sud-Est département

—729 46 Sud and Grand'Anse départements

—729 462 Sud département

—729 466 Grand'Anse département

—729 5 Puerto Rico

—729 51 San Juan district

Class here San Juan

—729 52 Bayamón district

—729 53 Arecibo district

—729 54 Aguadilla district

—729 56 Mayagüez district

—729 57 Ponce district

—729 58 Guayama district

—729 59 Humacao district

Including Vieques Island

—729 6 Bahama Islands

—729 61 Turks and Caicos Islands

> —729 7–729 8 Lesser Antilles (Caribbees)

Class comprehensive works in —729

—729 7 Leeward Islands

For Dominica, see —729841

—729 72 Virgin Islands

—729 722 Virgin Islands of the United States

Including Saint Croix, Saint John, Saint Thomas islands; Virgin Islands National Park

—729 725 British Virgin Islands

Including Tortola, Virgin Gorda islands

—729 73 Anguilla and Saint Kitts-Nevis

Class here West Indies Associated States

For Antigua, see —72974; for Windward Islands, see —72984

—729 74 Antigua and Barbuda

—729 75 Montserrat

—729 76 Guadeloupe

Overseas department of France

Including islands of Désirade, Guadeloupe, Les Saintes, Marie Galante, Saint Barthélemy, part of Saint Martin

Class here French West Indies, comprehensive works on Saint Martin

For Netherlands part of Saint Martin, see —72977; for Martinique, see —72982

—729 77 Leeward Netherlands islands

Including Saba, Saint Eustatius, part of Saint Martin

Class comprehensive works on Netherlands Antilles in —72986

—729 8 Windward and other southern islands

For Nueva Esparta, Venezuela, see —8754

—729 81 Barbados

—729 82 Martinique

Overseas department of France

—729 83 Trinidad and Tobago

—729 84 Windward Islands

—729 841 Dominica

—729 843 Saint Lucia

—729 844 Saint Vincent and the Grenadines

For Carriacou, see —729845

—729 845 Grenada and Carriacou

—729 86 Netherlands islands

Including Aruba, Bonaire, Curaçao

Class here Netherlands Antilles

For Leeward Netherlands islands, see —72977

—729 9 Bermuda

—73 United States

For specific states, see —74–79

See Manual at T2—73 vs. T2—71

—(734–739) Specific states

(Optional numbers; prefer —74–79)

Add to base number —73 the numbers following —7 in notation 74–79 of this table, e.g., Pennsylvania —7348

> **—74–79 Specific states of United States**

Class comprehensive works in —73

For Hawaii, see —969

(Option: Class in —734–739)

—74 Northeastern United States (New England and Middle Atlantic states)

Class here United States east of Allegheny Mountains, east of Mississippi River; *Appalachian Mountains; *Connecticut River

For southeastern United States, see —75; for south central United States, see —76; for north central United States, see —77

SUMMARY

—741	**Maine**
—742	**New Hampshire**
—743	**Vermont**
—744	**Massachusetts**
—745	**Rhode Island**
—746	**Connecticut**
—747	**New York**
—748	**Pennsylvania**
—749	**New Jersey**

> —741–746 New England

Class comprehensive works in —74

—741 Maine

—741 1 Aroostook County

—741 2 Northwestern counties of Maine

Including Moosehead Lake

—741 22 Somerset County

Class here *Kennebec River

—741 25 Piscataquis County

—741 3 Penobscot County

Including Bangor

Class here *Penobscot River

—741 4 Southeastern counties of Maine

*For a specific part of this jurisdiction, region, or feature, see the part and follow instructions under —4–9

—741 42 Washington County

Class here *Saint Croix River

—741 45 Hancock County

Including Mount Desert Island

Class here Acadia National Park

For Acadia National Park in Knox County, see —74153

—741 5 South central counties of Maine

—741 52 Waldo County

—741 53 Knox County

—741 57 Lincoln County

—741 6 Kennebec County

Including Augusta

—741 7 West central counties of Maine

Class here *Rangeley Lakes

—741 72 Franklin County

—741 75 Oxford County

—741 8 Southwest central counties of Maine

Class here *Androscoggin River

—741 82 Androscoggin County

—741 85 Sagadahoc County

—741 9 Southwestern counties of Maine

—741 91 Cumberland County

Class here Portland

—741 95 York County

—742 New Hampshire

—742 1 Coos County

—742 2 *White Mountains

—742 3 Grafton County

—742 4 Counties bordering *Lake Winnipesaukee

—742 42 Carroll County

—742 45 Belknap County

*For a specific part of this jurisdiction, region, or feature, see the part and follow instructions under —4–9

—742 5 Strafford County

—742 6 Rockingham County

Including Portsmouth

—742 7 West central counties of New Hampshire

—742 72 Merrimack County

Including Concord

Class here *Merrimack River

—742 75 Sullivan County

—742 8 Hillsborough County

Including Manchester

—742 9 Cheshire County

—743 Vermont

Class here *Green Mountains

—743 1 Northwestern counties of Vermont

Class here *Lake Champlain in Vermont

—743 12 Grand Isle County

—743 13 Franklin County

—743 17 Chittenden County

Including Burlington

Class here *Winooski River

—743 2 Northeastern counties of Vermont

—743 23 Orleans County

—743 25 Essex County

—743 3 North central counties of Vermont

—743 34 Caledonia County

—743 35 Lamoille County

—743 4 Washington County

Including Montpelier

—743 5 Addison County

—743 6 East central counties of Vermont

—743 63 Orange County

*For a specific part of this jurisdiction, region, or feature, see the part and follow instructions under —4–9

—743 65 Windsor County

—743 7 Rutland County

—743 8 Bennington County

—743 9 Windham County

—744 Massachusetts

—744 1 Berkshire County

Class here *Berkshire Hills

—744 2 Connecticut River counties

—744 22 Franklin County

—744 23 Hampshire County

—744 26 Hampden County

Including Springfield

—744 3 Worcester County

—744 4 Middlesex County

Including Cambridge, Lexington, Lowell; *Charles River

—744 5 Essex County

—744 6 Suffolk County

—744 61 Boston

—744 7 Norfolk County

—744 8 Southeastern counties of Massachusetts

For counties bordering Nantucket Sound, see —7449

See also —16345 for Cape Cod Bay

—744 82 Plymouth County

—744 85 Bristol County

—744 9 Counties bordering Nantucket Sound

See also —16346 for Nantucket Sound

—744 92 Barnstable County (Cape Cod)

See also —16345 for Cape Cod Bay

—744 94 Dukes County

Including Elizabeth Islands, Martha's Vineyard

*For a specific part of this jurisdiction, region, or feature, see the part and follow instructions under —4–9

—744 97 Nantucket County

Class here Nantucket Island

—745 Rhode Island

See also —16346 for Rhode Island Sound, Narragansett Bay

—745 1 Providence County

For Providence, see —7452

—745 2 Providence

—745 4 Kent County

—745 5 Bristol County

—745 6 Newport County

For Newport, see —7457

—745 7 Newport

—745 8 Block Island

—745 9 Washington County

For Block Island, see —7458

—746 Connecticut

See also —16346 for Long Island Sound

—746 1 Litchfield County

—746 2 Hartford County

For Hartford, see —7463

—746 3 Hartford

—746 4 Northeastern counties of Connecticut

—746 43 Tolland County

—746 45 Windham County

—746 5 New London County

—746 6 Middlesex County

—746 7 New Haven County

For New Haven, see —7468

—746 8 New Haven

—746 9 Fairfield County

Including Stamford

> —747–749 Middle Atlantic states

Class comprehensive works in —74

—747 New York

—747 1 New York Borough of Manhattan (Manhattan Island, New York County)

For borough of Brooklyn, see —74723; for borough of Queens, see —747243; for borough of Richmond, see —74726; for borough of the Bronx, see —747275

See also —16346 for New York Bay

—747 2 Other parts of New York metropolitan area

For Fairfield County, Connecticut, see —7469; for New Jersey counties of metropolitan area, see —7493

—747 21 Long Island

For specific parts of Long Island, see —74723–74725

See also —16346 for Long Island Sound

> —747 23–747 25 Specific parts of Long Island

Class comprehensive works in —74721

—747 23 Borough of Brooklyn (Kings County)

—747 24 Queens and Nassau Counties

—747 243 Borough of Queens (Queens County)

—747 245 Nassau County

—747 25 Suffolk County

—747 26 Staten Island (Borough of Richmond, Richmond County)

—747 27 Borough of the Bronx and Westchester County

—747 275 Borough of the Bronx (Bronx County)

—747 277 Westchester County

—747 28 Rockland County

—747 3 Other southeastern counties of New York

Class here *Hudson River

—747 31 Orange County

—747 32 Putnam County

*For a specific part of this jurisdiction, region, or feature, see the part and follow instructions under —4–9

—747 33 Dutchess County

—747 34 Ulster County

—747 35 Sullivan County

—747 36 Delaware County

—747 37 Greene County

—747 38 *Catskill Mountains

—747 39 Columbia County

—747 4 Middle eastern counties of New York

—747 41 Rensselaer County

—747 42 Albany County

For Albany, see —74743

—747 43 Albany

—747 44 Schenectady County

—747 45 Schoharie County

—747 46 Montgomery County

—747 47 Fulton County

—747 48 Saratoga County

—747 49 Washington County

—747 5 Northern counties of New York

Class here *Adirondack Mountains

—747 51 Warren County

Including *Lake George

—747 52 Hamilton County

—747 53 Essex County

—747 54 Clinton County

Class here *Lake Champlain

—747 55 Franklin County

—747 56 Saint Lawrence County

Including *Saint Lawrence River in New York

—747 57 Jefferson County

—747 58 *Thousand Islands

*For a specific part of this jurisdiction, region, or feature, see the part and follow instructions under —4–9

—747 59 Lewis County

—747 6 North central counties of New York

Class here *Mohawk River

—747 61 Herkimer County

—747 62 Oneida County

Including *Oneida Lake

—747 64 Madison County

—747 65 Onondaga County

For Syracuse, see —74766

—747 66 Syracuse

—747 67 Oswego County

—747 68 Cayuga County

Including *Cayuga Lake

—747 69 Seneca County

—747 7 South central counties of New York

—747 71 Tompkins County

Class here Ithaca

—747 72 Cortland County

—747 73 Chenango County

—747 74 Otsego County

—747 75 Broome County

—747 77 Tioga County

—747 78 Chemung County

—747 8 West central counties of New York

Class here *Finger Lakes

—747 81 Schuyler County

—747 82 Yates County

Class here *Keuka Lake

—747 83 Steuben County

—747 84 Allegany County

—747 85 Livingston County

*For a specific part of this jurisdiction, region, or feature, see the part and follow instructions under —4–9

—747 86 Ontario County

—747 87 Wayne County

—747 88 Monroe County

Class here *Genesee River

For Rochester, see —74789

—747 89 Rochester

—747 9 Western counties of New York

Class here *Lake Ontario

—747 91 Orleans County

—747 92 Genesee County

—747 93 Wyoming County

—747 94 Cattaraugus County

—747 95 Chautauqua County

—747 96 Erie County

For Buffalo, see —74797

—747 97 Buffalo

—747 98 Niagara County

Including Niagara Falls (city)

Class Niagara Falls (physiographic feature) in —74799

—747 99 Niagara Falls in New York

Physiographic feature

—748 Pennsylvania

Class here *Susquehanna River

—748 1 Southeastern counties of Pennsylvania

Class here *Schuylkill River

—748 11 Philadelphia County (Philadelphia)

—748 12 Montgomery County

—748 13 Chester County

—748 14 Delaware County

—748 15 Lancaster County

—748 16 Berks County

*For a specific part of this jurisdiction, region, or feature, see the part and follow instructions under —4–9

—748 17 Schuylkill County

—748 18 Dauphin County

Including Harrisburg

—748 19 Lebanon County

—748 2 Eastern counties of Pennsylvania

Class here *Pocono Mountains

—748 21 Bucks County

—748 22 Northampton County

—748 23 Wayne County

Including *Lake Wallenpaupack

—748 24 Pike County

—748 25 Monroe County

Including *Delaware Water Gap

—748 26 Carbon County

—748 27 Lehigh County

—748 3 Northeastern counties of Pennsylvania

—748 31 Northumberland County

—748 32 Luzerne County

—748 34 Susquehanna County

—748 35 Wyoming County

—748 36 Lackawanna County

For Scranton, see —74837

—748 37 Scranton

—748 38 Columbia County

—748 39 Montour County

—748 4 Southeast central counties of Pennsylvania

—748 41 York County

—748 42 Adams County

—748 43 Cumberland County

—748 44 Franklin County

*For a specific part of this jurisdiction, region, or feature, see the part and follow instructions under —4–9

—748 45 Perry County

Class here *Juniata River

—748 46 Mifflin County

—748 47 Juniata County

—748 48 Union County

—748 49 Snyder County

—748 5 Northeast central counties of Pennsylvania

Class here *West Branch of Susquehanna River

—748 51 Lycoming County

—748 53 Centre County

—748 54 Clinton County

—748 55 Potter County

—748 56 Tioga County

—748 57 Bradford County

—748 59 Sullivan County

—748 6 Northwest central counties of Pennsylvania

Class here *Allegheny River

—748 61 Clearfield County

—748 62 Jefferson County

—748 63 McKean County

—748 65 Elk County

—748 66 Cameron County

—748 67 Warren County

—748 68 Forest County

—748 69 Clarion County

—748 7 Southwest central counties of Pennsylvania

Class here *Allegheny Mountains

—748 71 Bedford County

—748 72 Fulton County

—748 73 Huntingdon County

—748 75 Blair County

*For a specific part of this jurisdiction, region, or feature, see the part and follow instructions under —4–9

—748 77 Cambria County

—748 79 Somerset County

—748 8 Southwestern counties of Pennsylvania

Class here *Monongahela River

—748 81 Westmoreland County

—748 82 Washington County

—748 83 Greene County

—748 84 Fayette County

—748 85 Allegheny County

For Pittsburgh, see —74886

—748 86 Pittsburgh

—748 88 Armstrong County

—748 89 Indiana County

—748 9 Northwestern counties of Pennsylvania

—748 91 Butler County

—748 92 Beaver County

—748 93 Lawrence County

—748 95 Mercer County

—748 96 Venango County

—748 97 Crawford County

—748 99 Erie County

—749 New Jersey

Class here *Delaware River

—749 2 Northeastern counties of New Jersey

—749 21 Bergen County

Class here *Hackensack River

—749 23 Passaic County

—749 26 Hudson County

For Jersey City, see —74927

—749 27 Jersey City

*For a specific part of this jurisdiction, region, or feature, see the part and follow instructions under —4–9

—749 3 *Counties of New Jersey in New York metropolitan area

Class here *Passaic River

—749 31 Essex County

For Newark, see —74932; for The Oranges, see —74933

—749 32 Newark

—749 33 The Oranges

Including East Orange, Maplewood, Orange, South Orange, West Orange

—749 36 Union County

—749 4 East central counties of New Jersey

See also —16346 for New York Bay

—749 41 Middlesex County

For New Brunswick, see —74942

—749 42 New Brunswick

—749 44 Somerset County

Class here *Raritan River

—749 46 Monmouth County

—749 48 Ocean County

—749 6 West central counties of New Jersey

—749 61 Burlington County

Including *Mullica River

Class here *Pine Barrens

—749 65 Mercer County

For Trenton, see —74966

—749 66 Trenton

—749 7 Northwestern counties of New Jersey

—749 71 Hunterdon County

—749 74 Morris County

—749 76 Sussex County

—749 78 Warren County

—749 8 South central counties of New Jersey

*For a specific part of this jurisdiction, region, or feature, see the part and follow instructions under —4–9

—749 81 Gloucester County

—749 84 Atlantic County

For Atlantic City, see —74985

—749 85 Atlantic City

—749 87 Camden County

—749 9 Southern counties of New Jersey

See also —16346 for Delaware Bay

—749 91 Salem County

—749 94 Cumberland County

—749 98 Cape May County

—75 Southeastern United States (South Atlantic states)

Class here southern states, *Piedmont, *Atlantic Coastal Plain

For south central United States, see —76

SUMMARY

— 751	**Delaware**
— 752	**Maryland**
— 753	**District of Columbia (Washington)**
— 754	**West Virginia**
— 755	**Virginia**
— 756	**North Carolina**
— 757	**South Carolina**
— 758	**Georgia**
— 759	**Florida**

—751 Delaware

See also —16346 for Delaware Bay

—751 1 New Castle County

For Wilmington, see —7512

—751 2 Wilmington

—751 4 Kent County

Including Dover

—751 7 Sussex County

—752 Maryland

Class here *Potomac River

See also —16347 for Chesapeake Bay

*For a specific part of this jurisdiction, region, or feature, see the part and follow instructions under —4–9

—752 1 Eastern Shore

Class here *Delmarva Peninsula

For southern counties of Eastern Shore, see —7522; for northern counties of Eastern Shore, see —7523

—752 2 Southern counties of Eastern Shore

—752 21 Worcester County

Including *Assateague Island

—752 23 Somerset County

—752 25 Wicomico County

—752 27 Dorchester County

—752 3 Northern counties of Eastern Shore

—752 31 Caroline County

Class here *Choptank River

—752 32 Talbot County

—752 34 Queen Annes County

Class here *Chester River

—752 36 Kent County

—752 38 Cecil County

> —752 4–752 9 Maryland west of Chesapeake Bay

Class comprehensive works in —752

—752 4 Southern counties of Maryland

Class here *Patuxent River

—752 41 Saint Marys County

—752 44 Calvert County

—752 47 Charles County

—752 5 South central counties of Maryland

—752 51 Prince George's County

—752 55 Anne Arundel County

For Annapolis, see —75256

—752 56 Annapolis

—752 6 Independent city of Baltimore

*For a specific part of this jurisdiction, region, or feature, see the part and follow instructions under —4–9

—752 7 North central counties of Maryland

Class here *Piedmont in Maryland

—752 71 Baltimore County

—752 74 Harford County

Including *Susquehanna River in Maryland

—752 77 Carroll County

—752 8 West central counties of Maryland

—752 81 Howard County

—752 84 Montgomery County

—752 87 Frederick County

—752 9 Western counties of Maryland

—752 91 Washington County

—752 94 Allegany County

—752 97 Garrett County

—753 District of Columbia (Washington)

—754 West Virginia

—754 1 Northern Panhandle counties

Class here *Ohio River in West Virginia

—754 12 Hancock County

—754 13 Brooke County

—754 14 Ohio County

Class here Wheeling

—754 16 Marshall County

—754 18 Wetzel County

—754 19 Tyler County

—754 2 Little Kanawha Valley counties

Class here *Little Kanawha River

—754 21 Pleasants County

—754 22 Wood County

—754 24 Ritchie County

—754 26 Wirt County

*For a specific part of this jurisdiction, region, or feature, see the part and follow instructions under —4–9

—754 27 Gilmer County

—754 29 Calhoun County

—754 3 Kanawha Valley counties

Class here *Kanawha River

—754 31 Jackson County

—754 33 Mason County

—754 35 Putnam County

—754 36 Roane County

—754 37 Kanawha County

Including Charleston

—754 39 Boone County

—754 4 Southwestern border counties of West Virginia

Including *Tug Fork

Class here *Guyandotte River

—754 42 Cabell County

—754 43 Lincoln County

—754 44 Logan County

—754 45 Wyoming County

—754 47 Wayne County

Including *Big Sandy River

—754 48 Mingo County

—754 49 McDowell County

—754 5 Monongahela Valley counties

Class here *Monongahela River in West Virginia

—754 52 Monongalia County

—754 54 Marion County

—754 55 Taylor County

—754 56 Doddridge County

—754 57 Harrison County

—754 59 Barbour County

—754 6 Central counties of West Virginia

*For a specific part of this jurisdiction, region, or feature, see the part and follow instructions under —4–9

—754 61 Lewis County

—754 62 Upshur County

—754 65 Webster County

—754 66 Braxton County

—754 67 Clay County

—754 69 Nicholas County

Class here *Gauley River

—754 7 New River Valley counties

Class here *New River

—754 71 Fayette County

—754 73 Raleigh County

—754 74 Mercer County

—754 76 Summers County

—754 78 Monroe County

—754 8 Allegheny Crest counties

Class here *Allegheny Mountains in West Virginia; *Cheat River

—754 82 Preston County

—754 83 Tucker County

—754 85 Randolph County

—754 87 Pocahontas County

—754 88 Greenbrier County

Class here *Greenbrier River

—754 9 Eastern Panhandle counties

Class here *Potomac Valley of West Virginia

—754 91 Pendleton County

—754 92 Grant County

—754 93 Hardy County

—754 94 Mineral County

—754 95 Hampshire County

—754 96 Morgan County

—754 97 Berkeley County

*For a specific part of this jurisdiction, region, or feature, see the part and follow instructions under —4–9

—754 99 Jefferson County

—755 Virginia

Class here *Blue Ridge

—755 1 Northampton and Accomack counties and Chesapeake Bay Region

Class here *Tidewater Virginia

—755 15 Northampton County

—755 16 Accomack County

—755 18 *Chesapeake Bay Region

See also —16347 for Chesapeake Bay

—755 2 Potomac-Rappahannock region

Including Northern Neck

Class here *Rappahannock River

—755 21 Northumberland County

—755 22 Lancaster County

—755 23 Richmond County

—755 24 Westmoreland County

—755 25 King George County

—755 26 Stafford County

—755 27 Prince William and Fauquier Counties, Manassas, Manassas Park

—755 273 Prince William County, Manassas, Manassas Park

—755 273 2 Prince William County

—755 273 4 Independent city of Manassas

—755 273 6 Independent city of Manassas Park

—755 275 Fauquier County

—755 28 Loudoun County

—755 29 Washington metropolitan area of Virginia

—755 291 Fairfax County

—755 292 Independent city of Fairfax

—755 293 Independent city of Falls Church

—755 295 Arlington County

—755 296 Independent city of Alexandria

*For a specific part of this jurisdiction, region, or feature, see the part and follow instructions under —4–9

—755 3 Rappahannock-York region

—755 31 Mathews County

—755 32 Gloucester County

—755 33 Middlesex County

—755 34 Essex County

—755 35 King and Queen and King William Counties

—755 352 King and Queen County

—755 355 King William County

—755 36 Caroline and Spotsylvania Counties, Fredericksburg

—755 362 Caroline County

—755 365 Spotsylvania County

—755 366 Independent city of Fredericksburg

—755 37 Orange and Greene Counties

—755 372 Orange County

—755 375 Greene County

—755 38 Madison County

—755 39 Culpeper and Rappahannock Counties

—755 392 Culpeper County

—755 395 Rappahannock County

—755 4 York-James region

Class here *James River

—755 41 Hampton and Newport News

—755 412 Independent city of Hampton

—755 416 Independent city of Newport News

—755 42 York and James City Counties, Poquoson, Williamsburg

—755 422 Independent city of Poquoson

—755 423 York County

—755 425 James City County and Williamsburg

—755 425 1 James City County

—755 425 2 Independent city of Williamsburg

—755 43 New Kent County

*For a specific part of this jurisdiction, region, or feature, see the part and follow instructions under —4–9

—755 44 Charles City County

—755 45 Henrico and Goochland Counties, Richmond

—755 451 Independent city of Richmond

—755 453 Henrico County

—755 455 Goochland County

—755 46 Hanover and Louisa Counties

—755 462 Hanover County

—755 465 Louisa County

—755 47 Fluvanna County

—755 48 Albemarle County and Charlottesville

—755 481 Independent city of Charlottesville

—755 482 Albemarle County

—755 49 Nelson and Amherst Counties

—755 493 Nelson County

—755 496 Amherst County

—755 5 Southeastern region of Virginia

—755 51 Independent city of Virginia Beach

—755 52 Norfolk, Portsmouth, Chesapeake

—755 521 Independent city of Norfolk

—755 522 Independent city of Portsmouth

—755 523 Independent city of Chesapeake

Class here *Dismal Swamp

—755 53 Independent city of Suffolk

—755 54 Isle of Wight County

—755 55 Southampton County and Franklin

—755 552 Southampton County

—755 553 Independent city of Franklin

—755 56 Surry and Sussex Counties

—755 562 Surry County

—755 565 Sussex County

—755 57 Greensville and Brunswick Counties and Emporia

*For a specific part of this jurisdiction, region, or feature, see the part and follow instructions under —4–9

—755 572 Greensville County

—755 573 Independent city of Emporia

—755 575 Brunswick County

—755 58 Dinwiddie and Prince George Counties, Petersburg, Hopewell

—755 581 Independent city of Petersburg

—755 582 Dinwiddie County

—755 585 Prince George County

—755 586 Independent city of Hopewell

—755 59 Chesterfield County and Colonial Heights

—755 594 Chesterfield County

—755 595 Independent city of Colonial Heights

—755 6 South central region of Virginia

Class here *Piedmont in Virginia; *Roanoke River in Virginia

—755 61 Powhatan and Cumberland Counties

—755 612 Powhatan County

—755 615 Cumberland County

—755 62 Buckingham and Appomattox Counties

—755 623 Buckingham County

—755 625 Appomattox County

—755 63 Prince Edward, Amelia, Nottoway Counties

—755 632 Prince Edward County

—755 634 Amelia County

—755 637 Nottoway County

—755 64 Lunenburg and Mecklenburg Counties

—755 643 Lunenburg County

—755 645 Mecklenburg County

—755 65 Charlotte County

—755 66 Halifax and Pittsylvania Counties and Danville

—755 661 Halifax County

Including South Boston [*formerly* —755662]

*For a specific part of this jurisdiction, region, or feature, see the part and follow instructions under —4–9

—[755 662] South Boston
Relocated to —755661
—755 665 Pittsylvania County
—755 666 Independent city of Danville
—755 67 Campbell and Bedford Counties, Lynchburg, Bedford
—755 671 Independent city of Lynchburg
—755 672 Campbell County
—755 675 Bedford County
—755 676 Independent city of Bedford
—755 68 Franklin County
—755 69 Henry and Patrick Counties and Martinsville
—755 692 Henry County
—755 693 Independent city of Martinsville
—755 695 Patrick County
—755 7 Southwestern region of Virginia
—755 71 Floyd, Carroll, Grayson Counties and Galax
—755 712 Floyd County
—755 714 Carroll County
—755 715 Independent city of Galax
—755 717 Grayson County
—755 72 Smyth and Washington Counties and Bristol
—755 723 Smyth County
—755 725 Washington County
—755 726 Independent city of Bristol
—755 73 Scott and Lee Counties
—755 732 Scott County
—755 735 Lee County
—755 74 Wise and Dickenson Counties and Norton
—755 743 Wise County
—755 744 Independent city of Norton
—755 745 Dickenson County
—755 75 Buchanan and Russell Counties
—755 752 Buchanan County

—755 755 Russell County

—755 76 Tazewell and Bland Counties

—755 763 Tazewell County

—755 765 Bland County

—755 77 Wythe and Pulaski Counties

—755 773 Wythe County

—755 775 Pulaski County

—755 78 Giles and Montgomery Counties and Radford

—755 782 Giles County

—755 785 Montgomery County

—755 786 Independent city of Radford

—755 79 Roanoke and Craig Counties, Roanoke, Salem

—755 791 Independent city of Roanoke

—755 792 Roanoke County

—755 793 Independent city of Salem

—755 795 Craig County

—755 8 Central western region of Virginia

—755 81 Alleghany County, Clifton Forge, Covington

—755 811 Independent city of Clifton Forge

—755 812 Independent city of Covington

—755 816 Alleghany County

—755 83 Botetourt County

—755 85 Rockbridge County, Buena Vista, Lexington

—755 851 Independent city of Buena Vista

—755 852 Rockbridge County

—755 853 Independent city of Lexington

—755 87 Bath County

—755 89 Highland County

—755 9 Northwestern region of Virginia

Class here *Shenandoah National Park; *Shenandoah Valley

—755 91 Augusta County, Staunton, Waynesboro

*For a specific part of this jurisdiction, region, or feature, see the part and follow instructions under —4–9

—755 911 Independent city of Staunton

—755 912 Independent city of Waynesboro

—755 916 Augusta County

—755 92 Rockingham County and Harrisonburg

—755 921 Independent city of Harrisonburg

—755 922 Rockingham County

—755 94 Page County

—755 95 Shenandoah County

—755 97 Warren County

—755 98 Clarke County

—755 99 Frederick County and Winchester

—755 991 Independent city of Winchester

—755 992 Frederick County

—756 North Carolina

—756 1 Northeast coastal plain counties of North Carolina

Class here *Coastal Plain in North Carolina; *Outer Banks

See also —16348 for Albemarle, Pamlico Sounds

—756 13 Currituck and Camden Counties

—756 132 Currituck County

—756 135 Camden County

Including *Dismal Swamp in North Carolina

—756 14 Pasquotank, Perquimans, Chowan Counties

—756 142 Pasquotank County

—756 144 Perquimans County

—756 147 Chowan County

—756 15 Gates and Hertford Counties

Class here *Chowan River

—756 153 Gates County

—756 155 Hertford County

—756 16 Bertie and Washington Counties

Class here *Roanoke River

*For a specific part of this jurisdiction, region, or feature, see the part and follow instructions under —4–9

—756 163 Bertie County

—756 165 Washington County

—756 17 Tyrrell and Dare Counties

—756 172 Tyrrell County

—756 175 Dare County

Including Roanoke Island; Cape Hatteras

—756 18 Hyde and Beaufort Counties

—756 184 Hyde County

—756 186 Beaufort County

—756 19 Craven, Pamlico, Carteret Counties

Class here *Neuse River

—756 192 Craven County

—756 194 Pamlico County

—756 197 Carteret County

—756 2 Southeast coastal plain counties of North Carolina

Class here *Cape Fear River

—756 21 Jones County

—756 23 Onslow County

—756 25 Pender County

—756 27 New Hanover County

Class here Wilmington

—756 29 Brunswick County

—756 3 Southwest coastal plain counties of North Carolina

—756 31 Columbus County

—756 32 Bladen County

—756 33 Robeson and Scotland Counties

—756 332 Robeson County

—756 335 Scotland County

—756 34 Richmond County

—756 35 Moore and Lee Counties

—756 352 Moore County

*For a specific part of this jurisdiction, region, or feature, see the part and follow instructions under —4–9

—756 355 Lee County

—756 36 Harnett and Hoke Counties

—756 362 Harnett County

—756 365 Hoke County

—756 37 Cumberland and Sampson Counties

—756 373 Cumberland County

—756 375 Sampson County

—756 38 Duplin and Lenoir Counties

—756 382 Duplin County

—756 385 Lenoir County

—756 39 Greene and Wayne Counties

—756 393 Greene County

—756 395 Wayne County

—756 4 Northwest coastal plain counties of North Carolina

—756 41 Johnston County

—756 43 Wilson County

—756 44 Pitt County

—756 45 Martin County

—756 46 Edgecombe County

—756 47 Nash County

—756 48 Halifax County

—756 49 Northampton County

—756 5 Northeast Piedmont counties

Class here *Piedmont in North Carolina

—756 52 Warren County

—756 53 Vance and Granville Counties

—756 532 Vance County

—756 535 Granville County

—756 54 Franklin County

—756 55 Wake County

Class here Raleigh

*For a specific part of this jurisdiction, region, or feature, see the part and follow instructions under —4–9

—756 56 Durham and Orange Counties

—756 563 Durham County

—756 565 Orange County

—756 57 Person and Caswell Counties

—756 573 Person County

—756 575 Caswell County

—756 58 Alamance County

—756 59 Chatham County

—756 6 Northwest Piedmont counties

—756 61 Randolph County

—756 62 Guilford County

—756 63 Rockingham County

—756 64 Stokes County

—756 65 Surry County

—756 66 Yadkin County

—756 67 Forsyth County

—756 68 Davidson County

Class here *Yadkin River

—756 69 Davie County

—756 7 Southern Piedmont counties

—756 71 Rowan County

—756 72 Cabarrus County

—756 73 Stanly County

—756 74 Montgomery County

—756 75 Anson and Union Counties

—756 753 Anson County

—756 755 Union County

—756 76 Mecklenburg County

Class here Charlotte

—756 77 Gaston and Cleveland Counties

—756 773 Gaston County

*For a specific part of this jurisdiction, region, or feature, see the part and follow instructions under —4–9

—756 775 Cleveland County

—756 78 Lincoln and Catawba Counties

—756 782 Lincoln County

—756 785 Catawba County

—756 79 Iredell and Alexander Counties

—756 793 Iredell County

—756 795 Alexander County

—756 8 Northern Appalachian region counties

Class here *Blue Ridge in North Carolina, *Appalachian region in North Carolina

—756 82 Wilkes County

—756 83 Alleghany and Ashe Counties

—756 832 Alleghany County

—756 835 Ashe County

—756 84 Watauga and Caldwell Counties

—756 843 Watauga County

—756 845 Caldwell County

—756 85 Burke County

—756 86 Avery and Mitchell Counties

—756 862 Avery County

—756 865 Mitchell County

—756 87 Yancey and Madison Counties

—756 873 Yancey County

—756 875 Madison County

—756 88 Buncombe County

Including Asheville

—756 89 McDowell County

—756 9 Southern Appalachian region

—756 91 Rutherford and Polk Counties

—756 913 Rutherford County

—756 915 Polk County

*For a specific part of this jurisdiction, region, or feature, see the part and follow instructions under —4–9

—756 92 Henderson County

—756 93 Transylvania County

—756 94 Haywood County

—756 95 Jackson County

—756 96 Swain County

Class here *Great Smoky Mountains in North Carolina

—756 97 Graham County

—756 98 Macon and Clay Counties

—756 982 Macon County

—756 985 Clay County

—756 99 Cherokee County

—757 South Carolina

—757 2 Mountain counties of South Carolina

Class here *Blue Ridge in South Carolina

—757 21 Oconee County

—757 23 Pickens County

—757 25 Anderson County

—757 27 Greenville County

—757 29 Spartanburg County

—757 3 Southwest Piedmont counties

Class here *Piedmont in South Carolina

—757 31 Laurens County

—757 33 Greenwood County

—757 35 Abbeville County

—757 36 McCormick County

—757 37 Edgefield County

—757 38 Saluda County

—757 39 Newberry County

—757 4 Northeast Piedmont counties

Class here *Broad River

—757 41 Union County

*For a specific part of this jurisdiction, region, or feature, see the part and follow instructions under —4–9

—757 42 Cherokee County

—757 43 York County

—757 45 Lancaster County

Class here *Catawba River

—757 47 Chester County

—757 49 Fairfield County

—757 6 Northeast counties of sand hills and upper pine belt of South Carolina

Class here *Coastal Plain in South Carolina

—757 61 Kershaw County

—757 63 Chesterfield County

—757 64 Marlboro County

—757 66 Darlington County

—757 67 Lee County

—757 69 Sumter County

—757 7 Southwest counties of sand hills and upper pine belt of South Carolina

—757 71 Richland County

Class here Columbia

—757 72 Calhoun County

—757 73 Lexington County

—757 75 Aiken County

—757 76 Barnwell County

—757 77 Allendale County

—757 78 Bamberg County

—757 79 Orangeburg County

—757 8 Northeast counties of lower pine belt of South Carolina

Including *Black, *Santee Rivers

Class here *Pee Dee River

—757 81 Clarendon County

—757 83 Williamsburg County

—757 84 Florence County

*For a specific part of this jurisdiction, region, or feature, see the part and follow instructions under —4–9

—757 85 Dillon County

—757 86 Marion County

—757 87 Horry County

—757 89 Georgetown County

—757 9 Southwest counties of lower pine belt of South Carolina

Including *Edisto River; *Savannah River in South Carolina

—757 91 Charleston County

—757 915 Charleston

—757 93 Berkeley County

—757 94 Dorchester County

—757 95 Colleton County

—757 97 Hampton County

—757 98 Jasper County

—757 99 Beaufort County

Class here *Sea Islands

—758 Georgia

Class here *Chattahoochee River

—758 1 Northeastern counties of Georgia

Class here *Savannah River

—758 12 Rabun and Habersham Counties

—758 123 Rabun County

—758 125 Habersham County

—758 13 Stephens and Franklin Counties

—758 132 Stephens County

—758 135 Franklin County

—758 14 Banks and Jackson Counties

—758 143 Banks County

—758 145 Jackson County

—758 15 Madison and Hart Counties

—758 152 Madison County

—758 155 Hart County

*For a specific part of this jurisdiction, region, or feature, see the part and follow instructions under —4–9

—758 16 Elbert and Lincoln Counties

—758 163 Elbert County

—758 165 Lincoln County

—758 17 Wilkes and Oglethorpe Counties

—758 172 Wilkes County

—758 175 Oglethorpe County

—758 18 Clarke County

Class here Athens

—758 19 Oconee and Barrow Counties

—758 193 Oconee County

—758 195 Barrow County

—758 2 North central counties of Georgia

Class here *Blue Ridge in Georgia

—758 21 Walton and Rockdale Counties

—758 212 Walton County

—758 215 Rockdale County

—758 22 Gwinnett and De Kalb Counties

—758 223 Gwinnett County

—758 225 De Kalb County

—758 23 Fulton County

—758 231 Atlanta

—758 24 Douglas and Cobb Counties

—758 243 Douglas County

—758 245 Cobb County

—758 25 Cherokee and Pickens Counties

—758 253 Cherokee County

—758 255 Pickens County

—758 26 Dawson and Forsyth Counties

—758 263 Dawson County

—758 265 Forsyth County

—758 27 Hall, Lumpkin, White Counties

*For a specific part of this jurisdiction, region, or feature, see the part and follow instructions under —4–9

—758 272	Hall County
—758 273	Lumpkin County
—758 277	White County
—758 28	Towns and Union Counties
—758 282	Towns County
—758 285	Union County
—758 29	Fannin and Gilmer Counties
—758 293	Fannin County
—758 295	Gilmer County
—758 3	Northwestern counties of Georgia
—758 31	Murray County
—758 32	Whitfield and Catoosa Counties
—758 324	Whitfield County
—758 326	Catoosa County
—758 33	Walker County
—758 34	Dade and Chattooga Counties
—758 342	Dade County
	Class here *Lookout Mountain in Georgia
—758 344	Chattooga County
—758 35	Floyd County
—758 36	Gordon and Bartow Counties
—758 362	Gordon County
—758 365	Bartow County
—758 37	Paulding and Polk Counties
—758 373	Paulding County
—758 375	Polk County
—758 38	Haralson County
—758 39	Carroll County
—758 4	West central counties of Georgia
	Class here *Piedmont in Georgia
—758 42	Heard, Coweta, Fayette Counties

*For a specific part of this jurisdiction, region, or feature, see the part and follow instructions under —4–9

—758 422 Heard County

—758 423 Coweta County

—758 426 Fayette County

—758 43 Clayton and Henry Counties

—758 432 Clayton County

—758 435 Henry County

—758 44 Spalding and Lamar Counties

—758 443 Spalding County

—758 446 Lamar County

—758 45 Pike and Meriwether Counties

—758 453 Pike County

—758 455 Meriwether County

—758 46 Troup and Harris Counties

—758 463 Troup County

—758 466 Harris County

—758 47 Muscogee and Chattahoochee Counties

—758 473 Muscogee County

—758 476 Chattahoochee County

—758 48 Marion, Talbot, Upson Counties

—758 482 Marion County

—758 483 Talbot County

—758 486 Upson County

—758 49 Taylor and Schley Counties

—758 493 Taylor County

—758 495 Schley County

—758 5 Central counties of Georgia

—758 51 Macon and Houston Counties

—758 513 Macon County

—758 515 Houston County

—758 52 Pulaski and Bleckley Counties

—758 523 Pulaski County

—758 525 Bleckley County

—758 53 Dodge and Laurens Counties

—758 532 Dodge County

—758 535 Laurens County

—758 54 Wilkinson and Twiggs Counties

—758 543 Wilkinson County

—758 545 Twiggs County

—758 55 Bibb and Peach Counties

—758 552 Bibb County

Class here Macon

—758 556 Peach County

—758 56 Crawford, Monroe, Jones Counties

—758 562 Crawford County

—758 563 Monroe County

—758 567 Jones County

—758 57 Baldwin and Putnam Counties

—758 573 Baldwin County

—758 576 Putnam County

—758 58 Jasper and Butts Counties

—758 583 Jasper County

—758 585 Butts County

—758 59 Newton and Morgan Counties

—758 593 Newton County

—758 595 Morgan County

—758 6 East central counties of Georgia

Including *Oconee River

Class here *Ogeechee River

—758 61 Greene and Taliaferro Counties

—758 612 Greene County

—758 616 Taliaferro County

—758 62 Hancock and Warren Counties

—758 623 Hancock County

—758 625 Warren County

*For a specific part of this jurisdiction, region, or feature, see the part and follow instructions under —4–9

—758 63 McDuffie and Columbia Counties

—758 632 McDuffie County

—758 635 Columbia County

—758 64 Richmond County

Class here Augusta

—758 65 Burke County

—758 66 Jefferson and Glascock Counties

—758 663 Jefferson County

—758 666 Glascock County

—758 67 Washington and Johnson Counties

—758 672 Washington County

—758 676 Johnson County

—758 68 Treutlen and Emanuel Counties

—758 682 Treutlen County

—758 684 Emanuel County

—758 69 Jenkins and Screven Counties

—758 693 Jenkins County

—758 695 Screven County

—758 7 Southeastern counties of Georgia

Including *Sea Islands of Georgia

—758 72 Effingham and Chatham Counties

—758 722 Effingham County

—758 724 Chatham County

Class here Savannah

—758 73 Bryan, Liberty, McIntosh Counties

—758 732 Bryan County

—758 733 Liberty County

—758 737 McIntosh County

—758 74 Glynn and Camden Counties

—758 742 Glynn County

—758 746 Camden County

*For a specific part of this jurisdiction, region, or feature, see the part and follow instructions under —4–9

—758 75	Charlton, Brantley, Wayne Counties
—758 752	Charlton County
	Class here *Okefenokee Swamp
—758 753	Brantley County
—758 756	Wayne County
—758 76	Long, Evans, Bulloch Counties
—758 762	Long County
—758 763	Evans County
—758 766	Bulloch County
—758 77	Candler and Tattnall Counties
—758 773	Candler County
—758 775	Tattnall County
—758 78	Toombs, Appling, Bacon Counties
—758 782	Toombs County
—758 784	Appling County
—758 787	Bacon County
—758 79	Pierce and Ware Counties
—758 792	Pierce County
—758 794	Ware County
—758 8	South central counties of Georgia
—758 81	Clinch, Echols, Lanier Counties
—758 812	Clinch County
—758 814	Echols County
—758 817	Lanier County
—758 82	Atkinson, Coffee, Jeff Davis Counties
—758 822	Atkinson County
—758 823	Coffee County
—758 827	Jeff Davis County
—758 83	Montgomery and Wheeler Counties
—758 832	Montgomery County
—758 835	Wheeler County

*For a specific part of this jurisdiction, region, or feature, see the part and follow instructions under —4–9

—758 84	Telfair and Wilcox Counties
—758 843	Telfair County
—758 845	Wilcox County
—758 85	Ben Hill and Irwin Counties
—758 852	Ben Hill County
—758 855	Irwin County
—758 86	Berrien and Lowndes Counties
—758 862	Berrien County
—758 864	Lowndes County
—758 87	Brooks and Cook Counties
—758 874	Brooks County
—758 876	Cook County
—758 88	Tift and Turner Counties
—758 882	Tift County
—758 885	Turner County
—758 89	Crisp and Dooly Counties
—758 893	Crisp County
—758 895	Dooly County
—758 9	Southwestern counties of Georgia
	Class here *Flint River
—758 91	Sumter and Webster Counties
—758 913	Sumter County
—758 916	Webster County
—758 92	Stewart, Quitman, Clay Counties
—758 922	Stewart County
—758 924	Quitman County
—758 927	Clay County
—758 93	Randolph and Terrell Counties
—758 932	Randolph County
—758 935	Terrell County
—758 94	Lee and Worth Counties

*For a specific part of this jurisdiction, region, or feature, see the part and follow instructions under —4–9

—758 943 Lee County

—758 945 Worth County

—758 95 Dougherty and Calhoun Counties

—758 953 Dougherty County

—758 956 Calhoun County

—758 96 Early, Miller, Baker Counties

—758 962 Early County

—758 964 Miller County

—758 967 Baker County

—758 97 Mitchell and Colquitt Counties

—758 973 Mitchell County

—758 975 Colquitt County

—758 98 Thomas and Grady Counties

—758 984 Thomas County

—758 986 Grady County

—758 99 Decatur and Seminole Counties

—758 993 Decatur County

—758 996 Seminole County

—759 Florida

—759 1 Northeastern counties of Florida

Class here *Saint Johns River

—759 11 Nassau County

Class here *Saint Marys River

—759 12 Duval County

Class here Jacksonville

—759 13 Baker County

—759 14 Union County

—759 15 Bradford County

—759 16 Clay County

—759 17 Putnam County

—759 18 Saint Johns County

*For a specific part of this jurisdiction, region, or feature, see the part and follow instructions under —4–9

—759 19 Flagler County

—759 2 East central counties of Florida

—759 21 Volusia County

—759 22 Lake County

—759 23 Seminole County

—759 24 Orange County

—759 25 Osceola County

—759 27 Brevard County

—759 28 Indian River County

—759 29 Saint Lucie County

—759 3 Southeastern counties of Florida

—759 31 Martin County

—759 32 Palm Beach County

—759 35 Broward County

Including Fort Lauderdale

—759 38 Dade County

—759 381 Miami and Miami Beach

—759 39 *The Everglades and *Lake Okeechobee

Class here *Everglades National Park

—759 4 Southwestern counties of Florida

—759 41 Monroe County

Including Key West

Class here *Florida Keys

—759 44 Collier County

Including *Ten Thousand Islands

Class here *Big Cypress Swamp

—759 46 Hendry County

—759 48 Lee County

Class here *Caloosahatchee River

—759 49 Charlotte County

—759 5 South central counties of Florida

*For a specific part of this jurisdiction, region, or feature, see the part and follow instructions under —4–9

—759 51 Glades County

—759 53 Okeechobee County

Class here *Kissimmee River

—759 55 Highlands County

—759 57 Hardee County

Class here *Peace River

—759 59 De Soto County

—759 6 Southern west central counties of Florida

—759 61 Sarasota County

—759 62 Manatee County

—759 63 Pinellas County

—759 65 Hillsborough County

Class here Tampa

—759 67 Polk County

—759 69 Pasco County

—759 7 Northern west central counties of Florida

Class here *Withlacoochee River

—759 71 Hernando County

—759 72 Citrus County

—759 73 Sumter County

—759 75 Marion County

—759 77 Levy County

—759 78 Gilchrist County

—759 79 Alachua County

—759 8 North central counties of Florida

Class here *Suwannee River

—759 81 Dixie and Lafayette Counties

—759 812 Dixie County

—759 816 Lafayette County

—759 82 Suwannee County

—759 83 Columbia County

*For a specific part of this jurisdiction, region, or feature, see the part and follow instructions under —4–9

—759 84	Hamilton County
—759 85	Madison County
—759 86	Taylor County
—759 87	Jefferson County
—759 88	Leon County
	Including Tallahassee
—759 89	Wakulla County
—759 9	Panhandle counties
—759 91	Franklin County
—759 92	Liberty and Gadsden Counties
	Including *Apalachicola River
—759 923	Liberty County
—759 925	Gadsden County
—759 93	Jackson County
—759 94	Calhoun and Gulf Counties
—759 943	Calhoun County
—759 947	Gulf County
—759 95	Bay County
—759 96	Washington and Holmes Counties
—759 963	Washington County
—759 965	Holmes County
—759 97	Walton County
—759 98	Okaloosa and Santa Rosa Counties
—759 982	Okaloosa County
—759 985	Santa Rosa County
—759 99	Escambia County
	Including Pensacola
—76	**South central United States Gulf Coast states**
	Class here Old Southwest

*For a specific part of this jurisdiction, region, or feature, see the part and follow instructions under —4–9

SUMMARY

— 761	**Alabama**
— 762	**Mississippi**
— 763	**Louisiana**
— 764	**Texas**
— 766	**Oklahoma**
— 767	**Arkansas**
— 768	**Tennessee**
— 769	**Kentucky**

> —761–764 Gulf Coast states

Class comprehensive works in —76

For Florida, see —759

—761 Alabama

—761 2 Gulf and Lower Coastal Plain counties

Class here *Alabama, *Tombigbee Rivers

—761 21 Baldwin County

Class here *Perdido River

—761 22 Mobile County

Including *Mobile River

Class here Mobile

—761 23 Lime Hills counties

For specific counties, see —76124–76127

> —761 24–761 27 Specific Lime Hills counties

Class comprehensive works in —76123

—761 24 Washington and Clarke Counties

—761 243 Washington County

—761 245 Clarke County

—761 25 Monroe County

—761 26 Conecuh and Escambia Counties

—761 263 Conecuh County

—761 265 Escambia County

—761 27 Covington County

*For a specific part of this jurisdiction, region, or feature, see the part and follow instructions under —4–9

—761 29	Lime sink counties of Alabama (Wire-grass region of Alabama)
—761 292	Geneva County
—761 295	Houston County
—761 3	Southern red hills counties of Alabama
—761 31	Henry County
—761 32	Barbour County
—761 33	Dale County
—761 34	Coffee County
—761 35	Pike County
—761 36	Crenshaw County
—761 37	Butler County
—761 38	Wilcox County
—761 39	Marengo and Choctaw Counties
—761 392	Marengo County
—761 395	Choctaw County
—761 4	Black Belt counties
—761 41	Sumter County
—761 42	Greene County
—761 43	Hale County
—761 44	Perry County
—761 45	Dallas County
—761 46	Autauga and Lowndes Counties
—761 463	Autauga County
—761 465	Lowndes County
—761 47	Montgomery County
	Class here Montgomery
—761 48	Bullock and Russell Counties
—761 483	Bullock County
—761 485	Russell County
—761 49	Macon County

—761 5 *Piedmont counties

Class here *Tallapoosa River

—761 52 Elmore County

—761 53 Tallapoosa County

Class here *Lake Martin

—761 55 Lee County

—761 56 Chambers County

—761 57 Randolph County

—761 58 Clay County

—761 59 Coosa County

—761 6 Coosa Valley counties

Class here *Coosa River

—761 61 Talladega County

—761 63 Calhoun County

—761 64 Cleburne County

—761 65 Cherokee County

—761 66 De Kalb County

—761 67 Etowah County

—761 69 Saint Clair County

—761 7 Central plateau and basin counties of Alabama

—761 72 Blount County

—761 73 Cullman County

—761 74 Winston County

—761 76 Walker County

—761 78 Jefferson County

—761 781 Birmingham

—761 79 Shelby County

—761 8 Central pine belt counties of Alabama

—761 81 Chilton County

—761 82 Bibb County

—761 84 Tuscaloosa County

*For a specific part of this jurisdiction, region, or feature, see the part and follow instructions under —4–9

—761 85 Pickens County

—761 86 Lamar County

—761 87 Fayette County

—761 89 Marion County

—761 9 Tennessee Valley counties

Class here *Tennessee River in Alabama

—761 91 Franklin and Colbert Counties

—761 913 Franklin County

—761 915 Colbert County

—761 92 Lawrence County

—761 93 Morgan County

—761 94 Marshall County

Class here *Guntersville Lake

—761 95 Jackson County

—761 97 Madison County

Class here Huntsville

—761 98 Limestone County

Class here *Wheeler Lake

—761 99 Lauderdale County

—762 Mississippi

—762 1 Southeastern counties of Mississippi

—762 12 Jackson County

—762 13 Harrison County

—762 14 Hancock County

—762 15 Pearl River County

—762 16 Stone and George Counties

—762 162 Stone County

—762 165 George County

—762 17 Greene and Perry Counties

—762 173 Greene County

—762 175 Perry County

*For a specific part of this jurisdiction, region, or feature, see the part and follow instructions under —4–9

—762 18 Forrest County

—762 19 Lamar County

—762 2 Southwestern counties of Mississippi

—762 21 Marion County

—762 22 Walthall County

—762 23 Pike County

—762 24 Amite County

—762 25 Wilkinson County

—762 26 Adams County

Class here Natchez

—762 27 Franklin County

—762 28 Jefferson and Claiborne Counties

—762 283 Jefferson County

—762 285 Claiborne County

—762 29 Warren County

—762 4 West central counties of Mississippi

Class here *Big Black, *Yazoo Rivers; Yazoo Mississippi Delta

—762 41 Issaquena and Sharkey Counties

—762 412 Issaquena County

—762 414 Sharkey County

—762 42 Washington County

—762 43 Bolivar County

—762 44 Coahoma County

—762 45 Quitman and Tallahatchie Counties

—762 453 Quitman County

—762 455 Tallahatchie County

—762 46 Leflore County

—762 47 Sunflower County

—762 48 Humphreys County

—762 49 Yazoo County

*For a specific part of this jurisdiction, region, or feature, see the part and follow instructions under —4–9

—762 5 South central counties of Mississippi

Class here *Piney Woods (region), *Pearl River

—762 51 Hinds County

Class here Jackson

—762 52 Copiah County

—762 53 Lincoln and Lawrence Counties

—762 534 Lincoln County

—762 536 Lawrence County

—762 54 Jefferson Davis and Covington Counties

—762 543 Jefferson Davis County

—762 545 Covington County

—762 55 Jones County

—762 57 Wayne and Jasper Counties

—762 573 Wayne County

—762 575 Jasper County

—762 58 Smith and Simpson Counties

—762 582 Smith County

—762 585 Simpson County

—762 59 Rankin County

—762 6 Central and east central counties of Mississippi

—762 62 Madison and Holmes Counties

—762 623 Madison County

—762 625 Holmes County

—762 63 Carroll and Grenada Counties

—762 633 Carroll County

—762 635 Grenada County

—762 64 Montgomery and Attala Counties

—762 642 Montgomery County

—762 644 Attala County

—762 65 Leake and Scott Counties

—762 653 Leake County

*For a specific part of this jurisdiction, region, or feature, see the part and follow instructions under —4–9

—762 655 Scott County

—762 67 Newton, Clarke, Lauderdale Counties

—762 672 Newton County

—762 673 Clarke County

—762 676 Lauderdale County

For Meridian, see —762677

—762 677 Meridian

—762 68 Kemper and Neshoba Counties

—762 683 Kemper County

—762 685 Neshoba County

—762 69 Winston, Choctaw, Webster Counties

—762 692 Winston County

—762 694 Choctaw County

—762 697 Webster County

—762 8 Northwestern counties of Mississippi

—762 81 Calhoun County

—762 82 Yalobusha County

—762 83 Lafayette County

—762 84 Panola County

—762 85 Tate County

—762 86 Tunica County

—762 87 De Soto County

—762 88 Marshall County

—762 89 Benton County

—762 9 Northeastern counties of Mississippi

—762 92 Tippah and Union Counties

—762 923 Tippah County

—762 925 Union County

—762 93 Pontotoc and Lee Counties

—762 932 Pontotoc County

—762 935 Lee County

—762 94 Chickasaw and Clay Counties

—762 942 Chickasaw County

—762 945 Clay County

—762 95 Oktibbeha and Noxubee Counties

—762 953 Oktibbeha County

—762 955 Noxubee County

—762 97 Lowndes and Monroe Counties

—762 973 Lowndes County

—762 975 Monroe County

—762 98 Itawamba and Prentiss Counties

—762 982 Itawamba County

—762 985 Prentiss County

—762 99 Alcorn and Tishomingo Counties

—762 993 Alcorn County

—762 995 Tishomingo County

—763 Louisiana

—763 1 Eastern parishes of Louisiana

—763 11 Washington Parish

—763 12 Saint Tammany Parish

—763 13 Tangipahoa Parish

—763 14 Livingston Parish

—763 15 Saint Helena Parish

—763 16 East Feliciana Parish

—763 17 West Feliciana Parish

—763 18 East Baton Rouge Parish

Class here Baton Rouge

—763 19 Ascension Parish

—763 3 Southeastern parishes of Louisiana

Class here Mississippi Delta

—763 31 Saint James Parish

—763 32 Saint John the Baptist Parish

Including *Lake Maurepas

—763 33 Saint Charles Parish

*For a specific part of this jurisdiction, region, or feature, see the part and follow instructions under —4–9

—763 34	*Lake Pontchartrain
—763 35	Orleans Parish (New Orleans)
—763 36	Saint Bernard Parish
—763 37	Plaquemines Parish
—763 38	Jefferson Parish
—763 39	Lafourche Parish
—763 4	South central parishes of Louisiana
—763 41	Terrebonne Parish
—763 42	Saint Mary Parish
—763 43	Assumption Parish
—763 44	Iberville Parish
—763 45	West Baton Rouge and Pointe Coupee Parishes
—763 452	West Baton Rouge Parish
—763 454	Pointe Coupee Parish
—763 46	Saint Landry Parish
—763 47	Lafayette Parish
—763 48	Saint Martin Parish
—763 49	Iberia Parish
—763 5	Southwestern parishes of Louisiana
—763 51	Vermilion Parish
—763 52	Cameron Parish
	Including Calcasieu, *Sabine Lakes
—763 54	Calcasieu Parish
—763 55	Jefferson Davis Parish
—763 56	Acadia Parish
—763 57	Evangeline Parish
—763 58	Allen Parish
—763 59	Beauregard Parish
—763 6	West central parishes of Louisiana
	Class here *Red River in Louisiana
—763 61	Vernon Parish

*For a specific part of this jurisdiction, region, or feature, see the part and follow instructions under —4–9

—763 62 Sabine Parish

Class here *Toledo Bend Reservoir

—763 63 De Soto Parish

—763 64 Red River Parish

—763 65 Natchitoches Parish

—763 66 Winn Parish

—763 67 Grant Parish

—763 69 Rapides Parish

—763 7 East central parishes of Louisiana

Class here *Ouachita River

—763 71 Avoyelles Parish

—763 73 Concordia Parish

—763 74 Catahoula Parish

—763 75 La Salle Parish

—763 76 Caldwell Parish

—763 77 Franklin Parish

—763 79 Tensas Parish

—763 8 Northeastern parishes of Louisiana

—763 81 Madison Parish

—763 82 East Carroll Parish

—763 83 West Carroll Parish

—763 84 Morehouse Parish

—763 86 Richland Parish

—763 87 Ouachita Parish

—763 89 Union Parish

—763 9 Northwestern parishes of Louisiana

—763 91 Lincoln Parish

—763 92 Jackson Parish

—763 93 Bienville Parish

—763 94 Claiborne Parish

—763 96 Webster Parish

*For a specific part of this jurisdiction, region, or feature, see the part and follow instructions under —4–9

—763 97 Bossier Parish

—763 99 Caddo Parish

Including *Caddo Lake

Class here Shreveport

—764 Texas

Class here *Brazos, *Colorado Rivers

—764 1 Coastal plains of Texas

For East Texas timber belt and blackland prairie, see —7642; for Rio Grande Plain, see —7644

—764 11 Nueces and neighboring counties

Class here *Nueces River

—764 113 Nueces County

Class here Corpus Christi

—764 115 San Patricio County

—764 117 Bee County

—764 119 Refugio County

—764 12 Calhoun and neighboring counties

Class here *Guadalupe, *San Antonio Rivers

—764 121 Calhoun County

—764 122 Aransas County

—764 123 Goliad County

—764 125 Victoria County

—764 127 Jackson County

—764 13 Matagorda and neighboring counties

—764 132 Matagorda County

—764 133 Wharton County

—764 135 Fort Bend County

—764 137 Brazoria County

—764 139 Galveston County

—764 14 Harris and neighboring counties

Class here *East Texas; *Sabine, *Trinity Rivers

*For a specific part of this jurisdiction, region, or feature, see the part and follow instructions under —4–9

—764 141 Harris County

—764 141 1 Houston

—764 143 Chambers County

—764 145 Jefferson County

—764 147 Orange County

—764 15 Montgomery and neighboring counties

Class here *Neches River

—764 153 Montgomery County

—764 155 Liberty County

—764 157 Hardin County

—764 159 Jasper County

—764 16 Newton and neighboring counties

—764 162 Newton County

—764 163 Tyler County

—764 165 Polk County

—764 167 San Jacinto County

—764 169 Walker County

—764 17 Trinity and neighboring counties

—764 172 Trinity County

—764 173 Angelina County

—764 175 San Augustine County

—764 177 Sabine County

—764 179 Shelby County

—764 18 Nacogdoches and neighboring counties

—764 182 Nacogdoches County

—764 183 Cherokee County

—764 185 Rusk County

—764 187 Panola County

—764 189 Gregg County

—764 19 Harrison and neighboring counties

—764 192 Harrison County

*For a specific part of this jurisdiction, region, or feature, see the part and follow instructions under —4–9

—764 193 Marion County

—764 195 Cass County

—764 197 Bowie County

—764 2 East Texas timber belt and blackland prairie

For Austin-San Antonio region, see —7643

—764 21 Red River and neighboring counties

—764 212 Red River County

—764 213 Franklin County

—764 215 Titus County

—764 217 Morris County

—764 219 Camp County

—764 22 Upshur and neighboring counties

—764 222 Upshur County

—764 223 Wood County

—764 225 Smith County

—764 227 Henderson County

—764 229 Anderson County

—764 23 Freestone and neighboring counties

—764 232 Freestone County

—764 233 Leon County

—764 235 Houston County

—764 237 Madison County

—764 239 Robertson County

—764 24 Burleson and neighboring counties

—764 241 Burleson County

—764 242 Brazos County

—764 243 Grimes County

—764 245 Washington County

—764 247 Lee County

—764 249 Waller County

—764 25 Fayette and neighboring counties

—764 251 Fayette County

—764 252 Austin County

See also —76431 for Austin (city)

—764 253 Colorado County

—764 255 Lavaca County

—764 257 Gonzales County

—764 259 De Witt County

—764 26 Lamar and Fannin Counties

Class here *blackland prairie

—764 263 Lamar County

—764 265 Fannin County

—764 27 Hunt and neighboring counties

—764 272 Hunt County

—764 273 Delta County

—764 274 Hopkins County

—764 275 Rains County

—764 276 Van Zandt County

—764 277 Kaufman County

—764 278 Rockwall County

—764 28 Dallas and neighboring counties

—764 281 Dallas and Ellis Counties

—764 281 1 Dallas County

For Dallas, see —7642812

—764 281 2 Dallas

Class here Dallas-Fort Worth metropolitan area

For Fort Worth, see —7645315

—764 281 5 Ellis County

—764 282 Navarro County

—764 283 Hill County

—764 284 McLennan County

—764 285 Limestone County

—764 286 Falls County

*For a specific part of this jurisdiction, region, or feature, see the part and follow instructions under —4–9

—764 287 Bell County

—764 288 Milam County

—764 289 Williamson County

—764 3 Austin-San Antonio region

For Comal County, see —764887; for Hays County, see —764888

—764 31 Travis County

Class here Austin

See also —764252 for Austin County

—764 32 Bastrop County

—764 33 Caldwell County

—764 34 Guadalupe County

—764 35 Bexar County

—764 351 San Antonio

—764 4 Rio Grande Plain (Lower Rio Grande Valley)

Class here *Rio Grande

—764 42 Medina County

—764 43 Uvalde and neighboring counties

—764 432 Uvalde County

—764 433 Kinney County

—764 435 Maverick County

—764 437 Zavala County

—764 44 Frio and neighboring counties

—764 442 Frio County

—764 443 Atascosa County

—764 444 Karnes County

—764 445 Wilson County

—764 447 Live Oak County

—764 45 McMullen and neighboring counties

—764 452 McMullen County

—764 453 La Salle County

—764 455 Dimmit County

*For a specific part of this jurisdiction, region, or feature, see the part and follow instructions under —4–9

—764 46 Webb and neighboring counties

—764 462 Webb County

—764 463 Duval County

—764 465 Jim Wells County

—764 47 Kleberg and neighboring counties

Class here *Padre Island

—764 472 Kleberg County

—764 473 Kenedy County

—764 475 Brooks County

—764 48 Jim Hogg and neighboring counties

—764 482 Jim Hogg County

—764 483 Zapata County

—764 485 Starr County

—764 49 Hidalgo and neighboring counties

—764 492 Hidalgo County

—764 493 Willacy County

—764 495 Cameron County

—764 5 North central plains of Texas

For Burnet-Llano region, see —7646; for northwestern lowland counties, see —7647

—764 51 Mills and neighboring counties

Class here *Grand Prairie

—764 512 Mills County

—764 513 Lampasas County

—764 515 Coryell County

—764 518 Bosque County

—764 52 Somervell and neighboring counties

—764 521 Somervell County

—764 522 Hood County

—764 524 Johnson County

—764 53 Tarrant and neighboring counties

*For a specific part of this jurisdiction, region, or feature, see the part and follow instructions under —4–9

—764 531 Tarrant County

—764 531 5 Fort Worth

Class comprehensive works on Dallas-Fort Worth metropolitan area in —7642812

—764 532 Wise County

—764 533 Cooke County

—764 54 Montague and neighboring counties

—764 541 Montague County

—764 542 Clay County

—764 543 Archer County

—764 544 Jack County

—764 545 Young County

—764 546 Stephens County

—764 547 Eastland County

—764 548 Brown County

—764 549 Hamilton County

—764 55 Erath and neighboring counties

—764 551 Erath County

—764 552 Palo Pinto County

—764 553 Parker County

—764 554 Comanche County

—764 555 Denton County

—764 556 Collin County

—764 557 Grayson County

—764 6 Burnet-Llano region

—764 62 Llano County

—764 63 Burnet County

—764 64 Blanco County

—764 65 Gillespie County

—764 66 Mason County

—764 67 McCulloch County

—764 68 San Saba County

—764 7 Northwestern lowland counties of Texas

—764 71 Concho County
—764 72 Tom Green and neighboring counties
—764 721 Tom Green County
—764 723 Coke County
—764 724 Runnels County
—764 725 Coleman County
—764 726 Callahan County
—764 727 Taylor County
—764 728 Nolan County
—764 729 Mitchell County
—764 73 Scurry and neighboring counties
—764 731 Scurry County
—764 732 Fisher County
—764 733 Jones County
—764 734 Shackelford County
—764 735 Throckmorton County
—764 736 Haskell County
—764 737 Stonewall County
—764 738 Kent County
—764 74 Dickens and neighboring counties
—764 741 Dickens County
—764 742 King County
—764 743 Knox County
—764 744 Baylor County
—764 745 Wichita County
—764 746 Wilbarger County
—764 747 Hardeman County
—764 748 Foard County
—764 75 Cottle and neighboring counties
—764 751 Cottle County
—764 752 Motley County
—764 753 Hall County
—764 754 Childress County

—764 8 Great Plains

Class here *Llano Estacado

> —764 81–764 83 Panhandle counties

Class comprehensive works in —7648

—764 81 Northern Panhandle counties

—764 812 Dallam County

—764 813 Sherman County

—764 814 Hansford County

—764 815 Ochiltree County

—764 816 Lipscomb County

—764 817 Hemphill County

—764 818 Roberts County

—764 82 Middle Panhandle counties

—764 821 Hutchinson County

—764 822 Moore County

—764 823 Hartley County

—764 824 Oldham County

—764 825 Potter County

—764 826 Carson County

—764 827 Gray County

—764 828 Wheeler County

—764 83 Southern Panhandle counties

—764 831 Collingsworth County

—764 832 Donley County

—764 833 Armstrong County

—764 834 Randall County

—764 835 Deaf Smith County

—764 836 Parmer County

—764 837 Castro County

—764 838 Swisher County

*For a specific part of this jurisdiction, region, or feature, see the part and follow instructions under —4–9

—764 839	Briscoe County
—764 84	Floyd and neighboring counties
—764 841	Floyd County
—764 842	Hale County
—764 843	Lamb County
—764 844	Bailey County
—764 845	Cochran County
—764 846	Hockley County
—764 847	Lubbock County
—764 848	Crosby County
—764 849	Yoakum County
—764 85	Lynn and neighboring counties
—764 851	Lynn County
—764 852	Garza County
—764 853	Borden County
—764 854	Dawson County
—764 855	Gaines County
—764 856	Andrews County
—764 857	Martin County
—764 858	Howard County
—764 859	Terry County
—764 86	Midland and neighboring counties
—764 861	Midland County
—764 862	Ector County
—764 863	Upton County
—764 87	*Edwards Plateau counties
—764 871	Sterling County
—764 872	Glasscock County
—764 873	Reagan County
—764 874	Irion County
—764 875	Crockett County

*For a specific part of this jurisdiction, region, or feature, see the part and follow instructions under —4–9

—764 876 Schleicher County

—764 877 Menard County

—764 878 Kimble County

—764 879 Sutton County

—764 88 Val Verde and neighboring counties

—764 881 Val Verde County

—764 882 Edwards County

—764 883 Real County

—764 884 Kerr County

—764 885 Bandera County

—764 886 Kendall County

—764 887 Comal County

—764 888 Hays County

—764 9 Western mountain and basin region of Texas

Class here *Pecos River

—764 91 Pecos Basin counties

—764 912 Loving County

—764 913 Winkler County

—764 914 Ward County

—764 915 Crane County

—764 92 Stockton Plateau counties

—764 922 Terrell County

—764 923 Pecos County

—764 924 Reeves County

—764 93 Big Bend Region counties

—764 932 Brewster County

Including Big Bend National Park

—764 933 Presidio County

—764 934 Jeff Davis County

*For a specific part of this jurisdiction, region, or feature, see the part and follow instructions under —4–9

—764 94 Culberson County

Including Guadalupe Mountains National Park

For Guadalupe Mountains National Park in Hudspeth County, see —76495

—764 95 Hudspeth County

—764 96 El Paso County

Class here El Paso; *upper Rio Grande of Texas

—766 Oklahoma

Class here *Canadian River

—766 1 Northwestern counties of Oklahoma

Class here former *Oklahoma Territory; *North Canadian River

—766 13 Panhandle counties

For Beaver County, see —76614

—766 132 Cimarron County

—766 135 Texas County

—766 14 Beaver County

—766 15 Harper and Ellis Counties

—766 153 Harper County

—766 155 Ellis County

—766 16 Roger Mills County

—766 17 Custer County

—766 18 Dewey County

—766 19 Woodward County

—766 2 North central counties of Oklahoma

—766 21 Woods County

—766 22 Alfalfa County

—766 23 Grant County

—766 24 Kay County

—766 25 Osage County

—766 26 Pawnee County

766 27 Noble County

*For a specific part of this jurisdiction, region, or feature, see the part and follow instructions under —4–9

—766 28	Garfield County
—766 29	Major County
—766 3	Central counties of Oklahoma
—766 31	Blaine County
—766 32	Kingfisher County
—766 33	Logan County
—766 34	Payne County
—766 35	Lincoln County
—766 36	Pottawatomie County
—766 37	Cleveland County
—766 38	Oklahoma County
	Class here Oklahoma City
—766 39	Canadian County
—766 4	Southwestern counties of Oklahoma
—766 41	Caddo County
—766 42	Washita County
—766 43	Beckham County
—766 44	Greer and Harmon Counties
—766 443	Greer County
—766 445	Harmon County
—766 45	Jackson County
—766 46	Tillman County
—766 47	Kiowa County
—766 48	Comanche County
—766 49	Cotton County
—766 5	South central counties of Oklahoma
	Class here former *Indian Territory; *Arbuckle Mountains; *Washita River
—766 52	Jefferson County
—766 53	Stephens County
—766 54	Grady County

*For a specific part of this jurisdiction, region, or feature, see the part and follow instructions under —4–9

—766 55 McClain County

—766 56 Garvin County

—766 57 Murray County

Including Platt National Park

—766 58 Carter County

—766 59 Love County

—766 6 Southeastern counties of Oklahoma

Class here *Ouachita Mountains; *Red River

—766 61 Marshall County

Class here *Lake Texoma

—766 62 Bryan County

—766 63 Choctaw County

—766 64 McCurtain County

—766 65 Pushmataha County

—766 66 Atoka County

—766 67 Coal County

—766 68 Johnston County

—766 69 Pontotoc County

—766 7 Southeast central counties of Oklahoma

—766 71 Seminole County

—766 72 Hughes County

—766 73 Okfuskee County

—766 74 McIntosh County

—766 75 Pittsburg County

—766 76 Latimer County

—766 77 Haskell County

—766 79 Le Flore County

—766 8 Northeast central counties of Oklahoma

Class here *Ozark Plateau in Oklahoma; *Boston Mountains in Oklahoma; *Arkansas River in Oklahoma

—766 81 Sequoyah County

*For a specific part of this jurisdiction, region, or feature, see the part and follow instructions under —4–9

—766 82 Muskogee County

—766 83 Okmulgee County

—766 84 Creek County

—766 86 Tulsa County

Class here Tulsa

—766 87 Wagoner County

Class here *Fort Gibson Reservoir

—766 88 Cherokee County

—766 89 Adair County

—766 9 Northeastern counties of Oklahoma

—766 91 Delaware County

—766 93 Mayes County

—766 94 Rogers County

—766 96 Washington County

—766 97 Nowata County

—766 98 Craig County

—766 99 Ottawa County

—767 Arkansas

—767 1 Northwestern counties of Arkansas

Class here *Ozark Mountains, *Ozark Plateau

—767 13 Benton County

—767 14 Washington County

—767 15 Madison County

—767 16 Newton County

—767 17 Carroll County

—767 18 Boone County

—767 19 Marion and Searcy Counties

—767 193 Marion County

Class here *Bull Shoals Lake

—767 195 Searcy County

*For a specific part of this jurisdiction, region, or feature, see the part and follow instructions under —4–9

—767 2 North central counties of Arkansas

Class here *White River

—767 21 Baxter County

—767 22 Fulton County

—767 23 Sharp County

—767 24 Randolph County

—767 25 Lawrence County

—767 26 Independence County

—767 27 Izard County

—767 28 Stone and Cleburne Counties

—767 283 Stone County

—767 285 Cleburne County

—767 29 Van Buren County

—767 3 Northwest central counties of Arkansas

Class here *Arkansas River

—767 31 Conway County

—767 32 Pope County

—767 33 Johnson County

—767 34 Franklin County

—767 35 Crawford County

—767 36 Sebastian County

—767 37 Logan County

—767 38 Yell County

—767 39 Perry County

—767 4 Southwest central counties of Arkansas

Class here *Ouachita Mountains in Arkansas

—767 41 Garland County

Including Hot Springs National Park

—767 42 Hot Spring County

—767 43 Montgomery County

—767 44 Scott County

*For a specific part of this jurisdiction, region, or feature, see the part and follow instructions under —4–9

—767 45 Polk County

—767 47 Sevier County

—767 48 Howard and Pike Counties

—767 483 Howard County

—767 485 Pike County

—767 49 Clark County

—767 5 Southwestern counties of Arkansas

—767 52 Nevada County

—767 54 Hempstead County

—767 55 Little River County

—767 56 Miller County

—767 57 Lafayette County

—767 59 Columbia County

—767 6 South central counties of Arkansas

—767 61 Union County

—767 63 Bradley County

—767 64 Calhoun County

—767 66 Ouachita County

—767 67 Dallas County

—767 69 Cleveland County

—767 7 Central counties of Arkansas

—767 71 Grant County

—767 72 Saline County

—767 73 Pulaski County

Class here Little Rock

—767 74 Faulkner County

—767 76 White County

—767 77 Prairie County

—767 78 Lonoke County

—767 79 Jefferson County

—767 8 Southeastern counties of Arkansas

Class here *Mississippi River in Arkansas

*For a specific part of this jurisdiction, region, or feature, see the part and follow instructions under —4–9

—767 82 Lincoln and Drew Counties

—767 823 Lincoln County

—767 825 Drew County

—767 83 Ashley County

—767 84 Chicot County

—767 85 Desha County

—767 86 Arkansas County

—767 87 Monroe County

—767 88 Phillips County

—767 89 Lee County

—767 9 Northeastern counties of Arkansas

—767 91 Saint Francis County

—767 92 Woodruff County

—767 93 Cross County

—767 94 Crittenden County

—767 95 Mississippi County

—767 96 Poinsett County

—767 97 Jackson County

—767 98 Craighead County

—767 99 Greene and Clay Counties

—767 993 Greene County

—767 995 Clay County

—768 Tennessee

Class here *Tennessee River

—768 1 Mississippi Valley counties

—768 12 Lake County

Including *Reelfoot Lake

—768 13 Obion County

—768 15 Dyer County

—768 16 Lauderdale County

*For a specific part of this jurisdiction, region, or feature, see the part and follow instructions under —4–9

—768 17 Tipton County

—768 19 Shelby County

Class here Memphis

—768 2 West Tennessee Plain counties

—768 21 Fayette County

—768 22 Haywood and Crockett Counties

—768 223 Haywood County

—768 225 Crockett County

—768 23 Gibson County

—768 24 Weakley County

—768 25 Carroll County

—768 26 Henderson and Chester Counties

—768 263 Henderson County

—768 265 Chester County

—768 27 Madison County

—768 28 Hardeman County

—768 29 McNairy County

—768 3 Western Tennessee River Valley counties

—768 31 Hardin County

—768 32 Decatur County

—768 33 Benton County

—768 34 Henry County

—768 35 Stewart County

—768 36 Houston County

—768 37 Humphreys County

—768 38 Perry County

—768 39 Wayne County

—768 4 West Highland Rim counties

Class here comprehensive works on Highland Rim counties

For east Highland Rim counties, see —7686

—768 42 Lawrence County

—768 43 Lewis and Hickman Counties

—768 432 Lewis County

—768 434 Hickman County

Class here *Duck River

—768 44 Dickson County

—768 45 Montgomery County

—768 46 Cheatham and Robertson Counties

—768 462 Cheatham County

—768 464 Robertson County

—768 47 Sumner County

—768 48 Trousdale and Macon Counties

—768 482 Trousdale County

—768 484 Macon County

—768 49 Clay County

Class here *Dale Hollow Lake

—768 5 Central Basin counties

Class here *Cumberland River

—768 51 Jackson County

—768 52 Smith County

—768 53 De Kalb and Cannon Counties

—768 532 De Kalb County

Class here *Center Hill Lake

—768 535 Cannon County

—768 54 Wilson County

—768 55 Davidson County

Class here Nashville

—768 56 Williamson County

—768 57 Rutherford County

—768 58 Bedford and Marshall Counties

—768 583 Bedford County

—768 585 Marshall County

—768 59 Maury County

—768 6 East Highland Rim counties

*For a specific part of this jurisdiction, region, or feature, see the part and follow instructions under —4–9

—768 61 Giles County

—768 62 Lincoln and Moore Counties

—768 624 Lincoln County

—768 627 Moore County

—768 63 Franklin County

—768 64 Coffee County

—768 65 Warren and Van Buren Counties

—768 653 Warren County

—768 657 Van Buren County

—768 66 White County

—768 67 Putnam County

—768 68 Overton and Pickett Counties

—768 684 Overton County

—768 687 Pickett County

—768 69 Fentress County

—768 7 *Cumberland Plateau counties

—768 71 Scott County

—768 72 Campbell County

—768 73 Anderson County

Class here *Clinch River

—768 74 Morgan County

—768 75 Cumberland County

—768 76 Bledsoe County

—768 77 Sequatchie County

Class here *Sequatchie River

—768 78 Grundy County

—768 79 Marion County

—768 8 Southeastern counties of Tennessee

—768 82 Hamilton County

Including *Lookout Mountain

Class here Chattanooga; *Chickamauga Lake

*For a specific part of this jurisdiction, region, or feature, see the part and follow instructions under —4–9

—768 83 Rhea and Meigs Counties

—768 834 Rhea County

—768 836 Meigs County

—768 84 Roane County

—768 85 Knox County

Including *Fort Loudoun Lake

Class here Knoxville

—768 86 Loudon and McMinn Counties

—768 863 Loudon County

—768 865 McMinn County

—768 87 Bradley and Polk Counties

—768 873 Bradley County

—768 875 Polk County

—768 88 Monroe and Blount Counties

—768 883 Monroe County

—768 885 Blount County

—768 89 *Great Smoky Mountains area

Class here *Great Smoky Mountains National Park

—768 893 Sevier County

—768 895 Cocke County

Class here *French Broad River

—768 9 Northeastern counties of Tennessee

—768 91 Greene County

—768 92 Hamblen and Jefferson Counties

—768 923 Hamblen County

—768 924 Jefferson County

—768 93 Grainger and Union Counties

—768 932 Grainger County

—768 935 Union County

Class here *Norris Lake

—768 94 Claiborne and Hancock Counties

*For a specific part of this jurisdiction, region, or feature, see the part and follow instructions under —4–9

—768 944 Claiborne County

Class here *Cumberland Mountains in Tennessee

—768 946 Hancock County

—768 95 Hawkins County

—768 96 Sullivan County

—768 97 Washington County

—768 98 Unicoi and Carter Counties

—768 982 Unicoi County

—768 984 Carter County

—768 99 Johnson County

—769 Kentucky

—769 1 Southern mountain region counties of Kentucky

Including *Cumberland Plateau in Kentucky

Class here *Cumberland Mountains

—769 12 Bell and Knox Counties

—769 123 Bell County

—769 125 Knox County

—769 13 Whitley and McCreary Counties

—769 132 Whitley County

—769 135 McCreary County

—769 14 Laurel and Clay Counties

—769 143 Laurel County

—769 145 Clay County

—769 15 Leslie and Harlan Counties

—769 152 Leslie County

—769 154 Harlan County

—769 16 Letcher and Knott Counties

—769 163 Letcher County

—769 165 Knott County

—769 17 Perry and Owsley Counties

—769 173 Perry County

*For a specific part of this jurisdiction, region, or feature, see the part and follow instructions under —4–9

—769 176 Owsley County

—769 18 Jackson and Lee Counties

—769 183 Jackson County

—769 185 Lee County

—769 19 Breathitt County

—769 2 Northern mountain region counties of Kentucky

Class here *Big Sandy River and *Tug Fork in Kentucky

—769 21 Wolfe and Magoffin Counties

—769 213 Wolfe County

—769 215 Magoffin County

—769 22 Floyd County

—769 23 Pike County

—769 24 Martin and Johnson Counties

—769 243 Martin County

—769 245 Johnson County

—769 25 Morgan and Elliott Counties

—769 253 Morgan County

—769 255 Elliott County

—769 26 Lawrence County

—769 27 Boyd County

—769 28 Carter County

—769 29 Greenup and Lewis Counties

—769 293 Greenup County

—769 295 Lewis County

—769 3 Northern Bluegrass counties

Class here *Bluegrass region, *Kentucky River

—769 32 Mason and Bracken Counties

—769 323 Mason County

—769 325 Bracken County

—769 33 Pendleton County

—769 34 Campbell County

*For a specific part of this jurisdiction, region, or feature, see the part and follow instructions under —4–9

—769 35 Kenton County

—769 36 Boone and Gallatin Counties

—769 363 Boone County

—769 365 Gallatin County

—769 37 Carroll and Trimble Counties

—769 373 Carroll County

—769 375 Trimble County

—769 38 Oldham and Henry Counties

—769 383 Oldham County

—769 385 Henry County

—769 39 Owen and Grant Counties

—769 393 Owen County

—769 395 Grant County

—769 4 Southern Bluegrass counties

—769 41 Harrison, Robertson, Nicholas Counties

—769 413 Harrison County

—769 415 Robertson County

—769 417 Nicholas County

—769 42 Bourbon and Scott Counties

—769 423 Bourbon County

—769 425 Scott County

—769 43 Franklin and Shelby Counties

—769 432 Franklin County

Including Frankfort

—769 435 Shelby County

—769 44 Jefferson County

Class here Louisville

—769 45 Bullitt and Spencer Counties

—769 453 Bullitt County

—769 455 Spencer County

—769 46 Anderson and Woodford Counties

—769 463 Anderson County

—769 465 Woodford County

—769 47 Fayette County

Class here Lexington

—769 48 Jessamine and Mercer Counties

—769 483 Jessamine County

—769 485 Mercer County

—769 49 Washington and Nelson Counties

—769 493 Washington County

—769 495 Nelson County

—769 5 The Knobs counties

—769 51 Marion County

—769 52 Boyle and Garrard Counties

—769 523 Boyle County

—769 525 Garrard County

—769 53 Madison County

—769 54 Clark County

—769 55 Montgomery and Bath Counties

—769 553 Montgomery County

—769 555 Bath County

—769 56 Fleming County

—769 57 Rowan County

—769 58 Menifee and Powell Counties

—769 583 Menifee County

—769 585 Powell County

—769 59 Estill County

—769 6 Eastern Pennyroyal counties

Class here *Highland Rim in Kentucky, *Pennyroyal Plateau

—769 62 Rockcastle and Lincoln Counties

—769 623 Rockcastle County

—769 625 Lincoln County

—769 63 Pulaski County

Class here *Lake Cumberland

*For a specific part of this jurisdiction, region, or feature, see the part and follow instructions under —4–9

—769 64	Wayne County
—769 65	Clinton and Russell Counties
—769 653	Clinton County
—769 655	Russell County
—769 66	Casey County
—769 67	Taylor and Adair Counties
—769 673	Taylor County
—769 675	Adair County
—769 68	Cumberland and Monroe Counties
—769 683	Cumberland County
—769 685	Monroe County
—769 69	Metcalfe and Green Counties
—769 693	Metcalfe County
—769 695	Green County
—769 7	Western Pennyroyal counties
—769 71	Larue and Hart Counties
—769 713	Larue County
—769 715	Hart County
—769 72	Barren County
—769 73	Allen and Simpson Counties
—769 732	Allen County
—769 735	Simpson County
—769 74	Warren County
—769 75	Edmonson and Butler Counties and Mammoth Cave National Park
—769 752	Edmonson County
—769 754	*Mammoth Cave National Park
—769 755	Butler County
—769 76	Logan County
—769 77	Todd County
—769 78	Christian County

*For a specific part of this jurisdiction, region, or feature, see the part and follow instructions under —4–9

—769 79 Trigg County

Class here *Land Between the Lakes; *Lake Barkley

—769 8 Western basin counties of Kentucky

Class here *Green River

—769 81 Lyon and Caldwell Counties

—769 813 Lyon County

—769 815 Caldwell County

—769 82 Hopkins and McLean Counties

—769 823 Hopkins County

—769 826 McLean County

—769 83 Muhlenberg and Ohio Counties

—769 832 Muhlenberg County

—769 835 Ohio County

—769 84 Grayson and Hardin Counties

—769 842 Grayson County

—769 845 Hardin County

—769 85 Meade and Breckinridge Counties

—769 852 Meade County

—769 854 Breckinridge County

—769 86 Hancock and Daviess Counties

—769 862 Hancock County

—769 864 Daviess County

Class here Owensboro

—769 87 Henderson County

—769 88 Webster and Union Counties

—769 883 Webster County

—769 885 Union County

—769 89 Crittenden and Livingston Counties

—769 893 Crittenden County

—769 895 Livingston County

Class here *Kentucky Lake

*For a specific part of this jurisdiction, region, or feature, see the part and follow instructions under —4–9

—769 9 Counties west of Tennessee River

—769 91 Marshall County

—769 92 Calloway County

—769 93 Graves County

—769 95 McCracken County

—769 96 Ballard County

—769 97 Carlisle County

—769 98 Hickman County

—769 99 Fulton County

—77 North central United States Lake states

Class here *Middle West; *Mississippi, *Ohio Rivers; *Great Lakes

SUMMARY

—771 Ohio
—772 Indiana
—773 Illinois
—774 Michigan
—775 Wisconsin
—776 Minnesota
—777 Iowa
—778 Missouri

> —771–776 Lake states

Class comprehensive works in —77

For New York, see —747; for Pennsylvania, see —748

—771 Ohio

—771 1 Northwestern counties of Ohio

Class here *Maumee River

—771 11 Williams and Fulton Counties

—771 113 Williams County

—771 115 Fulton County

—771 12 Lucas County

For Toledo, see —77113

—771 13 Toledo

—771 14 Defiance County

*For a specific part of this jurisdiction, region, or feature, see the part and follow instructions under —4–9

—771 15 Henry County

—771 16 Wood County

—771 17 Paulding County

—771 18 Putnam County

—771 19 Hancock County

—771 2 North central counties of Ohio

Class here *Lake Erie

—771 21 Ottawa and Sandusky Counties

—771 212 Ottawa County

—771 214 Sandusky County

Class here *Sandusky Bay

—771 22 Erie County

—771 23 Lorain County

—771 24 Seneca County

—771 25 Huron County

—771 26 Wyandot County

—771 27 Crawford County

—771 28 Richland County

—771 29 Ashland County

—771 3 Northeastern counties of Ohio

—771 31 Cuyahoga County

Class here *Cuyahoga River

For Cleveland, see —77132

—771 32 Cleveland

—771 33 Lake and Geauga Counties

—771 334 Lake County

—771 336 Geauga County

—771 34 Ashtabula County

—771 35 Medina County

—771 36 Summit County

Class here Akron

*For a specific part of this jurisdiction, region, or feature, see the part and follow instructions under —4–9

—771 37 Portage County

—771 38 Trumbull County

—771 39 Mahoning County

Class here Youngstown; *Mahoning River

—771 4 West central counties of Ohio

—771 41 Van Wert and Mercer Counties

—771 413 Van Wert County

—771 415 Mercer County

Class here *Grand Lake (Lake Saint Marys)

—771 42 Allen County

—771 43 Auglaize County

—771 44 Hardin County

—771 45 Shelby County

—771 46 Logan and Champaign Counties

—771 463 Logan County

—771 465 Champaign County

—771 47 Darke County

—771 48 Miami County

—771 49 Clark County

—771 5 Central counties of Ohio

Class here *Scioto River

—771 51 Marion and Morrow Counties

—771 514 Marion County

—771 516 Morrow County

—771 52 Knox County

—771 53 Union and Delaware Counties

—771 532 Union County

—771 535 Delaware County

—771 54 Licking County

—771 55 Madison County

*For a specific part of this jurisdiction, region, or feature, see the part and follow instructions under —4–9

—771 56 Franklin County

For Columbus, see —77157

—771 57 Columbus

—771 58 Fairfield County

—771 59 Perry County

—771 6 East central counties of Ohio

—771 61 Wayne County

—771 62 Stark County

—771 63 Columbiana County

—771 64 Holmes County

—771 65 Coshocton County

—771 66 Tuscarawas County

—771 67 Carroll County

—771 68 Harrison County

—771 69 Jefferson County

—771 7 Southwestern counties of Ohio

Class here *Miami River

—771 71 Preble County

—771 72 Montgomery County

For Dayton, see —77173

—771 73 Dayton

—771 74 Greene County

—771 75 Butler County

—771 76 Warren and Clinton Counties

—771 763 Warren County

—771 765 Clinton County

—771 77 Hamilton County

For Cincinnati, see —77178

—771 78 Cincinnati

—771 79 Clermont and Brown Counties

—771 794 Clermont County

*For a specific part of this jurisdiction, region, or feature, see the part and follow instructions under —4–9

—771 796 Brown County

—771 8 South central counties of Ohio

—771 81 Fayette and Pickaway Counties

—771 813 Fayette County

—771 815 Pickaway County

—771 82 Ross County

—771 83 Hocking and Vinton Counties

—771 835 Hocking County

—771 837 Vinton County

—771 84 Highland and Pike Counties

—771 845 Highland County

—771 847 Pike County

—771 85 Jackson County

—771 86 Adams County

—771 87 Scioto County

—771 88 Lawrence County

—771 89 Gallia County

—771 9 Southeastern counties of Ohio

—771 91 Muskingum County

Class here *Muskingum River

—771 92 Guernsey County

—771 93 Belmont County

—771 94 Morgan County

—771 95 Noble County

—771 96 Monroe County

—771 97 Athens County

Class here *Hocking River

—771 98 Washington County

—771 99 Meigs County

—772 Indiana

—772 1 Southeastern counties of Indiana

*For a specific part of this jurisdiction, region, or feature, see the part and follow instructions under —4–9

—772 11 Dearborn County

—772 12 Ohio and Switzerland Counties

—772 123 Ohio County

—772 125 Switzerland County

—772 13 Jefferson County

—772 14 Ripley County

—772 15 Franklin County

—772 16 Decatur County

—772 17 Jennings County

—772 18 Scott and Clark Counties

—772 183 Scott County

—772 185 Clark County

—772 19 Floyd County

—772 2 South central counties of Indiana

—772 21 Harrison County

—772 22 Washington County

—772 23 Jackson County

—772 24 Bartholomew County

—772 25 Brown and Monroe Counties

—772 253 Brown County

—772 255 Monroe County

—772 26 Lawrence County

—772 27 Orange County

—772 28 Crawford County

—772 29 Perry County

—772 3 Southwestern counties of Indiana

Class here *White River

—772 31 Spencer County

—772 32 Warrick County

—772 33 Vanderburgh County

—772 34 Posey County

*For a specific part of this jurisdiction, region, or feature, see the part and follow instructions under —4–9

—772 35 Gibson County

—772 36 Pike County

—772 37 Dubois County

—772 38 Martin and Daviess Counties

—772 382 Martin County

—772 385 Daviess County

—772 39 Knox County

—772 4 West central counties of Indiana

Class here *Wabash River

—772 41 Sullivan County

—772 42 Greene County

—772 43 Owen County

—772 44 Clay County

—772 45 Vigo County

—772 46 Vermillion and Parke Counties

—772 462 Vermillion County

—772 465 Parke County

—772 47 Fountain County

—772 48 Montgomery County

—772 49 Putnam County

—772 5 Central counties of Indiana

—772 51 Morgan and Johnson Counties

—772 513 Morgan County

—772 515 Johnson County

—772 52 Marion County

Class here Indianapolis

—772 53 Hendricks County

—772 54 Boone County

—772 55 Clinton and Tipton Counties

—772 553 Clinton County

—772 555 Tipton County

*For a specific part of this jurisdiction, region, or feature, see the part and follow instructions under —4–9

—772 56 Hamilton County

—772 57 Madison County

—772 58 Hancock County

—772 59 Shelby County

—772 6 East central counties of Indiana

—772 61 Rush County

—772 62 Fayette and Union Counties

—772 623 Fayette County

—772 625 Union County

—772 63 Wayne County

—772 64 Henry County

—772 65 Delaware County

Including Muncie

—772 66 Randolph County

—772 67 Jay County

—772 68 Blackford County

—772 69 Grant County

—772 7 Northeastern counties of Indiana

—772 71 Huntington County

—772 72 Wells County

—772 73 Adams County

—772 74 Allen County

Class here Fort Wayne

—772 75 Whitley County

—772 76 Noble County

—772 77 De Kalb County

—772 78 Steuben County

—772 79 Lagrange County

—772 8 North central counties of Indiana

—772 81 Elkhart County

—772 82 Kosciusko County

—772 83 Wabash County

—772 84 Miami County

—772 85 Howard County

—772 86 Cass County

—772 87 Fulton County

—772 88 Marshall County

—772 89 Saint Joseph County

Class here South Bend

—772 9 Northwestern counties of Indiana

—772 91 La Porte County

—772 92 Starke and Pulaski Counties

—772 923 Starke County

—772 925 Pulaski County

—772 93 White County

—772 94 Carroll County

—772 95 Tippecanoe County

—772 96 Warren County

—772 97 Benton, Newton, Jasper Counties

—772 972 Benton County

—772 974 Newton County

—772 977 Jasper County

—772 98 Porter County

—772 99 Lake County

Including Gary

—773 Illinois

—773 1 Cook County

—773 11 Chicago

—773 2 Northeastern counties of Illinois

Class here *Des Plaines River

For Cook County, see —7731

—773 21 Lake County

—773 22 McHenry County

—773 23 Kane County

*For a specific part of this jurisdiction, region, or feature, see the part and follow instructions under —4–9

—773 24 Du Page County

—773 25 Will County

—773 26 Kendall and Grundy Counties

—773 263 Kendall County

—773 265 Grundy County

—773 27 La Salle County

—773 28 De Kalb County

—773 29 Boone County

—773 3 Northwestern counties of Illinois

Class here *Rock River

—773 31 Winnebago County

—773 32 Ogle County

—773 33 Stephenson County

—773 34 Jo Daviess and Carroll Counties

—773 343 Jo Daviess County

—773 345 Carroll County

—773 35 Whiteside County

—773 36 Lee County

—773 37 Bureau and Putnam Counties

—773 372 Burcau County

—773 375 Putnam County

—773 38 Henry County

—773 39 Rock Island and Mercer Counties

—773 393 Rock Island County

Class comprehensive works on Davenport-Rock Island-Moline tri-city area in —77769

—773 395 Mercer County

—773 4 West central counties of Illinois

—773 41 Henderson and Warren Counties

—773 413 Henderson County

—773 415 Warren County

*For a specific part of this jurisdiction, region, or feature, see the part and follow instructions under —4–9

—773 42 McDonough County

—773 43 Hancock County

—773 44 Adams County

—773 45 Pike and Scott Counties

—773 453 Pike County

—773 455 Scott County

—773 46 Morgan and Cass Counties

—773 463 Morgan County

—773 465 Cass County

—773 47 Brown and Schuyler Counties

—773 473 Brown County

—773 475 Schuyler County

—773 48 Fulton County

—773 49 Knox County

—773 5 Central counties of Illinois

Class here *Illinois River

—773 51 Stark and Marshall Counties

—773 513 Stark County

—773 515 Marshall County

—773 52 Peoria County

—773 53 Woodford County

—773 54 Tazewell County

—773 55 Mason and Menard Counties

Class here *Sangamon River

—773 553 Mason County

—773 555 Menard County

—773 56 Sangamon County

Including Springfield

—773 57 Logan County

—773 58 Macon and De Witt Counties

—773 582 Macon County

*For a specific part of this jurisdiction, region, or feature, see the part and follow instructions under —4–9

—773 585 De Witt County

—773 59 McLean County

—773 6 East central counties of Illinois

—773 61 Livingston County

—773 62 Ford County

—773 63 Kankakee County

—773 64 Iroquois County

—773 65 Vermilion County

—773 66 Champaign County

—773 67 Piatt and Moultrie Counties

—773 673 Piatt County

—773 675 Moultrie County

—773 68 Douglas County

—773 69 Edgar County

—773 7 Southeastern and south central counties of Illinois

> —773 71–773 78 Southeastern counties of Illinois

Class comprehensive works in —7737

—773 71 Clark County

—773 72 Coles County

—773 73 Cumberland County

—773 74 Jasper County

—773 75 Crawford County

—773 76 Lawrence County

—773 77 Richland County

—773 78 Wabash County

—773 79 South central counties of Illinois

—773 791 Edwards County

—773 792 Wayne County

—773 793 Jefferson County

—773 794 Marion County

—773 795 Clay County

—773 796 Effingham County

—773 797	Fayette County
—773 798	Shelby County
—773 8	Southwestern counties of Illinois
—773 81	Christian County
—773 82	Montgomery County
—773 83	Macoupin County
—773 84	Greene County
—773 85	Calhoun and Jersey Counties
—773 853	Calhoun County
—773 855	Jersey County
—773 86	Madison County
—773 87	Bond and Clinton Counties
—773 873	Bond County
—773 875	Clinton County
—773 88	Washington County
—773 89	Saint Clair County
—773 9	Southern counties of Illinois
—773 91	Monroe County
—773 92	Randolph County
—773 93	Perry County
—773 94	Franklin County
—773 95	Hamilton County
—773 96	White County
—773 97	Gallatin County
—773 98	Hardin County
—773 99	Southernmost counties of Illinois
—773 991	Pope County
—773 992	Saline County
—773 993	Williamson County
—773 994	Jackson County
—773 995	Union County
—773 996	Johnson County
—773 997	Massac County

—773 998 Pulaski County

—773 999 Alexander County

—774 Michigan

Class here Lakes *Huron, *Michigan

> —774 1–774 8 Lower Peninsula

Class comprehensive works in —774

—774 1 Southwestern counties of Lower Peninsula

—774 11 Berrien County

—774 12 Cass County

—774 13 Van Buren County

—774 14 Allegan County

—774 15 Ottawa County

Class here *Grand River

—774 16 Barry County

—774 17 Kalamazoo County

—774 19 Saint Joseph County

—774 2 South central counties of Lower Peninsula

—774 21 Branch County

—774 22 Calhoun County

—774 23 Eaton County

—774 24 Clinton County

—774 25 Shiawassee County

—774 26 Ingham County

For Lansing and East Lansing, see —77427

—774 27 Lansing and East Lansing

—774 28 Jackson County

—774 29 Hillsdale County

—774 3 Southeastern counties of Lower Peninsula

—774 31 Lenawee County

—774 32 Monroe County

*For a specific part of this jurisdiction, region, or feature, see the part and follow instructions under —4–9

—774 33 Wayne County

Including Dearborn; *Detroit River

For Detroit, see —77434

—774 34 Detroit

—774 35 Washtenaw County

Including Ann Arbor

—774 36 Livingston County

—774 37 Genesee County

Including Flint

—774 38 Oakland County

—774 39 Macomb County

Including *Lake Saint Clair

—774 4 Southeast central counties of Lower Peninsula

—774 41 Saint Clair County

Including *Saint Clair River

—774 42 Lapeer County

—774 43 Sanilac County

—774 44 Huron County

—774 45 Tuscola County

—774 46 Saginaw County

—774 47 Bay County

Class here *Saginaw River; *Saginaw Bay

—774 48 Midland County

—774 49 Gratiot County

—774 5 Southwest central counties of Lower Peninsula

—774 51 Isabella County

—774 52 Mecosta County

—774 53 Montcalm County

—774 54 Ionia County

—774 55 Kent County

For Grand Rapids, see —77456

*For a specific part of this jurisdiction, region, or feature, see the part and follow instructions under —4–9

—774 56 Grand Rapids

—774 57 Muskegon County

—774 58 Newaygo County

—774 59 Oceana County

—774 6 Northwest central counties of Lower Peninsula

—774 61 Mason County

—774 62 Manistee County

—774 63 Benzie and Leelanau Counties

—774 632 Benzie County

—774 635 Leelanau County

—774 64 Grand Traverse County

Class here *Grand Traverse Bay

—774 65 Kalkaska County

—774 66 Missaukee County

—774 67 Wexford County

—774 68 Lake County

—774 69 Osceola County

—774 7 Northeast central counties of Lower Peninsula

Class here *Au Sable River

—774 71 Clare County

—774 72 Gladwin County

—774 73 Arenac County

—774 74 Iosco County

—774 75 Ogemaw County

—774 76 Roscommon County

—774 77 Crawford County

—774 78 Oscoda County

—774 79 Alcona County

—774 8 Northern counties of Lower Peninsula

—774 81 Alpena County

—774 82 Presque Isle County

*For a specific part of this jurisdiction, region, or feature, see the part and follow instructions under —4–9

—774 83	Montmorency County
—774 84	Otsego County
—774 85	Antrim County
—774 86	Charlevoix County
—774 87	Cheboygan County
—774 88	Emmet County
—774 9	Upper Peninsula
	Class here *Lake Superior
—774 91	Chippewa County
	Including *Saint Marys River; *Whitefish Bay
—774 92	Mackinac and Luce Counties
—774 923	Mackinac County
	Including *Straits of Mackinac
—774 925	Luce County
—774 93	Alger and Schoolcraft Counties
—774 932	Alger County
—774 935	Schoolcraft County
—774 94	Delta County
—774 95	Menominee and Dickinson Counties
—774 953	Menominee County
—774 955	Dickinson County
—774 96	Marquette County
—774 97	Baraga and Iron Counties
—774 973	Baraga County
—774 975	Iron County
—774 98	Gogebic and Ontonagon Counties
—774 983	Gogebic County
—774 985	Ontonagon County
—774 99	Houghton and Keweenaw Counties
	Class here Keweenaw Peninsula
—774 993	Houghton County

*For a specific part of this jurisdiction, region, or feature, see the part and follow instructions under —4–9

—774 995 Keweenaw County

For Isle Royale, see —774997

—774 997 Isle Royale (Isle Royale National Park)

—775 Wisconsin

Class here *Wisconsin River

—775 1 Northwestern counties of Wisconsin

Class here *Saint Croix River

—775 11 Douglas County

Including Superior

Class comprehensive works on Duluth and Superior in —776771

—775 13 Bayfield County

—775 14 Burnett County

—775 15 Washburn County

—775 16 Sawyer County

—775 17 Polk County

—775 18 Barron County

—775 19 Rusk County

—775 2 North central counties of Wisconsin

—775 21 Ashland County

—775 22 Iron County

—775 23 Vilas County

—775 24 Price County

—775 25 Oneida County

—775 26 Taylor County

—775 27 Lincoln County

—775 28 Clark County

—775 29 Marathon County

—775 3 Northeastern counties of Wisconsin

—775 31 Forest County

—775 32 Florence County

—775 33 Marinette County

*For a specific part of this jurisdiction, region, or feature, see the part and follow instructions under —4–9

—775 35 Langlade and Menominee Counties

—775 354 Langlade County

—775 356 Menominee County

—775 36 Shawano County

—775 37 Oconto County

—775 38 Waupaca County

—775 39 Outagamie County

—775 4 West central counties of Wisconsin

Class here *Chippewa River

—775 41 Saint Croix County

—775 42 Pierce County

—775 43 Dunn County

—775 44 Chippewa County

—775 45 Eau Claire County

—775 47 Pepin County

—775 48 Buffalo County

—775 49 Trempealeau County

—775 5 Central counties of Wisconsin

—775 51 Jackson County

—775 52 Wood County

—775 53 Portage County

—775 54 Monroe County

—775 55 Juneau County

—775 56 Adams County

—775 57 Waushara County

—775 58 Marquette County

—775 59 Green Lake County

—775 6 East central counties of Wisconsin

Class here *Fox River

*For a specific part of this jurisdiction, region, or feature, see the part and follow instructions under —4–9

—775 61 Brown County

Including Green Bay (city)

See also —77563 for Green Bay (physiographic feature)

—775 62 Kewaunee County

—775 63 Door County

Class here *Green Bay (physiographic feature)

See also —77561 for Green Bay (city)

—775 64 Winnebago County

Class here *Lake Winnebago

—775 66 Calumet County

—775 67 Manitowoc County

—775 68 Fond du Lac County

—775 69 Sheboygan County

—775 7 Southwestern counties of Wisconsin

—775 71 La Crosse County

—775 73 Vernon County

—775 74 Crawford County

—775 75 Richland County

—775 76 Sauk County

—775 77 Grant County

—775 78 Iowa County

—775 79 Lafayette County

—775 8 South central counties of Wisconsin

—775 81 Columbia County

—775 82 Dodge County

—775 83 Dane County

Class here Madison

—775 85 Jefferson County

—775 86 Green County

—775 87 Rock County

—775 89 Walworth County

*For a specific part of this jurisdiction, region, or feature, see the part and follow instructions under —4–9

—775 9 Southeastern counties of Wisconsin

—775 91 Washington County

—775 92 Ozaukee County

—775 93 Waukesha County

—775 94 Milwaukee County

For Milwaukee, see —77595

—775 95 Milwaukee

—775 96 Racine County

—775 98 Kenosha County

—776 Minnesota

—776 1 Southeastern counties of Minnesota

—776 11 Houston County

—776 12 Winona County

—776 13 Wabasha County

—776 14 Goodhue County

—776 15 Dodge and Olmsted Counties

—776 153 Dodge County

—776 155 Olmsted County

—776 16 Fillmore County

—776 17 Mower County

—776 18 Freeborn County

—776 19 Steele and Waseca Counties

—776 193 Steele County

—776 195 Waseca County

—776 2 Southwestern counties of Minnesota

—776 21 Blue Earth County

—776 22 Faribault County

—776 23 Martin and Jackson Counties

—776 232 Martin County

—776 235 Jackson County

—776 24 Nobles County

—776 25 Rock County

—776 26 Pipestone County

—776 27 Murray County

—776 28 Cottonwood County

—776 29 Watonwan County

—776 3 Southwest central counties of Minnesota

Class here *Minnesota River

—776 31 Brown County

—776 32 Nicollet County

—776 33 Sibley County

—776 34 Renville County

—776 35 Redwood County

—776 36 Lyon and Lincoln Counties

—776 363 Lyon County

—776 365 Lincoln County

—776 37 Yellow Medicine County

—776 38 Lac qui Parle County

—776 39 Chippewa County

—776 4 West central counties of Minnesota

—776 41 Swift County

—776 42 Stevens County

—776 43 Big Stone and Traverse Counties

—776 432 Big Stone County

—776 435 Traverse County

—776 44 Grant County

—776 45 Douglas County

—776 46 Pope County

—776 47 Stearns County

—776 48 Kandiyohi County

—776 49 Meeker County

—776 5 Southeast central counties of Minnesota

—776 51 Wright County

—776 52 McLeod County

*For a specific part of this jurisdiction, region, or feature, see the part and follow instructions under —4–9

—776 53 Carver County

—776 54 Scott County

—776 55 Le Sueur and Rice Counties

—776 553 Le Sueur County

—776 555 Rice County

—776 56 Dakota County

—776 57 Hennepin County

—776 579 Minneapolis

Class here Twin Cities

For Saint Paul, see —776581

—776 58 Ramsey County

—776 581 Saint Paul

Class comprehensive works on Twin Cities in —776579

—776 59 Washington County

—776 6 East central counties of Minnesota

—776 61 Chisago County

—776 62 Pine County

—776 63 Kanabec County

—776 64 Isanti County

—776 65 Anoka County

—776 66 Sherburne County

—776 67 Benton County

—776 68 Mille Lacs County

—776 69 Morrison County

—776 7 Northeastern counties of Minnesota

—776 71 Crow Wing County

—776 72 Aitkin County

—776 73 Carlton County

—776 75 Cook County

—776 76 Lake County

—776 77 Saint Louis County

Including Voyageurs National Park; *Mesabi Range

For Voyageurs National Park in Koochiching County, see —77679

—776 771 Duluth

Class here comprehensive works on Duluth and Superior, Wisconsin

For Superior, see —77511

—776 78 Itasca County

—776 79 Koochiching County

Including *Rainy River; *Rainy Lake

—776 8 North central counties of Minnesota

—776 81 Lake of the Woods County

Class here *Lake of the Woods

—776 82 Beltrami County

—776 83 Clearwater County

—776 84 Becker County

—776 85 Hubbard County

—776 86 Cass County

—776 87 Wadena County

—776 88 Todd County

—776 89 Otter Tail County

—776 9 Northwestern counties of Minnesota

Class here *Red River of the North in Minnesota

—776 91 Wilkin County

—776 92 Clay County

—776 93 Norman County

—776 94 Mahnomen County

—776 95 Polk County

—776 96 Red Lake and Pennington Counties

—776 963 Red Lake County

—776 965 Pennington County

*For a specific part of this jurisdiction, region, or feature, see the part and follow instructions under —4–9

—776 97 Marshall County

—776 98 Roseau County

—776 99 Kittson County

—777 Iowa

Class here *Des Moines River

—777 1 Northwestern counties of Iowa

Including *Big Sioux River in Iowa

—777 11 Lyon and Osceola Counties

—777 114 Lyon County

—777 116 Osceola County

—777 12 Dickinson and Emmet Counties

—777 123 Dickinson County

—777 125 Emmet County

—777 13 Sioux County

—777 14 O'Brien County

—777 15 Clay and Palo Alto Counties

—777 153 Clay County

—777 155 Palo Alto County

—777 16 Plymouth County

—777 17 Cherokee County

—777 18 Buena Vista County

—777 19 Pocahontas County

—777 2 North central counties of Iowa

—777 21 Kossuth County

—777 22 Winnebago County

—777 23 Worth and Mitchell Counties

—777 232 Worth County

—777 234 Mitchell County

—777 24 Hancock County

—777 25 Cerro Gordo County

—777 26 Floyd County

*For a specific part of this jurisdiction, region, or feature, see the part and follow instructions under —4–9

—777 27 Humboldt and Wright Counties
—777 272 Humboldt County
—777 274 Wright County
—777 28 Franklin County
—777 29 Butler County
—777 3 Northeastern counties of Iowa
—777 31 Howard and Chickasaw Counties
—777 312 Howard County
—777 315 Chickasaw County
—777 32 Winneshiek County
—777 33 Allamakee County
—777 34 Bremer County
—777 35 Fayette County
—777 36 Clayton County
—777 37 Black Hawk County
—777 38 Buchanan and Delaware Counties
—777 382 Buchanan County
—777 385 Delaware County
—777 39 Dubuque County
—777 4 West central counties of Iowa
—777 41 Woodbury County
Including Sioux City
—777 42 Ida and Sac Counties
—777 422 Ida County
—777 424 Sac County
—777 43 Calhoun County
—777 44 Monona County
—777 45 Crawford County
—777 46 Carroll and Greene Counties
—777 465 Carroll County
—777 466 Greene County
—777 47 Harrison County
—777 48 Shelby and Audubon Counties

—777 484 Shelby County

—777 486 Audubon County

—777 49 Guthrie County

—777 5 Central counties of Iowa

—777 51 Webster County

—777 52 Hamilton County

—777 53 Hardin and Grundy Counties

—777 535 Hardin County

—777 537 Grundy County

—777 54 Boone and Story Counties

—777 544 Boone County

—777 546 Story County

—777 55 Marshall County

—777 56 Tama County

—777 57 Dallas County

—777 58 Polk County

Class here Des Moines

—777 59 Jasper and Poweshiek Counties

—777 594 Jasper County

—777 596 Poweshiek County

—777 6 East central counties of Iowa

Class here *Iowa River

—777 61 Benton County

—777 62 Linn County

—777 63 Jones County

—777 64 Jackson County

—777 65 Iowa and Johnson Counties

—777 653 Iowa County

—777 655 Johnson County

—777 66 Cedar County

—777 67 Clinton County

*For a specific part of this jurisdiction, region, or feature, see the part and follow instructions under —4–9

—777 68 Muscatine County

—777 69 Scott County

Class here Davenport-Rock Island-Moline tri-city area

For Rock Island County, Illinois, see —773393

—777 7 Southwestern counties of Iowa

—777 71 Pottawattamie County

—777 72 Cass County

—777 73 Adair County

—777 74 Mills County

—777 75 Montgomery County

—777 76 Adams County

—777 77 Fremont County

—777 78 Page County

—777 79 Taylor County

—777 8 South central counties of Iowa

—777 81 Madison County

—777 82 Warren County

—777 83 Marion County

—777 84 Mahaska County

—777 85 Union and Clarke Counties

—777 853 Union County

—777 856 Clarke County

—777 86 Lucas and Monroe Counties

—777 863 Lucas County

—777 865 Monroe County

—777 87 Ringgold and Decatur Counties

—777 873 Ringgold County

—777 875 Decatur County

—777 88 Wayne County

—777 89 Appanoose County

—777 9 Southeastern counties of Iowa

—777 91 Keokuk County

—777 92 Washington and Louisa Counties

—777 923 Washington County

—777 926 Louisa County

—777 93 Wapello County

—777 94 Jefferson County

—777 95 Henry County

—777 96 Des Moines County

—777 97 Davis County

—777 98 Van Buren County

—777 99 Lee County

—778 Missouri

Class here *Missouri River in Missouri

—778 1 Northwestern counties of Missouri

—778 11 Atchison and Holt Counties

—778 113 Atchison County

—778 115 Holt County

—778 12 Nodaway and Andrew Counties

—778 124 Nodaway County

—778 126 Andrew County

—778 13 Buchanan and Platte Counties

—778 132 Buchanan County

—778 135 Platte County

—778 14 Worth and Gentry Counties

—778 143 Worth County

—778 145 Gentry County

—778 15 De Kalb and Clinton Counties

—778 153 De Kalb County

—778 155 Clinton County

—778 16 Clay County

—778 17 Harrison County

—778 18 Daviess and Caldwell Counties

—778 183 Daviess County

*For a specific part of this jurisdiction, region, or feature, see the part and follow instructions under —4–9

—778 185 Caldwell County

—778 19 Ray County

—778 2 North central counties of Missouri

Class here *Chariton, *Grand Rivers

—778 21 Mercer and Grundy Counties

—778 213 Mercer County

—778 215 Grundy County

—778 22 Livingston and Carroll Counties

—778 223 Livingston County

—778 225 Carroll County

—778 23 Putnam and Sullivan Counties

—778 232 Putnam County

—778 235 Sullivan County

—778 24 Linn County

—778 25 Chariton County

—778 26 Schuyler and Adair Counties

—778 262 Schuyler County

—778 264 Adair County

—778 27 Macon County

—778 28 Randolph and Howard Counties

—778 283 Randolph County

—778 285 Howard County

—778 29 Boone County

—778 3 Northeastern counties of Missouri

—778 31 Scotland and Knox Counties

—778 312 Scotland County

—778 315 Knox County

—778 32 Shelby and Monroe Counties

—778 323 Shelby County

—778 325 Monroe County

—778 33 Audrain and Callaway Counties

*For a specific part of this jurisdiction, region, or feature, see the part and follow instructions under —4–9

—778 332 Audrain County

—778 335 Callaway County

—778 34 Clark and Lewis Counties

—778 343 Clark County

—778 345 Lewis County

—778 35 Marion and Ralls Counties

—778 353 Marion County

—778 355 Ralls County

—778 36 Pike County

—778 37 Lincoln County

—778 38 Montgomery and Warren Counties

—778 382 Montgomery County

—778 386 Warren County

—778 39 Saint Charles County

—778 4 West central counties of Missouri

—778 41 Jackson County

—778 411 Kansas City

Class here Greater Kansas City

For Wyandotte County, Kansas, see —78139

—778 42 Cass County

—778 43 Bates County

—778 44 Vernon County

—778 45 Lafayette and Johnson Counties

—778 453 Lafayette County

—778 455 Johnson County

—778 46 Henry and Saint Clair Counties

—778 462 Henry County

—778 466 Saint Clair County

—778 47 Saline County

—778 48 Pettis County

—778 49 Benton and Hickory Counties

—778 493 Benton County

Class here *Lake of the Ozarks

*For a specific part of this jurisdiction, region, or feature, see the part and follow instructions under —4–9

—778 496 Hickory County

—778 5 Central counties of Missouri

—778 51 Cooper County

—778 52 Moniteau County

—778 53 Morgan County

—778 54 Camden County

—778 55 Cole County

Including Jefferson City

—778 56 Miller County

—778 57 Pulaski County

—778 58 Osage County

—778 59 Maries and Phelps Counties

—778 592 Maries County

—778 594 Phelps County

—778 6 East central counties of Missouri

—778 61 Gasconade County

—778 62 Crawford County

—778 63 Franklin County

—778 64 Washington County

—778 65 Saint Louis County

—778 66 Independent city of Saint Louis

—778 67 Jefferson County

—778 68 Saint Francois County

—778 69 Sainte Genevieve and Perry Counties

—778 692 Sainte Genevieve County

—778 694 Perry County

—778 7 Southwestern counties of Missouri

—778 71 Barton County

—778 72 Jasper County

—778 73 Newton and McDonald Counties

—778 732 Newton County

—778 736 McDonald County

—778 74 Cedar and Dade Counties

—778 743 Cedar County

—778 745 Dade County

—778 75 Lawrence County

—778 76 Barry County

—778 77 Polk County

—778 78 Greene County

—778 79 Christian, Stone, Taney Counties

—778 792 Christian County

—778 794 Stone County

—778 797 Taney County

—778 8 South central counties of Missouri

Class here *Ozark Plateau in Missouri

—778 81 Dallas and Laclede Counties

—778 813 Dallas County

—778 815 Laclede County

—778 82 Webster and Wright Counties

—778 823 Webster County

—778 825 Wright County

—778 83 Douglas and Ozark Counties

—778 832 Douglas County

—778 835 Ozark County

—778 84 Texas County

—778 85 Howell County

—778 86 Dent County

—778 87 Shannon and Oregon Counties

—778 873 Shannon County

—778 875 Oregon County

—778 88 Iron and Reynolds Counties

—778 883 Iron County

—778 885 Reynolds County

—778 89 Carter and Ripley Counties

*For a specific part of this jurisdiction, region, or feature, see the part and follow instructions under —4–9

—778 892 Carter County

—778 894 Ripley County

—778 9 Southeastern counties of Missouri

—778 91 Madison County

—778 92 Wayne County

—778 93 Butler County

—778 94 Bollinger County

—778 95 Stoddard County

—778 96 Cape Girardeau County

—778 97 Scott County

—778 98 Mississippi and New Madrid Counties

—778 983 Mississippi County

—778 985 New Madrid County

—778 99 Dunklin and Pemiscot Counties

—778 993 Dunklin County

—778 996 Pemiscot County

—78 Western United States

Class here the West; *Great Plains; *Rocky Mountains; *Missouri River

For Great Basin and Pacific Slope region, see —79

SUMMARY

— 781	**Kansas**
— 782	**Nebraska**
— 783	**South Dakota**
— 784	**North Dakota**
— 786	**Montana**
— 787	**Wyoming**
— 788	**Colorado**
— 789	**New Mexico**

—781 Kansas

Class here *Arkansas River in Kansas

—781 1 Northwestern counties of Kansas

—781 11 Cheyenne and Sherman Counties

—781 112 Cheyenne County

—781 115 Sherman County

*For a specific part of this jurisdiction, region, or feature, see the part and follow instructions under —4–9

—781 12 Wallace and Rawlins Counties

—781 123 Wallace County

—781 125 Rawlins County

—781 13 Thomas and Logan Counties

—781 132 Thomas County

—781 135 Logan County

—781 14 Decatur and Sheridan Counties

—781 143 Decatur County

—781 145 Sheridan County

—781 15 Gove and Norton Counties

—781 152 Gove County

—781 155 Norton County

—781 16 Graham and Trego Counties

—781 163 Graham County

—781 165 Trego County

—781 17 Phillips County

—781 18 Rooks County

—781 19 Ellis County

—781 2 North central counties of Kansas

Class here *Republican, *Solomon Rivers

—781 21 Smith and Osborne Counties

—781 213 Smith County

—781 215 Osborne County

—781 22 Jewell County

—781 23 Mitchell County

—781 24 Republic County

—781 25 Cloud County

—781 26 Ottawa County

—781 27 Washington and Clay Counties

—781 273 Washington County

—781 275 Clay County

*For a specific part of this jurisdiction, region, or feature, see the part and follow instructions under —4–9

—781 28	Riley County
—781 29	Geary County
—781 3	Northeastern counties of Kansas
	Class here *Kansas (Kaw) River
—781 31	Marshall County
—781 32	Pottawatomie County
—781 33	Nemaha and Jackson Counties
—781 332	Nemaha County
—781 335	Jackson County
—781 34	Brown County
—781 35	Doniphan County
—781 36	Atchison County
—781 37	Jefferson County
—781 38	Leavenworth County
—781 39	Wyandotte County
	Class here Kansas City
	Class comprehensive works on Greater Kansas City in —778411
—781 4	West central counties of Kansas
—781 41	Greeley and Hamilton Counties
—781 413	Greeley County
—781 415	Hamilton County
—781 42	Wichita and Kearny Counties
—781 423	Wichita County
—781 425	Kearny County
—781 43	Scott County
—781 44	Finney County
—781 45	Lane County
—781 46	Ness County
—781 47	Hodgeman County
—781 48	Rush County
—781 49	Pawnee County

*For a specific part of this jurisdiction, region, or feature, see the part and follow instructions under —4–9

—781 5 Central counties of Kansas

—781 51 Russell County

—781 52 Barton County

—781 53 Lincoln and Ellsworth Counties

—781 532 Lincoln County

—781 535 Ellsworth County

—781 54 Rice and Saline Counties

—781 543 Rice County

—781 545 Saline County

—781 55 McPherson County

—781 56 Dickinson County

—781 57 Marion County

—781 58 Morris County

—781 59 Chase County

—781 6 East central counties of Kansas

—781 61 Wabaunsee County

—781 62 Lyon County

—781 63 Shawnee County

Class here Topeka

—781 64 Osage and Coffey Counties

—781 643 Osage County

—781 645 Coffey County

—781 65 Douglas County

—781 66 Franklin County

—781 67 Anderson and Johnson Counties

—781 672 Anderson County

—781 675 Johnson County

—781 68 Miami County

—781 69 Linn County

—781 7 Southwestern counties of Kansas

—781 71 Stanton and Morton Counties

—781 712 Stanton County

—781 715 Morton County

—781 72	Grant and Stevens Counties
—781 723	Grant County
—781 725	Stevens County
—781 73	Haskell and Seward Counties
—781 732	Haskell County
—781 735	Seward County
—781 74	Gray County
—781 75	Meade County
—781 76	Ford County
—781 77	Clark County
—781 78	Edwards and Kiowa Counties
—781 782	Edwards County
—781 785	Kiowa County
—781 79	Comanche County
—781 8	South central counties of Kansas
—781 81	Stafford and Pratt Counties
—781 813	Stafford County
—781 815	Pratt County
—781 82	Barber County
—781 83	Reno County
—781 84	Kingman and Harper Counties
—781 843	Kingman County
—781 845	Harper County
—781 85	Harvey County
—781 86	Sedgwick County Class here Wichita
—781 87	Sumner County
—781 88	Butler County
—781 89	Cowley County
—781 9	Southeastern counties of Kansas
—781 91	Greenwood, Elk, Chautauqua Counties
—781 913	Greenwood County
—781 915	Elk County

—781 918 Chautauqua County

—781 92 Woodson and Wilson Counties

—781 923 Woodson County

—781 925 Wilson County

—781 93 Montgomery County

—781 94 Allen County

—781 95 Neosho County

—781 96 Labette County

—781 97 Bourbon County

—781 98 Crawford County

—781 99 Cherokee County

—782 Nebraska

Class here *Platte River

—782 2 Missouri River lowland counties

—782 22 Dixon, Dakota, Thurston Counties

—782 223 Dixon County

—782 224 Dakota County

—782 227 Thurston County

—782 23 Cuming and Dodge Counties

—782 232 Cuming County

—782 235 Dodge County

—782 24 Burt and Washington Counties

—782 243 Burt County

—782 245 Washington County

—782 25 Douglas and Sarpy Counties

—782 254 Douglas County

Class here Omaha

—782 256 Sarpy County

—782 27 Cass and neighboring counties

—782 272 Cass County

—782 273 Otoe County

*For a specific part of this jurisdiction, region, or feature, see the part and follow instructions under —4–9

—782 276 Johnson County

—782 278 Nemaha County

—782 28 Richardson, Pawnee, Gage Counties

—782 282 Richardson County

—782 284 Pawnee County

—782 286 Gage County

—782 29 Lancaster and Saunders Counties

—782 293 Lancaster County

Class here Lincoln

—782 296 Saunders County

—782 3 South central counties of Nebraska

—782 32 Butler, Seward, Saline Counties

—782 322 Butler County

—782 324 Seward County

—782 327 Saline County

—782 33 Jefferson and Thayer Counties

—782 332 Jefferson County

—782 335 Thayer County

—782 34 Fillmore and York Counties

—782 342 Fillmore County

—782 345 York County

—782 35 Polk, Hamilton, Clay Counties

—782 352 Polk County

—782 354 Hamilton County

—782 357 Clay County

—782 37 Nuckolls, Webster, Franklin Counties

Class here *Republican River in Nebraska

—782 372 Nuckolls County

—782 374 Webster County

—782 377 Franklin County

—782 38 Harlan, Furnas, Gosper Counties

*For a specific part of this jurisdiction, region, or feature, see the part and follow instructions under —4–9

—782 382 Harlan County
—782 384 Furnas County
—782 387 Gosper County
—782 39 Phelps, Kearney, Adams Counties
—782 392 Phelps County
—782 394 Kearney County
—782 397 Adams County
—782 4 Central counties of Nebraska
—782 41 Hall County
—782 42 Merrick and Nance Counties
—782 423 Merrick County
—782 425 Nance County
—782 43 Howard County
—782 44 Sherman County
—782 45 Buffalo County
—782 46 Dawson County
—782 47 Custer County
—782 48 Valley County
—782 49 Greeley County
—782 5 Northeast central counties of Nebraska
—782 51 Boone County
—782 52 Platte County
—782 53 Colfax and Stanton Counties
—782 532 Colfax County
—782 535 Stanton County
—782 54 Madison County
—782 55 Antelope County
—782 56 Pierce County
—782 57 Wayne County
—782 58 Cedar County
—782 59 Knox County

—782 7 North central counties of Nebraska

Class here *Niobrara River

—782 72 Boyd and Keya Paha Counties

—782 723 Boyd County

—782 725 Keya Paha County

—782 73 Cherry and Brown Counties

—782 732 Cherry County

—782 736 Brown County

—782 74 Rock and Holt Counties

—782 743 Rock County

—782 745 Holt County

—782 76 Wheeler, Garfield, Loup Counties

—782 762 Wheeler County

—782 764 Garfield County

—782 767 Loup County

—782 77 Blaine, Thomas, Hooker Counties

—782 772 Blaine County

—782 774 Thomas County

—782 777 Hooker County

—782 78 Grant and Arthur Counties

—782 783 Grant County

—782 785 Arthur County

—782 79 McPherson and Logan Counties

—782 793 McPherson County

—782 795 Logan County

—782 8 Southwestern counties of Nebraska

—782 82 Lincoln County

—782 83 Hayes and Frontier Counties

—782 832 Hayes County

—782 835 Frontier County

—782 84 Red Willow and Hitchcock Counties

*For a specific part of this jurisdiction, region, or feature, see the part and follow instructions under —4–9

—782 843	Red Willow County
—782 845	Hitchcock County
—782 86	Dundy County
—782 87	Chase County
—782 88	Perkins County
—782 89	Keith County
—782 9	Panhandle counties
—782 91	Deuel and Garden Counties
—782 913	Deuel County
—782 915	Garden County
—782 92	Sheridan County
—782 93	Dawes County
—782 94	Box Butte County
—782 95	Morrill County
—782 96	Cheyenne County
—782 97	Kimball and Banner Counties
—782 973	Kimball County
—782 975	Banner County
—782 98	Scotts Bluff County
—782 99	Sioux County
—783	South Dakota
—783 1	Northeastern counties of South Dakota
—783 12	Roberts County
—783 13	Marshall County
—783 14	Day and Brown Counties
—783 142	Day County
—783 144	Brown County
—783 15	Edmunds County
—783 16	McPherson County
—783 17	Campbell County
—783 18	Walworth County
—783 19	Potter County
—783 2	East central counties of South Dakota

—783 21 Faulk and Spink Counties

—783 213 Faulk County

—783 217 Spink County

—783 22 Clark County

—783 23 Codington County

—783 24 Grant County

—783 25 Deuel County

—783 26 Hamlin County

—783 27 Brookings, Kingsbury, Beadle Counties

—783 272 Brookings County

—783 273 Kingsbury County

—783 274 Beadle County

—783 28 Hand, Hyde, Sully Counties

—783 282 Hand County

—783 283 Hyde County

—783 284 Sully County

—783 29 Hughes County

Including Pierre

—783 3 Southeastern counties of South Dakota

Class here *Missouri River in South Dakota, *James River

—783 31 Buffalo County

—783 32 Jerauld County

—783 33 Sanborn County

—783 34 Miner County

—783 35 Lake County

—783 36 Moody County

—783 37 Minnehaha and neighboring counties

—783 371 Minnehaha County

Including Sioux Falls

—783 372 McCook County

—783 373 Hanson County

*For a specific part of this jurisdiction, region, or feature, see the part and follow instructions under —4–9

—783 374 Davison County

—783 375 Aurora County

—783 38 Brule and neighboring counties

Class here *Lake Francis Case

—783 381 Brule County

—783 382 Charles Mix County

—783 383 Douglas County

—783 384 Hutchinson County

—783 385 Turner County

—783 39 Lincoln and neighboring counties

Class here *Big Sioux River

—783 391 Lincoln County

—783 392 Union County

—783 393 Clay County

—783 394 Yankton County

—783 395 Bon Homme County

—783 4 Northwestern counties of South Dakota

—783 42 Harding County

—783 43 Butte County

—783 44 Meade County

—783 45 Perkins County

—783 5 Central counties of South Dakota

Class here *Lake Oahe

—783 52 Corson County

—783 53 Ziebach County

—783 54 Dewey County

—783 55 Stanley County

—783 56 Haakon County

—783 57 Jackson and Jones Counties

—783 572 Jackson County

—783 577 Jones County

*For a specific part of this jurisdiction, region, or feature, see the part and follow instructions under —4–9

—783 58 Lyman County

—783 59 Gregory County

—783 6 South central counties of South Dakota

—783 61 Tripp County

—783 62 Todd County

—783 63 Mellette County

—783 64 Washabaugh County

—783 65 Bennett County

—783 66 Shannon County

—783 9 Southwestern counties of South Dakota

Class here *Black Hills

—783 91 Lawrence County

—783 93 Pennington County

Including Badlands National Park

For Badlands National Park in Jackson County, see —783572; for Badlands National Park in Shannon County, see —78366

—783 95 Custer County

Including Wind Cave National Park

—783 97 Fall River County

—784 North Dakota

—784 1 Red River Valley counties

Class here *Red River of the North

—784 12 Richland County

—784 13 Cass County

Including Fargo

—784 14 Traill County

—784 16 Grand Forks County

—784 18 Walsh County

—784 19 Pembina County

—784 3 Sheyenne River Valley and adjacent counties

Class here *Sheyenne River

*For a specific part of this jurisdiction, region, or feature, see the part and follow instructions under —4–9

—784 31 Sargent and Ransom Counties

—784 314 Sargent County

—784 315 Ransom County

—784 32 Barnes County

—784 33 Steele County

—784 34 Griggs County

—784 35 Nelson County

—784 36 Ramsey County

—784 37 Cavalier County

—784 38 Towner County

—784 39 Benson County

—784 5 James River Valley and adjacent counties

Class here *James River in North Dakota

—784 51 Eddy and Foster Counties

—784 512 Eddy County

—784 516 Foster County

—784 52 Stutsman County

—784 53 La Moure County

—784 54 Dickey County

—784 55 McIntosh County

—784 56 Logan County

—784 57 Kidder County

—784 58 Wells County

—784 59 Pierce and Rolette Counties

—784 591 Pierce County

—784 592 Rolette County

—784 6 Souris River Valley counties

Class here *Souris River

—784 61 Bottineau County

—784 62 McHenry County

—784 63 Ward County

*For a specific part of this jurisdiction, region, or feature, see the part and follow instructions under —4–9

—784 64 Renville County

—784 7 Counties of North Dakota north and east of Missouri River

Class here *Missouri River in North Dakota

—784 71 Divide County

—784 72 Burke County

—784 73 Williams County

—784 74 Mountrail County

—784 75 McLean County

Class here *Lake Sakakawea (Garrison Reservoir)

—784 76 Sheridan County

—784 77 Burleigh County

Including Bismarck

—784 78 Emmons County

—784 8 Counties of North Dakota south and west of Missouri River

For Badlands counties, see —7849

—784 81 McKenzie County

—784 82 Dunn County

—784 83 Mercer County

—784 84 Oliver and Stark Counties

—784 843 Oliver County

—784 844 Stark County

—784 85 Morton County

—784 86 Hettinger County

—784 87 Grant County

—784 88 Sioux County

—784 89 Adams County

—784 9 Badlands counties

—784 92 Bowman County

—784 93 Slope County

—784 94 Billings County

—784 95 Golden Valley County

*For a specific part of this jurisdiction, region, or feature, see the part and follow instructions under —4–9

> —786–789 Rocky Mountains states

Class comprehensive works in —78

For Idaho, see —796

—786 Montana

Class here *Missouri River in Montana

—786 1 North central counties of Montana

Class here *Great Plains in Montana; *Milk River

—786 12 Toole County

—786 13 Liberty County

—786 14 Hill County

—786 15 Blaine County

—786 16 Phillips County

—786 17 Valley County

Class here *Fort Peck Lake

—786 2 Northeastern and central plains counties of Montana

—786 21 Daniels and Sheridan Counties

—786 213 Daniels County

—786 218 Sheridan County

—786 22 Roosevelt County

—786 23 Richland County

—786 24 Dawson County

—786 25 Prairie County

—786 26 McCone County

—786 27 Garfield County

—786 28 Petroleum County

—786 29 Fergus and Chouteau Counties

—786 292 Fergus County

—786 293 Chouteau County

*For a specific part of this jurisdiction, region, or feature, see the part and follow instructions under —4–9

—786 3 Southeastern counties of Montana

Class here *Yellowstone River

—786 31 Golden Valley, Musselshell, Treasure Counties

—786 311 Golden Valley County

—786 312 Musselshell County

—786 313 Treasure County

—786 32 Rosebud County

—786 33 Custer County

—786 34 Wibaux County

—786 35 Fallon County

—786 36 Carter County

—786 37 Powder River County

—786 38 Big Horn County

—786 39 Yellowstone County

—786 5 Northwest central counties of Montana

Class here *Rocky Mountains in Montana

—786 52 Glacier County

Including *Glacier National Park, *Waterton-Glacier International Peace Park

—786 53 Pondera County

—786 55 Teton County

—786 6 Southwestern and central mountain counties of Montana

—786 61 Cascade, Meagher, Lewis and Clark Counties

—786 611 Cascade County

—786 612 Meagher County

—786 615 Lewis and Clark County

Including Helena

—786 62 Judith Basin County

—786 63 Wheatland County

—786 64 Sweet Grass County

—786 65 Stillwater and Carbon Counties

*For a specific part of this jurisdiction, region, or feature, see the part and follow instructions under —4–9

—786 651 Stillwater County

—786 652 Carbon County

—786 66 Park and neighboring counties

—786 661 Park County

Including Yellowstone National Park in Montana

For Yellowstone National Park in Gallatin County, see —786662

—786 662 Gallatin County

—786 663 Madison County

—786 664 Broadwater County

—786 67 Jefferson County

—786 68 Silver Bow County

Including Butte

—786 69 Beaverhead County

—786 8 Northwestern counties of Montana

Class here *Bitterroot Range

—786 81 Lincoln County

—786 82 Flathead County

—786 83 Lake and Sanders Counties

—786 832 Lake County

Class here *Flathead Lake

—786 833 Sanders County

—786 84 Mineral County

—786 85 Missoula County

—786 86 Powell County

—786 87 Deer Lodge County

—786 88 Granite County

—786 89 Ravalli County

—787 Wyoming

—787 1 Eastern counties of Wyoming

Class here *Great Plains in Wyoming

*For a specific part of this jurisdiction, region, or feature, see the part and follow instructions under —4–9

—787 12 Campbell County

—787 13 Crook County

—787 14 Weston County

—787 15 Niobrara County

—787 16 Converse County

Class here *North Platte River

—787 17 Platte County

—787 18 Goshen County

—787 19 Laramie County

Including Cheyenne

—787 2 *Rocky Mountains in Wyoming

—787 3 *Big Horn Mountains counties

—787 32 Sheridan County

—787 33 Big Horn County

—787 34 Washakie County

—787 35 Johnson County

—787 4 *Absaroka Range counties

—787 42 Park County

—787 43 Hot Springs County

Including *Owl Creek Mountains

—787 5 Yellowstone National Park and Teton County

—787 52 *Yellowstone National Park

—787 55 Teton County

Including Grand Teton National Park; *Teton Range

Class here *Snake River in Wyoming

—787 6 *Wind River Range counties

—787 63 Fremont County

—787 65 Sublette County

—787 8 Southwestern counties of Wyoming

—787 82 Lincoln County

—787 84 Uinta County

*For a specific part of this jurisdiction, region, or feature, see the part and follow instructions under —4–9

—787 85 Sweetwater County

Including *Green River in Wyoming

—787 86 Carbon County

Class here *Medicine Bow Range

—787 9 *Laramie Mountains counties

—787 93 Natrona County

—787 95 Albany County

—788 Colorado

Class here *Rocky Mountains in Colorado

—788 1 Northern Colorado Plateau counties

Class here *Colorado Plateau

—788 12 Moffat County

Class here Dinosaur National Monument

For Dinosaur National Monument in Uintah County, Utah, see —79221

—788 14 Routt County

—788 15 Rio Blanco County

—788 16 Garfield County

—788 17 Mesa County

Class here *Colorado River in Colorado

—788 18 Delta County

—788 19 Montrose County

Including Black Canyon of the Gunnison National Park

—788 2 Southern Colorado Plateau counties

—788 22 Ouray County

—788 23 San Miguel County

—788 25 San Juan County

—788 26 Dolores County

—788 27 Montezuma County

Including Mesa Verde National Park

—788 29 La Plata County

*For a specific part of this jurisdiction, region, or feature, see the part and follow instructions under —4–9

—788 3 Southern Rocky Mountains counties

Class here *San Juan Mountains; *San Luis Valley; *Rio Grande in Colorado

—788 32 Archuleta County

—788 33 Conejos County

—788 35 Costilla County

—788 36 Alamosa County

—788 37 Rio Grande County

—788 38 Mineral County

—788 39 Hinsdale County

—788 4 West central Rocky Mountains counties

—788 41 Gunnison County

—788 43 Pitkin County

—788 44 Eagle County

—788 45 Summit County

—788 46 Lake County

—788 47 Chaffee County

—788 49 Saguache County

Including Great Sand Dunes National Park; *Sangre de Cristo Mountains

For Great Sand Dunes National Park in Alamosa County, see —78836

—788 5 East central Rocky Mountains counties

—788 51 Huerfano County

—788 52 Custer County

—788 53 Fremont County

—788 55 Pueblo County

—788 56 El Paso County

Class here Colorado Springs

—788 58 Teller County

—788 59 Park County

*For a specific part of this jurisdiction, region, or feature, see the part and follow instructions under —4–9

—788 6 Northern Rocky Mountains counties

Class here *Front Range

—788 61 Clear Creek County

—788 62 Gilpin County

—788 63 Boulder County

Northwestern Broomfield County, formerly part of Boulder County, relocated to —78864

—788 64 Broomfield County

Including northwestern Broomfield County [*formerly* —78863]; northeastern Broomfield County [*formerly* —78872]; southeastern Broomfield County [*formerly* —78881]; southwestern Broomfield County [*formerly* —78884]

—788 65 Grand County

—788 66 Jackson County

Class here *Park Range

—788 68 Larimer County

—788 69 *Rocky Mountain National Park

—788 7 Northern Great Plains counties

Class here *Great Plains in Colorado; *South Platte River

—788 72 Weld County

Northeastern Broomfield County, formerly part of Weld County, relocated to —78864

—788 74 Morgan County

—788 75 Logan County

—788 76 Sedgwick County

—788 77 Phillips County

—788 78 Yuma County

—788 79 Washington County

—788 8 Central Great Plains counties

—788 81 Adams County

Southeastern Broomfield County, formerly part of Adams County, relocated to —78864

—788 82 Arapahoe County

—788 83 Denver County (Denver)

*For a specific part of this jurisdiction, region, or feature, see the part and follow instructions under —4–9

—788 84 Jefferson County

Southwestern Broomfield County, formerly part of Jefferson County, relocated to —78864

—788 86 Douglas County

—788 87 Elbert County

—788 89 Lincoln County

—788 9 Southern Great Plains counties

Class here *Arkansas River in Colorado

—788 91 Kit Carson County

—788 92 Cheyenne County

—788 93 Kiowa County

—788 94 Crowley County

—788 95 Otero County

—788 96 Las Animas County

—788 97 Bent County

—788 98 Prowers County

—788 99 Baca County

—789 New Mexico

—789 2 Northeastern counties of New Mexico

Class here *Great Plains in New Mexico

—789 22 Colfax County

—789 23 Union County

—789 24 Harding County

—789 25 Guadalupe County

—789 26 Quay County

—789 27 Curry County

—789 3 Roosevelt and Lea Counties

Class here *Llano Estacado in New Mexico

—789 32 Roosevelt County

—789 33 Lea County

*For a specific part of this jurisdiction, region, or feature, see the part and follow instructions under —4–9

—789 4 Pecos Valley counties

Class here *Pecos River in New Mexico

—789 42 Eddy County

Including Carlsbad Caverns National Park

—789 43 Chaves County

—789 44 De Baca County

—789 5 *Rocky Mountains counties

—789 52 Rio Arriba County

—789 53 Taos County

—789 54 Mora County

—789 55 San Miguel County

—789 56 Santa Fe County

Class here Santa Fe

—789 57 Sandoval County

—789 58 Los Alamos County

—789 6 Basin and Range region counties

Class here *Rio Grande in New Mexico

—789 61 Bernalillo County

Class here Albuquerque

—789 62 Socorro County

Including *Elephant Butte Reservoir

—789 63 Torrance County

—789 64 Lincoln County

—789 65 Otero County

Including White Sands National Monument; *Sacramento Mountains

For White Sands National Monument in Doña Ana County, see —78966

—789 66 Doña Ana County

—789 67 Sierra County

Class here *San Andres Mountains

—789 68 Luna County

*For a specific part of this jurisdiction, region, or feature, see the part and follow instructions under —4–9

—789 69 Grant and Hidalgo Counties

—789 692 Grant County

—789 693 Hidalgo County

Class here *Peloncillo Mountains

—789 8 Northwestern counties of New Mexico

—789 82 San Juan County

—789 83 McKinley County

—789 9 West central counties of New Mexico

—789 91 Cibola County

—789 92 Valencia County

—789 93 Catron County

—79 Great Basin and Pacific Slope of United States Pacific Coast states

Class here new Southwest

SUMMARY

—791	**Arizona**
—792	**Utah**
—793	**Nevada**
—794	**California**
—795	**Oregon**
—796	**Idaho**
—797	**Washington**
—798	**Alaska**

—791 Arizona

—791 3 Colorado Plateau region

Class here *Colorado River

—791 32 *Grand Canyon National Park

—791 33 Coconino County

Class here *Painted Desert; *Little Colorado River

—791 35 Navajo County

—791 37 Apache County

Including Petrified Forest National Park

For Petrified Forest National Park in Navajo County, see —79135

—791 5 Mountain region of Arizona

*For a specific part of this jurisdiction, region, or feature, see the part and follow instructions under —4–9

—791 51 Greenlee County

—791 53 Cochise County

—791 54 Graham County

—791 55 Gila County

—791 57 Yavapai County

—791 59 Mohave County

—791 7 Plains region of Arizona

Class here *Sonoran Desert in United States, *Gila River

—791 71 Yuma County

—791 72 La Paz County

—791 73 Maricopa County

Class here Phoenix

—791 75 Pinal County

—791 77 Pima County

—791 776 Tucson

—791 79 Santa Cruz County

—792 Utah

—792 1 Wyoming Basin region

—792 12 Cache County

—792 13 Rich County

—792 14 Summit County

Including *Uinta Mountains

—792 15 Daggett County

—792 2 Rocky Mountains region

Class here *Wasatch Range

—792 21 Uintah County

—792 22 Duchesne County

—792 23 Wasatch County

—792 24 Utah County

—792 25 Salt Lake County

—792 258 Salt Lake City

*For a specific part of this jurisdiction, region, or feature, see the part and follow instructions under —4–9

—792 26 Morgan County

—792 27 Davis County

—792 28 Weber County

—792 4 Great Basin region

—792 42 Box Elder County

Class here *Great Salt Lake

—792 43 Tooele County

Class here *Great Salt Lake Desert

—792 44 Juab County

—792 45 Millard County

—792 46 Beaver County

—792 47 Iron County

—792 48 Washington County

Class here Zion National Park

For Zion National Park in Iron County, see —79247; for Zion National Park in Kane County, see —79251

—792 5 Colorado Plateau region

Class here *Colorado River in Utah, *Green River

—792 51 Kane County

Including Grand Staircase-Escalante National Monument

For Grand Staircase-Escalante National Monument in Garfield County, see —79252

—792 52 Garfield County

Including Bryce Canyon National Park

For Bryce Canyon National Park in Kane County, see —79251

—792 53 Piute County

—792 54 Wayne County

Including *Capitol Reef National Park

—792 55 Sevier County

—792 56 Sanpete and Carbon Counties

—792 563 Sanpete County

—792 566 Carbon County

*For a specific part of this jurisdiction, region, or feature, see the part and follow instructions under —4–9

—792 57 Emery County

—792 58 Grand County

Including Arches National Park

—792 59 San Juan County

Including Canyonlands National Park; *Glen Canyon National Recreation Area; *San Juan River; *Lake Powell

Class here *Four Corners Region

For Canyonlands National Park in Wayne County, see —79254

—793 Nevada

—793 1 Eastern region of Nevada

—793 12 *Lake Mead National Recreation Area

—793 13 Clark County

—793 135 Las Vegas

—793 14 Lincoln County

—793 15 White Pine County

Including Great Basin National Park

—793 16 Elko County

Class here *Humboldt River

—793 3 Central region of Nevada

—793 32 Eureka County

—793 33 Lander County

—793 34 Nye County

—793 35 Esmeralda County

—793 5 Western region of Nevada

—793 51 Mineral County

—793 52 Churchill County

—793 53 Pershing County

—793 54 Humboldt County

Including *Black Rock Desert

—793 55 Washoe County

Including Reno

*For a specific part of this jurisdiction, region, or feature, see the part and follow instructions under —4–9

—793 56 Storey County

Including Virginia City

—793 57 Carson City

Including *Lake Tahoe in Nevada

—793 58 Lyon County

—793 59 Douglas County

—794 California

—794 1 Northwestern counties of California

Class here *Coast Ranges in California

—794 11 Del Norte County

—794 12 Humboldt County

Including Redwood National Park

For Redwood National Park in Del Norte County, see —79411

—794 14 Trinity County

—794 15 Mendocino County

—794 17 Lake County

—794 18 Sonoma County

—794 19 Napa County

—794 2 Northeastern counties of California

Class here *Cascade Range in California

—794 21 Siskiyou County

Including Lava Beds National Monument

Class here *Klamath Mountains in California

For Lava Beds National Monument in Modoc County, see —79423

—794 23 Modoc County

—794 24 Shasta County

Including *Lassen Volcanic National Park

—794 26 Lassen County

—794 27 Tehama County

—794 29 Plumas County

*For a specific part of this jurisdiction, region, or feature, see the part and follow instructions under —4–9

—794 3 North central counties of California

—794 31 Glenn County

—794 32 Butte County

—794 33 Colusa County

—794 34 Sutter County

—794 35 Yuba County

—794 36 Sierra County

—794 37 Nevada County

—794 38 Placer County

Including *Lake Tahoe

—794 4 East central counties of California

Class here *Sierra Nevada

—794 41 El Dorado County

—794 42 Amador County

—794 43 Alpine County

—794 44 Calaveras County

—794 45 Tuolumne County

—794 46 Mariposa County

—794 47 *Yosemite National Park

—794 48 Mono County

—794 5 Central counties of California

Class here *Central Valley (Great Valley); *Sacramento River

—794 51 Yolo County

—794 52 Solano County

—794 53 Sacramento County

For Sacramento, see —79454

—794 54 Sacramento

—794 55 San Joaquin County

—794 57 Stanislaus County

—794 58 Merced County

*For a specific part of this jurisdiction, region, or feature, see the part and follow instructions under —4–9

—794 6 West central counties of California

Class here *San Francisco Bay Area

See also —16432 for San Francisco Bay

—794 61 San Francisco County (San Francisco)

—794 62 Marin County

—794 63 Contra Costa County

—794 65 Alameda County

For Oakland, see —79466; for Berkeley, see —79467

—794 66 Oakland

—794 67 Berkeley

—794 69 San Mateo County

—794 7 Southern Coast Range counties

—794 71 Santa Cruz County

—794 73 Santa Clara County

For San Jose, see —79474

—794 74 San Jose

—794 75 San Benito County

—794 76 Monterey County

Class here *Salinas River

See also —16432 for Monterey Bay

—794 78 San Luis Obispo County

Class here *Santa Lucia Range

—794 8 South central counties of California

Class here *San Joaquin River

—794 81 Madera County

—794 82 Fresno County

Including Kings Canyon National Park

For Fresno, see —79483; for Kings Canyon National Park in Tulare County, see —79486

—794 83 Fresno

—794 85 Kings County

*For a specific part of this jurisdiction, region, or feature, see the part and follow instructions under —4–9

—794 86 Tulare County

Including Sequoia National Park; *Mount Whitney

—794 87 Inyo County

Class here *Death Valley National Park

—794 88 Kern County

—794 9 Southern California

—794 91 Santa Barbara County

Including Channel Islands National Park; *Santa Barbara Islands

For Anacapa Island, see —79492

—794 92 Ventura County

—794 93 Los Angeles County

Including Pasadena; *San Gabriel Mountains

For Los Angeles, see —79494

—794 94 Los Angeles

—794 95 San Bernardino County

Including *San Bernardino Mountains

Class here *Mojave Desert

—794 96 Orange County

Including *Santa Ana Mountains

—794 97 Riverside County

Including Joshua Tree National Park

For Joshua Tree National Park in San Bernardino County, see —79495

—794 98 San Diego County

—794 985 San Diego

—794 99 Imperial County

Including *Salton Sea

Class here *Imperial Valley; *Colorado Desert

—795 Oregon

Class here Pacific Northwest; *Cascade Range

For British Columbia, see —711; for Idaho, see —796; for Washington, see —797

*For a specific part of this jurisdiction, region, or feature, see the part and follow instructions under —4–9

—795 1 *Western Oregon

Class here *Coast Ranges

—795 2 Southwestern counties of Oregon

Class here *Klamath Mountains

—795 21 Curry County

Class here *Rogue River

—795 23 Coos County

—795 25 Josephine County

—795 27 Jackson County

—795 29 Douglas County

Class here Umpqua River

—795 3 West central counties of Oregon

Class here *Willamette River

—795 31 Lane County

—795 33 Lincoln County

—795 34 Benton County

—795 35 Linn County

—795 37 Marion County

Including Salem

—795 38 Polk County

—795 39 Yamhill County

—795 4 Northwestern counties of Oregon

Class here *Columbia River in Oregon

—795 41 Clackamas County

—795 43 Washington County

—795 44 Tillamook County

—795 46 Clatsop County

—795 47 Columbia County

—795 49 Multnomah County

Class here Portland

—795 5 *Eastern Oregon

*For a specific part of this jurisdiction, region, or feature, see the part and follow instructions under —4–9

—795 6 North central counties of Oregon

—795 61 Hood River County

Including *Mount Hood

—795 62 Wasco County

Class here *Deschutes River

—795 64 Sherman County

—795 65 Gilliam County

—795 67 Morrow County

—795 69 Umatilla County

—795 7 Northeastern counties of Oregon

Class here *Blue Mountains; *Snake River in Oregon

—795 71 Union County

—795 73 Wallowa County

Including *Wallowa Mountains

—795 75 Baker County

—795 78 Grant County

—795 8 Central counties of Oregon

—795 81 Wheeler County

—795 83 Crook County

—795 85 Jefferson County

—795 87 Deschutes County

—795 9 Southeastern counties of Oregon

—795 91 Klamath County

—795 915 Crater Lake National Park

—795 93 Lake County

—795 95 Harney County

—795 97 Malheur County

—796 Idaho

—796 1 *Southern Idaho

Class here *Snake River

—796 2 Southwestern counties of Idaho

*For a specific part of this jurisdiction, region, or feature, see the part and follow instructions under —4–9

—796 21 Owyhee County

—796 23 Canyon County

—796 24 Payette County

—796 25 Washington County

—796 26 Adams County

—796 27 Gem County

—796 28 Ada County

Including Boise

—796 29 Elmore County

Including *Sawtooth Range

Class comprehensive works on Sawtooth Mountains in —79672

—796 3 South central counties of Idaho

—796 31 Camas County

—796 32 Blaine County

—796 33 Minidoka County

—796 34 Lincoln County

—796 35 Jerome County

—796 36 Gooding County

—796 37 Twin Falls County

—796 39 Cassia County

—796 4 Southeastern counties of Idaho

—796 41 Oneida County

—796 42 Franklin County

—796 44 Bear Lake County

Including *Wasatch Range in Idaho

—796 45 Caribou County

—796 47 Bannock County

—796 49 Power County

—796 5 Northeastern counties of southern Idaho

—796 51 Bingham County

—796 53 Bonneville County

*For a specific part of this jurisdiction, region, or feature, see the part and follow instructions under —4–9

—796 54 Teton County

—796 55 Madison County

—796 56 Fremont County

—796 57 Clark County

—796 58 Jefferson County

—796 59 Butte County

Including Craters of the Moon National Monument

For Craters of the Moon National Monument in Blaine County, see —79632

—796 6 *Central Idaho

Class here *Bitterroot Range in Idaho

—796 7 South central counties of Idaho

Class here *Salmon River Mountains

—796 72 Custer County

Including *Sawtooth Mountains

See also —79629 for Sawtooth Range

—796 74 Boise County

—796 76 Valley County

—796 78 Lemhi County

—796 8 North central counties of Idaho

—796 82 Idaho County

Class here *Salmon River

—796 84 Lewis County

—796 85 Nez Perce County

Including *Clearwater River

—796 86 Latah County

—796 88 Clearwater County

—796 9 Northern Idaho

—796 91 Shoshone County

Including *Coeur d'Alene Mountains

—796 93 Benewah County

*For a specific part of this jurisdiction, region, or feature, see the part and follow instructions under —4–9

—796 94 Kootenai County

—796 96 Bonner County

—796 98 Boundary County

—797 Washington

Class here *Columbia River

—797 1 *Eastern Washington

—797 2 Northeastern counties of Washington

—797 21 Pend Oreille County

—797 23 Stevens County

Including *Franklin D. Roosevelt Lake

—797 25 Ferry County

—797 28 Okanogan County

—797 3 East central counties of Washington

—797 31 Douglas County

—797 32 Grant County

—797 33 Franklin County

—797 34 Adams County

—797 35 Lincoln County

—797 37 Spokane County

Class here Spokane

—797 39 Whitman County

Class here *Palouse River

—797 4 Southeastern counties of Washington

Class here *Snake River in Washington

—797 42 Asotin County

—797 44 Garfield County

—797 46 Columbia County

Including *Blue Mountains in Washington

—797 48 Walla Walla County

—797 5 Central counties of Washington

Class here *Cascade Range in Washington

*For a specific part of this jurisdiction, region, or feature, see the part and follow instructions under —4–9

—797 51 Benton County

—797 53 Klickitat County

—797 55 Yakima County

Class here *Yakima River

—797 57 Kittitas County

—797 59 Chelan County

—797 6 *Western Washington

—797 7 Puget Sound counties

See also —16432 for Puget Sound

—797 71 Snohomish County

—797 72 Skagit County

—797 73 Whatcom County

Including North Cascades National Park

For North Cascades National Park in Chelan County, see —79759; for North Cascades National Park in Skagit County, see —79772

—797 74 San Juan County

—797 75 Island County

—797 76 Kitsap County

—797 77 King County

—797 772 Seattle

—797 78 Pierce County

—797 782 Mount Rainier National Park

For Mount Rainier National Park in Lewis County, see —79782

—797 788 Tacoma

—797 79 Thurston County

Including Olympia

—797 8 Southwest central counties of Washington

—797 82 Lewis County

Class here *Cowlitz River

—797 84 Skamania County

*For a specific part of this jurisdiction, region, or feature, see the part and follow instructions under —4–9

—797 86 Clark County

—797 88 Cowlitz County

—797 9 Coastal counties of Washington

Class here *Coast Ranges in Washington

—797 91 Wahkiakum County

—797 92 Pacific County

—797 94 *Olympic Peninsula

Class here *Olympic Mountains

—797 95 Grays Harbor County

—797 97 Mason County

—797 98 Jefferson County

Class here Olympic National Park

For Olympic National Park in Mason County, see —79797; for Olympic National Park in Clallam County, see —79799

—797 99 Clallam County

See also —16432 for Strait of Juan de Fuca

—798 Alaska

—798 2 Panhandle region

Including Haines, Juneau, Ketchikan Gateway, Sitka, Yakutat Boroughs; Glacier Bay National Park and Preserve, Misty Fjords National Monument

—798 3 South central region of Alaska

Pacific Coast area from Icy Bay to Cape Douglas, inland to crest of Alaska and Aleutian Ranges

Including Kenai Peninsula, Matanuska-Susitna Boroughs; *Denali National Park and Preserve, Kenai Fjords National Park, *Wrangell-Saint Elias National Park and Preserve; Kenai Peninsula; *Alaska Range

See also —16434 for Gulf of Alaska, Cook Inlet; also —7986 for Denali Borough

—798 35 Greater Anchorage Area Borough

*For a specific part of this jurisdiction, region, or feature, see the part and follow instructions under —4–9

—798 4 Southwestern region of Alaska

Area from Cape Douglas to Stuart Island

Including Aleutians East, Bristol Bay, Kodiak Island, Lake and Peninsula Boroughs; Katmai National Park and Preserve; Aleutian, Kodiak Islands; *Kuskokwim River

See also —16434 for Bristol Bay

—798 6 Central region of Alaska

Area from the crest of Alaska Range to North Slope Borough

Including Denali, Fairbanks North Star, Northwest Arctic Boroughs; Gates of the Arctic National Park and Preserve, Kobuk Valley National Park, Lake Clark National Park and Preserve; Seward Peninsula

Class here *Yukon River

Class comprehensive works on Denali National Park and Preserve in —7983

For Gates of the Arctic National Park and Preserve in North Slope Borough, see —7987

See also —16434 for Norton Sound

—798 7 North Slope Borough

Including Brooks Range

—8 South America

Class here Latin America, Spanish America, the *Andes

For Middle America, see —72

SUMMARY

— 81	**Brazil**
— 82	**Argentina**
— 83	**Chile**
— 84	**Bolivia**
— 85	**Peru**
— 86	**Colombia and Ecuador**
— 87	**Venezuela**
— 88	**Guiana**
— 89	**Paraguay and Uruguay**

—81 Brazil

—811 Northern region of Brazil

Class here *Amazon River

—811 1 Rondônia state

*For a specific part of this jurisdiction, region, or feature, see the part and follow instructions under —4–9

—811 2 Acre state

—811 3 Amazonas state

—811 4 Roraima state

—811 5 Pará state

—811 6 Amapá state

—811 7 Tocantins state

—812 Maranhão and Piauí states

—812 1 Maranhão state

—812 2 Piauí state

—813 Northeastern region of Brazil

For Maranhão and Piauí states, see —812; for Sergipe and Bahia states, see —814

—813 1 Ceará state

—813 2 Rio Grande do Norte state

—813 3 Paraíba state

—813 4 Pernambuco state

Including Fernando de Noronha archipelago

—813 5 Alagoas state

—814 Sergipe and Bahia states

—814 1 Sergipe state

—814 2 Bahia state

Class here *São Francisco River

—815 Southeastern region of Brazil

For São Paulo state, see —8161

—815 1 Minas Gerais state

—815 2 Espírito Santo state

—815 3 Rio de Janeiro state

Class here Rio de Janeiro

—816 São Paulo state and southern region of Brazil

Class here *Paraná River in Brazil

Subdivisions are added for São Paulo state and southern region of Brazil together, for southern region of Brazil alone

*For a specific part of this jurisdiction, region, or feature, see the part and follow instructions under —4–9

—816 1 São Paulo state

Class here São Paulo

> —816 2–816 5 Southern region of Brazil

Class comprehensive works in —816

—816 2 Paraná state

—816 4 Santa Catarina state

—816 5 Rio Grande do Sul state

—817 West central region of Brazil

—817 1 Mato Grosso do Sul state

—817 2 Mato Grosso state

—817 3 Goiás state

—817 4 Federal District of Brazil

Including Brasília

—82 Argentina

—821 South central region of Argentina

—821 1 Capital Federal

Including Buenos Aires

—821 2 Buenos Aires province

See also —16368 for Bahía Blanca Estuary, Río de la Plata

—821 3 La Pampa province

—822 Mesopotamian provinces

Class here *Paraná, *Uruguay Rivers

—822 1 Entre Ríos

—822 2 Corrientes

—822 3 Misiones

—822 4 Santa Fe

—823 Northeastern provinces of Argentina

—823 4 Chaco

—823 5 Formosa

—824 Northwestern provinces of Argentina

*For a specific part of this jurisdiction, region, or feature, see the part and follow instructions under —4–9

—824 1 Jujuy

—824 2 Salta

—824 3 Tucumán

—824 5 Catamarca

—824 6 La Rioja

—825 North central provinces of Argentina

—825 2 Santiago del Estero

—825 4 Córdoba

—826 Central Highland provinces

—826 2 San Luis

—826 3 San Juan

—826 4 Mendoza

—827 Patagonian region

Class here comprehensive works on Patagonia

For Patagonian region in Chile, see —83644

—827 2 Neuquén province

—827 3 Río Negro province

See also —16368 for Gulf of San Matias

—827 4 Chubut province

See also —16368 for Gulf of San Jorge

—827 5 Santa Cruz province

See also —16368 for Bahia Grande, Gulf of San Jorge

—827 6 Tierra del Fuego province

Class here comprehensive works on Tierra del Fuego archipelago, Isla Grande de Tierra del Fuego

Class south Atlantic Ocean islands claimed by Argentina in —9711

For Tierra del Fuego province of Chile, see —83646

—83 Chile

—831 Tarapacá, Antofagasta, Atacama regions

—831 2 Tarapacá region

—831 23 Arica province

—831 27 Iquique province

—831 3 Antofagasta region

—831 32 Tocopilla province

—831 35 El Loa province

—831 38 Antofagasta province

—831 4 Atacama region

—831 42 Chañaral province

—831 45 Copiapó province

—831 48 Huasco province

—832 Comquimbo and Valparaíso regions

—832 3 Coquimbo region

—832 32 Elqui province

—832 35 Limarí province

—832 38 Choapa province

—832 4 Valparaíso region

For Quillota, Valparaíso, San Antonio provinces, see —8325; for Easter Island, see —9618

—832 42 Los Andes province

—832 45 San Felipe province

—832 48 Petorca province

—832 5 Quillota, Valparaíso, San Antonio provinces

Class comprehensive works on Valparaíso region in —8324

—832 52 Quillota province

—832 55 Valparaíso province

—832 58 San Antonio province

—833 Central regions

—833 1 Metropolitana region

—833 15 Santiago

—833 2 Cachapoal province

Class here Libertador General Bernardo O'Higgins region

For Colchagua province, see —8333

—833 3 Colchagua province

—833 4 Curicó province

—833 5 Talca province

Class here Maule region

For Curicó province, see —8334; for Linares province, see —8337

—833 7 Linares province

—833 8 Ñuble province

—833 9 Concepción province

—834 Bíobío and Araucanía regions

—834 1 Bíobío (Bío-Bío) region

For Ñuble province, see —8338; for Concepción province, see —8339; for Arauco province, see —8342; for Bío-Bío province, see —8343

—834 2 Arauco province

—834 3 Bío-Bío province

—834 5 Malleco province

—834 6 Cautín province

Class here Araucanía region

For Malleco province, see —8345

—835 Los Lagos region

—835 2 Valdivia province

—835 3 Osorno province

—835 4 Llanquihue province

—835 6 Chiloé province

—836 Aisén del General Carlos Ibáñez del Campo and Magallanes y Antártica Chilena regions

—836 2 Aisén del General Carlos Ibáñez del Campo region

—836 22 Aisén province

—836 25 General Carrera province

—836 28 Capitán Prat province

—836 4 Magallanes y Antártica Chilena region

—836 42 Ultima Esperanza province

—836 44 Magallanes province

See also —1674 for Strait of Magellan

—836 46 Tierra del Fuego province

Class comprehensive works on Tierra del Fuego archipelago in —8276

—836 48 Antártica Chilena province

—84 Bolivia

—841 Mountain region departments of Bolivia

—841 2 La Paz

Class here La Paz, *Lake Titicaca

—841 3 Oruro

—841 4 Potosí

—842 Valley region departments of Bolivia

—842 3 Cochabamba

—842 4 Chuquisaca

Including Sucre

—842 5 Tarija

—843 Santa Cruz department

Class here plains region

—844 Amazon region departments

—844 2 El Beni (Beni)

—844 3 Pando

—85 Peru

—851 Northern departments of Peru

—851 2 Tumbes department

Class here Grau region

For Piura department, see —8513

—851 3 Piura department

—851 4 Lambayeque department

Class here Nor Oriental del Marañón region

For Cajamarca department, see —8515; for Amazonas department, see —8546

—851 5 Cajamarca department

—851 6 La Libertad department (La Libertad region)

*For a specific part of this jurisdiction, region, or feature, see the part and follow instructions under —4–9

—852 Central departments of Peru

—852 1 Ancash department (Chavín Region)

—852 2 Huánuco department

Class here Andrés Avelino Cáceres region

For Pasco department, see —8523; for Junín department, see —8524

—852 3 Pasco department

—852 4 Junín department

—852 5 Lima department

Class here Lima

—852 6 Callao constitutional province

—852 7 Ica department

Class here Los Libertadores Wari region

For Huancavelica department, see —8528; for Ayacucho department, see —8529

—852 8 Huancavelica department

—852 9 Ayacucho department

—[852 92] Ayacucho department

Number discontinued; class in —8529

—[852 94] Apurímac department

Relocated to —8538

—853 Southern departments of Peru

—853 2 Arequipa department (Arequipa region)

—853 4 Moquegua department

Class here Mariátegui region

For Tacna department, see —8535; for Puno department, see —8536

—853 5 Tacna department

—853 6 Puno department

Including Lake Titicaca in Peru

—853 7 Cuzco department

Class here Inca region

For Apurímac department, see —8538; for Madre de Dios department, see —8542

—853 8 Apurímac department [*formerly* —85294]

—854 Eastern departments of Peru

—854 2 Madre de Dios department

—854 3 Ucayali department (Ucayali region)

—854 4 Loreto department (Amazonas region)

Class here *Amazon River in Peru

See also —8546 for Amazonas department

—854 5 San Martín department (San Martín region)

—854 6 Amazonas department

See also —8544 for Amazonas region

—86 Colombia and Ecuador

—861 Colombia

Class here *Magdalena River

—861 1 Caribbean Region

—861 11 San Andrés y Providencia [*formerly* —8618]

Islands in Caribbean Sea

—861 12 Córdoba

Including *San Jorge River

—861 13 Sucre

—861 14 Bolívar

—861 15 Atlántico

—861 16 Magdalena

Including *Sierra Nevada de Santa Marta National Park

—861 17 La Guajira

—861 18 Cesar [*formerly* —86123]

> —861 2–861 4 Andean Region

Class comprehensive works in —8612

*For a specific part of this jurisdiction, region, or feature, see the part and follow instructions under —4–9

—861 2 Northern departments of Andean Region

Class here Andean Region

Comprehensive works on Pacific Coast Region relocated to —8615

For southwestern departments of Andean Region, see —8613; for southeastern departments of Andean Region, see —8614

—[861 23] Cesar

Relocated to —86118

—861 24 Norte de Santander

Including *Tama National Park

—861 25 Santander

—861 26 Antioquia

Including *Paramillo National Park

—[861 27] Chocó

Relocated to —86151

—861 3 Southwestern departments of Andean Region

—861 32 Risaralda

—861 34 Quindío

—861 35 Caldas

—861 36 Tolima

—[861 37] Boyacá

Relocated to —86144

—[861 38] Arauca

Relocated to —86198

—861 39 Huila [*formerly* —86154]

Including *Nevado del Huila National Park

Vichada relocated to —86192

—861 4 Southeastern departments of Andean Region

—[861 43] Casanare

Relocated to —86196

—861 44 Boyacá [*formerly* —86137]

Including *El Cocuy National Park; *Cocuy Range

*For a specific part of this jurisdiction, region, or feature, see the part and follow instructions under —4–9

—861 46 Cundinamarca

Including *Sumapaz National Park

—861 48 Capital District of Santa Fe de Bogotá

Class here Bogotá

—861 5 Pacific Coast Region

Class here comprehensive works on Pacific Coast Region [*formerly* —8612]; *Cordillera Occidental

—861 51 Chocó [*formerly* —86127]

Including *Atrato River

—861 52 Valle del Cauca

Including Farallones de Cali National Park

—861 53 Cauca

Including *Puracé National Park; *Coconucos Range

—[861 54] Huila

Relocated to —86139

—[861 56] Meta

Relocated to —86194

—861 58 Nariño [*formerly* —86162]

Including Sanquianga National Park

—861 6 Amazon Region

For Amazonas, see —8617

—[861 62] Nariño

Relocated to —86158

—861 63 Putumayo

—861 64 Caquetá

—861 65 Vaupés

—861 66 Guaviare

—861 67 Guainía

—861 7 Amazonas

—[861 8] San Andrés y Providencia

Relocated to —86111

*For a specific part of this jurisdiction, region, or feature, see the part and follow instructions under —4–9

—861 9 Orinoquia Region

—861 92 Vichada [*formerly* —86139]

Including El Tuparro National Park

—861 94 Meta [*formerly* —86156]

Including *Los Picahos National Park, Serrania de La Macarena National Park

—861 96 Casanare [*formerly* —86143]

—861 98 Arauca [*formerly* —86138]

—866 Ecuador

—866 1 Sierra Region

For southern provinces of Sierra Region, see —8662

—866 11 Carchi

—866 12 Imbabura

—866 13 Pichincha

Including Quito

—866 14 Cotopaxi

—866 15 Tungurahua

—866 16 Bolívar

—866 17 Chimborazo

—866 2 Southern provinces of Sierra Region

—866 23 Cañar

—866 24 Azuay

—866 25 Loja

—866 3 Costa Region

—866 31 El Oro

—866 32 Guayas

See also —1641 for Gulf of Guayaquil

—866 33 Los Ríos

—866 34 Manabí

—866 35 Esmeraldas

—866 4 Oriente Region

*For a specific part of this jurisdiction, region, or feature, see the part and follow instructions under —4–9

—866 41 Sucumbíos and Napo provinces

—866 412 Sucumbíos

—866 416 Napo

—866 42 Pastaza

—866 43 Morona-Santiago

—866 44 Zamora-Chinchipe

—866 5 Galapagos Islands (Colón)

—87 Venezuela

Class here *Orinoco River

—871 Southwestern states of Venezuela

—871 2 Táchira

—871 3 Mérida

—871 4 Trujillo

—872 Northwestern states of Venezuela

—872 3 Zulia

Class here *Lake Maracaibo

—872 4 Falcón

See also —16365 for Gulf of Venezuela

—872 5 Lara

—872 6 Yaracuy

—873 North central states of Venezuela

Including Federal Dependencies

For Distrito Federal, see —877

—873 2 Carabobo

—873 4 Aragua

—873 5 Miranda

—874 Central states of Venezuela

—874 2 Apure

—874 3 Barinas

—874 5 Portuguesa

—874 6 Cojedes

*For a specific part of this jurisdiction, region, or feature, see the part and follow instructions under —4–9

—874 7 Guárico

—875 Northeastern states of Venezuela

—875 2 Anzoátegui

—875 3 Sucre

See also —16366 for Gulf of Paria

—875 4 Nueva Esparta

—875 6 Monagas

—876 Southeastern states of Venezuela

—876 2 Delta Amacuro

—876 3 Bolívar

—876 4 Amazonas

—877 Distrito Federal

Including Caracas

—88 Guiana

—881 Guyana

—881 1 Barima-Waini Region

Class here former North West district

—881 2 Pomeroon-Supenaam Region

Class here former Essequibo district

—881 3 Essequibo Islands-West Demerara Region

Including northwestern part of former West Demerara district [*formerly* —8814], former Essequibo Islands district

—881 4 Upper Demerara-Berbice Region

Including northwestern part of former East Berbice district [*formerly* —8817], northeastern part of former Rupununi district [*formerly* —8818], former Mazaruni-Potaro district east of Essequibo River [*formerly* —8819], comprehensive works on former West Demerara district

Northwestern part of former West Demerara district relocated to —8813; northeastern part of former West Demerara district relocated to —8815

—881 5 Demerara-Mahaica Region

Including northeastern part of former West Demerara district [*formerly* —8814]; Georgetown; comprehensive works on former East Demerara district

Eastern part of former East Demerara district relocated to —8816

—881 6 Mahaica-Berbice Region

Including eastern part of former East Demerara district [*formerly* —8815], former West Berbice district

—881 7 East Berbice-Corentyne Region

Including eastern part of former Rupununi district [*formerly* —8818], comprehensive works on former East Berbice district

Northwestern part of former East Berbice district relocated to —8814

—881 8 Upper Takutu-Upper Essequibo and Potaro-Siparuni regions

Class here comprehensive works on former Rupununi district

Northeastern part of former Rupununi district relocated to —8814; eastern part of former Rupununi district relocated to —8817

—881 84 Upper Takutu-Upper Essequibo Region

—881 87 Potaro-Siparuni Region

Including southern part of former Mazaruni-Potaro district [*formerly* —8819]

—881 9 Cuyuni-Mazaruni Region

Class here comprehensive works on former Mazaruni-Potaro district

Former Mazaruni-Potaro district east of Essequibo River relocated to —8814; southern part of former Mazaruni-Potaro district relocated to —88187

—882 French Guiana (Guyane)

Overseas department of France

Including Cayenne and Saint-Laurent du Maroni arrondissements

Class here Inini

—883 Suriname

This development reflects the political divisions established in 1985. Relatively minor changes between this development and the Edition 21 development, which reflects the previous political divisions, are not indicated

—883 1 Nickerie district

Western part of Sipaliwini district, formerly part of Nickerie district, relocated to —88395

—883 2 Coronie district

—883 3 Saramacca district

West central part of Sipaliwini district, formerly part of Saramacca district, relocated to —88395

—883 4 Para district

Including southern part of former Suriname district [*formerly* —8836]

—883 5 Paramaribo and Wanica districts

—883 52 Paramaribo district

Class here Paramaribo

—883 57 Wanica district

—[883 6] Suriname district

Southern part of former Suriname district relocated to —8834; northern part of former Suriname district relocated to —8837

—883 7 Commewijne district

Including northern part of former Suriname district [*formerly* —8836]

—883 8 Marowijne district

Eastern part of Sipaliwini district, formerly part of Marowijne district, relocated to —88395

—883 9 Brokopondo and Sipaliwini districts

—883 92 Brokopondo district

—883 95 Sipaliwini district

Including western part of Sipaliwini district [*formerly* —8831]; west central part of Sipaliwini district [*formerly* —8833]; eastern part of Sipaliwini district [*formerly* —8838]

—89 Paraguay and Uruguay

—892 Paraguay

Class here Paraguay River

—892 1 Oriental region

—892 12 Asunción Capital District and southern departments of Oriental region

Subdivisions are added for Asunción Capital District and southern departments of Oriental region together, for southern departments of Oriental region alone

—892 121 Asunción Capital District

> —892 122–892 128 Southern departments of Oriental region

Class comprehensive works in —89212

—892 122 Central

—892 123 Paraguarí

—892 124 Ñeembucú

—892 125 Misiones

—892 126 Itapúa

—892 127 Caazapá

—892 128 Guairá

—892 13 Northern departments of Oriental region

—892 132 Alto Paraná

—892 133 Canindeyú

—892 134 Caaguazú

—892 135 Cordillera

—892 136 San Pedro

—892 137 Amambay

—892 138 Concepción

—892 2 Occidental region

Class here *Chaco Boreal

—892 23 Presidente Hayes

—892 24 Boquerón

Including former Nueva Asunción department [*formerly* —89225]

—[892 25] Nueva Asunción

Relocated to —89224

—[892 26] Chaco

Relocated to —89227

—892 27 Alto Paraguay

Including former Chaco department [*formerly* —89226]

—895 Uruguay

Class here *Uruguay River in Uruguay

—895 1 Coastal departments of Uruguay

See also —16368 for Río de la Plata

—895 11 Colonia

—895 12 San José

—895 13 Montevideo

Class here Montevideo

—895 14 Canelones

—895 15 Maldonado

*For a specific part of this jurisdiction, region, or feature, see the part and follow instructions under —4–9

—895 16 Rocha

—895 2 Central departments of Uruguay

—895 21 Lavalleja

—895 22 Treinta y Tres

—895 23 Cerro Largo

—895 24 Durazno

—895 25 Florida

—895 26 Flores

—895 27 Soriano

—895 28 Río Negro

—895 3 Northern departments of Uruguay

—895 31 Paysandú

—895 32 Tacuarembó

—895 34 Rivera

—895 35 Salto

—895 36 Artigas

—9 Other parts of world and extraterrestrial worlds

Class here Australasia, *Pacific Ocean islands

SUMMARY

—93	**New Zealand**
—94	**Australia**
—95	**Melanesia New Guinea**
—96	**Other parts of Pacific Ocean Polynesia**
—97	**Atlantic Ocean islands**
—98	**Arctic islands and Antarctica**
—99	**Extraterrestrial worlds**

> **—93–96 Australasia and Pacific Ocean islands**

Class comprehensive works in —9

—93 New Zealand

See Manual at T2—93

*For a specific part of this jurisdiction, region, or feature, see the part and follow instructions under —4–9

SUMMARY

—931	**North Island**
—932	**Auckland Region**
—933	**Waikato Region**
—934	**Bay of Plenty, Gisborne, Hawke's Bay, Taranaki Regions**
—935	**Manawatu-Wanganui Region**
—936	**Wellington Region**
—937	**South Island**
—938	**Canterbury Region**
—939	**Otago and Southland Regions and outlying islands**

—931 *North Island

—931 2 Former *Auckland Province

> —931 3–931 8 Northland Region

Class comprehensive works in —9313

—931 3 Far North District

Class here Northland Region

For Whangarei District, see —9316; for Kaipara District, see —9318

—931 6 Whangarei District

—931 8 Kaipara District

—932 Auckland Region

—932 1 Rodney District

Including Kawau Island

—932 2 North Shore City

Class here Takapuna

—932 3 Waitakere City

—932 4 Auckland City

Including Little Barrier, Great Barrier, Waiheke Islands

Class here Auckland

—932 5 Manukau City

—932 6 Papakura District

—932 7 Franklin District in Auckland Region

—933 Waikato Region

*For a specific part of this jurisdiction, region, or feature, see the part and follow instructions under —4–9

—933 1 Franklin District

For Franklin District in Auckland Region, see —9327

—933 2 Thames Coromandel and Hauraki districts

—933 23 Thames Coromandel District

Class here Coromandel Peninsula

—933 27 Hauraki District

—933 3 Waikato District

—933 4 Hamilton City

Class here Hamilton

—933 5 Matamata Piako and Waipa districts

—933 53 Matamata Piako District

—933 57 Waipa District

—933 6 South Waikato District, and Rotorua District in Waikato Region

—933 63 South Waikato District

—933 67 Rotorua District in Waikato Region

—933 7 Otorohanga District

—933 8 Waitomo District

For Waitomo District in Manawatu-Wanganui Region, see —93517

—933 9 Taupo District

Including Lake Taupo

For Taupo District in Bay of Plenty Region, see —93424; for Taupo District in Hawke's Bay Region, see —93463; for Taupo District in Manawatu-Wanganui Region, see —93513

—934 Bay of Plenty, Gisborne, Hawke's Bay, Taranaki Regions

—934 2 Bay of Plenty Region

—934 21 Tauranga District

—934 22 Western Bay of Plenty District

—934 23 Rotorua District

For Rotorua District in Waikato Region, see —93367

—934 24 Taupo District in Bay of Plenty Region

—934 25 Whakatane District

Including Urewera National Park

For Urewera National Park in Wairoa District, see —93462

—934 26 Kawerau District

Class here Kawerau

—934 28 Opotiki District

—934 4 Gisborne Region (Gisborne District)

—934 6 Hawke's Bay Region

—934 62 Wairoa District

—934 63 Taupo District in Hawke's Bay Region

—934 64 Rangitikei District in Hawke's Bay Region

—934 65 Hastings District

—934 67 Napier City

—934 69 Central Hawke's Bay District

—934 8 Taranaki Region

—934 82 New Plymouth District

Including Egmont National Park

For Egmont National Park in Stratford District, see —93485; for Egmont National Park in South Taranaki District, see —93488

—934 85 Stratford District

For Stratford District in Manawatu-Wanganui Region, see —9353

—934 88 South Taranaki District

—935 Manawatu-Wanganui Region

For Taupo District, see —9339

—935 1 Taupo and Waitomo districts in Manawatu-Wanganui Region

—935 13 Taupo District in Manawatu-Wanganui Region

—935 17 Waitomo District in Manawatu-Wanganui Region

—935 2 Ruapehu District

Including Tongariro National Park, Whanganui National Park

For Tongariro National Park in Taupo District, see —9339; for Whanganui National Park in Wanganui District, see —9354

—935 3 Stratford District in Manawatu-Wanganui Region

—935 4 Wanganui District

—935 5 Rangitikei District

For Rangitikei District in Hawke's Bay Region, see —93464

—935 6 Manawatu District

—935 7 Tararua District

For Tararua District in Wellington Region, see —9369

—935 8 Palmerston North City

Class here Palmerston North

—935 9 Horowhenua District

—936 Wellington Region

—936 1 Kapiti Coast District

—936 2 Porirua City

—936 3 Wellington City

Class here Wellington

—936 4 Lower Hutt City

—936 5 Upper Hutt City

> —936 6–936 9 Wairarapa

Class comprehensive works in —9366

—936 6 South Wairarapa District

Class here Wairarapa

For Carterton District, see —9367; for Masterton District, see —9368; for Tararua District in Wellington Region, see —9369

—936 7 Carterton District

—936 8 Masterton District

—936 9 Tararua District in Wellington Region

—937 South Island

For Canterbury Region, see —938; for Otago and Southland Regions, see —939

> —937 1–937 4 West Coast Region

Class comprehensive works in —9371

—937 1 Westland District

Including *Mount Aspiring National Park, Westland National Park

Class here West Coast Region, *Southern Alps

For Grey District, see —9372; for Buller District, see —9373; for Tasman District in West Coast Region, see —9374

*For a specific part of this jurisdiction, region, or feature, see the part and follow instructions under —4–9

—937 2 Grey District

—937 3 Buller District

Including Paparoa National Park

For Paparoa National Park in Grey District, see —9372

—937 4 Tasman District in West Coast Region

Including Nelson Lakes National Park

> —937 5–937 9 Nelson-Marlborough Region

Class comprehensive works in —9375

—937 5 Marlborough District

Class here Nelson-Marlborough Region

For Nelson City, see —9376; for Tasman District, see —9377; for Kaikoura District, see —9378; for Hurunui District in Nelson-Marlborough Region, see —9379

—937 6 Nelson City

—937 7 Tasman District

Including Abel Tasman National Park

For Tasman District in West Coast Region, see —9374

—937 8 Kaikoura District

—937 9 Hurunui District in Nelson-Marlborough Region

—938 Canterbury Region

—938 1 Hurunui District

Including Arthur's Pass National Park

For Arthur's Pass National Park in Grey District, see —9372; for Arthur's Pass National Park in Selwyn District, see —9385; for Hurunui District in Nelson-Marlborough Region, see —9379

—938 2 Waimakariri District

—938 3 Christchurch City

Class here Christchurch

—938 4 Banks Peninsula District

Class here Banks Peninsula

—938 5 Selwyn District

—938 6 Ashburton District

—938 7 Timaru District

—938 8 MacKenzie District

Including Mount Cook National Park; Lake Pukaki

For Mount Cook National Park in Westland District, see —9371

—938 9 Waimate District, and Waitaki District in Canterbury Region

—938 93 Waimate District

—938 97 Waitaki District in Canterbury Region

Including Lake Ohau

—939 Otago and Southland Regions and outlying islands

> —939 1–939 5 Otago Region

Class comprehensive works in —9391

—939 1 Waitaki District

Class here Otago Region

For Waitaki District in Canterbury Region, see —93897; for Dunedin City, see —9392; for Clutha District, see —9393; for Central Otago District, see —9394; for Queenstown-Lakes District, see —9395

—939 2 Dunedin City

—939 3 Clutha District

—939 4 Central Otago District

—939 5 Queenstown-Lakes District

Including Lakes Hawea, Wakatipu, Wanaka

> —939 6–939 8 Southland Region

Class comprehensive works in —9396

—939 6 Southland District

Including Fiordland National Park; Stewart Island; Lakes Manapouri, Te Anau

Class here Southland Region

For Gore District, see —9397; for Invercargill District, see —9398

—939 7 Gore District

—939 8 Invercargill District

—939 9 Outlying islands

Including Chatham Islands, Kermadec Islands, Subantarctic Islands (Antipodes, Auckland, Bounty, Campbell, Snares, Traps Islands)

—94 Australia

Class here *Great Dividing Range

SUMMARY

—941 Western Australia

—941 1 Perth metropolitan district

Including Fremantle

—941 2 Southwestern district

Including Albany, Bunbury, Collie, Geraldton, Katanning, Manjimup, Narrogin, Northam; Kalbarri, Nelson and Hay, Nornalup, Stirling Range National Parks; Darling, Stirling Ranges; Blackwood, Swan Rivers

For Perth metropolitan district, see —9411

—941 3 Northwestern district

Including Port Hedland; Barrow Island, Bernier and Dorre Islands, Cape Range National Parks; Gascoyne River

—941 4 Kimberley district

Including Broome, Wyndham; Ord River

—941 5 North central district

Class here Gibson, Great Sandy, *Great Victoria Deserts

—941 6 South central district

Including Coolgardie, Kalgoorlie

—941 7 Southern district

Including Esperance, Norseman; Cape Le Grand, Esperance National Parks

—942 Central Australia

—942 3 South Australia

—942 31 Adelaide metropolitan district

*For a specific part of this jurisdiction, region, or feature, see the part and follow instructions under —4–9

—942 32 Central district

Including Angaston, Clare, Gawler, Murray Bridge, Port Pirie, Salisbury, Victor Harbour; Chaunceys Line Reserve National Park; Mount Lofty Ranges

For Adelaide metropolitan district, see —94231

—942 33 Eastern district

Including Barmera, Berri, Loxton, Renmark

—942 34 Southern district

Including Mount Gambier; Canunda National Park

—942 35 West central district

Including Flinders Chase National Park; Yorke Peninsula; Kangaroo Island

—942 36 North central district

Including Quorn

—942 37 Northern district

Class here *Flinders Ranges; *Coopers Creek

—942 38 Western district

Including Port Augusta, Port Lincoln, Whyalla; Lincoln National Park; Eyre Peninsula; Lakes Eyre, Gairdner

—942 9 Northern Territory

Class here northern Australia

For Western Australia, see —941; for Queensland, see —943

—942 91 Southern district

Including Alice Springs; Ormiston Gorge, Palm Valley, Uluru (Ayers Rock)-Mount Olga National Parks; Davenport Range; Ayers Rock

—942 95 Northern district

Including Darwin, Katherine, Tennant Creek; Cobourg Peninsula, Katherine Gorge National Parks; Arnhem Land; Groote Eylandt; Daly, Roper Rivers

—943 Queensland

Class here *Great Barrier Reef

—943 1 Brisbane metropolitan district

*For a specific part of this jurisdiction, region, or feature, see the part and follow instructions under —4–9

—943 2 Southeastern district

Including Bundaberg, Gympie, Ipswich, Kingaroy, Maryborough, Southport, Surfers Paradise; Bunya Mountains, Cooloola, Lamington, Mount Barney National Parks; Fraser Island

Class here *Brisbane River

For Brisbane metropolitan district, see —9431

—943 3 Downs district

Including Dalby, Millmerran, Oakey, Stanthorpe, Toowoomba; Granite Belt National Park; Darling Downs

—943 4 Southwestern district

Including Charleville, Mitchell

—943 5 Central district

Including Barcaldine, Blackall, Clermont, Gladstone, Longreach, Monto, Rockhampton, Yeppoon; Carnarvon, Dipperu, Isla Gorge, Robinson Gorge, Salvator Rosa National Parks; Fitzroy River

—943 6 Northeastern district

Including Atherton, Bowen, Cairns, Charters Towers, Ingham, Innisfail, Mackay, Mareeba, Townsville; Bellenden Ker, Conway Range, Eungella, Hinchinbrook Island, Mount Elliott, Mount Spec, Whitsunday Island, Windsor Tableland National Parks; Whitsunday Islands; Burdekin River

—943 7 Northwestern district

Including Mount Isa; Simpson Desert National Park

See also —16475 for Gulf of Carpentaria

—943 8 Peninsula and Torres Strait Islands

Including Cape York Peninsula

—944 New South Wales

Class here *Australian Alps; *Murray River

—944 1 Sydney metropolitan district

Including Parramatta, Penrith; Ku-ring-gai Chase National Park

—944 2 Lower north coast district

Including Cessnock, Forster, Gloucester, Gosford, Maitland, Muswellbrook, Newcastle, Port Macquarie, Singleton, Taree; Brisbane Water National Park; Hawkesbury, Hunter Rivers

*For a specific part of this jurisdiction, region, or feature, see the part and follow instructions under —4–9

—944 3 Upper north coast district

Including Ballina, Casino, Coffs Harbour, Grafton, Kempsey, Kyogle, Lismore, Murwillumbah; Gibraltar Range National Park; Richmond River

Class here *Macleay Rivers

—944 4 North central district

Including Armidale, Coonabarabran, Glen Innes, Inverell, Tamworth, Tenterfield; Mount Kaputar, New England National Parks

Class here *Gwydir River

—944 5 Central district

Including Bathurst, Cowra, Dubbo, Forbes, Gilgandra, Katoomba, Lithgow, Mudgee, Orange, Wellington; Blue Mountains National Park; *Blue Mountains

—944 6 Upper south coast district

Including Camden, Campbelltown, Port Kembla, Wollongong; Morton, Royal National Parks; Nepean River

—944 7 Southeastern district

Including Batemans Bay, Bega, Bombala, Eden, Goulburn, Moruya, Narooma, Nowra, Queanbeyan, Yass; Kosciusko, Shoalhaven National Parks; Shoalhaven River

Class here *Snowy Mountains

Class Australian Capital Territory in —947

—944 8 Southern district

Including Albury, Cootamundra, Corowa, Griffith, Junee, Leeton, Wagga Wagga; Cocoparra National Park; Wakool River

Class here Murrumbidgee River

—944 9 Western district

Including Bourke, Broken Hill, Cobar, Nyngan, Walgett, Warren; Menindee Lake

Class here *Lachlan River

—945 Victoria

—945 1 Melbourne metropolitan district

*For a specific part of this jurisdiction, region, or feature, see the part and follow instructions under —4–9

—945 2 Central district

Including Geelong, Healesville, Mornington, Queenscliff, Sorrento, Sunbury, Torquay, Werribee; Kinglake National Park; French, Phillip Islands

Class here Yarra River

For Melbourne metropolitan district, see —9451

—945 3 North central district

Including Castlemaine, Creswick, Daylesford, Heathcote, Maldon, Maryborough, Woodend

—945 4 Northern district

Including Bendigo, Echuca, Inglewood, Kyabram, Nathalia, Rushworth, Shepparton

Class here *Goulburn River

—945 5 Northeastern district

Including Beechworth, Benalla, Corryong, Euroa, Rutherglen, Wangaratta, Wodonga; Mount Buffalo National Park

Class here *Ovens Rivers

—945 6 Gippsland district

Including Bairnsdale, Lakes Entrance, Moe, Morwell, Traralgon, Warragul; Mallacoota Inlet, Wilsons Promontory National Parks

—945 7 Western district

Including Ararat, Ballarat, Colac, Hamilton, Port Fairy, Portland, Warrnambool

—945 8 Wimmera district

Including Horsham, Stawell

—945 9 Mallee district

Including Merbein, Mildura, Swan Hill; Hattah Lakes, Wyperfeld National Parks; *Wimmera River

—946 Tasmania

—946 1 Hobart metropolitan district

—946 2 Southern district

Including Kingston, New Norfolk, Port Cygnet; Hartz Mountains, Lake Pedder, Mount Field National Parks; Bruny Island

For Hobart metropolitan district, see —9461

*For a specific part of this jurisdiction, region, or feature, see the part and follow instructions under —4–9

—946 3 Central district

Including Deloraine, Oatlands; Cradle Mountain-Lake Saint Clair National Park; Cradle Mountain; Great Lake; Lake Saint Clair

—946 4 Eastern district

Including Port Arthur, Scottsdale; Ben Lomond, Freycinet, Maria Island National Parks; Tasman Peninsula

—946 5 Northwestern district

Including Beaconsfield, Burnie, Devonport, Launceston, Smithton, Stanley, Wynyard

Class here *Tamar River

—946 6 Western district

Including Queenstown; Frenchmans Cap National Park

—946 7 Bass Strait Islands

Including Furneaux Islands

—947 Australian Capital Territory

—947 1 Canberra

—948 Outlying islands

Including Christmas Islands, Coral Sea Islands

For Cocos Islands, see —699

—948 1 Lord Howe Island

—948 2 Norfolk Island

—95 Melanesia New Guinea

Class here Oceania

For Polynesia, Micronesia, see —96

> —951–957 New Guinea

Class comprehensive works in —95

—951 Papua

Former name: Irian Jaya

Province of Indonesia

*For a specific part of this jurisdiction, region, or feature, see the part and follow instructions under —4–9

—953 Papua New Guinea New Guinea region

Class here former German New Guinea, former territory of New Guinea

For Papuan region, see —954; for Highlands region, see —956; for Momase region, see —957; for Bismarck Archipelago, see —958; for North Solomons Province, see —9592

—954 Papuan region of Papua New Guinea

—954 1 Milne Bay Province

Including D'Entrecasteaux Islands, Murua (Woodlark) Island, Trobriand Islands

—954 2 Northern (Oro) Province

—954 5 National Capital District

Class here Port Moresby

—954 6 Central Province

Including Bereina

—954 7 Gulf Province

Class here *Purari River

—954 9 Western (Fly River) Province

—956 Highlands region of Papua New Guinea

Class here *Bismarck Range

—956 1 Southern Highlands Province

—956 3 Enga Province

—956 5 Western Highlands Province

Class here Jimi River

—956 7 Simbu (Chimbu) Province

—956 9 Eastern Highlands Province

Including Goroka

—957 Momase (Northern coastal) region of Papua New Guinea

—957 1 Morobe Province

Including Lae; Siassi Islands; Markham River

—957 3 Madang Province

—957 5 East Sepik Province

Class here *Sepik, *Yuat Rivers

*For a specific part of this jurisdiction, region, or feature, see the part and follow instructions under —4–9

—957 7 West Sepik (Sandaun) Province

—958 Bismarck Archipelago

Part of Papua New Guinea

—958 1 Manus Province

Including Admiralty Islands

—958 3 New Ireland Province

Including Kavieng

—958 5 East New Britain Province

Including Rabau

Class here comprehensive works on New Britain

For West New Britain Province, see —9587

—958 7 West New Britain Province

—959 Other parts of Melanesia

—959 2 North Solomons Province

Part of Papua New Guinea

Including Bougainville, Buka islands

—959 3 Solomon Islands

Independent nation

—959 31 Western Province

—959 33 Guadalcanal Province

—959 35 Central Province

—959 36 Isabel Province

—959 37 Malaita Province

—959 38 Makira and Ulawa Province

—959 39 Temotu Province

—959 5 Vanuatu

—959 7 New Caledonia

Including Loyalty Islands

—96 Other parts of Pacific Ocean Polynesia

—961 Southwest central Pacific Ocean islands, isolated islands of southeast Pacific Ocean

Subdivisions are added for southwest central Pacific Ocean islands, isolated islands of southeast Pacific Ocean together; for southwest central Pacific Ocean islands alone

—961 1 Fiji

—961 2 Tonga (Friendly Islands)

—961 3 American Samoa

Class here comprehensive works on Samoan Islands

For Samoa, see —9614

—961 4 Samoa

Former name: Western Samoa

Class comprehensive works on Samoan Islands in —9613

—961 5 Tokelau (Union) Islands

—961 6 Wallis and Futuna Islands

—961 8 Isolated islands of southeast Pacific Ocean

Including Easter, Oeno, Pitcairn

—962 South central Pacific Ocean islands

Class here French Polynesia

For Marquesas Islands, see —9631; for Tuamotu Islands, see —9632

—962 1 Society Islands

—962 11 Tahiti

—962 2 Gambier and Tubuai (Austral) Islands

—962 3 Cook Islands

For Manihiki Atoll, see —9624

—962 4 Manihiki Atoll

Part of Cook Islands

—962 6 Niue

—963 Southeast central Pacific Ocean islands

For isolated islands of southeast Pacific Ocean, see —9618

—963 1 Marquesas Islands

Part of French Polynesia

—963 2 Tuamotu Islands (Low Archipelago)

Part of French Polynesia

For Gambier Islands, see —9622

—964 Line Islands (Equatorial Islands)

Including Kiritimati (Christmas)

For Palmyra, see —9699

—965 *West central Pacific Ocean islands (Micronesia) *Trust Territory of the Pacific Islands

Including Wake Island

—966 Federated States of Micronesia and Republic of Palau

Including Truk Islands

Class here Caroline Islands

—967 Mariana Islands

Including Guam, Saipan, Tinian

Class here Commonwealth of the Northern Mariana Islands

—968 Islands of eastern Micronesia

—968 1 Kiribati

Including Gilbert Islands

For Line Islands, see —964

—968 2 Tuvalu

Class here Ellice Islands

—968 3 Marshall Islands

Including Bikini, Enewetak, Kwajalein Atolls

—968 5 Nauru (Pleasant Island)

—969 North central Pacific Ocean islands Hawaii

> —969 1–969 4 Hawaii

State of the United States of America

Class comprehensive works in —969

—969 1 Hawaii County (Hawaii Island)

—969 2 Maui County

—969 21 Maui Island

—969 22 Kahoolawe Island

—969 23 Lanai Island

—969 24 Molokai Island

Including Kalawao County

—969 3 Honolulu County (Oahu Island)

—969 31 Honolulu

*For a specific part of this jurisdiction, region, or feature, see the part and follow instructions under —4–9

—969 4 Kauai County

—969 41 Kauai Island

—969 42 Niihau Island

—969 9 Outlying islands

Including Howland, Johnston, Midway, Palmyra Islands

—97 *Atlantic Ocean islands

—971 Falkland Islands, South Georgia and South Sandwich Islands, Bouvet Island

—971 1 Falkland Islands (Islas Malvinas)

—971 2 South Georgia and South Sandwich Islands

Subdivisions are added for either or both topics in heading

—971 3 Bouvet Island

—973 Saint Helena and dependencies

Including Ascension Island; Tristan da Cunha Islands

Subdivisions are added for Saint Helena and dependencies together, for Saint Helena alone

—98 Arctic islands and Antarctica

Subdivisions are added for Arctic islands and Antarctica together, for Arctic islands alone

---

> —981–988 *Arctic islands

Class comprehensive works in —98

—981 Svalbard

Including Spitsbergen Island

—982 Greenland

—983 Jan Mayen Island

—985 Franz Josef Land

Part of Arkhangel´sk province of Russia

—986 Novaya Zemlya

Part of Arkhangel´sk province of Russia

—987 Severnaya Zemlya

Part of Krasnoyarsk territory of Russia

*For a specific part of this jurisdiction, region, or feature, see the part and follow instructions under —4–9

—988 New Siberian Islands

Part of Yakutia republic of Russia

—989 Antarctica

Including British Antarctic Territory; Dronning Maud (Queen Maud), Ellsworth, Enderby Lands; South Orkney, South Shetland Islands; South Pole

—99 Extraterrestrial worlds

Worlds other than Earth

Class space in —19

See Manual at T2—99 vs. T2—19

> —991–994 Solar system

Class comprehensive works in —99

—991 Earth's moon

—992 Planets of solar system and their satellites

—992 1 Mercury

—992 2 Venus

—992 3 Mars

—992 4 Asteroids (Planetoids)

—992 5 Jupiter

—992 6 Saturn

—992 7 Uranus

—992 8 Neptune

—992 9 Pluto and transplutonian planets

Subdivisions are added for Pluto and transplutonian planets together, for Pluto alone

—993 Meteoroids and comets

—994 Sun

Table 3. Subdivisions for the Arts, for Individual Literatures, for Specific Literary Forms

Notation from Table 3 is never used alone, but may be used as required by add notes under subdivisions of individual literatures or with base numbers for individual literatures identified by * under 810–890. It is never used for individual literatures that lack instructions to add from Table 3; the number for works of or about such literatures ends with the language notation, e.g., Newari poetry 895.49

Notation from Table 3 may also be used where instructed in 700.4, 791.4, 808–809

Table 3 is divided into three subtables:

Table 3A for description, critical appraisal, biography, single or collected works of an individual author

Table 3B for description, critical appraisal, biography, collected works of two or more authors; also for rhetoric in specific literary forms

Table 3C for additional elements used in number building within Table 3B and as instructed in 700.4, 791.4, 808–809

Turn to Table 3A or 3B for full instructions on building numbers for individual literatures, to 808–809 for other uses of Table 3B and 3C for literature, to 700.4 for uses of Table 3C for the arts, to 791.4 for uses of Table 3C for motion pictures, radio, television

See Manual at Table 3

Table 3A. Subdivisions for Works by or about Individual Authors

Procedures for building numbers for individual authors:

1. Look in the schedule 810–890 to find the base number for the language. The base number may be identified in an add note, e.g., at 820.1–828 ("add to base number 82") or another note, e.g., at 896 ("896.392 Swahili"); otherwise, it is the number given for the literature, e.g., Dutch-language literature 839.31. If there is a specific literary form, go to step 2; if not, go to the instructions under —8 in Table 3A

2. In Table 3A find the correct subdivision for the literary form, e.g., poetry —1. Add this to the base number, e.g., Swahili poetry 896.3921, Dutch poetry 839.311. If the literary form appears as a subdivision of —8 Miscellaneous writings, go to the instructions under —8 in Table 3A; otherwise, go to step 3

3. Turn back to the appropriate number in the schedule 810–890 to see whether there is an applicable period table. If there is one, go to step 4; if not, complete the class number by inserting a point between the third and fourth digits, e.g., Khmer (Cambodian) poetry by a 20th-century author 895.9321
   (Option: Where optional period tables are available for countries that share the same language, either [1] use initial letters to distinguish the separate countries, or [2] use the special number designated for literature of those countries that are not preferred. Then use the optional period tables, e.g., drama in English by a 20th-century New Zealand author NZ822.2 or 828.993322. Full instructions for optional period tables appear under 810.1–818, 819, 820.1–828, 828.99, 840.1–848, 848.99, 860.1–868, 868.99, 869, 869.899. If the option is used, go to step 4)
   (Option: Where optional period tables are not available for countries that share the same language, use initial letters to distinguish the separate countries. Then use the standard period table for the language if one is available. If a period table is available, go to step 4)

4. Select the appropriate period number. Add this number to the number already derived; always insert a point after the third digit. The class number is complete (*except* for William Shakespeare), since standard subdivisions are never added for individual authors, e.g., Spenser's *Faerie Queene* 821.3 (821 English poetry + 3 Elizabethan period)

See Manual at Table 3A; also at 800: Literary criticism

> —1–8 Specific forms

Unless other instructions are given, observe the following table of preference for works combining two or more literary forms, e.g., drama written in verse —2 (*not* —1):

Drama	—2
Poetry	—1
Class epigrams in verse in —8	
Fiction	—3
Essays	—4
Speeches	—5
Letters	—6
Miscellaneous writings	—8

A single work of humor or satire, or a collection of humor or satire by an individual author in one form is classed with the form, e.g., satirical fiction —3. Humor or satire without identifiable form is classed according to the instructions at —8, plus notation 07 from the table under —81–89 if there is an applicable period table. A collection of humor or satire by an individual author in more than one form is classed according to the instructions at —8, plus notation 09 from the add table under —81–89 if there is an applicable period table

Class comprehensive works (description, critical appraisal, biography, or collected works that cover two or more forms of literature by an individual author) with the form with which the author is chiefly identified, e.g., a biography that discusses the poetry and fiction of a mid-19th-century American writer known primarily as a novelist 813.3

If the author is not chiefly identified with any one form, class comprehensive works as instructed at —8, plus notation 09 from the table under —81–89 if there is an applicable period table, e.g., the collected poetry and fiction of a mid-19th-century American writer not chiefly identified with any one form 818.309

See Manual at Table 3A

(Option: Class description, critical appraisal, biography, single and collected works of all individual authors regardless of form in —8)

—1 Poetry

Class epigrams in verse in —8

See Manual at T3A—2, T3B—2 vs. T3A—1, T3B—102

—11–19 Poetry of specific periods

Add to —1 notation from the period table for the specific literature in 810–890, e.g., earliest period —11; do not add standard subdivisions. If there is no applicable period table, add nothing to —1, e.g., Mongolian poetry by an author of the earliest period 894.231 (*not* 894.2311)

(Option: Where two or more countries share the same language, follow one of the options given after step 3 at beginning of Table 3A, e.g., poetry in English by an Australian author of the earliest period A821.1 or 828.993411)

—2 Drama

Class here closet drama, drama written in poetry

See Manual at T3A—2, T3B—2 vs. T3A—1, T3B—102

—21–29 Specific periods

Add to —2 notation from the period table for the specific literature in 810–890, e.g., earliest period —21; do not add standard subdivisions. If there is no applicable period table, add nothing to —2, e.g., Mongolian drama by an author of the earliest period 894.232 (*not* 894.2321)

(Option: Where two or more countries share the same language, follow one of the options given after step 3 at beginning of Table 3A, e.g., drama in English by a New Zealand author of the earliest period NZ822.1 or 828.993321)

—3 Fiction

Class here novels, novelettes, short stories

Class graphic novels (cartoon or comic strip novels) in 741.5

—31–39 Specific periods

Add to —3 notation from the period table for the specific literature in 810–890, e.g., earliest period —31; do not add standard subdivisions. If there is no applicable period table, add nothing to —3, e.g., Mongolian fiction by an author of the earliest period 894.233 (*not* 894.2331)

(Option: Where two or more countries share the same language, follow one of the options given after step 3 at beginning of Table 3A, e.g., fiction in French by a Canadian author of the colonial period C843.3 or 848.99233)

—4 Essays

Texts, collections, discussions of works with literary value

See Manual at 800: Choice between literature and nonliterary subject

—41–49 Specific periods

Add to —4 notation from the period table for the specific literature in 810–890, e.g., earliest period —41; do not add standard subdivisions. If there is no applicable period table, add nothing to —4, e.g., Macedonian essays by an author of the earliest period 891.8194 (*not* 891.81941)

(Option: Where two or more countries share the same language, follow one of the options given after step 3 at beginning of Table 3A, e.g., essays in Spanish by a 19th-century Mexican author M864.2 or 868.992142)

—5 Speeches

Texts, collections, discussions of works with literary value

See Manual at 800: Choice between literature and nonliterary subject

—51–59 Specific periods

Add to —5 notation from the period table for the specific literature in 810–890, e.g., earliest period —51; do not add standard subdivisions. If there is no applicable period table, add nothing to —5, e.g., Mongolian speeches by an author of the earliest period 894.235 (*not* 894.2351)

(Option: Where two or more countries share the same language, follow one of the options given after step 3 at beginning of Table 3A, e.g., speeches in Spanish by a 19th-century Chilean author Ch865.2 or 868.993352)

—6 Letters

Texts, collections, discussions of works with literary value

Class collections of the letters of an individual author as biography with the form with which the author is chiefly identified, e.g., letters of a mid-19th-century American known primarily as a novelist 813.3

See Manual at 800: Choice between literature and nonliterary subject

—61–69 Specific periods

Add to —6 notation from the period table for the specific literature in 810–890, e.g., earliest period —61; do not add standard subdivisions. If there is no applicable period table, add nothing to —6, e.g., Tibetan letters by an author of the earliest period 895.46 (*not* 895.461)

(Option: Where two or more countries share the same language, follow one of the options given after step 3 at beginning of Table 3A, e.g., letters in Portuguese by a 20th-century Brazilian author B869.64 or 869.899264)

—8 Miscellaneous writings

Procedures for building numbers:

1. To the base number add notation 8, e.g., miscellaneous writings in English 828. Go to step 2

2. Turn back to the appropriate number in the schedule 810–890 to see whether there is an applicable period table. If there is one, go to step 3; if not, complete the class number by inserting a point between the third and fourth digits, e.g., miscellaneous writings in Khmer (Cambodian) by a 20th-century writer 895.9328

(Option: Where optional period tables are available for countries that share the same language, either [1] use initial letters to distinguish the separate countries, or [2] use the special number designated for literature of those countries that are not preferred. Then use the optional period tables, e.g., miscellaneous writings in English by a 20th-century New Zealand author NZ828.2 or 828.993382. Full instructions for optional period tables appear under 810.1–818, 819, 820.1–828, 828.99, 840.1–848, 848.99, 860.1–868, 868.99, 869, 869.899. If the option is used, go to step 3)

(Option: Where optional period tables are not available for countries that share the same language, use initial letters to distinguish the separate countries. Then use the standard period table for the language if one is available. If a period table is available, go to step 3)

3. Select the appropriate period number, e.g., the Victorian period in the English literature of Great Britain 8. Then follow the instructions under —81–89

(Option: Class here description, critical appraisal, biography, single and collected works of all individual authors regardless of form; prefer —1–8)

—81–89 Specific periods

Add to —8 notation from the period table for the specific literature in 810–890, e.g., earliest period —81; then add further as follows, but in no case add standard subdivisions:

02 Anecdotes, epigrams, graffiti, jokes, quotations

Including riddles that are jokes

Class riddles as folk literature, interdisciplinary works on riddles in 398.6

See Manual at T1—0207 vs. T3B—7, T3A—8 + 02, T3B—802, T3B—8 + 02, T3A—8 + 07, T3B—807, T3B—8 + 07; also at T3A—8 + 02, T3B—802, T3B—8 + 02 vs. 398.6, 793.735

03 Diaries, journals, notebooks, reminiscences

See Manual at T3A—8 + 03 and T3B—803, T3B—8 + 03

07 Works without identifiable literary form

Class here experimental and nonformalized works

Class experimental works with an identifiable literary form with the form, e.g., experimental novels —3

See Manual at T1—0207 vs. T3B—7, T3A—8 + 02, T3B—802, T3B—8 + 02, T3A—8 + 07, T3B—807, T3B—8 + 07

08 Prose literature

Collections or discussions of works in more than one prose form

Class here collections and criticism of selected prose works of an individual author that do not include the author's main literary form, e.g., a collection of the prose works of an English Victorian poet 828.808, a collection of the stories and plays of an English essayist of the romantic period 828.708

Class prose without identifiable literary form in 07. Class a specific form of prose literature with the form, e.g., essays —4; class comprehensive collections or criticisms of an author's work with the the author's main literary number, either with the predominant literary form or in 09 for individual authors not limited to or chiefly identifiable with one specific form, e.g., a comprehensive collection of the works of an English Victorian writer known primarily as a novelist 823.8

09 Individual authors not limited to or chiefly identifiable with one specific form

Class here description, critical appraisal, biography, collected works

If there is no applicable period table, add nothing to —8, e.g., Mongolian prose literature by an author of the later 20th century 894.238 (*not* 894.23808)

(Option: Where two or more countries share the same language, follow one of the options given after step 2 under —8, e.g., prose literature in English by an Indian author of the later 20th century In828.308 or 828.99358308)

Table 3B. Subdivisions for Works by or about More than One Author

Table 3B is followed and supplemented by Table 3C, which provides additional elements for building numbers within Table 3B

Procedures for building numbers for works by or about more than one author, limited to literatures of specific languages:

1. Look in the schedule 810–890 to find the base number for the language. The base number may be identified in an add note, e.g., at 820.1–828 ("add to base number 82") or another note, e.g., at 896 ("896.392 Swahili"); otherwise, it is the number given for the literature, e.g., Dutch-language literature 839.31. If there is a specific literary form, go to step 2; if not, go to step 8

2. In Table 3B find the subdivision for the literary form, e.g., poetry —1. Add this to the base number, e.g., English poetry 821, Dutch poetry 839.311. If the literary form appears as a subdivision of —8 Miscellaneous writings, go to the instructions under —8 in Table 3B. If the work deals with poetry, drama, fiction, or speech of specific media, scopes, kinds for which there is special notation in Table 3B (e.g., —1042 sonnets), go to step 3. For other works that deal with or fall within a limited time span, go to step 4. A limited time span is (1) fewer than three literary periods or (2) a single century. For other works not limited by time period, go to step 7

3. Use the notation in Table 3B for the kind of poetry, drama, fiction, or speech, e.g., sonnets in English literature 821.042. Insert a point after the third digit. Check whether the specific form is (1) the sole kind in a heading identified by * or (2) is named in a subdivisions-are-added note as a kind for which subdivisions may be added or (3) appears in a class-here note under a heading identified by *. If none of these conditions holds, the number is complete, e.g., collections of English-language clerihews 821.07

If one of the three conditions does hold, follow the instructions in the table under —102–107 in Table 3B. Following these instructions will involve using Table 3C for literature of specific periods, literature displaying specific features or emphasizing specific subjects, and literature for and by specific kinds of persons, e.g., collections of English sonnets 821.04208, collections of English sonnets about love 821.042083543

(continued)

Table 3B. Subdivisions for Works by or about More than One Author (continued)

4. Turn back to the appropriate number in the schedule 810–890 to see whether there is an applicable period table. If there is one, go to step 5; if not, complete the class number by inserting a point between the third and fourth digits, e.g., Khmer (Cambodian) poetry by 20th-century authors 895.9321

(Option: Where optional period tables are available for countries that share the same language, either [1] use initial letters to distinguish the separate countries, or [2] use the special number designated for literature of those countries that are not preferred. Then use the optional period tables, e.g., 20th-century drama in English by New Zealand authors NZ822.2 or 828.993322. Full instructions for optional period tables appear under 810.1–818, 819, 820.1–828, 828.99, 840.1–848, 848.99, 860.1–868, 868.99, 869, 869.899. If the option is used, go to step 5)

(Option: Where optional period tables are not available for countries that share the same language, use initial letters to distinguish the separate countries. Then use the standard period table for the language if one is available. If a period table is available, go to step 5)

5. Select the appropriate period number. Add this number to the number already derived, e.g., English poetry of the Elizabethan period 821.3; always insert a point after the third digit. Go to step 6

6. Under the number for the literary form in Table 3B, go to the subdivisions for specific periods, e.g., under —1 for poetry go to —11–19. Follow the instructions given there, which will lead to use of the table under —1–8. For literature displaying specific features, literature emphasizing subjects, and literature for and by specific kinds of persons, the instructions at —1–8 will lead to use of Table 3C, e.g., critical appraisal of idealism in English Elizabethan poetry 821.30913

7. If the work is not limited by time period, go to the first subdivisions under the particular form in Table 3B, e.g., under —1 for poetry go to —1001–1009. Follow the instructions given there, which will lead to use of the table under —1–8. For literature displaying specific features, literature emphasizing subjects, and literature for and by specific kinds of persons, the instructions at —1–8 will lead to use of Table 3C, e.g., collections of English poetry about war 821.0080358, collections of English poetry by rural authors 821.008091734

(continued)

Table 3B. Subdivisions for Works by or about More than One Author (continued)

8. If the work is not limited to a specific literary form, consult —01–09 in Table 3B. Follow the instructions at the number selected, making use of Table 3C when specified, e.g., collections of English literature in many forms about holidays 820.80334. Use period notation 08001–08009 and —09001–09009 only if there is an applicable period table

(Option: Where optional period tables are available for countries that share the same language, either [1] use initial letters to distinguish the separate countries, or [2] use the special number designated for literature of those countries that are not preferred. Then use the optional period tables, e.g., 20th-century drama in English by New Zealand authors NZ822.2 or 828.993322. Full instructions for optional period tables appear under 810.1–818, 819, 820.1–828, 828.99, 840.1–848, 848.99, 860.1–868, 868.99, 869, 869.899)

(Option: Where optional period tables are not available for countries that share the same language, use initial letters to distinguish the separate countries. Then use the standard period table for the language if one is available)

The procedures described above require the use of schedule 810–890, Table 3B, and Table 3C in varying order. Sometimes also other tables are used. Example:

82	English (810–890)
1	poetry (Table 3B)
914	of later 20th century (810–890)
080	collections (Table 3B)
32	about places (Table 3C)
4253	Lincolnshire (Table 2)

Thus, collections of contemporary English-language poetry about Lincolnshire 821.914080324253

Note that literary form —8 Miscellaneous writings is arranged first by period and then by specific miscellaneous forms

Instructions in the use of notation from Table 3B for rhetoric in specific literary forms, collections of literary texts from more than two literatures, and history, description, critical appraisal of more than two literatures are found in 808–809

See Manual at Table 3B; also at 800

SUMMARY

— 01–09	**[Standard subdivisions; collections; history, description, critical appraisal]**
— 1	**Poetry**
— 2	**Drama**
— 3	**Fiction**
— 4	**Essays**
— 5	**Speeches**
— 6	**Letters**
— 7	**Humor and satire**
— 8	**Miscellaneous writings**

—01–07 Standard subdivisions

Standard subdivisions are used for general works consisting equally of literary texts and history, description, critical appraisal, e.g., a serial consisting equally of literary texts and history, description, critical appraisal of a variety of literature in English 820.5. Works limited to specific topics found in Table 3C are classed in —08, plus notation from Table 3C

Class collections of literary texts in —08; class history, description, critical appraisal in —09

—08 Collections of literary texts in more than one form

Class history, description, critical appraisal of a specific literature in —09

See Manual at T3B—08 and T3B—09

—080 001–080 99 Standard subdivisions; specific periods; literature displaying specific features, or emphasizing subjects, or for and by specific kinds of persons

Add to —080 notation 001–99 from Table 3C, e.g., collections of literary texts about holidays —080334

Works consisting equally of literary texts and history, description, critical appraisal of a specific literature are classed here if limited to specific topics found in Table 3C, e.g., texts and criticism of English-language literary works about war 820.80358

—09 History, description, critical appraisal of works in more than one form

Class here collected biography

See Manual at T3B—08 and T3B—09

—090 001–090 008 Standard subdivisions

—090 009 Historical and geographic treatment

—[090 009 01–090 009 05] Historical periods

Do not use; class in —09001–09009

—090 009 3–090 009 9 Treatment by specific continents, countries, localities

Do not use for literature for and by persons resident in specific continents, countries, localities; class in —0993–0999

—090 01–090 09 Literature from specific periods

Add to —0900 notation from the period table for the specific literature, e.g., earliest period —09001. If there is no applicable period table, this provision for indicating period cannot be used, e.g., history of early Cornish literature 891.6709

(Option: Use notation from an optional period table, e.g., history of literature in Spanish by Chilean authors of early 20th century Ch860.90042 or 868.9933090042; prefer —0993–0999, e.g., history of literature in Spanish by Chilean authors 860.9983, history of literature in Spanish by Chilean authors of early 20th century 860.998309041. Full instructions appear under 810.1–818, 819, 820.1–828, 828.99, 840.1–848, 848.99, 860.1–868, 868.99, 869, and 869.899)

See Manual at T3B—091–099 vs. T3B—09001–09009

—091–099 Literature displaying specific features or emphasizing subjects, and for and by specific kinds of persons

Add to —09 notation 1–9 from Table 3C, e.g., history and description of literature on Faust —09351, history of literature in Spanish by Chilean authors 860.9983, history of literature in Spanish by Chilean authors of early 20th century 860.998309041

See Manual at T3B—091–099 vs. T3B—09001–09009

(Option: Class literature from specific periods in —09001–09009, using notation from an optional period table)

> —1–8 Specific forms

Unless other instructions are given, observe the following table of preference for works combining two or more literary forms, e.g., poetic drama —2 (*not* —1):

Drama	—2
Poetry	—1
Class epigrams in verse in —8	
Fiction	—3
Essays	—4
Speeches	—5
Letters	—6
Miscellaneous writings	—8
Humor and satire	—7

When told to add as instructed under —1–8, add as follows:

1–7 Standard subdivisions

Standard subdivisions are used for general works consisting equally of literary texts and history, description, critical appraisal, e.g., a serial consisting equally of literary texts and history, description, critical appraisal of poetry in English 821.005. Works limited to specific topics found in Table 3C are classed in 801–809

Class collections of literary texts in 8; class history, description, critical appraisal in 9

(continued)

> **—1–8 Specific forms (continued)**

8 Collections of literary texts

General works consisting equally of literary texts and history, description, critical appraisal are classed in 1–7, in the number for the specific form, or the specific form plus literary period. Works limited to specific topics found in Table 3C are classed in 801–809

8001–8007 Standard subdivisions

[8008] History and description with respect to kinds of persons

Do not use; class in 808–809

[8009] Historical, geographic, persons treatment

Do not use; class in 9

801–809 Collections displaying specific features or emphasizing specific subjects, for and by specific kinds of persons

Add to 80 notation 1–9 from Table 3C, e.g., collections dealing with places 8032

Works consisting equally of literary texts and history, description, critical appraisal are classed here if limited to specific topics found in Table 3C

9 History, description, critical appraisal

Class here collected biography

Follow the instructions under 8 for works consisting equally of literary texts and history, description, critical appraisal

901–907 Standard subdivisions

[908] History and description with respect to kinds of persons

Do not use; class in 98–99

[909] Historical, geographic, persons treatment

Do not use for historical and persons treatment; class in 9. Do not use for geographic treatment; class in 99

91–99 History, description, critical appraisal of texts displaying specific features or emphasizing specific subjects, for and by specific kinds of persons

Add to 9 notation 1–9 from Table 3C, e.g., critical appraisal of works by children 99282

Class comprehensive works on prose literature in —808. Class comprehensive works on two or more forms with the base number for the individual literature, plus notation 01–09 from Table 3B if applicable, adding 0 when required to make a three-figure number, e.g., comprehensive works on English poetry and fiction 820

—1 Poetry

Including greeting card verse

Class here prose poems

See Manual at T3B—1

—100 1–100 9 Standard subdivisions; collections; history, description, critical appraisal

Add to —100 as instructed under —1–8, e.g., collections of poetry dealing with places —1008032

> —102–107 Specific kinds of poetry

Limited to the kinds provided for below

Except for modifications shown under specific entries, add to each subdivision identified by * as follows:

01–07 Standard subdivisions
Standard subdivisions are used for general works consisting equally of literary texts and history, description, critical appraisal, e.g., a serial consisting equally of literary texts and history, description, critical appraisal of narrative poetry in English —10305. Works limited to specific topics found in Table 3C are classed in 08, plus notation from Table 3C
Class collections of literary texts in 08; class history, description, critical appraisal in 09

08 Collections of literary texts
Add to 08 notation 001–99 from Table 3C, e.g., collections dealing with places 0832, collections of English sonnets of the Elizabethan period 821.0420803
Works consisting equally of literary texts and history, description, critical appraisal of the form in a specific kind are classed here if limited to specific topics found in Table 3C, e.g., texts and criticism of narrative poems about war —10308358

09 History, description, critical appraisal
Class here collected biography
Add to 09 notation 001–99 from Table 3C, e.g., critical appraisal of works by children 099282, critical appraisal of 20th century French lyric poetry 841.0409091
Follow the instructions under 08 for works consisting equally of literary texts and history, description, critical appraisal

Class epigrams in verse in —8; class comprehensive works in —1

See Manual at T3B—102–107, T3B—205, T3B—308 vs. T3C—1, T3C—3

—102 *Dramatic poetry

Including dramatic monologues

See also —2 for poetic plays

See Manual at T3A—2, T3B—2 vs. T3A—1, T3B—102

—103 *Narrative poetry

Including fabliaux

For ballads, see —1044

—103 2 *Epic poetry

—103 3 *Medieval metrical romances

See also —3 for prose versions of medieval romances

*Add as instructed under —102–107

—104 *Lyric and balladic poetry

Including concrete poetry

Class here poetry of minnesingers and troubadours

Subdivisions are added for lyric and balladic poetry together, for lyric poetry alone

Class dramatic lyric poems in —102

—104 1 *Haiku

—104 2 *Sonnets

—104 3 *Odes

—104 4 *Ballads

—105 *Didactic poetry

—107 *Humorous and satirical poetry

Including clerihews

Class here light verse [*formerly* —108]

Subdivisions are added for either or both topics in heading

Class humor and satire in two or more literary forms, including both verse and prose, in —7

—107 5 *Limericks

—[108] Ephemeral and light verse

Use of this number for ephemeral verse that is not light or humorous verse discontinued; class in —1

Light verse relocated to —107

—11–19 Poetry of specific periods

Add to —1 notation from the period table for the specific literature in 810–890, e.g., earliest period —11; then add 0 and to the result add further as instructed under —1–8, e.g., collections from the earliest period dealing with places —1108032

If there is no applicable period table, add nothing to —1, e.g., collections of Mongolian poetry by authors of the earliest period 894.231 (*not* 894.231108)

Class specific kinds of poetry from specific periods in —102–107

(Option: Where two or more countries share the same language, follow one of the options given after step 4 at beginning of Table 3B, e.g., collections of poetry in English by Australian authors of the earliest period A821.108 or 828.99341108)

*Add as instructed under —102–107

—2 Drama

Class here closet drama, drama written in poetry

See Manual at T3B—2; also at T3A—2, T3B—2 vs. T3A—1, T3B—102

—200 1–200 9 Standard subdivisions; collections; history, description, critical appraisal

Add to —200 as instructed under —1–8, e.g., collections of drama dealing with places —2008032

> —202–205 Drama of specific media, scopes, kinds

Add to each subdivision identified by * as instructed under —102–107, e.g., collections of comedies dealing with places —205230832

Class comprehensive works in —2

> —202–203 Drama for mass media

Class comprehensive works in —2

—202 Drama for radio and television

—202 2 *Drama for radio

—202 5 *Drama for television

—203 *Drama for motion pictures

—204 Drama of restricted scope

Class drama of restricted scope for mass media in —202–203

—204 1 *One-act plays

Including interludes, sketches

—204 5 *Monologues

—205 Specific kinds of drama

Limited to the kinds provided for below

Including masques

Class specific kinds of drama for mass media in —202–203; class specific kinds of drama of restricted scope in —204

See Manual at T3B—102–107, T3B—205, T3B—308 vs. T3C—1, T3C—3

—205 1 *Serious drama

Class here Nō plays

*Add as instructed under —102–107

—205 12 *Tragedy

Class tragicomedy in —20523

—205 14 *Historical drama

—205 16 *Religious and morality plays

Not limited to medieval plays

Class here miracle, mystery, passion plays

Subdivisions are added for either or both topics in heading

—205 2 *Comedy and melodrama

—205 23 *Comedy

Including tragicomedy

Class humor and satire in two or more literary forms, including both verse and prose, in —7

—205 232 *Farce

—205 27 *Melodrama

Including modern detective and mystery (suspense) drama

—205 7 *Variety drama

—21–29 Drama of specific periods

Add to —2 notation from the period table for the specific literature in 810–890, e.g., earliest period —21; then add 0 and to the result add further as instructed under —1–8, e.g., critical appraisal of drama of earliest period —2109

If there is no applicable period table, add nothing to —2, e.g., collections of Mongolian drama by authors of the earliest period 894.232 (*not* 894.232108)

Class drama of specific media, scopes, kinds from specific periods in —202–205

(Option: Where two or more countries share the same language, follow one of the options given after step 4 at beginning of Table 3B, e.g., collections of drama in English by New Zealand authors of the earliest period NZ822.108 or 828.99332108)

*Add as instructed under —102–107

—3 Fiction

Class here novelettes and novels

Class graphic novels (cartoon or comic strip novels) in 741.5

See Manual at T3B—3

—300 1–300 9 Standard subdivisions; collections; history, description, critical appraisal

Add to —300 as instructed under —1–8, e.g., collections of fiction dealing with places —3008032

> —301–308 Fiction of specific scopes and kinds

Add to each subdivision identified by * as instructed under —102–107, e.g., collections of short stories dealing with places —3010832

Class comprehensive works in —3

—301 *Short stories

Class short stories of specific kinds in —308

—308 Specific kinds of fiction

Limited to the kinds provided for below

Unless other instructions are given, observe the following table of preference, e.g., historical adventure fiction —3081 (*not* —3087):

Historical and period fiction	—3081
Adventure fiction	—3087
Love and romance	—3085
Psychological, realistic, sociological fiction	—3083

See Manual at T3B—102–107, T3B—205, T3B—308 vs. T3C—1, T3C—3

—308 1 *Historical and period fiction

Subdivisions are added for either or both topics in heading

—308 3 *Psychological, realistic, sociological fiction

Subdivisions are added for any or all topics in heading

—308 5 *Love and romance

Modern romantic fiction

Subdivisions are added for either or both topics in heading

Class medieval prose romances in —3

*Add as instructed under —102–107

—308 7 *Adventure fiction

Unless other instructions are given, observe the following table of preference, e.g., Gothic horror fiction —308729 (*not* —308738):

Science fiction	—308762
Gothic fiction	—308729
Western fiction	—30874
Detective, mystery, suspense, spy fiction (*except* —308729)	—30872
Ghost fiction	—308733
Horror fiction	—308738
Fantasy fiction	—308766
Picaresque fiction	—30877

—308 72 *Detective, mystery, suspense, spy, Gothic fiction

Subdivisions are added for a combination of two or more topics in heading, for detective fiction alone, for mystery fiction alone, for suspense fiction alone, for spy fiction alone

—308 729 *Gothic fiction

Class modern romantic fiction in which the supernatural has little or no role in —3085

—308 73 *Ghost and horror fiction

—308 733 *Ghost fiction

—308 738 *Horror fiction

—308 74 *Western fiction

—308 76 *Science and fantasy fiction

—308 762 *Science fiction

—308 766 *Fantasy fiction

—308 77 *Picaresque fiction

—31–39 Fiction of specific periods

Add to —3 notation from the period table for the specific literature in 810–890, e.g., earliest period —31; then add 0 and to the result add further as instructed under —1–8, e.g., critical appraisal of fiction of earliest period —3109

If there is no applicable period table, add nothing to —3, e.g., collections of Mongolian fiction by authors of the earliest period 894.233 (*not* 894.233108)

Class specific scopes and kinds from specific periods in —301–308

(Option: Where two or more countries share the same language, follow one of the options given after step 4 at beginning of Table 3B, e.g., collections of fiction in French by Canadian authors of the earliest period C843.108 or 848.9923108)

*Add as instructed under —102–107

—4 Essays

Collections or discussions of works with literary value

See Manual at 800: Choice between literature and nonliterary subject

—400 1–400 9 Standard subdivisions; collections; history, description, critical appraisal

Add to —400 as instructed under —1–8, e.g., collections of essays dealing with places —4008032

—41–49 Essays of specific periods

Add to —4 notation from the period table for the specific literature in 810–890, e.g., earliest period —41; then add 0 and to the result add further as instructed under —1–8, e.g., critical appraisal of essays of the earliest period —4109

If there is no applicable period table, add nothing to —4, e.g., collections of Mongolian essays by authors of the earliest period 894.234 (*not* 894.234108)

(Option: Where two or more countries share the same language, follow one of the options given after step 4 at beginning of Table 3B, e.g., collections of essays in Spanish by Mexican authors of the 19th century M864.208 or 868.99214208)

—5 Speeches

Collections or discussions of works with literary value

See Manual at 800: Choice between literature and nonliterary subject

—500 1–500 9 Standard subdivisions; collections; history, description, critical appraisal

Add to —500 as instructed under —1–8, e.g., collections of speeches dealing with places —5008032

> —501–506 Specific kinds of speeches

Limited to the kinds provided for below

Add to each subdivision identified by * as instructed under —102–107, e.g., collections of recitations dealing with places —5040832

Class comprehensive works in —5

—501 *Public speeches (Oratory)

Including after-dinner, platform, television speeches; speeches and toasts for special occasions

For debates, see —503

—503 *Debates

Class here public discussion of opposing views

*Add as instructed under —102–107

—504 *Recitations

—505 *Texts for choral speaking

—506 *Conversations

—51–59 Speeches of specific periods

Add to —5 notation from the period table for the specific literature in 810–890, e.g., earliest period —51; then add 0 and to the result add further as instructed under —1–8, e.g., critical appraisal of speeches of the earliest period —5109

If there is no applicable period table, add nothing to —5, e.g., collections of Mongolian speeches by authors of the earliest period 894.235 (*not* 894.235108)

Class specific kinds from specific periods in —501–506

(Option: Where two or more countries share the same language, follow one of the options given after step 4 at beginning of Table 3B, e.g., collections of speeches in Spanish by Chilean authors of the 19th century Ch865.208 or 868.99335208)

—6 Letters

Collections or discussions of works with literary value

See Manual at 800: Choice between literature and nonliterary subject

—600 1–600 9 Standard subdivisions; collections; history, description, critical appraisal

Add to —600 as instructed under —1–8, e.g., collections of letters dealing with places —6008032

—61–69 Letters of specific periods

Add to —6 notation from the period table for the specific literature in 810–890, e.g., earliest period —61; then add 0 and to the result add further as instructed under —1–8, e.g., critical appraisal of letters of the earliest period —6109

If there is no applicable period table, add nothing to —6, e.g., collections of Tibetan letters by authors of the earliest period 895.46 (*not* 895.46108)

(Option: Where two or more countries share the same language, follow one of the options given after step 4 at beginning of Table 3B, e.g., collections of letters in Portuguese by Brazilian authors of the 20th century B869.6408 or 869.89926408)

*Add as instructed under —102–107

—7 Humor and satire

Limited to collections and criticism of works in two or more literary forms including both verse and prose

Class here parody

See also —808 for humor and satire in two or more prose forms

See Manual at T1—0207 vs. T3B—7, T3A—8 + 02, T3B—802, T3B—8 + 02, T3A—8 + 07, T3B—807, T3B—8 + 07

(Option: Give precedence to humor and satire over all other literary forms)

—700 1–700 9 Standard subdivisions; collections; history, description, critical appraisal

Add to —700 as instructed under —1–8, e.g., collections of humor and satire dealing with places —7008032

—71–79 Humor and satire of specific periods

Add to —7 notation from the period table for the specific literature in 810–890, e.g., earliest period —71; then add 0 and to the result add further as instructed under —1–8, e.g., critical appraisal of humor and satire of the earliest period —7109

If there is no applicable period table, add nothing to —7, e.g., collections of Turkmen humor and satire by authors of the earliest period 894.3647 (*not* 894.3647108)

(Option: Where two or more countries share the same language, follow one of the options given after step 4 at beginning of Table 3B, e.g., collections of humor and satire in English by Australian authors of the earliest period A827.108 or 828.99347108)

—8 Miscellaneous writings

Procedures for building numbers:

1. To the base number for the literature add notation 8, e.g., miscellaneous writings in English 828. If the work covers a limited time span (fewer than three literary periods, unless a single century spans three periods, then a single century), go to step 2; if not, go to step 4

2. Turn back to the appropriate number in the schedule 810–890 to see whether there is an applicable period table. If there is one, go to step 3; if not, go to step 4
(Option: Where optional period tables are available for countries that share the same language, either [1] use initial letters to distinguish the separate countries, or [2] use the special number designated for literature of those countries that are not preferred. Then use the optional period tables, e.g., miscellaneous writings in English by 20th-century New Zealand authors NZ828.2 or 828.993382. Full instructions for optional period tables appear under 810.1–818, 819, 820.1–828, 828.99, 840.1–848, 848.99, 860.1–868, 868.99, 869, 869.899. If the option is used, go to step 3)
(Option: Where optional period tables are not available for countries that share the same language, use initial letters to distinguish the separate countries. Then use the standard period table for the language if one is available. If a period table is available, go to step 3)

3. Select the appropriate period number, e.g., the Victorian period in English literature 8. Then follow the instructions under —81–89

4. If the work does not cover a limited time period, or if there is no applicable period table, consider whether the work is limited to one of the forms of miscellaneous writing listed in —802–808. If it is limited to one of those forms, go to step 5; if not, complete the class number by inserting a point between the third and fourth digits, e.g., miscellaneous writings in Russian from many time periods 891.78, miscellaneous writings in Khmer (Cambodian) by 20th-century authors 895.9328

5. Class the work in the appropriate number from the span —802–808, then complete the number by inserting a point between the third and fourth digits, e.g., prose literature in Russian from many time periods 891.7808, prose literature in Khmer (Cambodian) by 20th-century authors 895.932808

See Manual at Table 3B: Number building

—800 1–800 9 Standard subdivisions; collections; history, description, critical appraisal

Add to —800 as instructed under —1–8, e.g., critical appraisal of miscellaneous writings from more than one period —8009

> —802–808 Specific kinds of miscellaneous writings

Limited to kinds provided for below

Class in each number without further subdivision history, description, critical appraisal, biography, collections of works of authors from more than one period

Class comprehensive works in —8

—802 Anecdotes, epigrams, graffiti, jokes, quotations

Standard subdivisions are added for any or all topics in heading

Including riddles that are jokes

Class humor and satire in two or more literary forms, including both verse and prose, in —7; class riddles as folk literature, interdisciplinary works on riddles in 398.6

See Manual at T1—0207 vs. T3B—7, T3A—8 + 02, T3B—802, T3B—8 + 02, T3A—8 + 07, T3B—807, T3B—8 + 07; also at T3A—8 + 02, T3B—802, T3B—8 + 02 vs. 398.6, 793.735

—803 Diaries, journals, notebooks, reminiscences

Class interdisciplinary collections of diaries in 900. Class diaries, journals, notebooks, reminiscences of nonliterary authors with the appropriate subject, e.g., diary of an astronomer 520.92

See Manual at T3A—8 + 03 and T3B—803, T3B—8 + 03

—807 Works without identifiable literary form

Class here experimental and nonformalized works

Class experimental works with an identifiable literary form with the form, e.g., experimental novels —3

See Manual at T1—0207 vs. T3B—7, T3A—8 + 02, T3B—802, T3B—8 + 02, T3A—8 + 07, T3B—807, T3B—8 + 07

—808 Prose literature

Collections and discussions of works in more than one literary form

Class prose without identifiable literary form in —807. Class a specific form of prose literature with the form, e.g., essays —4

—81–89 Miscellaneous writings of specific periods

Add to —8 notation from the period table for the specific literature in 810–890, e.g., earliest period —81; then add further as follows:

001–009 Standard subdivisions; collections; history, description, critical appraisal

Add to 00 as instructed under —1–8, e.g., collections 008

02 Anecdotes, epigrams, graffiti, jokes, quotations

Standard subdivisions are added for any or all topics in heading

Including riddles that are jokes

Class humor and satire in two or more literary forms, including both verse and prose, in —7; class anecdotes, epigrams, graffiti, jokes, quotations from specific periods in —802 if there is no applicable period table; class riddles as folk literature, interdisciplinary works on riddles in 398.6

See Manual at T1—0207 vs. T3B—7, T3A—8 + 02, T3B—802, T3B—8 + 02, T3A—8 + 07, T3B—807, T3B—8 + 07; also at T3A—8 + 02, T3B—802, T3B—8 + 02 vs. 398.6, 793.735

0201–0209 Standard subdivisions; collections; history, description, critical appraisal

Add to 020 as instructed under —1–8, e.g., collections 0208

03 Diaries, journals, notebooks, reminiscences

Class diaries, journals, notebooks, reminiscences from specific periods in —803 if there is no applicable period table

See Manual at T3A—8 + 03 and T3B—803, T3B—8 + 03

0301–0309 Standard subdivisions; collections; history, description, critical appraisal

Add to 030 as instructed under —1–8, e.g., collections 0308

07 Works without identifiable literary form

Class here experimental and nonformalized works

Class works without identifiable literary form from specific periods in —807 if there is no applicable period table. Class experimental works with an identifiable literary form with the form, e.g., experimental novels —3

See Manual at T1—0207 vs. T3B—7, T3A—8 + 02, T3B—802, T3B—8 + 02, T3A—8 + 07, T3B—807, T3B—8 + 07

0701–0709 Standard subdivisions; collections; history, description, critical appraisal

Add to 070 as instructed under —1–8, e.g., collections of stream of consciousness writings 0708025

(continued)

—81–89 Miscellaneous writings of specific periods (continued)

08 Prose literature

Collections and discussions of works in more than one literary form

Class prose without identifiable literary form in 07. Class a specific form of prose literature with the form, e.g., essays —4

0801–0809 Standard subdivisions; collections; history, description, critical appraisal

Add to 080 as instructed under —1–8, e.g., collections 0808

Class prose literature from specific periods in —808, e.g., collections of 20th-century Albanian prose literature 891.991808

(Option: Use the notation from an optional period table with either option given after step 2 under —8 in Table 3B, e.g., prose literature in English by Australian authors of early 20th century A828.20808 or 828.9934820808)

Table 3C. Notation to Be Added Where Instructed in Table 3B, 700.4, 791.4, 808–809

See Manual at Table 3B: Preference order

SUMMARY

— 001–009	**Standard subdivisions**
— 01–09	**Specific periods**
— 1	**Arts and literature displaying specific qualities of style, mood, viewpoint**
— 2	**Literature displaying specific elements**
— 3	**Arts and literature dealing with specific themes and subjects**
— 4	**Literature emphasizing subjects**
— 8	**Literature for and by persons of ethnic and national groups**
— 9	**Literature for and by other specific kinds of persons**

—001–008 Standard subdivisions

—009 Historical and geographic treatment

—009 01–009 05 Historical periods

Do not use for literature of a specific language; class in —01–09

—01–09 Specific periods

Add to —0 notation from the period table for the specific literature, e.g., earliest period —01

—1 Arts and literature displaying specific qualities of style, mood, viewpoint

Do not use if redundant, e.g., horror (—164) in horror fiction (—308738 in Table 3B)

Class literature displaying specific elements and specific qualities in —2; class arts and literature dealing with specific themes and subjects and displaying specific qualities in —3

See Manual at T3B—102–107, T3B—205, T3B—308 vs. T3C—1, T3C—3

—11 Nontraditional viewpoints

Including impressionism

Class here avant-garde, experimental approaches in the arts

For a specific type of avant-garde or experimental approach not provided for here, see the type, e.g., experimental literary works without identifiable literary form —807 in Table 3B

—112 Modernism

—113 Postmodernism

—114 Futurism

—115 Expressionism

—116 Dadaism and surrealism

—116 2 Dadaism

—116 3 Surrealism

—12 Realism and naturalism

Including determinism

—13 Idealism

—14 Classicism and romanticism

Class pastoral arts and literature in —321734

—142 Classicism

—145 Romanticism

Including primitivism

—15 Symbolism, allegory, fantasy, myth

Standard subdivisions are added for any or all topics in heading

Including the grotesque, science fiction in the arts

Class symbolism, allegory, fantasy, myth associated with a specific style or viewpoint with the style or viewpoint, e.g., surrealism —1163

For science fiction as a type of fiction, see —308762 in Table 3B

See Manual at T3C—37 vs. T3C—15

—16 Tragedy and horror

—162 Tragedy

For tragedy as a kind of drama, see —20512 in Table 3B

—164 Horror

For horror fiction, see —308738 in Table 3B

—17 Comedy

Comic style or viewpoint

Class collections and criticism of humor and satire in two or more literary forms in —7 in Table 3B; class jokes in —802 in Table 3B

For comedy as a kind of drama, see —20523 in Table 3B

—18 Irony

—2 Literature displaying specific elements

Class literature dealing with specific themes and subjects and displaying specific elements in —3

—22 Description

Including setting

—23 Narrative

—24 Plot

—25 Stream of consciousness

—26 Dialogue

—27 Characters

Including the "double" (Doppelgänger) in literature

—3 Arts and literature dealing with specific themes and subjects

Do not use if redundant, e.g., historical themes (—358) in historical fiction (—3081 in Table 3B)

See Manual at T3B—102–107, T3B—205, T3B—308 vs. T3C—1, T3C—3

—32 Places

Class here travel [*formerly* —355], landscapes, civilization of places

Add to —32 notation 1–9 from Table 2, e.g., the sea —32162, pastoral themes —321734, the American West —3278, California —32794

Class western fiction as a type of fiction in —30874 in Table 3B; class historical and political themes, historical events in specific places in —358

For supernatural, mythological, legendary places, see —372

—33 Times

Including seasons; parts of day, e.g., dawn

Class time as a philosophic concept in —384

—334 Holidays

Including religious holidays, e.g., Christmas

—35 Humanity

Class here human existence, works dealing with contemporary viewpoints

Unless other instructions are given, observe the following table of preference, e.g., artistic themes associated with artists —357 (*not* —35287):

Specific persons	—351
Historical and political themes	—358
Life cycle	—354
Social themes	—355
Artistic, recreational, literary themes	—357
Technical themes	—356
Human characteristics and activities	—353
Specific kinds of persons	—352

—351 Specific persons

Real, fictional, legendary, mythological persons

Including Count Dracula, Don Juan, Faust, Joan of Arc, Job, Julius Caesar, King Arthur, Odysseus, Pierrot

See also —382 for specific gods and goddesses

—352 Specific kinds of persons

Including heroes

Add to —352 the numbers following —08 in notation 081–089 from Table 1, e.g., women —3522

The numbers following —08 in notation 081–089 from Table 1 replace notation 03–99 from Table 7 with the result that many numbers have been reused with new meanings

See also —375 for paranatural beings of human and semihuman form; also —8–9 for literature for and by specific kinds of persons

See Manual at T3C—353–358 vs. T3C—352

> —353–358 Specific human, social, scientific, technical, artistic, literary, historical, political themes

Class comprehensive works in —35

See Manual at T3C—353–358 vs. T3C—352

—353 Human characteristics and activities

Including alienation, chivalry, dreams, fear, friendship, happiness, heroism, justice, melancholy, personal beauty and ugliness, pride, sexual orientation, snobbishness, success, vices, virtues

Class here moral and psychological themes

Mental illness relocated to —3561

Class legal justice in —3554; class comprehensive works on human body in —3561

—353 8 Sex

Class here erotica, sexuality

Class sexual orientation in —353

—354 Life cycle

Including birth, youth, aging

—354 3 Love and marriage

—354 8 Death

—355 Social themes

Class here adventure, everyday life

Travel relocated to —32; social welfare problems of and services for persons with physical illness, mental illness, substance abuse, mental retardation, physical disabilities relocated to —3561; dancing, sports relocated to —357

Class adventure fiction in literature in —3087 in Table 3B

For political themes, see —358. For a specific kind of adventure, see the kind, e.g., historical adventure —358

—355 2 Sociology and anthropology

Standard subdivisions are added for either or both topics in heading

Including exile, violence

Class sex in —3538; class life cycle in —354; class war and peace in —358

—355 3 Economics

Including commerce, environment, industry, labor

—355 4 Law

—355 6 Social problems and services

Standard subdivisions are added for either or both topics in heading

Including crime, poverty

For social welfare problems of and services for persons with physical illness, mental illness, substance abuse, mental retardation, physical disabilities, see —3561

—355 7 Education

—355 9 Customs

Including costume, dwellings, food

—356 Technical themes

Including flight, ships

Agriculture, scientific themes, comprehensive works on scientific and technical themes relocated to —36

—356 1 Medicine, health, human body

Including mental illness [*formerly* —353]; social welfare problems of and services for persons with physical illness, mental illness, substance abuse, mental retardation, physical disabilities [*formerly* —355]; human anatomy, physiology, diseases; human form and shape, nudity

For personal beauty and ugliness, see —353

—357 Artistic, recreational, literary themes

Including dancing, sports [*both formerly* —355], architecture, books, music, painting

Class gardens in —364

—358 Historical and political themes

Standard subdivisions are added for either or both topics in heading

Including nationalism, peace, war

Class here historical adventure, historical events in specific places

Class nonhistorical adventure in —355; class historical fiction in literature in —3081

—36 Physical and natural phenomena

Including fire, weather

Class here agriculture, scientific themes, comprehensive works on scientific and technical themes [*all formerly* —356], nature

Class science fiction in literature in —308762 in Table 3B; class science fiction in the arts in —15; class landscapes in —32; class times (e.g., seasons, times of day) in —33. Class animals or plants for a specific purpose with the purpose, e.g., medicinal plants —3561

For human anatomy, physiology, diseases, see —3561

—362 Animals

Class here pets

Add to base number —362 the numbers following 59 in 592–599, e.g., cats —3629752

Class supernatural, mythological, legendary animals in —374

See Manual at 800, T3C—362 vs. 398.245, 590, 636

—364 Plants

Class here gardens

Class supernatural, mythological, legendary plants in —37

—37 The supernatural, mythological, legendary

Standard subdivisions are added for any or all topics in heading

Including spiritualism

Class here monsters

Class specific legendary and mythological persons in —351; class specific kinds of legendary and mythological persons in —352; class religious mythology in —382013

See Manual at T3C—37 vs. T3C—15

—372 Places

Including Atlantis, dystopias, utopias

Class religious treatment of places associated with life after death in —382023

See also —382035 for religious treatment of sacred places

—374 Animals

Including dragons, werewolves

—375 Paranatural beings of human and semihuman form

Including centaurs, fairies, ghosts, vampires

Class gods, goddesses, other objects of worship and veneration in —382

For ghost fiction as a kind of fiction, see —308733 in Table 3B; for specific paranatural beings of human and semihuman form, see —351; for werewolves, see —374

—377 Magic and witchcraft

Standard subdivisions are added for either or both topics in heading

—38 Philosophic and abstract themes

—382 Religious themes

Add to base number —382 the numbers following 2 in 201–290, e.g., Buddhism —382943; however, for religious holidays, see —334; for specific natural persons connected with religion, see —351; for kinds of natural persons associated with religion, see —35282

See also —42 for religious works not basically belletristic but discussed as literature

—384 Philosophic themes

Including existentialism, humanism, nihilism, self, time, transcendentalism

Class times (e.g., seasons, times of day) in —33; class human moral qualities and activities in —353

—4 Literature emphasizing subjects

Works not basically belletristic discussed as literature, where the real interest is in the literary quality of the text rather than the subject of the text

Add to —4 notation 001–999, e.g., religious works as literature —42, biography as literature —492

Class literary examination of a text in order to reach conclusions about its meaning, structure, authorship, date, where the real interest is in the subject of the text with the text, e.g., literary criticism of Bible 220.66

> —8–9 Literature for and by specific kinds of persons

Do not use if redundant, e.g., collections of English-language poetry for and by the English 821.008 (*not* 821.0080821)

Unless other instructions are given, observe the following table of preference, e.g., literature for or by Roman Catholic girls —92827 (*not* —921282 or —9287):

Persons of specific age groups	—9282–9285
Persons of specific sexes	—9286–9287
Persons by relationships, persons by miscellaneous social characteristics, persons with disabilities and illnesses, gifted persons	—9205–9207
Persons of specific occupational and religious groups	—921
Persons of ethnic and national groups	—8
Persons resident in specific continents, countries, localities	—93–99
Persons resident in specific regions	—91

Class literature displaying specific features for and by specific kinds of persons in —1–3; class comprehensive works in the appropriate number in Table 3B

—8 Literature for and by persons of ethnic and national groups

Add to —8 notation 05–99 from Table 5, e.g., literature by Africans and persons of African descent —896, literature by Africans and persons of African descent in Brazil —896081

Class literature for and by persons of ethnic and national groups in continents, countries, localities where the groups predominate in —93–99

See Manual at T3C—93–99, T3C—9174 vs. T3C—8

—9 Literature for and by other specific kinds of persons

—91 Literature for and by persons resident in specific regions

Not limited by continent, country, locality

Add to —91 the numbers following —1 in notation 11–19 from Table 2, e.g., literature by rural authors —91734

See Manual at T3C—93–99, T3C—9174 vs. T3C—8

—92 Literature for and by persons of specific classes

This table is extensively revised, —9205, —9207, and —921 in particular having been prepared with little reference to earlier editions

—920 5–920 7 Persons by relationships, persons by miscellaneous social characteristics, persons with disabilities and illnesses, gifted persons

Miscellaneous social characteristics not provided for elsewhere

Add to —920 the numbers following —08 in notation 085–087 from Table 1, e.g., literature by mothers —92052, literature by convicts —9206927
The numbers following —08 in notation 085–087 from Table 1 replace notation 043–046, 06–08 from Table 7 with the result that many numbers have been reused with new meanings

—921 Persons of specific occupational and religious groups

Add to —921 notation 001–999, e.g., literature by Catholics —921282, literature by painters —92175
Notation 001–999 replaces notation 09–99 from Table 7 with the result that many numbers have been reused with new meanings

—928 Persons of specific age groups and sexes

> —928 2–928 5 Age groups

Class comprehensive works in —928

—928 2 Children

—928 26 Boys

—928 27 Girls

—928 3 Young people twelve to twenty

—928 36 Males twelve to twenty

—928 37 Females twelve to twenty

—928 5 Persons in late adulthood

> —928 6–928 7 Sexes

Class comprehensive works in —928

—928 6 Men

—928 7 Women

—93–99 Literature for and by persons resident in specific continents, countries, localities

Class here literature for and by persons of ethnic and national groups in continents, countries, localities where the groups predominate

Add to —9 notation 3–9 from Table 2, e.g., literature (other than in Japanese language) by residents of Japan —952, a collection of Japanese-language literature by residents of Hokkaidō 895.60809524, a collection of English literature by residents of Australia 820.80994

See Manual at T3C—93–99; also at T3C—93–99, T3C—9174 vs. T3C—8

(Option: Do not use for literatures of specific countries if the literatures are separately identified in accordance with options given under 810, 819, 820, 828.99, 840.1–848, 848.99, 860.1–868, 868.99, 869, 869.899)

Table 4. Subdivisions of Individual Languages and Language Families

The following notation is never used alone, but may be used as required by add notes under subdivisions of specific languages or language families, or with the base numbers for individual languages identified by * as explained under 420–490, e.g., Norwegian (base number 439.82) grammar (—5 in this table): 439.825. A point is inserted following the third digit of any number thus constructed that is longer than three digits

Notation from Table 1 is added to the notation in Table 4 when appropriate, e.g., —509 history of grammar, 439.82509 history of Norwegian grammar

See Manual at 410

SUMMARY

— 01–09	**Standard subdivisions**
— 1	**Writing systems, phonology, phonetics of the standard form of the language**
— 2	**Etymology of the standard form of the language**
— 3	**Dictionaries of the standard form of the language**
— 5	**Grammar of the standard form of the language Syntax of the standard form of the language**
— 7	**Historical and geographic variations, modern nongeographic variations**
— 8	**Standard usage of the language (Prescriptive linguistics) Applied linguistics**

—01 Philosophy and theory

Class schools and theories of linguistics in —018

—014 Language and communication

Class here lexicology, terminology

For dictionaries, see —3; for lexicography, see —3028; for discursive works on terminology intended to teach vocabulary, see —81; for spelling and pronunciation in applied linguistics, see —813. For terminology (including pronunciation and spelling) of a specific subject or discipline, see the subject or discipline, plus notation 014 from Table 1, e.g., terminology of accounting 657.014

See Manual at T4—3 vs. T4—81

—014 1 Discourse analysis

Class here content analysis, semiotics

Class discourse analysis of a specific subject with the subject, plus notation 014 from Table 1, e.g., discourse analysis of science 501.4

For semantics, see —0143

—[014 2] Etymology

Do not use; class in —2

—014 3 Semantics

For history of word meanings, see —2

See Manual at 401.43 vs. 306.44, 401.9, 412, 415

—[014 8] Abbreviations and symbols

Do not use for abbreviations and symbols as part of writing systems; class in —11. Do not use for dictionaries of symbols; class in —31. Do not use for dictionaries of abbreviations; class in —315

—018 Schools and theories of linguistics

Including functionalism, structural linguistics

For works on schools and theories of linguistics that stress syntax, or syntax and phonology, see —5

—019 Psychological principles

Including language acquisition

Class here psycholinguistics

Class language acquisition, psychological principles, psycholinguistics of a specific topic with the topic, e.g., acquisition of grammar of a specific language —5019

See Manual at 407.1, T1—071 vs. 401.93, T4—019, 410.71, 418.0071, T4—80071

—02 Miscellany

—03 Encyclopedias and concordances

Do not use for dictionaries of standard form of language; class in —3. Do not use for dictionaries of historical and geographic variations, of modern nongeographic variations in the language; class in —7

—04 Special topics of subdivisions of individual languages and language families

—042 Bilingualism

Class here multilingualism

Add to —042 notation 2–9 from Table 6 for the language that is not dominant in the area in which the linguistic interaction occurs, e.g., works dealing with the dominant language and English —04221, works dealing with French as the dominant language and English 440.4221

See also 306.446 for sociology of bilingualism and multilingualism

—05–08 Standard subdivisions

See Manual at 407.1, T1—071 vs. 401.93, T4—019, 410.71, 418.0071, T4—80071

—09 Historical, geographic, persons treatment

Do not use for works that stress distinctive characteristics of historical and geographic variations from the standard form of the language; class in —7

> —1–5 Description and analysis of the standard form of the language

Class writing systems, phonology, etymology, dictionaries, grammar of historical and geographic variations, of modern nongeographic variations of the language in —7; class standard usage, prescriptive and applied linguistics in —8; class comprehensive works in the base number for the language (adding 0 when required to make a three-figure number), e.g., comprehensive works on phonology, etymology, dictionaries, grammar of standard French 440

See Manual at T4—1–5, T4—8 vs. T4—7

—1 Writing systems, phonology, phonetics of the standard form of the language

—11 Writing systems

Including alphabets, ideographs, syllabaries; braille; abbreviations, acronyms, capitalization, punctuation, transliteration

Class here paleography and epigraphy in the narrow sense of study of ancient and medieval handwriting and inscriptions

Class dictionaries of abbreviations and acronyms in —315; class paleography in the broad sense of all aspects of early writings in the base number for the language (adding 0 when required to make a three-digit number), e.g., Latin paleography 470; class paleography (in both broad and narrow senses) of historical and geographic variations, of modern nongeographic variations of the language in —7, e.g., paleography of postclassical Latin 477; class books meant to teach the alphabet in —813; class manual alphabets in —891

For spelling, see —152

—15 Phonology, phonetics, spelling

Standard subdivisions are added for phonology, phonetics, spelling together; for phonology and phonetics together; for phonology alone

Class comprehensive works on phonology and morphology, on phonology and syntax, or on all three in —5

For suprasegmental features, see —16

See also —3 for dictionaries

—152 Spelling (Orthography) and pronunciation

Standard subdivisions are added for either or both topics in heading

Class here description and analysis of the nature, history, and function of spelling and pronunciation

Class specialized spelling and pronouncing dictionaries in —31; class training in standard spelling and pronunciation in —81; class fingerspelling in —891; class speech training for public speaking, debating, conversation in 808.5; class comprehensive works on writing systems in —11

—158 Phonetics

—16 Suprasegmental features

Phonology and phonetics of vocal effects extending over more than one sound segment

Including juncture (pauses), pitch, stress

Class here intonation

—2 Etymology of the standard form of the language

—24 Foreign elements

Add to —24 notation 1–9 from Table 6, e.g., French words in the language —2441, French words in English 422.441

—3 Dictionaries of the standard form of the language

See Manual at T4—3 vs. T4—81

—302 8 Techniques, procedures, apparatus, equipment, materials

Class here lexicography

—31 Specialized dictionaries

Including dictionaries of clichés, eponyms, homonyms, paronyms; reverse dictionaries; speller-dividers (in the sense of ready-reference lists of words)

Crossword-puzzle dictionaries relocated to 793.73203

Class etymological dictionaries in —203; class reverse dictionaries in the sense of dictionaries of synonyms and antonyms in —312; class bilingual specialized dictionaries in —32–39; class spellers in the sense of spelling books with exercises to teach how to spell in —813

—312 Dictionaries of synonyms and antonyms

Standard subdivisions are added for either or both topics in heading

—313 Dictionaries of idioms

—315 Dictionaries of abbreviations and acronyms

Standard subdivisions are added for either or both topics in heading

—317 Picture dictionaries

—32–39 Bilingual dictionaries

Add to —3 notation 2–9 from Table 6, e.g., dictionaries of the language and English —321, dictionary of French and English 443.21

A bilingual dictionary with entry words in only one language is classed with that language, e.g., an English-French dictionary 423.41. A bilingual dictionary with entry words in both languages is classed with the language in which it will be more useful; for example, most libraries in English-speaking regions will find English-French, French-English dictionaries most useful classed with French in 443.21, Chinese-French, French-Chinese dictionaries with Chinese in 495.1341. If classification with either language is equally useful, give priority to the language coming later in 420–490, e.g., French-German, German-French dictionaries 443.31

—5 Grammar of the standard form of the language
Syntax of the standard form of the language

Class here sentences, topic and comment; grammatical categories; word order; comprehensive works on phonology and morphology, on phonology and syntax, or on all three

Unless other instructions are given, class a subject with aspects in two or more subdivisions of —5 in the number coming last, e.g., number expressed by verbs —56 (*not* —55)

For phonology, see —15; for prescriptive grammar, see —82

—501 Philosophy and theory

—501 8 Schools and theories

Including case, categorial, relational grammar

—501 82 Generative grammar

—501 84 Dependency grammar

\> **—55–57 Word classes**

Class here parts of speech

Class comprehensive works in —5

—55 Nouns, pronouns, adjectives, articles

Including case, number, person

Class here noun phrases

—554 Nouns

—555 Pronouns

—56 **Verbs**

Including modality, mood, voice; comprehensive works on words derived from verbs, on infinitives, on participles

Class here verb phrases

Class works that treat a specific function (other than the verb function) of words derived from verbs with the function, e.g., gerunds as nouns —554

—562 Tense

—563 Aspect

—57 **Miscellaneous word classes**

Including conjunctions, interjections, particles, prepositions, prepositional phrases

—576 Adverbs

Including adverbials

—59 **Morphology**

Class morphophonology, morphophonemics in —15

For morphology of specific word classes, see —55–57

—592 Word formation

Including prefixes, suffixes

Class here derivational morphology

Class derivational etymology in —2

—595 Inflection

For inflectional schemata designed for use as aids in learning a language, see —82

—7 Historical and geographic variations, modern nongeographic variations

Class here early forms; dialects, pidgins, creoles; slang

Subdivisions of —7 are given under some individual languages in 420–490

Use notation 7 only for works that stress differences among the forms of a language

Topics classed in —1–5 and —8 when applied to standard forms of the language are classed here when applied to historical and geographic variations, to modern nongeographic variations, e.g., the distinctive grammatical characteristics of a particular dialect

See Manual at T4—7; also at T4—1–5, T4—8 vs. T4—7

—8 Standard usage of the language (Prescriptive linguistics) Applied linguistics

General, formal, informal usage

Class here works for persons learning a second language, works for native speakers who are learning the acceptable patterns of their own language

Class purely descriptive linguistics in —1–5; class prescriptive and applied linguistics applied to historical and geographic variations, to modern nongeographic variations of the language in —7

For dictionaries, see —3; for rhetoric, see 808.04

See Manual at T4—1–5, T4—8 vs. T4—7; also at 410

—800 1–800 9 Standard subdivisions

See Manual at 407.1, T1—071 vs. 401.93, T4—019, 410.71, 418.0071, T4—80071

—802 Translating to and from other languages

Class here interpreting

Use the base number for the language being translated into

Add to —802 notation 2–9 from Table 6 for the language being translated from, e.g., translating from Chinese —802951, translating from Chinese into English 428.02951

—81 Words

Class formal presentation of vocabulary for those whose native language is different in —824; class audio-lingual presentation of vocabulary for those whose native language is different in —834

See also —3 for dictionaries

See Manual at T4—3 vs. T4—81

—813 Spelling (Orthography) and pronunciation

Standard subdivisions are added for either or both topics in heading

Including books meant to teach the alphabet

Class here spellers in the sense of spelling books with exercises to teach how to spell

Class spellers in the sense of ready-reference spelling dictionaries in —31

See also —152 for nonprescriptive treatment of spelling and pronunciation; also 783.043 for pronunciation for singing

—82 Structural approach to expression

Formal (traditional) presentation of grammar, vocabulary, reading selections

Class here prescriptive grammar, verb tables and inflectional schemata designed for use as aids in learning a language

For words, see —81; for reading, see —84

—824 Structural approach to expression for persons whose native language is different

Add to —824 notation 2–9 from Table 6, e.g., the language for Spanish-speaking people —82461, English for Spanish-speaking people 428.2461

—83 Audio-lingual approach to expression

Class here the "hear-speak" school of learning a language

For pronunciation, see —81

—834 Audio-lingual approach to expression for persons whose native language is different

Class here bilingual phrase books

Add to —834 notation 2–9 from Table 6, e.g., the language for Spanish-speaking people —83461, English for Spanish-speaking people 428.3461

—84 Reading

For readers, see —86

—842 Remedial reading

Correcting faulty habits and increasing the proficiency of poor readers

—843 Developmental reading

Including reading power and efficiency of good readers

—843 2 Rapid reading (Speed reading)

—86 Readers

Graded selections with emphasis on structure and vocabulary as needed

Including readers compiled for training college students in reading comprehension

Class here texts intended primarily for practice in reading a language

(Option: Class elementary readers in 372.4122)

—862 Readers for new literates

Regardless of subject or discipline

—864 Readers for persons whose native language is different from the language of the reader

—864 024 Readers for persons in specific occupations

Class here readers intended to instill a knowledge of the special vocabulary of a specific subject or discipline

Add to base number —864024 notation 001–999, e.g., engineering readers for persons whose native language is different —86402462, English-language engineering readers for persons whose native language is not English 428.6402462

—864 2–864 9 Readers for specific native language speakers

Add to —864 notation 2–9 from Table 6, e.g., readers (in language other than Spanish) for Spanish-speaking people —86461, English-language readers for Spanish-speaking people 428.6461; then add further as follows:

024 Readers for persons in specific occupations

Class here readers intended to instill a knowledge of the special vocabulary of a specific subject or discipline

Add to base number 024 notation 001–999, e.g., engineering readers (in language other than Spanish) for Spanish-speaking people —8646102462, English-language engineering readers for Spanish-speaking people 428.646102462

—89 Use of a spoken language or a manually coded form of a spoken language for communication with and by deaf persons

—891 Manually coded language

Class here use of signs and fingerspelling to represent specific standard spoken languages [*formerly* 419]

Class signs and fingerspelling used as part of sign languages in 419

See also —8955 for cued speech

—891 4–891 9 Specific systems of manual coding

Add to base number —891 notation 4–9 from Table 2 for supranational region or country only, e.g., British systems of signing and fingerspelling —89141

—895 Lipreading, cued speech, oral interpretation (lipspeaking)

—895 4 Lipreading

—895 5 Cued speech

Table 5. Ethnic and National Groups

The following numbers are never used alone, but may be used as required (either directly when so noted or through the interposition of notation 089 from Table 1) with any number from the schedules, e.g., civil and political rights (323.11) of Navajo Indians (—9726 in this table): 323.119726; ceramic arts (738) of Jews (—924 in this table): 738.089924. They may also be used when so noted with numbers from other tables, e.g., notation 174 from Table 2

In this table racial groups are mentioned in connection with a few broad ethnic groupings, e.g., a note to class Blacks of African origin at —96 Africans and people of African descent. Concepts of race vary. A work that emphasizes race should be classed with the ethnic group that most closely matches the concept of race described in the work

Except where instructed otherwise, and unless it is redundant, add 0 to the number from this table and to the result add notation 1 or 3–9 from Table 2 for area in which a group is or was located, e.g., Germans in Brazil —31081, but Germans in Germany —31; Jews in Germany or Jews from Germany —924043. If notation from Table 2 is not added, use 00 for standard subdivisions; see below for complete instructions on using standard subdivisions

Notation from Table 2 may be added if the number in Table 5 is limited to speakers of only one language even if the group discussed does not approximate the whole of the group specified by the Table 5 number, e.g., Bavarians in Brazil —31081 (because German is the primary language spoken by Bavarians), but Amhara in United States —928 (*not* —928073 because Amharic is not the only language spoken by the peoples included in —928)

Notation from Table 2 may be added for either present or past specific location of the group discussed if only one specific location is relevant, e.g., sociology of Jews from many different countries now in United States 305.8924073, contributions to music around the world of Jews who previously lived in Poland 780.899240438

If both present and past specific locations of the group discussed are relevant, then notation from Table 2 is added only for present location of the group, e.g., Jews from Germany in the United States —924073 (*not* —924043). An exception occurs when the present location of the group is defined by the class number to which ethnic or national group notation is added, e.g., Jews in United States history 973.04924. The area notation added to Table 5 numbers is then available to show the past location of the group, e.g., Jews from Germany in United States history 973.04924043, Jews from Germany in United States higher education 378.73089924043

Standard subdivisions may be added to Table 5 notation when that notation is added directly to the base number, e.g., periodicals about sociology of Irish Americans 305.8916207305. However, standard subdivisions are not added to Table 5 notation when that notation is used through interposition of notation 089 from Table 1, e.g., an exhibition of ceramic arts of Russian Jews 738.089924047 (*not* 738.089924047074)

(continued)

Table 5. Ethnic and National Groups (continued)

When Table 5 notation is not followed by 0 plus notation from Table 2, use 00 for standard subdivisions, e.g., periodicals about sociology of Japanese 305.8956005, collected biography of Irish Americans in New York City 974.71004916200922. When Table 5 notation is followed by 0 plus notation from Table 2, however, use 0 for standard subdivisions, e.g., periodicals about sociology of Japanese Americans 305.895607305. (For the purpose of this rule, notation 96073 African Americans is treated as Table 5 notation, e.g., periodicals on sociology of African Americans 305.896073005, periodicals on sociology of African Americans in Ohio 305.896073077105)

Except where instructed otherwise, give preference to ethnic group over nationality, e.g., United States citizens of Serbian descent —91822073 (*not* —13). In this table "ethnic group" most often means a group with linguistic ties, but it can also mean a group with other cultural ties

Except where instructed otherwise, when choosing between two ethnic groups, give preference to the group for which the notation is different from that for the nationality of the people, e.g., a work treating equally Hispanic and native American heritage of bilingual Spanish-Guaraní mestizos of Paraguay —983820892 (*not* —68892)

Except where instructed otherwise, when choosing between two national groups, give preference to the former or ancestral national group, e.g., people from the former Soviet Union who became United States citizens —917073 (*not* —13)

See Manual at Table 5

SUMMARY

— 05–09	**[Persons of mixed ancestry with ethnic origins from more than one continent; Europeans and people of European descent]**
— 1	**North Americans**
— 2	**British, English, Anglo-Saxons**
— 3	**Germanic people**
— 4	**Modern Latin peoples**
— 5	**Italians, Romanians, related groups**
— 6	**Spanish and Portuguese**
— 7	**Other Italic peoples**
— 8	**Greeks and related groups**
— 9	**Other ethnic and national groups**

—[03] Basic races

Provision discontinued because without meaning in context

—[034] Europeans and people of European descent

Relocated to —09

—[04] Persons of mixed ancestry with ethnic origins from more than one continent

Relocated to —05

—05 **Persons of mixed ancestry with ethnic origins from more than one continent [*formerly* —04]**

Limited to works that emphasize such mixed ancestry

Add to base number —05 notation 09–9 from Table 5 for the group only, e.g., American native peoples of mixed ancestry with ethnic origins from more than one continent —0597; then, for each group having its own number, add 0* and to the result add notation 09–9 from Table 5, e.g., persons of mixed American native and European ancestry —0597009, persons of mixed American native and European ancestry in Canada —0597009071, persons of mixed Aleut and Russian ancestry —05971909171; however, for persons of mixed North and South American native ancestry, see —97

Give priority in notation to the ethnic group emphasized. If emphasis is equal, give priority to the one coming last in Table 5

Class works about persons of mixed ancestry that do not emphasize mixture with the ethnic groups stressed in the works or with the groups with which the people are most closely identified, e.g., works about Métis that emphasize their North American native roots —97 (*not* —0597009); class works that stress the kind of mixed ethnic heritage (e.g., language, customs, food, but not genetics) that results when people of one continent move to another continent and raise their children in the new location with the ethnic group of origin, plus notation from Table 2 as instructed at beginning of Table 5 to show the new location, e.g., persons who have Chinese parents and were raised in the United Kingdom —951041

—09 **Europeans and people of European descent [*formerly* —034]**

Class here people who speak or whose ancestors spoke languages traditionally spoken in Europe; comprehensive works on Indo-European peoples; comprehensive works on whites

Class works that emphasize mixed ancestry with origins from more than one continent in —05, e.g., works emphasizing mixed Hindi-English ancestry —059143021

For a specific ethnic or regional group, see the group, e.g., Germans —31, Bengali —9144, Arabs —927, people of Middle Eastern origins —94

> **—1–9 Specific ethnic and national groups**

By origin or situation

Class comprehensive works on Europeans, on Indo-European peoples in —09; class comprehensive works in 001–999 without adding notation from Table 5

See Manual at Table 5

(Option: To give local emphasis and a shorter number to a specific group, place it first by use of a letter or other symbol, e.g., Arabs —A [preceding —1]. Another option is given at —1)

*Add 000 for standard subdivisions; see instructions at beginning of Table 1

—1 North Americans

For Spanish Americans, see —68; for North American regional and national groups of largely African descent, see —9697, e.g., West Indians —969729, Haitians —9697294; for North American native peoples, see —97. For North Americans of other origins, see the ethnic group of origin, e.g., North Americans of Celtic (Irish, Scots, Manx, Welsh, Cornish) origin —91607

(Option: To give local emphasis and a shorter number to a specific group, e.g., Sinhalese, class it in this number; in that case class North Americans in —2. Another option is given at —1–9)

—11 Canadians

Class here people of Canada as a national group

For Canadians not of British or French origin, see the ethnic group of origin, e.g., Canadians of German origin —31071, Inuit —9712071

—112 Canadians of British origin

See Manual at T5—112, T5—114 vs. T5—2, T5—41

—114 Canadians of French origin

See Manual at T5—112, T5—114 vs. T5—2, T5—41

—13 People of United States ("Americans")

Class here United States citizens of British origin, people of United States as a national group

For United States citizens of other origins, see the ethnic group of origin, e.g., German Americans —31073, African Americans —96073

See Manual at T5—13 vs. T5—2073, T5—21073

—2 British, English, Anglo-Saxons

Subdivisions are added for British, English, Anglo-Saxons together; for British as an ethnic group; for English as an ethnic group

For North Americans of British origin, see —1; for Anglo-Indians (Indian citizens of British origin), see —91411; for people of Celtic (Irish, Scots, Manx, Welsh, Cornish) origin, see —916

See Manual at Table 5; also at T5—112, T5—114 vs. T5—2, T5—41; also at T5—13 vs. T5—2073, T5—21073; also at T5—201–209 vs. T5—2101–2109

—21 **People of British Isles**

Class here United Kingdom citizens of British origin, people of United Kingdom as a national group

Class New Zealanders of British origin in —23; class Australians of British origin in —24; class South Africans of British origin in —28

For United Kingdom citizens of other origins, see the ethnic group of origin, e.g., United Kingdom citizens of Indian origin —91411041

See Manual at T5—13 vs. T5—2073, T5—21073; also at T5—201–209 vs. T5—2101–2109

—23 **New Zealanders**

Class here New Zealanders of British origin, New Zealanders as a national group

For New Zealanders of other origins, see the ethnic group of origin, e.g., New Zealanders of Irish origin —9162093, Maori —99442

—24 **Australians**

Class here Australians of British origin, Australians as a national group

For Australians of other origins, see the ethnic group of origin, e.g., Australians of Italian origin —51094, Aboriginal peoples of Australia —9915

—28 **South Africans of British origin**

Class South Africans as a national group in —968

See also —2106891 for Zimbabweans of British origin

—3 Germanic peoples

For English, Anglo-Saxons, see —2

—31 **Germans**

—35 **Swiss**

Class here Swiss Germans, comprehensive works on people of Switzerland as a national group

For Swiss citizens of other ethnic groups, see the ethnic group, e.g., French-speaking Swiss —410494, Romansh-speaking Swiss —5, Italian-speaking Swiss —510494

—36 **Austrians**

—39 **Other Germanic peoples**

Including Goths, Vandals

—392 Friesians

—393 Netherlandish peoples

—393 1 Dutch

—393 2 Flemings (Flemish)

Class here comprehensive works on Belgians as a national group

For Walloons, see —42

—393 6 Afrikaners

Class South Africans as a national group in —968

—395 Scandinavians

Class here comprehensive works on peoples of the Nordic countries

For Icelanders and Faeroese, see —396; for Swedes, see —397; for Danes and Norwegians, see —398; for Finns, see —94541; for Sami, see —9455

—396 Icelanders and Faeroese

Former heading: West Scandinavians

—396 1 Icelanders

—396 9 Faeroese

—397 Swedes

—398 Danes and Norwegians

—398 1 Danes

—398 2 Norwegians

—4 Modern Latin peoples

For Italians, Romanians, related groups, see —5; for Spanish and Portuguese, see —6

—41 French

Class Canadians of French origin in —114

For Corsicans, see —58; for Basques, see —9992

See Manual at T5—112, T5—114 vs. T5—2, T5—41

—42 Walloons

—49 Catalans

—5 Italians, Romanians, related groups

Including Rhaetians

—51 Italians

—56 Sardinians

—57 Dalmatians

—58 Corsicans

—59 Romanians

—6 Spanish and Portuguese

—61 People of Spain

For Catalans, see —49; for Basques, see —9992

—68 Spanish Americans

Class here comprehensive works on Latin Americans

For Latin American peoples not provided for here, see the people, e.g., Brazilians —698

See also —9141 for people of Guyana and Suriname as national groups; also —96972 for Central American and Caribbean national groups of majority African origin, e.g., —9697282 for Belizeans, —9697294 for Haitians

—687–688 Regional and national groups

Citizens of independent and partly independent jurisdictions having a Spanish-speaking majority or Spanish as an official language; former citizens and descendants of citizens of these jurisdictions

Add to base number —68 notation 7–8 from Table 2, e.g., Central Americans —68728, Puerto-Ricans —687295, Chileans —6883; then add further as instructed at beginning of Table 5, e.g., Chileans in United States and U.S. citizens of Chilean origin —6883073; however, for comprehensive works on Spanish Americans in jurisdictions where they are a minority, see —6804–6809, e.g., Spanish Americans in United States —68073

—69 Portuguese-speaking peoples

—691 People of Portugal

—698 Brazilians

Class here Brazilians of Portuguese origin, Brazilians as a national group

For Brazilian citizens of other origins, see the ethnic group of origin, e.g., Brazilians of Italian origin —51081, Brazilians of African origin —96081

—7 Other Italic peoples

For Etruscans, see —9994

—71 Ancient Romans

—79 Osco-Umbrians

—8 Greeks and related groups

Subdivisions are added for Greeks and related groups together, for Greeks as an ethnic group alone

See also —91819 for Slavic Macedonians

—81 Ancient Greeks

Class here comprehensive works on ancient Greeks and Romans

For ancient Romans, see —71

—89 Modern Greeks and related groups

—893 Greek nationals

—895 Cypriots

Class here comprehensive works on people of Cyprus

For Turkish Cypriots, see —943505693

—9 Other ethnic and national groups

SUMMARY

—91	Other Indo-European peoples
—92	Semites
—93	Non-Semitic Afro-Asiatic peoples
—94	Peoples of North and West Asian origin or situation; Dravidians
—95	East and Southeast Asian peoples; Mundas
—96	Africans and people of African descent
—97	North American native peoples
—98	South American native peoples
—99	Aeta, Andamanese, Semang; Papuans; Aboriginal people of Australia and Tasmania; Malayo-Polynesian and related peoples; miscellaneous peoples

—91 Other Indo-European peoples

SUMMARY

—914	South Asians
—915	Peoples who speak, or whose ancestors spoke, Iranian languages
—916	Celts
—917	East Slavs
—918	Slavs
—919	Balts and other Indo-European peoples

—914 South Asians

Class here Indic peoples (peoples who speak, or whose ancestors spoke, Indic languages), Indo-Aryans

For Dravidians and Scytho-Dravidians, see —948; for South Asians who speak, or whose ancestors spoke, languages closely related to East and Southeast Asian languages, see —95

See also notation 08621 in Table 1 for Brahmans as an elite social group; also notation 0882945 in Table 1 for Brahmans as a religious group

—914 1 National groups

Citizens of independent and partly independent jurisdictions of South Asia and of largely South Asian origin; former citizens and descendants of citizens of these jurisdictions

Including Guyanese, Maldivians, Mauritians, Surinamers

For nationals of specific ethnolinguistic groups, see —9142–9149; for Nepalese national group, see —91495; for Trinidadians of South Asian origin, see —96972983054; for Fijians of South Asian origin, see —995

—914 11 Indians

Including Anglo-Indians (Indian citizens of British origin), post-1975 Sikkimese

Class comprehensive works on Sikkimese in —91417

—914 12 Pakistanis and people of Bangladesh

—914 122 Pakistanis

—914 126 People of Bangladesh

—914 13 Sri Lankans (Ceylonese)

For Sinhalese as an ethnic group, see —9148; for Tamil as an ethnic group, see —94811

—914 17 Sikkimese

For post-1975 Sikkimese, see —91411

—914 18 Bhutanese

Class Bhotia as an ethnic group in —954

—914 2 Punjabis

—914 3 Hindis

—914 4 Bengali

For Bengali of Bangladesh, see —914126

—914 5 Assamese, Bihari, Oriya

—914 7 Gujar, Gujarati; Bhil; people who speak, or whose ancestors spoke, Rajasthani

—914 8 Sinhalese

—914 9 Other Indic peoples

Including Nuri

—914 95 Nepali

Class here Nepali as an ethnic group, comprehensive works on people of Nepal as a national group

For citizens of Nepal belonging to other ethnic groups, see the ethnic group, e.g., Bihari —9145, Chepang and Newar —95

—914 96 Pahari

—914 97 Romany people

—914 99 Dardic peoples

Including Kashmiris, Kohistanis

Class Romany people in —91497

—915 Peoples who speak, or whose ancestors spoke, Iranian languages

Including Kushans, Scythians

—915 5 Persians

Class here Persians as an ethnic group, comprehensive works on people of Iran as a national group

For citizens of Iran belonging to other ethnic groups, see the ethnic group, e.g., Azerbaijani —94361055

—915 7 Tajik

Including Galcha

—915 9 Other Iranian peoples

Including Ossets, Pamiri

—915 93 Afghans (Pashtun)

Class here Afghans as an ethnic group, comprehensive works on people of Afghanistan as a national group

For citizens of Afghanistan belonging to other ethnic groups, see the ethnic group, e.g., Tajik —91570581

—915 97 Kurds

—915 98 Baluchi

—916 Celts

Including Gauls

—916 2 Irish

—916 3 Scots

—916 4 Manx

—916 6 Welsh (Cymry)

—916 7 Cornish

—916 8 Bretons

—917 East Slavs

Class here people of Commonwealth of Independent States, of former Soviet Union as national groups

Class comprehensive works on Slavs in —918

For a specific ethnic group of Commonwealth of Independent States or former Soviet Union, see the group, e.g., Uzbek —94325

—917 1 Russians

—917 14 Cossacks

—917 9 Ukrainians, Ruthenians, Belarusians

—917 91 Ukrainians and Ruthenians

Subdivisions are added for Ukrainians and Ruthenians together, for Ukrainians alone

See also notation 0882815 in Table 1 for Ruthenians as a religious group

—917 99 Belarusians

—918 Slavs

For East Slavs, see —917

—918 1 Bulgarians and Macedonians

Class here comprehensive works on South Slavs

For Serbs, Montenegrins, Croats, Bosnian Muslims, see —9182; for Slovenes, see —9184

—918 11 Bulgarians

—918 19 Macedonians

—918 2 Serbs, Montenegrins, Croats, Bosnian Muslims

Class here peoples who speak, or whose ancestors spoke, Serbo-Croatian; people of former Yugoslavia (1918–1991) as a national group

Class people of former Yugoslavia (1991–2003) as a national group in —91822; class comprehensive works on South Slavs in —9181

For citizens of former Yugoslavia (1918–1991) of other ethnic groups, see the ethnic group, e.g., Albanians —919910497

See also notation 088297 from Table 1 for Muslims as a religious group

—918 22 Serbs and Montenegrins

Class here people of Serbia and Montenegro as a national group, people of former Yugoslavia (1991–2003) as a national group

Subdivisions are added for Serbs and Montenegrins together, for Serbs alone

Class people of former Yugoslavia (1918–1991) as a national group in —9182

For citizens of Serbia and Montenegro of other ethnic groups, citizens of former Yugoslavia (1991–2003) of other ethnic groups, see the ethnic group, e.g., Hungarians —9451104971

—918 23 Croats

—918 4 Slovenes

—918 5 West Slavs Poles

Including Kashubs

For Cossacks, see —91714; for Czechs and Moravians, see —9186; for Slovaks, see —9187; for Wends, see —9188

—918 6 Czechs and Moravians

Class here Czechoslovaks

Subdivisions are added for either or both topics in heading

For Slovaks, see —9187

See also notation 0882846 in Table 1 for Moravians as a religious group

—918 7 Slovaks

—918 8 Wends (Lusatians, Sorbs)

—919 Balts and other Indo-European peoples

Subdivisions are added for Balts and other Indo-European peoples together, for Balts alone

—919 2 Lithuanians

—919 3 Latvians (Letts)

—919 9 Albanians, Armenians, Hittites

—919 91 Albanians

—919 92 Armenians

—92 Semites

Class here comprehensive works on Afro-Asiatic peoples

For non-Semitic Afro-Asiatic peoples, see —93

—921 Akkadians, Amorites, Assyrians, Babylonians

—922 Aramaeans

—924 Hebrews, Israelis, Jews

Class here Beta Israel

Subdivisions are added for any or all topics in heading

See also notation 088296 in Table 1 for Jews as a religious group

—926 Canaanites and Phoenicians

For Amorites, see —921

—927 Arabs and Maltese

Subdivisions are added for Arabs and Maltese together, for Arabs alone

—927 2 Bedouins

See also —933 for Berbers and Tuareg

—927 4 Palestinian Arabs

—927 5–927 6 Regional and national groups of Arabs

Citizens of independent or partly independent jurisdictions having an Arab or Arabic-speaking majority or Arabic as the official language; former citizens and descendants of citizens of these jurisdictions

Add to base number —927 notation 5–6 from Table 2, e.g., Iraqis —927567, North Africans —92761, Sudanese —927624; then add further as instructed at beginning of Table 5, e.g., Sudanese in Ethiopia and Ethiopian citizens of Sudanese ancestry —927624063; however, for comprehensive works on Arabs as a minority group in a country of Asia or Africa where Arabic is not the official language, see —92705–92706, e.g., Arabs in Iran —927055; for Mauritanians as a national group, see —9661

Class Palestinian Arabs as an ethnic group in —9274

—927 61 Arabs of North Africa

Number built according to instructions under —9275–9276

Class here comprehensive works on North Africans [*formerly* —93]

For a specific North African group not provided for here, see the group, e.g., Algerians —92765, Berbers —933

—927 9 Maltese

—928 Persons who speak, or whose ancestors spoke, Ethiopian languages

Including Amhara, Gurage, Harari, Tigre, Tigrinya

Class here comprehensive works on people of Ethiopia as a national group

For Beta Israel, see —924; for Cushitic and Omotic peoples of Ethiopia, see —935; for Nilo-Saharan peoples of Ethiopia, see —965

—928 9 Eritreans

Class here comprehensive works on people of Eritrea as a national group

Class Eritreans who speak, or whose ancestors spoke, a specific Ethiopian language in —928

For Cushitic peoples of Eritrea, see —935; for Nilo-Saharan peoples of Eritrea, see —965

—929 Mahri and Socotrans

Class here South Arabic peoples

—93 Non-Semitic Afro-Asiatic peoples

Class here peoples who speak, or whose ancestors spoke, non-Semitic Afro-Asiatic languages

Comprehensive works on North Africans relocated to —92761

—931 Ancient Egyptians

—932 Copts

See also notation 08828172 in Table 1 for Copts as members of the Coptic Church

—933 Berbers and Tuareg

—935 Cushitic and Omotic peoples

Including Afar, Beja, Oromo, Somali

Class Beta Israel in —924; class Ethiopians as a national group in —928; class Eritreans as a national group in —9289; class Djiboutians as a national group in —96771; class Somali as a national group in —96773

—937 Hausa

Class the people of Niger as a national group in —96626

—94 Peoples of North and West Asian origin or situation; Dravidians

Class here comprehensive works on peoples of Middle Eastern origin

For Cypriots, see —895; for Indo-European peoples of these regions, see —91; for Semites, see —92

—941 Tungusic peoples

Including Evenki, Nanai

—942 Mongols

—943 Turkic peoples

Add to base number —943 the numbers following —943 in notation 9431–9438 from Table 6, e.g., Turks —9435, Uzbek —94325; then add further as instructed at beginning of Table 5, e.g., Turks in Germany —9435043; however, for Chuvashes, see —9456

Class Cossacks in —91714

See Manual at T5—9435

—944 Samoyed

—945 Finno-Ugrians

—945 1 Ugrians

Including Ostyaks, Vogul

—945 11 Hungarians

—945 3 Permiaks, Votyak, Komi (Zyrian)

—945 4 Finnic peoples

Including Karelians, Livonians, Veps

For Permiaks, Votyak, Komi, see —9453; for Sami, see —9455; for Cheremis, Chuvashes, Mordvin, see —9456

—945 41 Finns

—945 45 Estonians

—945 5 Sami

—945 6 Mari, Chuvashes, Mordvin

—946 Paleo-Asiatic (Paleosiberian) peoples

Including Ainu (Utari); peoples who speak or whose ancestors spoke Chukotko-Kamchatkan (Luorawetlin), Yukaghir languages; Nivkh (Gilyak), Ket (Yenisei Ostyak)

—948 Dravidians and Scytho-Dravidians

Including Maratha (Mahratta), Sindhi

Subdivisions are added for Dravidians and Scytho-Dravidians together, for Dravidians alone

See also —914 for speakers of Indic languages who are not Scytho-Dravidians; also —915 for Scythians

—948 1 South Dravidians

Including Toda

Class here peoples who speak, or whose ancestors spoke, South Dravidian languages

—948 11 Tamil

—948 12 Malayalis

—948 14 Kanarese

—948 2 Central Dravidians

Including Gond, Kandh

Class here peoples who speak, or whose ancestors spoke, central Dravidian languages

—948 27 Telugu

—948 3 North Dravidians Brahui

Including Kurukh

Class here peoples who speak, or whose ancestors spoke, North Dravidian languages

—95 East and Southeast Asian peoples; Mundas

Including Chepang, Karen, Naxi, Newar

Class here East Asians; South Asian peoples who speak, or whose ancestors spoke, languages closely related to East and Southeast Asian languages; comprehensive works on Asian peoples

For a specific Asian people not provided for here, see the people, e.g., Persians —9155, Aeta and Andamanese —9911, Malays —9928

—951 Chinese

—954 Tibetans

Class here Bhotia as an ethnic group

See also —91418 for Bhutanese as a national group

—956 Japanese

Including Ryukyuans

For Ainu, see —946

—957 Koreans

—958 Burmese

—959 Miscellaneous southeast Asian peoples; Mundas

Only those peoples provided for below

Including peoples who speak, or whose ancestors spoke, Kadai languages, Kam-Sui languages

Class here peoples who speak, or whose ancestors spoke, Daic languages

—959 1 Tai peoples

Class here peoples who speak, or whose ancestors spoke, Tai languages

—959 11 Thai (Siamese)

—959 19 Other Tai peoples

—959 191 Lao

—959 2 Viet-Muong peoples Vietnamese

Class here peoples who speak, or whose ancestors spoke, Viet-Muong languages

Class comprehensive works on Montagnards of Vietnam in —9593

—959 3 Mon-Khmer peoples Khmer (Cambodians)

Including comprehensive works on Montagnards of Vietnam

Class here peoples who speak, or whose ancestors spoke, Mon-Khmer languages

Class Montagnards of a specific ethnic group with the ethnic group, e.g., Rhade —9922

For Semang, see —9911

—959 4 Miao and Yao peoples

Class here peoples who speak, or whose ancestors spoke, Miao-Yao languages

—959 42 Miao (Hmong) people

—959 5 Mundas

—96 Africans and people of African descent

Class here Blacks of African origin

For people who speak or whose ancestors spoke Ethiopian languages, see —928; for non-Semitic Afro-Asiatic peoples, see —93; for Malagasy, see —993

—960 67 Africans of Central Africa and offshore islands

Number built according to instructions at beginning of Table 5

Class here comprehensive works on African pygmies

For specifc groups of African pygmies, see the specific ethnic group, e.g., Baka —96361

—960 73 African Americans (United States Blacks)

Unless it is redundant, add 0* to —96073 and to the result add notation 1–9 from Table 2 for area, e.g., African Americans in England —96073042, African Americans in New York —960730747, but African Americans in United States —96073

See Manual at T5—96073

—961 Khoikhoi and San

*Add 00 for standard subdivisions; see instructions at beginning of Table 5

—963 Peoples who speak, or whose ancestors spoke, Niger-Congo languages

Including peoples who speak, or whose ancestors spoke, Ijoid languages, Kordofanian languages; Dogon

Add to base number —963 the numbers following —963 in notation 9632–9639 from Table 6, e.g., Zulu —963986; then add further as instructed at beginning of Table 5, e.g., Zulu in Malawi —96398606897

—965 Peoples who speak, or whose ancestors spoke, Nilo-Saharan languages

Including Nilotic peoples, Nubians, Luo, Songhai

Class here peoples who speak or whose ancestors spoke Chari-Nile (Macrosudanic) languages

—966–968 Regional and national groups in Africa

Citizens of independent and partly independent jurisdictions; former citizens and descendants of citizens of these jurisdictions

Add to base number —96 the numbers following —6 in notation 66–68 from Table 2, e.g., West Africans —966, Nigerians —9669; then add further as instructed at beginning of Table 5, e.g., Nigerians in the United Kingdom and British citizens of Nigerian origin —9669041

Class nationals of a specific ethnolinguistic group with the group, e.g., South Africans of British origin —28, Nigerian Hausa —9370669, Nigerian Igbo —963320669

See also —9276 for national groups of African Arabs, e.g., modern Egyptians —92762, Sudanese —927624; also —928 for Ethiopians as a national group; also —9289 for Eritreans as a national group; also —931 for ancient Egyptians as a national group

—969 Other regional and national groups of largely African descent

Citizens of independent and partly independent jurisdictions outside Africa; former citizens and descendants of citizens of these jurisdictions

Add to base number —969 notation 4–9 from Table 2, e.g., West Indians —969729, Haitians —9697294, Virgin Islanders —96972972; then add further as instructed at beginning of Table 5, e.g., Haitians in the United States —9697294073

Class Cubans in —687291; class Dominicans (Dominican Republic) in —687293; class Puerto Ricans in —687295; class minority groups of African descent in —9604–9609, plus notation from Table 2 as instructed at beginning of Table 5 to show where the groups are located, e.g., persons of African descent in Canada —96071. Class nationals of a specific ethnolinguistic group with the group, e.g., Bahamians of English origin —2107296

—97 North American native peoples

Class here people who speak, or whose ancestors spoke, North American native languages; comprehensive works on Woodland Indians, on North and South American native peoples

Add to base number —97 the numbers following —97 in notation 971–979 from Table 6, e.g., Cherokee —97557; then add further as instructed at beginning of Table 5, e.g., Cherokee in Oklahoma —975570766

Class national groups of modern Central America where Spanish is an official language in —68728 even if the majority of their population is of North American native origin, e.g., Guatemalans as a national group —687281. Class a specific group of Woodland Indians with the group according to the language that the Indians speak or their ancestors spoke, e.g., Iroquois Indians —9755

For South American native peoples, see —98

—970 78 Indians of Western United States

Number built according to instructions at beginning of Table 5

Class here Plains Indians

For a specific group of Plains Indians, see the group according to the language that the Indians speak or their ancestors spoke, e.g., Cheyenne Indians —97353

—972 5 Apachean Indians

Number built according to instructions under —97

Including Jicarilla Indians, Kiowa Apache Indians

Class here Apache Indians

—974 Peoples who speak, or whose ancestors spoke, Penutian, Mayan, Mixe-Zoque, Uto-Aztecan, Kiowa-Tanoan languages

Number built according to instructions under —97

Class here Pueblo Indians

Class a specific group of Pueblo Indians with the group according to the language that the Indians speak or their ancestors spoke, e.g., Hopi —97458

—98 South American native peoples

Class here peoples who speak, or whose ancestors spoke, South American native languages

Add to base number —98 the numbers following —98 in notation 982–984 from Table 6, e.g., Quechua —98323; then add further as instructed at beginning of Table 5, e.g., Quechua in Bolivia —98323084

Class national groups of modern South America where Spanish is an official language in —688 even if the majority of their population is of South American native origin, e.g., Peruvians as a national group —6885

—983 23 Quechuan (Kechuan) Indians

Number built according to instructions under —98

Class here Incas, Quechua (Kechuan) Indians

—99 Aeta, Andamanese, Semang; Papuans; Aboriginal people of Australia and Tasmania; Malayo-Polynesian and related peoples; miscellaneous peoples

—991 Aeta, Andamanese, Semang; Papuans; Aboriginal people of Australia and Tasmania

—991 1 Aeta, Andamanese, Semang

—991 2 Papuans

Class here peoples who speak, or whose ancestors spoke, Papuan languages; Papua New Guineans as a national group

Class peoples of New Guinea who speak, or whose ancestors spoke, Austronesian languages in —995

For Andamanese, see —9911

—991 5 Aboriginal people of Australia and Tasmania

Subdivisions are added for Aboriginal people of Australia and Tasmania together, for Aboriginal people of Australia alone

For peoples of Australia who speak, or whose ancestors spoke, Papuan languages, see —9912

—991 59 Aboriginal people of Tasmania

—992 Malayo-Polynesian and related peoples

Class here peoples who speak, or whose ancestors spoke, Malayo-Polynesian languages; comprehensive works on peoples who speak, or whose ancestors spoke, Austronesian languages

For Malagasy, see —993; for Polynesians, see —994; for Melanesians and Micronesians, see —995

—992 1 Filipinos

Class here people of the Philippines as a national group

For Aeta, see —9911. For Philippine citizens of non-Filipino ethnic groups, see the ethnic group, e.g., Philippine citizens of Chinese origin —9510599

—992 2 Peoples who speak, or whose ancestors spoke, Indonesian and Chamic languages

Including Jarai, Rhade

Class here people of Indonesia as a national group

Class comprehensive works on Montagnards of Vietnam in —9593

For Formosan native peoples, see —9925; for peoples who speak, or whose ancestors spoke, Malay, and Malaysians as a national group, see —9928

—992 5 Formosan native peoples

Including Ami, Atayal, Bunun, Paiwan, Thao, Yami

Class here peoples who speak, or whose ancestors spoke, Taiwan (Formosan) languages

See also —951 for peoples who speak, or whose ancestors spoke, Taiwanese dialect of Chinese

—992 8 Malays

Class here people who speak, or whose ancestors spoke, Malay (Bahasa Malaysia); people of Malaysia as a national group

For citizens of Malaysia belonging to other ethnic groups, see the ethnic group, e.g., Chinese —9510595

—993 Malagasy

—994 Polynesians

Class here peoples who speak, or whose ancestors spoke, Polynesian languages; national groups of Polynesia; comprehensive works on Pacific Islanders; former citizens and descendants of citizens of these jurisdictions

Add to base number —994 the numbers following —994 in notation 9942–9948 from Table 6, e.g., Tahitians —99444; then add further as instructed at beginning of Table 5, e.g., Tahitians in New Zealand —99444093

For Melanesians and Micronesians, see —995

—995 Melanesians and Micronesians

Including peoples who speak, or whose ancestors spoke, Austronesian languages of Melanesia; national groups of Melanesia; Fijians

For Papua New Guineans as a national group and peoples who speak, or whose ancestors spoke, Papuan languages, see —9912; for peoples of Polynesian descent, see —994

—995 2 Micronesian peoples

Class here peoples who speak, or whose ancestors spoke, Austronesian languages of Micronesia; national groups of Micronesia

—999 Miscellaneous peoples

Limited to peoples provided for below

—999 2 Basques

—999 3 Elamites

—999 4 Etruscans

—999 5 Sumerians

—999 6 Georgians, Ingush, Chechen, Circassians, related peoples

Class here peoples who speak, or whose ancestors spoke, Caucasian (Caucasic) languages

Add to base number —9996 the numbers following —9996 in notation 99962–99969 from Table 6, e.g., Georgians —99969; then add further as instructed at beginning of Table 5, e.g., Georgians in Canada —99969071

Table 6. Languages

The following notation is never used alone, but may be used with those numbers from the schedules and other tables to which the classifier is instructed to add notation from Table 6, e.g., translations of the Bible (220.5) into Dutch (—3931 in this table): 220.53931; regions (notation —175 from Table 2) where Spanish language (—61 in this table) predominates: Table 2 notation 17561. When adding to a number from the schedules, always insert a point between the third and fourth digits of the complete number

Unless there is specific provision for the old or middle form of a modern language, class these forms with the modern language, e.g., Old High German —31, but Old English —29

Unless there is specific provision for a dialect of a language, class the dialect with the language, e.g., American English dialects —21, but Swiss-German dialect —35

Unless there is a specific provision for a pidgin or creole, class it with the source language from which more of its vocabulary comes than from its other source language(s), e.g., Crioulo language —69, but Papiamento —68

The numbers in this table do not necessarily correspond exactly to the numbers used for individual languages in 420–490 and in 810–890. For example, although the base number for English in 420–490 is 42, the number for English in Table 6 is —21, not —2

(Option A: To give local emphasis and a shorter number to a specific language, place it first by use of a letter or other symbol, e.g., Arabic language –A [preceding –1]. Option B is described at –1)

See Manual at Table 6

SUMMARY

—1	**Indo-European languages**
—2	**English and Old English (Anglo-Saxon)**
—3	**Germanic languages**
—4	**Romance languages**
—5	**Italian, Sardinian, Dalmatian, Romanian, Rhaeto-Romanic**
—6	**Spanish and Portuguese**
—7	**Italic languages**
—8	**Hellenic languages**
—9	**Other languages**

—1 Indo-European languages

Including Nostratic hypothesis

For specific Indo-European languages, see —2–91

(Option B: To give local emphasis and a shorter number to a specific language, e.g., Ukrainian, class it in this number, and class Indo-European languages in —91. Option A is described in the introduction to Table 6)

\> —2–91 **Specific Indo-European languages**

Class comprehensive works in —1

—2 English and Old English (Anglo-Saxon)

—21 English

Including dialects

Class Old English in —29

—217 English-based pidgins and creoles

Including Bislama, Krio, Sea Islands Creole (Gullah), Tok Pisin

—219 Middle English, 1100–1500

—29 Old English (Anglo-Saxon)

See also —219 for Middle English

—3 Germanic languages

For English and Old English, see —2

—31 German

Class here comprehensive works on dialects of German

For specific dialects of German, see —32–38

See also —394 for Low German

\> —32–38 **German dialects**

Class comprehensive works in —31

For Low German, see —394

—32 Franconian dialect

—33 Swabian dialect

—34 Alsatian dialect

—35 Swiss-German dialect

—38 Pennsylvania Dutch (Pennsylvania German)

—39 Other Germanic languages

—391 Yiddish

\> —392–394 Low Germanic languages

Class here West Germanic languages

Class comprehensive works in —39

—392 Frisian

—393 Netherlandish languages

—393 1 Dutch

Including Old Low Franconian

Class here Flemish

—393 6 Afrikaans

—394 Low German (Plattdeutsch)

Including Old Saxon

—395 North Germanic languages (Nordic languages)

Including proto-Nordic language

Class here comprehensive works on West Scandinavian languages [*formerly* —396], comprehensive works on modern West Scandinavian languages [*formerly* —3969], comprehensive works on East Scandinavian languages, comprehensive works on languages in the Nordic countries

For specific North Germanic languages, see —396–398; for Finnish, see —94541; for Sami, see —9455

\> —396–398 Specific North Germanic languages

Class comprehensive works in —395

—396 Old Norse (Old Icelandic), Icelandic, Faeroese

Comprehensive works on West Scandinavian languages relocated to —395

—396 1 Old Norse (Old Icelandic)

—396 9 Icelandic and Faeroese

Comprehensive works on modern West Scandinavian languages relocated to —395

—396 91 Icelandic

—396 99 Faeroese

—397 Swedish

—398 Danish and Norwegian

—398 1 Danish

Class Dano-Norwegian in —3982

—398 2 Norwegian

Class here New Norse, Landsmål [*both formerly* —3983]; Dano-Norwegian, Riksmål, Bokmål

—[398 3] New Norse, Landsmål

Relocated to —3982

—399 East Germanic languages

Including Burgundian, Gothic, Vandalic

—4 Romance languages

Class comprehensive works on Italic languages in —7

For Italian, Romanian, Rhaeto-Romanic, see —5; for Spanish and Portuguese, see —6

—41 French

Class Franco-Provençal in —49; class Occitan in —491

—417 French-based pidgins and creoles

—49 Occitan, Catalan, Franco-Provençal

—491 Occitan

Standard subdivisions are added for "Provençal" in the sense of a synonym of Occitan, not for "Provençal" in the sense of one of the dialects of Occitan

Including Auvergnat, Gascon, Languedocien, Limousin, Provençal dialects

Class here Langue d'oc

See also —49 for Franco-Provençal

—499 Catalan

—5 Italian, Sardinian, Dalmatian, Romanian, Rhaeto-Romanic

Class comprehensive works on Romance languages in —4; class comprehensive works on Italic languages in —7

—51 Italian

—56 Sardinian

—57 Dalmatian

Class here Vegliote dialect

—59 Romanian and Rhaeto-Romanic

—591 Romanian

—599 Rhaeto-Romance languages

Including Friulian, Ladin, Romansh

—6 Spanish and Portuguese

Class comprehensive works on Romance languages in —4

—61 Spanish

Including Spanish-based pidgins and creoles

For Judeo-Spanish (Ladino), see —67; for Papiamento, see —68

—67 Judeo-Spanish (Ladino)

—68 Papiamento

—69 Portuguese

Including Galician (Gallegan); Portuguese-based pidgins and creoles, e.g., Crioulo

For Papiamento, see —68

—7 Italic languages

For Romance languages, see —4

—71 Latin

Class comprehensive works on Latin and Greek in —8

—79 Other Italic languages

—794 Latinian languages other than Latin

Including Faliscan, Lanuvian, Praenestian, Venetic

—797 Sabellian languages

Including Aequian, Marrucinian, Marsian, Paelignian, Sabine, Vestinian, Volscian

—799 Osco-Umbrian languages

Including Oscan, Umbrian

—8 Hellenic languages

Class here comprehensive works on classical (Greek and Latin) languages

For Latin, see —71

—81 Classical Greek

—87 Preclassical and postclassical Greek

Including the language of Minoan Linear B; Biblical Greek, Koine (Hellenistic Greek); Byzantine Greek

See also —926 for Minoan Linear A

—89 **Modern Greek**

Including Demotic, Katharevusa

—9 Other languages

Including language of Indus script

SUMMARY

—91 **East Indo-European and Celtic languages**
—92 **Afro-Asiatic languages Semitic languages**
—93 **Non-Semitic Afro-Asiatic languages**
—94 **Altaic, Uralic, Hyperborean, Dravidian languages**
—95 **Languages of East and Southeast Asia Sino-Tibetan languages**
—96 **African languages**
—97 **North American native languages**
—98 **South American native languages**
—99 **Non-Austronesian languages of Oceania, Austronesian languages, miscellaneous languages**

—91 East Indo-European and Celtic languages

SUMMARY

—911 **Indo-Iranian languages**
—912 **Sanskrit**
—913 **Middle Indic languages**
—914 **Modern Indic languages**
—915 **Iranian languages**
—916 **Celtic languages**
—917 **East Slavic languages**
—918 **Slavic (Slavonic) languages**
—919 **Baltic and other Indo-European languages**

—911 Indo-Iranian languages

Class here comprehensive works on South Asian languages

For Indo-Aryan languages, see —912–914; for Iranian languages, see —915; for Dravidian languages, see —948; for South Asian languages closely related to the languages of East and southeast Asia, see —95

> —912–914 Indo-Aryan (Indic) languages

Class comprehensive works in —911

—912 Sanskrit

—912 9 Vedic (Old Indic)

—913 Middle Indic languages

Class here comprehensive works on Prakrit languages

For modern Prakrit languages, see —914

—913 7 Pali

—914 Modern Indic languages

Class here modern Prakrit languages

Class comprehensive works on Prakrit languages in —913

—914 1 Sindhi and Lahnda

—914 11 Sindhi

—914 19 Lahnda

—914 2 Panjabi

—914 3 Western Hindi languages

—914 31 Standard Hindi

—914 39 Urdu

—914 4 Bengali

Class here comprehensive works on Bengali and Assamese

For Assamese, see —91451

—914 5 Assamese, Bihari, Oriya

—914 51 Assamese

—914 54 Bihari

Including Bhojpuri, Magahi, Maithili

—914 56 Oriya

—914 6 Marathi and Konkani

—914 61 Marathi

—914 69 Konkani

—914 7 Gujarati, Bhili, Rajasthani

—914 71 Gujarati

—914 79 Rajasthani

Including Jaipuri, Marwari

—914 8 Sinhalese-Maldivian languages Sinhalese

Including Divehi (Maldivian)

—914 9 Other Indo-Aryan (Indic) languages

Including Awadhi, Bagheli, Chattisgarhi, Eastern Hindi, Nuristani (Kafiri), Pahari

See also —948 for Dravidian languages; also —954 for Tibeto-Burman languages; also —9595 for Munda languages

—914 95 Nepali

—914 97 Romani

—914 99 Dardic (Pisacha) languages

Including Kashmiri, Khowar, Kohistani, Shina

—915 Iranian languages

—915 1 Old Persian

Class here ancient West Iranian languages

See also —9152 for Avestan language

—915 2 Avestan

Class here ancient East Iranian languages

—915 3 Middle Iranian languages

Including Khotanese (Saka), Pahlavi (Middle Persian), Sogdian

—915 5 Modern Persian (Farsi)

Class Dari in —9156; class Tajik in —9157

—915 6 Dari

—915 7 Tajik

—915 9 Other modern Iranian languages

Including Pamir languages; Ossetic

—915 93 Pashto (Afghan)

—915 97 Kurdish languages Kurdish (Kurmanji)

Including Kurdi

—915 98 Baluchi

—916 Celtic languages

Including Gaulish

—916 2 Irish Gaelic

—916 3 Scottish Gaelic

—916 4 Manx

—916 6 Welsh (Cymric)

—916 7 Cornish

—916 8 Breton

—917 East Slavic languages

Class comprchensive works on Slavic (Slavonic) languages in —918

—917 1 Russian

—917 9 Ukrainian and Belarusian

—917 91 Ukrainian

—917 99 Belarusian

—918 Slavic (Slavonic) languages

Including Common Slavic

Class here comprehensive works on Balto-Slavic languages

For East Slavic languages, see —917; for Baltic languages, see —919

—918 1 South Slavic languages

For Serbo-Croatian, see —9182; for Slovenian, see —9184

—918 11 Bulgarian

—918 17 Old Bulgarian (Church Slavic)

—918 19 Macedonian

—918 2 Serbo-Croatian

—918 4 Slovenian

—918 5 West Slavic languages

Including Kashubian

For Czech, see —9186; for Slovak, see —9187; for Wendish, see —9188; for Polabian, see —9189

—918 51 Polish

—918 6 Czech

Including Moravian dialects

—918 7 Slovak

—918 8 Wendish (Lusatian, Sorbian)

—918 9 Polabian

—919 Baltic and other Indo-European languages

Standard subdivisions are added for Baltic and other Indo-European languages together, for Baltic languages alone

---

> —919 1–919 3 Baltic languages

Class comprehensive works in —919

—919 1 Old Prussian

—919 2 Lithuanian

—919 3 Latvian (Lettish)

—919 9 Other Indo-European languages

—919 91 Albanian

—919 92 Armenian

—919 93 Illyrian and Thraco-Phrygian languages

Including Ligurian, Messapian, Phrygian, Thracian

—919 94 Tocharian

—919 98 Anatolian languages Hittite

Including Luwian, Lycian, Lydian, Palaic

See also —999 for Hurrian languages

—92 Afro-Asiatic languages Semitic languages

For non-Semitic Afro-Asiatic languages, see —93

—921 East Semitic languages Akkadian (Assyro-Babylonian)

Including Assyrian, Babylonian

For Eblaite, see —926

See also —9995 for Sumerian

> —922–929 West Semitic languages

Class comprehensive works in —92

—922 Aramaic languages

For Eastern Aramaic languages, see —923

—922 9 Western Aramaic languages

Including Biblical Aramaic (Chaldee) and Samaritan

—923 Eastern Aramaic languages Syriac

—924 Hebrew

—926 Canaanite languages

Including Ammonite, Eblaite, Moabite, Phoenician, language of Minoan Linear A

Class here comprehensive works on Canaanitic languages

For Hebrew, see —924

See also —87 for Minoan Linear B

See Manual at T6—926

—926 7 Ugaritic

—927 Arabic and Maltese

Standard subdivisions are added for Arabic and Maltese together, for Arabic alone

Including Judeo-Arabic

Class here classical Arabic

See also —929 for South Arabian languages

—927 9 Maltese

—928 Ethiopian languages

Including Gurage, Harari

Class here comprehensive works on South Semitic languages

For South Arabian languages, see —929

—928 1 Ge‘ez

—928 2 Tigré

—928 3 Tigrinya (Tigrigna)

—928 7 Amharic

—929 South Arabian languages

Including Mahri, Sokotri

Class comprehensive works on South Semitic languages in —928

See also —927 for Arabic

—93 Non-Semitic Afro-Asiatic languages

—931 Egyptian

Including Demotic Egyptian

For Coptic, see —932

—932 Coptic

—933 Berber languages

Including Rif, Siwa

—933 3 Tamazight

—933 4 Kabyle

—933 8 Tamashek

—935 Cushitic and Omotic languages

Standard subdivisions are added for Cushitic and Omotic languages together, for Cushitic languages alone

Including Afar, Beja

—935 4 Somali

—935 5 Oromo

—935 9 Omotic languages

—937 Chadic languages

Including Angas

—937 2 Hausa

—94 Altaic, Uralic, Hyperborean, Dravidian languages

SUMMARY

— 941	**Tungusic languages**
— 942	**Mongolian languages**
— 943	**Turkic languages**
— 944	**Samoyedic languages**
— 945	**Finno-Ugric languages**
— 946	**Hyperborean (Paleosiberian) languages**
— 948	**Dravidian languages**

> —941–943 Altaic languages

Class comprehensive works in —94

For Ainu, see —946; for Japanese, see —956; for Korean, see —957

—941 Tungusic languages

Including Even (Lamut), Evenki (Tungus), Manchu, Nanai (Goldi)

—942 Mongolian languages

Including Buriat, Kalmyk

—942 3 Mongolian Khalkha Mongolian

—943 Turkic languages

—943 1 Old Turkic and Chuvash

—943 15 Chuvash

> —943 2–943 8 Common Turkic languages

Class comprehensive works in —943

—943 2 Eastern Turkic languages

For Northeast Turkic languages, see —9433; for Southern Turkic languages, see —9436

—943 23 Uighur

—943 25 Uzbek

—943 3 Northern Turkic languages

Including Tuva-Altai languages

Class here Northeast Turkic languages

Class Old Turkic in —9431

For Eastern Turkic languages, see —9432

—943 32 Yakut languages Yakut

Including Dolgan

—943 4 Central Turkic languages

Including Kara-Kalpak, Nogai

—943 45 Kazakh

—943 47 Kyrgyz

—943 5 Turkish (Osmanli)

Class here Ottoman Turkish

—943 6 Southern Turkic languages

Including Gagauz, Khalaj, Salar

Class here Southwest Turkic languages

For Turkish, see —9435; for Western Turkic languages, see —9438

—943 61 Azerbaijani

—943 64 Turkmen

Including Chagatai

—943 8 Western Turkic languages

Including Bashkir, Karachay-Balkar, Karaim

Class here Northwest Turkic languages

For Northern Turkic languages, see —9433; for Kara-Kalpak, Nogai, see —9434; for Kazakh, see —94345; for Kyrgyz, see —94347

—943 87 Tatar

Class here comprehensive works on Tatar languages

For Crimean Tatar, see —94388

—943 88 Crimean Tatar

—944 Samoyedic languages

Including Nganasan, Ostyak Samoyed, Yenisei Samoyed (Enets), Yurak Samoyed (Nenets)

See also —9451 for Khanty (Ostyak); also —946 for Ket (Yenisei Ostyak)

—945 Finno-Ugric languages

Class here comprehensive works on Uralic languages, on Uralic and Yukaghir languages

For Samoyedic languages, see —944; for Yukaghir languages, see —946

—945 1 Ugric languages

Including Khanty (Ostyak), Vogul

See also —944 for Ostyak Samoyed; also —946 for Ket (Yenisei Ostyak)

—945 11 Hungarian (Magyar)

—945 3 Permic languages

Including Votyak (Udmurt), Zyrian (Komi)

—945 4 Finnic languages

Including Karelian, Livonian, Veps

For Permian languages, see —9453; for Sami, see —9455; for Middle Volga languages, see —9456

—945 41 Finnish (Suomi)

—945 45 Estonian

—945 5 Sami

—945 6 Middle Volga languages

Including Mari, Mordvin

—946 Hyperborean (Paleosiberian) languages

Including Chukotko-Kamchatkan (Luorawetlin), Yukaghir languages; Ainu, Nivkh (Gilyak), Ket (Yenisei Ostyak)

Class comprehensive works on the Uralic and Yukaghir languages in —945

See also —944 for Ostyak Samoyed, Yenisei Samoyed; also —9451 for Ostyak; also —9714 for Yupik languages; also —9719 for Aleut language

—948 Dravidian languages

—948 1 South Dravidian languages

Including Kota, Toda

Class here Dravida group

—948 11 Tamil

—948 12 Malayalam

—948 14 Kannada (Kanarese)

—948 2 Central Dravidian languages

—948 23 Gondi

—948 24 Khond (Kandh)

—948 27 Telugu

—948 3 North Dravidian languages Brahui

Including Kurukh (Oraon), Malto

—95 Languages of East and Southeast Asia Sino-Tibetan languages

Including Karen

Here are classed South Asian languages closely related to the languages of East and Southeast Asia

For Austronesian languages of East and Southeast Asia, see —992

—951 Chinese

—951 1 Mandarin (Putonghua)

Class here Beijing dialect

—951 7 Chinese dialects

Including Gan, Hakka, Min, Wu, Xiang, Yue (Cantonese) dialects

For Beijing, Mandarin dialects, see —9511

—954 Tibeto-Burman languages

Including Baric, Bodish, Loloish languages

Class Karen in —95

For Burmese, see —958

—954 1 Tibetan

—954 9 Eastern Himalayan languages

Including Chepang, Limbu, Magari, Sunwar; Newari

Class here Kiranti languages, Mahakiranti languages

See also —91495 for Nepali

—956 Japanese

—957 Korean

—958 Burmese

—959 Miscellaneous languages of Southeast Asia; Munda languages

Only those languages provided for below

Including Kadai languages, Kam-Sui languages

Class here Daic languages

Class Austroasiatic languages in —9593

For Austronesian languages, see —992

—959 1 Tai languages

—959 11 Thai (Siamese)

—959 19 Other Tai languages

Including Shan

For Viet-Muong languages, see —9592

—959 191 Lao

—959 2 Viet-Muong languages

—959 22 Vietnamese

—959 3 Austroasiatic languages Mon-Khmer languages

Including Semang, Senoic languages; Khasi, Mon, Sedang, Srê

For Viet-Muong languages, see —9592; for Munda languages, see —9595

—959 32 Khmer (Cambodian)

—959 5 Munda languages

Including Gadaba, Ho, Mundari, Santali

—959 7 Hmong-Mien (Miao-Yao) languages

—959 72 Hmong (Miao)

—96 African languages

Class an African creole having a non-African primary source language with the source language, e.g., Krio —217

For Afrikaans, see —3936; for Ethiopian languages, see —928; for non-Semitic Afro-Asiatic languages, see —93; for Malagasy, see —993

SUMMARY

— 961 Khoisan languages
— 963 Niger-Congo languages
— 965 Nilo-Saharan languages

—961 Khoisan languages

Including Khoikhoi, San

—963 Niger-Congo languages

Including Ijoid, Kordofanian languages; Dogon

SUMMARY

—963 2	**West Atlantic languages**
—963 3	**Igboid, Defoid, Edoid, Idomoid, Nupoid, Akpes, Oko, Ukaan languages; Kwa languages; Kru languages**
—963 4	**Mande languages**
—963 5	**Gur (Voltaic) languages**
—963 6	**Benue-Congo and Adamawa-Ubangi languages**
—963 9	**Bantu languages**

—963 2 West Atlantic languages

—963 21 Senegal group

Including Serer

For Fulani, see —96322

—963 214 Wolof

—963 22 Fulani (Fulah)

—963 3 Igboid, Defoid, Edoid, Idomoid, Nupoid, Akpes, Oko, Ukaan languages; Kwa languages; Kru languages

Class comprehensive works on Benue-Congo languages in —9636

—963 32 Ibo (Igbo)

—963 33 Yoruba group Yoruba

—963 37 Kwa languages

Including Adangme

For Volta-Comoe group, see —96338

—963 374 Ewe group Ewe

—963 378 Gã

—963 38 Volta-Comoe group

—963 385 Central Volta-Comoe (Tano) subgroup Akan

Including Anyi, Baoulé

Class here Fante, Twi

—963 4 Mande languages

—963 45 Mandekan languages

—963 452 Bambara

—963 48 Mende-Bandi group Mende

—963 5 Gur (Voltaic) languages

Including Dagomba, Moré, Senufo

Class Dogon in —963

—963 6 Benue-Congo and Adamawa-Ubangi languages

Standard subdivisions are added for Benue-Congo and Adamawa-Ubangi languages together, for Benue-Congo languages alone

Including Bamileke

Class here Bantoid languages

For Igboid, Defoid, Edoid, Idomoid, Nupoid, Akpes, Oko, Ukaan languages, see —9633; for Bantu languages, see —9639

—963 61 Adamawa-Ubangi languages

Including Gbaya, Zande

—963 616 Sango

—963 64 Cross River languages

Including Ibibio

—963 642 Efik

—963 9 Bantu languages

Bantu proper (Narrow Bantu)

See also —9636 for Bantoid languages other than Bantu proper

See Manual at T6—9639

—963 91 Central Bantu languages Central eastern Bantu languages

Including Bena-Kinga, Gogo, Pogoro, Shambala, Zigula-Zaramo groups (from zone G); Bisa-Lamba, Fipa-Mambwe, Lenje-Tonga, Nyakyusa, Nyika-Safwa groups (from zone M); Manda, Senga-Sena, Tumbuka groups (from zone N)

For Swahili group, see —96392; for central western Bantu languages, see —96393

—963 915 Bemba group Bemba

Including Bwile

—963 918 Nyanja group Nyanja

Class here Chichewa (Chewa)

—963 92 Swahili group Swahili

—963 93 Central western Bantu languages

Including Hungana, Yaka groups (from zone H); Holu, Mbala, Salampasu-Ndembo groups (from zone K); Kaonde, Luba, Nkoya, Songye groups (from zone L)

Class Bwile in —963915; class Chokwe-Luchazi, Diriku, Kwangwa, Subia groups in —96399

—963 931 Kikongo group Kongo

—963 932 Mbundu group Mbundu (Kimbundu)

Limited to zone H

—963 94 Northern Bantu languages Northeastern Bantu languages

Including Bembe, Bira-Huku, Enya, Lega-Kalanga, Nyanga groups (zone D); Nyilamba-Langi, Sukuma-Nyamwezi, Tongwe groups (zone F); Konzo, Shi-Havu groups (from zone J)

For north northeastern Bantu languages, see —96395; for northwestern Bantu languages, see —96396

—963 946 Rwanda-Rundi group

—963 946 1 Rwanda (Kinyarwanda)

—963 946 5 Rundi

—963 95 North northeastern Bantu languages

Including Chaga, Kuria, Nyika groups (from zone E); Haya-Jita, Masaba-Luyia groups (from zone J)

Class Konzo, Shi-Havu groups in —96394

—963 953 Kikuyu-Kamba group

For Kikuyu, see —963954

—963 954 Kikuyu

—963 956 Nyoro-Ganda group

Including Chiga, Nyankore

For Ganda (Luganda), see —963957

—963 957 Ganda (Luganda)

—963 96 Northwestern Bantu languages

Including Bafia, Basaa, Bube-Benga, Kako, Lundu-Balong, Makaa-Njem, Sanaga, Yaunde-Fang groups (from zone A); Kele, Mbere, Myene, Njebi, Sira, Teke, Tsogo, Yanzi groups (zone B); Bushong, Kele, Mbosi, Mongo, Ngando, Ngombe, Ngundi, Tetela groups (from zone C)

—963 962 Duala group Duala

—963 968 Bangi-Ntomba group

—963 968 6 Lusengo cluster Lingala

—963 97 Southern Bantu languages Southeastern Bantu languages

Including Makua, Matumbi, Yao groups (zone P); Chopi group (from zone S)

For Nguni group, see —96398; for southwestern Bantu languages, Lozi, see —96399

—963 975 Shona group Shona

—963 976 Venda (Tshivenda)

—963 977 Sotho-Tswana group

Class here Sotho languages

Ndebele (South Africa) relocated to —963989

Class Lozi in —96399

—963 977 1 Northern Sotho

Class comprehensive works on northern and southern Sotho in —963977

—963 977 2 Southern Sotho

—963 977 5 Tswana

—963 978 Tswa-Ronga group Tsonga

—963 98 Nguni group

Including Ndebele (Zimbabwe)

—963 985 Xhosa

Class Fanakalo in —963986

—963 986 Zulu

Including Fanakalo

—963 987 Swazi (siSwati)

—963 989 Ndebele (South Africa) [*formerly* —963977]

—963 99 Southwestern Bantu languages

Including Chokwe-Luchazi, Diriku, Kwangwa, Subia groups (from zone K); Herero, Ndonga, South Mbundu, Yeye groups (zone R); Lozi

Class Holu, Mbala, Salampasu-Ndembo groups in —96393

—965 Nilo-Saharan languages

Including Nilotic, Nubian languages; Luo, Songhai

Class here Chari-Nile (Macrosudanic) languages

—97 North American native languages

Class here comprehensive works on North and South American native languages

For South American native languages, see —98

—971 Inuit, Yupik, Aleut languages

Class here Eskimo languages

—971 2 Inuit (Inuktitut) languages

Including Inupiatun, Kalâtdlisut (Greenlandic)

Class comprehensive works on Inuit and Yupik languages in —971

—971 24 Eastern Canadian Inuktitut

—971 4 Yupik languages

Including Siberian Yupik languages; Yuit

—971 9 Aleut

—972 Na-Dene languages

Including Chipewyan, Hupa, Koyukon

Class here Athapascan languages

—972 5 Apachean languages

Including Jicarilla Apache, Kiowa Apache

For Navajo, see —9726

See also —97492 for Kiowa

—972 56 Mescalero-Chiricahua Apache

Class here Chiricahua, Mescalero

—972 6 Navajo (Diné)

—972 7 Tlingit

—972 8 Haida

—973 Algic and Muskogean languages

Standard subdivisions are added for Algic and Muskogean languages together, for Algic languages alone

Including Lumbee, Yurok

Class here Algonquian languages

> —973 1–973 5 Algonquian languages

Class comprehensive works in —973

—973 1 Central Algonquian languages

For Cree-Montagnais-Naskapi languages, see —9732; for Ojibwa languages, see —9733

—973 12 Kickapoo

—973 13 Menomini

—973 14 Mesquakie

Class here Fox

—973 149 Sauk (Sac)

—973 15 Miami

Including Illinois

—973 16 Potawatomi

—973 17 Shawnee

—973 2 Cree-Montagnais-Naskapi languages

—973 23 Cree

—973 3 Ojibwa languages

—973 33 Ojibwa

Class here Chippewa

—973 36 Ottawa

—973 4 Eastern Algonquian languages

Including Abnaki, Malecite-Passamaquoddy

—973 43 Micmac

—973 44 Mohegan-Montauk-Narragansett

Class here Mohegan, Montauk, Narragansett, Pequot

—973 449 Stockbridge

—973 45 Unami and Munsee

Standard subdivisions are added for Unami and Munsee together, for Unami alone

Variant names for Unami: Delaware, Lenni Lenape

Variant name for Munsee: Delaware

—973 47 Powhatan

—973 48 Wampanoag

Including Massachuset

—973 5 Plains Algonquian languages

—973 52 Blackfoot

Class here Siksika

—973 53 Cheyenne

—973 54 Arapaho languages

Including Gros Ventre (Atsina)

Class here Arapaho

—973 8 Muskogean languages

Including Koasati, Mikasuki

—973 85 Muskogee (Creek) and Seminole

Standard subdivisions are added for Muskogee and Seminole together, for Muskogee alone

—973 859 Seminole

—973 86 Chickasaw

—973 87 Choctaw

—974 Penutian, Mayan, Mixe-Zoque, Uto-Aztecan, Kiowa-Tanoan languages

—974 1 Penutian languages

Including Chinook, Maidu

Mixe-Zoque languages relocated to —9743

Class Zuni in —97994; class Araucanian languages in —9872; class Uru-Chipaya languages in —989

—974 12 Plateau Penutian languages, Tsimshian languages

Including Umatilla

—974 122 Klamath-Modoc

Class here Klamath, Modoc

—974 124 Nez Percé

—974 127 Yakama

—974 128 Tsimshian

—974 13 Yok-Utian languages

Including Costanoan, Yokuts

—974 133 Miwok

—[974 15] Mayan languages

Relocated to —9742

—974 2 Mayan languages [*formerly* —97415]

Including Kekchí, Mam, Tzutujil

Class here Quichean-Mamean, Quichean languages

—974 22 Cakchikel

—974 23 Quiché

—974 27 Yucatecan languages

Including Itzá, Lacandón, Mopán

Class here Maya, Yucatec Maya

—974 28 Cholan-Tzeltalan languages

Including Tzeltal

—974 287 Tzotzil

—974 3 Mixe-Zoque languages [*formerly* —9741]

—974 5 Uto-Aztecan languages

Including Cahuilla, Luiseño

—974 52 Aztecan languages

Class here Nahuatl (Aztec)

—974 54 Sonoran languages

For Tepiman languages, see —97455

—974 542 Yaqui

—974 544 Huichol

—974 546 Tarahumaran languages

Class here Tarahumara

—974 55 Tepiman languages

—974 552 Tohono O'Odham and Akimel O'Odham

Standard subdivisions are added for Tohono O'Odham and Akimel O'Odham together, for Tohono O'Odham alone

—974 552 9 Akimel O'Odham (Pima)

—974 57 Numic languages

Including Mono

—974 572 Comanche

—974 574 Shoshoni

—974 576 Ute and Southern Paiute

Standard subdivisions are added for Ute and Southern Paiute together, for Ute alone

Including Chemehuevi

—974 576 9 Southern Paiute

Class here comprehensive works on Paiute

For Northern Paiute, see —974577

—974 577 Northern Paiute

Class here Bannock

Class comprehensive works on Paiute in —9745769

—974 58 Hopi

—974 9 Kiowa-Tanoan languages

Variant name: Tanoan languages

—974 92 Kiowa

See also —9725 for Kiowa Apache

—974 94 Tewa

—974 96 Northern Tiwa

Class here Taos, comprehensive works on Northern and Southern Tiwa

For Southern Tiwa, see —97497

—974 97 Southern Tiwa

Class here Isleta

Class comprehensive works on Northern and Southern Tiwa in —97496

—975 Siouan, Iroquian, Hokan, Chumash, Yuki languages

Class Keresan languages in —979; class Caddoan languages in —9793

See also —979 for Yuchi

—975 2 Siouan languages

Including Catawba, Iowa, Oto

—975 22 Mandan

—975 24 Dakota languages

Including Assiniboine

—975 243 Dakota

—975 244 Lakota

—975 25 Dhegiha languages

—975 253 Omaha and Ponca

Standard subdivisions are added for Omaha and Ponca together, for Omaha alone

—975 253 9 Ponca

—975 254 Osage

—975 26 Winnebago

—975 27 Missouri Valley Siouan languages

—975 272 Crow

—975 274 Hidatsa

—975 5 Iroquoian languages

Including Tuscarora

—975 54 Five Nations languages

Including Cayuga, Onondaga

—975 542 Mohawk

—975 543 Oneida

—975 546 Seneca

—975 55 Wyandot

Class here Huron

—975 57 Cherokee

—975 7 Hokan languages

—975 72 Yuman languages

Including Maricopa, Quechan (Yuma)

—975 722 Mohave

—975 724 Havasupai-Walapai-Yavapai

Class here Havasupai, Walapai, Yavapai

—975 74 Pomo languages

—975 76 Washo

—975 8 Chumash languages

—976 Oto-Manguean languages

Including Otomí

—976 3 Mixtecan languages

Class here Mixtec

—976 8 Zapotecan languages

Class here Zapotec

—978 Chibchan languages of North America, Misumalpan languages

Standard subdivisions are added for Chibchan languages of North America and Misumalpan languages together, for Chibchan languages of North America alone

Class comprehensive works on Chibchan languages in —982

—978 3 San Blas Kuna (San Blas Cuna)

—978 8 Misumalpan languages

—978 82 Mískito

—979 Other North American languages

Including Chimakuan, Coahuiltecan, Gulf, Huavean, Keres, Subtiaba-Tlapanec, Totonacan languages; Choco languages of Central America; Cuitlateco, Lenca, Xinca, Yuchi

Class comprehensive works on Choco languages in —989

See also —975 for Yuki languages

—979 2 Arawakan languages of Central America and West Indies

Including Garífuna (Black Carib)

Class comprehensive works on Arawakan languages in —9839

See also —9842 for Carib languages

—979 22 Taino

—979 3 Caddoan languages

Including Caddo, Wichita

—979 32 Arikara

—979 33 Pawnee

—979 4 Salishan languages

—979 43 Interior Salish languages

Including Coeur d'Alene (Skitswish), Shuswap, Spokane

—979 435 Kalispel-Pend d'Oreille (Salish)

Class here Kalispel, Pend d'Oreille

—979 5 Wakashan languages

—979 53 Kwakiutl

—979 54 Makah

—979 55 Nootka

—979 6 Tarascan languages

Class here Purépecha (Tarasco)

—979 9 Kutenai and Zuni

—979 92 Kutenai

—979 94 Zuni

—98 South American native languages

—982 Chibchan, Barbacoan, Paezan languages

Class Warao in —989; class Yanomam languages in —9892

For Chibchan languages of North America, see —978

—983 Quechuan, Aymaran, Tucanoan, Tupí, Arawakan languages

—983 2 Quechuan and Aymaran languages

—983 23 Quechuan (Kechuan) languages

Class here Quechua (Kechua)

Class Aymaran languages in —98324

—983 24 Aymaran languages

Class here Aymara

—983 5 Tucanoan languages

Including Tucano

—983 7 Jivaroan languages

Class Yaruro in —989

—983 72 Shuar

—983 8 Tupí languages

—983 82 Narrow Tupí group

Class here Guaraní

—983 829 Tupí (Nhengatu)

—983 9 Arawakan languages

Class here comprehensive works on Arawakan languages of South America and of Central America and West Indies

Class Guahiban languages in —989

For Arawakan languages of Central America and West Indies, see —9792

—984 Carib, Macro-Gê, Nambiquaran, Panoan languages

Class Mataco-Guaicuru languages in —987; class Tacanan, Witotoan languages in —989

—984 2 Carib languages

See also —9792 for Island Carib, Black Carib

—984 22 Carib (Galibi)

—987 Araucanian, Alacalufan, Chon, Lule-Vilela, Mataco-Guaicuru languages

—987 2 Araucanian languages

Class here Mapudungun (Mapuche)

—989 Other South American languages

Including Arauan, Arutani-Sape, Cahuapanan, Chapacura-Wanham, Choco, Guahiban, Harakmbet, Katukinan, Maku, Mascoian, Mosetenan, Mura, Peba-Yaguan, Salivan, Tacanan, Uru-Chipaya, Witotoan, Zamucoan, Zaparoan languages; Warao, Yaruro

For Choco languages of Central America, see —979

—989 2 Yanomam languages

Class here Yanomamo

—99 Non-Austronesian languages of Oceania, Austronesian languages, miscellaneous languages

—991 Non-Austronesian languages of Oceania

Including Bayono-Awbono, Lower Mamberamo languages

—991 2 Papuan languages

Non-Austronesian languages of New Guinea and related languages spoken nearby

Including Amto-Musan, East Bird's Head, Geelvink Bay, Kwomtari-Baibai, Left May, Sepik-Ramu, Sko, Torricelli, Trans-New Guinea languages

See also —995 for Austronesian languages of New Guinea

—991 5 Australian and Tasmanian languages

Standard subdivisions are added for Australian and Tasmanian languages together, for Australian languages alone

Aboriginal languages of Australia and Tasmania, and related languages of adjacent islands

Class Papuan languages spoken in Australia in —9912

—991 59 Tasmanian languages

—992 Austronesian languages

Including Taiwan (Formosan) languages

Class here Malay languages, Malayo-Polynesian languages

For Malagasy, see —993; for Polynesian languages, see —994; for Austronesian languages of Melanesia and Micronesia, see —995

—992 1 Philippine languages

—992 11 Tagalog (Filipino)

—992 2 Indonesian and Chamic languages

Standard subdivisions are added for Indonesian and Chamic languages together, for Indonesian languages alone

Including Borneo languages; Balinese, Madurese, Sundanese

For Malay, see —9928

—992 21 Indonesian (Bahasa Indonesia)

Class comprehensive works on Indonesian (Bahasa Indonesia) and Malay (Bahasa Malaysia) in —9928

—992 22 Javanese

—992 8 Malay (Bahasa Malaysia)

Including Melayu Asli (Proto-Malay) languages; Jakun

Class here comprehensive works on Malay (Bahasa Malaysia) and Indonesian (Bahasa Indonesia)

Class Semang, Senoic languages in —9593

For Indonesian, see —99221

—993 Malagasy

—994 Polynesian languages

Including Rapanui

Class here comprehensive works on Oceanic languages

For Austronesian languages of Melanesia and Micronesia, see —995

—994 2 Marquesic languages Hawaiian

Including Marquesan

—994 4 Tahitic languages

Including Rarotongan

—994 42 Maori

—994 44 Tahitian

—994 6 Samoic Outlier languages

Including Nukuoro, Rennellese, Tuvalu

—994 62 Samoan

—994 8 Tongic languages

Including Niuean, Tonga

—995 Austronesian languages of Melanesia and Micronesia

Including Fijian class Polynesian languages of Melanesia and Micronesia, comprehensive works on Oceanic languages in —994

See also —9912 for Non-Austronesian languages of Melanesia

—995 2 Austronesian languages of Micronesia

—999 Miscellaneous languages

Only those named below

Including Hurrian languages

—999 2 Basque

—999 3 Elamite

—999 4 Etruscan

—999 5 Sumerian

See also —926 for Eblaite language

—999 6 Caucasian (Caucasic) languages

> —999 62–999 64 North Caucasian languages

Class comprehensive works in —9996

—999 62 Abkhazo-Adyghian (Northwest Caucasian) languages

Including Abazin, Ubykh

—999 623 Abkhaz

—999 624 Circassian languages

Including Kabardian

For Adyghe, see —999625

—999 625 Adyghe

—999 64 Nakho-Daghestan (Northeast Caucasian) languages

Including Avaro-Andi-Dido group; Avaric, Dargwa, Lak, Lezghian, Tabasaran

Class here Daghestan languages

—999 641 Nakh languages

Including Chechen, Ingush

Class here north central Caucasian languages

—999 68 Kartvelian (South Caucasian) languages

Including Laz, Svan

For Georgian, see —99969

—999 69 Georgian

—999 9 Artificial languages

Including Afrihili, Klingon

—999 92 Esperanto

—999 93 Interlingua

Relocations and Discontinuations

The following two lists show all the relocations and discontinuations since Edition 21.

The column headed *Edition 21* indicates in numerical order each number in that edition from which a topic or group of topics has been shifted; the column headed *Edition 22* indicates each corresponding number in the present edition to which those topics or groups of topics have been shifted. If two or more topics have been shifted from one number to two or more numbers, each separate shift is shown.

Numbers in the *Edition 21* column enclosed in square brackets are no longer in use; those not enclosed in brackets have lost part of their original meaning through relocation or discontinuation, but still retain some of their meaning.

In the following lists, the same abbreviations employed in the Relative Index are used for Tables 1–6, e.g., T1 means Table 1 Standard Subdivisions.

Relocations

In a relocation, one or more topics are shifted to a number differing from the old in respects other than length. If the relocation is partial, the original number remains valid; but if it is total, the original number is no longer used. Relocations are described and explained in the Introduction.

Relocations that have appeared previously in an interim update prior to the publication of Edition 22 are indicated by * next to the Edition 21 number. Relocations that eliminate dual provision for the same topic or topics are indicated by † next to the Edition 21 number.

For example, in Table 2 one of the topics that was in —16533 in Edition 21 has been relocated to —6215 in Edition 22; all of the topics in —4112 have been relocated to —4113. All the topics in —4434 have been relocated to —4436 to eliminate dual provision.

"Scattered within 543" means that the topic has been relocated to so many numbers throughout 543.1–543.8 that it is not feasible to name them all.

An indented number is an element of an add table. The number or span under which it is indented shows the location of the add table or the add instruction related to an add table. For example, the [09] and 009 under 299.683–.685 indicate that the [09] and 009 are elements of the add table at 299.683–.685.

Table 7 Groups of Persons has been deleted and replaced by direct use of notation already available in the schedules and in notation 08 from Table 1. Relocations resulting from this deletion and replacement are not given. The following list gives the numbers with add instructions where notation from Table 7 was previously added:

T1—024
T1—088001–088999
T2—1762–1769
T3C—352
T3C—9205–9207
T3C—921
174.9
303.388
305.43
305.6
305.908
305.909
305.91–.99
390.4
781.711–.719
781.74–.79
782.3221–.3229
782.34–.39

For details of the specific relocated topics the classifier should consult the appropriate entries in the tables and schedules.

Edition 21	*Edition 22*
T2—145†	T2—153
T2—16533	T2—6215
[T2—4112]*	T2—4113
[T2—4116]*	T2—41152
[T2—4117]*	T2—41156
[T2—41172]*	T2—41152
[T2—4118]*	T2—41154
[T2—41182]*	T2—41154
[T2—41185]*	T2—41154
[T2—41185]*	T2—41156
[T2—4119]*	T2—41158
[T2—4121]*	T2—41158
[T2—4121]*	T2—4124
[T2—41225]*	T2—4124
[T2—41232]*	T2—4124
[T2—4125]*	T2—4126
[T2—4125]*	T2—4128
T2—4127*	T2—4126
[T2—4132]*	T2—4133
[T2—4138]*	T2—4137
[T2—4139]*	T2—4137
[T2—41425]*	T2—41432
[T2—41428]*	T2—41431
[T2—41434]*	T2—41436
T2—41436*	T2—41452
[T2—41438]*	T2—41452
[T2—41441]*	T2—41437
[T2—41441]*	T2—41439
[T2—41443]*	T2—41457
[T2—41446]*	T2—41452
[T2—41449]*	T2—41452
[T2—41451]*	T2—41439
[T2—41454]*	T2—41457
[T2—41463]*	T2—41467
[T2—41469]*	T2—41457
[T2—4148]*	T2—4147
[T2—4149]*	T2—4147
[T2—42254]*	T2—42256
[T2—42394]*	T2—42391
[T2—42397]*	T2—42398
[T2—42444]*	T2—4242
[T2—42444]*	T2—42447
[T2—42445]*	T2—4242
[T2—42446]*	T2—4242
T2—42447*	T2—4242
[T2—42831]*	T2—42832
[T2—42833]*	T2—42834
[T2—42835]*	T2—42832
[T2—42835]*	T2—42839
[T2—42836]*	T2—42839
[T2—42838]*	T2—42839
[T2—42923]*	T2—42925
[T2—42929]*	T2—42925
[T2—42931]*	T2—42927
[T2—42932]*	T2—42937
[T2—42936]*	T2—42933
T2—42937*	T2—42939
T2—42937*	T2—42951
[T2—42954]*	T2—42951
[T2—42963]*	T2—42962
[T2—42967]*	T2—42965
[T2—42968]*	T2—42965
T2—42971*	T2—42989
[T2—42972]*	T2—42978
[T2—42973]*	T2—42978
T2—42978*	T2—42987
[T2—42981]*	T2—42982
[T2—42983]*	T2—42982
[T2—42983]*	T2—42985
[T2—42984]*	T2—42985
[T2—42986]*	T2—42987
[T2—42993]*	T2—42976
T2—42995*	T2—42998
[T2—43157]	T2—43154
T2—43172	T2—43178
T2—43174	T2—43178
T2—43182	T2—43186
T2—43184	T2—43186
T2—4337	T2—4346
[T2—434646]	T2—4346452
T2—4381*	T2—43822
T2—4382*	T2—43832
T2—4384*	T2—43866
T2—4386*	T2—43858
[T2—4414]*	T2—44167
[T2—4434]*†	T2—4436
[T2—44345]*	T2—44266
[T2—4435]*	T2—44264
[T2—443825]*	T2—44385
[T2—44383]*	T2—4439
T2—4439*	T2—44389
[T2—4444]*	T2—44583
[T2—4448]*	T2—44585
[T2—4449]*	T2—44584
[T2—4456]*	T2—44416
[T2—4457]*	T2—44597
[T2—4461]*	T2—44169
[T2—4476]*	T2—44718
T2—4477*	T2—4473
[T2—44772]*	T2—44715

*Previously published
†Eliminates dual provision

Edition 21	*Edition 22*	*Edition 21*	*Edition 22*
[T2—4479]*	T2—44716	[T2—6821]*	T2—68223
[T2—44813]*	T2—44595	T2—6822*	T2—68277
[T2—4482]*	T2—44589	[T2—6823]*	T2—68228
[T2—4485]*	T2—44737	[T2—6823]*	T2—68229
[T2—4486]*	T2—4473	[T2—6823]*	T2—68241
[T2—4486]*	T2—44736	[T2—6823]*	T2—68248
[T2—4488]*	T2—44735	[T2—6823]*	T2—68251
T2—4489*	T2—4473	[T2—6823]*	T2—68275
T2—449*	T2—4458	[T2—68235]*	T2—68227
T2—4492*	T2—44588	[T2—68235]*	T2—68228
[T2—44945]*	T2—4499	[T2—6826]*	T2—68259
[T2—4496]*	T2—44586	[T2—6826]*	T2—68271
[T2—4498]*	T2—44587	[T2—6826]*	T2—68272
T2—4499*	T2—44586	[T2—6826]*	T2—68273
T2—45781*	T2—45782	[T2—6826]*	T2—68274
T2—45781*	T2—45787	T2—6827*	T2—6842
T2—542	T2—5451	[T2—68291]*	T2—68257
T2—543	T2—54137	[T2—68292]*	T2—68257
[T2—54796]	T2—5476	[T2—68292]*	T2—68259
[T2—54799]	T2—5477	[T2—68293]*	T2—68253
[T2—54799]	T2—5478	[T2—68293]*	T2—68255
T2—54912	T2—54911	[T2—68293]*	T2—68256
T2—549142	T2—549149	[T2—68293]*	T2—68257
T2—54923	T2—54927	[T2—68293]*	T2—68259
T2—54923	T2—54929	[T2—68294]*	T2—6824
T2—54925	T2—54926	[T2—68294]*	T2—68241
T2—5523	T2—5522	[T2—68294]*	T2—68244
T2—5523	T2—5524	[T2—68294]*	T2—68246
T2—5527	T2—5526	[T2—68294]*	T2—68247
T2—553	T2—5512	[T2—68294]*	T2—68248
T2—5552	T2—5556	[T2—68294]*	T2—68275
T2—5552	T2—5558	[T2—68294]*	T2—6855
T2—5575	T2—5574	[T2—68295]*	T2—68275
T2—5595	T2—5594	[T2—68296]*	T2—68271
T2—5595	T2—5597	[T2—68296]*	T2—68272
T2—5662	T2—5667	[T2—68491]*	T2—6841–6847
T2—56958	T2—569562	[T2—6859]*	T2—6851
T2—5986*	T2—5987	[T2—68591]*	T2—6851
T2—642	T2—641	T2—68711*	T2—68246
T2—642	T2—6432	T2—68713*	T2—68756
T2—642	T2—6433	[T2—68714]*	T2—68751
T2—643	T2—645	[T2—68714]*	T2—68753
T2—643	T2—6462	[T2—68714]*	T2—68754
T2—66928	T2—66927	[T2—68714]*	T2—68755
T2—66942	T2—66941	[T2—68714]*	T2—68756
T2—66945	T2—66947	[T2—68715]*	T2—68739
T2—66949	T2—66947	[T2—68715]*	T2—68751
T2—66952	T2—66953	[T2—68715]*	T2—68754
T2—66962	T2—66961	[T2—68716]*	T2—68738
T2—66982	T2—66984	[T2—6872]*	T2—68719

*Previously published

Edition 21	*Edition 22*	*Edition 21*	*Edition 22*
[T2—6872]*	T2—68731	T2—78872*	T2—78864
[T2—6874]*	T2—68737	T2—78881*	T2—78864
[T2—6874]*	T2—68738	T2—78884*	T2—78864
[T2—6874]*	T2—68751	[T2—85294]	T2—8538
[T2—6876]*	T2—68755	T2—8612*	T2—8615
[T2—6876]*	T2—68756	[T2—86123]*	T2—86118
[T2—6876]*	T2—68757	[T2—86127]*	T2—86151
[T2—6879]*	T2—6875	[T2—86137]*	T2—86144
[T2—68791]*	T2—68756	[T2—86138]*	T2—86198
[T2—68791]*	T2—68758	T2—86139*	T2—86192
[T2—68791]*	T2—68759	[T2—86143]*	T2—86196
[T2—68792]*	T2—68755	[T2—86154]*	T2—86139
T2—71137	T2—71133	[T2—86156]*	T2—86194
T2—71336	T2—71337	[T2—86162]*	T2—86158
[T2—71383]	T2—71384	[T2—8618]*	T2—86111
T2—714115	T2—714117	T2—8814	T2—8813
T2—71421	T2—714224	T2—8814	T2—8815
T2—714221	T2—714223	T2—8815	T2—8816
T2—714221	T2—714224	T2—8817	T2—8814
[T2—714225]	T2—714241	T2—8818	T2—8814
T2—71424	T2—714412	T2—8818	T2—8817
[T2—71433]	T2—71434	T2—8819	T2—8814
T2—71437	T2—714365	T2—8819	T2—88187
T2—714451	T2—714453	T2—8831	T2—88395
T2—714451	T2—714455	T2—8833	T2—88395
T2—714455	T2—714451	[T2—8836]	T2—8834
T2—71448	T2—714476	[T2—8836]	T2—8837
T2—7145	T2—7146	T2—8838	T2—88395
[T2—71451]	T2—71439	[T2—89225]	T2—89224
T2—714573	T2—714712	[T2—89226]	T2—89227
[T2—71461]	T2—71438	[T3B—108]	T3B—107
T2—714771	T2—714773	T3C—353	T3C—3561
T2—714775	T2—714778	T3C—355	T3C—32
T2—7192*	T2—7195	T3C—355	T3C—3561
[T2—7194]*	T2—7193	T3C—355	T3C—357
[T2—7194]*	T2—71958	T3C—356	T3C—36
[T2—7196]*	T2—7193	T4—31†	793.73203
[T2—7197]*	T2—7193	[T5—034]	T5—09
[T2—7197]*	T2—71955	[T5—04]	T5—05
T2—728532*	T2—728537	T5—93	T5—92761
T2—728711*	T2—728717	T6—396*	T6—395
T2—728712*	T2—728717	T6—3969*	T6—395
T2—728722*	T2—728717	[T6—3983]*	T6—3982
T2—72873*	T2—728772	T6—963977*	T6—963989
T2—728731*	T2—728773	T6—9741	T6—9743
[T2—72874]*	T2—728774	[T6—97415]	T6—9742
[T2—72874]*	T2—728776	[004.3585]	004.357
[T2—72874]*	T2—728778	005.3	005.5
[T2—755662]*	T2—755661	[005.3042]	005.5
T2—78863*	T2—78864	[005.424]	005.434

*Previously published

†Eliminates dual provision

Edition 21	*Edition 22*
[005.425]	005.435
[005.426]	005.436
[005.6]	005.18
[011.77]†	016.0053
[013]	011.8
[013.9]†	015
023.8†	020.7155
[028.5342]	028.532
[028.5343]	028.533
070.18†	070.43
070.194†	070.43
070.195†	070.43
070.4833	070.4834
153	006.3
[174.24]	179.7
[174.25]*	174.29
[174.25]*	174.297954
[174.25]*	174.295895
215.7	218
[261.834]	270.08
261.836	261.88
284.143	284.0943
[291]	200
[291.042]	201.42
[291.046]	200.9034
[291.1]	201
[291.17]	201.7
[291.171]	201.7
[291.172]	201.5
[291.175]	201.6
[291.175]	201.7
[291.177]	201.72
[291.178]	201.76
[291.1783]	201.76
[291.178326]	201.7638
[291.178327]	201.7628292
[291.1783271]	201.76276
[291.1783272]	201.76276
[291.1783273]	201.762764
[291.178328]	201.76287
[291.17833]	201.764
[291.17834]	200.8
[291.17835]	201.7
[291.178362]	201.77
[291.178366]	201.7
[291.1785]	201.73
[291.1787]	201.727
[291.2]	202
[291.3]	203
[291.4]	204
[291.5]	205
[291.6]	206
[291.7]	207
[291.8]	208
[291.9]	209
[299.62]	299.6113
[299.62]	299.67
[299.62]	299.68
[299.63]	299.612
[299.63]	299.67
[299.63]	299.68
[299.64]	299.613
[299.64]	299.6138
[299.64]	299.67
[299.64]	299.675
[299.64]	299.68
299.683–.685	299.683–.685
01–08	001–008
09	009
[299.72]	299.7113
[299.72]	299.78
	013
[299.73]	299.712
[299.73]	299.78
	02
[299.74]	299.713
[299.74]	299.7138
[299.74]	299.78
	03
[299.74]	299.78
	038
[299.82]	299.8113
[299.82]	299.88
	013
[299.83]	299.812
[299.83]	299.88
	02
[299.84]	299.813
[299.84]	299.8138
[299.84]	299.88
	03
[299.84]	299.88
	038
303.388	303.386
305.3894	306.87
[305.389652]	306.8152
[305.3896523]	306.734081
[305.389653]	306.892
305.389654	306.882
[305.389655]†	306.8722

*Previously published
†Eliminates dual provision

Edition 21	*Edition 22*
305.38966	306.76
305.389664	306.7662
[305.4894]	306.87
[305.489652]	306.8153
[305.4896523]	306.734082
[305.489653]	306.893
305.489654	306.883
[305.489655]†	306.8723
305.48966	306.76
305.489664	306.7663
305.4896947	306.87432
[305.555]†	305.963
305.563	305.963
305.563	306.365
[305.567]	306.362
[305.904]	306.87
[305.9063]	305.5
[305.90631]	305.552
[305.90632]	305.55
[305.90633]	305.565
[305.9065]	306.81
[305.90652]	306.815
[305.906523]	306.734
[305.90653]	306.89
[305.90654]	306.88
[305.90655]	306.872
[305.90659]	306.8423
[305.9066]	306.76
[305.906923]	305.2308692
305.90694	305.56
[305.906945]	305.23086945
[305.906945]†	306.874
[305.906949]	305.90695
[305.906949]	362.88
[305.90696]	306.38
[306.08]	305.8
[306.089]	305.805–.89
306.2–.6	
[08]	T1—08
306.364	305.963
[306.484208]†	780.8
[306.485]†	302.234
[306.489]	306.47
[306.608]†	200.8
[306.735]	306.841
[306.735]	306.8423
320.019	320.6
321	352.23
[323.636]	323.62
[324.023]†	324.22

Edition 21	*Edition 22*
324.243082	324.24304
324.243083	324.24303
324.274703	324.274708
324.274707	324.274708
[324.274709]	324.274708
[324.2747093]	324.274703
[324.2747097]	324.274707
325.21	305.906914
[327.093–.099]	327.3–.9
[327.1093–.1099]	327.3–.9
[328.094–.099]†	328.4–.9
[328.333]†	331.28132833
[330.90092]†	330.092
331.136	331.137
331.21†	339.5
331.38†	331.318
[331.714]†	331.761658
[331.88041]	331.8836
331.8892	331.8896
[331.8894]	331.8896
[331.8915]	331.8912
331.898†	331.8892
[332.02403]†	332.0240089
[332.02404–.0249]	332.0240081–.0240088
[332.02404–.0249]	332.02401081–.02401088
[332.02404–.0249]	332.02402081–.02402088
332.1†	368.854
332.5	332.4
332.6042†	332.0240145
[332.6712]	332.6722
[332.6715]	332.6725
332.672	332.678
332.67253	332.678
332.67254	332.67253
332.6732093–.6732099†	332.67322
332.6732093–.6732099†	332.67324
[333.91601–.91609]†	333.91001–.91009
[334.6068]†	658.87
334.6813801–.681382	334.682–.688
[335.9]	307.77
[336.0068]†	352.4
[336.11]	336.12
[336.11]	336.16
[336.32]	336.31
[338.009]	338.09
[339.3093–.3099]	339.33–.39
[339.31093–.31099]	339.33–.39

†Eliminates dual provision

Edition 21	*Edition 22*
[339.32093–.32099]	339.33–.39
339.41†	339.42
341.2–.7	342–347
026	0261
0267	02632
0268	0264
341.48†	342.08
341.48†	346.047
[341.482]†	342.083
[341.484]†	342.083
[341.484]†	346.0408691
[341.4842]†	342.082
[341.4844]†	343.0526
[341.4846]†	343.0252
341.486	342.083
[341.488]†	342.083
[341.488]†	345.01
[341.488]†	345.052
341.72†	343.01
341.72†	344.0535
[341.725]†	343.0157
[341.728]†	342.0412
[341.75]	343.07
[341.7506]	343.07
[341.750614]	343.2407
[341.751]	343.03
[341.751]†	343.034
[341.7511]†	346.082
[341.75115]†	346.073
[341.75115]†	346.08215
[341.7512]†	346.0822
[341.7513]†	346.0823
[341.7514]†	343.032
[341.752]†	346.092
[341.7522]†	346.0926
[341.75232]†	346.0922
[341.75242]†	346.0926
[341.75244]†	343.08
[341.7526]†	346.0662
[341.753]†	343.072
[341.753]†	343.0723
[341.753]†	346.065
[341.753]†	346.07
[341.754]†	343.075
[341.754]†	343.07891
[341.754]†	343.087
[341.7543]†	343.056
[341.7547]†	343.056
[341.7547]†	343.0871–.0875
[341.755]†	343.0925
[341.755]†	346.04679
[341.756]†	343.093
[341.756]†	343.0932
[341.756]†	343.0933
[341.7565]†	343.095
[341.7566]†	343.096
[341.75662]†	343.0962
[341.7567]†	343.097
[341.75676]†	343.0976
[341.75679]†	343.0979
[341.7568]†	343.094
[341.7569]†	343.0932
[341.757]†	343.099
[341.7573]†	343.0992
[341.7577]†	343.0994
[341.7577]†	343.09943
[341.7577]†	343.09944
[341.7577]†	343.09945
[341.7577]†	343.09946
[341.758]†	346.048
[341.759]†	343.074
[341.7592]†	343.076
[341.76]†	344.01
[341.76]	344.0327
[341.762]	341.4
[341.762]†	344.046
[341.762]†	344.0955
[341.762]†	346.044
[341.7621]	341.455
[341.7622]†	343.07692
[341.7622]†	343.076928
[341.7622]†	343.076929
[341.7622]†	343.07694
[341.7622]†	346.046956
[341.7623]†	344.04632
[341.7623]†	344.046336
[341.7625]†	344.04634
[341.7625]†	346.046
[341.76252]†	344.046342
[341.76253]†	344.046343
[341.763]†	344.01
[341.765]†	344.04
[341.765]†	344.047
[341.766]†	344.03
[341.766]†	344.0534
[341.767]†	344.07
[341.767]†	344.09
[341.7672]	344.09
[341.7673]†	344.08
[341.7675]†	344.095

†Eliminates dual provision

Edition 21	Edition 22
[341.7677]†	344.094
[341.7677]†	344.097
[341.77]	345
[341.77]†	345.0235
[341.77]	345.052
[341.772]†	345.02552
[341.772]†	345.0264
[341.773]†	345.02
[341.775]†	345.0277
[341.778]†	345.0251
[341.78]†	345.052
[341.78]†	347.012
343.013†	343.0153
343.013†	343.0155
343.076†	344.0957
[343.088]	343.0815
[343.0881–.0885]	343.0851–.0855
[343.0887]	343.0811
[343.0888]	343.0812
343.094	343.093
346.042	346.01664
348.001–.003	348.0201–.0203
348.001–.003	348.02501–.02503
348.005	348.0205
348.005	348.02505
348.006	348.0206
348.006	348.02506
348.007–.008	348.0207–.0208
348.007–.008	348.02507–.02508
362.16†	362.61
362.61†	362.16
362.87*†	940.53187
362.88	613.66
362.883	613.663
[363.20683]†	363.22
370.153	370.1528
[371.9127]*	371.91246
[371.9127]*	418
371.93	371.94
372.82	372.373
374.22†	361.4
378.1543	373.238
[380.1]	381
[381.1401–.1409]	381.101–.109
[381.148]	381.149
[381.148]†	381.456413
381.149	381.15
[388.10223]†	912
[390.001–.007]	390.01–.07
[390.008]	390.08

Edition 21	Edition 22
[390.009]	390.09
[392.36001]	392.3601
[392.36002]	392.3602
[392.36003]	392.3603
[392.36005–.36007]	392.3605–.3607
[392.36008]	392.3608
[392.360088]	392.360882
[392.36009]	392.3609
392.3601	392.360862
392.3602	392.360862
[392.3604]	392.36088
394.25†	394.26
398.356	398.36
413.1†	793.73203
419*	418
419*	T4—891
427.1–.9	427.02094–.02099
437.1–.9	437.01094–.01099
437.1–.9	437.02094–.02099
439.6*	439.5
439.69*	439.5
439.7701*	439.77001
[439.7702–.7708]*	439.77002–.77008
[439.7709]*	439.77009
[439.770902]*	439.7701
[439.77094–.77099]*	439.776–.779
439.81701*	439.817001
[439.81702–.81708]*	439.817002–.817008
[439.81709]*	439.817009
[439.8170902]*	439.81701
[439.817094–.817099]*	439.8171–.8179
[439.82701]*	439.827001
439.82702*	439.827002
[439.82703–.82708]*	439.827003–.827008
[439.82709]*	439.827009
[439.8270902]*	439.82702
[439.827094–.827099]*	439.8272–.8279
[439.83]*	439.82
447.1–.9	447.01094–.01099
447.1–.9	447.02094–.02099
457.1–.9	457.01094–.01099
457.1–.9	457.02094–.02099
467.1–.9	467.01094–.01099
467.1–.9	467.02094–.02099
469.71–.79	469.701094–.7099
469.71–.79	469.702094–.702099
491.467	491.469
491.774–.779	491.7701094–.7701099
491.774–.779	491.7702094–.7702099

*Previously published
†Eliminates dual provision

Edition 21	*Edition 22*
[511.22]	511.36
511.3	512.62
511.32	511.332
511.33	511.326
511.5	511.66
511.5	518.23
511.8	518.1
512	518.42
512.2	512.46
[512.24]	512.4
[512.24]	512.44
[512.24]	512.46
[512.24]	512.48
512.55	512.482
512.55	512.62
512.55	512.64
512.55	512.66
512.72†	511.64
512.72	512.73
512.74	512.72
[512.925]†	511.64
[512.93]	515.24
512.9434	512.9436
513.24†	511.4
[513.25]†	511.64
[513.4]	515.24
[514.32001]	514.3201
[514.32002]	514.3202
[514.32003]	514.3203
[514.32005–.32009]	514.3205–.3209
514.74	515.39
515	518
515.35	515.392
515.352	515.39
515.42	515.48
[515.623]	518.53
[515.624]	518.54
[515.783]	515.42
[516.05]	516.154
[516.06]	516.156
516.35	516.158
[516.36001–.36009]	516.3601–.3609
516.362†	514.224
519.282	518.282
519.287	519.236
519.3	519.6
[519.4]	518
[537.67]*	530.1433
[541.221]†	541.220212
541.24	546.8
[541.301–.303]†	541.01–.03
[541.305–.309]†	541.05–.09
[543.001]	543.01
[543.002]	543.02
[543.003–.006]	543.03–.06
[543.007]	543.07
[543.008]	543.08
[543.009]	543.09
543.01	543.0284
543.02	543.19
543.07	543.19
543.08	543.2–.8
[544]	543.1
[544]	Scattered within 543
[545]	543.1
[545]	Scattered within 543
546.3	543
547	
[0459]	547.2
547.01–.08†	547.2
[547.139]	547.2
547.21	547.27
[547.223]	547.27
[547.225]	547.27
[547.24]	547.27
[547.25]	547.27
[547.26]	547.27
[547.3]	543.17
[547.3]	Scattered within 543
547.4–.8	547.2
[547.7704593]	547.27
[551.46001]	551.4601
[551.46002–.46006]	551.4602–.4606
[551.46007]	551.4607
[551.46008]	551.4608
[551.46009]	551.4609
551.4601	551.465
551.4601	551.466
551.4608	551.468
551.4609	551.4618
551.4609	551.4829
551.462	551.46138
[551.4634]	551.461364
[551.4635]	551.461365
551.464	551.46135
[551.4646]	551.46136
[551.4647]	551.46137
551.465	551.4614
551.466	551.46142
[551.4661]	551.46141

*Previously published
†Eliminates dual provision

Edition 21	*Edition 22*
[551.4663]	551.46143
[551.467]	551.4615
551.468	551.46132
[551.469]	551.4617
[551.47]	551.462
[551.4701]	551.462
[551.4702]	551.463
[551.4708]	551.464
551.559*	551.556
561.13	571.8452
571.64	572.3
571.81	591.56
576.542	572.838
576.58†	576.86
578.47†	591.472
580†	630
[597.92177]	597.928
[597.96177]	597.965
598.64	598.74
[610.6953]	610.737069
[610.6953]	610.7372069
[610.7361]	616.025
[610.7361]	616.028
[610.7361]	616.029
[610.7362]	618.9200231
[610.7365]	618.970231
[610.73677]	616.70231
[610.73677]	617
	0231
[610.73677]	617.0231
[610.73677]	617.70231
[610.73678]	618.10231
[610.73678]	618.20231
[610.7368]	616.804231
[610.7368]	616.85880231
[610.7368]	616.890231
[610.7369]	616.1–.9
	0231
611.0184	611.41
[612.01573]	612.01577
[612.491]	612.41
[612.6001–.6009]	612.601–.609
612.78	612.82336
[613.13]	613.11
[613.14]	613.11
[614.517]	614.593427
[614.5266]	614.5263
[614.571]	615.58852
[614.5742]	614.588
[614.575]	614.58
614.577	614.59523
[615.373]	615.372
615.39	615.37
[615.42]†	615.19
[615.43]†	615.19
[615.45]†	615.19
[615.75]	615.783
[615.8043]†	616.025
615.842	615.8315
[615.886]†	615.1
[615.899]	615.880901
[615.899]	615.880902
[616.01]	616.9041
[616.014]	616.9201
[616.015]	616.96901
[616.016]	616.93601
[616.019]	616.9101
[616.0192]	616.92201
[616.0194]	616.9101
616.047	616.901–.96
616.1–.9	616.1–.9
[0192]	014
05	061–069
[616.156]	616.99442
[616.3423]*	616.399
[616.521]	616.51
[616.524]	616.523
616.57	616.523
[616.837]	616.842
616.84	616.89
616.851	616.83
[616.857]	616.84912
616.85884	616.85889
[616.87]	616.856
[616.88]	616.8569
[616.892]	616.83
[616.8982]	616.85882
[616.8983]	616.83
[616.917]	616.92987
[616.921]	616.91852
[616.9226]	616.9223
[616.9242]	616.918
[616.925]	616.91
[616.928]	616.91854
[616.942]	616.523
[616.992]	616.994
617	617
052	061–069
[617.01]	617.919
[617.124]	616.9897

*Previously published
†Eliminates dual provision

Edition 21	Edition 22
617.143	617.13
[617.6009]	617.609
617.692	617.693
[617.97059]	617.05
[617.98059]	617.05
[617.99059]	617.05
618.1–.8	618.1–.8
052	061–069
[618.13]	618.14
[618.173]	618.15
[618.32078]†	618.392
618.39201–.39209	618.392001–.392009
618.39701–.39709	618.397001–.397009
[618.73]	618.74
[618.75]	618.36132
[618.83]	618.88
[618.92000832]	618.9202
[619]*	616.027
[621.3125]	621.31243
[621.872]	621.873
[624.253]	624.283
[624.254]	624.284
624.257	624.20284
[624.3]	624.2
[624.3]	624.21
[624.4]	624.21
[624.4]	624.215
[624.5]	624.23
[624.6]	624.22
[624.7]	624.2
[624.8]	624.24
632.8*	632.32
[640.42]	332.024
[640.49]	613.69
[641.333]	641.3565
[641.50284]†	643.3
641.51	641.5024
[641.576]	641.575
[641.633]	641.6565
[645.042]	645.029
646.7	650.1
[646.71]†	613.4
[646.75]	613.41
[646.75]	613.71
[646.75]	613.72
[646.75]	796.41
[647.3]	647.2
647.94	910.46
647.94	910.462
647.94	910.464
647.94	910.466
647.94	910.468
647.94025	910.46
[647.943–.949]	647.940253–.940259
[647.943–.949]	647.94093–.94099
[647.943–.949]	913–919
[01]	06
[01]	062
[02]	06
[03]	064
[06–07]	066
[09]	068
649.1†	649.6
649.58	649.68
[652.5]	005.52
657.48	657.7
[658.3126]†	658.31424
[658.3127]	658.3144
658.3128†	658.4022
[658.3226]	658.3225
[658.8103]	658.8102
[658.8104]	658.8102
[658.8105]	658.8102
658.84	658.87
658.84†	658.872
658.86	658.87
[658.8703]	658.8702
[658.878]†	381.4564130068
[658.878]	658.879
658.879	658.8705
659.13	659.19
659.131	659.19
659.14	659.19
[659.1932473]†	324.73
[659.293247]†	324.7
666.44	666.328
[704.043–.046]	704.085
[704.05]	704.083–.084
[704.06]	704.086
[704.09–.87]	704.088
[704.94963]	704.943
709.04	776
726.4	726.5
[739.227]	738.2209
[739.237]	739.2309
[739.37]	739.309
[739.47]	739.409
743.5	743.4
[745.44]	745.409
[747.2]	747.09

*Previously published
†Eliminates dual provision

Edition 21	*Edition 22*
[748.29]	748.209
[748.59]	748.509
[749.2]	749.09
[758.963]	758.5
[790.0132]	790.019
[790.0135]	790.1
[799.166]	799.1609163–.1609167
808.06665*	650.142
808.066651*	650.142
839.6*	839.5
839.69*	839.5
[839.83]*	839.82
895.6	895.6
4	34
[930.2]†	930.1
[930.3]†	930.15
[930.4]†	930.16
936.3	943.6022
936.3	943.648
[940.4143]	940.4144
[940.4143]	940.4147
940.5317094*	940.53185
940.531743–.531749*	940.531853–.531859
940.5423	940.5424
943.026	943.027
943.053	943.054
943.076	943.074
943.081	943.083
943.0876	943.0875
943.0878	943.0877
[943.0879]	943.0881
[943.0879]	943.0882
[943.10876]	943.10875
943.10877	943.10875
[943.10878]	943.10877
943.10879	943.10881
943.10879	943.10882
943.603	943.6025
943.6044	943.60511
943.702	943.7102
948.022*	948.023
948.05*	948.04
948.06*	948.04

Edition 21	*Edition 22*
948.07*	948.05
[948.08]*	948.06
[948.09]*	948.07
948.102*	948.101
[948.1045]*	948.1043
[948.1046]*	948.1043
[948.1047]*	948.1044
[948.1048]*	948.1044
[948.1049]*	948.1044
948.5014*	948.5018
[948.502]*	948.5032
948.503*	948.504
[948.5055]*	948.5053
[948.5056]*	948.5053
[948.5057]*	948.5054
[948.5058]*	948.5054
[948.5059]*	948.5054
948.9015*	948.9014
948.903*	948.902
[948.9055]*	948.9053
[948.9056]*	948.9053
[948.9057]*	948.9054
[948.9058]*	948.9054
[948.9059]*	948.9054
949.1204*	949.1203
949.1204*	949.1205
949.1205*	949.1206
949.7103	949.702
959.603	959.601
959.603	959.602
959.86*	959.87
963.506*	963.5071
971.9102	971.9101
[972.0837]*	972.0841
[973.623]	973.624
[973.623]	973.6242
[973.625]	973.6245
985.0631*	985.0632
987.061*	987.062
987.0632*	987.06314
987.0632*	987.06315
987.0632*	987.0633
994.065*	994.066

*Previously published
†Eliminates dual provision

Discontinuations

A discontinuation is the result of shifting one or more topics to a number shorter than the previous one but otherwise not differing from it. If all topics in a given number are thus shifted, the number is no longer valid. Discontinuations are described and explained in the Introduction.

In addition, several numbers have been dropped because their content in Edition 21 was meaningless within the context of Edition 22.

Discontinuations that have appeared previously in an interim update prior to the publication of Edition 22 are indicated by * next to the Edition 21 number.

"Main number" means that the provision for the topic within a table has been discontinued to the numbers to which the table number would previously have been added.

For example in Table 2, —[41223] has been discontinued and all of its contents moved up to the broader number —4122, while only some of the topics in —41425 have been moved up to —4142. In Table 5, —[03] has been discontinued because it is without meaning.

An indented number is an element of an add table. The number or span under which it is indented shows the location of the add table. For example, [64–65] and 6 under 546 indicate that [64–65] and 6 are elements of the add table at 546.

Table 7 Groups of Persons has been deleted and replaced by direct use of notation already available in the schedules and in notation 08 from Table 1. Discontinuations resulting from this deletion and replacement are not given. The list giving the add instructions where notation from Table 7 was previously added is located in the introduction to list of relocations.

For details of the specific discontinued topics the classifier should consult the appropriate entries in the tables and schedules.

Edition 21	*Edition 22*	*Edition 21*	*Edition 22*
[T1—013]	T1—01	[004.71]	004.7
[T1—0142]	T1—014	[005.304]	005.3
[T1—0221]	Without meaning	[005.369]	005.36
T1—0294	T1—029	[005.752]	005.75
T1—0296	T1—029	[005.7592]	005.759
T1—0297	T1—029	[005.7598]	005.759
T1—0299	T1—029	[028.5344]	028.534
[T1—0753–0755]	T1—075	133	130
[T1—077]	T1—07	[153.932–.933]	153.93
[T1—08632]	T1—0863	[154.22–.24]	154.2
T1—088001–088009	T1—088	[155.81]	155.8
[T2—4118]*	Without meaning	[200.13]	200.1
T2—4122*	Without meaning	[291.04]	Without meaning
[T2—41223]*	T2—4122	[299.77]	299.7
T2—4123*	Without meaning	[299.87]	299.8
[T2—41235]*	T2—4123	302.234	302.23
[T2—41292–41298]*	T2—4129	[302.25]	302.2
[T2—4141]*	T2—414	[302.52]	302.5
T2—4142*	Without meaning	[303.3231–.3232]	303.323
[T2—41423]*	T2—4142	303.327	303.32
[T2—41425]*	T2—4142	[304.634]	304.63
T2—4143*	Without meaning	[305.5222]	305.522
T2—4144*	Without meaning	[305.5223]	305.522
[T2—41443]*	T2—4144	[305.906941]	305.90694
T2—4145*	Without meaning	[306.344]	306.34
T2—4146*	Without meaning	[306.347]	306.34
[T2—422323]*	T2—42232	[306.366]	306.36
[T2—422325]*	T2—42232	306.44089	306.44
[T2—42282]*	T2—4228	[306.735]	306.73
[T2—42285]*	T2—4228	[306.773]	306.77
[T2—435958]	T2—43595	[306.853]	306.85
T2—443823*	T2—44382	306.874	306.87
[T2—44771]*	T2—4477	[323.622]	323.62
[T2—44815]*	T2—4481	[323.629]	323.62
T2—44941*	T2—4494	[323.632–.634]	323.63
[T2—449414]*	T2—44941	[323.636]	323.63
T2—4831*	T2—483	330.154	330.15
T2—4841*	T2—484	330.155	330.15
T2—4971	T2—497	[330.9009]	330.9
T2—54792	T2—5479	[331.11424]	331.1142
[T2—547923]	T2—54792	331.119042	331.11
[T2—6849]*	T2—684	331.129042	331.12
[T2—68491]*	T2—684	[331.1374]	331.137
T2—714115	T2—71411	331.2572	331.257
[T2—85292]	T2—8529	331.25722	331.257
[T3B—108]	T3B—1	[331.348]	331.34
[T5—03]	Without meaning	[331.712]	331.71
[004.338]	004.33	[331.8804]	331.88
[004.358]	005.35	[331.88042]	331.88
[004.368]	004.36	[331.8921]	331.892

*Previously published

Edition 21	*Edition 22*
[331.8922–.8924]	331.892
[331.8926]	331.892
[331.8982]	331.898
332.02402	332.024
332.04154	332.0415
332.34	332.3
[332.4048]	332.404
[332.4204]	332.42
[332.424–.427]	332.42
[332.454]	332.45
332.63	332.6
332.632044	332.632
[332.63223]	332.6322
[332.671]	332.67
[332.67153]	332.6
332.672	332.6
332.67253	332.6
332.67314	332.673
332.67314	332.6731
[332.82]	332.8
333.916	333.91
336.2432	336.243
338.47	338.4
340.58	340.5
[341.481]	341.48
343.013	343.01
[343.0532]	343.053
[343.088]	343.08
[343.09942]	343.0994
[346.062]	346.06
370.153	370.15
[382.782–.788]	382.78
[384.352–.354]	384.35
491.487	491.48
[511.2]	Without meaning
[512.925]	Without meaning
[513.25]	Without meaning
[513.54]	513.5
[513.56–.57]	513.5
514.3202	514.32
514.3203	514.32
[515.223]	515.22
[515.232–.235]	515.23
[515.254]	515.25
[515.74]	515.7
[515.784]	515.78
[516.17]	516.1
[516.184–.186]	516.18
[516.372]	516.37
[526.0221]	526
[540.118]	540.1

Edition 21	*Edition 22*
541.3	541
541.393	541.39
546	546
[64–65]	6
[546.2242–.2248]	546.224
[546.2253–.2259]	546.225
[546.252–.258]	546.25
[546.263–.269]	546.26
[546.342–.345]	546.34
547	547
[0464–0465]	046
[547.071–.077]	547.07
547.21	547.2
[547.22]	547.2
[547.225]	547.2
547.28	547.2
[547.72–.76]	547.7
[547.781–.783]	547.78
[547.79]	547.7
551.4607	551.46
551.559*	551.55
599.784	599.78
610.695	610.69
[610.6952]	610.695
[610.7361]	610.736
[612.014452]	612.01445
[612.01572]	612.0157
612.015756	612.01575
[612.01576]	612.0157
[612.1122]	612.112
612.492	612.49
[613.67]	613.6
614.52	614.5
[614.5266]	614.526
614.59994	614.5999
[615.362]	615.36
[615.367]	615.36
[615.373]	Without meaning
[615.375]	615.37
[615.531]	615.53
[615.731]	615.73
[615.733–.735]	615.73
[615.804]	Without meaning
615.822	615.82
[615.824]	615.82
[615.8322]	615.832
[615.8325]	615.832
[615.882]	615.88
616.1–.9	616.1–.9
[0142–0149]	014
[0194]	019

*Previously published

Edition 21	Edition 22
616.212	616.21
[616.3434]	616.343
616.51	616.5
616.52	616.5
[616.633]	616.63
[616.838]	616.83
616.85223	616.8522
616.85232	616.8523
[616.85845]	616.8584
616.85884	616.8588
[616.8982]	616.898
616.91	616.9
616.9223	616.922
[616.9226]	616.922
[616.977]	616.97
[617.025]	617
[617.0262]	617.026
[617.08]	617
[617.122]	617.12
617.14	617.1
[617.146]	617.1
[617.9172]	617.917
[618.143]	618.14
[618.51–.53]	618.5
[618.56–.58]	618.5
[618.73]	618.7
[618.75]	618.7
[618.77]	618.7
[618.87]	618.8
[618.89]	618.8
[618.92012]	618.9201
[621.31916]	621.3191
[621.3212–.3213]	621.321
[621.3612–.3617]	621.361
[621.38489]	621.3848
[621.384892–.384893]	621.3848
[621.3894]	621.389
[621.465–.466]	621.46
[621.837]	621.83
[621.983]	621.98
[641.47]	641.4
[641.5634]	641.653
649.4	Without meaning
[652.325]	652.32
[653.421–.423]	653.42
[653.4242–.4245]	653.424
[653.425–.426]	653.42
[653.4272–.4273]	653.427
657.48	657
[657.99]	657.9
[658.3151]	658.315
[658.566]	658.56
[658.576]	658.57
[658.7886]	658.788
[658.835]	658.83
[658.848]	658.84
[658.8701]	658.87
[658.8704]	658.87
[658.8706–.8707]	658.87
[658.873–.876]	658.87
[660.28441–.28442]	660.2844
[660.28444–.28448]	660.2844
[940.5318089924]*	940.5318
[973.5275]	973.527
[973.5285]	973.528
[973.6275]	973.627
[973.8975]	973.897

*Previously published

Reused Numbers

A reused number is a number with a total change in meaning from one edition to another. The list of reused numbers shows all Edition 21 numbers immediately reused in Edition 22 with the exception of reused numbers resulting from the deletion and replacement of Table 7 Groups of Persons. The list giving the add instructions where notation from Table 7 was previously used is located in the introduction to the list of relocations.

T1—0294
T1—0296
T1—0297
T1—0299
T2—4439
T2—4499
T2—86139
299.683–.685
    01–08
324.274703
324.274707
392.3601
392.3602
439.7701
439.81701
439.82702
514.3202
514.3203
543.01
543.02
543.03–.06
543.07
543.08
543.09
551.4601
551.4607
551.4608
551.4609
551.462
551.463
551.464
551.465
551.466
551.468
616.91
618.39201–.39209
618.39701–.39709
948.05
948.06
948.07

The 22nd edition of the Dewey Decimal Classification was designed by Lisa Hanifan of Lisa Hanifan/Graphic Design, Albany, New York. The cover was designed by Nola Burger. Edition 22 was generated from an online database management system developed by OCLC Online Computer Library Center, Inc. Composition was done in Times Roman and Arial under the supervision of Lisa Hanifan. The book was printed and bound by Edwards Brothers, Inc., Ann Arbor, Michigan.